Children
and Parents:
PSYCHOANALYTIC STUDIES
IN DEVELOPMENT

JUDITH S. KESTENBERG, M.D.

in collaboration with

Esther Robbins, M.D. (Chapters 8, 16, 17, 18)

and

Jay Berlowe, M.D., Arnhilt Buelte and
Hershey Marcus, M.D. (Chapter 8)

With a Foreword by Phyllis Greenacre

Children
and Parents:
Psychoanalytic Studies
in Development

JASON ARONSON   NEW YORK

ISBN: 0-87668-106-2

Library of Congress Catalog Number: 73-81391

To
My Husband
and
Children

Classical Psychoanalysis and Its Applications:
A Series of Books
Edited by Robert Langs, M.D.

Langs, Robert—"THE TECHNIQUE OF PSYCHOAN-ALYTIC PSYCHOTHERAPY" VOL. I AND II

Kestenberg, Judith—"CHILDREN AND PARENTS: PSYCHOANALYTIC STUDIES IN DEVELOPMENT

Sperling, Melitta—"THE MAJOR NEUROSES AND BEHAVIOR DISORDERS IN CHILDREN"

Giovacchini, Peter—"PSYCHOANALYSIS OF CHA-RACTER DISORDER"

Kernberg, Otto—"BORDERLINE CONDITIONS AND PATHOLOGICAL NARCISSISM"

Nagera, Humberto—"FEMALE SEXUALITY AND THE OEDIPUS COMPLEX"

Hoffer, Willie—"THE EARLY DEVELOPMENT AND EDUCATION OF THE CHILD"

Meissner, William—"THE PARANOID PROCESS"

Classical Psychoanalysis and Its Applications:
A Series of Books
Edited by Robert Langs, M.D.

Series Introduction

Judith Kestenberg is a rare and singular psychoanalyst—a true pioneer in her field. Having gained a unique and remarkable panoramic in-depth view of infantile functioning, she has translated her rich findings into formulations and insights that are relevant for all who study or attempt to modify human behavior. Her searching investigations into the contributions of bodily functions and sensations, hormonal changes, and the mother-child interaction to the development of psychic structures, object relationships, and conscious and unconscious fantasy formations. In fact, to all aspects of human functioning—are original sojourns into a much-neglected dimension of human adaptation. The reader will be richly rewarded by her comprehenension of the nuances of the developmental vicissitudes of both boys and girls as they grow into men and women. Human sexuality, movements, maternal feelings, and problems of aggression—and both the anxieties and conflicts that they can create and their contribution to healthy psychological growth—become deeply meaningful and understandable on these pages. Her work provides valuable landmarks for future students of human development, and offers a sound framework for psychotherapeutic and psychoanalytic endeavors with both children and adults. In fact, anyone who is interested in the psychotherapy and the growth and development of infants, children, adolescents, and adults will be richly rewarded by Dr. Kestenberg's insights.

In all, this is a book that boldly demonstrates the unique and universal value of classical psychoanalysis and its applications, as molded by the mind of an unusual and gifted psychoanalyst.

Robert J. Langs, M.D.

Contents

Foreword

The period surrounding World War II—roughly beginning in the mid-thirties and extending into the fifties—was one of extraordinarily significant development in psychiatry and psychoanalysis in America. Earlier there had been a considerable and widening interest in psychoanalysis, but little training was available. For some time, a steady but small stream of young professional people (psychiatrists, psychologists, teachers, and social workers) found their way to the European centers of psychoanalytic training. As the threat of war came closer, this small tide was reversed, as established analysts began to emigrate and locate in the United States. As this number increased, psychoanalytic education began to be more thoroughly organized, and simultaneously there was some enrichment in and from allied fields, especially in academic and professional circles in which psychoanalysis found an increasing acceptance.

In this setting I first met Judith Silberpfennig, as a fellow student in a private seminar conducted by Dr. Herman Nunberg. I soon heard of her as a young, gifted, and devoted student, already well trained in neurology in Vienna, where she also had begun her psychoanalytic training. These traits and this background combined with an enduring concern for the study of infant development, presented a rare combination of interests and capabilities, which I was to see more and value highly when she joined the psychiatric clinic outpatient staff of which I was then the senior member.

In 1941, Dr. Silberpfennig's first paper was entitled "Mother-Types Encountered in Child Guidance Clinics." About twenty-five years later we find her concerned with adolescence in an especially noteworthy treatise, written in three sections, dealing with "Phases of Adolescence, with Suggestions for a Correlation of Psychic and Hormonal Organization." In the years in between and after, she had written about various aspects of infant and child development as well as problems of parent-child interactions.

Always attentive to the infant's growing self-realization through the maturational body changes, she has carried on a series of significant research studies. These have been focused on movement patterns, especially on the tension-flow and shape-flow and on the emergence of ego-controlled motion factors as the infant responds and adapts to the surrounding forces of space, weight, and time, and experiences these in relationships to people and things in the environment. These and other studies carried on over a period of years furnish an invaluable addition to the knowledge of the preverbal and nonverbal aspects of infant and child development and of mother-infant interaction.

The range of Dr. Kestenberg's interest and exploring scrutiny is impressive and fascinating in what it brings to view of these maturational processes and concomitant activities, especially the part these play in psychic development. In her untiring interest in how patterning and integrative organization take place, she never loses the stance of the analyst. Thus she is able to widen the scope of our vision and deepen our feeling for and our understanding of the manifestations of psychic disturbances with which we must work in treating neuroses.

It is especially felicitous that the papers, originally published in a variety of places are now drawn together, and their content as well as their extensive bibliographies are made readily available. One feels that some of the papers might be supplemented and published as separate volumes. In their range and their implicit point of view in regard to the field of psychoanalytic research, they represent a stage of development in the very vision of psychoanalysis. They emphasize the usefulness of a wider understanding of the total individual, an understanding which adds to but does not disavow the important and necessary restrictions of the psychoanalytic technical method itself.

PHYLLIS GREENACRE

Preface

My interest in child development started early. When Europe began to recuperate from the ravages of World War I, a great number of children were orphaned and homeless. In my small hometown in Poland there was an institution in which hundreds of children of all ages grew up under the watchful eye of an authoritarian director. It was my mother who helped me realize that the infants and toddlers among them desperately needed a homelike atmosphere. We both persuaded my generous father to create a small home for ten young children. My mother took me there often; while she discussed matters of policy with the nurses, I played with the babies.

I was an avid reader of Korczak's books on children and for children. This gifted psychologist and writer was to perish later in the Warsaw ghetto. Although allowed his freedom he preferred to lead "his children" with a song to the train which brought them to the site of their extermination.

My grammar-school teacher, Miss T., was another source of inspiration. She not only liked children but she understood them as well. Many years later, when I applied to the Vienna Psychoanalytic Institute and was interviewed by Anna Freud, I found all the good features of Miss T. embodied in her.

In adolescence, I became temporarily estranged from child development. Instead, I spent many precious hours, choreographing thoughts and stories in fantasy. No doubt, this was good practice for my future research on movement patterns. In medical school, I became fascinated with brain anatomy. In the last year before graduation I began to work in the Neurological Institute under Marburg and in the Neuropsychiatric University Klinik under Poetzl, Hoff, and Urban. Looking back at this part of my life I am reminded of the horror I felt as a little girl when I peered into the empty head of a decapitated doll. No doubt, I wanted to make sure that there was something precious and important inside all heads.

Among the many papers on neurology, which I published since 1935, were three which laid a foundation for my future research on the correlation between movement patterns and psychic functions. A child who could not move his eyes because of a medulla-lesion, learned to move his head sideways to overcome his deficit, and thus make contact with people. Two women with extensive cortical lesions simply did not react when approached from the left side. For them, space had become constricted into a narrow strip from the midline to the right side, and people on the left side did not exist. To study the developmental sequences of various types of eye movement, I examined them in successive stages of awakening from insulin coma. During this research I began to appreciate the genetic nature of transference when one of the patients called me "mama" just as her eye movements began to show the first signs of ego control.

Upon my arrival in New York in 1937 I had the opportunity to work with Schilder who had brought me over to the United States. Despite our differences on the subject of psychoanalysis, I was fascinated by Schilder's approach to the borderland between organic and psychic phenomena. In his house I met many people who brought with them a Viennese atmosphere. Among them were Sandor Lorand and Fritz Wittels. Sandor became a good friend who helped me in many ways.

Although still a student in the New York Psychoanalytic Institute, I was invited to Herman Nunberg's private seminar. Beyond supervising me he was most helpful, not only in scientific and professional matters, but also personally. His death was a great loss to psychoanalysis and to his students, who admired his scientific and personal integrity. In Nunberg's seminar I met Norvelle C. LaMar whose warm friendship we still miss. Phyllis Greenacre, who had a profound influence on my research, was just then writing her pioneering paper "The Predisposition to Anxiety" (1941). By introducing the concept of "organic imprints," she opened up the road toward the understanding of the continuity of soma and psyche. Working with her and LaMar in the Payne Whitney Clinic, I formulated a longitudinal study of infants which I could not pursue until many years later. In the clinic I saw a great many infants and there I collected the data for my papers on mother types (Chapter 3 in this book), which Margaret Mahler discussed. My previous association with her dated from Vienna, where she taught me the Rorschach method we applied to the study of the brain-damaged. Before I left, in 1937, we could complete only one paper of the projected series (1938). This inspiring collaboration marked the shift in my interest from neurology to psychoanalysis. When Margaret first came to New York in 1938, the vicissitudes of daily living under the shadow of the holocaust did not permit scientific work. However, Margaret's feelings and knowledge of babies communicated itself effortlessly in her courses at the institute and in the many hours we spent discussing various problems.

With the influx of European colleagues in 1938 and 1939, the atmosphere in the New York Institute began to change. At the same time, almost all my former Viennese teachers were assembled at Nunberg's seminar. Engrossed in Hartmann's paper on "Ego Psychology and the Problem of Adaptation" (1939), I was especially struck by the way he applied the Jacksonian concept of "change of function" to the psychoanalytic theories on development. I found Hartmann most receptive to my early ideas on development from which my movement studies evolved.

Although I disagreed with him regarding his concept of primary autonomy (Kestenberg, 1953),[1] he was always ready to read my papers and outlines and helped me to formulate thoughts that were to become the basis for my developmental research.

The revision of psychoanalytic theory, especially regarding the formation of psychic structure, by Hartmann, Kris, and Loewenstein, were then at the center of our interest. At the same time, Bertha Bornstein and Marianne Kris brought to us their distinctive ways of teaching child analysis. Listening to the information given by parents, I became keenly aware of the impact the child's analysis had on them. Each psychoanalytic patient opened up new vistas for the understanding of individual development through transference. Anna Freud's monthly reports from the Hampstead Nursery brought into sharp focus how infants felt when separated from their mothers. Periodically, we were presented with the responsibility for similar suffering, thrust upon us when we took a vacation, and saw our adult patients behave like abandoned children. Mothers of young infants asked our guidance, hoping to find ways of child-rearing that would ensure lasting happiness for their children and a guilt-free fulfillment of the parental task for themselves. All these experiences, and others of a more personal nature, combined to evoke my lasting interest in the "enigma of motherhood." In my endeavor to derive traits of maternality from early infantile sources (Chapters 1, 2, 5, 9, 11, and 13), I was greatly encouraged by Marjorie Brierley. She was forever ready to read my manuscripts and comment on them and helped me put the data I gathered in perspective. Her lucid discussion of the subject, her approach to "integration" as a principal factor on the organization of femininity were a great help to me personally and in research. I still hope to meet her some day and thank her for past guidance.

Writing on "Early Fears and Early Defenses" (Chapter 7) in the mid-forties, I was concerned with the nonverbal aspects of mother-child interaction and with the motor prototypes of defense mechanisms which, early in life, set the tone for future development. I treated a girl who used masturbation as a soothing method since earliest infancy. At the same time I tried to find new ways of treating an "autistic" child who immobilized his arms rather than let them do what they wanted. I had not been able to analyze his fears until I could help him release his tension by exercises (1953). I was becoming increasingly aware of the need to record the attitudes, movement, and tensions of mother and child. In trying to explain data regarding cryptic tensions, obtained from the anal-

---

[1]Years later, Rapaport (1959) and Gill (1963) modified this concept and renamed it "relative autonomy" of the ego.

yses of young children and older girls (Chapters 1, 2, 4, 5, 10, 11, 13, and 14), I found it difficult at first to report what was conveyed to me. By 1955 and 1956, when my first three papers (Chapters 1, 2, and 4) on female sexuality were finally formulated, I was already engaged in a longitudinal study that eventually led to a construction of a comprehensive movement profile, suitable for the assessment of parents and children (1965, 1967a).

In the summer of 1953 I selected several newborn infants for a pilot project, with the purpose of devising a method of movement notation that would obviate impressionistic descriptions of nonverbal transactions between mothers and babies. Today these children have grown to be adults; some are married and have children themselves. I am most grateful to them and their mothers and fathers for their unswerving cooperation in my study, their lasting friendship and understanding of the nature of my work. They most generously provided the information that made movement notation meaningful within a clinical framework. They gave me the first clues that my original method of notation of tension changes did not suffice for the scoring of ego-controlled motility.

Through the good offices of my friend, Maria Piscator—a dancer, drama teacher, and writer—I was introduced to the work of Laban. This outstanding choreographer discovered that ethnic dances were composed of everyday work-movements. He devised the "effort-shape" notation which is now extensively used in behavioral research (1947).[2] I was fortunate enough to study with his pupils Irma Bartenieff in New York and Warren Lamb in London, and had some contact with Marion North and Valerie Preston. After seven years of training, I began to meet regularly with the Sands Point Movement Study Group, composed of Dr. Jay Berlowe, Arnhilt Buelte, Dr. Hershey Marcus, and Dr. Esther Robbins. In later years, Martha Soodak joined our group. Through years of personal retraining and practicing my own and Laban's movement notation, our more refined kinesthetic awareness allowed us to classify movement patterns that were used to express specific modalities (Chapters 10 and 17). We modified Lamb's aptitude assessment so that all patterns were covered in a movement profile that could be correlated with a psychoanalytic evaluation. We were eager to verify our findings, but were not able to do so until 1965, when I visited the Hampstead Clinic and became acquainted with

[2]Effort-shape notation should not be confused with Labanotation. The former notates style of movement while the latter prepares scores in which every motion is located precisely in space. Both methods can be learned in the Dance Notation Bureau in New York. Our own system is taught under the auspices of Child Development Research in Port Washington, N.Y.

the practical application of Anna Freud's assessment. In London I had the unusual opportunity to test our movement profile in two ways. Observing in the Hampstead Nursery I met Mrs. Friedman, the nursery-school teacher who was very interested and helpful. I notated movement patterns of several children, sitting far enough away so I would not hear what they were saying. Mrs. Friedmann meticulously avoided giving me information about the children. At last, I finished the first profile and attempted, for the first time, to correlate it with categories of Anna Freud's development assessment. Then I showed the movement data to two Laban pupils, who worked with effort-shape in different ways: Marion North, who has developed a children's profile of her own, and Warren Lamb, the originator of the aptitude test for executives. Even though their experience and methods were different, their interpretations of my data were approximately the same. Moreover, my own interpretation, although couched in psychoanalytic terms, did not essentially differ from theirs. The final and the most important test was to see whether my formulations came anyway near the developmental assessment done in the Hampstead Clinic. I handed my results over to Mrs. Friedmann and hastened to read the clinic profile of the first child. I was very pleased with what I read, but became disheartened when I attended a conference during which a participant suggested that the child in question was compulsive. My record indicated that she had an oral fixation and was depressive. The few moments until Dr. Freud corrected the discussant and thus, without knowing it, saved the movement profile from abandonment and oblivion, seemed like years. I am most grateful to Dr. Freud for the courtesy extended to me in the clinic and for the kind words she had for the results of the metapsychological assessment, based on a movement profile. I am also most grateful to Mrs. Burlingham for allowing me to make notations in the blind nursery and letting me know where my conclusions had been erroneous. I subsequently notated movement patterns of blind and deaf children in America and came to realize that assessments of handicapped children required a knowledge of their special type of developmental progression (Burlingham and Goldberger, 1968, Fraiberg, 1968; Wills, 1965). One of the most important things I learned from these profiles was that when the ability to create meaningful configurations in space was lacking, object constancy was considerably delayed and object relationships were simplified and flattened (see Chapters 8, 10, 17).

Encouraged by our good results with the normal children in the Hampstead nursery, we notated movements of three-year-old children in the Child Development Center in New York. Dr. Peter Neubauer kindly put at out disposal the developmental assessments of these children. There was substantial agreement between the interpretations, derived from movement profiles, and the clinical assessments. Once we found a means for validating the movement profile, we needed to establish more data on developmental norms. To do so, I visited several kibbutzim in 1968 and 1970. There, I amassed about 150 observations and notations of children between the ages of two months and six years. The raw data of these notations are still being scored. All members of the Movement Study Group observed and notated in the New-Born Nursery of Long Island Jewish Hospital and some of us made notations of mothers and children in the Well Baby Clinic. We observed three- and four-year-old children in the Merklee Nursery in Port Washington. Our latest sphere of operation is an organization chartered under the name of Child Development Research, under whose auspices we pursue two developmental projects:[3]

(1) The Center for Parents and Children in Port Washington, N.Y., where parents and children under the age of four participate in joint sessions. The center is devoted to the prevention of emotional disorders. It enlists the cooperation of parents and staff in joint efforts to study development in a parent-centered curriculum. Mothers participate in center activities as caretakers of babies, as teachers of high school trainees, and as professionals engaged in special projects (see footnote 4 on page 00). Data from social interaction of babies and toddlers derived through observations in the center are included in Chapters 10 and 17.

(2) A prenatal project, dedicated to the memory of Sidney L. Green, who gave the first course on child development in the Child-Analysis Division of Down-State-University, Brooklyn, N.Y. Headed by Dr. Esther Robbins, this program offers instructions to nurses and prospective parents regarding the movement repertoire of the infant. The courses are designed by Robbins and Soodak to help those engaged in child care attune to the child's preferred rhythms and become sensitive to his nonverbal cues. Some of the data on which this program is based are included in Chapter 6.

One of our most recent studies concerns the notation of fetal movement. We hope to learn from them about the way mother and fetus attune to one another and how, through the palpation of fetal movement, not only mothers but fathers and siblings learn to anticipate the movement of the baby. It is possible that we shall learn to predict prenatally the ways in which mothers and infants will fit and how they might clash after the child is born. At this time, we can help novice mothers increase their kinesthetic sensitivity to a variety of ways in which a baby might move. We can help a mother detect her most comfortable method of holding a baby or, through widening her arms, and broadening her lap,

[3]The royalties of this book are donated to Child Development Research.

accommodating to the baby and an older sibling as well. We can help parents find means of aiding a child to readjust to the adult. These methods of "infant therapy" have just begun. We are grateful to the chiefs of the departments of psychiatry, pediatrics, and obstetrics, to the obstetricians and nurses, as well as the expectant parents, in Long Island Jewish Hospital, who have given us encouragement and help in our work. Although we have engaged in individual movement training since the center open in 1972, 1974-75 is the first year in which we conduct classes by means of which we hope to foster a more harmonious relationship between center parents and children through nonverbal interaction. Jody Zacharias teaches the group, with Arhilt Buelte and myself acting as consultants. We welcome as our collaborators the parents and children of the Center for Parents and Children, who have begun to participate in our research and training program.

Some of the results of our movement research are incorporated in three chapters (8, 10, 17). Much of what I have described in other chapters, written after 1960, has been inspired by our group discussions. Through the solitary and joint interpretations of profiles I was forced, so to speak, to appraise each developmental phase from a great many points of view (Freud, A., 1965). It was no longer possible to refer to libidinal phases and think only in terms of phase-specific drives. Since 1905, when Freud first introduced the concept of a drive organization, we have come a long way in recognizing that there was a great deal more to a so-called "libidinal phase" than libido alone. To cite only the most important aspects of a phase, we must include: the predominant forms of libido, aggression, their directions and related affects; phase-adequate ego functions, especially coping methods serving adaptation to external reality, defense mechanisms, building of the body-image, and self-representations and ways of relating to objects, be they external or internal; the precursors of the superego or its mature components and forms; harmonies between various functions and conflicts, intersystemic or intrasystemic (Hartmann, 1939). Over and above these intrinsic factors that converge in a specific way to become dominant components and modalities (Erikson, 1950) of a developmental phase, I learned to pay attention to the type of organization that was used preferentially in a given phase.

My conviction that there is a great need to explore the intrinsic unity between soma and psyche led me to formulate suggestions regarding a correlation between hormonal, anatomic, and psychic organizations (Chapters 12, 13, 14, 15, and 16) in childhood and adolescence. The data on which these suggestions were based are in themselves inconclusive. Thus, what has been hypothesized is mainly an attempt to show what kind of correlation could be made on the basis of more reliable data. Newer methods of hormonal assays will make it possible to conduct interdisciplinary, cross-sectional, and longitudinal studies. These should also take into consideration subtle differences in quantities of precursors of adult hormonal mechanisms which, through their special rhythms, trigger off physical and psychic changes in children. The latest findings on hormonal rhythmicity (Chapter 16) have drawn our attention to other rhythmic organizations in adolescence, presented in Chapters 17 and 18.

As pointed out by Greenacre, the data gathered from movement studies and from hormonal literature became meaningful to me within the framework of my primary interest and daily occupation: *The psychoanalysis of adults and children.* The extra-analytic sources helped me to classify organizations in specific developmental phases, which proved to be significant technical guides for the analyses of patients of all ages. I found it especially useful to detect the predominant organization in the behavior of child patients. By formulating my interpretation in keeping with a phase-specific organizational trend, I could enlist the child's cooperation. In states of disequilibrium, I would refrain from making specific interpretations and would point out the confusion which the patient felt. I watched the way in which he would try to reorganize his thinking and responded by describing what he was doing only when he chose a regressive method. I found it very useful to point out to adult patients that they were reacting with aggression to a change in the organization of their child's behavior that presaged his transition into a new developmental phase (Chapter 11). These interventions opened up for me new ways of looking at the development of children and parents under analysis.

My classification of phases arose from analyses of children and adults and from the supplementary studies of movement patterns and hormones. This division had to be presented in a schematic way but was not meant to be rigid. Development proceeds in periods of progression and regression and each phase is interspersed with various trends and counter-trends that are sometimes difficult to classify. As long as there is a prevailing direction that serves the attainment of a developmental task, we can speak of a phase without expecting a day-to-day, minute-to-minute conformity to the task. Movement profiles are especially useful in the appraisal of phases because they show ratios of qualities rather than absolute measures. Thus, we can see the predominance of isolation in latency, but will rely more on a balance between isolation and synthesis as characteristic for this phase (Chapter 10).

When I first heard Benedek speak of "Parenthood as a Developmental Phase" (1959), it brought back to me a whole gamut of observations on parents I have analyzed, mothers in my longitudinal study, mothers and fathers whose children I had analyzed, and the impact parenthood had on my husband and myself. Only then could I begin to link up the antecedents of parenthood with its final fulfillment in adulthood (Chapter 11). I tried to show that, in certain phases, the prevailing organizational trend must be shared by mother and child to allow for developmental changes in both. For instance, the three-year-old who tries to integrate the past with the present invites his mother's participation in this enterprise. As she aids him in this task, she too reintegrates her own past with the present. In examining male parenthood, I have been primarily concerned with the sources of "male maternality" and, thus, have put much more stress on the father's identification with his mother in the preoedipal phase than on his identification with his father in the preoedipal and oedipal phases, (Chapter 2).

We have just begun to be concerned with sources of the adult community spirit in the family group that is composed of father, mother, and several children (Chapter 18). As we encounter mothers who bring two children to our center, we are becoming aware of the role of the parent in the development of cohesive group attitudes instead of unadulterated sibling rivalry. This in turn makes us listen with a new interest to productions of patients who tend to speak about their children or families as a group and of those who speak of one child at a time.

Both my classification of phases and my movement studies, have been subject to controversy. At the same time, they have been accepted and used for instruction and research. An anecdote may illustrate this point. One colleague, who regularly assigns my papers on adolescence to students of psychoanalysis, complimented me on my work and then added: "But I don't like your nomenclature, could you perhaps change the term 'inner-genital' to another? It is so unwieldy." This reminded me of a conversation I had in 1956 with a prominent professional woman and mother whom I queried about the widespread usage of the word *vagina* in explaining to little girls what they had instead of a penis. After a brief period of amazement she realized that parents really meant "vulva" when they said "vagina." They did not really intend to tell the girl what she had inside. On the contrary, the real vagina, whose name has been purloined, has remained nameless, leaving an anonymous gap between the outer genitals and the accepted container of the baby, the uterus. My informant thought for a while and then told me musingly that she could not tell her daughter that she had a vulva because "this was such an ugly word."

Although not spelled out in each chapter, it is evident that I have classified three phases as "inner-genital": (1) the neonatal phase; (2) that which occurs in transition from pregenital interests to phallic dominance; and (3) prepuberty. Hormonal data and the appearance of the genitalia support this classification in the neonatal and prepuberty phases. The material supporting such a nomenclature in the three-year-old is largely based on the analyses and observations of young children and on movement studies (Chapters 2, 5, and 10). Hormonal assays on young children are too unreliable to be used as a positive corroboration or refutation. I have coined the terms for each phase and for the rhythms of tension-changes, predominant in it, in the tradition of naming phases after their primary erotogenic zones. It must be noted, however, that each of the three phases in which "inner genitality" is dominant in childhood share the following characteristics: in each there is a progression from an initial disequilibrium to a new integration, and in each, there is a trend toward externalization of internal tensions and impulses. At first I discovered the neonate's and the three-year-old child's "inner-genital" phase in the girl. Only more detailed observations and analyses of boys and men convinced me that newborn boys had "genital crises" of their own and that in the preoedipal phase both sexes externalized genital impulses on babylike objects. Lastly, both sexes are capable of maternal feelings early in life (Chapter 2). This recognition prompted our research group to rename the rhythm, originally called "feminine," as "inner-genital." The inner genitalia of the men are male structures which should not be confused with female organs. The externalization of impulses arising from male reproductive organs takes on a different form than that arising from their female counterparts. As documented in Chapter 5, these anatomical facts tend to be obscured and terms referring to cryptic genital structures are neither welcomed by parents nor by researchers. For the same reason, it took me fourteen years after I formulated the equation "baby=genital" in 1941 to write about its antecedents in childhood; it took another decade before I could begin to acknowledge the impact of inner-genital tensions on the male child and allow for the "legitimacy" of maternal feelings in men (1975).

Critics of my work sometimes complain that I favor the study of the id over the ego. I have found that the id has been thoroughly forgotten and is hardly ever used in psychoanalytic papers. Instead we have begun to speak of drives. However, once drives are differentiated, they come under the control of the ego. I concur with Gill who says:

> But id and ego are a continuum and not a dichotomy, and the antithesis drive-defense cannot be divided up into major structures but exists at all levels of psychic organization (1963, p. 164; *see also* Kestenberg, 1953).

I have always tried to include all aspects of psychic functioning in the sphere of investigation. This becomes inevitable when one uses psychoanalytic types of assessment. It is true that, in introducing my movement studies, I began by describing rhythms of tension-flow that are the outstanding apparatus available to the id and are only partially controlled by the ego. Once one begins to notate the advanced patterns of effort and shaping, one notes the dependence of these motor patterns on the ego's control over external reality and relationships to objects (Chapters 10 and 17).

Another source of criticism I have encountered is concerned with the validation of movement studies. Sometimes I hear that I am the only one who can notate and interpret the notations of movement patterns. The fact is that every one of the original members of the Movement Study Group can notate and interpret. In addition, there are several students who have taken a course with us and have learned the method. One of them is Penny Bernstein, who used tension-flow notation in the study of mother-child interaction in Pittsburgh. The method must be learned to be practiced. The interpretation of the profile depends greatly on the expertise of a given researcher. Movement profiles speak for themselves, in a language of their own. One can correlate them with a metapsychological assessment for which they are designed. However, one can also compare them with results of a Rorschach test and with clinical appraisals.

Finally, I must stress that only three chapters of this book are devoted to movement studies. All others are concerned with development, as it can be gleaned from psychoanalytic observation and analyses of adults and children. It is not necessary to read the chapters on movement to understand the other chapters. Much of what I have said in those chapters is not new; the way I organized and classified what I have seen is my own. Where Dr. Esther Robbins collaborated with me, we based our views on our respective clinical experiences and we wrote only what we could agree on.

When this book was divided into parts, I asked myself where to include those chapters which dealt with the development of maternal feelings in childhood. Each of the papers I selected for this volume is concerned with development. Even where I singled out for discussion special developmental lines (Freud, A., 1963), such as the development of female sexuality (Chapter 1) or the changes in self- and object-representations (Chapter 9), the theme of parenthood was foremost in my mind. Nevertheless, I concluded that a paper dealing primarily with the development of maternal feelings (Chapter 2) should be included under the heading "development of sexuality," provided we could think of it in its primary and derivative forms. When I discuss phase-specific forms of maternality, from infancy to adulthood, I attempt a metapsychological assessment of this quality without losing sight of the fact that its ultimate origin lies in the reproductive drive (Benedek, 1970a).

The chapters in this book were reprinted as faithfully as possible, but not in chronological order. The slight revisions that were made and the sequence selected were guided by the plan of this particular book. More substantial revisions were necessary where I had changed my opinion since writing the original papers. Thus, in Chapter 1, I have replaced the passage on "activity and passivity," and in Chapters 1 and 2, I have included newer formulations regarding the development of maternal feelings in boys. Because I have written on the same topics from various points of view, a repetition could not be avoided. Where it concerned the introduction of new ideas, I decided to leave similar passages as they were. This made it possible to preserve each chapter as an entity that can be read without preparation. I thought it would be easier to gloss over repetitions than to have to look back for a clarification to a preceding chapter. For that reason my classification of phases is repeated several times and definitions of movement patterns are reiterated in each chapter, dealing with movement. Rather than disrupt the attempted model for a correlation between hormonal and psychic organizations in childhood and adolescence, I left entire passages in Chapters 12, 13, 14, and 15 as they were, and summarized newer data, gathered between 1967 and 1974, in Chapter 16.

I am grateful to the editor of this series, Dr. Robert Langs, for suggesting the reprinting of my papers, for his advice, encouragement, and patience. It is not possible to list all who assisted me including my collaborators in Chapters 8, 16, 17, and 18. Our special thanks go to Dr. Elliot Robbins who helped clarify many issues. I am especially indebted to my friend, Judith Werner, who edited all my papers from 1964 to 1971 (this includes Chapters 5, 9, 11, 13, 14, and 15). Her special gift in understanding psychoanalysis as well as movement studies and her ability to shorten, rewrite, and correct made it possible for me to formulate material which was difficult to express in words. Chapter 8 has been edited by my friend Jo Jordan, a psychotherapist and a poet of unusual sensitivity. From Judith and Jo I learned to write without help, but I have never been able to conquer my tendency to include three thoughts in one sentence, long enough to fill half a page. I am grateful for the help in editing given to me by Mrs. Janelle Lysenko, Mrs. Jan Blakeslee,[4] and many others. However, where the sentences have remained too long and thoughts too condensed, it is due entirely to my own short-coming. Sylvia Weinblum not only typed large sections of this manu-script but also collated the extensive bibliography, sometimes working long hours to meet a dead line. Lisa Dryman also typed and collated some of the material for this book and Alex Pushkin indefatigably pho-tostated pages and put them in order.

JUDITH KESTENBERG

Preface to the Second Printing

The papers comprising this book, those revised and reprinted in 1975 and those published here originally (Chapters 6, 10, 16, 17 and 18), do not need to be revised. (An exception are hormonal studies, updated in Chapter 16 and once more in a new paper on preadolescence, the second inner genital phase in development [1980d]. The third inner genital phase occurs during pregnancy [1976b] and is expanded into the rest of human generavity [1979b].) They are still the basic studies on which my developmental theories and my clinical practice of psychoanalysis and prevention are built. Most of my new work since 1975 constitutes a continuation of these studies.

In the area of female sexuality, I have given further thought to feminine integration (1976b) and have successively turned my attention to the amalgamation of the two (1976) and then three *"Face of Femininity"* (1980b). These are the maternal, the determined and the sensual "faces of woman which emerge in the early genital phases (the maternal, inner-genital, preoedipal; the phallic, negative-oedipal; and the phallic positive-oedipal). Their successive integration and differentiation within a given culture are the subject of my ongoing work.

Revisions of the concepts of activity and passivity in Chapter 1 led us to suggest to Warren Lamb that he report on the differences between mens' and womens' movement. This enabled us to distinguish between a hypothetical monosex (the macho-man and its female counterpart) and the average bisexual man and woman in our culture (1979a).

[4]Mrs. Lysenko is the mother of five children. When in 1973-74 she and her two youngest babies attended the center, she was engaged in research for her M.A. on early childhood education. She enlisted several mothers to establish interobserver reliability for a temperament scale which is a part of a clinical assessment, devised as a clinical method for the validation of the movement profile. In this connection she read and corrected chapter 10. Her work is an example of our endeavour to provide opportunities for mothers to pursue their interests without having to separate from their young children.

Revisions in Chapter 2 arose within the context of our new understanding of the development of male sexuality and its influence on the epigenesis of parenthood (1979b), 1980a, 1981). A paper devoted entirely to a description of the inner-genital phase in girls is now in press (1980c). A similar paper on the male inner genital phase is not yet written.

Working as analyst and movement observer, I have become impressed with the relevance infant-observation and infant-therapy to adult psychotherapy (1977a, b, c; 1978d; 1979c). A study of the Rat-Man's movement patterns and of Freud's influence on his adaptation helped me to reconstruct the Rat Man's early development and to extract from Freud's technique at the time the ingredients of today's therapeutic alliance, based as it is on the analyst's constancy in space, gravity and time (1979d). In a related project, the expansion of our understanding of the influence of the early "holding environment" (1878a and b), prompted the study of the origins of work and to a distinction between work and play in the earliest phases of human development (1980a).

Our attempts to introduce music, dance and visual art to infants and toddlers led us to a tentative formulation of the role of artistic expression in the child's creation of objects (1979f), a theme suggested, but not developed in Chapters 9 and 10. The study of id, ego and superego functions through the medium of movement (Chapters 6, 8, 10 and 17) continued as longitudinal studies made successive movement profiles accessible to interpretation. This was expanded in the second volume of my "Movement Studies in Development" which contains a glossary of movement terms and a detailed account of a multitude of conflicts, intra- and intersystemic, vertical and horizontal (as expressed through clashing of movement patterns). The difference between gestures and postures, defined in Chapter 17 is taken up in detail and its role in the interpretation of adult movement profiles specified (1979c).

A number of projects originated in Child Development Research was partially financed by the royalties from this book (1976a, 1977d, 1977e, 1978c, d, e). An ongoing "Father Project" is headed by Dr. Hershey Marcus and staffed by Mark Sossin, Richard Stevenson and Susan Tross (1980c, 1981). We now provide an internship program for expressive art therapists, under the guidance of Susan Loman. We continue to enlist parents' participation in research. Among those who practice the integration of research and maternal child care are Elaine Schenee, Joan Weinstein, Bayla Silbert, Dr. Gazala Javaid and Dr. Carmel Foley (1978-1979).

My renewed thanks to the inspiring editor of this series, Dr. Robert Langs and to his wife Joan who is now president of CDR. I am also grateful to the trustees and directors of CDR, to the parents and children who work with us, to the staff, and volunteers without whom our work would not be possible.

PART ONE

Development of Sexuality

CHAPTER 1

Vicissitudes of Female Sexuality

The divergent psychoanalytic theories of feminine sexuality center upon the disputed question of early vaginal sensations. Freud (1932-36) consistently maintained that the vagina is discovered at puberty and true femininity accepted only then. A number of other authors—among them Brierley (1932; 1936), Greenacre (1950), Horney (1926; 1933), Jacobson (1937), Jones (1927), Klein (1932; 1948), Lorand (1939), Muller (1932), Payne (1935)—modified this view, some finding a good deal of evidence for the occurrence of vaginal sensations in early childhood. In a later paper Freud (1938) expressed pessimism concerning the resolution of penis envy in women and of feminine wishes in men. This opinion seems primarily based on Freud's respect for constitutional and anatomic differences. The question why femininity is difficult to accept may have its ultimate answer in constitutional hormonal differences. The anatomy of organs representing femininity, however, undoubtedly shapes the vicissitudes of feminine sexual development.

This chapter is devoted to a reconstruction of feminine genital development on the basis of direct observation of children as well as on analyses of adults and children. An attempt is made to unify and reconcile the seemingly divergent theories of the role of the vagina in early development. Mechanisms leading to the rejection of the vagina and enhancing penis envy as well as ways and means of early preparations for the

First published in the *Journal of the American Psychoanalytic Association* 4 (1956), 453–75, and revised for publication here. Reproduced by permission.

feminine role are traced back to childhood. The outcome of these early struggles appears to depend on the ability to accept and use one's own bisexuality without fear and guilt. This presupposes the full acceptance of the total genital region and the assuming of responsibility for sensations and urges arising in this region.

Before attempting to explore the influence of vaginal sensations upon feminine development, it is necessary to examine the problem of activity and passivity, which is inextricably connected with the question of femininity. More specifically, before we can explore sensations stemming from an organ, we need to define what is meant by activity or passivity of that organ.

The Activity-Passivity Problem[1]

Freud (1932) pointed out that, despite their intrinsic association, passivity cannot be fully identified with femininity. He singled out maternal behavior as an example of feminine activity. Most of the discussion below is centered on the activity of the vagina as an organ. Therefore, one needs to clarify the concept of activity versus passivity of an organ. When is an organ active or used actively? When is it passive or used passively?

Webster's International Dictionary (1955) defines activity as "Any process which an organism carries on or participates in by virtue of being alive, as digesting, moving, thinking, desiring" (p. 27). In some of the examples listed, one can recognize the existence of a rhythmic alternation between the active and passive componets of an ongoing process.[2] For instance, active swallowing is followed by the passive passage of food through the digestive canal; all movement alternates active and passive motion factors. Successively or simultaneously the organism acts upon the environment and the environment acts upon the organism. Thus, when we speak of activity in general, we do not really make a distinction between active and passive trends, but subsume under this generic term a process of variation which includes both. When we speak of "activity" specifically we imply that acting upon predominates over being acted upon. The reverse is true of "passivity." For instance, the intrusive phallus is the foremost symbol of active masculinity, but the passivity with which it fills with blood to become erect is understood but not stressed. The receptive vagina is a foremost symbol of passive femininity, but the fact that it actively encloses and holds the penis is acknowledged but not emphasized.

Movement observation teaches us that activity and passivity are not opposites but rather polarities (Kestenberg & Marcus, 1973). The opposite of activity is inactivity and the opposite of passivity is impassivity. The term "inactive" is sometimes used in lieu of saying "not discernibly active"; used in its literal meaning it implies a state of inertia, close to death. The term "impassive" is sometimes used to connote "insensibility"; used in its literal meaning it suggests a lack of emotion due to inanimateness (Webster's, 1955. p. 1247).

Applying these formulations to Freud's instinct theory, we can correlate inactivity and/or impassivity with a waning drive tension. Once drives gain sufficient impetus, their active and passive aims need not be mutually exclusive. There may be evidence of two drive components, operating simultaneously with two divergent aims, or of a temporal change in aims within the operational realm of one drive only. Within this general framework, we can concede that active aims are more compatible with male forms of functioning and passive aims with female modes. At the same time, we can also accept Freud's repeated correlation between activity, aggression, and maleness. To be consistent, we should go a step further and assume a correlation, not only between passivity and femininity, but also between these qualities and libido. No doubt, intrusive aims require the activation of more aggression than receptive aims. The latter are more clearly associated with general libidinal aims than the former. Bearing these differences in mind, we can say that the rhythmic interplay, between intrusion and withdrawal in the male and between receiving and letting go in the female, encompasses various degrees of activity and passivity which harmonize to achieve a successful union between man and woman.

Through the studies of Kinsey et al. (1953) and Masters and Johnson (1966) and from patients' reports, we have come to recognize how responses from different parts of the genitals become integrated in successive phases of the sexual cycle. In addition to the individual integration of responses, there is a biological fit between the activity and passivity patterns of the male and female. For instance, the upper part of the vagina dilates and moves in an almost imperceptible way, allowing a transudate to infiltrate the vagina, which acts as a homologue to man's erection. The lower portion of the vagina adjusts its size and the level of tension to fit the activity of the intruding penis. It opens to receive and holds to give support. During orgasm, the lower portion of the vagina as well as the uterus assume a more active role, abruptly increasing and lowering the intensity of tension, in synchrony with the male's contractions. The decongestion of female genitalia and the reduction of the size of the upper part of the vagina proceed at a much more gradual pace than the corresponding processes in the male. As a result, there is a more prolonged period of passivity in the resolution of the female cycle than in that of the male.

The model used for the discussion of activity and passivity has been largely derived from adult sexual functioning, at a time when a satisfactory sex partner is already available. In mammals, the male is more active in seeking an object and the female is more prone to submit to the wooing. However, she too may be active as a seductress and latently active as a receiver and incorporator of the penis. The normal adult woman accepts the sequences and cycles of activity and passivity and integrates them in such a way that passivity becomes the prime but not the only organizer of her experiences. When she is unable to find satisfaction and her tension mounts to great heights, she begins to experience passivity as a burden, and sometimes even as pain. She interprets the increasing lubrication, congestion, radiation of heat, and waves of pulsation from within, as if they were imposed upon her against her will. When she is sexually excited, she becomes aware of identifiable representations of her inside and outside that help organize her behavior in a way appropriate to her gender. She becomes intensely aware of her wish to be penetrated. When her excitement subsides, her genitalia lose their cathexis. Returning to what might be called a neutral state, they may temporarily lose their psychic representation. In contrast, there is a continuity of psychic representation of the phallus even though sexual excitement has abated and the nature of the sensations has changed.

During the development of sexual functioning from childhood to adulthood, one or another part of the female genital becomes dominant. Before dominance can be achieved, different genital regions may vie with one another. Various types of sensations and various sources of their localization, overlap, come and go, and only rarely can the vagina gain a permanent representation as an organ before a solid integration of all component parts of the genitals is accomplished in adulthood (Brierley, 1936).

From the psychoanalytic point of view, organ activity and passivity presuppose aggressive and libidinal organ-cathexis, respectively. Activity of the organ enhances its localization and sharpens its boundaries, thus creating a foundation for its representation in conjunction with a passive object. An organ, experienced passively, that is, primarily experienced as acted upon, gains a representation in which the active object plays a prominent part. Active and passive experiences combine to leave permanent imprints on organ-, object-, and self-representations (see Chapter 9). However, a preponderance of passive components in the tension variations of an organ detracts from a clear formation of its boundaries until

6

an active object delineates them. The question arises whether the vagina gains a clear representation before a repeated experience of coitus. Does the child's vagina receive any representation at all? A great many internal organs function continuously without attaining a place in the body image. Is the vagina one of them before menarche gives the girl proof of its existence as a purveyor of blood from the uterus to the outside? Is the sexual tension arising from the vagina only a rare and exceptional occurrence in childhood? Or is the vagina, as all other organs opening to the outside, activated since birth, becoming absorbed into the body schema in the process of ego development? Does it finally reach the status of an ego-syntonic, central part of the body, cathected at times and uncathected at other times?

Because it connotes low tension, relaxation[3] is generally used as a model for passivity. Contraction of muscles with its concomitant innervation and vascularization serves as a model for activity. The only activity recognized by children as true activity is visible and movement-producing. A moving object seems active and alive while a stationary one appears inanimate and dead. Therefore, invisible activity, such as contractions of perineal and laminal muscles, is recognized as such only by the individual who feels the contraction and knows that he is instrumental in producing it. Still the lack of visual confirmation detracts from its activity value. Muscle tension and all innervation that does not lead to movement is experienced in various, not clearly defined ways as swelling, pulling, jitteriness, a funny feeling, heat or pain. The activity of the organ may not be recognized. From the viewpoint of the ego, the experience is a passive one, as if something were inflicted upon the person by an alien force. The tension of one's own muscles, produced voluntarily in an experiment, is often interpreted as "being pulled or being hurt." In dreams, such an activity is often assigned to animals, worms and snakes, roaming inside the sleeper. Nunberg (1947, 1949) calls an activity caused by tension and resulting in rigid immobility an "inner activity" in contradistinction to genuine passivity.

Inner activity of an organ creates an urge for relaxation which is experienced as a need to shake off the aggressor. When discharge is not forthcoming, the impulse to move visibly increases, as latent activity rarely is followed by complete relaxation. Yearning for the passive experience concomitant with the abating of contraction, decrease of blood supply and release of innervation mounts with growing awareness of one's own inability to discharge tension.

Such seems to be the feeling arising from latent vaginal activity, prior to acceptance of the vagina as an organ, a part of one's own body: a sensation of something being inflicted upon oneself, an inability to dis-

7

charge tension (identified with an aggressor) and a yearning for relaxation (identified with passive dependence). A swelling of the mucous membranes, a muscle contraction or both create a persistent need for release. This need stimulates various activities to accomplish discharge. As a last resort, passive dependence on someone else's visible activity is accepted as the only effective means of relaxation. At that point, the ego can shift all its available resources toward the wooing of another person who might, by manifest activity, gratify the urgent need. The ego gives up its prerogative of mastery over the body, and contents itself with the feeling of mastery over people who can provide satisfaction and thus effect relaxation.

Analysis of children reveals that they do not have an awareness of the vagina as an organ yet, but they do react to sexual tensions arising in the vagina with a great need for discharge and relaxation, without being able to point to the source of the tension. Latent activity of the vagina seems to permeate the personality of the growing girl. Yearning for passivity dominates her, but true passivity is only attained with the experience of relaxation of genital tension in adulthood.

What are then the ways and means that the young girl employs to cope with vaginal excitations?

The Neonate

In many newborns, either the inner or the outer labia or the clitoris are engorged; the vagina may be crimson or covered with a whitish layer. It is generally thought that this genital crisis of the newborn is produced by flooding with maternal hormones, which are gradually discharged in the urine of the infant (Pratt, 1954; Talbot *et al.*, 1952). Only in some instances does the genital engorgement lead to premature genital activity of the young infant.

In one case where the post-partum swelling of the genital was quite pronounced, the infant started masturbation by means of thigh pressure at the age of about six weeks (Kestenberg, 1945). She accompanied the activity by grunts, giving the impression of almost reaching an orgasm. She was constipated early. Her mother tried to relieve "the gas which gave the baby a belly ache" by raising the child's legs. It was the theory of the mother that the child's masturbation was initiated by this action. The question remains open as to whether the abdominal distress was due to constipation or to a combination of vaginal and rectal stimulations. Was the constipation already an early response to vaginal stimulation? Was pressure of the full rectum used to obtain vaginal release, as seen in older children?

In the neonate, tensions arising from the genitals may cause distress and shock reactions. They easily overflow onto other regions (Greenacre, 1950b). The observer may be able to tell whether the baby's abdominal distress has been alleviated by sucking, pressure on the abdomen, raising of legs, or urination. However, he cannot detect a specific source of excitation unless he is cognizant of rhythms of tension-discharge that are optimal for specific sources of tension (Kestenberg, 1965, 1967 a; Chapters 8 and 9). Many neonates become red in their face as they strain to defecate; they have very clear anal patterns from the start. Others, or the same infants at other times, indicate their urination by shuddering. Not only oral, anal and urethral discharge forms can be noted in the neonate, but one can also identify phallic-clitoric as well as inner-genital modes of tension reduction. The latter are quite frequent in the first days of life when the maternal hormones are still very high, as they have not been sufficiently excreted. No doubt, infants like the one described above do use many genital discharge forms which may even subordinate others and thus, distort subsequent developmental phases. However, early genital excitations usually spread upward and become modified, merging with the prevailing oral rhythms of the suckling. When a child in the first six weeks of life is not unduly burdened by non-oral endogenous or exogenous demands, frequent feedings help him shift his attention to the mouth and subordinate various stimulations to the dominant oral gratification. One can sometimes see how inner-genital (feminine) rhythms of the nursing mother, spreading upward from the pelvic region to the upper part of her body, become modified when they merge with the oral rhythms of her suckling (Buelte and Kestenberg, 1971). For the infant, this may well be the external model for the displacement of genital tensions upward.

The Oral Stage of Development

We assume that oral libidinous zones dominate the first year of life. Other libidinous zones are absorbed by orality at that time, and sensations stemming from them are treated as if they were oral. We can therefore surmise that vaginal tensions of moderate degree, which exist in early infancy, combine with other tensions to produce frustration. This in turn may enhance the increase of mechanisms available for consolation at the oral stage, such as sucking. Analysis of late thumb suckers reveals that the sucking urge appears as a response to every type of

9

frustration. Frequently, in the repressed fantasies accompanying the sucking, mouth and vagina, thumb and penis are equated. The fantasies merely give ideational content to an earlier shift of focus from pelvic tension to the oral zone. Early frustrations are mastered more readily via the oral zone, as the mouth-head-eyes-hand syndrome is the first resource available to the ego for the purpose of regulating tensions in an organized pattern (Hoffer, 1949, 1950).

From the viewpoint of function, the mouth goes through various vicissitudes during which it serves as a sucking, apprehensive and exploratory organ and last but not least, the mouth becomes a model for an opening and closing device. The ability to open or close the mouth at volition establishes permanent boundaries between oneself and the outside. Such oral experiences are used by analogy in the body-image formation of other openings. As each opening landmarks the boundaries of the body, it successively influences the image of the next opening that the infant surveyor stakes out. The mouth, however, as the model opening, becomes the symbol of all "holes" of the body (Spitz, 1955). Thus the vaginal opening becomes endowed with oral representations stemming from a direct equation with the mouth as well as from an indirect one, which emerges from oral admixtures incorporated in the image of other openings with which the introitus is successively equated.

Early sensations stemming from body cavities are almost invariably externalized upon the openings of the body. Throughout life the opening remains the symbol of the cavity to which it provides access (Schilder, 1935). The confusion resulting from this penetrates our language to the point that indentations, cavities and openings are expressed by the common word "hole." This language confusion contributes in great measure to the child's difficulty in understanding his own body.

By the time the child reaches the second half of his first year, he has begun to explore and detect the lower part of his body. The boy frequently not only discovers his penis by then, but is also aware of the pleasant sensation its handling can evoke (Kleeman, 1965). Girls seem to discover their external genital later, simply because of its lesser accessibility to manual exploration. Early and current sensations lay the foundation for the development of the organ concept of the external genital. But it is only the visual experience (compare the excellent description of the discovery of the penis by Lowenstein (1950) which makes it possible for the child to accept the organ as his own. It is the visual experience that supplies the feeling of belonging and organ constancy. Other sensations come and go, but only the ability to see the organ at volition at all times supplies the feeling of permanent togetherness with the whole body. Only later, tactile manipulation by the entire surface of the hand

10

can substitute for the visual experience of perceiving the organ as a whole. It is extremely rare that the girl can attain the organ constancy of her external genital in the first or even the second year of life as the boy can. As he begins to stand and to walk, the boy can further fixate the image of the penis by observation and mastery of its function. The girl, at the same age, has only a vague, unclear idea that the urine comes from below as the feces do. The cloacal concept of the genitals pervades the girl's anal stage of development.

The Anal Stage of Development

It is a frequent observation that girls are toilet trained earlier and speak earlier than boys. While the boy is still busy experimenting with his body and getting an intimate knowledge of it, the girl, frustrated in her efforts to master bodily sensations of the lower part of the body, is already more dependent on the mother than the boy and therefore more in need of communication and obedience. Thus she develops ego resources of a higher level early, without the secure foundation of clear, fixed body boundaries on which the boy is still working. But, for her too, as for the boy, what comes out of the bodily openings gives evidence of the size and shape of the bodily cavities. Both boys and girls experiment with concave and convex objects; the control over opening of cabinets, boxes, etc., is practiced and creates the intellectual foundation for future understanding of one's own complex of cavities. By that time the girl has explored her external genital, but has not discovered the vagina or even the opening of the vagina. She often interprets the introitus as one of the many indentations of her external genital. Vaginal sensations are merged with rectal sensations and experienced as one. Exploration and experimentation with feces and sphincter control provide a clue to what is happening in the mysterious abdominal cavity. It seems that vaginal stimulations are intensified now by the cathexis of the cloacal sphere. Retention of feces and of urine can already serve for stimulation or alleviation of the sensation of inner swelling which seems to stem from the vagina. The theory of anal delivery, which alternates with the theory of bursting open and delivering the baby through the navel, is based on the imprints of early shifts from and to genital and anal organs. The pressure of feces can be eventually mastered by voluntary release of the sphincter contraction and by a contraction of the abdominal muscles. The additional feeling of fullness which is produced by vaginal swellings gives rise to the helpless feeling of ballooning out, bursting and being torn to pieces without hope of help. This derivation is frequently ob-

11

scured by a condensation of rectal, bladder and vaginal fullness under the dominance of prevailing anal libido.

The temper tantrums of this period may evidence a stubborn protest against giving up of the feces. At last the child has become master of his own body by the achievement of sphincter control. Before he can properly enjoy the newfound freedom of retaining or releasing at will, his mother steps in and tells the child when and where to do it. The mother thus becomes the symbolic successor of abdominal pressures which had been overwhelming to the ego and were experienced as attacks from the inside of one's own body before sphincter control mastered the attacker. The anal-sadistic fight with the mother is the prototype of the fight for independence which was foreshadowed by the determination of the young infant to eat what he wants, how much he wants, and when he wants it.

The anal struggle can be resolved satisfactorily by way of trade. The boy gives up part of his anal independence for the now won freedom of the penis. He begins to urinate standing up, holding his penis, and is able to cathect this organ as his own with the approval of his mother. Depending on external circumstances, at the end of the anal period, the girl may have already developed a pregenital form of penis envy which may cast its shadow upon the next stage she enters before she can reach the phallic phase[4] (Galeuson and Roiphe, 1971).

The Early Maternal[5] Stage of Development

In the process of experimentation, the two-to-three-year-old seems to have gotten a hazy idea of inside pressure unrelieved by anal or urethral maneuvers. This unrelieved pressure is now identified with a baby inside. Thus the baby-genital equation receives its foundation. The inside of the body is inaccessible to visual and tactile explorations, but the product of this inside can be handled and scrutinized in substitution for the yearned-for handling of the inside. Vaginal tension is often experienced as an attack from the inside. Turning from passivity to activity, the girl projects her wish to counterattack upon the baby-doll, on whom mastery can be achieved. Thus, some degree of illusory control over the vagina is practiced by the indirect route of domination of the baby.

Maternal behavior is based on identification with the mother (Freud, 1932; Mack Brunswick, 1940). Children of both sexes play the role of the all-powerful, preoedipal maternal figure, reducing the real mother in fantasy to the status of a helpless baby. The boy too develops parental feelings and wants to play with dolls. It is also true that he has been discouraged from such play while the girl has been invited by her own mother and other caretakers to play with her "baby." However, the most powerful source of the girl's maternal interest is the externalization of vaginal impulses upon the baby,[6] and the equation of the inside of the body with the baby (Klein, 1932). The oral concept of the vagina as devouring, biting, and spitting is succeeded by its anal image (retaining, expelling, tossing away, pressing, torn into pieces, dirty, and bad-smelling). But the now-developing "baby concept" of the vagina makes it a precious organ: "smooth like the baby's skin, crying out for satisfaction and falling asleep when satiated." The baby-doll, which can be carried everywhere and can be held close to the body during sleep, substitutes for the lack of organ entity and organ constancy inherent in early vaginal tensions. As an expression of her fear of genital injury, the girl worries whether she will be able to keep her baby safe and wholesome. Precursors of these worries can be already seen in the second year of life.

I have been able to observe the play of a fourteen-month-old who has been encouraged by her mother to play with dolls for several months. She was fretful and upset, trying to cover the face of a little brown doll with a blanket and never satisfied with the result. Her mother would cover the doll for her and the child would remove the cover impatiently and try again to cover the doll's face which would again produce only discomfort. When, at my request, her mother handed the child a white doll, the child became tremendously relieved and had no further preoccupation with the blanket. After some time I gave her a little blanket. She took it very quickly, proceeded to the doll carriage, removed the dark doll and her blanket. She placed the white doll in the carriage, covered it with the new blanket and handed the dark doll and its blanket to her mother as if to say: "You can have that baby." The worry about the doll's color and its presentation to the mother implied anal concerns (as suggested to me by B. Bornstein, 1956).

Pregenital types of worries merge with and reinforce the three-year-old-girl's preoccupation with the welfare of her "child." Such early worries are repeated in adulthood, during pregnancy and actual motherhood. From the fantasies of women, one can sometimes reconstruct their origin from the prephallic period, a time in which doubts about the reality of the baby alternate with complete assurance that the baby-doll is alive, perfect, and a real baby.

The prephallic maternal phase seems to correspond in time with the passive prephallic stage described by H. Deutsch (1925 b). The girl at that time is passive as compared with her activity during the later phallic phase. However, she is active inasmuch as she acts out the part of a busy, active mother, and she does in effect look like a miniature mother. She takes possessive pride in her doll. Where a doll may not be readily available, another toy or a younger sibling may substitute for it. The mother herself is often required to play the role of a baby. The relationship to the doll is symbiotic. A constant companion, it almost seems to be part of the child. While the treatment of the doll is greatly influenced by the girl's identification with the real mother, it always shows traces of a sadistic type of mastery, which illustrates the girl's relationship both to her mother and to her own body. The sadistic component of mothering is especially pronounced in the latter part of this phase, at about three and a half to four. At first, the affectionate solicitude represents dramatically the way in which the child herself would like to be treated. When frustration and dissatisfaction increase, the doll is often subjected to cruel mistreatment. It is punished severely when the girl displaces her hateful feelings toward the mother onto it. But the doll is also chastised for the girl's own hateful qualities, such as oral greed and anal stubbornness. Foremost, however, loom the qualities of nagging and argumentativeness with the doll, dramatizing the feelings produced by unsatisfied vaginal urges (see Chapter 4). We recognize derivations of these sado-masochistic impulses in the much later fantasy of a powerful master driving the girl to continuous sexual acts without hope for deliverance. At this time these urges are only dimly perceived heirs of earlier discomforts, for which the girl blamed her mother. Past and present merge in current play. The little girl acts the exasperated, harassed mother who is being attacked by the bad demandingness of the child-doll (equating mother = the girl herself = vagina = doll). But she also loves her doll and wants to gratify the doll's wishes with a fullness which only the magic of play can provide. But the child-doll seems never satisfied and makes her poor "mother" suffer. This scene is subject to abrupt changes, as if the child and mother suddenly would change places. The doll becomes the victim and the girl-mother the persecutor. The obedient and dainty little girl transforms herself into a "monster-victim unit" in her doll play. However, she is inseparable from her doll not only for the purpose of perpetuating the persecution-victim drama, but also because she is fond of it and keenly aware of its helplessness without "mommy." During the play it is evident that the child has little awareness of the unreality value of the transactions.

The doll is frequently brought in contact with the genitals and held there as if it were part of them. Masturbation on the doll externalizes the vagina and makes it accessible to unification with the outer genital. It is important to note that the doll of this stage is most frequently a girl doll. The image of a small baby girl or a girl doll appears later in dreams as a symbol of the vagina. The doll is an object on which the girl child can achieve the feeling of organ belonging, organ constancy and of mastery over it that she can later transfer back to the vagina, once she has discovered its existence. At this stage there may already be a foreboding of the future vagina image, but certainly not a firsthand knowledge of it. Klein (1932), who assumes phylogenetically determined congenital knowledge of the vagina, may be referring to such early vaginal forebodings. Because of their vagueness and because of the continuous shift of boundaries associated with tumescence and detumescence of the vaginal walls, such forebodings cannot lead to the awareness of the vagina as an organ. The closest one could come to a formulation of this prestage of vaginal feelings may be as follows: an inside fullness, a feeling of emptiness, a desire to be filled.[7] Fantasies of older patients that seem to belong to this stage of development range from ideas of having nothing at all inside or being nothing themselves to the opposite feeling of intolerable fullness and of inner swelling to the bursting point. Such verbalizations seem to correspond to thickening and shrinking of the vaginal wall respectively. Occasionally a wavelike excitement, symbolized by the image of a snake or a worm crawling inside, appears to belong to this period, although from the theoretical point of view, one would assume that it is associated with vaginal tensions occurring in the phallic stage.[8] The pressure for discharge is sometimes described as incessant nagging, at other times as a fear of being torn to pieces by an avalanche of simultaneous demands. Retention of urine and feces may be used to "squeeze" the vagina out and to reduce it to nothing. These methods are doomed to failure as they often increase the vaginal stimulation instead of reducing it.

While there is still considerable confusion between all sensations stemming from the inside of the body, there seems to be already a differentiation between pressures which are relieved by a discharge of contents and those which disappear only when a swelling abates. This differentiation is sometimes expressed when vaginal excitations are transferred to the nose. On the nose, expriments with swelling, shrinkage and dryness of mucous membranes can be performed. With increased vaginal excitement, psychosomatic symptoms of that kind are likely to appear because neither the handling of the doll nor the retention of feces and urine can be satisfactorily released. The early maternal stage, however, ends with disappointment, no matter what methods are employed to gain vaginal release. In this respect this stage shows certain similarities with late latency and prepuberty. In both stages a number of divergent methods are used to obtain release, while all the time the little girl gives a ladylike

15

appearance on the surface. Yet all efforts end with disappointment, and in the end distress breaks through the façade of polite poise.

The doll play loses its reality value as the little girl discovers that the doll is not a live baby. From the physical point of view, frustration persists, as no relief of vaginal tensions is forthcoming. Once again the little girl is angry at her mother and disappointed in her. At the same time, she doubts her own ability to become a mother, which results in permanent decrease in self-esteem. The little girl becomes genuinely depressed. The net gain for the ego, however, is the increased ability to test reality. The play with dolls, if continued, takes on the characteristics of real play in contrast to the earlier make-believe games which were more comparable to acting out of an adult than to a child's play.

A three-year-old, inseparable from her two baby dolls, lost interest in one of the dolls completely after the doll's head came off. Even though the head was put back, this doll was spoiled for the child. Soon afterward she disfigured the face of her second doll by painting it. She refused every offer to restore the doll's face in the doll clinic and renounced all doll play for several years. In both instances, the dolls lost the appearance of real babies and became lifeless, inanimate objects, not worthy of attention. While some elements of penis envy and disappointment in her own castration played a role in the child's distress, the main factor was a depression over the loss of her illusory babies.

At times the early maternal stage ends dramatically with the "death of the baby," more frequently the inanimate quality of the doll is recognized in a gradual process. Later fears connected with pregnancy, delivery and child care draw from this stage in which the ego makes the transition from psychic to objective reality. Fears that either the child or the mother will die during delivery, or that one of them will be injured, fears of delivering a monster, of having the baby exchanged in the hospital, kidnapped, lost or attacked, repeat the early shock of the loss of the baby-doll. Inasmuch as the baby represents the girl's own inside genital, such fears are also castration fears. Because of the equation baby = mother, the death of the girl's own mother is anticipated with the delivery of the baby. An intense fear that the baby will be only an inanimate doll again makes a mother experience a tremendous feeling of relief and elation at the sight of her newborn moving and breathing. For the little girl, the discovery of the lifelessness of the doll often means that the doll, previously alive, is now dead simply by virtue of her discovery. Self-accusations of having injured and killed the baby alternate with accusations of the mother. The child feels defeated by the mother, who, like the witch in Hansel and Gretel, only fattened up the illusions about the baby-doll in order to kill her. Suspicion that the doll was never alive creates an even greater distrust of the mother who frequently had encouraged the child in the belief that the doll was a baby. This early mourning for the dead baby is reevoked in a mild way during menstruations, which psychologically represent the death of the unborn child. The irritability and increased sensitivity of the premenstrual period paves the way for projection of guilt upon others. Most of these conflicts have a double representation as they are reexperienced in the phallic phase directly in relation to the external genitals. The shift from the inside out in the phallic stage externalizes vaginal tensions again, but this time concentrates them on the clitoris. As is well known, the phallic phase ends in the renewal of the wish for a baby, who now is the successor of a desired penis.

The Phallic Phase of Development

The maternal stage ends with a temporary renunciation of the baby. Guilt is not only projected upon the mother but also upon men, especially upon the father. If penis envy has occurred early, the little girl will not go through a very active clitoris masturbation but may start the phallic period with a projection of all her genital feelings upon the penis of the man. The fantasy of an illusory penis may start immediately after the renouncing of the baby. Such a fantasy frequently results in the belief of a hidden penis inside the body (Jacobson, 1936). A similar effect is produced by very early prohibitions that deter the child from focusing upon her clitoris. More frequently the girl, disappointed in her mother, becomes rebellious, disobedient and tries to find direct genital release despite her mother. She turns to her own genital and begins to explore it actively.

The little girl's masturbation now changes from gingerly genital touch to a violent, impatient handling of her external genital region. The depression ending the maternal stage is lifted by an onslaught of aggression which brings about a weakening or resolution of earlier reaction formations against aggression and dirt. The good little girl feels cheated by her mother and no longer expects that good behavior will bring a reward. She identifies with the image of an aggressive, frustrating mother who wants all the babies and gratification for herself. The little girl yearns for the power to give or withhold from her mother in turn.

During the repeated explorations of the genital region, the introitus

17

is frequently discovered and identified with the injured baby. The tearing of the introitus in the final stage of delivery and the earlier tearing of the hymen seem to represent the just punishment for the injury to the baby as well as a repetition of this injury on the basis of the equation baby = genital. When the girl discovers her introitus, she is convinced of her own injury, as she considers it to be a self-inflicted tear. This frequently coincides with the deanimation of the doll (Chapter 5). Denial of the introitus, which now ensues, of necessity leads to the future denial of the not yet discovered vagina. A further defense reinforces this denial as the girl isolates the introitus from the rest of the external genital. The urethro-clitoric region is now overcathected to uphold the withdrawal of cathexis from the introitus. Experimentation with urine retention and irritation of the urethra are preferred regressive activities. The swelling and the detumescence of the clitoris as well as urethral sensations substitute for similar vaginal sensations. The urethra is particularly suitable for this substitution, as in adulthood it undergoes the same epithelial changes as the vagina does with hormone fluctuations. Yet satisfaction is not attained and penis envy increases in proportion to the amount of frustration experienced now. The smallness and inadequacy of the clitoris is blamed for lack of satisfaction, and a great desire to possess a penis draws not only from present but also from past frustrations.

With the onset of the negative oedipus complex, the father, who until now was looked upon as if he were an older sibling preferred by the mother, becomes transformed in the child's mind into a most powerful, godlike figure, the only one who can satisfy the mother. Insight into the fact that the mother does not possess a penis either reconciles the little girl with her mother. She forgives her for past injuries and pities her. She competes with her father and would like to have his penis to satisfy her poor mother. In an upsurge of generosity, she wants now to give her mother all the babies that she herself had wanted so badly before. This type of identification is based on similarity. It seems to be the least ambivalent of all the identifications with the mother.

"We mistreated women" is a slogan born at that time. Fantasies of growing a penis outside alternate with despair over having nothing at all. Unverifiable consolations about the existence of an inner hidden penis are connected with wishes to incorporate the father's penis, which in turn lead to fears of retaliation by the castrated father. But this "inner penis" fantasy also represents a useful step in the development toward femininity, as it cathects the inside of the body and paves the way for the future acceptance of the vagina.[9] The fear of punishment, however, prevails and the girl eventually "evicts" her inner feelings (symbolized at this time by the "inner penis") and projects them on a wholesale basis upon the man's penis. In this process, guilt is projected upon men too and the little girl can feel free of her guilt-producing "inside."

The Projection Phase of the Phallic Girl

Making a virtue out of a shortcoming, the little girl who has "nothing" with which to satisfy herself and her mother pretends to have nothing at all that might crave her satisfaction. The image of the innocent little girl, who must submit to brutal male urges without any pleasures of her own, reawakens earlier masochistic fantasies of being tortured, this time as a slave of men. All genital urges by which the girl had felt enslaved, can now be represented by the cruel enslaving master. The argumentativeness, acted out earlier in the doll play and practiced on the mother, now shifts toward men. The central point of the argument is the insistence on fixing the responsibility for all evil upon men. While the anal-sadistic fight with the mother was a struggle for independence, the present fight seems to be a violent plea for acquittal.

The powerful father must now assume responsibility for the girl and thus raise her self-esteem by taking all her sins upon himself and transforming her into a saint, a pure, good, long-suffering mother. Under such conditions, the idealized father is to give the girl a baby as a reward for goodness and suffering. This feeling is much more acceptable than the earlier wish to attack the father and take the penis away from him. The vaginal feelings are taboo before the vagina is recognized as an organ. In the last part of the maternal phase or in the beginning of the phallic phase, ground was laid for the denial and isolation of the vagina, with the ensuing hope that the clitoris would grow into a penis. Now the whole genital region is rejected and treated as nonexistent or inanimate. Lack of satisfaction is blamed on the father. The nagging excitement is rationalized as justified because of injuries inflicted by men or boys. The verbal torrents and tears, however, provide a discharge for genital excitement. Where clitoris dominance persists because of constitutional factors, the clitoris is similarly blamed and condemned as if all excitation and all dissatisfaction was due to this organ. At this stage the inanimate doll is often substituted for by live pets who come to represent the unknown wildness of vaginal feelings and, on another level, the jumping clitoris and the yearned-for penis.

The active competition with the father for the love of the mother has ended with a projection of the sexual urges upon the father. The hostile accusations of the father gave rise to fears and renewed guilt feelings.

At this point the hostility toward the father is deflected toward boys and other men and to some extent to the mother again. The little girl becomes self-righteous both toward her mother and toward boys. She turns to her father hopefully and affectionately with relatively little guilt. Since she has ejected the responsibility for her yearnings and placed them upon the father, she fantasies that he seduces her. She is sure that he prefers her to his wife and would surely show it more clearly if not prevented by the jealous mother. Death wishes toward the interfering rival take on a mild form in comparison with those stemming from the anal and maternal stages. "Mother lived long enough. Now it is my turn," is not even fully meant as a death wish, since the girl expects the reincarnation of her mother in the baby that she hopes to receive from her father. She merely wants to change places with her mother. In giving up the penis wish and hoping for a baby in lieu of a penis, she can love her father now without ambivalence. She wishes to be dependent on him and loved by him. Her fears are now centered in her concern that she might not achieve or may lose the father's love. She yearns for the full possession of the idealized father who can give satisfaction of all needs. She projects upon him her own feelings of love and waits for the day he will be free to show them to her. The disappointment in the father who seems to reject her after raising her hopes terminates the Oedipus complex with greater force than fears of the rival mother.

The Latency Period

The girl enters the latency period disappointed in both parents, but less so in her mother. She identifies with her mother but is not as dependent on her as she used to be. She is reaching out for independence from both parents. Once again, as in the beginning of the phallic phase, she is trying out her own resources. She may feel virtuous, because she tries to lessen the narcissistic injury of the rejection by her father by the fantasy that she has given him up for the sake of her mother. Her greatest source of narcissistic satisfaction is being a good girl. This reaction formation helps her to compensate for her feelings of inferiority stemming from penis envy, from the rejection by both parents and from lack of genital satisfaction.

The little girl at this time has a great many secrets, which she shares with her girl friends. The secrets are clearly sexual or turn out to be no real secrets. Thus the secret discovery of the vaginal opening is worked through on a higher level. The inspection of each others' genitals and mutual masturbation seems a dramatic representation of the shared secret. The boys are not admitted into the community of girls. Disdain for wild, stupid boys is a group reaction against penis envy and a group revenge for being rejected by men.

The identification with her group gives the child strength really to reject the masculine role and to prepare herself for the time when she can proudly and openly admit her vaginal secret, now shared with all women. A sense of fairness based on equality develops between girls but does not apply to boys. Toward adults there is distrustful politeness since they are expected to deceive and to disappoint.

In transition from latency, the group gives way more and more to pairing off and genuine friendships that become consolidated in that pre-puberty. Twin fantasies are common in this stage and the desire to be alike dominates conscious thinking. The difference between mother and child is accentuated by the girl's rejection of her parents as too old, un-like her, and therefore unable to understand her.

The latency girl performs well in academic subjects, but she approaches learning with an inhibition of exploratory curiosity. In creative activity she is restricted by her trend to suppress feelings and her inhibition of handling materials. She was creative in the maternal stage when she projected sexual feelings upon objects. She was explosively creative in the phallic stage when she was frantically exploring genitals but lapsed into inactivity and daydreaming at times when she felt frustrated and rejected. In latency, dancing becomes one of the preferred creative activities. In dancing the girl can relibidinize her body and gain control over it by perfection of movements. This exercise in body control compensates for the deplored lack of visual motility of the genital. As in dancing, in her skill games the girl reveals that she is preparing herself for the most important function of a woman: the adjustment and integration of several parts of her body so necessary for smooth functioning as a whole unit, despite a variety of divergent stimuli. Jacks, hopscotch, typical ball play are practiced to increase the ability to unify diverse sensations and motor acts. The girl perfects herself in the art of resynthesizing the scattered genital sensations on one level and in the art of taking care of several babies and her husband all at once on another level. The scattered jacks, for instance, represent vaginal sensations as well as number of babies. The little ball seems to symbolize the clitoris whose excitement initiates and accompanies all vaginal sensations. The little hand trains itself to grasp them all at once and hold them all at once. The gradual integration of all parts clearly shows its derivation from genital activity in the rule that only a certain specified number of jacks are to be touched at a given phase of the game.

The intellectual curiosity is satisfied academically, maternal behavior

21

continues in play, and in skill games integration of function is practiced. The latency girl prepares herself for the acceptance of her total genital and of herself as wife and mother.

Prepuberty

In late latency and prepuberty, interest in boys reawakens, at first with denial and later openly. Grooming and clothes become an important preoccupation. This expresses both the interest in the girl's body as well as the desire to please boys. The estrangement from the mother reaches its height and the desire for independence from parental authority increases. The increase in self-reliance goes hand in hand with increased narcissism. The precious girl friends represent duplications of oneself and thus expansions of the ego. Crushes on adults usually inaccessible to the girl seem like games of love. Being noticed and receiving attention assumes tremendous importance, as self-observation is projected upon men in a renewed effort to ward off curiosity about one's own body.

The early shocks are far removed now, blocked by defenses, elevated on a higher plane. A number of sublimations are now available, so that menstruation need not come as a tremendous shock comparable to the "death of the baby" or the discovery of the introitus. The conflict between masculine and feminine tendencies is intensified. The girl acts as if she had to make a decision whether or not to accept menstruation and the implied femininity. The narcissistic desire to be admired and wanted overcomes the penis envy to some extent. Boys are accepted again but primarily used to raise the girl's self-esteem. In her fantasies, the girl dreams of meeting glamorous strangers, but such a meeting with the idealized father figure never materializes. Vaginal sensations are heightened now and the glamorous stranger also represents the unknown organ from which the yearnings emerge. The never attained meeting seems to represent the inability to experience orgasm.

Toward the end of prepuberty, sex play with boys occurs. It seems to be dominated by curiosity in relation to the girl's own body, especially her genitals. At times the girl will allow the boy to discover her vagina for her. Her own sexual feelings are experienced as if her genitals were teasing her. The great desire to get rid of this feeling leads to the tendency to tease boys. Exciting boys without giving them satisfaction seems to be a favorite prepuberty pastime. This heightens the girl's feeling that she is desirable and powerful and reconciles her to her feminine role. She begins to look forward to menstruation and she measures the growth of her breasts from day to day. Where the preoccupation with breasts overshadows the desire for genital maturity, menstruation comes as a shock. The expectation of greater desirability with sexual maturity makes the dreaded menstrual pain palatable. At times, early concern with lipstick reveals the wish openly to display the bleeding introitus. Out of the shame and guilt of the bleeding genital, there emerges by reaction formation the virtue of attractiveness and the value of seduction by very red lips.

Puberty[10] and After

Nevertheless menstruation reawakens the earlier conflicts and both castration and the "death of the baby" problems are reexperienced in some form. As blood comes out of the opening, however, there can no longer be any question as to the existence of the opening. With the readmittance of the introitus as part of the girl's body, the vagina is truly discovered. Blood and bloody tissue prove the existence of a hidden container for it. Uterus cramps further help to localize the boundaries of the vagina, which however still remain hazy until the penetrating penis makes them distinct for the girl. Waves of intense penis envy alternate now with masochistic fantasies. Masturbation, if it occurs, is accompanied by rape fantasies in which the guilt is clearly placed upon the attacking male. In such fantasies, the girl renews the denial of the introitus and now denies the vagina as well. Only at the peak of the fantasy does she receive her organ back again because she is being penetrated by the penis which creates the vagina for her. Sexual feelings are again projected on men, and the desirability of the vagina is raised by assigning all need for intercourse to men. The girl is willing to trade again. She will surrender her vagina to men for the assurance of eternal love which implies continued satisfaction. The need for babies also represents the wish for gratification but seems more a successor of earlier unfulfilled wishes to explore, handle and master the vagina. The penetrating penis awakens the vagina and gives it boundaries. The baby makes up for the inability to master the vagina. Both intercourse and delivery are fraught with danger until the girl is able to accept full responsibility for the vagina as her own organ and take full responsibility for the sexual excitement arising from it. She can then cease the fight between masculinity and femininity, between clitoris and vagina, condemn none but accept and integrate all her bodily organs and their functions.

Conclusions

What seems to be the effect of the long period of vaginal frustration that is imposed upon the girl biologically? It is likely that the development of maternal feelings depends largely on the transformation of vaginal tensions into maternal urges. The early externalization of vaginal impulses upon the baby would most probably not occur if vaginal gratification was possible at that time.

But are not the masculinity complex and the intense penis envy unnecessary remnants to be condemned for the purpose of smooth development of femininity? Without them, it seems, and without masculine sublimations, the woman could not accept and tolerate the feminine wishes of the man, which may seem equally unnecessary and undesirable. But without feminine wishes and feminine sublimation, could the man understand a woman, identify with her and love her? By projecting his own femininity upon her, he can love her free from guilt and fear. Vice versa, by projecting her own masculinity upon the man, the woman can accept him and love him without fear, guilt or shame. It appears that bisexuality is a necessary prerequisite for the understanding and tolerance so important in sexual and social adjustment between sexes.

NOTES

[1]Since 1956, my views on activity and passivity have considerably changed. For that reason, the section from pp. 2–5 has been revised for this publication.

[2]The need to study and rhythmic alternation between activity and passivity has been suggested to me in a discussion by Dr. Paul Gray (1962).

[3]For a definition of relaxation see Kestenberg, 1967 a.

[4]An urethral stage which follows the anal is described in Chapters 5, 8, 9, and 13. It precedes the early maternal, "inner-genital" phase in both sexes (see Chapters 5, 9, and 13; also Kestenberg, 1966).

[5]Later called the "inner-genital" phase and described in both sexes (see Chapters 5, 9, and 13).

[6]Throughout the book, "externalization of sensations or tensions" refers to a displacement of perceptions from the inside of the body to the outside. "Externalization of impulses" refers to the displacement of responses to internal stimulation to the outside of the body or to a concrete, external object (see footnote 1, Chapter 5 which pertains to errors in terminology in the original publication of this chapter).

[7]See the description of drawings and designs that represent clitoric and vaginal sensations, in Chapter 9, and in Kestenberg (1969).

[8]Freud's assumption that worms wandering from the rectum to the vagina may produce early vaginal sensations is reinterpreted here to mean that recollections of worms may screen memories for vaginal sensations. The wavy pattern of worms' movements is reminiscent of vaginal waves of excitation.

[9]For a most lucid exposition of this phase of feminine development, see Jacobson.

[10]For a definition of puberty as the time when ovulatory cycles begin, see Chapters 13, 14, 15.

CHAPTER 2

On the Development of Maternal Feelings in Early Childhood

Introduction

Although Freud wrote several papers on the development of female sexuality, his references to maternal needs are few and far between. When they do occur, they disclose a concept of motherhood which is consistent with his interpretation of female development. Freud could readily accept new contributions of female analysts to this subject. He considered the female psyche quite enigmatic, possibly more accessible to understanding by women than by men. But he could never agree with theories of the universality of early vaginal sensations. In one case he did find a possible evidence of such an occurrence (Freud, 1925), but as a rule he thought that memories of early vaginal sensations were displacements from other libidinous zones. To Freud, the little girl was essentially masculine up to the time she turned to her father because of her disappointment in her mother, who had failed to give her a penis. The girl's early preoccupation with dolls was explained in terms of the young child's need to reverse the mother-child relationship. Freud consistently called activity masculine and passivity feminine, but conceded that the activity involved in the little girl's maternal play was "the activity of femininity" (1931). The question never arose whether the boy's early maternal play was of a similar nature. Neither was the source of fatherly feelings discussed in any detail.

While the relationship between maternal activity and femininity remained somewhat obscure, Freud discovered two sources of a baby image: the "anal-baby" associated with a passive feminine attitude, and the

First published in *The Psychoanalytic Study of the Child* (1956): 257–90, and revised for publication here. Reproduced by permission.

"penis-baby" derived from the active masculinity of the phallic phase. In discussing the fantasy "A Child Is Being Beaten," Freud (1919) made a fleeting reference to the girl's identification of her clitoris with a child. The vagina, emerging late in female development, was considered a successor to the rectum or its subtenant. Its symbolic representation was that of a receptacle for the penis. Inasmuch as the wish for the penis was eventually replaced by the wish for the child the vaginal cavity became also a host of the child.

Various authors enlarged, modified or contradicted some of Freud's views.[1] Two schools of thought emerged, one most consistently represented by Horney and the Kleinian school; the other, expounded by such adherents of Freud as Deutsch, Mack Brunswick and Bonaparte. The former believed in the existence of early vaginal sensations which were denied or repressed in time, thus assuming an early femininity; the latter followed Freud in his concept of the girl's initial masculinity. Klein drew attention to the child's concept of babies residing in the maternal abdomen, and consistently maintained that children had an unconscious, inherited "knowledge" of the vagina as an organ. Brierley and Payne, especially emphasized the equation of the vagina with the mouth, pointing out that vaginal contractions were sometimes associated with suckling. Deutsch described passive feminine masochism preceding the appearance of the vagina as an organ, while Payne spoke of receptivity rather than passivity, and of a capacity to tolerate and adapt to periodical variations rather than of masochism. It was Brierley who suggested that feminine normality depended on a particular kind of coordination between the clitoric and the vaginal functions, getting away from the idea that one supplanted the other.

One gets the impression that the proponents of early masculinity in women followed Freud's concept of maternal activity, while those who assumed early vaginal participation in female development were more inclined to see the mother's role as oscillating between activity and passivity, according to the changing needs of the child. It was Freud himself who drew our attention to the fundamental change of maternal attitude which occurs when the small infant grows up to be a child. In his paper on Leonardo da Vinci (1910b) he said: "The love of the mother for the suckling whom she nourishes and cares for is something far deeper reaching than her later affection for the growing child. It is of the nature of a fully gratified love affair, which fulfills not only all the psychic wishes but also all physical needs, and when it represents one of the forms of happiness attainable by man it is due, in no little measure, to the possibility of gratifying without reproach also wish feelings which were long repressed and designated as perverse" (pp. 92–93). The reference to all bodily needs may be taken as a hint that pregenital and genital desires find fulfillment in the care of the infant. In this reflection, Freud did not speak of any difference in the handling of male and female infants. Later he described the mother's need to realize her frustrated wishes for a penis in the achievements of her son (1932–36). Inasmuch as the male child substitutes for a penis, we have to expect that the mother's attitude toward her son will not change fundamentally when he grows up. She still will take narcissistic pride in his adult achievements. The maternal bliss in caring for her infant, regardless of sex, seems dependent on the child's smallness and helplessness. Freud's remarks can be developed further to mean that mothers enjoy the care of their infants in substitution of their early repressed wishes to handle their own genitals. I have suggested a similar interpretation of a mother's need for a small child, in the hypothesis that early undischarged vaginal excitations were the basic source of the girl's need for a child (see Chapter 1).

The localization of the vagina, its inaccessibility and the diffuseness of its excitations make it impossible for the child to explore it fully. The infant can be handled and fondled while the early vaginal tensions are not fully discharged on the organ itself. The young girl has to find substitute channels for discharge. Even in the rare cases where children do experience an orgastic vaginal discharge, it does not seem likely that the anxieties connected with the excitement can be fully mastered. Other libidinous zones are accessible to continuous experimentation and can become incorporated in the body scheme; their excitations cease to be sources of anxiety when their boundaries and functions have been sufficiently explored. The vaginal tensions can find a certain modicum of discharge by displacements to other parts of the body. This neither constitutes full discharge nor does it allow for the creation of an organ concept. In her search for an explorable object, the little girl, who identifies herself with her mother, chooses a baby as a suitable substitute. The wish for a child can thus be traced from a biological need. This need is, in turn, influenced by psychologically determined attitudes, such as the identification with the mother and the wish for a penis. With such speculations, we come closer to the subject of maternal "instinct."

Maternal "Instinct"

The question of instinct has been a long-standing bone of contention in the development of psychoanalytic theory. Hartmann, Kris, and Loewenstein (1946) clarified this issue by pointing out that instinct, as evident in animals, is largely lacking in the human species. Erikson (1950) stated: "Man's 'inborn instincts' are drive fragments to be assembled, given meaning, and organized during a prolonged childhood by methods of child training and schooling which vary from culture to culture and are determined by tradition." Helene Deutsch (1944–45)), evaluating the maternal instinct in the human female, found it difficult to decide "to what extent the complex emotional attribute that we call 'motherliness' expresses a biologic condition." In adult women, Benedek (1970a) was able to find an experimentally established correlate between maternal qualities and hormone fluctuations. Deutsch (1944–45) was inclined to stress the psychological meaning of motherhood in the present society. Still she said: "Possibly part of the deeply feminine quality of intuition is a remnant of that strong instinct, to which we are told woman once owed her dominant position in primitive society."

It is undoubtedly true that today's woman does not approach childbirth and infant care as if she were guided by a maternal instinct. She has no inner wisdom which would prompt her to find a nesting place, to bite off the cord, and to suckle the infant as long and as often as he needs it. She uses substitute equipment in the care of the child's excrements. She seems singularly unprepared for these maternal functions and often afraid to exercise them. Nevertheless, our ideal picture of a truly maternal woman is one of an omnipotent, all-knowing mother who knows what to do with her infant by sheer intuition. However, our present culture has contributed a great deal to the estrangement of the woman from her biological functions. While I shall return to the question of cultural influences later, I want to mention in passing that both vaginal sensibility and motherly behavior have suffered from the increasing masculinization of women, largely due to environmental changes.[2] Despite their flight from femininity, women cannot escape womanhood when, with the onset of puberty, they become subject to hormonal fluctuations that make fertilization possible. We have learned from psychoanalysis and from research on maturation that adult functions are foreshadowed in early development. We wonder, then, how the adult woman, whose psychological attitude undoubtedly depends on her specifically female hormonal cycle (see Chapters 13, 14, 15), has been prepared for the cyclic nature of her femininity as well as for the events of pregnancy and infant nursing, which periodically interrupt her cycles. We postulate a preparation, and doubt that such a preparation has only psychological determinants. We expect to find a biological substrate to maternal behavior which operates since early childhood. Whatever such a biological factor may be, we are inclined to think of it as a substitute for the animal instinct, and we expect to find a correlation between the biological factor and the specifically maternal intuition of women. Let us turn to observations of children to gather traces of later motherliness.

Vaginal Stimulations in the Oral Phase of Development

Early in his writings Freud (1905) drew our attention to the role of the mother as seductress of the infant who, ministering to his bodily needs, awakens such sexual urges as are attached to the erogenous zones of the infant's body. While there is a succession of dominant needs during infantile development, the infant's mother not only satisfies the phase-specific needs but also acts as premature stimulant of zones which are destined to become erogenous at a later time. Greenacre (1952) pointed to a possibility that genital discharge may occur prematurely when, under deprivation, the infant responds with an unspecific totality of discharge through all channels. More frequent is the genital stimulation that occurs when a mother cleanses the anal and the urethrogenital zones after a child has been fed, i.e., under conditions of oral satisfaction. Brierley and Payne thought in terms of spontaneous overflow of excitation from the oral to the vaginal zone. This is quite feasible in view of the fact that in the first few weeks the whole female genital is frequently enlarged and swollen, so that a local response of vaginal "sucking" may develop in association with oral sucking. The ministrations of the mother, such as bathing, oiling and diapering, may have a further stimulating effect not only upon the external but also on the internal genital of the girl. Soapy bathing water can flow into the vagina, wiping of the introitus mucosa can have an indirect effect on the vaginal mucosa which it adjoins. There are other sources of excitations in the vagina early in life. The pressures exerted on the adjoining vaginal walls by a full rectum or bladder are probably only fleeting, because in the average infant a discharge follows the fullness almost immediately. Such stimulations become more important with the establishment of sphincter controls. The pressing of the infant's abdomen, widely practiced calisthenics and the playful tossing up and down also contribute to vaginal excitations. Some girls recapture during analysis the memory of inner genital excitement produced by jumping up and down in early childhood. The attachment to transitional objects seems to have a connection with early genital sensations (Wulff, 1946; Greenacre, 1953, 1955).

Transitional Objects

Toward the end of the oral phase and sometimes earlier, children often get addicted to articles which they need to touch or rub while going to sleep (Wulff, 1946; Winnicott, 1953; Stevenson, 1954). Some of these objects are quite inappropriately called "baby," as they rarely resemble babies. Winnicott rightly pointed out that these possessions, to

29

which the child clings not only at moments of separation, represent both the mother and the child itself. One can easily recognize from the demeanor of the infants that they are repeating the nursing situation: they suck with one hand and clutch an article with the other. The fingers substitute for the breast or bottle, while the touching of the cherished item revives the sensation of handling the mother's clothes or breast. Yet one must not forget that the most frequent appearance of transitional objects coincides with the time when the child has already been able to reach his genitals. Not only has he already the awareness of the lower part of his body, but he is also beginning to recognize dimly the connection between abdominal sensations and elimination, a problem which has held his attention rather early in life. I am inclined to believe that the transitional object serves a multitude of needs. It represents an ideal solution for the infant who cannot cope with so many tensions stemming from the outside as well as the inside of his body, tensions which overcome him with greater force when the waking activity ceases and the immobility and aloneness of the sleep separation brings about a unique intimacy with his own body. Oral, anal and genital needs seem to be met in holding on to articles of special texture which feel like mother's breast, like the tissue cleansing the anal and genital regions, all areas where the "me" and the "not me" meet. At that stage, inner sensations are most probably still fused with and projected to the outside, so that they too can be mastered by the method of delineation of boundaries between oneself and others. Some children indicate that a special softness of the texture is important, as if they wanted to reproduce the feel of mucous membranes, which are the mediators between outside and inside. The connection with anality is indicated by a special smell important in some cases. A clear substitution of anal manipulation by rubbing of a silk fringe (changed later to silk pants) was observed in P. Her first action on lying down was putting her fingers into her mouth and scratching her anal region with her other hand. Only after the mother removed her hand from this place twice, did the child turn to handling the silk piece as a substitute.

The primary transitional objects lay the foundation for secondary preferred toys, many of whom represent anal babies. The child is entering an abdominal stage in which most probably all inner sensations are fused and predominantly externalized upon the anal orifice.

The Anal-Baby

The little girl develops sphincter control earlier than the boy. This is generally assigned to the girl's greater dependence on her mother, her more obedient and passive attitude. It is quite possible that the girl is more dependent on outside help because she has an additional inner tension which adds to her difficulties in coping with bodily stimulations. Also, the girl finds additional pleasures in the exercise of sphincter control which the boy does not have. There is a general tendency to contract vaginal muscles along with the contraction of sphincters. Contraction of laminal muscles, which we find so rigidly established in cases of vaginism, seems to be the girl's pastime of the anal phase, of which no conscious representation is possible because of the simultaneous contractions of sphincters and laminal muscles. Holding back of feces and urine for a good long time is a play preferred by girls. The resulting fullness of bladder and rectum may be kept up until abdominal pain develops. The feeling of fullness, experienced by the girl, seems to foreshadow the pleasure of a full vagina which she cannot really feel until much later. When boys hold back feces and urine, they often feel the pressure, exerted on their inner-genital organs, in the perineal-scrotal region or the groin. The period of holding back is often interpreted as production time. What is discharged after the withholding is considered "made" (formed) by the child, while immediate release is experienced as surrender to both bodily demands and mother's commands, in contrast to active voluntary "work." Feces are particularly suitable for the development of this concept, as the child apprehends that holding back will result in solid, formed bowel movements, while feces discharged in great urgency tend to be fluid or "torn" ("in pieces"). This work principle seems to be intimately connected with the "anal-baby" concept. Knowing clearly where the feces come from, and the experience of making them, is a practical creative process associated with the illusory creativeness of the transitory phenomena. The transitional object seems to lay a foundation for the baby concept in the sense of "something of me and something of mother." The anal baby is not only a possession but also a product from which the child parts with sorrow before he is able to give it away to his mother as a present.

Nelly, a two-and-a-half-year-old girl, came to analysis because she was not able to solve her oral and anal problems and was already overwhelmed by genital excitations. Nelly's difficulties with toilet training came into focus when she told me that she wanted to eat feces and was afraid of her mother, who would be displeased if Nelly soiled herself. After this session, Nelly withheld feces and urine, as she was prone to do on previous occasions. This time her mother was advised to allow the child to hold back her excrements as long as possible. Immediately after mother stopped reminding her to go to the bathroom, Nelly began to "work" at ironing and washing. Because of the long withholding, she developed abdominal cramps in the middle of her work. Mother then told her that going to the bathroom would relieve her pain. Nelly complied and seated herself on the toilet in such a way that she could observe how her feces would leave her anus. When a tiny piece of "b. m." adhered to her skin, she anxiously asked her mother why this piece kept dancing on her and would not go into the toilet. She quieted when her mother wiped the disobedient piece away. This incident detracted from the feeling of control over feces that she was about to acquire.

In the next analytic hour, Nelly indicated a preoccupation with an earlier, sexually tinged episode, the nature of which she either would not disclose or could not remember. Subsequently she became quite high in what seemed to be a generalized sexual excitement. At night she made several attempts to seduce her mother into bodily intimacy with her, asking her at the same time what "eat me up" meant. The following morning she wanted to know why her mother's "wee-wee" was brown. When told it was hair, which she would get when she was big, Nelly announced that she was big already. The same day she showed her mother her "b. m." Pointing to the big pieces, she called them "mommy-ballies" and the small pieces she named "brother-ballies" (her brother was then a small baby).

The following day Nelly jumped on her mother's bed and, in her excitement, urinated on it. The loss of urinary control distressed her greatly. In her session, she returned to what seemed to be a confession of seeing adults engaged in sex, but again she could not tell me the details. She made it quite clear, however, that she had reacted with a lot of "b. m." and urine (?) to the traumatic scenes she had witnessed. After leaving her session, she vomited her meal, as she was prone to do before she started her analysis.

Nelly had responded with a polymorph excitement to the primal scenes that she had watched in the anal phase. We found out much later that she had witnessed fellatio. Because of the unresolved pregenital problems that were connected with her premature genital excitement, Nelly tried to work out oro- and ano-urethral-genital excitations by retention of feces and urine, and by vomiting and urinating on her mother's bed, where she had seen her father in action (Kestenberg, 1972). As she worked out these problems in analysis, one could observe a distinct overlapping of anal and genital interests and theories. Nelly originated several explanations for sex relationships and childbirth. The clearest theory of all was that of the anal-baby, which solved a great many problems, such as sibling rivalry, fear of incontinence, and fear of the pain that resulted from retention of feces. After she had linked up the "triad" of withholding, work, and control over her abdominal content, Nelly developed the idea of an anal-baby. At the same time, her early genitality was liberated and this was linked up with the creation of another baby. Like her mother, she now had two babies. In identification with her mother, she delivered a fecal penis-boy (brother-ballie). The baby-making was intimately connected with her sexual feelings for her mother. In identification with her mother, and with a simultaneous reversal of roles, she gave birth to her mother-baby (mommy-ballie). Both babies appeared in the toilet, yet the mommy-ballie was a product of Nelly's genital excitement, which had occurred during defecation. This connection had been established during the primal scenes she had witnessed. The urethral jumping on mother's bed was a new addition to an old scene.

At an earlier time, Nelly had shown an interesting transition from the fear of loss of feces to a spurt of generosity in which she wanted to bestow a gift of feces upon her girl friend. She had identified herself with her own bowel movement and was afraid that she too would be flushed down the toilet. When the sewer system was explained to her, she listened carefully and then exclaimed cheerfully that the pipes which had carried her feces would land in the friend's house. Nelly could now share and give. The anal-baby had emerged as a product which Nelly wanted to control by herself. Possibly because of the recognition of her helplessness, she turned to her mother, inviting her to participate in the baby production and to admire what she expelled from three orifices. She seemed to present her mother with the ballies, the urine, and the vomit when she recognized her mother's usefulness and soon after she was confronted with her mother's anatomic superiority. These pregenital gifts, bestowed out of newly acquired generosity, were also an expression of her genital interest in competition with her father.

In summary, we may conclude that the production of pregenital babies emerges from feelings of possession, creativity, sharing, exhibiting, and generous altruistic surrender to a love object. It is intimately connected with withholding, with abdominal sensations and ejection of abdominal content. There is no direct evidence that vaginal excitations contribute to the prevailing abdominal-pelvic pressures. We know from analyses of older girls that abdominal fullness may lead to vaginal tensions that cannot be discharged adequately through the available oral, anal or urethral channels. When, as in the case of Nelly, the maturational spurt of genital drives is counteracted by anal wishes, the anal-baby becomes an especially pronounced fantasy. However, even in normal development, the prephallic, maternal stage which succeeds pregenital phases, shows at least some traces of the earlier anal-baby concept. Yet, the intensity of the two-to-four-year-old child's need for the baby cannot be due to a trace of anality alone. We may wonder about the nature of the organic tension which supplies the fuel for the ardent maternal urges of the toilet-trained, clean girl.

The Baby of the Early Maternal Stage[3]

I have the impression that with the passing of the pregenital phases vaginal excitations become an important, and at times discernible, source of tension. This could be deduced from direct observation of young children, and seems a very likely turn in development from the retrospective analysis of young girls and women.[4] In immediate observation it becomes evident that the girl's maternal interest in that stage is much more pronounced than that of the boy.

A, who distinguished himself early by his unusual independence and persistence in his own ways, initiated his self-feeding by first feeding his mother and then eating from his mother's plate rather than his own. Prior to this, he had gone through a difficult feeding period which seemed to end with complete recovery. He responded to weaning from the bottle by a spurt of independent behavior in keeping with his early self-containment. When A mastered walking, he became increasingly interested in his brother's and sister's toys. He loved to wheel his sister's doll carriage. On seeing his sister's doll he would kiss it and go off to other interesting play. To my knowledge, his mother never discouraged doll play. His siblings' refusal to give up their toys to A for a prolonged period would only increase his interest in them. Yet, A did not develop more than a fleeting interest in dolls. Before he reached his second year he became inseparable from a cap which he wore all day and hung on the bedpost at night. When he was about two he was given a rag doll of his own which he kept in his bed alongside with an array of other toys such as guns, but which he did not carry around with him.

Shortly before he was two and a half, A told his mother repeatedly that a dog had bitten his "boy" (his brother's term for the penis). He would assert this when she washed him and they could both view his intact penis. Even though completely toilet-trained, A was still dependent on his mother when he urinated standing up. She had to hold his penis to direct the stream of urine into the toilet bowl because A was too small to reach it. One day, he refused the mother's help stubbornly. However, after several experiences of spilling urine, he asked her to assist him again. Thus A was not yet in full control of his penis and needed his mother to help take care of his "boy."

Shortly after A's debacle with independent urinating, I visited him on a routine longitudinal-study follow-up. He greeted me with a large screwdriver in his hand, every inch a little repairman. His mother told me that, in the absence of his father, brother, and sister, he had taken his sister's doll out of her bed. Having lost interest in his rag doll, he liked to bottle-feed his sister's doll. I had brought him a set of tiny baby-dolls in bunk beds, a set of hollow cubes, and a tiny doll bottle. He became very interested in nursing the tiny dolls, but concentrated more on his sister's doll. He alternated between feeding her with the bottle and with a hollow cube which he used as a cup. He asked me to help him with such things as putting the nipple on the bottle and other menial tasks which he could not accomplish by himself. However, his whole demeanor showed that he shared the doll with the mother. For example, he would hand her the doll for feeding. He sat next to her and tried to alternate with her in the feeding process. At his mother's request, he would sit next to me, but then he would accompany his activities with gestures and phrases, designed to tell his mother what he did with the doll. He corrected her each time when she referred to the doll as "she" or "her." He would turn his intent face toward her and would reiterate "boy" in a tone of firmness and finality, even though the doll had braids and was dressed in girls' clothes. When I asked him to show me the doll's "boy," he uncertainly pointed to the navel and around the abdominal area. He knew where the "wee-wee" came from and pointed between the doll's legs. When his mother went to the kitchen to prepare a meal, he once more handed me the bottle, thinking that it was empty. To show him that there was still some water in it, I spilled some on my hand. He proceeded to spill water on the doll's hands, wiping them carefully each time. In an almost imperceptible transition, he began to sprinkle water on the rug, making progressively wider and more vigorous movements and getting away from doll-play.

When A's mother called him in to eat, he left the doll behind but then refused to eat until the doll was seated next to him and fed also. At times, he fed the doll and at other moments, he asked his mother to do so. He held the doll closely only when he bottle-fed her, and the only expression of affection for the doll was a gentle patting of its shoulder, which he did between spoonfuls of the soup he fed to her.

Quite different was the behavior of P, a little girl of two and a half. She already had a vast experience of playing with a number of dolls. To her, the affectionate hugging of the doll was the most important part of the play. She would be busy with the doll's clothing, bathe it, put it on the pottie, and lay it down to sleep, making sure that her "baby" had silk pants in bed with her, in imitation of P's own transitional object. All these were serious activities in which she would use the mother or me to help her, where her motor skill lagged behind her maternal ambitions. When embracing her doll, however, she would look blissfully happy, press it affectionately to her "bosom" and would repeat with great conviction "my baby." When she needed a helper in the doll care, she insisted that things be done exactly to her specification. Whenever I came to visit for the observational period, she looked for a baby doll in my bag, and was keenly disappointed and almost unbelieving when I gave her another present. On testing, she excelled early in all items in which a doll was used, losing interest quickly when the doll was removed.

When P was a little over one year old, she seemed quite worried about the face of a black doll. She clearly indicated that there was something wrong with her baby. It is likely that anal components played a role in P's distress at that time (see Chapter 1). Yet she was able to overcome her worries about the doll's appearance toward the end of her second year, at a time when her toilet training was far from being accomplished and long before she was able to express an equation of dark face and feces. When she was shown that the black face could be lightened with a white crayon, P immediately proceeded with the task, but also whitened her white doll's feet with the crayon. From that time on, she no longer minded her black doll, though she was still in the midst of her anal conflicts. Some months later, she was reminded of feces when she saw a little black boy and she indicated to her mother that she should not take a black baby home.

During P's second year of life, she called every doll "baby," a term suggested by her mother. Without mother's encouragement every doll was thought to be female. When P got a boy-doll for her second birthday, she carried it around with her incessantly, but was convinced that this doll too was a girl. Some weeks later, she understood that people referred to the new doll as "boy." When I asked her about the doll's sex, she answered "baby." When I repeated the question she answered "baby-doll." This term had been introduced to her recently. By the tone of her voice she revealed that, in using this term, she was making a concession to the demands of adults. In response to further questions about the doll's sex, she would ignore them or would repeat the question's last word in an echolalic, mechanistic way. After a few months, she devised a new answer. She called the male doll "girl-boy." Confronted with a real baby before she reached the age of two, she stroked and hugged it, as she did her dolls, but she also pinched the baby and poked at his eyes, as she used to do with her dolls. When the baby cried as a result of of these doings, P watched the baby's face with the curiosity of a scientific observer. This real, crying baby was clearly not her own. When, in the baby's presence, her doll was pre-

sented to her, she smiled with exalted happiness, pressed her doll and hugged it with great affection, saying tenderly: "baby, baby."

P, like A, was well acquainted with sex differences. Some time during her second year she had begun to pull her older brother's penis when she followed him into the bathroom. This seemed to be integrated into a phase in which she was very greedy, and in her mother's words "everything was hers." Similarly it was difficult for P to give things away, while she wanted to grab all of her brother's toys. Yet, even in this phase, P, given a definite choice between a gun and a doll, was primarily eager to keep the doll although she wanted the gun too. By the time she was two and a half P's interest in her brother's toys seemed to diminish, while her play with dolls not only persisted but also became more meaningful. At this age, she was preoccupied to some extent with cracks and "boo-boos" of different dolls. She treated such injuries with bandages and did not show undue concern over them. She wanted her mother to fix (glue together) broken things and also small items which she detached from dolls. She would, for instance, remove a bow from the head of a little doll, would demand that this be repaired, but would tear it off again as soon as the repair was done. Throughout such play she would remain placid. On seeing a paper doll which was headless and legless, P was not alarmed. When asked where the missing parts were, she pointed happily to the empty space where they should have been. In manipulating the head, which could be put in the empty space, she pulled it and almost tore it, on finding it in an upside-down position. The "injury" which she inflicted herself frightened her. The combination of the "upside-down head" and the twisted neck was too much for her. Again, it seemed that distortions of the body image (earlier through color difference, which the child could not correct until she was taught how to do it, now through reversal of accustomed configurations) were much more disquieting to P than injuries such as cracks or losses of limbs. Anal preoccupations at first played a role in P's experimentation with dolls. However, her main interest centered on efforts to preserve the baby image of her dolls. Cracks and limbs could be filled in fantasy, but distortions were too difficult to overcome, and therefore frightening.

Clearly, both children took on their mothers' roles in their doll play. Both identified the dolls with themselves. Both were in a stage where turning from passivity to activity was of paramount importance. A, however, acted out a special traumatic area of feeding, while P was universally maternal. To A, the bottle and the feeding cube were significant objects in the process. The identification of the bottle with the urinating penis broke through during the nursing game. A wanted to be in control of the mother's feeding activity, the feeding tools being of special oro-phallic significance to him. P wanted to possess a baby as her very own. A shared

the doll with the mother. He acted as if it was important to him that the child was his and his mother's, with the distributions of roles clearly indicating that A was the director, corrector and dictator of the whole affair. P wanted her dolls at all cost and would renounce masculine toys for them. She yearned to be given more and more babies, over which she wanted full control. Sharing was acceptable if necessary, and even that was tolerated for a short time only. Alongside with her possessive pride, P used dolls a great deal to solve her own body problems. She was not a child who frightened easily, yet she would get quite upset if something in a doll's countenance would detract from her baby qualities. When she was able to control the color of the doll's skin with crayons, which worried her at first, she proceeded to equalize her babies, making one doll whiter and some other dolls darker. Loss of control over her "baby's" bodies filled her with fear. Injuries, which did not distort the baby image of the doll, she could fix with ease. Neither was she compulsive about small matters like a doll's bow. She even enjoyed such little deprivations that she herself could inflict upon the doll. Important was that the "babies" were hers and that they were girl dolls, shaped like she was herself, treated the way she wanted to be treated. They were part of her. Castration fear and penis envy played a tangential role in the doll games of both children. To A, it was important to have a boy with his mother, although he knew that the doll was supposed to be a girl. To P, it was equally important that the doll was a girl like herself, compromising under pressure for a bisexual child, but certainly not for a boy. Nelly, who abandoned a transitional object in favor of a doll only after the birth of her brother, also insisted that her doll must be a girl. She would play with boy dolls only for very short periods, and would cling tenaciously to her girl doll. Only after she has been assured that in contrast to boys and men she had a "bottom" like mommy and all other women, did she permit her girl doll to play the role of a boy, for brief periods, in which she imitated her mother's behavior toward her brother. Before this, she would act out, on the distinctly female doll, her mother's activities on herself as well as those on her brother. She too, like P, had her doll very much on her mind. She would interrupt her play with other toys and would ask in a tone of anxious concern: "Where is Hedy?" She too made it quite clear that this baby was hers and nobody else's. She too, despite her penis envy, insisted that the doll was shaped in her image. Only when she knew that she had some kind of an organ, specifically feminine, could she unqualifiedly allow her girl doll to assume the role of a male, but only for a short time. The girl doll seemed to represent both the child herself as well as that part of her which she intuitively perceived as an organ important for her feminine identity. A identified the doll with his "boy," his penis (see page 35, eleventh sentence). P was adamant about

the female sex of the doll. Both identified the doll with themselves. No doubt, they looked upon the doll as a sex-specific genital, a *pars pro toto*. However, P and Nelly were attached to their dolls much more intensively and for a much longer period of time than A ever was.[5]

We recognize in the two-year-old girl's attachment to the doll not only the continuation of earlier oral and anal possessiveness, but also elements familiar to us from the behavior with transitional objects. Winnicott (1953) says that the transitional objects and phenomena belong to the realm of illusion, an illusion that what the infant creates really exists. He says further: "This intermediate area of experience, unchallenged in respect of its belonging to inner or external (shared) reality, constitutes the greater part of the infant's experience and throughout life is retained in the intense experiencing that belongs to the arts and to religion and to imaginative living, and to creative scientific work." While both sexes live for some time in this world of illusion where reality and imagination flow into each other freely, the little girl singles out the illusion of motherhood as her most cherished creative experience. What Winnicott describes seems to be identical with the intuitive quality inherent in creativeness. The peculiar transition from reality to irreality in the games of the two-year-old "mother" is an all-pervasive phenomenon of her acting out of the maternal role. It is not even quite correct to call her activity a play or game. It seems more like a creation of a dramatic role, in which reality and imagination merge.

Two-year-old P, surrounded by her dolls when I arrive for my periodic visits, is very happy to let me undress and dress her dolls. She understands a role game and participates in calling different dolls by such names as are familiar to her as titles of different members of her family. She also readily consents to my pretending that some of P's dolls are mine. Both P and I are sitting on the floor, each hugging a doll and saying to the respective "babies" with great affection "My baby." For a few minutes P is enjoying herself, then she gets up, runs to her mother, vocalizing plaintively, and pointing to me with an accusing finger. She condenses her complaint in a sentence that sounds like "Lady, my baby." Suddenly she has become afraid that the play is real, and that the lady is taking one of her babies away from her.

Nelly who frequently treats her analyst like a baby, demands that the analyst cry for various childish reasons. She puts the analyst to sleep, covers her, gives her candy or withholds it. But foremost she insists that the analyst should cry because some object is "not for you." In one such crying episode the analyst unwittingly begins to smile. Nelly runs to her mother and joyfully exclaims: "Dr. K. is only kidding." When presented with small pipe-cleaner dolls, Nelly insists that the analyst should put pants and shoes on them. One such doll has shoes painted on her feet. Nelly demands that the analyst take them off. When I explain to her that these are toys with which we can play make-believe games, but we cannot really do them, she consents with an air of an indulgent adult, who caters to the whims of a child. At another time she puts a big doll to sleep in another room. Upon her return to the analyst she insists that she hears Daisy's crying and it does not disturb her in the least that nobody can really hear a sound. She acts the role of an intuitive mother with an extrasensory perception. When she creates the crying, it exists. When the analyst wants her to imagine shoes on the dolls, she becomes a representative of reality and doubts the existence of something she cannot see. She does not take seriously the adult's assurances that the doll is only a toy. In patting a big doll, Nelly discovers a "crying whistle" in the doll's body. She repeatedly asks what this is and gets the same answer to the effect that the man who made the doll put a whistle in to imitate a real child's crying. Nelly listens to the explanation each time. Then she gives up asking and runs behind me, hugging me and asking me to cry (this time for no apparent reason). She presses me in the region corresponding to the same place on the doll in which she discovered the whistle. Obviously Nelly does not believe the story about the toy manufacturer. She wants to find my whistle to prove her belief in the doll's identity with a living being. Only her own imaginative creativeness becomes reality, she neither accepts the adult's make-believe nor the adult's reality when they interfere with her own magic world of pseudo-reality. For her, the doll is not a toy with a whistle, but just as alive as the analyst and built the same way.

Whence does the inanimate doll get the quality of aliveness, which permeates the "play" of the two-year-old girl? The answer sometimes comes from the analyses of older girls and women.

A young woman in analysis had great difficulties in understanding female anatomy. She had been fully enlightened as a child. She has read relevant books on the subject, both in her childhood and recently. Yet she could not grasp the shape and location of the vagina, uterus and tubes. She thought of the vagina as a line rather than an organ. Throughout her associations there were sporadic references to dolls from her childhood. A vague fantasy or screen memory of her mother throwing the head of a doll out of the window and into the garden, where the patient played, appeared as the first doll reference, and was repressed during the analysis. The doll theme vanished for a long time. The completely frigid patient was busy with castration fears, dreaded injuries of her inner genital, penis envy, and with fears of her mother and her sisters. Memories of exploration of the labia had occurred much earlier. Now, however, clitoric sensations became apparent to her, though not clearly remembered from childhood. A vague awareness of deeper genital sensations followed in time. She was uncertain whether she really felt anything inside, and was most uncertain about the localization of the sensations. Experimentation with retention of feces and urine seemed to be the main source of vaginal excitation. When she began to worry that she might get a baby, the doll theme reappeared. She used the recollection of one doll who had a very wide skirt for speculations about mechanisms of childbirth and pregnancy. She could not understand how a baby could come in one piece, and was afraid that her baby would be cut during delivery.

One of her persistent complaints in connection with dolls was a still intensely felt frustration because her mother would not let her have a doll which looked like a real baby. I had the distinct impression that she repressed the memory of an early doll which might have represented a real baby to her. Such a recollection did not appear and I abandoned my initial impression, assigning it to the realm of the "analyst's wishful thinking." After some weeks, a lucky set of circumstances uncovered a definite evidence of a "baby doll" which the patient had possessed at the age of about two. She reacted to this discovery with amazement, but could not yet remember this particular doll. But the associations which came up now were clearly connected with the phase of the patient's development in which she played with the forgotten doll. Her feelings of inadequacy in caring for a baby became adamant, and she came close to a state of panic when thinking of a possible pregnancy. At the same time her confusion about her vagina returned. She bought a children's book about female anatomy, studying the diagrams carefully. She had been irrationally preoccupied for some time with short-sleeved blouses, and it occurred to her now that the diagram of the vagina looked like a blouse, the fornix indicating the sleeves, the rest of the organ representing the main body of the blouse. The image was strikingly similar to shapes associated with the "wide-skirt doll." While working out the blouse-vagina equation, the patient measured in fantasy different-size breasts. She understood then why she had been preoccupied with blouses for such a long time. She associated motherlines with large breasts and was jealous of her motherly sisters and still doubted her ability to produce an uninjured, live baby. The anticipation of caring for an infant filled her with intense anxiety. She stressed particularly that she did not want to raise a boy at this time. Her confusion about vaginal sensations and the shape and localization of the vagina reigned supreme. Oral, anal and phallic representations distorted and confused her intellectual knowledge of anatomy as well as her memory of recent experiences in which the vagina played a role. Defensively she retreated to her past "feelings" that her inside was empty, her vagina virtually nonexistent, merely a line or at best two-dimensional. The defensiveness as well as the rapid stream of confused and contradictory representations of her genital ceased when she realized that she had accumulated several images of her vagina, which, superimposed over each other, created a chameleon-like object, and forever changing and impossible to fathom.[6] She would see in the diagram of the vagina a headless and legless baby. (Compare P's lack of concern when she saw the headless and legless paper doll picture.) She could also see the uterus as a head of a baby or as a headless and legless child, the tubes representing the arms.[7] Superimposed images of her mother's body as well as those of her own body were related to her blouse-vagina concept. She mistook the contours of the vagina diagram as well as those of the uterus for the outside of the female body. Conflicting with all these representations, there loomed the shape of the penis, giving content to the empty space created by the female outside. When she thought of the outer lines of the diagram as outlines of the female body, it seemed that the vagina and uterus were empty shells. When she thought of the vagina as a penis container the feeling of emptiness left. Earlier ideas of a connection between mouth and a vagina-rectum (cloaca) did not add too much to the confusion at this time. But her dread of the "mutilated baby" image could be linked up now with oral and anal aggressions. The "inner penis" fantasy elicited a fear that the baby would not have enough space for the development of its whole body. Many of the conflicting ideas were supported by various vague vaginal sensations, which fused with anal, clitoric and urethral sensations, and therefore could not be localized. The appearance of vaginal sensations would give her a feeling of having something inside. Disappearance of these sensations confirmed the ideas of having nothing inside. She seemed to feel that sensations could only come from a solid, moving, if not visible part of the body. It took her some time to realize that the walls of the vagina consisted of living tissue, capable of excitation. She linked up such inner sensations, as came from the vagina, with ideas of a solid baby or a solid penis inside, or else projected them outside when she shaped the baby after the outer contours of the mother. Sensations associated with "water waves" could be traced back to excitations of the anterior wall of the vagina. When she finally understood that there was a solid interior wall of the vagina adjoining the bladder, she still kept calling it bladder. Fears that she would defecate during intercourse led to the realization that the posterior wall of the vagina was separate from the rectum. She worried how the penis could reach the fornix where she seemed to feel a tension, expressed as a need for the penis to get in deeper. She thought of the fornix as a bilateral excrescence, identified with the tubes and the arms of the baby. The usual fears that the vagina was too small for the baby was easily worked out, as she herself experienced the vaginal wall as flexible ("can be pushed out"). Clitoric sensations seemed an easy challenge, as compared with vaginal excitations, which were scattered all over, unclear and unlocalizable. She never was quite sure where they were. In an effort to decide whether they were inside or outside, she would touch her clitoris. She deduced from lack of excitement in the clitoris, as determined by touch, that the sensations must be elsewhere. She was keenly dissatisfied with direct explorations of the vagina, as she could not find solid unshiftable boundaries, and could not get the image of the vagina as a whole organ, being unable to encompass the whole structure at once. Active experimentation would follow the passive perception of sensations, coming from different parts of the vagina as well as from the clitoris. She was less frightened by and surer of her vaginal contractions, which she could produce at will. Wonderment about the motility of the vagina was worked out in connection with mechanics of intercourse. These she associated with a contraption easily recognizable as a spinning top, a toy from her childhood. She speculated helplessly, asking like a very small child whether the whole body of the top moved or merely the outside, with the axle remaining stationary. She worried about not being able to spin the top if it fell sideways, an idea linked up with earlier lateral shifts of the vagina image. It was conspicuous that the patient's thinking showed unmistakable characteristics of a two-to-three-year-old child's reasoning. In one session she kept using the words *vagina* and *baby* interchangeably, so that I could not understand what she was saying. When I asked her what she meant, she glossed over the confusing aspect of this condensation in the same way a two-year-old ignores the gaps between reality and fantasy. When she finally got to understand that there was meaning to her using these terms as if she was speaking of one and the same object, her ego functions lifted to the level of an adult, but she could no longer remember what she had said.

Only after the vaginal confusion was thus worked through, did the patient express fantasies associated with the positive and negative oedipus complex, as they related to her wish for a child. She also returned then to a preoccupation with the mechanics of defecation, dwelling for some time on the withholding-work-production factor in anal birth, which she developed along lines identical with Nelly's ideas. Withholding was linked with vaginal excitations. Much earlier she was able to recover the memory of fused clitoric-vaginal sensations which occurred during the excited jumping in her childhood. Needless to say that castration wishes and fears as well as penis envy entered into the fantasies connected with the positive and negative oedipus wishes.

DEVELOPMENT OF SEXUALITY

A girl in late latency displayed conspicuous symptoms of penis envy in her analysis. She seemed forever arrested in the early maternal phase, woven through with anal sadistic and genital masochistic wishes. She too showed a confusion between a vagina and a baby, in her own drawings of the inside and in her understanding of diagrams. An extremely articulate child, she called her vaginal feelings "yearnings" in contradistinction to clitoric sensations which were associated with masochistic fantasies of being raped, enslaved herself, and enslaving others. In trying to explore her vagina through the small opening the hymen allowed, she fantasied that a child is coming out, and was keenly disappointed because she could not get very far with her finger, and could not touch anything tangible inside. The unfulfilled yearning and the disappointment after the fruitless exploration would enhance her penis envy as well as her resentment of her mother, who neither satisfied the yearnings nor gave her a penis. When she reached adolescence, she was able to stop clitoric masturbation, but her sadomasochistic genital fantasies were either acted out or filled her thinking to a point where effective functioning became impossible. When she understood that the new fantasies were replicas of her earlier "slave and torture" ideas, she found herself incapable of imagining them any longer. Instead painful vaginal sensations appeared for the first time. I reminded her how she used to interrupt her earlier clitoris masturbation each time when she felt that she had hurt herself. The physical part of her masturbation ran parallel to her stopping of masochistic fantasies, before the actual rape occurred. As a child, she had a habit of wetting her pants and holding her feces until she developed severe abdominal cramps. These cramps were continued into the phase of menstrual cramps. In the anal withholding as well as in the clitoris handling, excitement, pain, anxiety and relief were typical sequences which could not be adequately explained until the contribution of vaginal excitations to these processes became apparent. She had associated feces with inner little people, her slaves, and this had led to links with anal birth and anal penis ideas. Only when she could not continue her sadomasochistic daydreams any longer no matter how hard she tried, she found that instead of these fantasies there appeared unpleasant burning sensations in her vagina. She had no control over their coming and going, but the sequence of excitement, pain, fear and temporary relief remained. She was glad to cooperate to the utmost hoping to get rid of the uncontrollable feelings. She associated the burning with the pain of delivery. She wanted to stop the sensation before an injury would occur, while at the same time she could not wait to get the baby, she needed it so badly. Delivery would stop unbearable inner sensations, yet feelings of loss, injury (her vagina falling to pieces) and letdown were associated with continuing the sensation to the peak of delivery (equation of genital discharge with child delivery).

A similar set of fantasies interfered with the older patient's ability for orgastic discharge. To her, excitement was life; the end of excitement was death. Externalization of the life-giving vaginal impulses to the outside, to an already delivered baby, circumvented the feeling of vaginal loss and injury. That kind of solution was only temporarily successful in the life of the younger patient, when she had revived doll play shortly before the onset of her menstruation. She gave the new doll complete bodily care and fantasied that her boyfriend was the doll's father. Only when playing with dolls became unacceptable as too unreal, was she able to express the connection between vaginal sensations and her need for a baby. After the baby-doll experience, turning to penis envy and urgent but passive wishes toward her father could be seen. They were followed by a relapse to phallic, sadomasochistic wishes toward her mother, the analysis of which revealed again the underlying unbearable tensions, which she wanted to eject into the form of a baby.

Helene Deutsch (1945) recognized the importance of organ lack in the development of the girl. Both observation and analyses seem to indicate that the girl's first substitute, created to compensate for the organ lack, is a baby. Vaginal tensions appear to urge the girl on in her need for an organ of discharge. The difficulty in localization as well as the enigmatic quality and multilocality of fleeting vaginal sensations create a confusion in her, which she tries to solve in two ways. In one type of solution she fuses vaginal tensions with others, coming from the inside of her body, and displaces their common bulk to orifices with which she has become familiar, such as the mouth, the anus, and the urethral opening. A similar mechanism connects the genital to the nose. Such fusions and displacements are facilitated by the simultaneous occurrence of various sensations. The second, most important way, by which the girl tries to overcome her confusion about vaginal impulses, is to externalize them, at first to a baby and later, in the phallic phase, to a penis. Both are solid outer objects rather than parts of her own body. Fusions and externalizations do not give permanent relief and are, therefore, abandoned over and over again throughout the girl's development, thus creating a psychological readiness for the adult feminine cycles.

Externalization of inner sensations is reiterated in the cathecting of bodily orifices, in the attachment to transitional objects, and in the girl's creation of her very own "fetish," her doll-baby. The image of that baby is molded after the child's own body as well as after that of the mother. The vagueness of early vaginal sensations and the lack of differentiation of vaginal and sphincter contractions create a fertile atmosphere for the development of intuition, rather than knowledge, about the exis-

45

tence of a female inner organ.[8] This intuitive quality is displaced, alongside with the vague tensions, onto the relationship of the girl with her baby doll. The little mother intuits what is wrong with the baby and alleviates it. In a period in which turning of passivity into activity predominates, the little girl has a strong need for mastery which she can achieve in relation to her doll, while discharge on and mastery of the inner genital is not feasible.[9] Where the environment does not furnish a doll, siblings and the mother herself are used for the same purpose as the doll. Fantasies about making the mother small like a baby belong to this period (Deutsch, 1933; Freud, A., 1949). Children, who do play with dolls, alternately use people and dolls for the achievement of mastery. The intuitive quality of the early doll play is reinforced by the girl's identification with her own intuitive mother.

Where clearly localized vaginal sensations, introduction of foreign bodies into the vagina, and even orgastic masturbation in the vagina, have been reported as experiences of childhood, the published clinical material (Müller, 1932; Hann-Kende, 1933; Eissler, 1939; Kramer, 1954) does not lend itself to an evaluation of motherliness in such deviant development. A reverse relationship between vaginal sensitivity and maternal needs in adult women has been clearly elucidated by Helene Deutsch. Adult vaginal satisfaction in coitus and masturbation brings relief of sexual tension, but does not allow for active mastery of the organ. The girl has to yield the exploring, fear-conquering activity on her vagina to the man. This she normally does in her role as the receptive passive partner in intercourse. The active manipulation and mastery of her infant substitute for her inability to develop actively a clear image of her inner genital. Following Freud's concept of motherhood as an active occupation, Wittels (1933) suggested that motherhood was in part a sublimation of masculinity. Undoubtedly the wish for masculinity is operative in the desire to have a child.[10] However, underlying the wish for masculinity is the more fundamental urge to respond with active motor discharge to sensory stimuli. In the ego, this biological urge is represented in the wish to experiment actively with organ boundaries and organ qualities, crowned by the achievement of a secure body image. In terms of object relationship, the same sphere of interest is expressed in the small child's eagerness to show his discoveries to his mother, and to exhibit proudly not only what he or she had, but also what he has done to his possessions.[11]

The Passing of the Early Maternal Stage

Just as the real mother has to accept the giving up of her infant because he grows into a child, and countless times before had to renounce a hoped-for pregnancy with each return of menstruation, the illusory little mother goes through similar experiences. (See chapter 11) Various episodes in which the unreality of the doll-baby becomes apparent contribute to the girl's growing understanding that she is merely playing with a doll and has no baby. Sometime during the third or fourth year, traumatic incidences of doll mutilations are linked with ideas of the baby's death. In a way, with the "death of the doll,"[12] the world of unreality and magic creativity seems to die too. The girl may now pass through a phase of dull obedience and lack of productivity. Depressions varying from brief letdowns to prolonged periods of depressive inhibition occur now.[13] With the devaluation of the doll, the little girl's inside becomes devaluated too. She withdraws from the doll as well as from her mother, who neither gave her genital satisfaction nor a substitute for it, a real child. The "major withdrawal and shift of cathexis from the object to the self-representations" (Jacobson, 1954) leads her to transitory "inactivity or general inhibition of the ego activity." After the recovery from this depressive phase, in which the loss of the baby was equated with the loss of the mother, the little girl returns to her mother as a love object in the new phase of phallic orientation.

It is important to consider the role of aggressive impulses and actions in the behavior of the "little mother," because they have a decisive influence upon the form and length of her prephallic depressions. Needless to say, that unresolved oral and anal sadistic problems enhance a more regressive form of depression. In her maternal behavior, the little girl acts out on the doll her aggressions against the mother, as well as the hostility which her mother inflicts upon her. Parallel to these phenomena which belong to the realm of object relationships, there goes on in the girl a latent battle between herself and those parts of her body which disturb her equilibrium through increase of tensions. Deep-seated autotomic impulses to destroy the sources of unbearable itching, swelling, yearning, are associated with fears of bodily harm, which the small child gleefully projects upon the mother and her doll.

Nelly, whose bodily excitations made it difficult for her to fall asleep and once asleep to maintain sleep, accused her mother of waking her when she got out of bed or screamed for someone to come to her at night. She scolded her doll severely for screaming, and threatened to take her to the analyst if her bad behavior would not stop. Other children, who are freer in expressing their aggression and who show more intense sadism, sometimes attack a doll with a fury very similar to the rage expressed by a depressive adult patient who fantasied pulling out her excited vagina and losing it in the bloody menstrual discharge. She hoped that such a loss by

47

self-inflicted injury (which she also dreaded) would rid her of undischargea-
ble sexual tensions forever. She acted out this fantasy by repeatedly losing
her pocketbook. While in other phases of her analysis she wanted to be
a boy who could ret rid of sexual tensions on his penis, in the moments
of greatest excitement and rage she wished for aphanisis (Jones, 1927)
rather than for a penis. The young woman, described earlier, remembered
biting one of her early dolls. In her fears of delivery, the image of mutilation of the baby in the birth process was linked to memories of injuries
inflicted by herself upon various dolls and to fantasies of her mother who
threw the doll's head out of the window "and would take away her baby"
once it were safely delivered.

Spitz and Wolf (1949) described a typical group of depressed mothers
whose children developed coprophilic tendencies. They presented a picture of the self-sacrificing, self-debasing mother who envelops her child
with love. Their worries about their infants expressed themselves in anxious questioning whether the baby was blind or deaf. The incidence of
injury of the children at the hands of their mothers was great. Such a
maternal behavior is identical with the play behavior of the "little
mother who loves her doll to death" and examines it anxiously, worrying
about any little defect.

Nelly, for instance, playing with tiny dolls, asked the analyst compulsively what the side seam on the doll was. She was sure it was an
injury. On seeing a microscopic protuberance on the doll's foot, she
asked anxiously who pulled it out. She refused to let anyone play with
one of the little dolls who had a small hole in the foot. She ruminated
about the question who had broken the doll and how it was done. She
wondered whether she might have crashed it with her foot, as she remembered stepping carelessly over a number of small toys lying on the
floor and breaking some in the process. Her preoccupation with defects
was connected with the discovery of the introitus, and was not overlaid
with penis-envy yet. P dropped her dolls suddenly, and used to stick her
finger in the doll's eye, although she had a faint awareness that such an
act hurts people and can lead to a disfigurement of dolls. One must not
forget, in this context that not every careless action of the "little
mother" is due to an aggressive impulse. Much of it is a result of the
two-to-three-year-old girl's lack of skill, her poor sense of reality and her
sudden shifting of cathexis with which she reacts to new pleasurable
stimuli. A feeling of being a little child, incapable of handling a real
baby, might have contributed to a repetition of early lack of skill, in
the behavior of Spitz's depressive mothers. Such a self-evaluation is typical of infantile mothers, who have to be helped in every step of child

48

care. A transitory feeling that her own lack of qualification for infant care renders her helpless, confronts every new mother who grows up in our culture.

Further Developments of the Wish for the Baby

Except in cases of very early intense penis envy, the girl in the phallic phase not only explores her outer genital but also masturbates. She continues her interest in her genital, which had started sometime during the first year when she discovered it manually. In her first genital strivings she had passive aims and often expressed the wish to be handled by her mother in her genital region.[14] Now she frequently succeeds in getting a visual experience by bending down and looking between her legs. In the course of her handling of her genital, she experiments not only with the shape and consistency of all parts she can reach, but also tries out different movements which in turn produce different sensations. Just as the boy is worried about a possible self-injury, she too at that time develops castration fears in connection with present and past scratches and hurts.

Soon the clitoris is singled out as a more sensitive and distinct organ which conveys the qualities of aliveness she had lost earlier in the discovery of the inanimateness of the doll. Frequent complaints about the flabby consistency and the undefined borders of the rest of the genital highlight the clitoris as a very special organ, which the girl hopes to enlarge by various manipulations. Fantasies about growing a penis (illusory penis [Rado, 1933] seem to alternate with hopes to grow a baby externally. At the height of the phallic phase the girl cathects the clitoris in the sense of an active masculine organ. She develops a sense of organ belonging. Because this organ gives her a great deal of satisfaction she feels that it might satisfy her mother too. Both the baby and the penis which she wants to develop there are meant to be presented to her mother now. But the baby idea is mostly condensed with the penis representation, as the penis itself is valued as a baby-making organ. A frequent speculation of this time concerns impregnation with a penis which, deposited in a mother, transforms into a baby. This in turn leads to ideas of multiple penises, as many as necessary to produce a lot of babies. Such thoughts are also used for consolation about the smallness of the clitoris, which "was big once and will grow back to make another baby." The girl eventually gives up her mother attachment and this libidinous zone because of her disappointment in the zone itself and in the mother who failed to give her an organ more suitable for satisfaction and baby-

49

making. Many a time the clitoris is only given up as an organ of satisfaction for the mother and remains active in connection with fantasies directed toward the father.

During the play with the outer genital, the child is able to discharge a great many vaginal tensions, as the clitoris seems to draw from all genital zones. On the other hand, the handling of the clitoris, labia and the introitus region stimulates the vagina much more than earlier pregenital activities. Both the discovery of the introitus and the increase of vaginal stimulation connected with its explorations contribute to the denial of the introitus and vagina. The girl, who had become bolder and had come closer to the vagina in her explorations, now withdraws and goes further and further away from it. She will either retreat swiftly to the clitoris or else remain only active on the periphery of the labia and the skin around the genital. Her castration fears are denied along with the denial of the hole she has discovered on the genital. In her play with dolls, she may now act out her fears of injury. Pregenital fantasies contribute to her playing that the doll is being wet, soiled, stamped and torn. In this play, the doll represents the girl herself as well as her mother and father, but also her own genital. The preoccupation with castration fears occupies the child so much that the baby wish, latent in the early phallic phase, recedes more and more.

The long identification with the father prepares a fertile ground for the development of a positive relationship to him. However, when the girl hopes for genital gratification by the father, her castration fears frequently are transformed into a castration wish. The desire for the child is revived, as it substitutes for the missing penis and is considered a gift indicating the father's love for the girl. The fantasy of an incorporated penis has succeeded the idea that a penis will grow on the outside. Edith Jacobson (1937) recognized this fantasy as favorable for the development of femininity, as she found that it paved the way for the acceptance of an inner genital organ. This thought of vaginal ingestion of the penis, and the masochistic desire to be injured and penetrated, lead to a recathexis of the inside of the body. If the girl has stopped masturbation she has no discharge channels for external and internal excitations. She may revive the early doll play with added features, which indicate that the baby of this period is identified with a penis. Toward the end of the oedipal phase and carried through into latency, the games with dolls are used to express oedipal wishes. Teenage dolls are in vogue now. The girls play out fairy stories of princesses who, first persecuted by a mother figure, eventually marry the king, get children and live happily ever after.

In this phase the girl may come closest to an awareness of vaginal sensations. When resolution of oedipal wishes prompts her to repress it and to postpone her hope for marriage and children, she can express her wish for a baby with greater ease than her wish for sexual gratification. The baby image, and with it the doll play, has become desexualized. Preoccupation with dolls' clothes substitutes for the earlier baby care games. Costume dolls, sewing of dolls' dresses come into the foreground. As the girl grew, her child-doll has grown with her. Revivals of earlier forms of play occur both in latency and prepuberty, even in adolescence. The form the play takes in each individual instance reveals the phase that is being relived. Age-adequate modifications as acting out with puppets, marionettes, and costume dolls, contribute to such extensions of doll play. In each successive phase the girl acts on her doll what she wishes would happen to her. But she identifies herself with a mother of a growing child too. The doll is still used to express and act out genital wishes which the girl herself is unable to admit and experience. The externalization of genital impulses and the projection of genital wish fulfillment upon the doll continue. We can see here the similarity to the mother of a growing girl, who eventually has to give up her youthful sexual aspirations and tends to relive sexual gratification by identification with her daughter (Freud, 1913). She not only shares the daughter's gratifications, but also projects upon the girl her own forbidden or repressed sexual wishes. Where parents expect their children to fulfill their thwarted ambitions, the behavior of the father can be identical with that of the mother. But the boy rarely experiences as intense a yearning for a child as the girl does, nor does the father involve himself with his children to the extent a mother does.

The Boy's Wish for a Baby[15]

Benedek traces the origin of the wish to become a parent to an instinctual drive for survival (1970 a, b). The mother survives in her daughter and the father in his son. Children are also looked upon as reincarnations of their grandparents (see page 456). Both sexes, in their quest for a child, identify with the preoedipal and later with the oedipal mother, and both sexes hope to become impregnated by the father. Both identify with the father and wish to give the mother a phallic baby. Yet, the outcome of these early struggles is as different for boys and girls as they themselves differ in their anatomical and physiological makeup. The boy identifies with his father and wishes to become a father in the future; the girl identifies with her mother and looks forward to being a mother. Men are often maternal and women, especially of late, try to assume the role of the mother and father as well. Since the first signs of maternal preoccupation reveal themselves in the preoedipal phase of development, both sexes are primed for motherliness through their early relationship with their mother. As a result, motherliness is a trait of both sexes while women never quite succeed in being fatherly. A man's wish for a baby is sublimated in his creative work. Yet, he finds great satisfaction in being a father. What is the biological source of his parental feelings and how does it develop?

Through analyses of women and children I have come to the conclusion that inner-genital drives are the source of motherly feeling. Subsequently, the analyses of fathers and of men who could not beget children as well as the analyses of preoedipal boys, suggested to me that inner-genital drives are also the primary sources of male "motherliness." Their externalization and condensation on the penis in the phallic phase transforms the primarily male motherliness into fatherliness.

In the transitional object, common to both sexes, we have seen the early model for a child.[16] Both sexes derive the equations breast = food = baby = feces from the oral and anal phases respectively. The boy, more than the girl, looks upon the fecal column as a penis. This results in a double representation of the baby as feces and a feces-penis. More than the girl, does the boy look upon the urinating penis as a model for a baby. In transition from urethral to genital interests, he may alternate between feeding a baby-doll, like his mother feeds him, and using the "milk" as a substitute for urine and the bottle as substitute for the penis (see pp. 34-35). Equating his testicles with maternal breasts ("mine are down here and yours up there"), a boy will try to manipulate them trying to find a baby in them. In the phase in which he identifies with his mother and becomes motherly, the boy copes with inner-genital impulses by externalizing them upon baby objects, preferably toy animals, cars, and trains. Even if encouraged to play with dolls, he uses them less consistently and less possessively than the girl. Thus, from the beginning the boy's motherliness is diverted so that he functions like a part-time mother. Because of his particular genital deep sensibility and inner involuntary motility, his inner-genital tensions that some day will lead to the creation of a child's call for a greater degree of experimentation than doll play alone can provide. He endows his mother with a phallus and expects to grow up to be a phallic mother like her (Kestenberg, 1969, 1971). Nevertheless he has no intention of giving up his masculine identity; he does not wish to become a girl or woman, as he might later when he develops negative oedipal attitudes. He equates a baby to a penis, but to him the image of the penis encompasses all external and internal genital structures as an indistinct, yet anthropomorphic unit, with the testicles as eyes and the penis as a nose. He pictures himself and the baby inside his mother and he visualizes his mother in his own inner genital. Sometimes, an adult, who relives this phase in analysis, draws testicles as if they were maternal breasts and the penis as if it were mother's arm. Out of the double representation of the boy himself and his mother, there emerges the image of a shared baby. Toys that he endowed with a live quality are used to externalize impulses from the inner genitals and to project fantasies about the inside upon them.[17] He also experiments with retaining and expelling feces and urine to influence and dominate the mysteriously moving genital understructure. At the same time he tries to dominate his mother whom he identifies with his bossy inside. In his effort to disengage himself from his mother's body, he stresses that she has a penis of her own and does not need to treat him as her penis-boy. At the same time, severing the bonds to the mother represents a mutilation of his body and hers. He solves this problem by denying that he has an inner-genital structure (Chapter 13) and by externalizing inner-genital tensions upon his phallus. Because of the external and visceral sensibility of the penis, this organ lends itself especially for the interception and containment of externalized inner-genital impulses.

Giving up the preoedipal union with his mother, the boy has to accept that she is a separate person and has no penis. This makes him not only very frightened but also very angry. He finds himself in a double bind: growing up to be a mother will rob him of his precious organ and growing up to be a father will prevent him from having a baby inside (Van der Leeuwen, 1958). As he mourns the loss of his preoedipal, inner-genital (diffusely phallic) baby-mother, he also gives up his own babyhood. He recovers from this depression, not only through denying the existence of inner genitals in himself and in all males but also through isolating the penis from them. The glamour of the masculinity of the penis (Freud, A., 1952), which draws cathexes from the denigrated pregenital and inner-genital zones, becomes the center of the phallic boy's life. Hoping to take his father's place, in fantasy he adds his father's penis to his own and generously promises his mother to give her many bigger and better children. A small baby and a baby girl are disdained. The wish to give mother a very special baby has its roots in the overestimation of feces; the desire to make a baby all by himself (a homunculus) lingers on from the preceding maternal phase. These contribute to the phallic boy's wishes that a boy-child be born as an extension of his phallus. They, in turn, contribute their share to a father's feeling that his son is an extension of himself.

DEVELOPMENT OF SEXUALITY

Passive oedipal strivings bring on identification with the oedipal mother, a wish to be penetrated by the father, and given a child (Freud, 1923b). Pregenital, especially anal, fantasies of impregnation are regressively revived and elaborated. Inner-genital impulses fuse with anal-receptive urges and cease to be externalized on the phallus. As soon as the "grandeur of phallic narcissism" (Freud, A., 1952b) is restored, the boy scorns babies and dolls except in play with heroic, hypermasculine warriors or rescuers from evil deeds. When he becomes more secure in his male role, he accepts children and plays house with girls in the role of a father, who gives presents to his wife and provides for her (Benedek, 1970b). At the end of this phase, the boy projects his wishes for a child on the female sex and reinforces the denial of his own internal genital structures by assigning them to women rather than men (Chapter 13). In normal development, the predominance of phallic interests combines with cultural influences to perpetuate the estrangement of the growing boy from babies and dolls. But, in identification with his father he expects to marry and have children when he grows up. In young adulthood, the man's wish for a child is overdetermined by tendencies: to emulate the father and reproduce him, to reproduce himself as well and relive his own childhood. These ideas may be conscious while the continued need to externalize, and thus desexualize, inner-genital impulses upon the child is still denied and projected upon women.

From analyses of men who suffer from a strong identification with their mothers, we can learn about two distinct types of wishing for a baby in a feminine way: (1) The man who identifies with the preoedipal, phallic mother repeats the mother-child relationship when he chooses a person to represent himself while he takes on the role of the mother. He rarely wants a child as a result of this union; if he does produce one, he mothers the child instead of acting toward him like a father. He chooses people who stand for a boy-child for his love objects; if he fathers a daughter, he treats her like a boy. In such cases, there is usually an oral fixation which prevents the resolution of problems arising in the maternal phase of development. (2) The man who identifies with his mother on the basis of negative oedipal strivings has passive desires toward his father and vagina-uterus envy of his mother. He experiences genital sensations in the pelvis (Federn, 1913) or shifts their focus to abdominal tensions and anal sensations. Confusion and helplessness, analogous to that of women who respond in that way to vaginal sensations, is related to abdominal pain, distension, cramps, and countless other unfathomed inner sensations. There is difficulty in turning from passivity to activity which, in normal development, fosters a shift of cathexis to the outside, especially to the phallus. Instead of displacement onto the genitals, we see in such cases fusions of genital and anal sensations. Erections are tied with sphincter contractions and anal-pelvic representations become one with the image of the penis. A wish to be pregnant and deliver a baby is very pronounced (Van der Leeuwen, 1958).

> In the case of a patient of this type, periodic acting out of delivery during analytic sessions brought about extreme passivity, relaxation to the point of sleep and incoherent talk. During these episodes the penis was erected. Only bits of the incoherent, later repressed associations would betray abdominal sensations, wishes to be penetrated, and disguised hopes to deliver a baby safely. On one hand, the erection of the penis served as a signal that all this was only a game; on the other hand, the penis represented the child who came out uninjured and in one piece. At the end of the delivery game, the patient would jump up, practically sit up on the couch and would suddenly be able to act his usual masculine self. The erection would go down as soon as the sleepy period would end. The penis was used here as an accumulator, condensor and reactor for anal and inner-genital sensations; it also represented a child. Early in the analysis before the development of these sleep attacks, this patient brought his analyst a toy figure which was given to him by his mother. The statue was a symbolic representation of a little boy and was called by a nickname which was also used for the patient, hence an object equivalent to a doll.

In recent years, feminine identification and the enjoyment of baby care has been encouraged and declared compatible with the image of a young married father. Nevertheless, men still prefer playing with older children than caring for babies. Many are much more comfortable in their role as providers (Benedek, 1960, 1970b) and teachers than in the role of "maternal caretakers." However, the new trend that allows men to participate in deliveries has enriched male experience and has enhanced a more complex integration of bisexual impulses. Witnessing the delivery of his baby brings on a renewal of man's castration fear, but also provides an opportunity for the working through of the resolution of his castration complex. This in turn facilitates a better acceptance of women and babies.

The Influence of Tradition and Culture on the Choice of Baby Substitutes in Children's Play

In discussing the concept of doll-child = vagina in early childhood, Benedek (1952) emphasized the girl's identification with her pregnant mother and questioned the emphasis on dolls, as developed in my previ-

55

ous paper on female sexuality. Why children chose particular toys such as dolls to act out their libidinous problems, seemed to me a question well worth an investigation.

I am indebted to my husband for the suggestion that dolls of today may be descendants of idols, the formidable inanimate representations of parental figures. Many data from the spheres of language development, anthropology and fairy tales, tend to confirm this idea. For example, the word "doll," according to one theory of language development, is derived from the word "idol" (Daiken, 1953). The symbol of a child is traced from the symbol of a parent. In traditions and superstitions of many people, the female child appears to be a reincarnation of the grandmother, while the male child is taken for a reincarnation of the father. We are reminded here of unconscious fantasies which play a role in the early development of the wish for a baby in both sexes. ("When I grow big and you grow small.") In one tribal society, after a festival in which gods have been celebrated, the children are given the divine images to play with (Mead, M., 1956). In this aftermath of a ceremonial, we possibly encounter a condensed repetition of prehistory. Parents, through tradition and language, encourage the small child's belief that the doll is a baby. Thus, in the doll custom of today we may find the condensation of old theories of reincarnation of ancestors through the equations ancestor = child, ancestor = stone, child = doll. The mother, who calls her little girl's doll a baby, is not the deceiver the child believes her to be when she begins to appreciate the inanimate quality of the doll. In the language of the primary process, in the unconscious, the doll apparently is a child. How ingrained the doll-baby equation used to be in our language can be shown from the following examples taken from Daiken's book *Children's Toys Throughout the Ages* (1953). Until 1850 the word "dollhouse" was not used in England. The then existing term was "babyhouse." The dictionaries of that time defined a doll as a "child's baby," although some began to be more realistic and called the doll a "girl's toy baby." (Compare P's transition from calling her doll a "baby" to "baby doll.")

An alternate theory about the derivation of the word "doll" connects the doll with femininity. It has been thought that "doll" was derived from the name "Dolly." The doll as symbol of femininity also appears in the Japanese doll festival. The girls' festival is celebrated by a display of dolls, the boys' festival is distinguished by waving phallic symbols in the form of kites depicting fishes. Thus the boy's sex is defined by the phallus, while the girl's sex is defined by a doll. The size of the kite flown during the boy's festival is directed by the size of the child to be celebrated in the household. The fish kite seems to stand for the whole male child as well as for the phallus. By analogy, the doll probably represents the female child as well as the female genital. Freud was of the opinion that a "child" *(Kleines* = "little one") symbolically represents the genital, male or female. He also pointed out that raw material, such as wood, is a symbol of femininity, and objects made out of raw material, such as a wooden table, are also feminine. Primitive images are made of stone or wood. Thus, the inanimate wooden doll symbolically may stand for a child, for the genital and for femininity.

The theme of inanimateness of the stone image, as contrasted with the alive qualities of real babies, is preserved in such fairy tales as the one about the wolf who stole and ate the babies of the goat. The mother rescued her live children by cutting the wolf's belly open, and replaced the babies with stones. M. Klein believed that in the pebble play of toddlers, the little stones represent babies (personal communication). "Jacks" which are used in a typical girl's game of skill (Chapter 1) are successors of Jack-stones. Primitive jacks were small stones, the modern jack is made out of metal. An identical theme appears in the custom of primitive shamans, who in imitation of delivery, retire into the woods where they are supposed to deliver stones (Mead, 1949). The absence of the female genital in the male shaman prevents the delivery of live babies. Similarly, the inner genital of the little girl, which is not ready to deliver a live baby, psychologically appears inanimate, empty, dead, stonelike. In folklore, an intercourse in which the woman is frigid, is said to be incompatible with conception. The presumably lifeless, stone cold vagina of a child, when externalized, can be only transformed into an inanimate baby, not a live one.

The masculinization of the inner genital, which develops in the phallic stage, gives the little girl new hope for a real, live, now male baby. In Bali, where the phallus is overcathected, little girls carry cucumbers in the same position their mothers carry the babies (Mead, M., 1956). In a society like the Sioux (described by Erikson, 1950) where the relationship of a mother to her infant takes preference over her relation to her husband and great value is placed upon the preservation of the hymen (the guardian of the vagina) before marriage, little girls are given dolls to play with. Thus, the baby substitutes may differ from culture to culture. The environment may encourage the prolongation of one developmental phase and diminish the impact of another. Accordingly, the baby substitutes with which the children play will differ.

Discussion

The question of vaginal sensations in early childhood is still controversial. The average little girl seems to fuse her vaginal excitations with sensations stemming from other zones. In addition, she externalizes vaginal tensions to the outside of her body. Unable to experience a direct vaginal discharge and unable to master vaginal excitations by active exploration, she tends to externalize her wish for mastery. In the baby-doll she finds a suitable substitute for the lack of an organ of discharge. When the aforementioned mechanisms break down, denial sets in. When vaginal sensations threaten to invade consciousness, repressive forces may be set in operation, which can be lifted during analyses. At the end of phallic development during which the baby-wish has become attached to the penis-wish, the inside of the female child is recathected, as the girl wishes to be penetrated like her mother and hopes to receive a baby.

These vaginal desires undergo further repression at the time the girl abandons her oedipal wishes and enters the latency period. This seems to be the average development, while cases in which vaginal sensations became fully conscious in childhood appear to be few and exceptional.

Various fusions, projections and externalizations of early vaginal impulses seem to contribute to the changing image of the girl's inside, which is later used for the development of the image of the vagina as an organ. Successive oral, anal, baby and phallic representations eventually merge with the final, more realistic image of the vagina. Each of these developmentally fixed representations can contribute its useful share to the various functions of the adult woman in her role as a mother. The oral representation, modeled after the primal cavity (Spitz, 1955), can foster the vaginal incorporation wish, so necessary for the initiation of pregnancy. The anal image can contribute to the retentive aspects of pregnancy. Both the anal and urethral images may serve as a model for the expelling in delivery. The baby image seems to enhance the mother's need to take care of her infant. The early female-baby concept coupled with the later penis-baby image make it possible for a mother to accept female and male children. Clitoric representations and fantasies may underlie the maternal concern with the steady growth of her small child. The many times in which the girl gives up her hope for a baby during her early development may well prepare her not only for the cycles of her adulthood, but also for the time when she eventually has to give up her children, so that they may form intimate relationships with others.

The more the wish for the baby is based on the underlying desire to master the genital as an organ, the more desexualized are the maternal functions. If there is a predominance of a need for discharge of vaginal tensions over the wish for mastery, the child is primarily used for discharge purposes and treated like a sex object. If it is true that the unfulfilled need to discharge and master early vaginal tensions creates the typically feminine wish for a child, the hymen, specific only to the human species, may prove to be the necessary prerequisite for the acceptance of children and a safeguard for the preservation of the species. Possibly with the development of the anterior extremities into prehensile organs, the vagina became more accessible to exploration so that a new protective device was needed to prevent premature sexual involvement. Undischarged vaginal tensions may serve as the biological vector of motherhood, substituting for the animal instinct. The intuitive "knowledge" of the vagina, derived from the unclear, shifting vaginal tensions, may be the source of the mysterious maternal quality called intuition. The yearning of women for children of both sexes as the ultimate fulfillment seems to be due to a long preparation for that kind of satisfaction. Children gratify the mother's desire for a reunion with her parents, and for the perpetuation of the parent-child relationship. A child also represents an ideal solution for the problems arising from the inaccessibility and enigmatic quality of the inner genital.

How the boy's wish for a child fits into his psychosexual development is one of the cryptic problems in psychoanalysis that is, perhaps, more difficult to understand than the enigma of female sexuality (Van der Leeuwen, 1958). The infant boy cherishes babylike transitional objects and the male toddler plays with baby-dolls in identification with his preoedipal mother. The boy equates babies with breasts, food, feces, urine, and testicles and condenses all these representations in the image of the boy-child as a phallus. In a prephalic, maternal phase, he externalizes inner-genital impulses on toys which represent babies. However, his overt maternality is more sporadic and less intensely expressed than that of the girl. In the phallic phase, his penis intercepts and accumulates the externalized inner-genital impulses and becomes a distinct entity. In his active oedipal strivings, the phallic boy looks upon babies as an extension of his penis and creates them, in fantasy, from wished-for reserve penises, multiple and replaceable like machinery parts. He gives them to his oedipal mother who needs them as a consolation for her lack of a penis. In his passive oedipal strivings, the boy wants to receive a child from his father and he condenses anal and inner-genital wishes in the fantasy that he too has a special place for the baby like his mother. With the repression of oedipal wishes, the phallic and the inner-genital or pregenital babies all come under disrepute. In identification with his father, the boy expects, some day, to be a father himself, but not until adolescence, does he begin to accept his inside genital structures as instrumental in the production of the baby. Because of his need to affirm his male identity, man often denies his maternal interests. He frequently prefers boys to girls and older children to babies. Equating small babies and anal babies with girls and big ones as well as phallic babies with boys are male fantasies which prepare the growing boy for his role as a father of small and big girls and boys. Through externalization of inner-genital impulses and the sublimation of corresponding drives as well as through identification with his mother and his wife, man can accept the nurturing of children in a maternal way. His maternal feelings may be a better guarantee against infanticide than his fatherly concerns. The latter rest on identification with his father, and on reaction formations against the wish to eliminate the oedipal rival son—a reincarnation of his father or brother. His daughter, as reincarnation of his mother, is often identified with inner-genital organs rather than a phallus. When his inner-genital impulses are desexualized, he treats her tenderly like a precious object. He is more of a disciplinarian to the son to whose seductive overtures he responds with fear. When his paternal behavior is sexualized, he can be seductive in a phallic way to a son or daughter during their oedipal phase; or, he may use a child to satisfy his forbidden infantile curiosity about the inside of the body. However, because of his sublimatory activities outside the home and because of the reduced bodily contact between him and the child, he is less prone than the mother to attack him when he himself is beset by inner tensions.

Women and men derive their maternal attitude from identifications with their mothers. These are converted into paternal traits in successive phases of the boy's identification with his father. The need to be maternal has its biological roots in the inner-genital apparatus of both sexes. But the man's wish to reproduce himself (Benedek, 1960, 1970) is based on his masculine apparatus. Guided by tension from inside, the boy emulates his mother in her maternal behavior. But his typically male maternality allows much less time for child care than the more sustained female who needs to have and to hold, to carry and care for. The boy has more time than the girl for activities dealing with the exploration and alteration of external objects which are derived from baby images. He will become a full-time researcher, worker, or businessman and a part-time father. In contrast, his wife, even if she works full time outside the home, always remains primarily a mother and is only secondarily concerned with other forms of sublimations of her inner-genital drives.

NOTES

[1]See particularly Abraham (1920), Bonaparte (1935, 1953), Brierley (1932, 1936), Deutsch (1933, 1944–45), Fenichel (1934), Ferenczi (1919), Hitschmann and Bergler (1934), Horney (1926, 1932, 1933), Jacobson (1936, 1937), Jones (1927, 1933, 1934), Klein (1932), Lampl-de Groot (1928, 1933), Lorand (1939), Mack Brunswick (1940), Müller (1932), Payne (1935), Riviere (1934).

[2]This factor in itself contributes largely to the obscurity which envelops our understanding of feminine development.

[3]Later called the "inner-genital." For discussion of the "urethral" phase that follows the anal, and precedes the "inner-genital" phase, see Chapters 5 and 13 and Kestenberg (1966).

[4]For evidence derived from the analyses of small children, see Chapter 8 and Kestenberg (1969).

[5]The toy industry, which is usually quite sensitive to both permanent and transitory childhood needs, teaches us that boy dolls are items of small demand. Those boys who are allowed to play with dolls show little interest in them when they reach the phallic phase. Since this paper was written in 1956, men dolls (such as GI Joe) have become very popular. They are successors of soldiers, toys with which boys play traditionally. Baby-boy dolls are still items of small demand.

[6]Greenacre (1948) described an intuitive knowledge of the vagina. In what mea-influence of anatomical structures upon the development of the superego.

[7]The equation of womb and baby in the unconscious has been pointed out by Jacobson (1950).

[8]Greenacre (1948) described an intuitive knowledge of the vagina. In what measure the phylogenetically determined "unconscious knowledge" (Klein 1932) or rather, readiness for knowledge, contributes to intuition is difficult to say on the basis of clinical observation. The universality of such symbols as jewel boxes makes us inclined to believe that there is a readiness in the depth of the unconscious to accept the hollow quality of the female genital.

[9]Exceptions reported in literature will be discussed later.

[10]Bonaparte(1935) thought that the apparatus of maternity exercises an inhibiting influence upon the virility of the female organism. She considered female genital pleasures to be virile and stressed the feminine-masochistic aspects of pregnancy and delivery. Still she kept in mind the activity involved in baby care.

[11]Ferenczi(1919)illustrated this theme beautifully in his description of Cornelia, mother of the Gracchi, who felt the need to exhibit her children, saying: "These are my treasures, there are my jewels."

[12]Compare Stevenson's warm account(1954)of the death and funeral of Goggles, seven-year-old Janet's shapeless wooden doll. In my experience, such an incident during the latency period usually functions as a screen for much earlier doll events which occurred during a less realistic phase of development.

[13]The depression ending the early maternal stage requires further exploration. The greater proneness to depression in women, as compared with men, has been noted long ago (see Lewin [1950] and the literature cited in his book). The precipitating factors of such depressions are frequently severe labors or deliveries, but, paradoxically, easy deliveries as well. It may not be necessary to evoke the thesis of increased feminine orality (Gero, 1939) in all such cases. Depression, connected with childbearing and related functions, may turn out to have a history of a traumatic ending of the early maternal

stage of development. The resulting early depression may have been very severe in such cases, not necessarily because of an orally determined predisposition, but also because of the individual circumstances operating in this phase, which could have enhanced an oral regression. A loss of the baby would be anticipated in such cases, and the trauma of the early maternal stage repeated, regardless of the reality of a good delivery of a healthy baby.

Early penis envy, based on anal possessiveness or on urethral exhibitionistic needs, also fosters depression, as does the appearance of a rival, newborn sibling. Each of these depressions has its own distinctive features which overlap at times.

[14]Compare here the early passive strivings of the boy (Loewenstein, 1935).

[15]The subsection on the boy's wish for a baby and the discussion of this theme at the end of this paper have been rewritten for this publication.

[16]It is interesting to note that in the boy a continuation of transitional phenomena into adulthood leads to fetishism (Wulff, 1946; Greenacre, 1953, 1955). In the girl, such a continuation sometimes develops into a tendency to use her child like a fetish. Some such women need the presence of the child for sexual stimulation, although they are rarely conscious of the connection. They use various rationalizations to have the child sleep in one bed with the parents and, also by other means, continuously involve it in their sex relations. A mild variation of this fetishistic attitude is displayed by "saintly" women who consider intercourse, removed from the anticipation of a child, a sin.

[17]From such fantasies men derive material for stories about "My car is my baby" or "My mother, the car."

CHAPTER 3

Mother Types Encountered In
Child
Guidance Clinics

It is well known, both in child analysis and in child guidance, that an understanding of the mother's problem is of great importance for the treatment of the child. Insight into maternal characteristics can serve as a guideline in the approach to parents by the child's therapist. Mother-child relationships vary. Sometimes all of the children in a family, sometimes only one child, are treated in a special way. In this paper I shall discuss three types of mothers that can be most easily detected in child guidance clinics and those problems which have the most significant effect on the child's difficulties.

Freud (1914) drew attention to the role a child plays in a woman's life. He said that even narcissistic women who remain cool to their husbands find a way to full object-love when a part of their own bodies presents itself to them as an object in the child they have born.[1] Many authors have discussed the decisive influence which the expectation of a child in the future has on the development of the little girl. In female development, the child is a solution to the problem of how to accept the reality of being a woman. The way in which the idea of a child has been used in this connection affects the relation between mother and child.

During pregnancy mother and child are a biological unit. It takes time for the mother to become accustomed to the fact that her child belongs to the outside world after birth. As the child grows and severs his dependence on his mother, she gradually begins to accept it. Neverthe-

First published in *Amer. J. Orthopsychiat.* 11 (1941), 475–84. Copyright, the American Orthopsychiatric Association, Inc., and revised for publication here. Reproduced by permission.

less, residues of the original unity always remain in the mother-child relationship. Some mothers keep the psychological mother-child unity an unduly long time. Unconsciously they do not accept the fact that the child is no longer a part of their own bodies, and utilize this strong attachment to solve their own problems, which they project onto the child. Forced into this close relationship, the child does not want to give it up. He reacts to his mother's behavior, and his reactions are closely related to, and produced by, her problems. The child's symptoms may be products of the mother-child relationship, yet in the family circle they manifest themselves only in the child's difficulty. On the other hand, the mother's special conduct toward the child may be sufficiently alien to her personality to stand out like a symptom to the outside observer. Authors writing about the "anxious mother" (Rado, 1927) and "maternal overprotection" (Levy, 1939) indicate that the adjectives "anxious" or "overprotective" relate to the attitude of these women toward their children, and not necessarily to other human relationships.

Following are cases in which the mother-child relationship was predetermined by a displacement of the mother's affective relationship toward her own parents, siblings, or husband onto one of her children. As far as could be ascertained, only this child was treated in a special way.

The Openly Aggressive Mother[2]

A mother of a five-year-old boy complained that her son was very aggressive and she could not cope with him. She asked that he be removed from home temporarily. Her younger daughter she described as a very good child who suffered because of the boy's jealousy. The boy was a problem even before his sister was born. He was not nursed because he would not take the breast, and he never could get used to a new nipple.

At the age of two he began to be afraid of thunder; at three he started to be afraid of the dark. At the time of the younger sibling's birth he had whooping cough. The grandmother, with whom he stayed at the time, did not properly care for him because of her own illness. Furthermore, the grandmother believed the boy's bad behavior drove her own oldest son back to the insane asylum where he had previously been confined. The boy was sent to a nursery before his sister was born. At that time his mother told him he was a bad boy and, consequently, he had to be sent away from home. His bad behavior increased after his sister's birth.

This boy was intelligent, aggressive, and restless. He complained openly about his mother's treatment. He felt he would not grow up and be healthy because he was very thin as a result of the beatings the mother administered. He experienced real and imaginary fears and indulged in aggressive fantasies. In play school the teacher recognized his problems, but praised him for his handiness and intelligence, and found him likable. In the clinic while he played with his sister, he responded to suggestions as to how to treat her. In contrast to the mother's description of the situation, the little girl revealed herself as a constant nuisance to her brother, whose toys she took as often as possible. The mother asked how the psychiatrist could stand the boy and was peeved when she did not find him as annoying as did the mother.

While she had only hostile expressions for the boy, she complained about no other member of the family. She put all the blame on the boy and justified her own cruelty by explaining it as the only effective educational method. So unrestrained was her aggression toward the boy that, when she was advised not to beat him, she resorted to binding his hands and putting him in a dark cellar as punishment. Only much later, when she herself was sick and meek, could she relate that her father, a strict Italian, was cruel. He constantly harassed her gentle mother, who never revolted. Her brother had been in a state hospital three times; at one time he had been violent. She was glad to get out of this home in order to marry.

One can only guess that this woman resented her own father and brother and had shifted her hostility to her firstborn. She had not been able to express hostility toward her own family in the strict home of her father. Nor could she allow herself to be hostile toward her husband who had offered her escape from the bad home in which she lived before her marriage.

Why could a mother express in relation to her child what she could not express in relation to the adults of her family? The child, because of his biological dependence on his mother, is helpless and must endure what adults are able to ward off. A mother can take advantage of the child's inability to defend himself adequately. He is available at all times when she feels the need to aggress. One is reminded of tribes where it is permissible to kill a child and eat him if the mother is hungry (noted by A. Balint, 1939). The child is replaceable, can be reproduced or destroyed according to the mother's wishes at the moment. In our own culture only children are permitted to act out that way in their play (see Chapter 1). Adult aggression against children is considered a crime. The mother in our culture must find an excuse or a subterfuge for cruel behavior toward her child. In the case described above, as in so many others of the same kind, the mother provoked the child's aggression, and then had a welcome rationalization for her own cruelty—she was not guilty, the child was; she could be cruel toward him and project the blame on him. When the child grew up and began to show some independence, the situation developed into a constant battle between them. Consequently, the child was full of fears and aggression, the latter coming from two sources—the wish to retaliate, and out of fear.

The question remains: why did this mother mistreat her older boy and at the same time act overprotectively toward her younger daughter? One explanation might be that, being the firstborn, he was the first convenient object of displacement from the mother's father and brother. Furthermore, as a boy he was a more suitable object for this mechanism than the girl. When the girl was born, the mother provoked a situation which she, the mother, may have experienced in childhood in relation to her own brother.

The Anxious Mother

This type, as described by Rado (1927), overcompensates her aggression toward the child by her anxiousness about him. However, her hidden aggression comes through and reveals itself in the child's symptoms. Ferenczi (1929) claimed that unwanted children die easily. In less-severe instances they develop colds easily. Whether a mother is hostile to a child, or merely needs the child's sickness in order to resolve problems of her own, unknowingly she is able to provoke the child's ills in a subtle way.

The mother of a four-year-old boy asked for help because the child vomited at home and refused food, while he ate well in the nursery home. The mother was anxious about his health. The undernourished youngster was anxious too. He was unwilling to leave his mother, afraid she might leave him. In his very aggressive play, he indicated clearly that he was afraid of his mother and that feeding meant an aggressive act for him. For example, playing with a baby doll, he shot the doll before and after feeding it; after tearing a clay doll to pieces he said, "She is gone to eat supper." How did the child get this conception of feeding from his very anxious and seemingly loving mother? The clue was furnished by the mother's discussion of her husband. He was lazy and deserted her so that she had to support the children. Consequently she hated her husband and wanted to punish him. While discussing her child she showed no open hostility. However, an important factor in the history of the child's feeding difficulty revealed the mother's aggression toward him. She had fed him during his sleep since early childhood, because he refused food while awake and was undernourished. She was convinced that only fear could make the child eat voluntarily. She insisted that they scared him in the nursery, where he did eat. Yet, to her mind, the treatment she had given this child was not cruel; it was merely the means to make him eat and preserve his health.

This mother, who shifted her hostility from her husband, whom she could not reach, to her firstborn child, overcompensated her hostility by overanxious behavior. Yet she betrayed herself by methods of feeding her child. He understood his mother's behavior correctly and recognized her hostility, although it was not expressed in words. He knew that feeding him in his sleep was an aggressive act. He responded with fear and aggression, and was unwilling to take food from his mother. In contrast to the first child described, he did not express resentment openly; only his play revealed his feelings.

That the mother shifted her hostility from the husband whom she consciously hated to her son, is not surprising. It is a well-known and often described mechanism. Wulff (1932) pointed out that a normal mother's relation to her child is determined by her feeling toward her husband. If she hates her husband, she will hate the child. The question arises: why could this mother hate her husband openly, and yet be forced to overcompensate her hostility toward the child? Her family constantly stimulated her to hate her lazy husband, because they had to support her while he was gone. But it was not permissible to hate a child. When she decided to place him in a foster home, her own mother forbade it. Although her actions toward the child were not recognized by the family as hostile, the child recognized them as such very well.

In these two examples, the mothers shifted hostile impulses toward adult family members to one of their children. The form in which the hostility was expressed was predetermined by the relationship of these women to their families. The family conscience directed the mothers in their relationship to the children. The fact that one particular child is the recipient of the mother's hostility is important in such situations. The child knows this and suffers more than the children in families in which the mother is generally aggressive to all. It seems that a child recognizes such a situation in the family in early infancy.

It is interesting to note that both children, the one with the openly aggressive and the other with the latently aggressive mother, were retarded in their speech. Another source of speech retardation was described by Mahler (1942), who could demonstrate that the infantile mother-child relationship can be prolonged by the retention of nonverbal affective rapport beyond early infancy. In the cases described here, the difficulties in self-expression arose from problems of aggression.

Dorothy Burlingham (1935) described the increased capacity of observation and interpretation of behavior that children possess in contrast to adults. Their behavior since earliest infancy is a reaction to the mother's unconscious and conscious wishes in relation to the child. Because of the closeness between mother and child, the mother-child relationship in such cases becomes the crux of the treatment situation. A mother may be concerned with a symptom such as a feeding disturbance or a speech problem which may arise from different intrafamilial factors. Our task then is to work with the mother and convey to her an understanding of her own problems. This therapeutic procedure cannot be discussed in this paper.[3]

In the above cases, the mothers' conflicts about their own aggressive wishes were solved by utilizing the child as the object of aggression. In other less known types of cases, mothers have utilized children in order to solve their fears about their own bodies. In the cases of the aggressive mothers described, advantage was taken of the child's dependence on the mother, and the child was treated as a piece of property and not as a human being. The following cases deal with the situation in which the children were treated as if they were parts of their mothers' bodies—their sexual organs.

The Genuinely Anxious Mother

Case I.   A mother of a two-and-a-half-year-old girl complained because of the child's enuresis. Two older daughters as well as the patient were poor eaters, but this was of no great concern to the mother. She was anxious to get help for the youngest child's "bladder trouble." The child, besides being enuretic day and night, had fears of the dark, woke up at night asking to be changed, was afraid of strangers, and clung to her mother constantly. The mother kept the child near her day and night. In the clinic she held her on her lap. They sat together playing and talking as if they were a mother-child unit and not two separate human beings.

The mother's history revealed a difficult birth with this child and high blood pressure during pregnancy. She also suffered from a heart condition, was a poor eater and undernourished. In addition, she had a tubal inflammation which had been neglected. As a result, she had a bladder disturbance which necessitated going to the bathroom several times a night. She was afraid the children were uncovered at night, and, when she got up, made sure there were no drafts. In relating this, she showed no anxiety about her own physical condition. Except for the fear of drafts in relation to all children, she showed no clear anxiety other than about her youngest daughter's enuresis. The child was extremely dependent on her mother and happy in this relationship. Speech development was retarded; her relations to other people limited. She made some attempts to get into bed with her two older sisters, but her mother stopped this, saying she was afraid she might wet them. The child continued to wet, and had fears which she seemed to have borrowed from her mother.

It appeared probable that this mother treated her youngest child as if the child were part of herself. She succeeded in submerging her fears about her own bladder disturbance; instead she worried about her child's bladder. The child in turn enjoyed the closeness to her mother, maintaining her symptoms in order to retain her mother's attention.

This mother chose her youngest child on whom to project her fears about her sexual organs. Fears about her own body were stimulated by the tubal disorder. She was never prepared for marriage and considered relations with her husband as brutality on his part; she learned to accept and tolerate it. When the tubal inflammation occurred, her fears increased, and with them the feelings of guilt. She attempted to deny this problem by not acknowledging its importance. Instead, she cultivated her child's enuresis, and so transferred her fears to the child. She felt she must do something for her child but, at the same time, clung tenaciously to this child's enuresis because once the child were trained, she would have to recognize her own disorder.

Case 2. A harassed mother came to the clinic complaining that her six-year-old daughter wet and soiled the bed. She thought her child masturbated and was greatly concerned about it. She told the child that if she continued to masturbate she would injure herself and would not be able to marry when she grew up. When asked why she thought that, she related that she herself had masturbated during her childhood and thought she was the only one to have done such a thing. After marriage her husband observed that she did not bleed during the first intercourse. He resented this and accused her of a past incestuous relation with her brother. She protested, and recalled in her defense that at the age of five she had fallen and bled from the rectum, and at a later time she had been attacked by a boy and may have bled then. Her husband did not believe her and, as a result, her 15 years of marriage were unhappy. She devoted her life to her numerous children, but could not cope with their constant habit disorders.

This mother, like the first of this series, did not seek examination or treatment for herself, but was anxious to get help for her daughter. Only by questioning was her own problem revealed. When it was suggested that her husband come to the clinic and be reassured in his doubts about her, she refused, saying she was afraid he might get angry that the problem was discussed in the clinic. The child, in response to her mother's behavior, developed fears similar to her mother's. She was afraid her teacher might punish her severely for masturbation, yet she could not stop, seemingly because it was the only basis of a close relationship to her mother. This was very important in a household where numerous children competed for the mother's affection, mostly by developing habit disorders.

It is important to stress that not only the fear about the mother's genitals, and possibly the fantasies connected with it (incestuous relation to a brother), were transferred to the child, but guilt feelings were also transferred. The child's guilty masturbation was significant in the mother's mind; it helped to diminish thoughts of her own sins. The anticipated punishment for these sins was transmitted to the child. Her child, she threatened, would be spoiled in the future. In line with these thoughts, this mother was anxious to have as many children as possible. She warded off her own fears and guilt by denying her own problem, and by proving she was not spoiled by her masturbation, the proof being that she could have so many children.

Case 3. A mother of a two-and-a-half-year-old boy complained he had been a feeding problem since birth. He was frequently sick, developed colds, and displayed temper tantrums without provocation. Being anxious to get help for her child, she read numerous articles about child care and asked incessantly what to do for her baby. The child was afraid of strangers, ate poorly, and obviously responded to his mother's fears by displaying temper tantrums. On questioning, the mother related that she had had numerous spontaneous abortions, that she was pregnant at the present time, but could not lie in bed as the doctor told her to because she had to take care of her boy. Before delivery, she was disinclined to send the boy to a nursery home, but demanded that his tonsils be removed while she was at the hospital. She blamed his colds and feeding difficulties on his bad tonsils. On the way to the hospital to be delivered of her second child she thought only of the boy whom she had left at home. She worried about him, and not about the delivery. It was not what would happen to her, but what would happen to her boy that filled her with fear. After the delivery, she hardly talked about her recent experience, but related that while her son was sick some time ago, she had had dreams in which he died.

Her second child, a daughter, developed feeding difficulties immediately after birth. The pediatrician discovered that she had given the child great quantities of water. The mother defended herself saying that the doctor prescribed too little food for the newborn baby, and that she had to double the doses in order to satisfy the child. She later returned to the clinic with her son complaining he frequently had colds. She demanded a tonsillectomy for him, although she had been previously advised to wait until he was older. Asked repeatedly how *she* felt, she said she had been torn during delivery and not sewn, that her womb fell out, and that she had bladder trouble. She claimed the doctors had advised operation and sterilization, which worried her, because she wanted to have at least three children. Should something happen to one of them, she would still have the other two. Asked if she was afraid of the operation, she denied it vigorously.

This mother seems to have transferred her fears about her own genitals to her child. The child, in turn, responded by behavior which was most welcome to his mother. He had feeding difficulties and suffered from colds, and thus could substantiate her fears about him. He proved, in his way, that his mother had the right to be concerned with his health instead of being concerned with her own. With this displacement from the mother to the child accomplished—from genitals to tonsils— she could anticipate that the danger would come to the child and not to her. She could dream that he and not she would die. He needed an operation, not she. She could avoid danger, he could endure it.

In each of the three cases, the mothers revealed fears about their own sexual organs, but did not confess to such fears. Instead they developed anxieties in connection with the health of their children. It appears that these mothers considered their children as parts of their own bodies. The fearful thoughts of their own sins which may have led to the injury of their genitals were minimized. Instead of worrying about their own problems, they worried about the symptoms and behavior of their children, and possible consequences of such behavior. The children became a source of fearful concern, the bearers of the mothers' guilt feelings, and the prospective bearers of a punishment which, the mothers thought, they deserved for their own sins. The fearful concern about the children was not an overcompensation of aggression, but was real fear. Only in a broad sense, the shifting of guilt feelings and punishment to the child can be interpreted as a form of aggression. This aggression, however, is entirely different from the hostility of the mothers described in the first two cases.

The behavior of these genuinely anxious mothers reminds one of the mechanism of altruism described by Anna Freud (1936). The difference appears to be that in her cases the altruistic behavior was a character trait, a conduct constantly present in relation to other people, while in the mothers here described there was no question of altruistic behavior other than in relation to the children. Anna Freud points out for her cases that fear of the death of the altruistically loved person is the projected fear of the individual's own death. This is also true for the mothers described here.

71

In contrast to the aggressive mothers, the genuinely anxious mothers do not want the injury of death of their children. They are afraid of injury and death for them because they project their own fears in this respect on the children.[4] They project not only their fears, but their whole "castration-complex" onto their children. The children seem to understand their mothers' problems and respond to them. Karl Abraham (1920) stated that women who are influenced to a great extent by the castration complex consciously or unconsciously project it onto their children. This fear of the mother and child strengthens the bond between them. They have something very important in common, and both are unwilling to renounce the close relationship between them.

In some cases the mother-child relationship becomes a problem, not because this relationship is too intense, but because it is completely denied. An example of this kind is the *distant* mother. A mother of a fourteen-year-old boy complained that her usually stable son had set fire to a garage. On a later occasion, the boy developed a trancelike state, with an almost complete amnesia. The mother described him as very impersonal in relation to her and lacking in affection for her. Yet to his father and other members of the family he showed affection. The boy in turn described his mother as distant; he could not get near her. She did not take care of him when he was a baby, but left him entirely to the care of nurses. The mother revealed her resentment toward her husband and his children by a former marriage, and considered separation from him. In her own family circle she felt at home; in the house of her husband she felt like a stranger. She did not say she resented her child, she only complained he was impersonal and not entirely obedient. This annoyed her; she wanted his affection and wondered why he was so different from the younger son who was free and happy in his relation to her.

This mother had estranged herself from her older son since his birth. The child, in turn, felt it and responded similarly. In puberty the effort to keep away from his mother became too great for him, and impulsive outbreaks as well as conversion symptoms developed. The mother shifted her feelings from her husband to her son. She did not leave her husband, but psychologically, she left her son.

In summary, we may say that the mother-child unity is normal during pregnancy and persists psychologically to some extent after birth of the child. The close relation between mother and child decreases in intensity as the child grows older and becomes independent of his mother.[5] Where the close mother-child relationship is overemphasized and taken advantage of to solve the mother's own problems, this relationship becomes a problem in the treatment situation.

The child may be used to express his mother's hostility against an adult member of the family whom she cannot reach. The child may be regarded so strongly as a part of the mother's body that she is free to use him in order to solve her own genital fears. In some cases the problem arises when the natural mother-child relationship is reversed to the point of estrangement.

The child observes his mother's overt behavior and reacts to it with similar behavior. He concludes from his observation the nature of the mother's conscious and unconscious wishes in relation to him and others, and he reacts to them. The younger the child, the more apt he is to endeavor to keep in close relationship to his mother by reacting the way his mother unconsciously wishes him to.

The idea suggests itself that in their own childhood these mothers have attempted to solve their infantile problems by means of the fantasy that when they will have their own children, their difficulties will vanish. In the cases of the aggressive mothers, the fantasy may have been that when they have their children they will be able to do with them what they want; they will be able to treat them just as they themselves were treated by adults. The anxious mothers may have felt that their having children would show that their genitals were intact, for the children remain a living proof of it. They may also have felt that they, the mothers, would treat their children much better than they were treated in childhood.[5]

The insight developed into a particular mother's difficulty with a given child guides the child's therapist in his approach to her and to the child. However, the child's therapist must be aware that his interpretations of maternal behavior have been derived from a nontherapeutic relationship, and should be looked upon as tentative and devoid of the complexity that reveals itself in the analyses of mothers.

NOTES

[1]Helene Deutsch (1930) raised the question as to when a female child begins to be a woman and when a mother. Her answer, based on her psychoanalytic experience, was—"at the same time."

[2]Social workers in this and the following cases were: Alice Johnston, Elisabeth Hand, Ann Wilson (2 cases), and Mellie Simon (2 cases).

[3]A method of treating preschool children by way of parents (Furman, 1957) is based on the understanding of the mother's problems, but does not deal with them directly.

DEVELOPMENT OF SEXUALITY

[4]When one of the anxious mothers spoke of dreaming about her child's death and of the possibility that one of her children might die, for her death was nothing ultimate. For the unconsious, one's death is inconceivable. The child may die because he can be reproduced and can live again.

[5]In the discussion that followed the original delivery of this paper, Mahler described other maternal types, not mentioned specifically: narcissistic mothers who overestimate the child who came from their body; those who treat the child as a particular kind of property—a phallus; and the nagging mothers who struggle "to make up for their castration fears and imagined deficiency through the perfection of the child." Some fifteen years later, I returned to the problem of the origin of nagging in women (Chapter 4). Implied, in many of my subsequent papers, are attempts to establish a connection between specific developmental phases and typical maternal characteristics (see Chapters 2 and 11).

CHAPTER 4

NAGGING, SPREADING EXCITEMENT, ARGUING

In the history of psychoanalytic theory formation, the reconstruction of feminine development has been subject to frequent changes. At first there was a trend toward a masculinization of girls whose early development was said to be phallic, and their inner genitals physiologically and psychologically inactive until puberty (Freud, 1925). The clitoris, looked upon as a meager substitute for the phallus, had to be condemned before the vagina could take over (Bonaparte, 1953). This contradicted Freud's beliefs that the clitoris kindled the excitation in the adult women's vagina (1905a). Many authors described one or another part of the vagina as most sensitive to excitation, but no unified image emerged that would integrate sequences of sensations from different parts of the genitals. Brierley (1932) postulated a typical female integration, but herself added that oral representations are leading in adult female sexual performance (1936). In this she was joined by H. Deutsch (1944–45), Langer (1951), Heiman (1963) and others (see Moore, 1964, 1968, 1971).[1] Freud himself agreed with Andreas Lou Salome that the vagina was rented out *(abgemietet)* from the cloaca. Those who reported vaginal sensa-

This chapter is a revised version of a paper, "A Phase in the Development of Female Sexuality," which was read before the Psychoanalytic Study Group in Seattle in January, 1954. I am grateful to the members of the study group, and especially to Dr. Edith Buxbaum, for the stimulating discussion which prompted me to reexamine early development and correlate certain behavioral patterns and moods with prevailing sensations in early and later developmental phases.

The introductory remarks are partially taken from a discussion of Heiman's (1963) paper "Sexual Response in Women," given at the New York Psychoanalytic Institute on April 11, 1961.

First published in the *Int. J. Psychiat. Psychother.*, 2:265–297, 1973, and revised for publication here. Reprinted by permission.

75

tions in the posterior wall of the vagina (Reich, 1927), suggested by implication or directly that these are transferred from the rectum. Thus, even in adulthood, the vagina was said to respond vicariously rather than in its own right. A more recent idea which evolved from statistics (Kinsey *et al.*, 1953) and from the discovery of hormonal influences upon the sexual differentiation of the fetus (Sherfey, 1966) assigned a leading or even exclusive role to the clitoris as the only genital organ of the woman capable of sexual excitement and orgasm. Even though Masters and Johnson (1965) could show that in each sexual cycle all parts of the female genitals, including the vagina, are involved, individual preferences for one or another part as the organ of female sexuality still remain.

All these trends are probably due to the fact that, as psychoanalysts, we become aware of pathology first and have little opportunity to explore normal sexual behavior. It is undoubtedly true that the average adult has certain preferences for either oral, anal, or urethral modes which contribute to genitality to an individually varying degree. It is also true that many patients are fixated on a pregenital type of functioning which interferes with adult genital performance. Moreover, there is a special historical background to the representations of the vagina, which are successively modeled after the mouth, the rectum, the bladder, the baby, and the phallus. Eventually, under normal circumstances, all these images are subsumed under the dominance of the truly adult representation of the whole genital, and they cease to distort the adult feminine sexual response. The fusion experienced in the sexual act is a successor of the symbiotic oneness with the feeding mother, but is not identical with it. Fusion implies a temporary oneness which is preceded and followed by separation. The similarity between sucking and the vagina-uteral intake of semen is confined to the receptivity and the pumping action. However, in sucking, the tongue becomes actively involved, which, in itself, makes the mechanism and the experience different from the genital. Oral sucking is a part of foreplay activity and has only an indirect influence upon end play. Similarly, the retaining and expelling rhythm of the rectum has a certain similarity with the retention and the letting go of the penis, but they are not identical. The passive acceptance of wetting and the active contraction of urethral sphincters may act as prototype for the surrender and regaining of control in the sexual act but they are not identical. The participation of the sphincters in the sexual cycle (Masters and Johnson, 1965) has an important physiological function; it prevents loss of control over elimination and it is not a sign of pregenital fixation.

At times reports from patients give us most vivid examples of the differences between genital and pregenital experiences (Heiman, 1963).

At other times, we hear accounts of sensations for which words derived from pregenital representations have been used, but these can be better understood when they are correlated with different phases of the sexual cycle (Masters and Johnson, 1965). Feelings of wetness, dripping, losing the inside by dribs and drabs relate to the lubrication phase. Feelings of emptiness and a need to be filled relate to intravaginal distension; feelings of fullness, swelling to the point of bursting, as well as burning relate to the vasocongestive phase in the outer vaginal tube and outer genitalia. Representations of waves and worms relate to the rhythmic contractions of the vagina and uterus. Twitches and pulsations or knocking are terms frequently used to describe clitoric sensations. All of us can remember such examples. Yet, we hardly ever get the picture of an orderly, sequentially organized and unified memory of a sexual fulfillment. Synthesized, undisturbed sexual experiences are rarely brought to analysts' attention. In their fearful associations, patients bring to us scattered fragments which, genetically, belong to significant phases of their childhood, and have not been unified under adult genital dominance. Descriptions of sensations do not occur very often in analyses. Even if patients are admonished to include them in their associations, they are either reluctant or unable to verbalize what they sense in their bodies. More frequently than not, it is the patient's mood or form of excitement that reveals its origin in undisclosed sensations. In this paper, I shall describe certain modes of feminine affective behavior that originate in early developmental phases, and are responsive to specific sensations emanating from the inside of female genitalia.

Some years ago, when I analyzed a woman who suffered from a severe vaginism and a lack of genital sensitivity, I became keenly aware of the fallacy of the strict dualism of feminine erotogenic zones. When my patient became capable of sexual enjoyment and gave up her vaginism, I inquired whether her excitement centered on the clitoris or the vagina. She could hardly understand what I meant. Her feelings were all over the genitals and spread through her whole body. To localize it on the clitoris or any part of the vagina would be artificial and not in accordance with her experiences. Much later, three patients in various stages of preadolescence and adolescence helped me to understand that various, unintegrated genital sensations, reflected in their moods and in their behavior, were derived from early phases of their childhood.

All three patients were feminine in the sense that they were interested in men, attractive to them, and yet preoccupied with penis envy and competition with men. All three nagged me, each in a somewhat different way. Two of them were argumentative to the extreme and tended to create confusion and excitement by quarreling and demanding.

77

They were considered extremely aggressive by their families. The third one was highly confused, but very compliant and soft-spoken, almost incapable of expressing aggression of any kind. After some years of analysis, she too developed an argumentative side and became openly irritable like the others. To elicit a clear, precise statement from any of these highly intelligent girls was an exasperating task.

Magda, whom I analyzed from the end of her latency through her middle adolescence, talked so fast at first, and told so many things all at once that one could hardly follow her. (For other data on Magda's analysis see Chapter 1, pp. 44-45 and Chapter 5, pp. 117-119.) Her schoolwork suffered from her inability to separate one fact from the other. She invariably communicated the overflow of her excitement to anybody who stayed with her for a short while. She would, however, focus clearly on certain impossible demands over which she would quarrel and make scenes. Most of all, she wanted a real horse or a machine horse that would perform, as regulated by her.

Fern, whom I analyzed between sixteen and eighteen years of age, quarreled and sulked with such frequency and intensity that her family members began to avoid and isolate her, except for those who gladly participated in her excitement. (For further data on Fern's analysis see Chapter 5, pp. 119-120.) Her quarrels alternated with periods of silence. In her work and her thinking, this girl of superior intelligence could not draw logical conclusions and could not resolve problems without help. She would so isolate one thing from another that she lost all continuity and connection of events. She utilized the isolation in her frequent arguments in such a way that no sane reply or argument could reach her.

Sue, whom I analyzed through the better part of her adolescence, spoke at first like a broken record. Enunciating without excitement or even intonation, she also ignored punctuation. As a result, her sentences ran into each other, never beginning or ending. Words were often used for Klang-associations and mispronounced. When, after some time, she did begin to argue, Sue became utterly unreasonable and afraid of her own violent feelings.

All three patients were teasers of men, acutely aware of their feminine charm and the influence they could exert over their fathers. Magda was the youngest, and evidenced some of her manipulative behavior on male animals before she began to flirt with boys. Sue and Fern had at their disposal one or more boys or men in whom they evoked excitement, frustration, and helplessness by behaving as if males were marionettes, pulled by invisible strings. All three patients felt quite mistreated, both

by their mothers and by men. Sue and Magda had so-called slave fantasies in which they were either slaves or had slaves at their disposal. Being a slave, tied up and forced to do what the master bade, was clearly
related to rape wishes. Fern's fantasies abounded in men forcing women
to submit and in teachers punishing bad children, in which the punitive
act took the form of a sexual activity (Freud, 1917c). All three patients
went through life nagging, martyred, unsuccessful in their work, crying,
excited or depressed, argumentative or complaining. All three had a
great need to be helped or told what to do, and all could perform much
better under strict discipline. They were dependent on their mothers or
girl friends, dominated by them, and yet resentful of them. All three
yearned for children and were ready to care for them submissively. I have
described a woman as she appears in popular belief, in jokes and sayings:
an individual long suffering, argumentative, illogical, demanding, the
power behind the throne, complaining and dissatisfied and scheming; yet
enticing, easily dominated and led, self-sacrificing, a drudge and eternally
working for others to satisfy their bodily needs. Even the most masculine
women, who compete with men and give the impression of self-reliance,
show enough traces of this mixture of contradictory features to baffle their
families and friends. Magda, Sue, and Fern could each display distinctive
characteristics of masculine nature. There was ample evidence of their
penis envy, their competition with men, and their desire to castrate them.
Magda yearned for a big rifle with which she would cheerfully shoot her
father and then would live happily ever after with her enslaved mother.
Even in her affectless placid phase, Sue was forever ready to attack her
father; she loved to bite her uncle and one of her clearest fantasies was one
in which she cut off the arm of a boyfriend. Fern loved boys' games and
excelled in them. She was highly competitive with her father. During
intellectual competitions with him she could think best and perform best
intellectually.

It was Magda who in her great overflow of excitement virtually
spilled the information upon which this paper is based.

She discovered very soon that her excitement was genital and that it
was literally inside of her; that she could not stand the fact that she had
no direct access to it and therefore had to externalize it on the surface of
her body, pass it on to another person, or project it on him. On one hand
"he" would become the inciter, the slaveholder who took all responsibility
for her excitement, and on the other hand she would control "him" and
work on him, in the same way as she worked over the external parts of

her genitals. She named her excitement "Mr. Sit," and localized it very clearly inside her vagina and/or uterus. (For further material on "Sit" see Chapter 5, "Outside and Inside, Male and Female," pp. 117-118.)

Magda recognized very clearly that she wanted me to give her a penis as a solution to her problems. She was quite aware of the fact that her dissatisfaction and her depressed and sullen moods were related to her daily disappointments over not getting a penis. On one level "Mr. Sit," who was lame (castrated), desired to be cured of his lameness; on a deeper level he frantically wished to remain a cripple who could never truly walk out of the enclosure and thus would remain isolated and jailed. "He" seemed to enjoy the confinement, as if aware of the havoc he might create if he were to be let loose. On one hand he enslaved Magda, on the other he swallowed people whom she liked, such as her mother, her aunt, and her teacher, and made them do anything "he" pleased. Magda was quite aware of a concurrent fantasy in which she swallowed "little people" and carried them around with her in her abdomen and coerced them to obey her. This fantasy developed further into a story in which her parents would enslave her teacher, who would become a maid, forever obedient to the parents. The parents, in turn, would command the teacher to do things for Magda. She did not like to identify herself with the enslaver, whom she criticized severely. Thus she could never take full responsibility for her own wishes, especially if they stemmed from vaginal urges. Her vagina was ego-alien to her. She despised it and feared it and, therefore, either confined or rejected it. To substitute a penis for this dangerous, bad, and invisible part of her body appeared to be a desirable solution. The "inner penis" fantasy was personified in "Mr. Sit." His counterpart was the master who enslaved Magda from the outside. Alternating with her inner excitement was a clitoric, circumscribed masturbation which centered on a special sensate focus. She liked to masturbate with her mother sitting next to her and reading to her. This, too, relieved her from the responsibility for her excitement. She felt that there was a tacit agreement between her mother and herself, which meant that Magda had to play under the covers while mother supplied the stories to go with it. This arrangement did not prevent Magda from quarreling with her mother and getting her excited because of Magda's disobedience. A typical psychoanalytic session would begin with Magda's nagging me for something, becoming dissatisfied with my response, trying to get me excited by slamming doors, running out to the waiting room, complaining about me, screaming, and then, when she quieted down, explaining what kind of excitement she had experienced. She was keenly aware of the pulsation of the clitoris and of feeling hurt there, when she rubbed too long. She would give her clitoris a "rest" but she could not give her vagina a rest. She could not localize the throbbing and swelling she felt inside. She could describe it only in terms of breaking the box (the vagina) violently to let Mr. Sit out. She nagged me when she felt nagging feelings from inside. Her continuous arguing stemmed from her excited quarrel with more intense vaginal sensations, which threatened to overwhelm her like a torrent emanating from deep inside her. She would regressively resort to anal-sadistic forms of excitement and containment through temper tantrums and constipation. However, her only means of relieving her internal excitement was to find a sensate focus in clitoric masturbation (Masters and Johnson, 1965). When she felt very virtuous and renounced masturbation, the inner excitement externalized upon her skin and she would break out in hives. She would scratch them furiously and was subsequently covered with numerous scars. Since she quickly understood the reason for her hives, she attempted to blame me for the renewal of her masturbation and told her mother that at "my request" she had to cure the hives by masturbating.

In addition to masturbating, Magda coped with her excitement by: nagging people to alleviate "nagging" from within; spreading her excitement and passing it on to others, another form of externalization; and arguing, blaming others who made a slave out of her and subjected her to sexual excitement. The arguing was justified by a projection of her wishes to enslave others and make them gratify her. The projection was part of a general acting out in which Magda tried to get rid of her excitement and her guilt as well.

When Magda began to understand what she had inside that bothered her, she formed an image of her vagina, not on the basis of her inadequate finger exploration, but on the basis of the equation vagina = baby that stemmed from a prephallic, preoedipal, inner-genital phase (see Chapters 5 and 13). The renewal of this representation was due to her keen disappointment over her inability to explore the vagina more fully than the small opening allowed. Newly acquired knowledge about the role of the vagina in delivery also fostered the revival of the baby = vagina equation. In the following sessions she told me that she "most probably" wanted a penis as a Christmas present. Yet she rejected a cowboy outfit as babyish and not suitable. She recognized that the vagina could get excited by "remote control" (rubbing of the clitoris), like a hand puppet. Thoughtfully, she added that something had to be inside rather than nothing, because the baby came out by something pushing it out. This seemed to prove to her that there was a definite shape inside that followed the outlines of a baby's body. As the changing size of the vagina gave her some concern, we discussed the elasticity of the vaginal walls and the roles that muscles played in her own ability to influence its shape and size. In the sessions and at home, there was an increasing alteration of Magda's demands and moods. She had wanted a horse, or a dog of tremendous size, whom she would train to obedience, or else a tremendous rifle with BB ammunition. Now she wanted a life-size doll. In my office she asked for doll clothes, but became depressed because she did not know the exact size of the doll. She gave up her endeavor as quite useless and she said that she did not want anything at all. I offered to get material and sew doll clothes for her. She protested that she and she alone would choose the material and sew the clothes. It was quite clear that she was despondent because she did not know how to appraise the size of her vagina (and uterus?). She did not want to deal with the image of her inside on the basis of general information, but wanted to work it out on an individual basis. She wanted to establish the size and shape of her own vagina (and uterus?), not just anybody's. It was also clear that she wanted a big one that would accommodate a big baby.

Magda now used the acquisition of knowledge to reform her body image. Because this endeavor was colored by regressive demands for a tangible organ, a baby or a penis, we could reconstruct the developmental phases in which these demands had arisen. The baby = vagina equation was derived from a phase in which she must have been beset by nagging sensations from within, which she externalized on a baby-doll. Toward the end of this phase, which in her case was anally tinged, Magda seemed to have experienced increasing inner-genital excitement that came in waves and radiated out. Her need to excite her mother and pass the waves on to her seemed to have arisen before Magda could find a sensate focus in her clitoris. Once she could turn to her clitoris for comfort, she would deny that she had an inside and would concentrate on a special point on the crura which could be localized precisely. Her inability to achieve orgasm led to endless rubbing, which only ceased when she hurt herself. She wanted her mother to relieve her, and becamse very angry because she had no penis with which she could satisfy herself and her mother. At the height of the phallic phase, Magda had modeled the fantasy of an inner penis after oral and anal fantasies of swallowing and retaining little people. This pregenital fantasy allowed for a recathexis of her "inside" in a phallic mode. It was associated with guilt because it implied the castration of her father, with whom she felt competitive, at first. In the latter part of the phallic-oedipal phase, she had turned to her father in a positive oedipal relationship. At this point, she seemed to have projected all the responsibility for genital urges upon him and men or boys in general. Her argumentative mood supported the fantasy of being enslaved and tortured by men, while her own wishes to be penetrated could remain repressed. Latency brought some respite to Magda, but with the beginning of prepuberty changes, she regressed more and more, and became demanding, nagging, excited, and argumentative, spreading excitement. At the same time she felt guilty about her masturbation and needed to blame others even more.

It was interesting to follow her mood changes and discover what sensations emerged with the appearance of certain moods. Confusion and nagging seemed connected with diffuse, unlocalized vaginal sensations. Spreading of excitement went with feeling a swelling and throbbing inside which came and went in waves. Arguing and pinpointing guilt were connected with a clear representation of "Mr. Sit" inside her. Either he or another man or boy outside was responsible for Magda's inner-genital excitement. The sadomasochistic fantasy of being dominated and dominating had, as one of its roots, the pain on the clitoris which served as a screen for dissatisfaction inside the body.

Fern's problem was her argumentativeness, which she justified by projecting her guilt over sexual practices to father and boyfriends. Her primary fixation was in the phase which I had called the "projection phase of the phallic girl" (see Chapter 1). The projection was used to reinforce the denial of her inside and her wish to be empty of inner-genital sensations and discharge products. It was Fern who told me a great deal about the dangers lurking from vaginal excitement and about the irritability and quarrelsomeness with which she reacted to it. Her irritability was, no doubt, orally tinged. Her whole outlook on life was depressive and this colored her moods and gave them a touch of orality, no matter what occasioned them. In keeping with her orality, she used a great deal of simple denial. She claimed that she never masturbated, "or rarely." She never wanted a penis because it would be too much trouble to have one. She did not like to touch a penis but did not mind it when a boyfriend ejaculated on her thighs. She denied and then only grudgingly admitted that she did handle her boyfriend's genitalia. She veered between denials and admissions and acted out losing her insides by losses and recoveries of objects which she equated with her genitals. She lost bags and parcels. When she found something she had lost, she soon after incurred a new loss. Even though she believed that her hymen could get "used up," she could not resist the temptation of using tampons during menstrual periods. She would deny that there was an opening in the vagina and had to behave as if she created a new one each time she put in or removed the tampon. She suffered from a discharge but she would rather "kill herself" than go to the doctor, who could not do anything about it anyway. Her discharge was proof that she had an organ and she did not like to give it up. At a peak of sexual excitement, when she had to get along without a boyfriend on whom she could project her feelings, she informed me that the vagina was just a tunnel. There was nothing in it. The discharge could not possibly come from

83

there. She must have retained some water while bathing. When encouraged to go to a gynecologist, she became frantic, thinking the doctor would know that her discharge was due to sexual excitement and could do nothing about it. She accused me of being very harsh and repeating myself unnecessarily. The following day she complained bitterly because she failed a test. She could not understand the question after studying a great deal. She used to call a boyfriend, or for that matter, any available male, to confess her failure and to receive reassurance. She claimed that I had forbidden her to use men to get rid of uncomfortable feelings. She knew now what happened when she became frustrated, upset, and confused, when she could not understand things, when she needed directives and explanations to comfort her and then would invariably seek an argument to top this sequence. Her genitals became excited and from there the excitement spread over her whole body and made her irritated and uncomfortable to a degree that she wished to get rid of the feeling immediately. Her hostility to her own excitement and her fear of being overwhelmed by it became apparent to her. It was obvious that she quarreled with her excitement, not knowing who would get rid of whom. The excitement was personified and projected. It made her very angry that she was like a jellyfish and had no control over her own action. Like Magda on the inside, Fern personified her "inferiority" on the outside. She would have preferred men who were lame or deformed and would lean on her. However, this was just wishful thinking. In reality, each boyfriend was not any better than her inner excitement, which she could not control. Each had his own ways and his own initiative, which she could not change or control either. Each boyfriend's actions were unsatisfactory and she ended every yearned-for reunion by quarreling with him. Then she behaved as if it was he who had initiated her intolerable excitement. Not until Fern was able to take responsibility for her own body and its excitement was she able to integrate outer and inner excitement and experience peace without quarreling with her sex partner.

In contrast to Magda and Fern, Sue never got excited about anything. She kept her cool while her mother raised her voice and shouted at her. Only when her father was "a real pest" would she lose her temper, but that, she felt, was his fault, since she, Sue, was known for her exceedingly pleasant disposition, her great patience and tolerance. She felt that her father should know better than to start talking to her in the morning, which was her irritable period. She treated it as if it were a morning sickness from which she would recover after a short span of time. The mood was a reminder of her early inability to retain breakfast. Food had been a constant source of battle between herself and the rest of the family. For years she had refused to eat a sufficient amount of food until a doctor advised that she must go to bed very early and rest a lot to keep her strength. This measure "cured" her of her anorexia. However, eating breakfast had a price. She demanded to be left alone and not bothered at that very special time. Whenever she attacked her father she blamed him for not keeping to this rule. Other exceptions to her generally complacent disposition were occasional temper outbursts when she failed in trying to write a story or draw a picture. She would tear the paper in exasperation and erase her failure out of existence. When she reported such incidents, she appeared completely relaxed and pleasant. She was gentle and feminine in her movements, seemed to get along with friends and teachers, and was very popular with boys. Yet her teachers discovered during her absences from school that the class was much quieter when she was away. By some invisible means she seemed to create a continuous excitement around her.

Sue's monotone and lack of intelligibility became a source of frustration even to her analyst. This was explained to her in such a way that she could begin to help study the means by which she got people excited. At first this inquiry yielded primarily denial, negations, and projections. Discussing her lack of excitement, she professed that she never had sex play and had masturbated only a little, which, she added, "was normal." It gave her no particular pleasure, so she did not know why she did it. At twelve she began to go out on group dates and would describe gleefully to her girl friends and her analyst how much excitement she had produced in her date. She would describe the experience in all details with complete detachment, and she, for one, knew all about the male and female genitals, as a modern young lady should. She was fully acquainted with anatomical boundaries and could draw everything, but she really could not see any sense in it. When she did draw the uterus, she drew it asymmetrically, tilted to the side with one tube fully closed and vague outlines of what may have been ovaries. It was sketched in broken lines, especially in the outlines of the vagina and the contact points of uterus and vagina. Similarly, in her speech and her thinking there were no clear-cut boundaries between ideas, sentences, or events. She never focused clearly on anything. She could look in one direction and think that she was observing something which clearly lay in the field of her peripheral vision. While this lack of contact with reality was due in large measure to her form of adaptation to her mother, as described elsewhere, it was also a by-product of her feelings about her own body as a whole and her genitals in particular. As it turned out after a very long time, she was terribly afraid of being consumed by a fire that represented her mother on one level and her own genital excitement on the other.

When Sue grew up she was very annoyed by her lack of genital feelings, because she wanted to be proper at all times and sex was proper in the judgment of a modern girl. However, she fully identified sexual excitement with anger, and thus was afraid of what she might do if she yielded to any form of excitement. In her, there was no demarcation and difference or gradation of feelings. Every affect contained all affects. She was not able to cope even with the external parts of her genitals. Every small wave of excitation might become a sweeping fire and was dangerous. Eating had been dangerous when she was a child, as she might have eaten up everybody she wanted to retain. But resting in bed alone with her body was even more dangerous, and being different from the others, too intolerable. So she began to eat, and made up for sins even more by exaggerating her extreme obedience. In her early fantasies, she was a slave who endured hardships at the hand of the master until such time as the master fell in love with her. Through her influence over the all-powerful master she delivered all slaves. In everyday life, the master was the man to whom she yielded in a feminine way but through whom she exercised control over her body and over her own impulses. When she petted with a man she was excited and happy, fusing with him and sharing his excitement. She directed his actions in a subtle way and also used the whole relationship to evoke admiration in her girl friends and excitement in her parents. Sue's oral fixation and early deprivation was the primary source of her irritability and the flattening of her affect. These features colored the successive phases of her feminine development. Thus, she used boring repetitiousness to nag with senseless forms of communication. She acted as if she were trying to bend the listener's will to help her without understanding her needs. She was a master in spreading confusion and excitement in an amiable sort of way. Her projection of her own genital tensions on men was at first expressed in her slave fantasy. Here too, it was finally understood that the master would fall prey to her charms and serve not only her needs but those of all oppressed people (no doubt, women). Sue's argumentativeness, which arose mainly in relation to her father, had undergone a reaction formation and made her conforming and amiable. When this defense mechanism was analyzed, she began to understand the angry fire of her own excitement and her fear of perishing in its flames. When her nagging repetitiousness ceased, Sue began to feel maternal and became interested in helping young children. When her spreading of excitement was channeled into selective seductiveness to men, she still suffered for some time from her need to be enslaved. Not until she relinquished the massive projections upon men could she desist from seeking sadomasochistic relationships.

While each of the three patients reacted to their genital excitement in accordance with the development of their character and their preferences for certain pregenital fantasies and discharge forms, there were several features they had in common. They each nagged in their own way, each denied and yet spread excitement, and each projected inner-genital wishes and guilt over them upon others, primarily men. Each learned to correlate certain sensations, which became recognizable, with the occurrence of particular moods of nagging, spreading of excitement and arguing.

From the choice of defenses and the regressive features in ego functioning that accompanied these moods in these and other patients, one could reconstruct the role that inner-genital tensions play in the development of women. The reconstruction was made possible by the massive regressions to earlier phases that were part and parcel of these patients' adolescent development (see Chapters 5, 13, 14 and 15).

Typical feminine mood changes begin in early childhood. They can be traced to unrecognized inner-genital tensions in prelatency. These become very intense and invade consciousness in adolescence. During latency, the ways and means of coping with inner-genital tensions are covert. If they cannot be sublimated in games and stories, the child becomes moody and disturbed and may need treatment (Fraiberg, 1972). Analysis then reveals the genital wishes connected with the vagina that had been inadequately repressed. In early adolescence, nagging, passing excitement, and arguing become conspicuous again, as intense inner-genital impulses become rampant, and a great many regressive, yet newly elaborated fantasies and memories, begin to emerge from repression. The analyses of children, adolescents, and adults whose pathology serves to elucidate normal development, reveal not only the adverse effect of moodiness but also its outcome in feminine modes of adjustment. Much of what will be described about it below had been extrapolated from cases such as Magda's, Fern's, and Sue's.

It is not always easy to distinguish shifts in moods and correlate them with changes in sensations. Special attention to alterations of modes of excitement and to fantasies connected with them helps us to classify moods from the developmental point of view.

The newborn is characterized by changeability and unpredictability. It takes some time for him to coordinate various ways of crying appropriately according to needs. Once this has been accomplished, his mother can recognize whether he is hungry, ill, or sleepy. The impact of genital swelling in neonates has not been explored. There is so far no information available on the influence of early genital crises on infants' moods. There is no doubt that diffuse excitement diminishes at the same time as maternal hormones leave the body. Fussiness, crankiness, and irritability are typical for the oral phase; they often are linked up with teething pain. Abdominal distress, such as colics, are held responsible for rage reactions. It seems impossible to pacify an infant who screams and flails. Mothers feel helpless and blame themselves for their inability to offer relief. Temper and denigration of the frustrator are typical of the anal-sadistic phase. Repetitiveness, impatience, and interfering with the adult by incessant interruptions are the prevailing negative moods of the urethral phase. All these moods are related to internal discomfort. It is not known how soon an infant can distinguish between the sources of his distress. It is equally unexplored how early concepts of the inside as a contained hollow begin to develop. Spitz postulated that the mouth is experienced as "primal cavity" (1955). It is reasonable to assume that the tongue, which explores the inside of the mouth, eventually collaborates with the hand which explores both—the inside of the mouth and its outside. The hand, as a tool of externalization, aids the eyes in the task of creating the basis for the future concepts "cavity" and "inside." To this are added the feelings of fullness and emptiness that give internal spaces an affective meaning of comfort and discomfort. That an empty stomach is uncomfortable and a full one usually comfortable—but the rectum and bladder function in an opposite way—cannot be really experienced under normal circumstances until sphincter control has developed. It may well be that a cavity can never be properly understood unless it can be explored by tongue or hand or controlled by filling it, emptying it, opening and closing it. The ability to use a pincer movement gives the baby a personal understanding of "holes," as does cupping of the hand for holding without involuntary release. This prepares him for the understanding of indentations. Older infants play with boxes, open and close drawers, put things inside other things, and become acquainted with insides and outsides of external objects. Toward the end of the second year there develops a clear distinction between bladder and bowel function. This develops further into the comprehension of what is front and what is back. However, even though the young child had played inside his mouth and still does, has experienced "hollow" and "full" sensations, has ingested food and spit it out, has retained and excreted feces and urine, the concept of discrete structures inside his body is quite foreign to him. Boxes can be closed or open, full or empty, as far as the under-two-year-old is concerned, but they have no functional meaning as containers.

One fifteen-month-old toddler put a little toy into a large box, then strained to look inside to see whether the toy was there. An eighteen-month-old, while straining to defecate, could not point out the place where the feces would come out, but his two-year-old friend aimed right at his anus to supply the answer. Yet the eighteen-month-old was keenly aware that his feces were taken away from him when he was diapered. When his nurse told him they were "gone," he looked pained. An hour later, he put a paper plane, which I gave him, into the wastebasket. When asked where it was, he answered: "gone."

It may well be that, to the under-two, containers are things that make things go away. Two-year-old children are aware of sensations coming from inside the body, but they are not able to localize or interpret them adequately other than through the medium of openings and the content that goes in and out of these openings. The body is full of food, feces, and urine, and is often thought of as a tunnel through which things proceed after they have been put into it. The shape of the inside is judged mostly by the shape of things going in and out of the body. The sensations coming from inside, unless they are pain, are usually relegated to openings and even located there (Schilder, 1935). In the two-and-a-half-year-old, the process of transformation from food to excreta that goes on inside the body is frequently judged by analogy with cooking, mixing, and shaping until a solid becomes a mush or a mush a solid.

Two-year-old children are lovingly preoccupied with their bellies and rub them, pat them, and stick their fingers in their belly buttons. Some little girls of that age or even younger go around with their fingers pressed to the urethral opening or the clitoris. They discover that they can deal with external sensation which, in turn, can evoke internal tensions. However, even though the vagina has been subject to stimulation through activities of adjoining organs, it does not necessarily gain its own representation. From time to time, little girls play with "the cheese" which is excreted by the vagina and covers their vulva. They rub and smell it but, to my knowledge, they do not clearly connect it with the introitus or a separate inner structure.

With the passing of pregenital phases, the influx of genital sensations disquiets the little girl. She can no longer discharge the genital urges via pregenital routes alone. Increased handling of external genitalia evokes resonant chords inside the vagina. It seems that the little girl becomes increasingly harassed by nagging feelings inside, feelings she cannot reach by pressing, releasing, or manual manipulation. She learns to contract perineal and laminal muscles and experiments by squeezing her thighs. When she touches her vulva she gets "lost" in the irregular and changing tissues of the external genital and cannot identify the opening to the inside, although she feels something there.

DEVELOPMENT OF SEXUALITY

The two- or three-year-old tries to resolve her new problems with old methods. She retains feces and urine or lets them out to control utero-vaginal tensions. At this time of her life she creates meaningful contents for the vaguely developed ideas of oral and anal or urethral coitus and impregnation. Without localization, shape, or meaning, the vagina easily becomes a part of the body, ready to become ego-alien and threatening from within. However, the experience that genital sensations radiate in and out serves as a model for the externalization of vaginal impulses (Bradley, 1961) onto such objects as female baby-dolls or toy animals, which can be handled, cuddled and used to appraise by analogy the consistency and shape of the inner genital (see Chapter 1). Modelled after oral, anal and urethral images of the baby and yet different, the vagina = uterus becomes personified in the baby that came from inside.[2] Eventually, however, the little girl becomes disillusioned with her "maternal activities," with which she enlivens inanimate objects. As long as externalization helps to desexualize inner-genital feelings, she tends to nag the doll and need not feel nagged from inside her body. However, when vaginal infections, witnessing of primal scenes, birth of siblings and other, possibly even hormonal influences (see Chapter 13), increase the intensity of waves of excitation emanating from the inside, externalization fails. The characteristic fear attached to these flushes of feelings is that they will sweep over the whole body, becoming intolerable, all-consuming, and dangerous to the integrity of the body in toto. Sue's all-consuming fire was an exemplary illustration of it. Passing on of the dangerous excitement to others makes the recipient of the "gift" angry, and excited arguments may follow the initial defensive actions. Anger becomes confused with genital excitement and the roots of sadomasochistic relationships find a fertile ground in the three- or four-year-old girl's complaints that her mother does not alleviate her excitement and keeps real babies for herself. At the same time the child is afraid of losing her excitement and having "nothing." When free from inner-genital tensions, she will voluntarily reexcite herself. By the time she is four years old she may manipulate her genitals relentlessly and, in this process, she usually does discover the introitus. This then appears to be a proof that she had injured herself. In reality, she does frequently hurt herself by rubbing too hard or pulling and she may even bleed a bit from scratching, especially when she has a vulvoperineal rash or very sensitive mucous membranes. The discovery of the introitus is not only connected with fears of castration, but also with the image of a dead baby, a monster or a congenitally defective child. The "bad" inner-genital excitement generates a "bad" child. This fantasy, which originates at that time, is revived during pregnancy. Fetal movement and uterine contractions have a bearing on such ideas. I have no clinical evidence for uterine involvement in the inner-genital excitement of the child in the inner-genital phase. However, movement observation suggests that at least a minimal participation of uterine contractions does exist in childhood (Chapter 10).

Frustrated by her inability to satisfy herself or have her mother satisfy her by taking over her excitement, the disgruntled and frightened girl declares war on the vagina and its opening. She annihilates it in fantasy or reduces it to a thin line, "a nothing." A massive denial of the vagina (Horney, 1933) ensues and the denial is held in place by a number of mechanisms whose intensity and distribution vary individually. In contrast to children like Magda and Fern, who reinforce the denial of the inner genital by intense penis envy (characteristic of four-to-six-year-old girls), children like Sue deny their excitement rather than the organ that creates it. Feelings become shallow and subtle means are used to generate excitement in others. The representation of the inner genital becomes schematic, out of focus, flattened, fractionated, or distorted. Masturbation is then either short-lived or becomes mechanical, lest it produce a resurgence of inner feelings.

The organism has a natural tendency to transfer inner sensations to the outside of the body. The phallic-oedipal girl makes ample use of this mechanism to ignore what goes on inside while she masturbates outside. The waves of excitation have to be intercepted, prevented from spreading over the whole genital or the whole body, and localized carefully like a forest fire. The clitoris is a most useful organ for this because it pulsates in excitement and stops pulsating and even "disappears" at the peak of excitation (Masters and Johnson, 1965). The diffuse, confusing, and unlocalized inner-genital sensations can be safely transferred to pulsations which are identified with heartbeats and jumping jacks or even with the jumping of the whole phallic body. Moreover the erectile tissue of the clitoris, which grows and reappears from hiding in periodic intervals, makes the little girl feel a magic power to grow something and shrink it and bring it back when it has gone away. She fantasies that by pulling the clitoris out she can make it into a penis or that she can take what she has inside out and, unlike the boy, can hide it again. The girl's ability to use the "bone" as well as the "skin" to discharge her sexual tensions, her ability to pull the outer labia, rub them together, and close them, and her ways of handling the external labia to spread out or close, make her feel both special and discontented with the multiplicity of stimuli impinging upon her. The less she is capable of using masturbation for consolation, the less she is able to combat her feelings of inadequacy, the more she suffers from penis envy, which may have started already (Galenson *et al.*, 1972). However, early forms of penis envy are pregenital in character. Oral types of penis envy are based on a mama = penis equation; anal types are concerned with the possession of a large fecal penis; and urethral types deal with competition over the boy's ability to stand and aim while urinating, which the girl cannot do. In the phallic phase, the little girl covets the penis for its size, its ready availability for sexual discharge, and its recognized intrusiveness, which can fill hollows and thus satisfy the penisless mother. Girls are envious of boys because of the fact that the penis is movable, can get into things, and is covered with skin like a finger—in short, that there is so much more control over the penis than the girl can have over her genital organs. In addition, the girl perceives that her mother values the penis as a source of satisfaction and she becomes even more exasperated and unhappy.

Small children cannot go on suffering forever. A misfortune is soon turned into good fortune. There are several ways open to the girl at the height of phallic penis envy which help her overcome her miserable hopelessness. She can fantasy that she too has a penis, which grew in her like a baby; got into her through the castration of a man and has to be hidden; or is indeed growing on the outside and will be soon visible to all. Such fantasies keep her tied to her mother and identified with her rival father and/or brothers. It is the fantasy of the inner penis (Jacobson, 1936) which, transformed into a penis-baby, becomes the source of the wish for a baby boy. The baby boy now stands for the inner excitement which has been previously renounced. Before the phallic phase the coveted baby is a girl who represents the inside genitals (see Chapter 2).

When the little girl of four or five turns to her father, hoping that he will provide her with a baby, she gives up active intrusive wishes and represses negative oedipal fantasies. She turns from activity to passivity and wishes to be penetrated. Fantasies of being opened up and impregnated, then opened up to deliver, threaten to reawaken inner-genital sensations. Masochistic fantasies merge with recurring wishes sadistically to castrate the male. The little girl becomes afraid of pain, yet she may masturbate to the point of pain. This external, usually abrasive and stretch pain is used defensively to keep the hurting hand away from the introitus. Fear of the size of the penetrating penis and of the delivery of a huge baby overlie the more basic fears of all insides falling out and being broken up or torn. Attempts to reinforce the denial of the already isolated vagina by repression of penetration fantasies are disturbed by the repeated (maybe periodic) reemergence of inner-genital sensations. Continuous attempts to localize feelings externally are accompanied by projection of thoughts about the vagina upon the outside genital. Pulling the labia and the mons and using the clitoris as a sensate focus relieves the girl from genital excitation. The yearnings to be penetrated are displaced and projected in fantasies of being beaten by the father. The death wishes toward the mother participate in the masturbation fantasies and mingle with wishes to become "nothing" and to cease to struggle over excitement. The little girl, who began to argue and excite her mother before she entered the phallic-oedipal phase, revives these methods to activate the fantasy that her own excitement, equated with a phallus, can penetrate the mother. Very frequently such arguments center on challenging and correcting the mother about matters of daily routine. Sexual tension feeds the intrusive "why's" (Freud, 1907) of that time. Everything that exists and is not immediately apparent in a concrete way is questioned and the mother is expected to explain it. Argumentative debates threaten to disrupt family schedules, with the child poised for attack and the mother responding. Peace is restored when the girl can get rid of her masturbation guilt by blaming her father rather than her mother. The consequence of a successful projection which keeps the repression of inner genitality in place is a desexualization of the wish to be penetrated. Maternity becomes isolated from sex and from the inside, with the girl often denying any knowledge of the origin of babies. The charming, flirtatious little girl now becomes irrationally demanding of her father. She often succeeds in enticing him to become more and more attentive to her, thus proving that he is interested in her rather than the reverse. In subtle ways or in arguments she puts the blame on him for all her sexual wishes and all her angry accusations of the mother. In many cases, quarreling with the father is modeled after actual observations of the mother's arguments with him. The underlying excitement is tolerated and justified by the projection of sexual wishes upon the father. Disavowing guilt may be deflected from the father into arguments with a sibling. Displacements of blame from the father to burglars and attackers fosters elaborate fantasies and fears of being tied up, hurt, or abducted. Sometimes, the attacker is described as a male residing inside the girl; at other times boys are pictured as disturbers of peace who chase and annoy girls. Veering from fantasies of an inner penis to projecting all kinds of sexual fantasies upon men just before latency, the girl settles on the latter as a method of choice.

The latency girl becomes good and sedate, contrasting greatly with the wild little boys with whom she does not wish to associate. No doubt, she feels that she might succumb to contagion when she comes too close to boys who, in her mind, generate all forbidden impulses. During latency, the ways and means of coping with inner-genital excitement are covert. Games and stories reveal the hidden wishes to find what had been lost. In transition to prepuberty, the already intense inner-genital urges become rampant at times. Spurts of nagging, arguing, or passing on of excitement become more frequent and a great many fantasies begin to emerge from repression. What transpires in adolescent analyses, especially before menstruation sets in, are conglomerates of new and old thoughts and derivations of early forgotten events (Greenacre, 1952).

In prepuberty, when the impact of abrupt cyclic changes in intensity of feelings is added to internal and external bodily alterations, renewed exploration and clitoricolabial masturbation become the springboard for the "return of the inner-genital." The latency stories about hidden places and the reappearance of lost dolls may still be interesting, but they become superseded by horse and dog novels or detective stories in which girls assist their father substitutes to uncover hidden crimes. New features are immediately added when old fantasies emerge from repression. We see in them a mixture of naiveté of a small child and the increasing sophistication of the eleven-to-fourteen-year-old. Nobody really knows what is inside a surprise package. There may be a hidden penis inside or a baby may jump out like a jack-in-the-box. This was an important feature of Sue's surprise ending, when she became the master who delivered all slaves. However, she never once referred to herself as a master. It was the master's love which elevated her and gave her the relegated power to deliver all subjugated, suffering creatures. On one level, they were fellow women, mistreated by men, on another it was her mother whom she rescued, and on still another her own sensations were enclosed inside and waited to be liberated through a man's love. No doubt, the delivery of slaves was also equated with deliveries of babies. Magda assigned all her inner-genital urges to a male figure, "Mr. Sit," who resided in the uterus-vagina and directed the world from there. Thus he was a power behind the throne, compelling from inside and provoking attacks from the outside.

In prepuberty, the hidden penis and its predecessor, the monster-baby, assume a great many, regressively revived, threatening functions, such as biting, cutting, filling to the bursting point, twisting, tying into knots, burning, drowning, nagging, smashing and tearing the walls. The divergent feelings and fantasies merge into and interrupt one another, creating a diffusion of affect and thought. Out of the diffusion there emerge boundaries, already prepared for in the representation of the inner-genital as a baby or a penis. Drawing pains and cramps that begin with the onset of menstrual cycles reinforce and restructure the image of the inside genital as a shaped organ.

Listening to girls in prepuberty, one discovers how various forms of

94

excitation and shades of feelings come and go in waves until a focus is finally found and held on to. Monotonous nagging becomes tinged with irritability; feelings soar and excitement mounts as the girl recounts an argument with her mother; pouting or holding back is then used to provoke and get the analyst excited and, failing this, an avalanche is released to sweep over the analyst and make her excited with—or instead of—the girl. Eventually she confesses that she thinks she might get it (menstruate) because she has a funny feeling inside.

In puberty, one can observe periodic changes in feelings with nagging, passing on of excitement, or arguing becoming pronounced at separate times. When excitement becomes unbearable, old ideas about a hidden baby or penis recur. The girl sometimes feels that she must eject them and close up her vagina to gain peace. She contracts all sphincters, the laminal muscles of the vagina, even the circular muscles of the uterus and the perineal muscles. This closure, which recurs periodically, is a repetition of the motor counterpart of the original denial of the introitus (Chapter 10). At such times, the girl wishes to feel nothing, like Fern, or is indeed anesthetized by repression and feels nothing. When inner-genital feelings are milder in character, externalization helps to desexualize them.

While contractions of pelvic, laminal, and uterine muscles, clitoric masturbation, and manipulation through retention of feces and urine provide some means for active control of the vagina, engorgement and lubrication may give a sensation in the vagina for which there is no discharge and which cannot be controlled. The vagina may be experienced as bossy, independent, and demanding absolute obedience. This, added to the generally assumed childhood morality that genital excitement is bad and insides are disgusting, leads to the fantasy of the "bad" slave master. Through projection, this role is assigned to the male, who in the unconscious represents the father or the brother. The sleeping (anesthetized) vagina is being overwhelmed by a man. Here we can recognize the element of "revenge upon one's own body," acting as aggressor. The vagina is being treated as "badly" as it had treated the little girl. The personification of the vagina has its origin in its earlier equation with mother, baby, and the penis-father. It was the mother at first who seemed responsible for unbearable tensions, but it is the father with his well-controlled, large penis who assumes the final responsibility for the girl's genital excitation. In a way this is true inasmuch as at first the mother, and then the father, stimulated genital sensations. He was thus the last person responsible for the confusing goings-on in the vagina. If the vagina is dormant and there are no inner excitations through pressure from adjoining organs and muscle action, the mother, and later the father, can really "awaken it" by physical and verbal stimulations. The desire for control over one's own organ, so clearly expressed in external masturbation, reappears in those variations of slave fantasies in which the slave eventually wins over or controls the former slaveholder. This technique is also apparent in acting out with boys. The adolescent girl is coy and feminine with the boy and only at the insistence of his masculine demands does she yield to him and does for him "what she never wanted to do herself." In recent years, girls have become more open about sex. Because it has become fashionable to pursue boys, reaction formations against shyness have assumed almost bizarre proportions. Just recently I encountered a "liberated" fourteen-year-old girl who called a boy's mother asking for permission to go out with him. The modern, active adolescent girl is highly intellectual as she pursues an externally imposed "pseudomasculinity." Yet by manipulating his penis, by the control she gains over the man's excitement and gratification, the girl can achieve a measure of control over a body, even though not her own. The turning away from the mother in the preoedipal and oedipal phases and later, with even greater strength, in adolescence, is not only motivated by the girl's disappointment over loss of love, childlessness, and her "castrated" state, but also by the discovery that the mother herself does not possess the control over her own body that the girl yearns for. Mother is dependent on the father's generosity and love. The girl, competing with her mother, tries to be nice, good, patient, flirtatious, and long-suffering, hoping that her father will reward and rescue her. In the oedipal phase, and especially in its renewal in adolescence, she discovers that her father, far from allaying her tensions, does generate more excitement in her. She is disappointed in her father and finds fault with him, blaming him for her own lack of satisfaction and his lack of understanding. The argumentative disposition of the prelatency girl is revived and acted out in stormy altercations in mid-adolescence. Inner-genital tensions mount, adulthood beckons, and old, safely unattainable wishes are no longer unattainable childhood expectations. Escaping from her father, the girl tries to seduce boys, blaming them for all that she herself wishes. It is very important for her to prove that nothing is her fault. She has a difficult time accepting responsibility for failures, and this, in a great measure, helps her to avoid pressures from her superego.

Neither of the three patients could ever think of anything she had done badly without becoming excited. Others were to blame for all their misfortunes. This had to be proven by scenes, crying and shouting. The father was foremost to be blamed. Next in line was the mother, a brother, or a boyfriend. The feeling of being unloved because no gratification was forthcoming was the most prominent thought in these quarrels. Verbal torrents served to discharge sexual tension and tears represented vaginal discharge that could be displayed to the dismayed male. At times, crying was experienced as incontinence, especially by Fern, who leaked tears to dramatize her leaking discharge. On another level, the quarrels represented the inner argument between various parts of the genitals, especially clitoris and vagina.

The close alliance of the image of the vagina, first with the mother and then with the father image, makes this organ especially vulnerable to repression. Thus, the resolution of the oedipus complex in childhood is based on a repression of ties to the object and to the organ. In adolescence, the isolation of the genitals from primary objects is requisite for the successful giving up of incestuous wishes without giving up genital functioning. The guilt-free acceptance of sexual organs makes the adult woman less prone to the excessive mood changes adolescents suffer from. However, even under most favorable circumstances, there remains enough unrelieved, poorly localized excitement that is associated by the adult woman with inner-genital impulses to warrant repeated externalizations. These serve to foster and maintain desexualized maternal interest. When, as is often the case, the desexualization is not entirely successful, the adult woman resorts to nagging of her husband and children. This appears to be a universal feminine characteristic (Mead, 1956). Projection of sexual desires upon men helps woman combat her aggressive impulses toward those who do not satisfy her; it also provides the incentive for dependence upon man and for the assumption of a passive role to supplement the man's active strivings. Such an attitude becomes pathological when it leads to sexual anesthesia and an infantile type of dependence rather than to the realistic insight that biologically woman must depend on man for satisfaction and impregnation. A continuous need to project blame leads to argumentativeness as a means of discharging sexual tension.

Throughout development, feminine sublimations and adaptations counteract the severity of feminine moodiness. In the stage of maternal preoccupation before the phallic-oedipal phase, maternal care of dolls helps to desexualize the nagging inner-genital sensations. The need to pass on excitement is sublimated in adaptive communication through the free flow of speech. Out of the depression which occurs at the end of this phase (see Chapter 1) there arises the elation of phallic tomboyishness which promotes physical exercise and gross motor activity, affording permanent outlets for discharge. In the projective subphase of the phallic-oedipal phase, projection of wishes and guilt upon the male sex turns into compassion and other reaction formations. It contributes to the renouncing of physical aggression and encourages passive forms of adaptation. The argumentativeness of this period is a successor to the girlish talkativeness of the three–four-year-old. It provides a nonviolent avenue of discharge and prepares the girl for the future role of the judge and arbitrator she will assume as the mother of several children. Fixing the blame on the opposite sex prepares the girl for community ties with other girls and friendships, based on desexualized homosexual leanings. It also paves the way for feminine identity, which is protected by common disapproval of outsiders.

Latency is usually characterized by a steady disposition. A tendency to mood changes is still in evidence, but these are sporadic and transitory. Consolidating her feminine position, the latency girl never fully gives up her desire to attract her father. Especially when she is disappointed in him does she shift to a masculine identification. This may occasion attempts to seduce another girl, which revives passing on of excitement and arguing, as to who is to blame. Discriminating against peers and joint projections of blame on boys are frequent latency practices. When they do occur, they are fraught with less excitement than when prelatent and are self-limited in duration. The latency girl knows how to calm herself. She can even turn a seduction into a positive experience, serving the exploration of female or male anatomy. The former may pave the way toward a confirmation of feminine identity via the acceptance of another girl's body.

In prepuberty, the girl becomes capable of intense friendships. She still works on the adaptation of her body to her genital needs and still uses friendships for the purpose of increasing adaptive skills through common play and practice. The intense changes in the body bring narcissistic preoccupations to their height with renewal of mirroring and identification on the basis of sameness. The breaking through of unsublimated excitement may show itself in uncontrolled giggling, endless silly conversations and arguing, but it also leads to homosexual episodes. More than in latency, these can be used adaptively as preparations for heterosexual experiences. The outstanding achievement of the young adolescent is her increasing capacity to resolve problems posed by too many internal and external stimuli. She learns to integrate into new units a great many clashing sensations and feelings. Even when she is nagging, passing on excitement, and arguing, she can extract clarifications from externally or internally imposed traumatic events. In the midst of a domestic adversity, she comes up with new ideas to bring order into a chaotic situation. Similarly, she can cope with the "trauma of her menarche" by using it to reorganize her body image and her attitude toward femininity. She begins to accept the menstrual flow as a relief and takes it as conclusive proof of the existence of her inner-genital organs. She may elevate it from its secret and vague status to that of a precious jewel box, desired by men, active in its flow and creative in childbearing.

In mid-adolescence, the intensity of feelings singles out the sexual organs as unique. The girl may veer from condemning one or another of her genital parts and her moods change accordingly. Sometimes the acceptance of the vagina becomes exaggerated to the point that a "vagina-cult" is created at the expense of the now-rejected clitoris. However, the lack of sexual differentiation and genital integration betrays itself characterologically in competitiveness with man, alternating with argumentativeness and secretive gossiping or sullen resentment of men, whose orgastic experiences female organs cannot duplicate. In average development the seesawing of attitudes and moods in mid-adolescence becomes the basis for subsequent differentiations and for the renewal of reaction formations and sublimations. Through her capacity to modulate affects, the older adolescent can turn nagging into concern, passing on of excitement into seductiveness, and arguing into gentle persuasion. These become the enduring qualities of women in the last phase of adolescence which precedes adulthood.

The adapted adult woman accepts the participation of her total genital and her whole body in the sex act, but she also knows that there are shifts and variations in her sensations and feelings and she cannot always function the same way. She cannot gain minute control over the desexualization and resexualization of her vagina. Her ability to externalize varied inner-genital tensions and impulses makes her capable of desexualizing her activities for long periods of time and in various ways. Thus she can devote herself to being a mother, a wife, a homemaker, and a wage earner for the better part of the day. She is capable of giving up the externalization and can resexualize her activities in the time allotted to her for lovemaking. The transition from desexualization to resexualization is not always easy. There is hardly ever a day when woman's needs are perfectly synchronized with those of others. Resexualization occurring at the wrong time brings on nagging, passing on of excitement, or arguing. Many women are moody premenstrually and tend to spread excitement and yield to other typically feminine expressions of affect when gratification is withheld from them. When things get really rough and a woman feels tired out from the multiplicity of her tasks and from reaching the limits of her capacity to integrate, she may feel like a slave, a drudge, or an exploited victim of men on whom she projects her own masochistic fantasies.

99

Conclusions

The typically feminine moods of nagging, passing excitement on to others, and argumentatively trying to fix the blame on men have been correlated with female genital tensions and their origin traced back to early phases of girls' development. Nagging seems to originate in a phase which follows the pregenital and precedes the phallic-oedipal phase. It appears to be a response to nagging feelings from within. Passing on of excitement seems to originate in the end stages of this phase and is associated with feelings of swelling and intolerable spreading of waves of excitement, which give rise to feelings that the inside might get injured and fall out. Argumentativeness begins at that time also, but it becomes dominant in the late stage of phallic-oedipal development, when the need to project forbidden wishes and guilt upon men arises from inner-genital tensions, associated with oedipal fantasies. In adolescence, the increase of inner-genital sensations, the revival of old wishes and of early type of defenses intensifies nagging, passing on of excitement and argumentativeness. Even an adult woman capable of integration of many divergent simultaneous and successive needs and tasks is still at times subjected to the onslaught of these typically feminine types of moods. These can be correlated with the changes in her cycles and with other factors that produce inner-genital tensions without a possibility for gratification. The sublimation of inner-genital wishes and the typically feminine multiple forms of adaptation are the stabilizing influences in woman's development which rescue her from too frequent or excessive moodiness.

NOTES

[1]These views must be distinguished from the opinions of the British school, which maintains that an early oedipus complex is ushered in by oral dissatisfactions in infancy (Klein, 1928; Jones, 1935).

[2]In my view, the vagina-uterus image, modeled after a baby and externalized on dolls, develops in the preoedipal "inner-genital" phase, which precedes the phallic. The maternal behavior of the prephallic girl is based on her identification with her preoedipal mother. Moore (1968) assumes that the externalization of the vagina is connected with the feces = child equation and an identification with the phallic mother.

CHAPTER 5

OUTSIDE AND INSIDE, MALE AND FEMALE

Both in therapeutic and in character analyses we notice that two themes come into especial prominence and give the analyst an unusual amount of trouble. It soon becomes evident that a general principle is at work here. The two themes are tied to the distinction between the sexes; one is as characteristic of males as the other is of females. In spite of the dissimilarity of their content, there is an obvious correspondence between them. Something which both sexes have in common has been forced, by the difference between the sexes, into different forms of expression (Freud, S. 1937, p. 250).

We often have the impression that with the wish for a penis and the masculine protest we have penetrated through all the psychological strata and have reached bedrock, and thus our activities are at an end. This is probably true, since, for the psychical field, the biological field does in fact play the part of the underlying bedrock. The repudiation of feminity can be nothing else than a biological fact, a part of the great riddle of sex. It would be hard to say whether and when we have succeeded in mastering this factor in an analytic treatment. We can only console ourselves with the certainty that we have given the person analyzed every possible encouragement to reexamine and alter his attitude to it (Freud, S., 1937, pp. 252–53).

Ever since Freud tried to unravel the riddle of female sexuality, the interest of psychoanalysts has periodically turned to this subject (Barnett, 1966; Benedek, 1952, 1960; Bonaparte, M. 1953; Brierley, 1932; Deutsch, H., 1925a, 1944–45; Eissler, 1939; Erikson, 1950; Freud, S., 1905a, 1925, 1931, 1932, 1937; Greenacre, 1950b; Heiman, 1963;

Reprinted from *J. Amer. Psychoanal. Assoc.* 16 (1968):457–519. Slightly revised and reproduced by permission.

DEVELOPMENT OF SEXUALITY

Hitschmann and Bergler, 1934; Horney, K., 1933; Jacobson, 1936; Jones, 1927; Kestenberg (Chapters 1 & 2); Lampl-de Groot, 1928; Marmor, 1954; Moore, 1964, 1968; Müller, 1932). In contrast, Freud's theory of male development has remained essentially unchanged throughout decades of psychoanalytic experience. But the repudiation of femininity, common to both sexes, is still a riddle that poses a challenge to psychoanalysts and biologists.

In trying to do justice to the complexity of factors that cannot be reduced to a simple formula, I shall survey psychoanalytic literature and pertinent data from biology and expand on my own views on female sexuality (see Chapters 1, 2, 4, and 12). I shall propose that the universal repudiation of femininity is based on the anxiety-provoking nature of inner-genital sensations, and that, because man can more persistently externalize these sensations, he is less vulnerable than woman to fears of injury and loss of the inside genital.

Using clinical material from the analyses of children and adults, I shall compare the development of inner and outer genitality in women and men, distinguish adult from infantile genitality, and normality from pathology. After surveying similarities and dissimilarities in male and female development, I shall attempt to demonstrate the role of man in helping woman complete her sexual development. Lastly, I shall try to throw some light on the question why psychoanalysis cannot do more to help women achieve vaginal orgastic fulfillment than to restore her awareness of vaginal sensations.

Introduction

Psychoanalytic And Biological Views On Feminine Functioning

Freud persistently emphasized penis envy as a central feminine complex (Freud, S., 1925, 1931, 1933, 1937, 1940). He held that the vagina was awakened in puberty and not fully libidinized until adult genitality was established through the experience of coitus; the vagina was dormant in childhood and the occurrence of vaginal sensations before puberty was due to early seductions. The young boy, shocked by the discovery of the female opening, not only denied its existence but reinforced this denial by endowing women with a phallus. Beginning with Horney (1933), a great many, especially female analysts, could show that the "denial of the vagina" occurred regularly in feminine development as well, and that hyperchathexis of the clitoris as a small phallus, penis envy, and fantasies about an inner female phallus were all mechanisms that

102

reinforced this denial. There remained the controversy whether or not girls experienced vaginal sensations before puberty, whether they had to transfer their genital interest from the clitoris to the vagina and even had to condemn the clitoris to do so (Bonaparte, 1953).

Freud did acknowledge the role of the clitoris in adult genitality in a poetic reference to it as sparking the fire of the vagina (Freud, S., 1905). In discussing vaginal anesthesia, most analysts felt that the persistence of clitoral sensations was due to the typical feminine castration complex, to penis envy (Hitschmann and Bergler, 1934), and that the cultural suppression of women and the emphasis on phallic supremacy contributed in a great measure to the prevalence of frigidity. H. Deutsch (1925a, 1944–45) emphasized the complementary roles of maternality and sexuality and felt that much of feminine genitality was spent in reproductive functioning. Both she and Bonaparte (1953) stressed that feminine masochism led women to endure rather than enjoy coitus and contributed to the pain in reproductive functioning. Freud attributed woman's greater vulnerability to the more complex demands made on her, since she had to transfer her love from the mother to the father and her organ cathexis from the clitoris to the vagina.

Data from biology tended to confirm Freud's view on the role of the vagina in childhood. It is indeed an undeveloped organ in early childhood and its capacity to develop mucosal changes and vascularization is as limited as that of the "steroid-starved" postmenopausal woman (Huffman, 1959; Kestenberg, Chapters 13, 14, 15; Masters and Johnson, 1966). In addition, the surface of the vagina has few nerve endings and thus, compared to the clitoris, could not be considered a "live" organ even in adulthood. This view, especially propagated by Kinsey et al. (1953), became very popular and many a knowledgeable man spent time in trying to find the clitoris he was supposed to excite. The controversy became as intense as if there were two warring camps, the pro-vagina and the pro-clitoris factions (Bergler, 1947). Both women and men demanded vaginal orgasm as the ultimate achievement of female sexuality. Analysts stood by helplessly, acknowledging that they had not been too successful in helping patients to achieve vaginal orgasm (Benedek, 1961; Deutsch, H., 1961; Sherfey, 1966). Much of the hue and cry proved in analysis to be a renewal of the old demand that women should be given a penis, if not an outer one, at least an inner one (Jacobson, 1936; Rado, 1933).

Masters and Johnson's (1965, 1966) new discoveries about female sexuality help to correct the error made by Kinsey and others before him, who confused discriminatory sensibility dependent on somatic nerve endings with visceral sensibility, dependent on: sympathetic and parasympathetic innervations of genital organs; the nerve supply to the unique genital vascular system; and the mixed innervation of striate and non-striate muscles involved in orgastic experiences. Analysts were aware of this difference just as they were of the fact that feminine functioning depended on a specifically feminine integration rather than on simply quantitative variations in the importance of one organ or another (Barnett, 1966; Benedek, 1952; Bonaparte, 1953; Brierley, 1932, 1936; Deutsch, H., 1944–45, 1961; Erikson, 1950, 1964; Greenacre, 1950b; Harley, 1961b; Kestenberg, see Chapters 1–4 and 12–15; Moore, 1964, 1968; Payne, 1935).

Some analysts singled out orality as essential in feminine integration (Brierley, 1936; Deutsch, H., 1944–45; Heiman, 1963), but the claim of the latter two that the vagina has a sucking function has not been substantiated by Masters and Johnson (1966). Lorand (1939) and Langer (1951) presented cases of frigidity in which frustrated orality was an important factor. This is a frequent finding of experienced clinicians (Brierley, 1932). It may reflect an increasingly greater role of orality in both sexes rather than a selective influence of orality on vaginal functioning. With bottle feeding replacing breast feeding, the period of sucking has been extended beyond the oral phase. This mixture of deprivation and overindulgence of childhood oral needs has enhanced fixations in the oral phase. The vagina becomes endowed with the qualities of mouth, anus, urethra, baby, and phallus in fantasies derived from successive developmental phases, and individual differences in the importance of these representations stem from the individuality of constitution and early experience. Exaggerated emphasis on any one factor leads to an imbalance in feminine integration (see Chapter 4).

Whichever factor is singled out as cause of frigidity, there is a consensus that once denial and repression are removed, vaginal sensations impinge upon woman's awareness with full force. It does not necessarily follow that orgastic discharge will develop automatically.

The Orgastic Discharge

In normal development toward adult femininity, sensations from both clitoris and vagina become more integrated in an overall experience in which the inner genital is dominant (Masters and Johnson, 1966). But the vagina cannot achieve dominance in the same way as the clitoris and phallus. The latter organs can serve as "sensual foci" (Masters and Johnson, 1966) because of their abundant supply of superficial nerve endings. In contrast, visceral genital sensations are characterized by a "spreading" tendency, lack of localization, and refractoriness to verbal description. Diffusion of sensations, anesthesia to outer stimuli, and near or real loss of consciousness (Keiser, S. 1947, 1952; Masters and Johnson, 1966) involved in the total organismic response during orgasm break down the differentiation between inside and outside, between self and object. It is likely that at the peak of orgasm, both men and women who are not unduly afraid of surrender to primary-process functioning lose the awareness of a sensual focus. Nevertheless, a fundamental difference between the sexes remains: the female's sexual experience is inwardly oriented and is permeated more by purely visceral, inner genital sensations than by sensations from external genitals; the male's sexual experience is outwardly oriented and makes greater use of outer phallic sensations than of the purely visceral, inner genital sensations that initiate ejaculation.

The female orgasm may be felt as initiated by a clitoral sensation which resonates deep vaginal-pelvic feelings or as a diffuse spreading of inner general excitement over the entire genital. This culminates in rhythmic contractions of the "orgastic platform" (Masters and Johnson, 1965, 1966) that evolve from gradually ascending and descending waves of deep sensuous tension in the vagina, and merge with spasms and sensations from all over the body, ending in dimming of consciousness. The male orgasm may be experienced as initiated by the inner pelvic sensations of "ejaculatory inevitability" (Masters and Johnson, 1966), but is quickly transformed into a hypercathexis of the vascular and muscular changes in the phallus that occur during expulsion of the ejaculate. The generalized contractions and the merging of sensations from the whole body are shrouded by a loss of consciousness that is often equated with death—*le petit mort* (Keiser, 1947, 1952). A masterful presentation of fantasies of attack and injury, lust and fear, loss of identity between partners, and loss of distinction between life and death in orgasm is given in Ross's (1968) interpretations of Ahab's struggle with the whale in Melville's *Moby Dick:*

> The conflict culminates in a raging orgasm spewing forth "mountain torrents" and leaving as aftermath a "closing vortex . . . subsided into a creamy pool" out of which emerges a "coffin life buoy." It is orgasm yielding death, not life, or, if life, life is the object of death.

When the orgastic experience of partners coincides, boundaries between them break down as their outsides and insides unite, bringing them close to the yearned-for union with the mother or to the archaic image of hermaphroditic symbiosis (Ferenczi, 1924). The dimming of consciousness is akin to primary repression, which helps to repudiate

105

these fantasies when the ego's control reestablishes individual sexual identity. But the state of shock in the woman may be more intense and last longer than in the man, and the loss of body boundaries more readily evokes the image of loss of the sex organ (vagina), which at that moment merges with the self-representation. Not only women but also many men fail to reach such loss of control in orgasm, and even those individuals who can experience it do not do so always. Individual integration of pregenital, inner and outer genital drives under the dominance of a sex-specific zone (outer in the male and inner in the female) does not assure a high degree of orgastic fulfillment. An integrated relationship between love objects, based on mutual trust and predicated on successful identification with a nonincestuous partner, is an important prerequisite, especially for the woman. Furthermore, states of fatigue, anxiety, depressive feelings, and alertness to outer stimuli detract from the intensity of the orgastic experience or prevent its occurrence. Female object relationships and moods are more subject to fluctuation because women are more influenced by hormonal changes than men, more easily lose self-esteem, and more frequently feel a split between feelings for the mate and the children. Man's relationship to young children is more consistently desexualized than that of the woman; he is less tempted to regress to pregenital and early genital phases than is the woman, who is prone to relive the phase of childhood corresponding to the age of the child she is caring for. To be an "ordinary devoted mother" (Winnicott, 1949) she needs to desexualize her genital feelings and externalize her impulses upon her baby.[1] To fill her role as a sexual partner she needs to resexualize her genitals and give up externalization. Man can continue desexualization of his inside genitalia and externalization of inner genital impulses up to the moment of imminent ejaculation. Only for that brief moment does he cope with inner genital sensations and only then must he accept the passivity and helplessness that are brought about by the realization that he is losing control.

Man's adaptive task is easier and less subject to failure than that of woman; he can maintain ego control more consistently and more uniformly than she. His experience with orgastic discharge during masturbation is more successful. But the primary reason for his greater capability in orgastic discharge is his higher differentiation and his correspondingly lesser fear of an irreversible loss of control during orgasm. Nevertheless it is a fallacy to assume that frigidity is so much more frequent than impotence. It is more correct to say that total frigidity and vaginal anesthesia are more frequent than total impotence and failures of erections. Extreme denial of the "inside" makes the man unable to identify with women; it motivates him to seek out phallic women and makes him more prone to perversions based on externalization. Much of the present-day demand for woman's orgasm comes from man's feeling of failure; he feels that her deficiency may be due to his inability to delay ejaculation long enough. But the hyperpotent male, envied for his *ejaculatio retardata* or for his capacity to reinstate erection soon after ejaculation, is as much a victim of defensive externalization and compensatory overcathexis of the external genitals, as is the oversexed woman (Sherfey's [1966] "satiation in insatiation" type). Both are afraid of losing control and facing the sensations that are requisite for sexual fulfillment.

The similarity between the sexes is specific to *Homo sapiens*. It is based on externalization of inner sensations, without which secondary-process thinking and the formation of the human ego could not be achieved. Secondary-process thinking is derived from perceptions that aid localization, discrimination, and orientation in space, time, and in relation to gravity (Kestenberg, 1965); primary-process thinking is closer to visceral and protopathic global sensations. The repudiation of femininity (Freud, S., 1937) common to both sexes stems from the repudiation of the confusing visceral sensations from inside the body. Externalization of sensations from the inside protects the individual from overwhelming floods of excitation leading to regressions and states of shock.

The dissimilarity between the sexes is based on the higher differentiation of the male, leading to the enlargement of the outer genitalia and a greater development of musculature, both of which facilitate externalization and adjustment to reality. The fact that woman's reproductive organs are hidden helps her protect the young, but at the same time makes her more vulnerable to the breakdown of secondary-process thinking. Man, on the other hand, is more vulnerable to physical mishaps; engaged as he is in coping with the forces of nature and combating other males, he must remain aware of the danger to his exposed outer genitals.

Inner And Outer Genitality

Analysis of children and adults reveals that the outer and inner parts of the genitals play different roles in different developmental stages, that fantasies reinforce or diminish the cathexis of one or another genital zone, and that a transfer from inside to outside and vice versa occurs repeatedly. This two-way traffic between external and pelvic organs is not easily accessible to conscious awareness because its main connections are conducted by autonomic nerves:

> In the male, the extensions from the prostatic plexus reach the erectile tissues of the penis, and in the female similar nerves proceed to the clitoris

from the vaginal plexus. It is suggested that the pudental nerve also carries autonomic fibres, both sympathetic and parasympathetic, to the penis or clitoris (Cunningham, 1964, p. 780).

Throughout development there is a trend toward externalization of inner sensations which reaches its peak before sexual differentiation is accomplished. Puberty brings about a reversal in this trend in both sexes, but the cathexis of the inside genital plays a role in woman different from that in man. That woman's identity is based on her inner genital core is best expressed by Erikson (1964):

> When we speak of biologically given strengths and weaknesses in the human female, we may yet have to accept as one measure of all difference the biological rockbottom of sexual differentiation. In this, the woman's productive inner space may well remain the principal criterion whether she chooses to build her life partially or wholly around it or not (p. 598) . . . in women the basic schema exists within a *total optimum configuration* such as cultures have every reason to nurture in the majority of women, and this for the sake of collective survival as well as individual fulfillment (p. 599).

How this total configuration is achieved in development, and where fixations and distortions interfere, can best be shown through examples from literature and analytic practice. A presentation of the development of attitudes toward outside and inside in children, women, and men will serve to highlight sources of the repudiation of femininity.

Inside and Outside in Female Development

Infantile Genitality

Adult human genitality differs greatly from that of other mammals who respond only during estrus. Estral genitality is indiscriminate; any male will do. It is insatiable for the duration of the estrus. The engorgement of the sex skin of female animals persists after coitus, and full resolution of engorgement occurs only after the estrus. Some primate females solicit in a manner reminiscent of human prostitutes. They are "hypersexed" and demand repeated service from the male. Aberrant human genitality, because of its infantile traits, may retain traces of behavior of ancestral adults (Bradley, 1961).

The human female before puberty is safeguarded against indiscrimate genital activity by the concealed location of the vagina, its inanimate quality, the hymen that "locks the door," and the low hormonal supply in childhood, which keeps the vaginal mucosa as thin and bloodless as that of an aging female (Huffman, 1959; Masters and Johnson, 1966). However, the undeveloped genitals of the girl before puberty are as susceptible to sexual excitation as the target organs of the aging female (Masters and Johnson, 1966). When seduced, she may develop orgasms (Kramer, 1954). Under ordinary circumstances, maternal care brings about direct and indirect stimulation not only to the outside but to the inside genitals as well (as, for instance, through bath water). It is the task of the mother to stimulate and prime all bodily functions. Enough genital stimulation is provided during child care that, coupled with excitations triggered by small doses of hormones and those arising from pressure by adjoining organs, the genitals are prepared well enough for their use in adult genital behavior at the onset of sexual maturity.

Kittens and puppies that have not been licked by their mother in the appropriate zones will neither defecate nor urinate (Beach and Ford, 1952). Harlow's primates, raised by an artificial mother and isolated from playmates, did not know how to copulate or nurture their young (Harlow, 1965). Domesticated animals often require assistance from the breeder to perform coitus. Animals raised in zoos, deprived of the opportunity to observe adult mating (primal-scene deprivation), have to be taught how to copulate when they mature, but the vagina can be reawakened in maturity without exposure to mating behavior, as exemplified in the behavior of a young zoo primate who introduced twigs into her vagina, even though she did not know how to act in mating (Hediger, 1965). Conversely, in cases of congenital atresia of the vagina, the artificial vagina requires a great deal of priming before it becomes functional (Kaplan, 1963; Masters and Johnson, 1966). In normal development, maternal and hormonal priming of the vagina in childhood is reinforced in adulthood by successful coital techniques. These need to be taught in cultures characterized by "primal-scene deprivation."

Direct stimulation of the vagina during child care is minimal, but excitations of the external genitals spread to the inner genitals via nervous and vascular connections; in addition, nonstriate muscles of inner organs contract simultaneously with striate perineal muscles (Kinsey, *et al.,* 1953). Inner and outer genitals are also supplied with connections to other parts of the body, which participate in sexual excitement from early childhood (Cunningham, 1964).

DEVELOPMENT OF SEXUALITY

Modes of Genital Excitation in Childhood

Children usually do not masturbate to the point of orgasm, comparable to adult acme. Genital pleasure often occurs as a by-product of exploration or manipulation, designed to reaffirm the persisting presence of the organ. Lack of sensations makes the child fearful that the valuable organ is lost or changed.

Direct observation of masturbatory practices suggests that much of infantile genital handling is performed with rhythms that only rarely lead to orgasm comparable to that of an adult.

Light tapping or pulling of genitals has the character of an "oral" rhythm; playful tensing and releasing of perineal muscles evokes genital pleasure, associated with rhythmic sphincter contractions; prolonged contractions culminating in an explosive release may simulate orgasm, but this turns out to be an anal-sadistic type of discharge associated with holding and explosive discharge of feces; a passive surrender to dribbles of excitation is urethral in nature; a series of interruptions and cessations of contractions in which the control of continuity and discontinuity is the main source of pleasure is a urethral-sadistic discharge form (Kestenberg, 1965, 1967a). An "inner-genital" rhythm of discharge, I believe, is characteristic for children between two-and-a-half and four years of age. It can be discerned in wavelike and spreading movement of thighs or pelvis. The tension is low, it rises and falls gradually, and the rhythmic contractions are kept up for a long time. Sometimes it can be seen in slight pelvic writhing, reminiscent of the irregular rhythmic changes seen by Masters and Johnson (1966) in the expanding upper portion of the vagina of the adult woman.[2] In contrast, masturbation in the phallic phase is concentrated rather than spreading; it ends quickly, but is repeated quite often (Kestenberg, 1965, 1967a).

In latency, masturbation is either concealed or disguised and not accessible to direct observation. One can find its derivatives in latency stories which graphically represent the rhythmic inner genital discharge which is interspersed and coordinated with sudden spurts of activity derived from clitoral impulses. Direct communication about vaginal sensations and impulses occurs more frequently in prepuberty, but the "silent" organ of the latency girl is symbolized in accounts of dolls who are alive only when no one looks (Burnett, 1898). Of special import are the recurrent sudden initiations and cessations of all activity when the child pays attention to the doll. Both initiations and cessations seem to be derived from clitoral discharge forms that spark the "gentle fire" of the child's vaginal excitement or take over when the vagina yields to the clitoris, which acts as its resonance organ (Weiss, 1962).

110

OUTSIDE AND INSIDE, MALE AND FEMALE

Derivatives of Genital Discharge Forms Illustrated by the Theme in Children's Literature

The following excerpts from a popular story for girls illustrate the nature of the genital excitation processes which underlie fantasies of girls in latency and in transition to adolescence (Burnett, 1898). To distinguish between quotations from the story of nine-year-old Sara and my own comments, the latter will be bracketed.

The Vanishing Doll. "What I believe about dolls," she said, "is that they can do things they will not let us know about. Perhaps Emily [the doll] can read, talk and walk, but she will only do it when people are out of the room. That is her secret."

[As we shall see, Magda, whose case is presented later, complained that there was nothing in the vagina even though there was activity in it when she masturbated externally. Similarly, women who masturbate externally and do not allow themselves to acknowledge the activity "inside the room," even during coitus, are not aware of vaginal activity, whose existence during external genital excitation has been clearly established by Masters and Johnson.]

"You see [Sara continued], if people knew that dolls could do things, they would make them work. So, perhaps they have promised each other to keep it a secret. If you stay in the room, Emily will just sit there and stare; but if you go out, she will begin to read perhaps or go and look out of the window. Then if she heard either of us coming, she would just run back and jump into her chair and pretend she had been there all the time."

[In this passage we may recognize the well-known fear that once the vagina is discovered, its denial undone, and its representation freed from repression, it may be prematurely "put to work" by the adult seducer. "Looking out of the window" as if yearning to go outside may be taken as an invitation to come in, which stimulates the child to "open the door" and engage in sex play with a friend.]

"Let us go very quietly to the door" she whispered, "and then I will open the door quite suddenly; perhaps we may catch her."

She was half-laughing, but there was a touch of mysterious hope in her eyes which fascinated Ermengarde [the girl friend], though she had not the remotest idea what it meant, or whom it was she wanted to "catch," or why she wanted to catch her.

[We see here an instance of denial and virginal innocence of the seduced which, in the next passage, is followed by a gradual building up of anticipatory excitement, characteristic of sensations in the

111

labia minora and the introitus. An influx of a clitoral type of discharge initiates the entrance into the "room."]

Whatsoever she meant, Ermengarde was sure it was something delightfully exciting. So, quite thrilled with expectation, she followed her on tiptoe along the passage. They made not the least noise until they reached the door. Then Sara suddenly turned the handle, and threw the door wide open.

[We are reminded here of the widening of the vagina in response to stimulation, characteristic of the stage of excitation in adult women. But, as is often the case when adult women retain features of infantile genitality, the "gentle fire" of the vagina does not make up for the disappointment experienced when the budding awareness of its activity suddenly ceases, to be replaced by clitoral sensations.]

Its opening revealed the room quite neat and quiet, a fire gently burning in the grate, and a wonderful doll sitting in a chair by it, apparently reading a book.

"Oh, she got back to her seat before we could see her!" Sara exclaimed. "Of course, they always do. They are as quick as lightening." [This seems to symbolize the suddenness with which vaginal sensations can disappear when transferred to the clitoris.]

The Last Doll.   In prepuberty, pregenital, early vaginal, and phallic discharge forms are gradually reorganized under the primacy of a more mature form of genitality. The hormonal influx and the growth of inner-genital structures begun in latency (Freud, S., 1905; see also Chapter 13) bring on spurts of inside excitement, which contrast with the gentler activity of the vagina characteristic of latency. As early genital discharge forms become incorporated into phases of the menstrual cycle, initiated by the irregular influx of hormones in prepuberty, the girl retains a "respect" and a liking for the doll that helped her to desexualize cryptic vaginal excitations. Her early experiences with switching genital excitement on and off, in which the clitoris acts as a trigger and a shut-off valve, with fantasies of the live doll (sexualization of the vagina) and the quietly reading doll (desexualization of the vagina), prepare her not only for the impatient waiting in puberty, but also for adulthood, when she must alternate between sexualization of the vagina in coitus and its desexualization during the care of children and home. The last doll often signifies a turning point in the girl's life, a landmark that separates childhood sexuality from growing up to adult womanhood.

[In thanking her father for the last doll he gave her, Sara conveyed to him what it meant to be eleven:] "I am getting too old" she wrote, "you see, I shall never live to have another doll given to me. This will be my last doll. There is something solemn about it. . . . No one can take Emily's place. But I should respect the last doll very much, and I am sure the school would love it. They all like dolls, though some of the big ones—the almost fifteen ones—pretend they are too grown up."

The Lost Doll.   The detachment from the doll in prepuberty is preceded by several phases in which the girl's experiences with the loss and the recovery of a loved doll symbolize her struggles with the loss and recovery of the inner genital impulses which she had externalized upon the doll. A whole series of girls' stories deals with a long-lost doll that is found again (Gates, 1905; Lownsberry, 1946; McGinley, 1950). These show the despair of the child and the joy of finding what was once hers. Nothing comparable can be found in boys' literature. One may think that the "lost doll" represents the penis and in some passages of some stories it does. But this typically feminine theme relates to the loss and recovery of inner genital sensations.

In analysis, the recovery of memories about childhood dolls often precedes the recovery of vaginal sensations. It is then that one can see how diffuse inner sensations evoke a yearning for a focus that was once found in the "mothering" of dolls. The loss of the doll represents the loss of the inner genital. Vaginal sensations shift to the clitoris in an incomplete externalization that makes it possible for the patient to experience a sensual focus on an external part of the genital rather than on an external object. But the dominance of the clitoris also implies a loss of the vagina as an organ. Lost and recovered in the working through of repeated repudiations and reacceptances of femininity, vaginal sensations eventually unite and coordinate with sensations from the introitus, the labia, the prepuce, and the clitoris.

Most dramatic is the feeling of loss at the end of the early maternal (inner-genital) phase at the age of four. In repudiating her femininity the girl denies the existence of her introitus and recognizes with sorrow that the "live doll" she had treated like a real baby is only an inanimate object (Chapters 1 and 2). She transfers all feelings to the clitoris which, in the phallic phase, becomes hypercathected at the expense of inner genital sensations. In oedipal games, the girl plays house with dolls, girls and boys, acknowledging that babies need not only a mother but a father too. With her turning to her father, and her fantasies of being penetrated and delivering a baby, she comes very close to the recovery of vaginal sensations. But the denial of the vagina persists, and the reawakening of vaginal sensations is counteracted by the repression that ushers in

113

latency. In latency, genital feelings from inside and outside are expressed in drive-derivative fantasies, games, and stories. In prepuberty the on-rush of genital feelings calls for a renewed repudiation of the inside and once more the child gives up the doll. The theme of the lost and recovered doll in stories comes to an end; prepuberty stories shift from the loss of the doll to the loss and recovery of friendships. The cherished doll is replaced by the cherished girl friend.

Clashes Between Inside and Outside: Case Reports

The three-year-old integrates her pregenital and early genital urges before she can externalize her inner sensations upon the clitoris. This "inner-genital" phase is revived in prepuberty (Chapters 13 and 14). The return of the vaginal cathexis, which had been shifted to the clitoris, breasts, and other external parts of the body, ushers in periodic variations in the ratio of inside and outside genital excitations in various phases of the menstrual cycle. Adolescent genitality emerges from the integration of regressive pregenital, early genital, and new forms of sexuality. At the end of adolescence another phase of integration precedes the emergence of adult genitality (Chapter 15).

Examples from analyses in phases of transition from pregenitality to phallicity, from latency to adolescence, and from adolescence to adulthood will best illustrate the developmental crises which, though exaggerated and distorted by pathology, can give us insight into the struggles between inside and outside, between the acceptance and rejection of femininity that precede feminine integration in normal development.

Transition from Pregenitality to Phallicity

"My vagina hurts"

Gigi's case illustrates how excessive genital excitations in early childhood prevent externalization on substitute objects, interfere with the integration of pregenital, inner-genital, and phallic drive components, and produce an excitability comparable to that of adult women who are never satisfied.

Gigi was a delicate four-year-old girl who took on a witchlike quality when she quarreled, whined, and clung to her mother. Although very bright, Gigi had difficulties taming her pregenital drives. She was neither completely weaned nor trained before the age of three and a half. She demanded special foods and screamed to get what she wanted. She was a nail biter and also bit the inside of her mouth. She threw things around in a provocative way and staged temper tantrums. Gigi dealt with genitality directly and indirectly. She pulled her brother's penis and referred to the time "when I will be a man." At the same time she like to twirl like a ballerina and would amuse herself stuffing little things in her purse, but she never really enjoyed doll play for any length of time. She masturbated externally and vaginally, but also anally. During the day she seemed beset by divergent urges which interfered with her adjustment to reality. At night the focus of her distress was clearly centered on genital irritations. She would wake up and complain: "My vagina hurts."[3] She would be bathed in the middle of the night or else an ointment would be applied, outside and in the vagina, to alleviate the irritation that was due to congestion and aggravated by scratching and rubbing.

Gigi was beset by clashing pregenital, inner-genital, and outer-genital urges. Unable to bring order into this avalanche of confusing excitations, she repeatedly demanded relief from her mother. It was hard to know in advance when she would become excited, and it was not possible to help her when she attached the causes for her frustration to insignificant events of everyday life that could not be helped. When I suggested to her that she clung to her mother and pulled on her because she could not by herself alleviate what bothered her, she released her mother and proceeded to watch me for signs of excitement. She demonstrated to me dramatically that she expected me to get excited, which would take the excitement away from her. She tore up paper in tiny little strips and threw them all over the floor, all along looking up at me to see how I reacted. Turning from passivity to activity, she indicated that she would not pick anything up from the floor because she did not want to do it. This defensive anal-sadistic pattern was also used to express the wish to eject all the clashing stimuli from her body and transfer them outside. Everything was in pieces, beyond relief, and it was up to the adult to restore harmony in her body and mind by picking up the scattered fragments.

It was striking that Gigi seldom used play and toys to externalize inner-genital impulses, as children between three and four usually do. Because she used the genitals and pregenital zones as avenues of genital discharge, she was not able to desexualize any of her bodily functions. My first task was to eliminate current sources of genital excitement, which prevented externalization and interfered with the organizing forces that would enhance a transition into the phallic stage. Only after this was accomplished was I able to assist her in the process of the integration she herself was striving to achieve, as if driven by progressive developmental forces (Freud, A., 1965).

Among past sources of excitation was a fungus infection at the age of sixteen months which involved the genitals and the perianal area; recurrent sources of irritation were pinworms and very sensitive mucous membranes.

By the institution of proper medication Gigi's current genital distress was removed. When she calmed down, she became creative, could tell stories and draw, play with dolls and doctor sets, and thus became both analyzable and acceptable to her mother and playmates. This also helped her to renounce an imaginary companion, an alter ego who was responsible for all her misdeeds. She became maternal rather than ferociously jealous and destructive to her baby sister.

Instead of dealing with the inside genital directly, Gigi now produced memories of her third year of life, when she was frightened by workmen in her home who made windows and doors where none had existed before. The alteration of the house served to symbolize Gigi's discovery of her intoritus, which had prevented externalization on dolls, initiated intense penis envy and a depression. The mother had mistakenly interpreted Gigi's preoccupation with her vagina as due to a congenital absence of a hymen and, I suspect, was as distressed as Gigi when the walls of her house were taken down and gaping holes were exposed to view. With the working through of these and other memories and fantasies, Gigi's depression lifted and she was dismissed from treatment as she was entering the phallic-oedipal phase with a more successful denial of the introitus than she was able to achieve by herself.

Since describing the maternal preoccupation of the girl between two and four (Chapter 1), I have come to realize that the maternal play with dolls, in identification with the active mother, is only one of the manifestations of externalization, typical for that stage. Externalization on substitute objects (Chapter 9) serves the integration of pregenital, inner-genital, and phallic drives before a focused phallicity can be established as a safeguard against the intrusion of inner-genital sensations during the oedipal phase. Passive wishes to be penetrated and given a penis or a child are projected upon men before the repression of oedipal fantasies reinforces the denial of the vagina with the beginning of latency. But throughout these phases, the doll continues to be used as a preferred object on which inner-genital sensations can be externalized. When, toward the end of latency and in prepuberty, forbidden fantasies and impulses are lifted from repression, externalization once more becomes the principal mechanism by which reintegration of various drive components can be established. Prepuberty reorganization is least disturbed when previous attempts at externalization can be used as models for its more mature forms. Analysis of prepuberty fantasies often leads to the recovery of memories from the "inner-genital" phase between two and a half and four. In cases where earlier attempts at externalization were not satisfactory, the child must struggle with inner-genital strivings in latency.

OUTSIDE AND INSIDE, MALE AND FEMALE

Transition from Latency to Adolescence

"Sit" in the "upstairs room"

The account of Magda's analysis covers the period between the end of the latency at nine through her early teens.[4] Magda was an underachiever in school, did not get along with peers, and was persistently quarrelsome and excited at home. In the beginning, her analysis focused on her relationship to her parents, especially her mother, to the analyst, and to her girl friend, all of whom made her feel dissatisfied and frustrated. The solution to all her troubles, she felt, was either a large live horse (Freud, A., 1965; see also Chapter 14) or a hobbyhorse. This wish was connected with the feelings she had had as a child of about three when her father gave her piggyback rides and let her swing on his leg. Some of her current play with the girl friend, which always culminated in quarrels, was of a similar nature.

Magda's overwhelming excitement, unrelieved by masturbation, resembled that of Gigi, but was even more intense and spreading. It was contagious and disturbing to the environment. She herself could not tolerate her own disorganizing excitement and tried to discharge it by oral, anal, urethral, and clitoral routes, by nagging, sadistic attacks and masochistic surrender, by passing on her excitement to others, and by projecting all blame. As prepubertal changes occurred, she became at once more excited, more diffuse and disorganized. But she herself began to want to be better organized and could focus more clearly on the source of her excitement. She discovered that her excitement was "inside," and named it "Sit" in continuation of her fantasy of an illusory penis, of her need to blame all genital feelings on men, and in acknowledgment that her "inside" was foreign and frightening. "Sit" was a cripple who tortured and pursued her relentlessly. He tried to entice her to enter the "upstairs room"; he forced her to trap women to enter and be trapped there with him. He was very much afraid of me, the analyst, lest I catch him, take him out of hiding and cure him of his lameness. On one level he was an imperfect penis, unsatisfactory to women; on another level he represented inner-genital excitement, which Magda tried to "lame" for fear that it might go away and be lost. "Sit" also unified pregenital, inner-genital, and phallic urges, as he directed everything in the inside and outside of her body. Magda could not manage without his advice. In a way, he acted like a husband or father, cruel to be sure, but powerful and self-assertive. He enslaved Magda, swallowed people she liked, and made them do anything "he" pleased.

While "Sit" concealed from me what was going on inside, Magda was better able to describe what she experienced on the outside of her genitals.

117

She would shift her excitement further and further away from the introitus, upward and laterally and to a special focused point on the side of the clitoris where she could reach orgasm (see similar descriptions in Masters and Johnson, 1966). She called her clitoris "skin and bones," which probably referred to the foreskin and to the pressure she exerted on the pubic bone when she tried to reach the retracted clitoris (Masters and Johnson, 1966; Sherfey, 1966). Whenever she hurt herself or feared to do so, she shifted her manipulations lower down "to give the skin and bone rest," perhaps to lure it out from concealment. "Sit" was an occupant of the "inside" and there was no link between him and the clitoris. But her clitoral and labial masturbation fantasies were masochistic, about men who enslaved and tortured her, much as "Sit" did from inside.

When Magda demonstrated her image of her anatomy in a drawing, I helped her understand that her inside was structured and contained useful organs. She blamed me for her attempts to explore her inside and denied any "good feelings" there, but said she was playing "that I am getting a baby and it's coming out." Playing delivery, she succeeded in externalizing and desexualizing her vaginal excitement. But she complained that she could not penetrate very far, and once more she blamed it on "Sit": "He wants to stay there, he does not want the box in which he hides to be broken." She became sulky and responded to my remark that there was a door to the inside by telling me she did not want any Christmas present from me. Her wish for a penis became intensified as she refused to accept the "door" that would not open widely enough to admit her to the depth of the "box." She said sadly: "But when you put the tip of your finger there, there is nothing." She could not see how excitement could come from "nothing at all." When I told her that the inside had walls as she knew from her own drawings, she acknowledged that she knew she could control it by movements that made it tighter or wider. Through the puppets with which she played during these discussions, she made clear that rubbing the clitoris produced movement inside and vice versa, something inside made the clitoris move. "Look, look," she said with amazement, recognition, and exhilaration, "you don't even touch the tip of his nose, you must move your hand inside his neck and the nose moves. If you take his mane off, he will be a lioness. Look, look you can make his ears move and you don't even touch them." I agreed that unseen feelings and movements from inside influenced all parts of outer genitals. Yet she was still distressed by her inability to experience the vagina as an active, outer organ she could touch and feel. She demanded and received the "last doll," but rejected one as too small: "But that will be nothing at all, I need a baby-size doll which I can hold in my arms like a real baby." Sewing clothes for the doll, she worked through her worries about the size of the vagina, about its expansion and contraction. After entering puberty she ceased to masturbate, became calmer, and began to feel very intensely about boys whom she dated.

In the transition from adolescence to adulthood the young girl reexperiences more intensely the feelings, familiar to her from the later oedipal phase, that her sexual needs cannot be satisfied without the help of a man as guide and unifier of outside and inside genitality. Excerpts from the analysis of an eighteen-year-old girl show her struggles with the acceptance of her femininity, struggles that were greatly intensified because earlier attempts to integrate inner-genital impulses with more focused external sensations had failed. To alleviate her tensions she manipulated men rather than allowing them to teach her.

Transition from Adolescence to Adulthood

"I wish I were a doll"

Fern never masturbated by herself. Instead she quarreled with boyfriends and ended the mounting excitement by allowing them to masturbate her.[5] She limited their manipulations to genital zones furthest removed from the vagina. When a boy put his finger inside it, she became irritable and stopped him abruptly for fear that he would hurt her. She admitted sheepishly that boys had hurt her by rubbing the clitoris too violently, but that had not deterred her from sex play. She would prefer to have no genitals at all. "I wish I were a doll," she said repeatedly.

Fern insisted that she never wanted a penis, because its possession would bring even more trouble. She had masturbated boys and seemed to know that they were troubled too. When separated from a boyfriend for a short time, she began to masturbate on her own and achieved orgasm on the clitoris but claimed that there was no feeling in the vagina. With the vagina she maintained a continuous warfare. Every exercise, she believed, affected her hymen so that it eventually became all used up. Each time she had to remove a tampon, her vagina stubbornly refused to cooperate; it would not open on command and she had to use force. She tolerated the liquid menstrual blood, but the brown particles were "awful" and proof of being used up inside. Her vagina was always leaking somehow, spilling brown secretions when she "forgot" to remove the tampon, secreting a whitish discharge when she was not menstruating. Thus it was slowly approaching the state of nothingness which Fern yearned for and dreaded (Jones, 1927). She wanted relief from inner tensions, but was afraid that the loss of excitement would indicate the loss of her "inside." She maintained her excitement as if it were a precious possession she might lose if it slipped out of sight. She habitually lost articles of clothing, parcels, and handbags. She felt that she could not find them herself and waited until someone returned them. She demanded detailed and clear instructions as to how to go about the search. She never knew exactly what was in the parcel or bag she had lost. She gave few clues, but was never satisfied with any suggestions given. She constantly demanded directions and explanations and then refused to understand what she was told.

Although she was fully enlightened and knew anatomy, Fern felt that her ovary floated freely in the abdomen and there was no opening to the uterus. She closed up her uterus from above and her vagina from below to protect them from being used up or swelling into an unhealthy growth.

After an interpretation of the way she blamed men for everything she dreaded, she accused me of forbidding her the "use" of men to free herself from uncomfortable feelings. She now had to face what was going on inside of her. She became aware that her genitals were exciting her and the excitement spread all over her body, making her so irritable that she had to get rid of the feeling immediately. Her hostility to her own inner genital tension also became apparent to her. She quarreled with it and treated it as an adversary who would overwhelm her if she did not get rid of "him" first.[6] She yearned for a boy who would direct her, take responsibility for everything, and restore her balance. She began to realize that the boyfriend could not really do what she expected because she prescribed what he was to do and never really yielded control. She had to accept her vagina with all its qualities before she could allow a male to teach her how to use it.

All three of these patients had a trait that accounted for their dissatisfaction and their need for treatment: they were unteachable. It was the task of analysis to restore psychic balance so that they could function appropriately, in keeping with their developmental phases. Whether they would continue to develop their potentials depended in good measure on environmental forces to stimulate growth, hinder regression, and assist progressive reintegration toward adult functioning.

Pseudoadult and Adult Feminity Distinguished

With children, the role of the teacher and guide must be assumed by the parents; young adult women transfer their dependence on the parent to their new love objects, who become their teachers. Women who are teachable, but unsuccessful in meeting and attracting men able to teach and assume dominance in a relationship, frequently adapt to the habits, neurotic attitudes, and unconscious fantasies of the men they do find. Treatment of the husband may produce striking improvement in the wife. Conversely, overzealous men may chose doll-like infantile women, whose readily awakened sexuality appears to be very promising and satisfying until they realize that they are dealing with "playthings" rather than with teachable adults.

A case of a twenty-three-year-old woman will illustrate a pseudoacceptance of feminity, in which multiple orgasms simulated maturity but betrayed their source from infantile sexuality, not easily convertible into adult form.[7]

Multiple Orgasms

"We giggled a lot in bed"

Peg failed in everything she undertook, except in sex, which she professed to enjoy very much. She would always manage to lose the man who satisfied her and loved her. Yearning for children, she had to undergo an abortion and expended her maternal feelings in playing with dogs and watching horses she was "crazy about." She failed in her career despite great talent. Depressed, harassed, and forever badly treated by men, she failed even in a suicide attempt. After that she longed to sleep all day and have fun all night. The last of her lovers was an older, experienced man who seriously considered marrying her. But she clung to him so tenaciously that she exhausted his patience. She called him day and night demanding that he tell her where he was every minute. She felt well only when he embraced her and told her that she was a "good girl," not a tramp. Their relationship was so good, she said, that she could not understand why he would not marry her. He finally gave up explaining, saying that she ought to go to a psychiatrist. It seemed obvious that he loved her as a father might love a little girl but could not succeed in educating her to play the role of a grown woman, fit to be his wife.

When I asked how she felt about sex relations, she begged me not to tell her mother. With glee she reported that she had not only one orgasm but several during one coitus. She could not tell exactly where they were focused, but the implication was clear that her vagina played a role in the experience. Her face lit up and her depression lifted when she explained to me, as if in answer to my question about orgasms, that they giggled a lot in bed and rolled around, even fell on the floor. The playful nature of her multiple orgasms, which reflected her immaturity, attracted men who wanted to protect her and help her grow up. She made them feel powerful and her enjoyment of sex gratified them, but none of her suitors could really gratify the infantile needs which she presented under the guise of adult femininity.

DEVELOPMENT OF SEXUALITY

All patients described here felt mistreated and frustrated; all went through life martyred, unsuccessful in play and work, crying, excited, argumentative or depressed, driven, illogical, puzzles to their environment, and happy only when they could maneuver others into alleviating their excitement. In many ways their feelings were identical with those described in premenstrual distress, but their states were chronic. What I have described comes close to a caricature of woman as she appears in popular belief, cartoons, and jokes.[8] One can readily classify this syndrome as "satiation in insatiation" which, Sherfey (1966) postulates, is the prototype of womanhood. Every analyst is familiar with the complaints of dissatisfied women as well as with their nagging of husbands and children (see Chapter 4). There is usually some foundation for the complaints but they are aggrandized out of proportion to the misdeed, and the role of the patient in provoking others is obscured. These patients take a long time before they can realize that they externalize their need to control genital impulses and project the blame upon others. Quite often, penis envy and competition with men appear to be at the center of the dissatisfaction, but the analysis of the determinants of penis envy brings on manifestations of oral, anal, and urethral fantasies. A lack of integration between pregenital and genital drives becomes apparent, and attempts to discharge vaginal tensions through pregenital and phallic channels become especially noticeable in premenstrual phases. Diffusion of thought processes, physical discomfort, and states of psychic disequilibrium become intensified, and there is a corresponding urgency to find a focal form of discharge to escape the feeling of dissolution and annihilation of ego boundaries (Jones, 1927; Keiser, 1952; Lorand, 1939). Analysis of this typically feminine fear reveals *woman's dread of losing the "inside genital"—the core of the feminine body ego.*

Acceptance of the vagina as a source of pleasure without fear is an important, but not the only, factor in adult feminine integration. Throughout development, the girl goes through phases of sexualization and desexualization of the vagina, of transfers of cathexis from inside to outside or vice versa. These all converge in a unified image of external and internal genitals, in which parts of the genitals function in specific ways but in consonance with each other. Moreover, some parts become more dominant in sexual functions and others in reproductive functions. The more proximal, the more internal the organ, the more it serves reproductive functions and the more removed it is from sensuous awareness (ovaries, tubes). The more distal the genital organ, the more it serves as a "sensual focus," a "receptor," a "transformer" (Masters and Johnson, 1966) of vectors of genital discharge, a resonance organ (Weiss, 1962) of deep inner sensations, and the more removed it is from reproductive functioning (clitoris). The introitus, the labia, the distal and proximal portions of the vagina and the uterus participate, to varying degrees, in sexual discharge and reproduction. The vagina, as a middle organ with qualities of expansion and shrinking, and a readiness to be desexualized when it serves expulsion and to be sexualized when it serves reception, is uniquely and sensitively calibrated to shift from externalization to internalization and vice versa. The many transfers from inside to outside and outside to inside, which development provides before the vagina can assume its dual function in sexuality and reproduction, serve as preparations for optimal functioning. The transfer from the clitoris to the vagina in adolescence is only one instance of many similar earlier and later transfers. An adult woman must be able to desexualize her total genitals and to externalize her sexual impulses in adaptive and sublimatory activities. In optimal functioning, she becomes capable of resexualizing the genitalia under conditions of effective and undisturbed stimulation, which promotes an integrated unification of all portions of her genitalia. In order to achieve an adult feminine orgastic discharge, woman is just as dependent on man's performance as teacher and organizer of her sexuality as she is dependent on his performance as effective intruder into her body and giver of semen. This double dependence is anticipated in development in the many phases in which a girl yearns for an outside agent to relieve her genital tensions and to bring on an effective discharge.

The frequency of vaginal frigidity, statistically significant as it may be (Benedek, 1961; Deutsch, H., 1961; Kinsey *et al.,* 1953; Marmor, 1954; Moore, 1964), is a by-product of this organ's sensitive calibration and a by-product of its dependency on the man as organizer. The causes of frigidity range widely between phase-specific disturbances of the development of vaginal calibration and failures of men to act as final organizers of feminine sexuality.

Pathology and Normality in Women

Since the vagina's existence as an organ can be established only in states of sexual excitement, woman's feelings range from an overwhelming dread of loss to confident expectation that the "absent" organ will eventually return. Defense mechanisms, originated in childhood to counteract the fear of inner-genital excitation and of disintegration of the body ego, are perpetuated in adulthood in various forms of feminine pathology:

1. *Regressive shift of cathexis* from the genitals to pregenital zones

which may lead to somatization, persistence of infantile habits, and poor control over bodily functions. The genital itself may function as a zone of discharge for regressive pregenital discharge forms that invade genital functioning, as seen in pseudogenital multiple orgasms, vaginismus, profuse spontaneous lubrication, and spontaneous orgasm akin to spontaneous emissions (wet dreams) of immature men.

2. *Passing on excitement* to others by "contagion" or provocation leads to its perpetuation. Excitement is treated like an object that can be tossed back and forth between partners. This is expressed in teasing and arguments.

3. *Externalization of "inside" impulses* onto children or child substitutes in mildly seductive, adaptive mothering activities. When this mechanism is successful, the vagina becomes desexualized and maternal activities are sublimatory in nature; when it fails, maternal behavior becomes explicitly seductive and genital sensations and impulses break through in nursing, diapering and fondling activities (Heiman, 1963; Masters and Johnson, 1966; Sarlin, 1963).

Irreversible or only mildly reversible desexualization of the vagina creates a permanent split between maternality and sexual adjustment, as seen in women who are frigid, or only mildly interested in sex, but are truly maternal to their children and husbands (Deutsch, H., 1961).

Persistence of externalization on transitional objects (Chapters 1, 2 and 9), associated with infantile desexualization of the vagina, can be seen in certain forms of spinsterhood and infertility. Deficient externalization with desexualization of the vagina, or with its opposite, hypersexuality, weakens the integrative function of the ego, hinders adjustment to reality, and fosters the persistence of infantile genitality. Examples are: "child brides" (Greenacre, 1947), promiscuity (Glover, E., 1943), sexual delinquency, prostitution, and subordination to phallic women in overt homosexuality (Weiss, 1962; Kestenberg, 1962).

4. *Denial or isolation* of the vagina promotes: masculine identification and penis envy, transfer of inner sensations upon the clitoris, intolerance of passivity and repudiation of femininity. In extreme forms it leads to a condemnation of the clitoris not only as an inadequate penis substitute but also as a trigger and resonance organ of the vagina, whose phobic avoidance may progressively enlarge the area of "safe distance." This syndrome can be seen in cases of inveterate forms of total or partial genital anasthesia, voluntary spinsterhood, defensive devotion to careers away from the home, and agenital forms of homosexuality.

In some cases an illusory penis serves to aggrandize the clitoris or promotes the acceptance of the vagina as a hidden penis (Jacobson, 1936; Rado, 1933). These syndromes manifest themselves in a defensive insis-

124

tence that the clitoris is the prime organ of female sexuality (Bergler, 1947; Kinsey *et al.*, 1953) or in unattainable demands that the vaginal orgasm must be equivalent to the male orgasm. These mechanisms are grossly exaggerated in promiscuity, based on masculine identification, and in dominant forms of overt homosexuality.

5. *Projection* of aggressive and sexual wishes may lead to: masochistic surrender to men; provocation of attack; enduring all feminine functions as a burden rather than a pleasure; passive submissive attitudes toward men and children which only simulate true womanhood and motherhood. These syndromes are usually associated with a continuation of infantile dependency on preoedipal or oedipal objects, a failure of internalization, and an insufficient differentiation of the superego.

6. *Repression* of perceptions and representations of the genitalia and of connected fantasies leads to total frigidity. In partial frigidity the remainder of the genital is isolated from the cathected part. Where repression and isolation are weakened, a scattering of sensations and their displacement bring on conversion symptoms.

This classification has listed defense mechanisms in chronological order as they seem to appear during development from pregenitality to latency. In further development, drive derivatives undergo modifications, and temporary breakdowns of repression and regressions give the child a chance to reorganize constellations of defenses. In normal development the onset of sexual maturity enhances growth and differentiation of drives, adaptation to a new reality, and acceptance of femininity (Chapter 15).

Feminine integration is completed when woman learns to adjust to her role as wife and mother. In this she can succeed only if she is teachable and can accept her husband and children as organizers of her femininity.

A constellation of feminine defense mechanisms in an individually varying ratio of intensity, combination, and sequence is representative of woman's character formation. However, fluctuations and shifts in pattern occur in response to: internal and external changes, cyclic hormone fluctuations, states of alertness, fatigue and stress (Masters and Johnson, 1965).

Primacy of the inner genitalia cannot be achieved or maintained in face of the typically feminine castration anxiety that the inner genital will disappear (Benedek, 1961; Deutsch, H., 1961). This fear evokes denial and repression which, so to speak, put the vagina to sleep to safeguard its intactness. But through externalization of inner-genital sensations and impulses the activity of the vagina is perpetuated on substitute objects and organs.

DEVELOPMENT OF SEXUALITY

The vagina of the normal adult woman becomes fully functional and capable of being awakened by man without prolonged conditioning when the following requirements have been met:

There must be sufficient priming of the vagina in critical developmental phases. Denial and repression of genital-pelvic sensations and their reinforcement by hypercathexis of the clitoris must not be so strong as to become almost irreversible. Not only the vagina, but all other parts of the genitals must be accepted and allowed to function in coordination with each other.

The male's acceptance of his own inside genitals, projected on the woman, must be expressed in his fearless interest in the woman's inside genitals so that he will not defensively libidinize the clitoris as a homologue of his penis. To be regarded as a valuable organ and not an object of aggression, the vagina must be libidinized by the man's continuing interest in its penetration (Masters and Johnson, 1965, 1966), without intent to injure it.

Both partners must be relatively free of incestuous ties and capable of object constancy which motivates them to mutual adjustment and satisfaction.

Pregenital components in foreplay as well as in the three phases of the sexual cycle (Freud, S., 1905; Masters and Johnson, 1966) must be so encompassed within the dominant sphere of genitality that they cannot become dominant themselves. Their integration with the genital complex must not be so rigid, however, that they cannot be rearranged in intensity or sequence to adjust to the partner's needs.

There must be a flexible balance between desexualization and sexualization so that sexualization develops only under conditions appropriate in time and place.

There must be an ego-syntonic balance between activity and passivity and between inner- and outer-genital stimulation, so that masculine and feminine rhythms in each individual can operate in harmony with each other and with those of the partner. A conflict between partners or a competition between body parts leads to interruptions in excitation, shifts in cathexis, and scattering of sensations, all incompatible with a harmonious total genital experience. Mutual trust and identification must be based on sensitive attunement between sex partners so that foreplay is mutually satisfactory, rhythms of tension flow compatible, and body parts shaped in complementary alignment to each other (Kestenberg, 1967a).

For orgastic discharge, both men and women must be prepared for a regression in which the ego voluntarily and fearlessly relinquishes control and surrenders to drive pressure. Such a surrender must not be masochistic to the point that painful sensations sharpen the experience and prevent regressive abandon to visceral sensations; it must not be coupled with relegating sole responsibility to the partner for the timing of the discharge in substitution for mutual attunement.

Female sexuality cannot be understood in isolation from the sexuality of man; it is important to review male feelings toward inside and outside genitality. In the following section I shall confine myself to discussing those aspects of man's sexuality which influence his attitude toward woman. The case reports will illustrate how disturbances in these areas affect the quality of his performance as her teacher and his ability to help her achieve adult female integration.

Inside and Outside in Male Development

Male Dominance: The Shift from Inside to Outside

In his eternal quest for higher differentiation, man has consistently defended his status of dominance over other species and over females of his own species. In the social behavior of some primates, dominance is established by mounting or display, specific to the male but observed also in the female (Rosenblum, L., 1968). In higher mammals, male aggression and sexuality are the biological foundations of dominance. But the striving of women to emulate the male may not be unique to the human species.

The hierarchy of dominance which dictates social values demands that the immature child is subordinate to his mother. By holding and nurturing the young, the mother gains access to what was once inside of her, and she tends to identify the young with the inside whence it came.[9] Man tends to identify inside structures with femininity and immaturity. Women in their own way and children in another, yet similar, way are immature in comparison with him. But he bows to the woman in whose inside he once was. These attitudes are reflected in three types of offenses that enrage the boy and even the man: likening him to a woman and to a baby and denigrating the place of his origin, his mother.[10]

In the struggle between the sexes and the uneven battle for dominance, men taunt women with their inferior genital and encephalic differentiation (Sherfey, 1966), and women remind men that they were once babies, inside a woman, immature, and subordinate to their mothers. In religious cults one sees two opposing trends—worship of the outside and that of the inside genital: phallic cults and fertility cults. Women worship and envy man for his large phallus, while men worship and envy woman for her gestational capacity (Jacobson, 1950; Tausk, 1919).

127

DEVELOPMENT OF SEXUALITY

Powerful mythic women, be they goddesses or witches (Mead, 1949; Ro'Reim, 1945), are regarded as phallic. This may be based on ideas from the phallic phase that everything that is large and moving must be phallic, therefore the large object in the mother's abdomen must be a phallus shaped into a baby. In the evolution of universal ideas, it may be based on the awareness that female dominance is inconceivable without tribute to the phallus, essential to female reproduction.

By associating the inside of the body with femininity, man disposes of anxiety-provoking representations of his own inside. His fantasies about a penis inside a woman, frightening as they are, are reassuring by their implication that his own hidden structures are phallic, linked to the outside, and controllable from outside. Men are reluctant to talk about their testicles (Bell, 1961, 1964, 1965), but even more reluctant to acknowledge the role of the prostate, seminal vesicles or spermatic cords. Fears and fantasies connected with anal penetration tend to be expressed in terms of feminine identification and castration fear. The mysterious nature of vague prostatic sensations and secretions, associated with rectal pressure and linked with experiences of first emissions, fears of ejaculatory inevitability, and anticipation of prostatic hypertrophy of the aging male, are frequently ignored or isolated. The quality of the fears, fantasies, and misconceptions about the male inside genital structures has led me to believe that even in early childhood sensations of an uncanny nature may arise not only from testicles but also from accessory genital pelvic organs. Through analyses of children and adults I have become convinced that the externalization and the denial of the "inside" of the male is as much a requisite for the establishment of the phallic phase as it is in the female. The success of these mechanisms ensures man's libidinization of his phallus, his orientation toward the external world, and his greater tolerance for orgastic experiences, which shift so quickly from internal to external sensations. In puberty, the denial of the male inner genitals cannot be fully maintained without giving rise to serious pathology. In adulthood man tacitly acknowledges that male differentiation, which assures mature sexual fulfillment and reproduction, depends on the semi-internal male gonads, aided by the more hidden accessory organs inside the body. Curiosity about the "inside" framework gives rise to male sublimatory exploration of the unknown, often condensed with attempts to solve the riddle of femininity through derivatives of passive anal wishes.

It is important to distinguish between man's attitude toward his own inner-genital structures and his attitude toward femininity. The equation of all inside structures with femininity, the projection of feminine wishes upon women, and the displacement of curiosity about his own inside to that of woman obscure and distort man's awareness of inside tensions, diffuse sensations, and the fantasies that arise from them. In exploring women men try to find out what their own inside is like. In protecting them, they indirectly protect their own "inside." By projecting his fear of destruction of his inner-genital organs upon woman and by externalizing inner sensations upon the phallus, man rids himself of the archaic fear of attacks upon his inside. This enables him to concentrate his attention upon the outside world in order to protect his phallus and his women from external aggressors. The shift of emphasis from inside to outside in male genitality is reflected in myth and ritual. These are recapitulated in ontogenetic development. While there is no direct evidence for the conjectures that follow, they are used here to provide a background to clinical findings.

Ancient Hebrew mythology suggests that Jewish culture was predicated on the cult of the sperm that comes from the inside. There was much less emphasis on maleness as phallic than in the neighboring tribes. A bisexual deity (Nunberg, 1947) created man and promised him that his seed would spread all over the earth, as a symbol of fertility and dominance. Children were a blessing and childlessness a curse. Veracity was asserted by putting one's hand upon the groin, thus demonstrating that lying would bring on true castration—the loss of the testicle (Silving, 1964).

In the story of Adam and Eve, God took out a rib (*side*) from man's inside and converted it into a woman. Thus man could see outside what was once inside him, and Eve did indeed help him to satisfy his curiosity and to know how his outer genitalia were related to the inside. When God imposed circumcision on man, he gave sanction to the removal of a "feminine" covering and thus exposed the glans to inspection and easier manipulation (Nunberg, 1947). By fully exposing his phallus, man could symbolize his distinction from women, who represented the repudiated inside genital. Thus man's pact with God seemed to be based on the privilege and obligation that he must uncover what is hidden. By so doing he expiated the original sin of the Garden of Eden and established as his right what was once imposed as punishment: the exploration of progressively larger areas of the earth and toiling to conquer the forces of nature through experimentation and learning. The exposure of the penis also diverted the threat of real castration from the testicle to the penis, as it counteracted man's need to open himself—equated with death—and penetrate himself—equated with femininity. An upward shift of the cathexis from the inside genitals reinforced the taboo of the physical inside and protected it from shock and injury. God led his chosen people in quest for spiritual values rather than sexual knowledge, away from physical aggression to a high valuation of the mind as a masculine attribute. Women, as representatives of the forbidden "inside," were to serve men and leave them free to study the word of God. In this role they were dominant over other members of the household, but their position as childbearers was both sacrosanct and unclean. Men guarded the holy shrine of God, the home, and the book of wisdom whose etymology is feminine. The inside of the human body became a symbol of femininity and as such was repudiated.

External sexual pleasure was given to man as an inducement periodically to give up his avoidance of inner genitals and subject himself to the state of shock, akin to death (Keiser, 1947, 1952) in orgasm. But in the wished-for union of male and female insides, which brings man closer to the "hermaphroditic" state (Ferenczi, 1924) of Adam before his separation from the mother, Eve, exploration of the inside is circumvented by the anesthesia and dimming of consciousness that characterize adult genital sexual discharge. In the child, man was offered a mode of externalization of male and female insides and a substitute object for their exploration. But the temptation to kill his son was constant, not only because he anticipated oedipal dangers (Freud, S., 1913), but also because he wished to make the dangerous animate "inside" immobile and inanimate, harmless and accessible to study.

The continuous threat to the son's life—so clearly shown in the Isaac story, and revived, projected, and acted out on the Egyptians in Exodus—is evident in the early circumcision and the ceremonial redemption of the firstborn (pidyon haben). The emphasis on the importance of the seed and the protective measures against spermicide and infanticide reflected a more archaic type of castration fear than the castration anxiety related to the phallus.

Leaving the realm of conjecture and interpretation of the historical shift from fear of injury to the inside to castration fear centered on the phallus, we can now review how boys in today's culture cope with the fear-provoking nature of visceral genital tensions and sensations.

Developmental Sequence

The primary means by which the boy reacts to fears connected with inner genitality are:

1. *Regressive shift of cathexis* from the testicles and other, more hidden genital organs, not only to adjoining pregenital discharge zones (recto-anal and vesicourethral) but also to the oral zone.

2. *Externalization* from the inside upon its products and their substitutes whose exploration contributes to the formation of the image of inside structures.

130

3. *Denial* of the inside which is reinforced by: (a) externalization of inside genital tensions and impulses upon the phallus with a resulting shift of the content of castration anxiety; (b) equation of all inside genitals with femininity and immaturity; (c) repudiation of femininity not only in men but also in women, which maintains the fantasy of the phallic woman.

4. *Projection* of the wish to penetrate and destroy the inside (equated with women and children) upon strangers (oedipal father and brothers [Freud, S., 1973]). This reinforces the taboos against rape and killing of women, seduction of children, and infanticide.

Projection upon women of the wish to be penetrated counteracts feminine identification and masochistic homosexual impulses, arising from anorectal-prostatic excitations.

5. Phobic *avoidance* or *isolation* of male inside genitalia that may extend to those of the female and her offspring.

6. *Repression* of fantasies about the inside of the body that are connected with passive and active components of the oedipus complex.

7. *Displacement* of desexualized cathexis from the phallus upward, which serves to increase the distance from pelvic genitality, but also brings some of the externalized cathexis of inner genitals back into the body (brain, soul). The penis, as conveyor and transformer of diffuse visceral sensations, thus plays an important role in the internalization involved in concept formations, identifications, and codification of values and laws that bring about a progressive differentiation of the superego.

The defense mechanisms employed by man to free himself from the danger of being overwhelmed by genital-visceral sensations are listed in chronological order as they seem to appear in transitions from pregenitality to the phallic phase and from that to latency. Prepuberty brings on a crisis caused by the invasion of new sensations from outside and inside of the growing body and by the breakdown that liberates old fantasies and fears. Prepuberty reorganization is based on a renewed externalization, on a higher level (Chapters 13 and 14). If the boy is adequately prepared in this period for the events of puberty, he can accept the onrush of ejaculation and the involuntary nature of expulsory contractions without feeling that forces from his own inside are attacking and overwhelming him (Van Ophuijsen, 1920).

In optimal development, puberty growth and differentiation help the growing boy to enjoy the intensity of his sensation and to accept the transitory loss of control during orgasm, and the passivity involved, as an ego-syntonic phase of masculine functioning rather than a threat to his male identity. The conditional acceptance of his inside as important for his functioning allows him to accept women and identify with them.

131

It also allows for the recognition of the phallus's unique position as organizer of male and female sexuality.

The externalization of inner genital tensions upon the phallus makes use of neural and vascular connections that establish the continuity between outside and inside genital structures and their adjoining organs (rectum, bladder, and urethra). Because it is abundantly supplied with somatic and autonomic nerve endings, the phallus is an extension of the inside and an external organ as well. The dual capacity for erection and orgastic ejaculation and the combination of discriminatory perception with spreading intense sensations in an organ accessible to tactile and visual exploration not only affect man's concept of himself but have a profound effect on his image of woman.

The Avoidance of Male "Inside"

Adult male genitality, outwardly directed to be sure, is based on tolerance of the inside and of states of passive surrender. Only immature male genitality is completely phallocentric. Ellis (1936) observed that overt homosexuality rises in cultures condoning infanticide. Destruction of the "seed = child = inside" leads to renunciation of parenthood and erases the differences between the sexes. An excessively phallocentric attitude threatens the security of marriage and family as social institutions serving the perpetuation of the species.

Less extreme manifestations of phobic avoidance and denial of the importance of man's "inside" invade conventional behavior, hinder research, and, by preventing realistic enlightenment of children, sanction the persistence of infantile fantasies about the male body.

In teaching pediatricians I discovered that all of them routinely prepared girls for menarche and gave out literature on that subject. No literature was available to help prepare boys and their parents for ejaculation, but some physicians "prepared" adolescent boys for masturbation. The rationalizations given for this disregard of the ejaculate revealed fear of maternal reactions to interference. Thus the blame was shifted onto women, who themselves need support and explanations to deal with their sons' signs of maturity. A much more defensive guarding of the male secret confronted me when I asked a famous expert on male fertility for information or literature about histological studies of first emissions. The scientist's response was surprisingly indignant. He claimed that no data were available and it would be entirely improper and traumatizing to the young to examine his early ejaculate. I subsequently did find some data about the immaturity of sperm in eary adolescence (Talbot, et al., 1952) and became even more interested in the indignant protectiveness of the scientist (Chapter 13).[11]

Inquiries about the appearance of genitals of newborn males, some of whom manifest the genital crisis of the neonate, were equally unsuccessful. In addition to Robbins's 1964 observation on rhythmic contractions of the tunica Dartos, we found that many neonates had pigmented scrota with a thicker integument and a folded, loose skin quite unlike that of children before puberty. Although changes in the scrotum and testicles as well as the prostate of the neonate are documented in histological accounts, we have not yet found clinical descriptions of the syndrome. This stands in marked contrast to easily available descriptions of the swollen genitalia of newborn females (Talbot, et al., 1952).

Observations of Marcus and Berlowe (1965) of the appearance of the neonatal penis during erection drew our attention to the scanty knowledge about the dynamics of erections (Dickinson 1949; Masters and Johnson, 1966). Tumescence and erection have been used interchangeably, although there are differences between these phenomena, as there are between degrees and qualities of sensations from erectile and nonerectile engorgements in different parts of genitals (Dickinson, 1949). In the newborn, tumescence does not necessarily involve the whole penis; the distal part of the shaft may be enlarged and red but not the proximal, and vice versa, and most often it is the middle section that appears larger and swollen. Tumescence and erection do not always coincide. Some of these phenomena may be due to superficial swellings, to decrease of arterial muscle tonus in one part of the corpora cavernosa and not another, to flaccidity of some muscle fibers and tonicity in others, or to an irritability of the urethral muscles. They may be accounted for by the general immaturity of the nervous system or they may be an aftermath of delivery. They may be a result of intra-abdominal pressures (Halverson, 1938; Masters and Johnson, 1966) through distension of the bladder, the neonatal hypertrophy of the prostate, rectal fullness, or straining from crying.

These and other similar questions concern not only scientists but also children, who are baffled by the mysterious ways their penis and testicles act as if directed by unseen forces from within the body.[12]

The Models of the Male Inside

There seems to be a universal reluctance to acknowledge sensations from the inside of the body. Not only women, but men too, fear and distort the representations of their "insides." Many patients are afraid that their penis may be "torn out by its roots." Some of them blot out their knowledge of the crura of the penis and reveal that their imagery stems from the symbolic equation of the penis with a tree whose roots, spread under the earth, not only are essential to the tree's survival, but can also regenerate life if the tree trunk is cut off. Analyses of children and adolescents and reconstructions from adult analyses suggest that these and similar representations stem from fantasies in two phases of "internal genital" dominance which precede the phallic phase in childhood and puberty genitality in adolescence (Chapters 13, 14).

Through intensive and persistent interest in the dynamics of machinery (Elkisch and Mahler, 1959; Tausk, 1919) and of growth in plants and animals, boys study the working principles by which the testicles elevate and the penis moves. This interest is never really given up; it provides motivation for research in biology, physics, and mathematics. Young children rarely express their concern in words, but become lone investigators; they solicit the aid of adults by questions about the machinery of inanimate objects rather than direct questions about the inside of the body. Some of the many questions, familiar from open or disguised communications in analyses of children and adults are (Bell, 1961, 1964, 1965; Glenn, 1965; Yazmajian, 1966):

> What is in the scrotum that makes it move? Is it full of urine, live worms (epididymis) or feces? Will it go away when you have a child? Does it steer the penis and make it move? Why is one side lower than the other? Are testicles pulled up by cords inside the body? Are they weights to keep the penis in place? Fear that the penis can become retracted or pulled inwards, as it may have been in girls, brings on the idea that a bone in it protrudes to make erections and retracts, leaving flaccid skin. The "bone" may be connected in fantasy with the spinal column. The penis then appears to be securely held up by the entire bony structure, which gives rise to fears of skeletons. Another frequent fantasy is that electric wires or strings connect the eyes and brain to the penis, making it move in response to exciting sights or thoughts. All symmetrical "end organs" such as eyes, cheeks, breasts, hands, nates, and feet can be used for the externalization of scrotal-testicular sensations. When eyes are "invisibly connected" to the testicles, rubbing the eyes not only prevents seeing disturbing things, not only prevents erections, but also removes sensations from the scrotum and transfers masturbatory impulses upward. The wish to get inside the body to experiment with control from inside motivates disappearing behind curtains and certain enclosures, as in photography, puppeteering, stage setting and lighting.[13] Such experimentation is also derived from wishes to watch the primal scene from inside the mother and other elaborations of oedipal fantasies.

All external zones that had been stimulated by maternal touch are connected with early objects; representations of internal organs are also equated with early objects (Fenichel, 1945b; Nunberg, 1947). Fusions of object and organ representations account for fears of attack from the inside of the body (see Chapter 9 and Van Ophuijsen, 1920). Representations of inside genital structures are condensed with products from the inside, babies, and playthings. The fusion between drive objects, inner and outer organs, products and external objects is supported by the elusive way pelvic and abdominal sensations spread outward and inward, frequently preventing the hypercathexis necessary for conscious awareness. Because inner sensations are subject to primary rather than secondary processes, better insight into fears connected with images of inner structures can be obtained from dreams, psychosomatic symptoms, acting out, and drawings than from verbal descriptions.

Infantile Attitudes Toward Women

Often the way a patient nags others reveals that something within him is nagging him. Unable to cope with their inner genital tensions, women nag their children or husbands, a feminine trait observable in all cultures (Mead, M., 1956). Men hardly ever nag, complain, and argue as excessively as women do, but some male patients focus in analysis on a nagging dissatisfaction with their wives. My first attempts to understand this behavior were centered on the analysis of feminine identification, latent homosexual needs, passive wishes to be penetrated, and fixation in the anal stage, regressively revived to counteract negative oedipal fantasies. These men were all preoccupied with the inside of the body, but presented all discomfort as due to gastrointestinal or anal sensations. I wondered why some of these analyses were not as successful as I had anticipated. Symptoms would disappear, undesirable character traits would become ameliorated, yet the nagging dissatisfaction with the wife persisted. Eventually I became aware that the deficiency was due to my continued focus on pregenital regressions and fears of female insides, when I should also have analyzed the man's fears and fantasies about his own inside genitals. Much of this material reveals pregnancy wishes (Jacobson, 1950; Van der Leeuw, 1958). The analysis of these male fantasies reveals man's secret about his own male inside, which he tends to externalize and project upon women. By a perennial interest in feminine mystique man skillfully diverts his and other people's attention from his own secret. This form of endowing the woman with characteristics projected on her influences the image woman forms of herself.

DEVELOPMENT OF SEXUALITY

Case Reports

Orgasm Without Ejaculation

A successful veterinarian came for treatment because of marital discord. The marriage had been childless because of his low sperm count, but he did not mind because he disliked children and thought his wife would neglect him even more than she did if she had to care for a child. His wife was frigid and he found satisfaction only in his relations with a young actress. She enjoyed all kinds of sexual practices his wife would not tolerate.

Among his physical complaints were bouts of hemorrhoids. His masturbatory habits centered upon routine bodily care, and were so systematized that he could get rid of waste from inside all at once. With his wife he managed to have orgasms without releasing the ejaculate even though he felt it "coming."

He complained that his wife was rigid, all-knowing, conceited, repetitious, and neglectful of him and her duties. The girl friend on the other hand was a liar, irresponsible, oversexed, and clinging, but he always forgave her. Preoccupied with schemes of revenge on his wife, he would withhold semen from her as she withheld food from him. He had a conscious oral-urethral fantasy of having two containers inside (seminal vesicles) that he could tilt to spill semen out or tilt back to retain. The girl friend he fed directly and insisted that she swallow the ejaculate the same way his mother had insisted that his baby sister should swallow her food. His hemorrhoids came and went and he had as little success with curing them as he had with his infertility. He knew that the prostate could be reached through the anus and he toyed with the idea of going to the proctologist who, he fantasied, could look all the way through his body and into his mouth. Similarly, the dentist could see his anus through the mouth.

There were two levels to the fantasies that motivated his acting out and were expressed in dreams. One level concerned infantile objects and the other his own organs. The girl friend represented his bad, demanding baby sister who came out of his mother's belly, was his constant admirer, but also a pest. His wife represented his omnipotent mother who neglected him, took things away from him, and gave them to others. The dentist and doctor were identified with the doctor who attended his baby sister and with his father who did things to the mother to make the baby. He played with the girl friend as if she were a toy and manipulated her with a singular disregard for her feelings. She represented his "defective" testicles, his greedy seminal vesicles that withheld things from his wife, and she was his "lying" prostate who acted as if she would "tell" and then held back the "truth." On his wife he externalized his pelvic dissatisfaction, the diffusion of inside sensations, his lack of satiation, and his need to divert his attention from his genitals to delay ejaculation. The anorectal sensations which he painfully associated with his prostate were connected with fantasies of anal impregnation and bloody delivery. But he also associated the prostate with creativity and phallic power, a magic known only to men and not communicable to women.

With the exception of the contraptions in the seminal vesicles, specific representations of his inside were difficult for him to describe. They were modeled after toys, plants, animals he had dissected, machinery, maps and science fiction. Only when he drew maps or depicted his images of his inside was it possible to understand how he tried to work out an inside network which he controlled, and did not allow to control him. By this device he could maintain erections well and felt quite potent. But he had not externalized his control onto his penis and did not look upon it as a dominant, valuable motor of his actions. On the contrary, by acting out he demonstrated to me that his penis was a dangerous instrument which could not be controlled from outside.

When his mysterious inner controls were uncovered, he did not need the girl friend any longer and his wife improved because he now talked to her and explained what he expected of her. When he became her teacher he began to suffer from a transitory failure of erections, as he now transferred the misgivings about his inside upon the phallus. But he began to look forward to having a child and he began to play with children and could tolerate their behavior when they brought pets to his office. His sperm count improved considerably, so that he no longer felt infertile and no longer withheld the ejaculate from his wife. As his phallus became more central to his functioning than his inside, his masturbatory impulses decreased and his erections became dependable. He became bolder, more confident in his abilities, and more competitive with men; and he stopped feeling that he would injure himself or others if he released his full phallic aggression.

Developmental data revealed that he was fixated in the "inner-genital phase" that preceded phallic development. At that time, his mother disapproved of his independent exploits. His toys were ruined or disappeared and his little baby sister was born "injured." In prepuberty, he transferred his interest to animal experimentation in joint enterprises with a playmate. But his animals died or were killed and he gave up his research. These losses from his early and later childhood were linked to oral deprivations, sibling rivalry, and the disillusionment with his parents. They depressed and immobilized him. One important reason for his failures in externalization, which would have ensured phallic dominance, was his mother's continuous preoccupation with the defective "inside" of her second child, which was handled by doctors with drugs, injections, and operations. To protect himself from a similar assault he devised an inner control system and was compelled to repeat earlier forms of externalization, but was not able to externalize "inside" sensations successfully onto the phallus.

It was interesting to note the wife's improvement when the patient began to assume the role of a dominant male in the family. To the extent that she could adjust to him by learning from him, she did so; with only brief therapy, her sexual performance and her maternality improved.

Emission Without Orgasm

Another patient whose attempts at externalization were frustrated in early childhood and in prepuberty spent most of his analysis complaining about his wife. She was dirty, inadequate, a bad mother, and impossible to satisfy sexually. He acted as if he played at being a man. He failed in his musical career, was forever preoccupied with his son, and spent most of his time repairing the house. He presented himself in the transference as hyperpotent and hypererudite; he gave me long lectures on subjects I was deficient in. It took over two years of analysis before he realized that his hyperpotency was due to his dribbling the ejaculate rather than achieving an orgastic ejaculation. Up to that point he could never understand why his wife was dissatisfied and wanted to leave him.

In prepuberty this patient had a puzzling, incapacitating illness. Because of a misdiagnosis he was hospitalized and kept out of school for many months. The long immobilization intensified his passive-dependent needs and fostered feminine identification. He masturbated by pressing the base of his penis against a hard object and avoided the use of his hands. With the appearance of emissions he used to close up the urethral orifice with his fingers, waiting until he could dispose of his ejaculate where his mother could not find traces of it. During this practice he learned to seep his seminal fluid rather than discharge it all at once. As in the cases described by Federn (1914), his sensuousness was pelvic, but negative oedipal fantasies were less pronounced than his playful identification with the preoedipal mother. His behavior was reminiscent of boys between two and four who interchangeably play at being a man and a woman. He took care of his little son and his house and was very busy fixing things, deeply unhappy because his wife did not appreciate his earnest attempts to help. He nagged her and upset her, thus transferring upon her his self-dissatisfaction. He seemed arrested in a stage of externalization upon substitute objects and identification with the active mother. He could neither succeed in drawing the libido from his "inside" outward to his penis, nor was he able to displace his cathexis of external substitute objects (children, tools, machines) into adult forms of sublimation. He could not even successfully project blame for his feminine wishes upon his wife, but rather projected upon her his feeling that he failed as a man and could not really be a woman. His provocative behavior regularly evoked temper tantrums in his wife. Even more strikingly than in the preceding case the very disturbed wife would calm down when the patient himself showed signs of adult masculinity.

Sons of manipulative and seductive mothers may become dependent on women to protect their masculinity. Sometimes, fantasies that the penis and the testicles are connected to the inside by invisible strings evoke fears that the genitals will be pulled inward by an inner winding mechanism, unless an external agent (mother or wife) holds the external ends of the strings. There remains the fear that pulling the string from the outside will unwind the ball of string and eviscerate the secret machinery (Kestenberg, 1968).

The Hidden Cord, the Central Point Inside the Body, and the Ball of String

Two young men, each happily married to a supportive wife, failed in their senior year in college because they could only memorize and repeat rather than think problems through independently. Their knowledge was skin-deep and their approach to learning superficial.

Both these patients idealized and flattered me; they endowed me with magic powers which they continuously controlled by associations designed to influence my actions. One of them was afraid that his penis would be pulled inward by an invisible cord; the second was afraid that a central point within his body—roughly corresponding in location to the prostate—would become dislocated. I was supposed to exert a counterpull to keep the genitalia in their proper place, but my actions had to be controlled lest I pull too hard and expose the hidden network to male attackers.

A seven-year-old boy depended on his mother to take care of his bodily needs, to help him with his schoolwork, and to influence people to obey his commands. He sucked his thumb or pulled the left side of his shirt collar up to his mouth where he held it while he used his hands to play.

During one phase of the analysis he used thread to tie himself up. He fastened the end of the thread to furniture in my office, and moved it by remote control. He would throw torn pieces all around the room, would tie them up again and unwind them. At times, instead of tying up a chair, he invited his mother to come in and encircled her with the thread. All along I had to hold one end of the thread so that my movements mobilized furniture or made his mother move as he directed. He would not talk to me except to give me orders; if I disobeyed his instructions, he called his

139

mother to "make me" obey him. At the end of the session he would pull one end of the thread as he walked with his mother to the car. Thus, he hoped to make his presence felt in my office during his absence.

When he was nine, he felt ashamed because he could not refrain from thumb sucking in school; he allowed me to tell him what I thought of it. I explained that, whenever he was afraid or worried, he wanted his mother and that the thumb in his mouth substituted for her. Whereas before he had thrown things indiscriminately, crying out "shit" or "fuck" with each move, he now began to teach me how to throw planes into a container. He maneuvered to let me win the contest, although it was evident that his aim was better than mine. When I exposed his trick, he won the next game and then proceeded to teach me how to play ball with a ball of string.

During the ball game he laughed at my bad aim and poor control in catching. Intermittently he adjusted his genitals in a way which resembled his preparations for throwing. I told him that I did not have the things he had and so it was small wonder that I did not know how to handle balls. He reached for his "balls" below and showed me how to throw a ball by first rolling it. He reproduced exactly the movement executed by the cremasteric and instructed me to tie the end of the string so the ball would not unwind before I could throw it to him. In this and previous games he demonstrated his need to gain control over his testicles which might roll and unroll and entangle so that the strings composing them (epididymis and spermatic cords) might get twisted or broken. Pulling his shirt up on the left side served to pull up the left testicle, which, he feared, hung too low. By holding his thumb in his mouth he controlled his penis from above.

In the following sessions he seemed reassured about his testicles and pulled up the middle portion of his polo shirt, holding it in his mouth while he showed me new ways to throw the ball. When he waited to catch the ball, he protectively clutched his hand to his abdomen. When I asked him what he was protecting, he told me it was not a baby. It was clear from his play and the way he adjusted his genitals that he was concerned about his penis. He again laughed about my inadequacy as a player, but was reassured when I learned enough to help him in the game of catching and throwing. He then felt that he could look at the picture of a penis, scrotum and testicles. He reciprocated by drawing what was inside a boy's body, so that I could use this knowledge for teaching other children. He drew a giant ball which represented his chest and abdomen. In it he placed two intersecting diagonals. From the central point he drew a median line which was connected to the penis outside the ball; in addition, he connected the lower end points of the diagonals by a bar which appeared to hold the scrotum in place. Two balls representing the testicles in the scrotum were connected to the outside of the scrotum by two short "strings," even though he had just seen a drawing which showed the spermatic cords going upward inside the body. Both his penis and the end points on the scrotum gave out milk. Though associated to the "milky fluid" (semen), they betrayed the identification of penis and testicles with breasts. It was evident from this and other drawings that pregnancy wishes increased his fear that he would lose something from his inside. But the strings that held his body together and controlled his genitals were clearly masculine structures which safeguarded his penis. He was much less concerned about his testicles by that time and he showed me subsequently that he projected them into his mother by drawing twins inside his mother's body in the shape of testicles.

The fact that he could teach me to help him maneuver the externalized "ball and string network" inside of him allowed him to assert his masculinity and reassured him that with my help he could keep his genitals in place. Not only did he generously help me to improve my skills and my knowledge, but he felt confident enough to ask his mother to embrace him "the way you do daddy and let's call him so he can look."

The cases presented demonstrate man's concern with the inside of his body, and the ways man tries to achieve control over his genitals by interpreting his inside as a secure framework for the penis and by using women to externalize his inside or to supplement his own control system from outside. Once man rids himself of associating all inside control with femininity and works out problems concerning the foundations of masculinity, once he is satisfied with the way his own inside works, he reprojects his image of the inside as feminine onto the woman and can accept his role as organizer of woman's inside needs.

The adjustment between the sexes that completes development and establishes the adult sexual roles can be better understood when we survey the similarities and dissimilarities in the way sex-specific integration is achieved in male and female development.

Survey of Similarities and Dissimilarities in Male and Female Development

This brief survey is based on clinical material from analyses. The reconstruction of developmental stages and the views on the role of outer- and inner-genital organs in the development of sexuality fit into the framework of psychoanalytic theory and do not require an emendation of its basic principles. Where they differ in some respects from prevailing opinion they must be looked upon as tentative formulations subject to reevaluation and critical scrutiny by other investigators of psychoanalytic child psychology (Barnett, 1966; Bradley, 1961; Fraiberg, 1972.)[14]

Similarities

In the *pregenital* phases, both sexes cope with genital tensions by incorporating them into phase-specific pregenital discharge forms. The relief experienced after the intake of food or the expulsion of products from the inside provides a model for the child's wish to eat or expel all sources of tension.

> In identification with the preoedipal mother, children of both sexes feel that they too have babies. They animate the world around them with beings like themselves, "babies." At the same time, they preserve and enliven the lifeless products that gave rise to "live" sensations when they were inside or about to enter or leave the body. Images of babies are condensed with images of oral, anal, and urethral products but their derivation from early genital tensions becomes dominant only when pregenital wishes to play with food and excreta are repudiated.

The *"inner-genital"* phase is initiated by the spreading of genital excitement from the inside of the body, which increases the need for externalization. The toddler is vaguely familiar with sources of tension, unrelieved by intake or expulsion of visible products. The two- to three-year-old imagines that the inside is composed of food, feces, and urine. He is puzzled by the discovery that handling of external genitalia resonates vague sensations from the inside of his body. During this early "inner-genital" phase the child becomes more aware of genital tensions which come and go without leaving traces in the outside world. He begins to formulate the thought that there is something unknown inside him that he would like to take out and examine. In an effort to cope with this unknown "something" he externalizes the diffuse inner-genital impulses upon objects such as dolls, teddies, trucks, and trains, whose origin is to him equally mysterious, but which can be handled and examined. He animates these objects and pretends that they are babies that came from his inside. All things unknown seem to emanate from his inside, which is there although one can neither see nor touch it.

As the "inner-genital" phase progresses, the spreading of genital excitement from the inside of the body increases the need for externalization. This readily available mechanism is put in the service of integration of conflicting trends. Externalization helps the child to repudiate regressive pregenital wishes, to distinguish them from inner- and outer-genital impulses and, eventually, to coordinate them under the dominance of the outwardly oriented phallic drive. With the progressive increase of unfulfilled genital drives, the three- to four-year-old's externalization fails periodically. From time to time he becomes disillusioned with the inanimate objects which substituted for live babies and helped him create an image of his inside. He acknowledges periodically that they are only playthings and reinvests his genitals with the cathexis withdrawn from them. With the recathexis of the "inside," disquieting, unproductive, inner-genital tensions evoke fears of bursting, exploding, becoming eviscerated, empty, and "dead." To protect himself against attacks from the inside, the four-year-old focuses his excitement on the external genitals and denies the existence of the threatening inner-genital organs. The discovery of the difference between sexes reinforces the child's conviction that the inside is dangerous, dark, bloody, and full of strange attackers who must be locked up and not allowed out. Femininity becomes associated with bloody holes and masculinity with intactness. The phase of identification with the preoedipal mother is terminated by denial of femininity, renunciation of the wish for a live baby, and repudiation of the inside as babyish and feminine (Chapters 1, 13).

In the *phallic* phase, masturbatory activities allow for a focal form of discharge on the penis or clitoris which resonates deeper pelvic tensions, but prevents anxiety-provoking spreading and diffusion of sensations. The positive and negative oedipal fantasies that accompany masturbation reflect the child's conflicting wishes to penetrate sadistically and to be penetrated masochistically. The wish to give the mother a baby and the wish to receive one from the father arouse fears of injuring the mother and being injured by the father. The boy projects his wish to be penetrated onto women, and the girl projects all genital impulses onto men, who, she feels, want to penetrate and injure her.

The repression of sexuality in *latency* does not permit a direct expression of genital fantasies. It upholds the denial of feminity and perpetuates the trend toward externalization of inner-genital sensations in drive-derivative activities.

In *prepuberty,* the rapid growth of inner-genital structures increases inner tensions. The child tries to relieve them by a renewal of externalization, which protects him from overwhelming visceral sensations. But the onset of menses and emissions introduces new forms of discharge for inner-genital tensions and presents a concrete proof of the existence of inner-genital structures in both sexes. The renewed attempt to identify the inside with femininity and pregenitality and the outside with masculinity is counteracted by integration of pregenital, inner-genital, and outer-genital drives—a reorganization which initiates the sex-specific genital primacy in puberty.

In *biological puberty,* when reproduction becomes possible, the adolescent is faced with a reality which overshadows earlier fantasies. The boy projects infantile representations of his inside as feminine upon woman; the girl projects infantile representations of her inside structures as an inner phallus upon men.

At the end of puberty in a *preadult* developmental phase a reintegration of infantile and adolescent trends into adult genitality becomes the basis for sex-specific identity.

Dissimilarities

The sex-specific organs of the newborn are adultlike at birth and involute during the first weeks or months of extrauterine life. In the *pregenital* phases, the differences between the sexes are accentuated or blurred by maternal reactions evidenced in bodily care.

Internal genital organs are stimulated indirectly by pressures from the bladder and rectum. The exposed introitus of the baby girl accounts for the frequency of vaginal infections and inflammations in childhood (Nelson, 1959). Secretions from the vagina evidence the activity of this organ in childhood. Washing and swabbing of the introitus stimulate the vagina, urine may drip into it and bath waters suffuses it. Through the intrinsic nervous and vascular connections between clitoris, vestibular bulb, vagina and uterus, the continuity between inside and outside is maintained. There are similar connections in the male (Cunningham, 1964), but the spreading of pelvic sensations is counteracted by the continuous influence of epicritic sensibility in the skin covering of the penis which has no parallel in the female. The penis is accessible to manipulation and manual exploration earlier than the clitoris. Toward the end of the first year the boy discovers his penis as an organ by connecting what he can feel with what he can see. Very early he fuses scrotal and deep testicular sensations with the more acute and localizable sensations of his penis (Kleeman, 1965, 1966). The girl discovers her vulva later. She fuses it with anal and urethral images.

In the *"inner-genital"* phase, the boy erects an image of his inside based more on mechanical models than on baby-dolls. This representation is derived from experimentations on his own body and on outside objects (trains, balls, etc.); it constitutes the core of the "masculine inside." It condenses and overlaps with images of the inside, based on the identification with the preoedipal mother. In contrast, the girl's image of her own inside is more uniformly feminine, its principal model being the baby. The boy's fantasies about impregnation and delivery are repudiated because of their connection with regressive pregenital impulses and fears of injury.

Anorectal representations provide a connection between the scrotum, the perianal region, the rectum, and the prostate—a route which, by its discontinuity and organ division, is less suitable for access to the inside than the direct route from the external labia, the introitus, and the vagina, to the uterus. By identifying the rectoanal-scrotal route with the birth canal, the boy shifts his representation of the anal baby to the testicular baby; as he repudiates anality, equated to feminity, he denies the importance of the scrotum and testicles and transfers their cathexes to the adjoining phallus, which in its flaccid state also comes to represent a baby. The girl who fuses anal, perianal, and introital sensations also repudiates her inside genital as she repudiates anality and the anal baby; she derives from it not a fear of loss of the clitoris, but rather a fear that all of her inside will fall out during defecation (delivery), which parallels the fear of the boy that he may lose his testicles in the toilet (Bell, 1964).

The urethral route inside the boy's body is also associated with birth fantasies and culminates in the equation of the erect penis with a baby boy. Before he can establish his penis as symbol of activity and maleness, the boy is frightened by the invisible forces that stiffen the penis or soften it, erect it, or let it hang again. These are condensed with fears of testicular elevation, turgidity of the scrotum, and the unaccounted "falling" of the testicles with scrotal relaxation. The internal route from the testicles to the penis is equated with the female birth canal and with the tube that connects the bladder to the outside. But the boy recognizes the groin as the place of entry of the spermatic cord inside his body and also imagines that the baby is delivered on the *side* of the body through the inguinal ring which he equates with the birth canal. The girl fuses vesical-urethral sensations with clitoral, introital, and vaginal sensations and imagines being impregnated by urine entering her. She also thinks that the boy's bags may contain urine or babies and by identification with the boy may endow her external labia with these representations. But the boy's fantasy of the inguinal route (side, Nunberg, 1947) as passage of impregnation and delivery is unparalleled in the girl.

Girls externalize their dissatisfactions and inner tensions upon the preoedipal mother much more than boys, because they are more beset by "nagging" inner-genital tensions than boys. The denial of the inside and the transfer of cathexis to the outside genitals is much more successful in the boy than in the girl.

With the onset of the *phallic* phase, the connection between testicular movements and genital excitement is obscured, but the fear that the penis will be transformed into a baby and be cut off is perpetuated in oedipal fantasies of impregnation through the rectum. The phallic boy is satisfied that his whole body supports his penis; the phallic girl transfers her dissatisfactions with her inside to her clitoris. She dimly perceives that the clitoris arouses and resonates innermost tensions which are impossible to control.

> The girl envies the boy for his penis because he continues to have an organ before, during, and after sexual excitation. She can neither see nor feel her clitoris all the time; even that organ keeps appearing and disappearing in consonance with the arousal and abatement of diffuse inner-genital tensions. The fantasy that she will grow a penis is imparted to her by the boy, who feels more confident that he could grow a new penis if he lost the external end of it. The girl herself is more apt to think that she has an inside penis, connected to the clitoris, whose "jumpy" qualities, retractability, and sensory connections to pelvic organs promote such a fantasy. However, she readily gives up this imaginary organ in exchange for a penis introduced into her and making a baby there, which will come out. This wish helps her to think that she really has nothing inside, just as she has nothing outside, and that she is merely a carrier for the penis-baby her father will give her. He might lose his penis and she will gain a baby rather than lose what is inside of her. Her wish to penetrate her mother with a penis, as father can, is based on identification with the nursing mother. The intrusiveness, experienced as an active quality of the phallus, promotes positive oedipal fantasies in the boy. Since neither clitoris, tongue, finger or nipple have the intrusive qualities of the penis, the girl's negative oedipal fantasies lack the support from somatogenic sources. The girl does not know what it feels like to have a penis, although she continuously demands one in expression of her dissatisfaction with her sexual tensions, which cannot be fully resolved by clitoral masturbation.

The projection of sexual impulses upon men and the repression of sexuality make the girl's *latency* more peaceful than that of the boy. But the urgency of her feelings is expressed in her continued preoccupation with dolls, dogs, and horses, on which she can externalize her genital impulses. The two-way traffic between vaginal sensations and clitoral discharge forms is usually latent and becomes apparent only in typically feminine forms of sublimation. In latency, boys in our culture are surrounded by women who are in charge of taming their impulses. Feminine identification is fostered in both sexes, and in contrast to boys', girls' modes of externalization receive full support from the environment. The growth of internal and external reproductive organs in late latency is more apparent to the boy, and the increase of androgen production favors masculinization, independence, and outward orientation. The boy starts his battle to free himself from the feminizing influence of his home very early. In this process he repudiates femininity and denigrates feminine sexual organs. In the battle of the sexes in latency, the girl envies the boy's independence and is greatly influenced by the image of femininity imparted to her by the boy.

In *prepuberty,* the boy feels vague inner sensations—growing pains—which no one can explain satisfactorily. He regressively revives pregenital feminine representations of the inside of his body and connects them with the new internal sensations. Overwhelmed by fears that the understructure of his phallus has become endangered by mysterious forces from within, he looks to his peers and older boys for reassurance. By comparing himself with other boys, he finds out that emissions are masculine and not the result of injury to his inside. He tries out new forms of masturbation, plays tricks with his scrotum, his testicles, and exerts pressure on the perineum. Sometimes he attempts anal masturbation to see "what it is like to be a woman." He tries to squeeze out emissions or prevent them. He worries that someone, especially his mother, will discover that he is abusing himself and wasting himself. Although proud of his first emissions, he also worries that he is depleting his inside. The change in his scrotum and testicles bothers him greatly (Bell, 1965). The pendulousness of his scrotum seems to him a sure sign that his inside is "falling" lower. He externalizes his worries and his curiosity onto substitute objects. He uses pseudoscientific theorizations to conceptualize what is inside his body and to rid it of pregenital and feminine attributes, with which he has endowed his inside at the end of the early inner-genital phase. Eventually the boy succeeds in accepting the fact that the inside of his body contains structures essential to masculine functioning. He integrates pregenital inner- and outer-genital sensations in his masturbatory experience in such a way that they become subordinated to the genital primacy in puberty. He concentrates his libido on the phallus, but, instead of endowing the whole body with phallic qualities, he accepts the contribution of other parts of his body to the total genital experience.

The tremendous increase of estrogen production in prepuberty makes the girl especially vulnerable to inner-genital excitations. Shifting of libidinal cathexis from the vagina to the clitoris and to breasts reduces her fears and reinforces the equations of these organs with the penis. But neither nipples nor clitoris prove to be safe islands which remove her from the dreaded inner genitality. Genital sensations seem to float all over her body and shift rapidly from one organ to another. Externalization of genital impulses on substitute objects helps her to reestablish the image of her body and regain control over desexualization of her vagina. But menstruation forces her to accept the existence of the vagina and uterus as feminine organs.

The repeated experience of internal upheaval with resulting blood flow helps her to reorganize the image of her inside which she had erected in the early inner-genital phase. It is becoming clearer to her that what she has inside is neither a baby nor a penis but a container and a receptacle for both. She reorganizes her concepts about femininity and pregenitality. She looks to boys for the alleviation of her inner distress and for signs of admiration which imply the acceptance of her new-found femininity. But she still uses the clitoris as a sensual focus, as an organ that responds to stimulation from various parts of the body and resonates her inner-genital sensations, to which she cannot respond by direct manipulations.

With the onset of *biological puberty,* progesterone production regularizes the girl's cycles, brings on uterine cramps, and effects changes in the consistency of the menstrual flow. The regular changes in her vagina affect the girl's moods and attitudes. She becomes aware of feelings in the clitoris, whose association with deep vaginal sensations can no longer be ignored. The role of the clitoris recedes as the girl's wishes for penetration and direct contact with a penis increase. In sex play the girl allows the boy to help her find new discharge forms. When he manipulates and examines her, he gradually loses his fear of female genitalia.

In biological puberty, the boy seems to feel a new strength in the expulsive quality of his urethra and the strong contractions of pelvic muscles. He becomes proud of the ejectile propulsion of his semen but also worries about impregnating the girl. The new masculine experiences promote the identification with his father and reinforce the battle against infantilization (feminization) by the mother. The girl's approval of the boy as seducer and protector helps him to free himself from oedipal bonds.

To accept his inside genitality as masculine, the young man must weaken the link between the inside of his body and his mother. He can no longer hold on to her "apron strings" to keep him free from injury from within. In contrast to the girl, his detachment from his mother proceeds rather abruptly. The repression of his incestuous wishes is reinforced by his need to protect himself against his mother's persistent demands that he remain her baby.

Puberty brings the girl closer to her father. Deep vaginal sensations revive oedipal wishes to be penetrated and impregnated. But these wishes are now realizable and the girl intuitively understands that her projection of these wishes upon her father meets his own wishes halfway. To accept her vagina as a real organ, the girl needs the experience of being accepted by her father as a woman, when she has finally become one. Too strong a repression of adolescent ties to the father tends to desexualize the vagina. The more intolerant the woman's superego, the more difficult it is for man to relibidinize her vagina.

During the *preadult* reintegration period, the young man shifts his allegiance from his home to the social milieu he selects as his own. His ego-ideal and his actual place in society become the narcissistic core of his identity before he can safely invest his object-cathexis in a permanent relationship. In contrast, the preadult young woman molds and organizes her own identity to fit the ego-ideal and social aspirations of her love object. Her readiness for feminine object-ties evolves directly from her relationship to her parents. Her place in society is the niche created by man, who shelters her like her mother did, and provides for her like her father did.[15]

Vaginal sensations in childhood were linked to the wish for a baby, and thus were desexualized. To resexualize her vagina during coitus the adult woman must postpone her wish to receive a live baby when she feels the intromission of the phallus. The biological readiness of the vagina to accommodate the male organ in response to sexual stimulation and in preparation for impregnation is reflected in the woman's fears that she may become empty when exposed to vaginal excitement without impregnation. On the basis of past experiences she holds on to her excitement for fear that at the end of coitus she will again have nothing inside. Her fear lessens when she feels assured that man will neither injure her while she is helpless nor abandon her when her excitement subsides.

To fill the role of a lover and protector man must overcome fears of the inside as dangerous. Confident of his masculinity, he can doubly libidinize the vagina, which he has denied and dreaded for so long: as an organ essential to the full unfolding of male sexuality and as an organ which he yearned to explore in its deepest parts. If he has rid himself of the sadistic components of his curiosity and of his desire to attack and destroy what is foreign to him, he ceases to regard his semen as dangerous and can also accept and adjust to the retentive aspects of female orgasm.

Woman can accept the expulsive qualities of orgasm when she is ready to relinquish her own excitement and release the phallus. The end phase of female orgasm represents her struggle between expulsion and retention. The successive rise and ebb of excitement (sometimes confused with multiple orgasms) that distinguishes feminine orgasm from the abrupt release gained by man corresponds to the much less abrupt way woman relinquishes her oedipal ties as compared with man.

Woman's orgasm cannot be initiated without the participation of the vagina. Vaginal sensations are no longer dependent on their resonance in the clitoris when they can be directly experienced through repeated contact with the penis. In the process of reorganization of woman's sexuality the man unifies her past and present, her outside and her inside; thus he gives her a chance to incorporate all parts of her genitals in the sexual experience or to emphasize some and minimize the role of others. When woman loses confidence in the man as protector of her femininity, she safeguards her vagina from injury and loss by a rapid transfer of vaginal cathexis to the clitoris which acts as a safety valve.

Restoration of Function and Learning in Men and Women

Psychological impotence and frigidity can be successfully treated by psychoanalysis. But even men and women who have resolved the conflicts that had invaded genital functioning can achieve an adult form of constancy of self-representations and object-relatedness only in actual experience with real nonincestuous objects. This involves a learning process predicated on a freedom to learn which, if lost, can be restored by psychoanalysis. In psychoanalytic treatment, the patient becomes teachable, but the treatment situation does not allow for training, which only performance of function can give.[16] That must be relegated to the physical sphere of learning, practiced by mutually devoted men and women, or, if need be, taught by those practitioners who devise pedagogical methods to inculcate skills. But here we encounter significant differences in the learning process of men and women.

Not only do men in our culture create institutions and customs which allow them to learn the mechanics of sex before they teach them to their constant love objects, but by virtue of their outwardly oriented male sex anatomy and physiology they can learn much faster than women. Women require a great deal of priming of their principal sex zone, the vagina, because they lack direct experience with it earlier in life and because the vagina is an internal, visceral organ. Moreover, conditioning of the vagina in adulthood is more successfully accomplished with a constant love object so that the conflict-laden areas of unwanted pregnancy and the threat of infanticide do not impede the learning process.

It is too early to determine whether the premarital sexual activity of young women, freed from fear of pregnancy by the newly introduced contraceptive drugs, will facilitate vaginal conditioning and the achieving of orgasm. In predicting the outcome of these social changes one must be aware of the physical and psychological differences in ovulatory and anovulatory cycles. The latter may well enhance regression to early adolescence which is not compatible with adult genital functioning. Moreover, one must remember that contraception to the unconscious implies infanticide, equated with the loss of the inner-genital and with the loss of feminine identity. These deeply rooted feminine fears may not be easily counteracted by the conscious realization that prevention of ovulation does not constitute "germ killing."

Masters and Johnson (1966) report success in treating frigidity with the method of frequent and prolonged vaginal excitation, borrowed from techniques of awakening the artificial vagina. The setting for this form of physical therapy is conducive to conflict-free learning. It is taught to married women who desire children and are motivated to learn, with the full cooperation of their husbands whose role as conditioners of the vagina is sanctioned by parental figures, represented by the therapists.

Analysts treat their patients in an atmosphere of physical deprivation. By alleviation of conflicts analysis restores functions, but the ensuing improvement in these functions is to be sought in the patient's life experience. Analysis restores the awareness of tensions, sensations, and impulses emanating from the genitalia. It liberates infantile fantasies and fears and confronts the patient with the infantile demands of the superego which impede functioning on an adult level. By allowing the patient to reorganize his personality structure, analysis facilitates an adult sex-specific integration which, in the woman, is dominated by adult inner-genital drives and interests. Thus, analysis can remove the obstacles that psychological maladaptations pose in the way of orgastic fulfillment. It can neither teach nor institute the requisite setting for normal adult orgastic discharge, in which freedom from fear is provided by a constant love object. The self-imposed limitations, intrinsic to psychoanalytic technique, promote the therapeutic process. Analysts must leave methods of conditioning and teaching to the natural teachers of women, their adult love objects—men.

Summary and Discussion

Analyses of children and adults reveal the obstacles encountered in the development of the external orientation of men and inward orientation of women. Both sexes fear the destruction of their insides, but this more archaic form of the castration complex is typical for women.

There seem to be two "inner-genital" stages in which anxiety-provoking inner-genital impulses give rise to a reorganization of pregenital, inner-genital, and outer-genital component drives. The first "inner-genital" stage ends with the subordination of all component drives to phallic dominance. The second "inner-genital" stage in prepuberty ends with the integration of all component drives, including the phallic, in the sex-specific genital primacy that begins with the onset of biological puberty. Adult genital organization cannot be achieved without the acceptance of the role of internal genital organs in coitus and reproduction.

The developmental trend toward externalization, common to both sexes, promotes adjustment to reality and facilitates the formation of psychic structures at the expense of sexualization of internal genital organs. However, this very trend obscures and retards the developmental steps that prepare the acceptance of the vagina as the primary erotogenic zone of the adult woman.

Throughout development the girl depends on external objects to alleviate her inner-genital tensions. Completely to overcome her fear of losing her "inside," woman depends on man to protect her against the danger of ego dissolution, represented in the loss of contact with reality at the peak of orgastic experience.

Analysis can free man from the fears and defenses which prevent him from accepting and carrying out his role of teacher and organizer of feminine sexuality. Analysis can free woman from the defensive masculinization that supports her externalization, denial, and repression of the vagina, and prevents the cathexis of vaginal excitation. Analysis can make woman teachable, but it cannot teach her. Woman's orgastic capacity develops to its full potential only when man can help her to achieve it.

NOTES

[1]In my first accounts of externalization of inner genital tensions upon the baby-doll and later the child, I failed to realize that the tensions and vague sensations I was describing must evoke impulses that lead to maternal activity (see Chapter 1, p. 20). It was Bradley (1961) who pointed out my error. My early presentations also erred in the use of projection and externalization interchangeably. Inner genital impulses are externalized into maternal activities beginning with the early maternal stage, which I now subsume under the heading of an "inner-genital" stage or the early stage of integration (Kestenberg, 1966, see also Chapter 13). Sexual and aggressive wishes are projected upon the male in a late oedipal stage. Corresponding stages of development in the male are discussed in later sections of this chapter.

[2]A rhythm of this kind can also be observed in the scrotum of neonates. The movement appears wavelike or wormlike, spreads from one side of the scrotum to the other, and may be followed by rotatory movements in the testicles (Robbins, 1964).

[3]The reference to the vagina need not be taken as indication of inner sensations. "Modern" mothers, in their zeal to be enlightened parents, introduce this word for the female genital before the child is aware of her inner organ. As a result, they refer to the vulva as "vagina" and this semantic confusion serves the externalization of the vagina rather than enhancing its acceptance. Gigi called both inner and outer genitals "vagina."

[4]Magda's use of dolls and the image of a baby to represent her vagina was described in Chapter 2. The connection between her sensations and her moods was discussed in Chapter 4.

[5]The connection between Fern's sensations and her moods was discussed in Chapter 4.

[6]Reich's (1927) patient Lotte, whose feelings were even stronger than Fern's, talked to her vagina as if it were her child and promised it relief while she masturbated.

[7]Curves drawn to represent multiple orgasms (Reich, 1927) suggest that the rhythms involved are similar to pregenital and early inner-genital rhythms, characterized by small changes and a frequency of repetition that is unsuitable for adult genital discharge. Repeated high waves or peaks which eventually lead to disengorgement and relief (Dickinson, 1949) should not be construed as multiple orgasms but as phases of orgastic discharge, typical for women.

[8]Nagging women, who particularly blame their husbands and "pick" on them, sometimes become aware of their problem without analysis, as the following excerpt from a letter illustrates: "I swore if I ever found a good man I would be the best wife in the world. Well, I found a real jewel. . . . So, will you please tell me why my mouth is never shut? I nag constantly, I'm forever picking on this marvelous man and I'm so sick of listening to myself that I can't stand it. What is wrong with me anyway?"

[9]Animals prevented from licking their genitalia before they delivered acted as if estrangement from this zone made them incapable of mothering. Instead of licking the young to effect removal of embryonal covering, they behaved indifferently toward the newborns. (Beach and Ford, 1952).

[10]The resistance against the acceptance of the universal equation of woman = inside = vagina = uterus = baby = doll (Barnett, 1966; Bradley, 1961; Jacobson, 1936; Veszy-Wagner, 1965; see also Chapters 1, 2 and 15) is heightened by their connection to forbidden incestuous wishes, repudiated pregenital temptations, and defenses against the characterization of the mother as a prostitute.

Dolls, now used as child substitutes in play, were not long ago made to represent grown, elegant women. The word "doll" is derived not only from ancestral idols but also, as Bradley (1961) convincingly showed, from a common nickname that became applied to prostitutes (Daiken, 1953). In all languages known to me, "doll" is used both as a term of endearment, often revealing tolerant condescension toward the immature,

DEVELOPMENT OF SEXUALITY

and as a contemptuous epithet for empty-headed women who frivolously display on their clothes what they lack on their body.

[11]This experience and others parallel Sherfey's discovery of defensive attitudes toward cryptic parts of female genitals (1966).

[12]I am quite aware of the possibility that answers to our questions are already available and that we, who profess to investigate them, may be handicapped in our study by a resistance we share with others. However, revising this paper in 1972 and 1973 did not add to the knowledge obtained in 1967.

[13]The profession of puppeteer is traditionally a male one (Daiken, 1953). In some countries the handlers of marionettes may be clearly visible to the audience, but as a rule the secret of the puppeteer and magician remains his own. The audience identifies with the magician, who knows the secret but "won't tell."

[14]The primary differences pertain to the question whether inner-genital impulses and drives play a role in childhood sexuality. The reconstruction of "inner-genital" phases can be validated only by pooling psychoanalytic material and examining it for evidences of fantasies derived from inner-genital impulses and drives in early childhood and in prepuberty.

[15]Recurring protests against subjugations by men and calls for equalization of sexes, are based, no doubt, on the wish to abolish discriminatory practices against women. However, they are frequently reinforced by disappointments in men, who failed to provide for and shelter women and their children. Feeling unloved and unprotected, women tend to repudiate womanhood altogether and to identify with men who look down on child- and home-care as inferior.

[16]Child analysts are continuously faced with the fact that, once functions are restored, skills are not automatically acquired. Stutterers or asthmatics often require retraining by speech therapists or physiotherapists, once analysis frees them from conflicts that prevented normal breathing. An old joke may serve to clarify the dilemma of the analyst who cannot "teach" a patient a skill he never possessed. A patient asks a surgeon who put a cast on his fractured wrist: "Doctor, will I be able to play the piano?" Doctor: "Of course." Patient: "That's wonderful, I never could play before."

PART II

Phase Development from Infancy Through Latency

CHAPTER 6

Attunement and Clashing
in Mother-Child Interaction

Two interdependent trends have characterized psychoanalytic thinking since its early beginnings. One concerns the genetic continuity in individual development and the other concerns the orderly progression of phase-specific psychic organizations. In this and the next chapter I shall outline certain basic trends which, early in life, set the tone for the way individual development proceeds. All the subsequent chapters will be devoted to discussion of prevailing trends in successive developmental phases. Here I shall discuss the mother-child interaction as regards sensory intake, excitation, frustration, and tension-reduction. I shall try to give examples to show how attunement and clashing of modes can affect the child's present and future adaptations. By necessity, both the classification and the examples will be simplified for presentation. Even within the narrow framework of attunement versus clashing, it will not be possible to take into account the innumerable variables which mold each mother-child relationship and make each mother-infant couple unique.

Under optimal conditions of health, the needs of the fetus are taken care of by apparatus provided in his own and his mother's body. The mutual adjustment between mother and child becomes much less perfect when delivery brings about the first separation from the mother. For optimum postnatal development, the infant needs a quantitatively and qualitatively optimal stimulus intake, frustration doses, and corresponding tension reductions (Fries, 1947; Escalona, (1967).

The baby, through his very existence and through his particular behavior, stimulates and frustrates his mother and also provides her with his own innate modes of tension reduction of which she can make use herself.

Lecture to psychiatric residents of the Kings County Hospital, Brooklyn, N.Y., 1965.

We assume that the newborn's crying is an expression of physical frustration, which is often elicited by hunger. To the mother the baby's cry is an external stimulus. Regardless of how fast and well she can provide food for him, his crying becomes a source of frustration for her. Feeding the baby who ceases crying and sucks adequately is not only a source of physical gratification for the baby, but an emotional gratification for the mother. His behavior when put to the breast or bottle varies between evoking pleasant excitement, relief, pleasure, and frustration in the mother. When the baby stops sucking or reduces his vigor, this may coincide with the mother's need for a pause or for a reduction in activity, or it may become a source of frustration to her because, for reasons of her own temperament, she may want the activity to continue at the same pace. Her frustration elicits in her a need for tension reduction. She may shift her position, stimulate the baby's mouth or cheek, pull or push the nipple, or pick the baby up for burping. She can do all this in any number of ways characteristic of her own mode of functioning.

Mother and child each has certain preferences as regards stimulus intake and tension reduction methods. Each has individual thresholds which are responsible for certain stimuli being pleasurable, others being painful, and still others unnoticed (Benjamin, 1961). Both have individual degrees of frustration tolerance, which differ according to the states of mother or child at the time and according to their individual preferences (Escalona and Bergman, 1949; Kestenberg, 1965). A hungry child has less frustration tolerance when he has to wait for food. A tired or anxious mother becomes more frustrated by the child's crying than she would be in an alert or calm state of mind. One mother may be especially sensitive to auditory stimuli and she may complain that the child's crying hurts her ears. Another mother may feel pleasure in hearing the child's cry and exclaim joyfully "He is awake." One baby may have a great need for tactile stimuli and his mother may oblige him because of her equally strong need for tactile interaction. Her second baby may have a tendency to startle or even cry when handled by her. This may take her aback and she may feel rejected. If her preferred defense mechanisms are avoidance and withdrawal, she will stay away from the baby, not necessarily out of respect for his preference, but more to protect herself against feeling anxious and dejected. She may even withhold other stimuli from him saying: "He needs to be left alone," while all along this particular baby may hunger for visual or acoustic stimuli or both. Another mother may tend to be revengeful when feeling hurt. She keeps touching and startling the baby in an aggressive manner, so that "He will get used to things and not be such a scaredy-cat." As she talks to him thus she may simultaneously provide him with the stimuli he likes, while at the same time she frustrates him with her tactile approach. He may well learn to accept handling because he likes to be talked to. We do not know whether his startles necessarily connote displeasure or oversensitivity, but we tend to interpret them that way, because of the emotion we ourselves experience when we are startled.

There are so many facets to mother-child interaction that it becomes very difficult to isolate categories of interaction in a given mother-child couple. We have become familiar with gross maladaptations and their sources, but we have a long way to go in order to understand nuances in mutual adaptations that are contingent on a great many overlapping variables in the complex behavior of caretaker and infant. It would be easier if we could say that frustration is undesirable and gratification at a premium, as recent cultural attitudes prompt us to think. In our present-day Western culture we talk a great deal about happiness as a goal. We are very busy trying to make our children happy, and in turn we demand that our children, because of all this happiness we bestow upon them, must make us happy. We tend to forget that there is no gratification without preceding frustration. We tend to forget that stimulation from inner and outer sources that leads to either pleasure or unpleasure, frustration with its consequent unpleasure, and such tension reduction as produces pleasure, relief or peace are all part and parcel of an excitation process, with interdependent variables. Pleasure and pain are difficult to describe qualitatively and even more difficult to assess quantitatively. It is not possible to assay feeling tones from the study of reactive behavior. Many research projects were designed to study responses, both motor and autonomic (heart rate, respiration, skin resistance, and others), to well-defined stimuli in infants and adults (Eichhorn, 1970). To my knowledge, no attempt has been made to measure all these reactions in both subjects during mother-child interaction. To undertake such a study one would have to take into consideration not only the many variables such as thresholds, preferences for certain stimuli and modes of dealing with them, but also the manner in which they are organized in each individual and in the mother-child interaction. In addition, one would need to appraise the process units and their integration in terms of dependence on congenital givens, on states, and on the degrees of maturation and experience. At this time, one can make only very broad generalizations concerning the nature and sequel of mother-child interactions, the validity of which can be tested in most longitudinal studies. Judging from preliminary research on interaction of motor rhythms (Kestenberg, 1965) and from clinical observations, I can suggest the following general classification of mother-child interactions and their sequels:

159

PHASE DEVELOPMENT, INFANCY THROUGH LATENCY

1. The more complete the attunement between maternal and infantile characteristics (sensory thresholds, modes of perception, preferred motor rhythm, specific frustration tolerance, modes of tension rise, and preferred tension reduction modes), the more truly symbiotic the relationship (Mahler, 1968b).

2. The more disparate and desynchronized the maternal and infantile characteristics, the more we can expect early clashing and later conflict.

3. The road to normality is difficult to assess because it consists of both clashes and attunements in a complicated quantitative, qualitative, and sequential relationship.

Each new day and each new phase bring about new possibilities for mutual adaptation between mother and child. I can fully concur with Mahler (1963) in her observation about the resiliency of the infant and child. The infant's ability to recover from temporary setbacks is commensurate with his adaptive potential. Normality in infants can be described as overall good adaptation between mother and child on one hand, and the child and his wider environment on the other. This, of course, presupposes a fair adaptation of the mother to her wider environment also. In each so-called normal subject there are kernels of maladaptation that constitute pathogenic foci. These can develop into full pathology in conditions of general stress or in specific stress for which an appropriate mode of adaptation is not available. For instance, the child whose mother had left him alone, because he offended her by crying, may become quite capable of working out problems in solitude, but not be too adaptable to groups. Under conditions of general stress, such as illness, he may exaggerate his tendency to withdraw, want to be left alone at all costs and present a management problem to physicians and nurses. A specific stress may occur later in life when he will be asked to work on a committee. He may become irritable and anxious because his need for privacy has not been respected. Among the many variables that would change the child's pattern, we should consider the possibility that his father or siblings had assisted him when his mother absented herself. Or, that his mother would become more tolerant of his crying when she was not alone and could count on support from family and friends. This, of course, is an oversimplification, as are all such propositions that are useful only to illustrate a point.

With this qualification in mind, we can look at various developmental disorders from the viewpoint of attunement versus clashing in the mother-child interaction. The categories presented must of necessity overlap. The disorders range from mild developmental deviations to severe disturbances.

160

Complete Attunement

Complete attunement is based on mutual empathy or on an excessive similarity between partners. There is not only a sameness of needs and responses, but also a synchronization in rhythms. If such an attunement persists for a long time, it may lead to a prolongation and intensification of the symbiotic phase. This, in turn, may lead to: (1) defective ego boundaries and an exaggerated stranger anxiety; (2) intolerance to frustration, resulting from novel stimulations, with ensuing impulse disorders; (3) restriction of functions and refusal to practice skills long after maturation has made them available. As a result, the child has no incentive to learn to speak or walk independently. Instead he wants someone else to function with him. Generalized learning difficulties are often based on such a predicament: the child will not do on his own anything that requires considerable modification on his part ("I do not like to draw, count, read, write, etc.; I cannot do it by myself—you do it with me"). Two kinds of affect disorders are observed: either rages because things are not done exactly the way he wants them done, or a need to share excitement with others. The incorporation of parental objects occurs by fusion, and the patient has difficulty in distinguishing between his needs and such needs of other people as would prohibit the gratification of his own needs ("I had to take Johnny's truck because I needed it").

One-Sided Attunement

One-sided attunement between mother and child implies that only one of the two partners makes the bulk of the adjustment. In almost complete attunement, very little adjustment is necessary as both mother and child function in a very similar manner in most respects. In a one-sided attunement, one of the partners is extremely pliable and adjusts readily to the other's modes of functioning. We distinguish: (1) The so-called motherly mother who is equally successful with all infants, her own and others', and is capable of assuming the infant's modes of functioning no matter what they are. She intuitively fathoms whether he is hungry, wet, or just needs to be held, in what position, and so on. She holds, feeds, diapers, rocks, and walks the infant in complete synchronization with his rhythms of tension reduction. This presupposes an above-average ability to regress to early rhythms both in perception and motor performance. It is often associated with lack of initiative in relation to adults or older children and a deficiency in higher ego functions. An extreme of pliability is an asset in the care of very young babies but a liability in the care of older children. Some of these very maternal women become very disappointed when the baby grows up. They react with indifference, even rejection, when attunement to needs, and primitive tension reduction methods become inappropriate and more advanced forms of interaction are required. A child reared by such a caretaker, of which some of the southern mammies are a good examples, thrives in babyhood but may go through life feeling dejected and unloved when he is called to make active adjustments himself. The yearning for the lost bliss of passive babyhood interferes with his wish to grow up.

(2) The very pliable baby, who is capable of adjusting to his mother's needs. We hear that this is a "good baby," who cries very little and interferes singularly little with the household routine. These are the babies who can be taken to the movies at night, transferred from lap to car to crib without interference with their sleep. They can be fed at irregular intervals. They are less need-centered and more object-centered. They are very well acquainted with each changing facial expression, each new muscle tension of the mother. She may become the child's sole reality. Where external reality does not coincide with maternal representations, he will tend to deny what he sees or hears, so that he can continue to believe what mother wants him to believe. The attachment to the mother is one-sidedly symbiotic, inasmuch as the mother is not a partner to the symbiosis. She neither feels one with the child nor does she function for him or with him. The resulting picture resembles a *folie à deux* with the mother as dominant partner. A similar state can be also observed in twins. Sometimes a mother uses a pliable child to discharge her own tensions. She externalizes onto the baby in such a way that, when she is irritated, she knows it only after her baby has become irritated in response to her. At that point she observes that the baby is irritating her. She is incapable of finding the real source of her dissatisfaction. In such a case it is useful to follow the cycle of the mother; one may be able to observe that the baby's discontent coincides with the mother's premenstrual phase.

Pliable children depend a great deal in their mood on the moods of their love object. They tend to minimize internal or external clues in favor of what important people around them think and feel. Some such patients in adulthood may enter the analyst's office scrutinizing his face for clues to the analyst's emotional state. Their attunement to the analyst is such that they look upon each daily event, each problem in a manner in which the analyst looks upon it. If a student is unfortunate enough to have a patient like that as his first case, he may become highly gratified because the patient forever confirms the analyst's feelings and formulations. A treatment like that presents a problem in countertransference. The analyst does not suffer the frustration inherent in the psychoanalytic situation and may regress to feeling like the omnipotent child of an admiring mother.

Some of the children who have suffered from one-sided attunement in relation to their mothers find it very difficult to resolve oedipal conflicts. Trying to serve both masters, they are beset by bisexual temptations. Once a pattern of adjusting to everything and everybody is established, there is danger that a volatile, vague "as-if personality" will develop (Deutsch, H., 1937). Such people have a great facility in enacting different roles, and some of our very gifted performers are among them.

Complete attunement has very undesirable consequences if it continues beyond the symbiotic phase of the first few months of life. One-sided attunement of the mother to the child may become a burden to him rather than a pleasure when she fails to keep pace with him, as he develops advanced patterns that are alien to her. In some such cases, the child treats his mother as if she were a baby and allows her indulgently to play games with him that he no longer enjoys. In her absence, he practices and learns skills, becoming more dependent on self-esteem through achievement than on being cuddled and babied. Similarly, the overpliable children are frequently rescued by the spurt toward autonomy and individuation in the second year of life. Sometimes, the revolt of the anal-sadistic phase makes the mother aware of her own lack of adjustment to the child. She belatedly begins to attune to his needs. At other times, the identification with an active and demanding father helps the child to overcome his excessive desire to give in and please.

Functioning for the Other

Mother and child can function for each other by reciprocal arrangement, modeled after the child feeding the mother while she feeds him. They are simultaneously passive and active in relation to one another. The activity need not be the same for the two partners, especially when favors are exchanged. This can become an educational method whereby the child will do chores the mother dislikes and she will do the same for him. When exaggerated, a cooperative functioning of that kind leads to restrictions of certain functions and skills which must be relegated to others.

One-sided functioning for the other occurs when: (1) A child is reared to do things in lieu of the mother. From earliest infancy, she admonishes him to "go to sleep for mommy, eat for mommy, burp for

163

mommy." This implies that she need not put him to bed, feed, or burp him. The child becomes prematurely independent. Yet he may lose the pleasure in his own functioning and enjoy only when he does things for someone else. (2) The mother prevents the child from failing by stepping in before he can become frustrated. The child does not develop frustration tolerance and cannot learn by trial and error. However, this method is curative for children who become too excited to adapt, and suffer from organismic distress when they fail. They cannot learn under conditions of stress. For instance, the restless, hypertonic infant who has a hard time finding the nipple may not become frustrated at all if his mother anticipates him, and puts the nipple in his mouth and holds it there for him. A one-sided action of the mother is necessary before attunement in nursing becomes possible. A skillful mother will cease intervening as soon as the infant has learned to seize the nipple in peace. Sometimes, an autistic child or one with minimal neurological dysfunctions is raised happily because his mother camouflages his failures by functioning for him. The disorder becomes apparent when the child has to separate from the mother. At times, the mothers of these handicapped children cannot bear to see them frustrated and resist educational or therapeutic procedures. Many of them have become dependent on being the child's crutch and become disturbed themselves when the child improves. (3) The mother prevents the child's success by unnecessarily or prematurely functioning for him. She does not allow the baby to find the nipple but will put it in his mouth before he has a chance to try, even though he may be able to master the task without undue upset, or may need only a minimal amount of help. The child may accept this at the expense of his initiative or he may clash with her, as discussed on page 167-168.

Partial Attunement

Partial attunement can be all-pervasive or be only applicable to some interactions between mother and child. The needs of mother and child are met without complete fulfillment. The mother may nurse the child a bit longer than she can do in comfort, but not long enough to allow a complete satiation and relaxation. The flow of milk and the child's sucking rhythm may not be completely synchronized. The child may reduce his pumping action to low input at a time when the mother's breasts still need emptying. It is often difficult to know whether partial attunement is due to the mother's or the child's life-style or to both, unless one observes the child with another caretaker. Partial attunement frequently leads to selective or generalized low-key depressive constellations, and lowering of aspirations or underachieving. A mild depressive attitude can develop in one area of functioning only, as seen in some people who are generally cheerful but never relish food. Whether localized in specific segments of behavior or generalized, such a lowering of spirits is not based on contained aggression but rather on a diminished impetus of drives.

Selective Attunement

Selective attunement is the most common and best-known adaptation between mother and child. An attunement during feeding may not persist during play or sleep. A need for auditory stimuli in mother and child promotes musical interests and communication through speech. However, some motor patterns may be clashing so that the child, for instance, dawdles while feeding and the mother is made anxious by the delay. A mother and child may both enjoy a certain rhythm of rocking which becomes their principal method of tension reduction. On the other hand, in situations in which rocking cannot be used, mother and child may prefer disparate methods of soothing and releasing tension. For instance, the child brought for physical examination and placed on the examining table may merely need to see his mother in close proximity to feel comfortable. The mother, unable to rock him, may move out of his sight. She may be one of the women who cannot look on pain and must withdraw, in order to allay their own anxiety.

There are many examples of selective attunement, which is a familiar phenomenon in so-called normalcy and neurosis. The selection of symptoms and character traits is contingent on the vicissitudes of this type of mother-child interaction. The ways in which we get along with and choose people as companions are significantly related to the preferred areas of attunement, practiced in infancy.

Generalized Clashing

Generalized clashing encompasses all areas of functioning. It occurs most frequently:

(1) When children who are given to organismic distress early in life, live in an environment that tends to overstimulate them. Overwhelmed by inner and outer stimuli, they seem to be in a continuous state of distress for which there is no relief because the methods by which they are soothed are, in themselves, stimulating. In contrast, in dull, quiet

homes these children do not always become conspicuous in early infancy. Stimulus reduction in combination with monotonous routines for which, after a while, only already-learned automatic responses are needed, seem to provide sufficient means to cope with their excitability. However, they become disturbed in periods of rapid growth as well as at times of environmental changes.

(2) When babies have relatively few modes of functioning at their disposal, none of which coincide with those available to their mothers. One such example is that of the oversensitive baby who reacts unduly to normal stimuli. When a mother's thresholds are very much higher than the child's, she continually offers stimuli that jar him. Whether she talks to him, or picks him up, presents him with toys or food, her mode of activity is quantitatively more than he can endure. To him she practically yells when she says "shush, baby." She seems to jerk him when she holds him and when she rocks him she is overviolent for him. Since she cannot empathize with his sensitivity, she does not shield him from loud noises or strong visual stimuli unless specifically instructed to do so. She may get along fine with her next child, who likes her rough-and-ready approach to life (see, for an example, Freud, A., and Burlingham, 1943).

(3) When a child, though rich in endowment and not especially sensitive to stimuli, has an obligatory rhythm with which he perceives and acts. One such case from my pilot study on the development of movement patterns (1965) was that of a boy who from birth displayed a decided preference for deliberate-looking, gradually rising tension that could reach great heights. He could be handled roughly or gently, steadily or in a fluctuating manner, and he could respond with pleasure to all these approaches, provided he could prepare himself for the experiences in his own way. He had to be ready. Needless to say, if one approached him gradually, one could facilitate this readiness. His mother talked to him in an excited fashion, with a high-pitched voice and vigorous movements from the start. When he was ready, he responded in kind. Soon the observers noticed that she ceased feeding him in her arms and propped the bottle for him. It was a rather fortunate choice since, as it turned out later, the little boy became increasingly uncomfortable being fed in a noisy, crowded room with his mother attending to many things suddenly or all at once while feeding him. In the first few months the little boy began to stare in an absentminded fashion, especially when surrounded by a great many people with loud voices. At six months he finally withdrew to his crib and refused to stay in the noisy and forever shifting environment of the kitchen. He stopped reaching for things and stopped eating solids. But in his crib he was kingpin. He reached for

his toes in his own gradual way and they approached him in the same manner. Once he became excited in his own way and reached a peak of excitation, he could endure and even enjoy high-pitched, excited behavior in others. Later in life this child continued to withdraw by staring and would cease functioning altogether when shocked by approaches developing too suddenly. As a toddler he became a stutterer when the influx of excited genital libido clashed with his usually preferred approach. In grade school he became compulsive, and suffered from an incapacitating learning disturbance. It is interesting to note that, even though he used the method of total withdrawal, he could recover very easily if one adjusted to his mode of functioning. This held true even in latency. When he was changed from a rather rigid, uncompromising, and punitive school to a more progressive one, his scholastic achievement improved (Kestenberg, 1965, 1967a and b).

Total clashing may lead to a continuous fighting between mother and child. This can be observed rather early when the mother, for instance, while burping the baby, exclaims impatiently: "Oh, my, you are a bad boy, so stubborn, what are you keeping it for?" If both mother and child are uncompromising and there is no one else to take care of the child, a sado-masochistic relationship may develop quite early. A mother can clash with one child and accept another who has a different disposition. A clashing relationship need not be due to a dominating attitude of the mother. It is rather based on an incompatibility of temperaments. Sometimes, it occurs when an infantile mother has to deal with a child who, from start, refuses to be treated like a doll. Many such mothers learn from their babies and mature with them.

Partial Clashing

As in partial attunement, partial clashing can be all-pervasive or confined to one area only. This type of clashing does not lead to open battles, but rather to a generally tense emotional climate. The irritable mood is contagious. The irritable infant makes his mother irritable and vice versa. However, both may have the same disposition from the start, but not necessarily express it the same way. For instance, a baby can nurse with a perpetual frown on his face. The mother may look away from him and never meet his gaze. These are subtle forms of irritability and discord which often go by unnoticed. They may occur during feeding or before going to bed.

Among the many forms of partial clashing is one that overlaps with the category "functioning for the other." Paradoxically it is based on synchrony of action, and is often due to a persistence of mirroring as a form of identification. Mother and child are both inclined to be active; they irritate one another because they always do the same things at the same time and will not take turns. In such an atmosphere, the mother will forever give the child things for which he reaches. She puts a potty under him when he is starting to sit down on it, or shows him how to wave "bye-bye" when he has already begun to do it. Since the mother is more capable of organized actions than the baby, it often seems that she is the only one who initiates the clash. Close scrutiny reveals that the child himself has a great propensity for mirroring, over and above his developmental needs. He touches everything his mother touches, he must talk on the phone when she does and generally gets in her way in this manner. This can begin in early infancy and manifest itself in habits such as going to sleep only when mother does or eating only when mother does too. This type of clashing may become competitive under the guise of thoughtfulness or subservience. When the mother is the dominant member in such a relationship, she prevents the child from functioning without help. There are several ways open to him in this predicament. He may express his displeasure by pushing his mother away, crying, or withdrawing from her. He may contain his anger and function within the framework of general discontent, feeling that nothing ever goes quite the way he wants it to be. He may give up functioning independently and enjoy the omnipotence he gains through his mother's servitude. He may restrict functioning by inhibition of initiative and spitefully wait for his mother to start and then will continue what she had originated. A reverse inhibition may result in an aversion for completion of actions. These types of early inhibition provide the fuel for future strict superego-demands that the individual accomplish nothing that has not been started or completed by someone else. Such symptomatic behavior is always fraught with some form of irritability.

Selective Clashing

Selective clashing occurs in normal and neurotic development. It is the most common root of conflict in the areas of feeding and toilet-training, and the most frequent focus of deviant behavior that becomes encapsulated within an otherwise fairly adjusted person. It does not necessarily lead to symptoms, but rather to symptomatic actions and special habits. For instance, there are some people who retain remnants of early clashes in the harmless habit of leaving a bit of uneaten food on the plate at every meal. Others habitually defecate every second day or hold back urine for a very long time. Such clashes start early when mothers insist that the infant finishes all that is in the bottle, no matter what; put a child on the pottie every day at the same hour; or, admonish the child to go to the bathroom before every outing. Such battles may not persist on the surface but become evident later in selected superego defects, which reveal themselves in statements such as: "No one can force me to finish my food even if I *am* hungry," or "If I cheat on exams it does not count. It's like I used to eat so slowly that mother could not stand it and would leave the room, and then I would throw most of the stuff away or feed it to the cat. I cheated on her all right." The predecessor of this adult student is the young baby who allows his mother to feed him all the ounces she wants to put into him and then, quietly but surely, regurgitates a goodly amount of it.

Selective clashing usually begins within the framework of a particular developmental phase. Its persistence is largely responsible for fixations in this phase and a tendency to regress to it under stress. However, progressive developmental forces can help mitigate the results of early clashes. A mother may become less anxious about feeding when the child begins to feed himself. In phases of rapid growth, a child's hunger may overcome his aversion to "finishing all that is on the plate." The chivalry of the early phallic-oedipal phase changes the boy's attitude toward his mother and he may gladly relinquish feces and urine whenever his mother wishes him to do so. It may be possible to train him then whereas before he considered the bathroom a battlefield for his mother and himself.

Discussion

Surveying modes and areas of attunement and clashing in mother-child interaction, we recognize the broad outlines of two principles which govern developmental processes in each phase. They are the polarities of harmony and conflict that constitute the foundations of mental life. Attunement between mother and child reaches its peak at the height of each developmental phase, when clashes begin to be felt with increasing frequency (see Chapter 11). The latter are the prelude to the readjustment that mother and child must make to facilitate a successful transition into the next developmental phase.

There are many ways to attune, from doing the same thing the same way to harmonizing in rounds, sequences, and complementary phrasing. As we have seen, clashing may result not only from functioning in opposite ways, but also from inappropriate "doing the same thing at the same time" (see pages 167-168). In some phases, attunement in rhythms facilitates optimal functioning, for instance, when the rhythm of maternal milk-flow is identical with the rhythm of the infant's sucking. In other phases such an attunement is inappropriate, for instance when a mother strains with the toddler who defecates. Temporary bouts of clashing are characteristic of phases in which sadistic impulses begin to predominate, as when children bite or hit their mothers. Partial attunement or partial clashing are ways through which mother and child let each other know that certain needs are outdated or diminishing. For instance, the child who weans himself sucks less and less and his mother's breasts produce less and less milk. However, before these processes equalize there is an imbalance between them, leading to episodes of mild depression or irritability.

Generally speaking, attunement promotes symbiosis and clashing promotes separation. Exaggerated attunement fosters fears of engulfment and exaggerated clashing brings on excessive fears of separation. Too much attunement may lead to inhibition of independent functioning. Too much clashing enhances motor discharge as response to stress, but it may also lead to inhibition of function.

CHAPTER 7

Early Fears and
Early Defenses

The earliest basic fears of children are the fears of unpleasantness which are linked to the mother's absence and develop into fears of loss of love. Two basic defensive reactions are inhibition of movement and motor discharge. Isolated traumatic occurrences seem to lead more frequently to defensive motor discharge. Continuous frustrations which do not allow for the full development of motor discharge seem to pave the way for inhibitions. Such chronic frustrating situations may be confined to one aspect of the child's life and then produce inhibitions in this particular psychological area, or else frustrations may embrace all spheres of the child's everyday life and affect his total functioning.

Anxiety is an affect of unpleasant nature that signalizes danger. The individual is either aware of this affect or has succeeded in averting it by defensive activities. Inasmuch as anxiety is a signal of danger it does not manifest itself where the danger has either been conquered or has not been perceived. We may observe anxiety directly or we may conclude from the defensive activities that anxiety has been present. While anxiety pertains to the expectation of an undefined danger or danger in general, fear relates to a specific danger situation. For the development of anxiety a degree of maturity permitting anticipation of an unpleasant event is a prerequisite. An even higher degree of maturity is necessary for the development of fear, with its well-defined object (Freud, S., 1925).

Fears in Small Children[1]

The small child lacks the maturity required to describe fear as well as the relatively great strength of the ego needed to admit it; it is, there-

---

First published in *Nervous Child*. 5:56-70, 1946. Slightly revised for this publication, it is reproduced by permission.

fore, difficult to evaluate fear in small children. The mother is apt to confuse fear with fright in describing the behavior of her child. Fright is a shock reaction; the frightened child is not signaling danger but rather reacting to a very unpleasant experience that came as a surprise, for which he was consequently unprepared. The untrained observer is inclined to interpret the child's behavior by adult standards. It is fairly typical for a mother who sees her child recoil from a dog and cry to say: "Don't be afraid, the doggie won't bite you." She sees that her child withdraws, that he is upset, and she assumes that he is afraid of being bitten. When a two-year-old is asked what he fears at the sight of a dog he is rarely able to explain. Patient observation may reveal that he is afraid that the dog will jump on him, not that he will bite him. Direct questioning helps little since the small child's vocabulary is limited and he has little patience for prolonged discussion of such unpleasant problems. If he says: "Doggie won't jump," he has already succeeded in reassuring himself, but from the content of his denial one may infer the nature of his fear. However, if his mother has told him not to be afraid of being bitten he may repeat "Doggie won't bite" merely as a reassuring formula.

A little girl of two and a half gave concern to her anxious mother because she would not go into the ocean. The mother tried very hard to get the child to conquer this reluctance, but the girl looked at the waves with horror and kept away from them. She enjoyed playing with sand and wanted water for mud pies. She asked that water be brought to her in a pail. The mother kept saying "The water won't hurt you" and invited her to get the water herself. Whenever the child realized that in her play she had come quite close to the ocean she ran away quickly and renounced the pleasure of playing in the mud. The child could not explain what she feared despite her excellent ability to verbalize. At the end of her play she appeared tired of being questioned and said that she would not go near the ocean because the water would hurt her. At this point she may have accepted her mother's formulation, but this did not mean that she had really understood the content of her fear. The mother thought that the child was afraid that the water would hurt her; I thought that the child was afraid of the waves. Prolonged and patient observation might have given us a different and more satisfactory answer. Even more difficult was the situation of a fifteen-months-old boy who had no language yet at his disposal. He refused to sit on sand or to touch it, screaming when his body came in contact with it. Patiently his mother herself began to play with sand, from time to time putting small quantities on the child's hand. Within a short time the child began to play with the sand, throwing it in his hair and eyes. Although his eyes hurt, he continued throwing the sand with great pleasure His parents stepped in and cried, "No, no, don't throw sand." He looked in bewilderment from one to the other. It seemed a moment of conflict which passed quickly, and he turned to sand throwing again. One might speculate that the boy was afraid of sand because it was strange, or because it reminded him of dirt. Only from observation of the total situation of this child can one venture an interpretation that seems closer to the truth. This little boy crept a good deal and made attempts to get up and to walk a little. He felt secure only while creeping. An anxious expression appeared on his face whenever he pulled himself up to a standing position and after a while he would cry and sit down again. While he was happily creeping his mother followed him for a short time and then began to demand that he stay near her or stop all activity and go to sleep. "If you don't go to sleep right away I will spank you," she said. He looked at her as bewildered as when he was requested not to throw sand. The mother was trying to hamper his motility. The father complained that the child was backward and the mother denied it, but she made no attempt to encourage him to walk or get up. His actions were always subject to restraint. Judging from this whole picture it was possible to guess that the child was strongly tempted to throw sand but was afraid of the consequences and therefore avoided sand altogether. Induced to touch it, he could not resist the impulse to throw it.

These two examples illustrate the difficulty of understanding the child's fear in the second and third year of life. It is, of course, even more difficult to interpret his behavior in the first year. The question when fear and defenses begin is a rather complicated one. If we observe an infant screaming or getting excited, it is difficult to say what kind of affect we are about to witness. Even though infants cry differently with different needs, it is impossible to state with any reasonable assurance that crying expresses anger or fear or any other specific affect. Furthermore, pure unmixed affects are not too frequent even in adults. If we observe any anxiety attack we may find admixtures of sadness, fright, anger, pain, or rage; however, such components can be discerned as separate entities within a given affective situation in adults. Just how soon a child can differentiate between a variety of painful affects is an open question. We can only say that at first undifferentiated painful sensations appear in response to painful stimuli. As the child learns to recognize reality and to profit from repeated experiences and is mature enough to be able to anticipate an unpleasant occurrence, he is getting ready to use the signal of anxiety and somewhat later the signal of fear. Before this he has reacted in a number of different ways to painful stimuli. Early sensations and reactions slowly gain in psychic content. However, even in the earliest stages, where we can think only in terms of conditioning, traumatic situations and reactions to them leave imprints upon which later psychological patterns are formed (Greenacre, 1941).

The earliest known fear is that of missing the mother. This is linked up with the unpleasant somatic sensations accompanying lack of gratification. The child begins to be somewhat afraid of strangers and clings to his mother. The stranger seems to symbolize separation from the mother. Fear of being left alone and fear of the dark are variations of this basic fear. The child begins to make an effort to please the mother in order to gain her approval or in order to avoid disapproval, which in the extreme case means her leaving the child. This second phase is already a higher differentiation of the first, in which the child is afraid only of his mother's absence. It indicates an awareness that it is not only the mother's presence which brings about gratification but also the mother's willingness to provide such gratification. In order to insure his mother's inclination to satisfy him the child makes a good deal of effort to please. By the end of the first year, before there is any speech development, the baby becomes a serious student of his mother's features. He watches her facial expressions and thus interprets her moods. He becomes uncomfortable when his mother is sad or tense. Earlier he was able to sense fluctuations of his mother's mood by the nature of her touch, the way she held him, the intonation of her voice, the smile on her face. By now he has become expert in interpreting gestures. He is beginning to understand his mother's language, which he links up with his understanding of her motor behavior and expression. He is afraid that he might do something that will not please her and he watches her face for signs of approval or disapproval. The voice adults use with infants is usually much fuller of affect and expression than that used with older children and adults. This facilitates the development described above. A mother who is very careful not to prohibit but is naturally unable to control her expression of anger, fear, or disgust creates more tension than one who uses a slight intellectual "no." The small child who feels a prohibition is not able to understand the limitations of such a prohibition. The "no's" he acknowledges are frequently absolute rather than relative. Janusz Korczak, the Polish psychologist and author, expressed this problem well in one of his books for children. He said that the unhappy child feels that he will always be unhappy, will never have what he is deprived of at the moment. The unhappy adult can look forward to the time when he will have what he lacks at present. If a small child feels that his mother does not want him to be dirty it means to him that he must never be dirty. It is some time before he realizes the relativity of a prohibition. It is pathetic to observe a child of one or two or even three struggle with his impulse to do something in face of his apprehension of his mother's reaction. It is easy to discriminate between this struggle and that of older children who are afraid of their own consciences. The small child will look at his mother anxiously when he is about to play with something dirty, but do it as quickly as lightning when encouraged by his mother or when she is not looking. The older child, whose superego has developed fully, has a good deal of independence from his parents' current mood in choosing what to do.

A two-and-a-half-year-old boy was brought for consultation because of stuttering. His vocabulary far exceeded what is normally expected at his age. The parents, an intellectual couple, were anxious about his speech difficulty. Peter was well mannered, clean, inhibited in his motility, and adult in behavior. At times one could observe outbursts of motor impulses which he checked with great tension. In the office Peter's mother agreed verbally that Peter could play with clay and ink. However, every time Peter was about to dirty himself he looked toward his mother for silent approval. His mother would nod that he could do it and in turn would look a little anxiously at me. Both the mother's anxious look and her inability to continue her tolerance at home portrayed an indecisiveness which in turn made Peter look for approval with almost every "naughty" impulse. He finally helped himself by placing the blame on me. I became the "bad lady" who induced his mother to allow Peter certain things which she, the mother, considered bad.

A two-and-a-half-year-old girl was chronically constipated and developed a fear of going to the bathroom. In a room with her parents and myself she hesitated when offered toys. She continuously asked her mother whether she could touch certain toys. Even when her mother gave permission the child appeared somewhat doubtful. Experience showed that she was right to doubt her mother's seeming permissiveness. The mother had been encouraged to assure the child that it was not wrong to urinate or defecate in the panties or on the floor, that eventually she would grow up to be a bigger girl and do these things on the toilet. The mother reported great improvement in habits of urinating. After several "accidents" on the floor the child lost her fear of the bathroom and was able to urinate there; however the reluctance to defecate in the bathroom continued. At the end of one discussion with the mother, she admitted hesitantly that she did tell the child it was all right to urinate on the floor, but was not able to say that the same was true for the bowel movement. It became clear why the child, who in my office learned to enjoy throwing marbles out of a box, lost her interest in this play at home. Despite severe restriction of enjoyment in her home the little girl shunned other children and was only comfortable with her mother. Small children refuse to be separated from their mothers not only because they fear being left alone by them but also because they fear that in the mother's absence they might do something that will not meet with her approval. Where will they turn to find out whether they are doing the accepted thing?

It is not always easy to trace a small child's fear to the fear of displeasing a parent. A two-year-old, observed only casually, was an extremely active, outgoing, and noisy child. It was difficult to keep up with him: he was always running, investigating something, talking, repeating, and shouting. Consequently he was a source of disturbance to sleep or peace. By the time he was one year old all these characteristics were already in full bloom. At this time little Felix was already afraid of noisy machines. He did not want to go near them when they were in motion and making noise. When they were not in use and therefore quiet, motionless things, he was able to approach them. The hypothesis, that Felix identified the noisy machine in motion with the aggressor of whom he was afraid, becomes somewhat doubtful if one considers that Felix did not play that he was a machine or imitate the machine's noises. On the other hand, it was noticeable that Felix struggled against his "naughtiness" and did not suceed in overcoming it. When he threw dirt around he looked at adults "guiltily" and said: "look what I have done," and then proceeded to sweep it up. Before this task was finished, however, he turned his interest to something else. When reprimanded for running or shouting he made a visible effort to stop, but soon his good intentions were forgotten and he ran again. Thus, Felix' activity consisted of a succession of giving in to his impulses and of attempts to stop them. The incessant noise and motion of the machines may have impressed Felix as similar to his own "naughtiness." He did not mind approaching the machines when they were not in use. It is possible that he projected on to them his own problems which he was trying to overcome in order to please his parents.

Bertie, a two-and-a-half-year-old boy, had a particularly difficult first two years of life. Born under wartime conditions, he was taken on a long trip when only a few weeks old. Since his father was active in the war the child was left alone with the mother. When only a few months old he had to undergo an abdominal operation which involved staying in the hospital away from his mother. Before his hospitalization he suffered from feeding difficulties connected with the ailment which led to the operation. Upon his return home he had to be spoon-fed. Thus he never had the undisturbed pleasure of sucking. The love and patience of his unusually understanding mother made up to a great extent for all these deprivations. However, circumstances beyond her control forced the mother to leave Bertie alone in his playpen a number of times. She felt that her child was afraid to be left alone, but never once did he cry or express displeasure at her leaving. However, when she returned from her errands she invariably found him in the same position in which she left him. She reasoned that he was afraid to move in her absence. When Bertie was about eighteen months old he was reunited with his father, which at first "surprised" him. Soon after his father's return he was frightened by cackling hens while held above a fence to urinate. His mother felt that this was due to the fact that he had never seen hens before and was "surprised" by them. At two and a half Bertie had a very warm relationship with his father; they obviously loved each other very much. A few months earlier they developed a teasing game in which Bertie said that he, Bertie, was a good boy while his father laughingly asserted that Bertie was a bad boy. This went back and forth, instigated both by the father and the son. At one point in this play, possibly because the father for once kept a straight face, Bertie's face paled and a painful expression appeared; a mixture of surprise and hurt could be seen. Reassurance did not seem to help. Then, suddenly he found help for himself and declared laughingly: "Bertie bad boy." Apparently he identified with the father and undid the damage caused by his father by laughing the way his father usually laughed when he teased him. Also, he had turned from passivity to activity and this in itself brought relief. Observed a few months later while with his parents, Bertie did not cry once although he had plenty of reason to do so. He was tired and sleepy, he wanted to go home. He was disappointed because he had expected that the train ride he took would bring him to a little friend, whom he had seen the previous week after a similar train ride. He witnessed his mother throwing away his ice cream cone. At each such occasion his face would twist as if he were ready to cry and then he would stop himself. He looked after his ice cream cone in utter despair, yet he made no crying sound. In response to a question, the father explained that he had requested Bertie not to cry in his presence. The child was able to comply with this request admirably. Near the end of the day Bertie encountered a little puppy who jumped around lustily. Bertie, who had been afraid of dogs for some time, uttered a little scream, pulled away from the dog and looked at him with horror, but still he had not cried. He was afraid of losing his father's love. He wanted to please him and to be considered a "good boy." He had some earlier training in suppressing affects when he was left alone by his mother. However this pattern has not remained with Bertie. At the age of two and a half neither his motility nor his freedom to express his feelings were hampered when his father was absent. When he was alone with his mother he made up for lost crying time and displayed normal affective behavior at the appropriate occasions, because he knew that his mother did not object. With his father he was able to suppress crying so well that one must wonder whether this "ability" was not a direct descendant of his early reactions to frustrations. When afraid as a baby he neither cried nor moved. When afraid of his father's rebuke, he apparently used the old method and thus was capable of fulfilling his father's demand. In the light of this, what could have been the meaning of Bertie's fear of dogs? Unlike Freud's little Hans (1909), Bertie was not occupied with problems of the oedipus complex. Early fleeting castration fears may have been present when he was frightened by the hens while urinating. This event followed the father's arrival and one may conjecture that Bertie's castration fear was then linked with his father. It is possible that, like little Hans, Bertie shifted from his father to a dog and that his feat of dogs was representative of his fear that his father might castrate him. Yet it seemed that this was not Bertie's prime preoccupation. His main conflict centered upon his fear of losing his father's love. Bertie was an orally deprived child and has overcome these frustrations as far as one can see. It is likely that his fear of the dog was caused primarily by two important factors. The dog represented unrestrained behavior such as Bertie may have wished to display in response to his early deprivations. Secondly, Bertie's inclination to suppress such a behavior was recently reinforced by his father's demands. It seems likely that by avoiding the dog Bertie could control his "undesirable" impulses better and thus could avoid indirectly the disapproval of his father. The animal's presence, on the other hand, may have invited Bertie to act similarly, a temptation which filled him with fear. His current fears may have a great influence on the form and content of his future preoccupation with castration fears.

Early fears do not give way abruptly to castration fears, which bloom during the period of the oedipus complex. Fears of genital injury come up now and then during the preoedipal period, are linked with the fear of loss of love, and slowly gain in intensity. Their form and content are greatly influenced by the nature of earlier fears. A child who is afraid that biting will displease his parents later will be apt to express his castration fear in terms of his genitals being bitten off. Another child whose early problem was connected with jumping may later fear that he will be jumped on and injured genitally. An example of a child in the period of intensive castration fears may make this clearer. Harry, a boy of five, was afraid of a bogeyman. Standing on the roof-terrace of a building he looked down with great interest and inquired what would happen if a car drove down the steep wall. We agreed that the driver would get killed. Harry said quickly, "I would not send a man down there. I would not send my father down there." He felt, however, that he could send the bogeyman to his sure death. He was insatiable in a play in which he threw down a paper bogeyman. At my suggestion he drew a bogeyman to use in the play. He drew awkwardly and suddenly began to make disorganized movements with the pencil and scribbled all over the figure. He called the whole thing "duty," his word for feces. I knew from his parents that Harry was afraid to wipe himself lest some of his "duty" get on his hand. His favored terms of opprobrium were "stinky" and "duty." On the other hand he washed his hands very carefully and often, turning to adults to ask, "Are they clean?" In the office he was especially eager to wash his hands when his father was waiting for him. During one of his washing sprees he ran to the bathroom quickly, murmuring, "I will wash my wiwi." From Harry's total picture it was clear that he was suffering from castration fears and that he had aggressive wishes toward his father. Anal fears and wishes have become connected with the current problems. Harry's father, more than most fathers, had taken care of his bodily needs, washing him and dressing him and taking him to the bathroom. Also during the period in which Harry was overcoming his "dirty" habits he was threatened by an impending separation from his parents. Thus Harry's early wishes to be dirty were linked up with being left by his parents. When at the age of five he wished to remove his father, his methods of removal were not only the methods of a five-year-old but also earlier ways, such as removing his father by an attack with dirt. Consequently, he was not only afraid of the bogeyman to whom he shifted his problem; he was also afraid of dirt. Now, when his wish to injure his father and to get rid of him had become quite strong and he was afraid that his wish might come true, he connected the problem to his earlier fear: "My father may leave me because I am dirty." The new pressing concern, however, is that the father will not only leave but also punish Harry bodily for his "naughtiness." Every anticipated aggression against his body centered upon his fear of losing his genitals, while formerly anticipated dangers were mainly connected with the central fear of being left.

Following this trend of thought one can easily imagine that little Bertie, confronted with intensive castration fears, may in a year or two become afraid that a violent display of emotion on his part will cause his father not only to disapprove of him, but also to punish him by castration. The predominant early fear is the fear of loss of love. Very early frustrations are interpreted as results of loss of love and linked up with later threats and demands made by the parents. Slowly the emphasis shifts and the four- and five-year-old becomes preoccupied with castration fears, which in turn are linked up with earlier fears of loss of love.

Two Types of Early Defenses

The child uses a number of defenses against danger (Freud, A., 1936). Some of these are universal, as is turning from passivity to activity; others develop in specific developmental phases, as for instance, reaction formation in the anal-sadistic and repression in the phallic-oedipal phase. However, they are all based on the two earliest forms of reacting to frustration: inhibition and motor discharge. They may be looked upon as the earliest forms of defenses.

Inhibition

Inhibition of impulses that may bring about parental disapproval is a rather frequent early reaction. It is preventive and effective self-protection. To some extent it is useful and aids the child in the development of realistic behavior that makes him a social being considerate of others. Reference has been made to inhibition in Bertie's suppression of crying, in the fifteen-month-old boy's restriction of motility, in the case of the constipated girl and in other cases described earlier. In many children such an inhibition pattern is often supported by an organic trend toward inhibition. However, in many such instances there is an inhibition of function, not only because of organic disturbance but also because the child becomes aware of his lack of skill and understands the displeasure he causes his mother by his awkward performance. This may tend to inhibit still further the already-disturbed function. A seven-year-old retarded boy, who gave the impression of suffering from a birth injury, was asked to draw. He sat at the table for quite a long time holding the pencil. At first, he tried to distract my attention from the drawing by suggesting that he erase something. Then, with great effort he made himself draw two small lines which he erased quickly. Even though it was obvious that he was trying to please, he was unable to draw more than these two small lines. His only voluntary activity at home consisted of spinning various toys. In my office he was able, with great encouragement and help, to put some pieces of a puzzle together. It was noticeable that for every move of his hand to handle the pieces there were several moves to withdraw his hand and to abandon his task. Only continuous praise and encouragement, as well as guidance, kept him at this task. In normally developed children inhibition may at first sight stimulate constitutional lack of skill, and moderate disabilities may be aggrandized by psychological reactions to failure. Harry, the five-year-old boy mentioned earlier, hardly ever drew. When he did so he was awkward and very infantile in his performance, giving the impression that he simply was not talented in this direction. When he could be induced to draw, he invariably ended by drawing "duty." Since he had a fear connected with bowel movements and since he connected drawing with this function he was handicapped in his performance. Another of Harry's inhibitions was concerned with cutting out. This was due to his fear that he might cut off parts of the figures. On a higher level than the retarded boy, Harry tried to cover up what seemed to him a deficiency. He declared that he could cut out well and even tried to prove it, but soon discouraged by the meager results, he asked for help. He could not, however, bear to feel that someone else should be able to do something better than he. Therefore, he quickly declared my drawing and cutting out "stinky" and began to boast again. This interfered with his learning. When on one occasion he was more amenable to learning, it turned out that he intended to give the finished product to his mother. He realized that his mother would be pleased with his work, and this incentive helped him for a while to overcome his inhibition of drawing and cutting out. Because of his basic intolerance to frustration he was not able to continue his activity for a longer period of time. Every awkward or unsuccessful move of the pencil or scissors caused an intolerable tension. Harry's difficulty was reversible. By pointing out his reactions to his lack of skill, by making his lack of skill more acceptable to him and by the promise of future accomplishments through practice he could be helped to overcome his basic inhibition. It was very easy to help the fifteen-months-old boy combat his reluctance to play with sand; it was relatively easy to assist the little constipated girl to master her inhibition. However, where similar inhibitions are allowed to persist for years and a strong superstructure of reactions to the inhibition has been erected, the problem becomes quite difficult and is sometimes irreversible. The earlier the development of such mechanisms and the more they tend to be total rather than partial, the more serious the prognosis. The infant is less able to stand frustrations than the older child. His resources in the presence of frustrations are limited. When he resorts to inhibition in response to frustration and later in response to danger, his difficulties cannot be observed directly. In such cases we frequently get histories of "uneventful" first years. We may hear that the child cried for a while but on the whole was a rather quiet baby. We may hear that a child was weaned after a few months and accepted the bottle without difficulty, or that he even refused the breast when it was offered again and preferred the bottle. Certainly there are many cases where breast feeding is not satisfactory because of somatic or psychological difficulties of the mother while, in comparison, the bottle feeding is more pleasant. In many other instances the acceptance of the bottle on the part of the child does not seem to be a real acceptance but an inhibition of the desire for the breast. Various problems ranging from speech and breathing difficulties to disturbances of the relationship to women, develop from such a basic inhibition. Frequently it is possible to reconstruct from associations presented by adult patients an early, abrupt weaning and this history is then invariably confirmed by the mother. More often than not no noticeable disturbance is reported at the time of the weaning.

Motor Discharge

When the infant cries and frets in response to minor frustration and later shows distress in anticipation of slight unpleasantness, we can observe at firsthand his intolerance to frustration. Ordinarily the crying, at first a reflexlike action, develops into a signal of distress. The older infant uses the crying to summon his mother. The crying not only offers motor discharge but also helps to bring about real relief through the medium of the mother's help. Where such help is not forthcoming quickly, as for example in prolonged sickness or in the absence of steady mothering, crying in itself may remain the only relief and, of course, a not too satisfactory one. In neglected infants we see means of motor discharge, such as rocking or striking the head, which cannot develop into useful signals to summon help. When such a child begins to walk, his eagerness for motor discharge becomes a source of annoyance to others. Such toddlers run away, disregard dangers in climbing, or are so constantly on the go that it is difficult to keep them out of trouble. Another type of defensive motor discharge is the temper tantrum. Either one of two situations may develop when the dissatisfied infant grows up to be an excitable toddler. The environment may give in to him completely and he becomes the so-called "spoiled brat" who dominates the family; or a fight for control ensues in which the mother tries to subdue the child and the child fights for his opportunity to get relief in excitement. While originally the child was only seeking relief from tension or anxiety he may be forced into conflict by his mother when she tries to dam up his outlets. Soon he begins to derive vicarious satisfaction from exciting his mother; when afraid, he will now not necessarily get a motor discharge himself but try to get his mother to show annoyance. This gives him both pleasure and relief. A vicious cycle develops when the child becomes afraid of his mother's threats and punishments directed against his excitement and gets excited again as defense against the threats. Superficially the situation appears to be the same where the whole family is excitable and finds outlets in scenes. Here the child finds his place in the family as a participant in the general mood swings. As long as he is small, a change in the attitude of the family or a change in the environment produces a quick change in the child himself. When given the opportunity for other means to react, he is able to do so. But change of environment or improvement on the part of the mother does not produce an improvement in the excitable older child who has been a frustrated infant and has learned to find outlets in excitement during infancy. This may be the underlying problem in the so-called attention-getting of small children. The technique of not paying attention to the "attention seeker" yields desirable results only when the child is trying to produce excitement in the mother. If the child needs motor discharge in order to rid himself of his fears without regard to his mother's reaction, refusing attention to him may only increase his fears and thus increase his need for excitement.

It is difficult to say why, in one instance, the infant tends to develop inhibitions as response to tensions and in another tends to increase his motor discharge. It is easier to surmise why one function is chosen for inhibition rather than another; why in one case the motor discharge envelops the whole personality, such as in temper tantrums and generalized excitement, and why in still another case certain organs are chosen for discharge as, for example, in vomiting, diarrhea, etc. We assume that the selection of behavior and/or organs is influenced by constitutional factors. Also, trauma occurring at times when a certain function or organ is in the center of interest may have a deleterious effect, either by producing an inhibition of this function or by creating a greater need for discharge in the organ. A frustrating environment, not always manifested in the form of isolated incidents, but frequently expressed in constant attitudes of the mother, may have effects similar to trauma.

The Factor of Environment in the Development of Early Fears and Early Defenses

In trying to isolate what constitutes a traumatizing attitude in the environment there has been an overemphasis on what is generally called a "rejecting mother." The role of other relatives in producing similar situations has been greatly neglected. This is due partly to the fact that the child's contact with his mother is generally far more intensive than his relation to others. Furthermore, since mothers are often inclined to feel guilty whenever something is wrong with their children, they invite the educators and psychologists to put the blame on them. Last but not least, there seems to be a tendency in persons working with children to identify with them and to express some of their own grudges against their own mothers in terms of mothers in general. As a matter of fact, pure rejection on the part of a mother is an extremely rare phenomenon. More frequent is a deep clash between the needs of the child and the needs of the mother in which, from the viewpoint of the child at least, the mother emerges victorious. In cases of children who can already verbalize it becomes quite clear that they hold their mother fully responsible for any hardship they may incur. They tend to feel that their mother could bring about the alleviation of every tension if she only wanted to. This feeling is a direct descendant of the early experiences of hunger being satisfied at the appearance of the mother. Thus the mother comes to symbolize satisfaction and her absence lack of satisfaction. Imperceptibly, out of this simple feeling emerges the conviction that the mother's presence is identical with her approval, with her love of the child, and that her absence is indicative of the opposite. On the other hand, the mother's disapproval signifies a threat of leaving the child, and with it comes the threat of loss of satisfaction. Thus the mother's disapproval becomes enlarged to mean a far greater rejection than is felt by the mother. Long before language develops the baby studies the mother and learns to recognize her feelings. Facial expression is scrutinized, as indicated earlier in the paper. Also such subtle differences as the difference in tonus of the mother's arms when she picks up the baby, the rapidity or relative slowness of her movements, the pitch of her voice, are perceived. (Kestenberg, 1967a; see also Chapters 8 and 10). This is not accomplished by a conscious research into the mother's attitudes but develops from awareness of slight discomfort from being picked up differently from before and other such subtle occurrences. Worries of the mother find ready expression in the difficulties of tiny infants. Babies are fine thermometers of their mothers' feelings (Burlingham, 1935). It does not appear that any slight emotional upheaval of the mother is traumatic in itself. Where, however, there is a prolonged difficulty of this sort, the baby is traumatized. Any type of prolonged disturbance in the mother subjects the baby to prolonged frustrations. Every mother, like every individual, has some problems. A great number of mothers find it difficult to nurse a child. The fear of the primipara as to her ability to handle the baby is well known. There are individual differences in this too (Coleman *et al.*, 1953). One mother may fear that she will drop the tiny infant; another may be apprehensive as to the bath. One mother expressed her concern by asking: "What about my baby's emotional problem?" Underneath this remark was the feeling that she herself was nervous and was afraid that her baby would also be upset. The distaste for dirt is very common. No matter how enlightened and tolerant a mother may be, she may not be able to control her facial expression of disgust when she changes her baby's diapers. Others are disgusted by spitting, drooling, or vomiting. One mother was so sensitive to banging noises that she succeeded in preventing her baby from banging his spoon and cup while he was still in the high chair stage. When later he began to make up for this deprivation in babyhood and went through an orgy of banging plates on the table, the mother felt quite tortured by this practice. Enlightened pediatricians are keenly aware of such problems in mothers and stand ready for reassurance. They become mediators between the mother and child and smooth out their relationship. It is impossible to cover all difficulties of this sort which do not pertain to a general clash between the mother and the child but are limited to special problems. A few may be mentioned. Some mothers, generally even-tempered, lose their poise when their babies are sick. This may be due to a number of reasons. It is not always a reaction to the mother's hostility toward the child. A much more frequent cause for such anxiety is the mother's problem in relation to her own mother. Can she have a baby too or is this a privilege of her mother only? Can she take care of a baby properly or is this only her mother's prerogative? When the child is sick, it almost indicates that she should not have become a mother. Sometimes the mother identifies the infant with her own body and her own bodily fears become intensified when the baby is indisposed (see Chapters 1 and 3). In still other cases the child represents a compensation for all shortcomings in the mother. If something is wrong with him she begins to feel inferior all over again. A variation of overconcern with sickness is the exaggeration of preventive measures. Some parents, for example, worry unduly about their child not being sufficiently covered or clothed, both during the day and the night. Apart from sometimes overheating the baby, they unwittingly hamper his freedom of movement and make him uncomfortable. Without giving further examples I should like to point out the common denominator of the problems quoted above. In all of them it is an isolated difficulty of a parent which leads to the frustration of the child around one specific situation. The child frustrated in this one particular area develops associated fears. As an infant he becomes tense whenever he is disturbed in a special way, later he becomes afraid of similar circumstances.

Far more serious, because it envelops the whole personality structure of the child, is a clash between mother and child concerning everything that is going on. The mother's and the child's temperaments do not synchronize. Their personal rhythms differ greatly. Every little action is a source of difficulty. The child is too slow for the mother, or too quick, and vice versa. The natural rhythm of the child is constantly disturbed by the mother. She wakes him in order to feed him and is not ready to nurse him when he is hungry and cries. When he needs her most she is not there, and she wants him to smile and appreciate her when he is busy with something else. Modern pediatricians and psychologists emphasize the rhythm of sleep and feeding which the infant regulates himself and in which he feels most comfortable (Aldrich and Aldrich, 1944). Such a self-regulating schedule is most desirable for all functions of the infant. The environment should be adjusted to it. Where it can be carried through, the parents will be rewarded by the ability of the child to adjust to their demands when he reaches the toddler stage. Naturally it is much easier for the mother and the household to subject the infant to the routine arranged by adults than to adjust themselves to that geared to him. Household routines and habits of the adult members of the family constantly interfere with the infant's needs. Frustrations, such as waiting for some things, are unavoidable and sometimes have great constructive value in helping the child to recognize reality and its limitations. However, if such frustrations occur too early and too frequently, the child's relatively weak resources are not sufficient to cope with such a multitude of disagreeable situations. While in the cases discussed earlier a fear may develop around a certain aspect of life, babies subjected to constant frustrations in every sphere of life sometimes become unable to face reality easily and become restricted in their basic personality. They develop into inhibited individuals who have difficulty in coping with the little things which cause no concern to normal individuals. In some cases they escape into pleasant daydreams rather than face everyday tasks such as dressing, eating, washing, and going to school. In other cases they remain babyish, unwilling to take the risk of growing up. Their walking, their speech, their evaluation of dangers may be retarded considerably. Fortunately such a deep clash between mother and child, which envelops almost every daily happening, is a rare phenomenon. However, a similar result is obtained where the mother's urge to adjust to the child's needs is obstructed. This is sometimes due to the attitude of the father. He may actively discourage the mother from "giving in" to the child. He may be jealous of her attention to the child and interfere because of it. In some cases his own wish to be a mother is so strong that he makes it impossible for his wife to take care of the baby. Where he steps into her shoes and really takes over, he is unable to mother the child as well as a real mother can despite his great wish to do so. Interference by other relatives, especially by the mother's mother, occasionally spoils the pleasure of motherhood. Everything such a handicapped mother does is criticized by the husband, mother, or mother-in-law. If she wants to pick up her baby because he is crying, someone immediately tells her that this is not good for the baby. When she feeds him, one of the relatives volunteers the information that she does not know how to hold him. When she helps him in his effort to sit up, she is informed that this will undoubtedly curve his spine. If she permits him to suck his thumb, dire results are predicted by the solicitous onlooker. If the mother is attached to the interfering person, she is kept in continuous irritation which in turn produces frustration in the baby or else causes the mother to withdraw from the care of the child. Where nurses are employed in the care of the baby, there is not only the well-known difficulty resulting from a change of personnel handling the child, but also the frequent clash between the nurse and the mother brings about tense situations for the baby. In the first instance the baby who has become accustomed to one kind of handling has to readjust to another, and perhaps soon to a third type of care. He may become cranky, unhappy or retarded in his achievements, or else he may develop into an indifferent person, unable to form any permanent attachments. Where there is a clash between family members or the nurse and the mother as to the care of the baby, the child becomes involved in the discord. The persons taking care of him are tense, there is often a delay in satisfying his need, and the type of handling changes several times during the day.

Apart from such chronic or recurrent disturbances in the baby's rhythm or routine there are one-time traumata which occur during infancy, such as sudden weaning, necessitated by the mother's illness, sicknesses, accidents and operations of the child, and sudden departures of mothers or nurses. These traumata, however, seem to be less damaging than continuous frustrations. The child has a tendency to react to traumata. The infant has, of course, fewer means at his disposal than the older child who, after a traumatic incident, plays about it as long as he needs to in order to master it *a posteriori*. The infant, on the other hand, takes advantage of opportunities to make up for the injury. He may suck his thumb more vigorously or cry for days after the trauma. In a way he consoles himself. If he is freely permitted to do so, he may in his own way digest the trauma. However, if his own methods of coping with the trauma are interfered with, a readiness for tension and later for fear in connection with the anticipated trauma remains. In the continuous frustrations to which some babies are subjected, they are not given time to console themselves for one frustration, since the next one follows too quickly. It is likely that in these situations inhibitions rather than tendencies toward motor discharge develop. It goes without saying that no one child uses exclusively inhibitions or discharge patterns. All children use both methods. However, there may be a greater trend toward one reaction rather than the other.

Both inhibition and motor discharge are basic attitudes upon which a superstructure of defensive and nondefensive coping mechanisms are built. Inhibition need not lead to cessation of movement; it may delay, diminish, or help reverse the impact or course of movement. Thus, it becomes the motor counterpart and model for reaction formation, denial, isolation, repression, intellectualization (Fenichel, 1928), as well as for concentrated attention and internalization. Motor discharge implies a continuity of motion, on which are based such mechanisms as displacement, turning from passivity to activity, acting out, identification with the aggressor, as well as coping with reality and externalization.

NOTES

[1]By "small children" is meant children under three or four. The very fact that the word fear is used throughout indicates that only children who have attained sufficient maturity to be able to develop fear are included in this study. Occasional reference to children over four whose main problem is castration fear will be made only to show the links between the early fears and castration fear. Castration fear itself does not come within the limits of this discussion.

A PREVIEW: FORMS OF EXPRESSION AND ORGANIZATION IN DEVELOPMENT.

In the study of development we are concerned with the progression from early to later developmental structures and with the way this progression is organized in discrete developmental phases. The basic forms of reacting by attunement or clashing through motor discharge or its inhibition were outlined in the two preceding chapters. Throughout subsequent chapters phase development will be highlighted by emphasizing insights gained from the study of:

1. Motility as prototype and expression of mental functioning
2. Organization of developmental progression from states of disequilibrium to stabilization of structure

I

The problems involved in the correlation of nonverbal expressions of mental functioning has been stated by Laban in a succinct way:

> It is perhaps not too bold to introduce here the idea of thinking in terms of movement as contrasted with thinking in words . . . for a long time man has been unable to find the connection between his movement-thinking and his word-thinking (1960, pp. 17 and 19).

The two systems, the nonverbal and the verbal, supplement and reinforce one another.

There are periods in development when needs, drives, coping mechanisms, self-expression, and alliance with objects converge to serve a new developmental task—these periods being singled out as developmental phases. In studying them from the beginning of postnatal life, we cannot help but be concerned with the way motor apparatus are put into the service of developing mental structures.

In psychoanalysis we systematically extrapolate hidden meaning regarding mental patterning from verbal productions. In contrast, when we seek information regarding nonverbal behavior we discover or corroborate our findings by way of intuition. Freud's (1905) attempt to explain the means by which we understand movement and Deutsch's (1953) ingenious insight into the meaning of postures is yet to be pursued further by psychoanalytic researchers. Seeking to find connection between movement-thinking and word-thinking, psychoanalysts tend to translate man's gestures and facial expressions into the framework of verbal communication.

Students of movement have long been aware that language and motility are different means of self-expression and cannot substitute for one another. However, both systems are accessible to codification, decoding, and interpretation, and each of them, in its own way, can be used to make inferences regarding the nature of mental functioning. Both systems undergo developmental changes: Speech evolves from the infant's cry and vocalizations to the formation of words and sentences; movement evolves from rhythmic alterations of tension and body-shape to effort and spatial shaping, the motion factors used for coping with the environment and with objects (Bartenieff, 1962, 1970; Bartenieff and Davis, 1971; Laban and Lawrence, 1947; Lamb, 1961; Kestenberg, 1965, 1967a, 1973a).

Without a systematic classification of these movement patterns, students of early mother-child interaction have been confronted with two obstacles, each difficult to overcome. The first has been that, in comparing the adult behavior of the mother with that of the infant, one could not specify in what way attunement and mutual adjustment were accomplished and how these patterns differed from motor manifestations through which the mother acted as the infant's auxiliary ego. The second obstacle concerned the problem of outlining the differences in the child's modes of achieving specific developmental tasks at successive stages, when the data on which conclusions must be based have been of a different order. The verbal productions of the older child could not be compared wth the nonverbal behavioral characteristics of the infant. One needed to study the development of motor patterns in order to be able to compare data derived from infant motility with those pertaining to changes in motility in later phases of development. If movement profiles, derived from different developmental phases were to be made available, it would be necessary to find a means of interpreting them within the framework of metapsychology. This would enable us to find a connection between "movement-thinking and word-thinking."

With this aim in mind we spent many years inventing new and modifying old methods of movement notation and scoring in the process of constructing a movement profile that would allow for a comparison of the distribution of movement patterns in infants, children, and adults. We found that it was possible to correlate our findings with most of the items contained in Anna Freud's (1965) developmental assessment; however, the problem of how to make the new insights about development understandable and credible without explaining in great detail the methods by which we attain them has been a difficult obstacle to overcome. No one can duplicate our method of assessment without the knowledge gained from feeling it in one's body through movement and without time and effort spent learning the technique involved. We can only hope that through the convergence of our findings with those of other research groups, we can arrive at a shared conviction without the necessity of describing the technical details of our method. In this spirit, we introduce our views on development as we have derived them from our movement studies.

In Chapter 8, we describe the basic movement patterns whose extrapolation from motor behavior has played a decisive role in our understanding of the developmental tasks that the child accomplishes, with the aid of his mother, before the age of three. Excerpts from Mahler's discussion of our work are added to exemplify the "complementing value of psychoanalytically oriented developmental research" and to show what agreement can be reached by students of development who work with different methodologies.

The assumptions made about the development of self- and object-representations in Chapter 9 are based on Mahler's work and on data derived from psychoanalyses of young children. Rooted as they are in our special way of looking at clinical material—through the eyes of a movement observer—and evaluated as they are—from the psychoanalyst's point of view—these assumptions become more meaningful as a result of the perusal of Chapter 8.

Chapter 10 recapitulates briefly what was said about the correlation of basic movement patterns with psychological development in infancy, and extends the scope of the achievement of specific developmental tasks in childhood. Most of the preceding chapters have provided some justification for focusing on an inner-genital phase as a separate entity that must be distinguished from the phallic phase of development. Chapter 10 contains a documentation of this view, on the basis of data gleaned from movement studies and psychoanalyses. In extending this type of correlation up through the stage of latency, it is interesting to note that there are inferences from movement observation which yield new points of view regarding the balance of synthesis and isolation and about the special features of the superego during the latency period. A study of Chapter 10 will prepare the reader for the emphasis on transitions into and out of latency which is the theme of the subsequent chapter on latency. It might also be suggested that the reader refer back to Chapter 10 in order to gain a better understanding of adolescent rhythmicity and of the achievment of community spirit as the developmental task of adolescence contained in Chapters 17 and 18, which conclude this volume.

Finally, we must stress that our study of movement is only a beginning of understanding the body as "the instrument through which man communicates and expresses himself " (Laban, 1950, p. 56) and the messenger "of ideas and emotions which surpass thoughts expressible in words" (p. 156). We have not gone beyond Freud's definition of motor discharge as " . . . a means of unburdening the mental apparatus of accretions of stimuli, [and] which had carried out this task by sending innervations into the interior of the body [leading to expressive movements and the play of features and to manifestations of affect]," and had become "converted into *action*," once it could be employed in the "appropriate alterations of reality" (1911, p. 221). We have, however, made these and other forms of motility accessible to closer scrutiny and quantification. We have classified motor discharge in terms of tension- and shape-flow; the action, used in the appropriate alterations of reality, has been classified by Laban as "effort" (1947).

II

Through the use of developmental assessments we can characterize each phase in terms of a specific profile. We can observe which patterns are used more than others, which are intensifying or becoming more clearly differentiated. We can further observe how different patterns act upon each other, clashing or combining into more complex units. By comparing profiles from earlier to those of later developmental phases, we can assess the progress made and infer by what means it has been achieved. This enables us to discover not only which patterns are dominant but also what type of organization prevails in specific developmental phases.

If we subsume under "development" the processes of growth, differentiation, integration, and consolidation, we are mindful that these trends are continuous and thus operative in each phase. Nevertheless one of these developmental trends predominates over others in specific periods of development. Phases of predominant growth and differentiation may be followed by a disequilibrium from which there emerges a reintegration of various already differentiated but not yet coordinated patterns. A regression may initiate a period of consolidation of structures which become reinstated and settled (Kestenberg, 1963).

Attempts to correlate motor and psychic development suggested to us a division of consecutive phases in accordance with prevailing organizations. The following classification of developmental phases is implied in Chapters 8 and 9 and used in part in Chapters 10 and 11, 13, 14,

15, 17, and 18:

1. *Neonatal phase* which begins with a disequilibrium (the genital crisis of the newborn) that is followed by a progressive integration of functions
2. *Pregenital phases* (oral, anal, urethal), each subdivided into periods of growth and differentiation
3. *Inner-genital preoedipal phase* which begins with a disequilibrium that is followed by reintegration of functions to a higher level
4. *Phallic-oedipal phase* in which exuberant growth is followed by differentation
5. *Latency,* a phase of consolidation of previous gains, initiated by a regression
6. *Prepuberty,* a revival of the early inner-genital phase which begins with a diffusion that is followed by a reintegration of functions and structures
7. *Puberty* in which growth is followed by differentiation
8. *Preadult* phase of consolidation, initiated by regression

Developmental phases are discussed from various points of view and not all phases are considered in each chapter. For instance Chapter 8, which attempts to correlate psychic and motor development before the age of three emphasizes the differentiation of phase-specific tasks in pregenital phases. Chapters 9 and 11 cover all the phases from different clinical points of view while Chapter 10 gives a survey of psychomotor development within the framework of prevailing organization trends up to and including latency. A full discussion of organizations in successive phases of adolescence is contained in Chapters 14, 15, 17, and 18.

The study of rhythms from which we could infer the distribution of drives in a given individual in a given phase (Chapters 8 and 10; Kestenberg, 1965), prompted us to formulate the following propositions regarding the organizations in specific phases;

An increase in libidinal modes of discharge spurs on growth and an increase in aggression enhances differentiation (Hartman, 1939). In all phases in which prevailing growth is followed by prevailing differentiation there is at first a prevalence of libidinal discharge forms over aggressive forms and later the opposite is true.

In transition from one phase to the next, we frequently see an increase of genital discharge forms. This occurs, for instance, in transition from the oral to the anal and from the anal to the urethral phase. It seems that a mild influx of genitality counteracts the aggression generated at the end of a phase.

We have also observed that an increase in inner-genital impulses initiates states of disequilibrium which, however, are followed by periods of integration with other discharge forms (Chapters 10, 13).

Recovery from regression through sublimation is conducive to consolidation of old and newly acquired structures (see Chapters 10, 11, 17, and 18).

None of these propositions has been taken up directly or elaborated upon. They are enumerated here as a sample of what may be inferred from the study of motility regarding organizations and as an introduction to the specific descriptions of developmental phases that follow.

CHAPTER 8

Development of the Young Child as Expressed Through Bodily Movement, I

Coauthored by Hershey Marcus, M.D.; Esther Robbins, M.D.; Jay Berlowe, M.D.; and Arnhilt Buelte

In the newborn we can already discern two distinct mechanisms of self-regulation, which we have subsumed under the headings of: (1) *Flow of Tension* and (2) *Flow of Shape*. In this chapter we shall define the elements and attributes of these basic movement patterns, and will only allude to other movement categories without specifying them. This will serve as a springboard for an introductory presentation of the manner in which the study of movement patterns has enriched our understanding of development.

The Flow of Tension

When we refer to a movement pattern, we specify readily observable physical behavior. We do not look upon movement as a substitute for words. Neither do we try to discern content in a movement. We acknowledge that anxiety promotes tension, but we do not equate them.

This paper was first published in *J. Amer Psa. Assoc.*, 10:746–63, 1971. Slightly revised, it is reproduced here by permission.

When we speak of changes in the flow of tension in various parts of the body, we mean "muscle tension."

The simplest explanation for changes in muscle tension is the physiological interplay between agonist and antagonist muscle groups. A *free flow of tension* occurs when agonists are not met with counteraction by antagonists. The constraint in movement, called *bound flow of tension*, occurs when antagonists contract along with the agonistic muscles. In addition to the two basic elements of tension (free and bound flow), we can observe variations in such attributes of tension as frequency of change, degree of intensity, and rate of increase or decrease of tension *(Intensity Factors)* (Kestenberg, 1965).

The newborn infant's toes stiffen periodically in bound flow. His legs fling and bicycle in spurts of free flow. An influx of suddenly emerging free flow may bring his fist near his mouth, and the ensuing bound flow may enable him to hold his fist there for a brief moment. Soon, however, the repetition of free flow derails the hand. In every movement of child and adult alike, one can detect a regularly occurring alternation between free and bound flow of tension, as well as a repetition of their attributes, i.e., evenness or fluctuation of levels, high or low intensity, abrupt or gradual change of tension. This highly differentiated self-regulation is already present in the newborn.

The Flow of Shape

The shape of the body changes during movement. It grows and shrinks as does the simple configuration of the amoeba when it extends its pseudopodia and retracts them (Laban, 1960). We change our shape by alternately growing and shrinking as we inhale and exhale. We grow as we take in and shrink when we expel waste. We grow toward pleasant stimuli and shrink away from noxious ones. Spontaneous and reflexive rooting is based on the mechanism of changing one's body shape in response to a stimulus, be it internal or external. We use the terms "growing" and "shrinking," coined by Laban (1950), in preference to words which denote psychic functioning such as "turning to, advancing, turning away, and withdrawing."

Growing and *shrinking of body shape* are the basic elements of *shape-flow*. They alternate periodically. In addition one can also observe alternation in the attributes of shape-flow which we have called *"Dimensional Factors"* (Kestenberg, 1967a). They occur in specific dimensions (width, length, and depth of the body). For instance, in the upper part of the infant's body we observe narrowing when hand and mouth meet, and we notice widening when they move apart. We perceive how the baby's body lengthens when he extends his legs. His body shortens when his legs move toward the abdomen during bicycling. When the infant seizes the nipple, his mouth bulges (protrudes). Hollowing occurs when milk is being propelled back toward the larynx.

This rhythmic alternation between growing and shrinking and their dimensional attributes is another highly differentiated self-regulation. It provides a structure for the organism's interaction with the environment.

Affinity (Coordination) of Tension-Flow with Shape-Flow

Rhythms of tension-flow serve need satisfaction such as sucking, defecating, or urinating. With the onset of psychic functioning, the tension-flow apparatus is used for drive discharge in such a way that oral, anal, urethral, and genital drives find their expression in appropriate motor rhythms.

Rhythms of shape-flow give structure to changes in tension, by providing patterns for interaction with need-satisfying or frustrating stimuli and objects. With the onset of psychic functioning, the shape-flow apparatus is used for finding the drive object and for "losing" it when it is no longer needed. In later development, tension-flow and shape-flow are controlled by more advanced movement patterns, which are directed by the ego (Kestenberg, 1965, 1967a; Chapter 10).

In normal development there is an optimal correspondence between phase-specific drives and phase-specific objects. (Freud, A., 1965). The oral suckling seeks a feeding, giving mother, and the anal toddler wants his "training" mother not only to clean him but also generally assist him in his undertakings. It is noteworthy that rhythms of tension-flow which serve phase-specific drive discharge are closely related to corresponding shape-flow rhythms which are used in interaction with phase-specific objects.

We learn from movement studies that there is not only a correspondence between specific drives and specific objects, but also a correspondence between certain feeling tones and modes of expression. For instance, annoyance is expressed appropriately through the narrowing of the brow in frowning, while pleasure of recognition broadens the face in smiling. When certain attributes of tension-flow (intensity factors) are used at the same time as their counterparts in shape (dimensional factors), groundwork is laid not only for harmony between feelings and self-

197

expression, but also for conflict-free learning of new skills (Kestenberg, 1973a).

Over and above the biological affinity of free flow with growing of body shape and bound flow with shrinking, there is a more complex affinity of specific tension and shape variations. We note a hierarchic ascendancy in the development of control over the following combinations of tension and shape qualities:

1. a. Stabilizing the tension-level at a certain intensity and narrowing of body shape, as exemplified in the solemnly poised, narrow frame of the infant who has learned to hold his hand in his mouth.
   b. Adjusting of the tension level in adaptation to the widening of shape, as seen in the infant who has become capable of changing his position from prone to supine and is pleased with his new achievement.
2. a. Increasing the intensity of tension and shortening of the body, as seen in the concentrated self-containment of the older infant, who strains while stooping.
   b. Decreasing the intensity of tension and lengthening of the body, as seen in the quiet pleasure and demeanor of the infant who has learned to stand without pulling and straining.
3. a. Changing the intensity of tension abruptly and hollowing at the waist, as seen when the impatiently running toddler becomes capable of breaking his fall after he has stumbled.
   b. Changing the intensity of tension gradually and bulging out, as seen in the wistful contentment of the toddler, who has learned to climb stairs by pulling himself up step by step.

At first the infant is incapable of choosing the right combinations. Instead of poising his movement in bound flow, when he narrows and his hand nears his mouth, he may overshoot in free flow and bypass his mouth. Instead of flowing freely and gradually when he bulges out for inhaling, he may suddenly stiffen and hold his breath. Under his mother's tutelage, he will learn to integrate his motor patterns into biologically advantageous, expressive, and functional combinations which will form the basis for the successive development of his ego functions.

The Neonatal Phase

The developmental task of this phase calls for the achievement of *integration* of various patterns and their unification in functional adaptive sets. The mother acts as the organizer of this undertaking (Spitz, 1959). By helping the child to use his innate equipment in consonance with her own, she provides him with models for the coordination of tension-flow and shape-flow (Call, 1968).

In contrast to the experienced mother, a novice may not be able to attune to her infant's tension-flow rhythms or help him to attune to hers. She may become anxious each time the child loses his grip on the nipple. Her fear can cause such an overall tension that it may flock the flow of milk from the breast. By clashing with the infant's sucking rhythm the mother prevents him from achieving satisfaction. On the other hand, though she may attune to him in tension-flow rhythms, a young mother may fail to adjust to the infant's shape-flow. She may, for instance, in bending forward touch the child's left cheek at the time when his right cheek touches her breast during sucking. This initiates rooting to the left and release of the nipple. At times a mother cannot tolerate the slight separation of bodies that occurs when the infant shrinks away slightly during swallowing. Instead of shrinking away from him to facilitate deglutition, she may grow toward him, pushing the nipple deep into his mouth, squirting milk into it and causing the baby to choke or regurgitate.

The average new mother learns from her infant and allows the infant to learn from her. When he grows toward her, she grows toward him, using free flow and adjusting the degree of tension release in a finely modulated manner. When he shrinks away a bit, she shrinks from him, using bound flow evenly to ensure that he does not lose hold of the nipple. The baby fingers her breast and her back, using a rhythm similar or identical with the one he uses for sucking. This helps his mother to feel his mode of discharge throughout her body. When she changes position, he may squirm a bit until he finds a new nook for his most comfortable nursing shape. Through mutual attunement and harmonizing, the mother-child couple create the dual unity of the symbiotic relationship which characterizes the incipient oral phase (Mahler, 1968b). Mother and child relate and adjust through feelings of sameness or difference, but they are not yet able to communicate.

Oral Phase

The establishment of a primary system of *communication* is the *developmental task* of the oral phase. It replaces primary identification of the neonatal phase (Jacobson, 1964). By gaining control over oral rhythms of tension-flow and corresponding changes in shape-flow, the infant be-

199

comes partially independent of his mother and can erect the first edition of his body image. The oral body-ego serves prehension and release (introjection and projection). From it there evolves an oral ego organization in which attention and exploration of inner and outer space become the basis for the initial stage (see note 3) of object constancy. Only when self and object can be recognized as separated in space, can there be communication instead of communing.

Control Over Oral Forms of Tension- and Shape-Flow

The oral sucking rhythm is characterized by smooth transitions from free to bound flow. This rhythm is not only used for sucking but also for patting, rubbing, opening and closing of hands, and repetitious vocalization. The oral rhythm has a soothing quality. In contrast, the oral-sadistic rhythm (Abraham, 1924), is jerky and jarring. It has sharp transitions between free and bound flow and may also have the quality of holding through use of an even level of tension. It can be seen in biting, snapping, grasping and releasing, banging, and jerky rocking.

By gaining control over free and bound flow, the infant learns to initiate and stop these activities. By gaining control over the maintenance of certain tension levels and over adjustments of tension, and by combining them with affine shape-flow attributes, the infant becomes capable of communicating through gestures or facial expressions. Narrowing his brow and mouth and using a correspondingly even level of tension-flow to maintain this facial configuration, the infant creates the frown of disapproval. Widening his whole face in combination with finely modulated adjustments of tension, he produces various shades of smiling which successively denote feelings which adults interpret as: "I know you," "I am so happy," or "I won't cry, I'll smile." Through control of tension-flow the infant turns over from back to front and vice versa. In crawling he learns to coordinate his shape with the shape of things around him. Through these new controls over affects and skills, the infant progresses from the symbiotic-oral subphase to the oral-sadistic subphase in which drive differentiation is matched by differentiation between self and objects (Mahler, 1963).

Generally speaking, the oral sucking rhythms promote union with the object. In contrast, oral-sadistic biting rhythms serve separation and severing. When sucking rhythms predominate in the early oral phase, the attunement with the mother reaches its peak. At the time the child begins to bite his mother, she usually disengages herself from the dual unity. When she initiates distance feeding by placing him in a high chair for meals, he can accept this separation, because he has already acquired some self-reliance in distance from his mother's body.

200

The Oral Body Ego

The young infant who sucks after feeding tries to reestablish the feeling of unity with his mother by bringing his mouth and fingers close together through narrowing his shape (Kris, 1951). He maintains this position by poising his hand in evenly bound flow which prevents derailment. Alone in his crib, he creates conditions for sucking similar to those his mother had created, similar but not the same. When his mother reappears, he recognizes her by the "sameness" of her individual rhythms of tension- and shape-flow. He gradually begins to recognize himself by the "sameness" of his movement patterns, which are similar to those of his mother but not identical. In moments of complete synchronization and attunement with maternal rhythms, he loses the budding feeling of separateness. To regain his lost boundaries, he stiffens in the periphery of his body and interrupts the symbiotic fusion at will. In the words of Mahler (1968b) he "hatches." To do so, he creates his own hard shell of outer muscle tension.

At first the baby's uncertain body image encompasses the dual unity of the nursing couple. This image grows when the child is united with the mother and shrinks when he is alone and does not need her anymore. Such a fluctuating body image may veer from a feeling of being wide "as the whole world" to a feeling of being narrow "fenced in and all alone." The rhythmically fluctuating body image of the early oral phase is as labile as the anaclitic relationship to the need-satisfying object.

Once the infant gains control over narrowing and widening and over holding tension on an even keel (remaining quiet) and readjusting tension (settling himself), he can also master the rhythm of prehension and release. His hands substitute for his mother. Thus they gain a double representation: of belonging to his body as well as to the space into which they grow and reach. As mediators between the early "self " and the world of "not self" around him, the arms and hands become the foremost tools of the oral body ego (Hoffer, 1949, 1950; Almansi, 1964).

Through the interplay of growing and shrinking, of reaching and scooping, scattering and gathering (Laban, 1950), there develops between mother and child a *prehension-release* system. When, instead of enlarging himself by growing toward the mother, the infant reaches for her, or when, instead of narrowing to achieve union between mouth and hand, the infant puts things from "out there" into his mouth ("in here"), he becomes totally prehensile. Even his trunk and feet serve this purpose. The infant's oral body ego is functionally prehensile. From this early organization there emerge scanning, exploring, comprehending, and communicating.

201

Oral Ego Organization

Staring at his hands, exploring them, and playing with them, the infant makes them "his own." Hands gradually take over the exploring (tasting) qualities of the mouth. What was once widening of the body, which brought the hand passively into "reach space," becomes a differentiated approach. When the infant reaches out laterally, it almost seems that his mouth has sent his hand out to probe. What was once narrowing of the body, which brought mouth and hand together, becomes an action guided by eyes and tongue. The discriminating hand and the sensitive fingertips combine with the mouth to appraise, to savor, or spit out.

At first fingers and tongue explore each other and enjoy one another, so to speak. When teeth appear, fingers and tongue work together. The tongue pushes, and the fingers press. What hands learn in the oral cavity, they use outside of the mouth. Under the guidance of his eyes, hands transpose the child's actions from the confined space of the mouth ("the inner space") into the much wider, "outer space." The oral cavity is projected into the "outer cavity" which encloses the infant's whole body. For some time to come, the tongue will, from inside the mouth, direct and shape the movement outside.[1] The tongue will guide while hands try out and feel. Their trial actions are used as adjuncts of thought before ideation becomes independent of movement.

The tasting-licking tongue, the greedy eyes, and grabbing hands, all participate in the exploration of the horizontal plane of space, the table—or feeding—plane. In this plane the child interacts with the mother and with the objects she places before him. He takes and he gives, feeding from his mother's hands and putting things from his hands into her mouth.

Exploring primarily in the horizontal plane, the infant makes channeled pathways through space and learns to twist and wind around objects. He pays *attention* at first by staring with uniform tension. Then he learns to let his attention wander in free flow. Eventually he becomes capable of directing his attention or seeking and following through indirect pathways.[2] He explores by enclosing small areas of space, and he spreads himself through space to get the feel of its expanse. He familiarizes himself with the concepts of "here" and "there" as well as "not here" and "not there."

By recognizing *outer space* as a medium that separates him from objects, the infant defines his location in the "near" space and the location of objects in the "reach space." Once things get near to him ("here they are") they easily become part of him. Watching for his mother in the exact point of space at which she disappeared from sight, he not only begins to develop the concept of permanence of things in space (Piaget, 1937), but also the feeling of spatial constancy of the drive-object and of the object-seeking self (Kestenberg, 1967a and b). Thus, the need-satisfying object of the early oral phase is elevated to the status of a constant object (Freud, A., 1965). *Object constancy in space*[3] connotes that the object cathexis is controlled by the ego's internalized images of location and distance. Locating the mother internally reflects the child's capacity to bridge distance and make external space a medium of *communication* with his mother (Lamb, 1961; Ramsden, 1973).

Transition to the Anal Phase

In the second part of the first year, anal twisting and straining rhythms vie with oral sucking and biting rhythms (Kestenberg, 1966). Beginning with head control, antigravity muscles gradually attain a degree of tension which enables the infant to rise from the prone to the erect position. His interest shifts from the upper, prehensile, to the lower, stabilizing, part of his body. He discovers his legs and trunk and transforms them from prehensile to supportive tools. When he crawls even his hands become stabilizers instead of scoopers.

Extending his whole length into the vertical plane of space, the child begins to gain control over various intensities of tension. At first he strains to stand up. As he masters the pull of gravity, he needs to use less and less tension to keep himself erect without holding on. When he lowers himself and squats to play with things on the floor, he distinguishes more and more between little bits of things he picks up, and the big, heavy toys he pushes, pulls, and lifts. More and more, he recognizes things by the way they feel and by appraising what they are instead of merely knowing where they are. He discovers new objects and new body parts, his own and his mother's. Sometimes, the anal phase proper begins when he can create a transitional object. This helps him to retain the "feel" of various parts of the body, upper and lower, his own and his mother's (Winnicott, 1953). He cannot yet present his wants without the aid of concrete objects, neither can he yet represent them in the form of symbols.

Anal Phase

The developmental task of the anal phase is to attain a basis for *presenting oneself and objects* and for *representing them* in meaningful ideational content. The success in this task depends on the degree to which the infant can gain control over anal rhythms of tension-flow and their counterparts in shape-flow.

Control Over Anal Tension- and Shape-Flow

In their purest form, anal twisting rhythms are seen in contractions of the anus, but they are used quite frequently in other parts of the body as well. Characteristic for these rhythms are small adjustments of intensity, and preference for smoothness and low tension. This makes for gentleness which mitigates the sharp quality of biting rhythms. Through the use of anal rhythms, the fussy, teething baby transforms himself into a pleasant companion, who plays peek-a-boo and waves "bye-bye." He uses the same delicate mechanisms of tension control for adjusting to new positions, and for picking up small things with pincer movements.

When anal-sadistic straining rhythms begin to predominate, the child frequently pulls himself up by using high intensity of tension. He remains on an even level of tension for some time, then limps and falls or lets himself down. In typical anal-sadistic holding-expelling rhythms, he holds objects for a while and then throws them down. He learns to coordinate high tension with squatting (shortening of the body) and low tension with lengthening of the body. These sets of patterns are important for the acquisition of skills, for control over defecation, and control over affects as well. His body must remain tensed up when he squats and plays with toys, or else he will lose balance and topple over. Pressing while sitting down and releasing to get up, when pressing is no longer needed, is a coordinated set of tension- and shape-flow used during defecation. Gaining control over similar sets of patterns in body and face enables the toddler to display emotions like an actor. He not only can show how big or small he is, but also how happy or how angry he can get.

The preponderance of holding-expelling types of rhythms colors the toddler's total behavior. He holds onto his mother's legs, and unaccountably abandons her as if expelling her from his sight and touch. His mother must be there when he collapses from overdoing things. She must let him go when he needs to be on his own. The toddler needs a lot of time by himself in order to gain control over anal rhythms and get the feel of himself as an independent unit.

The Anal Body Ego

Standing a long time in a one-piece, erect position, the child feels that he is a steady, solid unit of resistance. He learns to stiffen on the periphery instead of holding on to things. He learns to stiffen inside to control his center of gravity. He holds himself up and he holds what is inside of him. Aligned in the vertical plane, he becomes part of the adult world. He seems to look down at the helpless things on the floor which cannot get up by themselves. Memories from the second year of life, obtained in the analysis of two- and three-year-old children, reveal that a child under two years of age frequently experiences his own falling as being thrown down, being expelled from his mother's arms and picked up again. No doubt, the more he gains control over his verticality, over shifts of weight, and over balance of trunk and limbs, the less he needs to throw things. The child under two years of age seems to think of his body as a solid vertical wall. When this wall collapses, the new firm body-image is in danger of dissolution. The child needs his mother's support to shield him at the right moment. When he feels capable of stabilizing himself again, he demands to be released at once. A harmonious mother-child couple develops a system of *stabilizing-releasing* (mobilizing) into which the previous prehension-release system is incorporated.

When he has to lie down alone in his bed, the toddler may lose the feeling of his whole body as being a unit of resistance against the pull of gravity. By using an object that has qualities of the upper and the lower part of his body as well as those of his holding mother (Winnicott, 1963), an object he can suck, taste, smell, lick, rub and twist, or squeeze and pluck, the toddler can reerect a functionally stabilizing and unifying body ego. From this early organization there emerge intentionality, evaluation, and confrontation on which presentation and symbolization are based (Lamb, 1961; Ramsden, 1973).

The Anal Ego Organization

Upon gaining control over various degrees of muscle tension and over the dimensions and directions (up and down) of the vertical plane, the child experiments with shifting his own weight as well as the weight of objects. By pushing, shoving, lifting, and throwing, he begins to differentiate between "heavy and light," "weak and strong" qualities. Experimenting with light touch and pressure, he evaluates textures; by lengthening and shortening, he evaluates sizes. In this manner objects become endowed with lasting qualities such as "big" or "strong." All objects are still related to the mother. In the oral phase the child felt that she put them "here" or "there." Now he feels that she made them "what" they are, firm or yielding, light or heavy, fluid or solid, rough or smooth. By gaining control over the weight of "this" and the size of "that," he makes them his own. When he discovers a new object, he lifts it high above his head to show it to his mother ("See that"). Her admiration makes the exhibited object a "thing of value," her disapproval makes it unworthy and expendable. In this manner all objects are in part transitional objects because they belong to mother and child (Winnicott, 1953; see Chapter 9). Knowing what are his body parts and what are objects gives the child a feeling of intentionality. He knows what he wants and he *confronts* his mother with a clear evidence of his *intent*.

At first the child may show what he wants through gestures and sound. Practicing stability and control over elimination, he may temporarily hold up word production, but he begins to *present* patterns which *symbolize* by representing. At first, he simply shows his mother what he did after he defecated. Then his grunts inform of his ongoing straining and expelling. At last he reproduces intentional grunts before he defecates, using a feature of his anal-sadistic rhythm to represent the intended activity and to let his mother know beforehand. He is becoming a reliable informant. Soon his capacity to present in the external world is matched by the capacity to represent internally. Not only sounds and words, but thoughts also become trial actions.

Once the child can create permanent symbols, he erects an image of his mother as an indestructible solid object, and he assumes the same qualities for himself. To constancy in space a *constancy in weight* (see note 3) is added. The anal toddler is highly ambivalent toward his mother. However, his ability to maintain "a positive inner image of his mother" (Freud, A., 1965) has advanced from the initial "internalized localization of the mother image" to a representation of the mother as a shaped *object* in space which is endowed with the quality of "belonging to the child" regardless of changes in his or her feeling tones. When the child becomes capable of internalizing the weight-volume qualities of objects, his ego begins to regulate object cathexis in accordance with lasting values. Through repeated shifts of weight and recoveries of balance in each new stance, he begins to recognize and accept those laws of gravity to which he must adjust. He compares relative weights and sizes and begins to attach value judgments to these aspects of reality. He begins to differentiate between the good and the bad, and he erects reaction formation to counteract self-devaluation. The newly acquired ego attitudes create a basis for the development of a set of values—the superego.

The anal toddler learns to show what he wants, but he is not yet able to decide and anticipate. He cannot carry out his intent in operations, and he still needs his mother to time, anticipate, and put order into his actions and thoughts. He himself will accomplish this only in the next phase, the urethral phase.

Transition to the Urethral Phase[4]

At the end of the second year the willful toddler becomes more pliable. His definite, rigid, anal-sadistic rhythms are mitigated by an influx of rhythms suitable for the discharge of passive urethral needs. *"Fluid,"* *"running"* types of changes in tension-flow are characterized by very gradually increasing and decreasing tension and by a smooth transition from free to bound flow. One moment the toddler will still strain, but the next moment he may allow his urine to drip out of him while he seems absentminded and dawdly. One moment he struts in self-importance, but the next moment he may linger. Playing at a distance from his mother, he still feels the need for "refueling" (Mahler and Furer, 1963). He comes close to his mother and lovingly lets himself go. He may place toys in her lap or settle in it himself (Mahler's [1963] "rapprochement").

The anal toddler's tenso- and morpho-static body image begins to give way to a new tenso- and morpho-mobile image.[5] Body boundaries become uncertain when the stable little fellow turns into a mobile and mobilizing entrepreneur. Even his patterns of defecation will change now. Instead of expelling feces, he may let go of them gradually or he may dribble them like urine. Conversely, he holds back urine, treating it like feces. He is confused. He not only wants to decide what to do and how to do it, he also wants to decide when to do it. But he is not yet capable of performing *timely* operations which have a definite beginning and a definite end (Lamb, 1961; Ramsden, 1973).

Urethral Phase

Development of the capacity for *operation* is the task of the urethral phase. This is accomplished when the child has gained control over urination and can master locomotion without interference from urethral needs. In the third year of life, the toddler changes from an aimless wanderer into a goal-directed initiator of games. He learns to control changes in urethral tension-flow and their counterparts in shape-flow. This helps him to become time-conscious, to gain initiative and make decisions as well as to anticipate people's reactions to his behavior.

Control Over Urethral Tension- and Shape-Flow

Urethral rhythms are characterized by a gradual rise and abatement of tension and by smooth transitions from free to bound flow. At first the child tries to control these rhythms by anal-sadistic holding and

207

straining.[6] Soon he will find out that urine cannot be treated as if it were feces. The flow of urine does not obey him, especially when he loses control over tension during sleep. In addition he enjoys flooding and being flooded. He savors the bulging fullness of his lower abdomen. He leads with it when he grows into space while giving into his propulsive wishes. He runs off, ahead of his mother, straight forward into the extension of his sagittal plane (the philobatic trend of Balint, M., 1959). He is in danger of hurting himself because he likes to run-walk and is unable to stop the free flow of his locomotor impulses. He yields to an inner mobility and loses himself in it. He is often falsely accused of being overactive because he moves so much and gets into everything. Not until urethral-sadistic types of tension-flow become dominant, can he arrest the flow of his movement and become master over it.

Urethral-sadistic rhythms are characterized by sharp transitions from free to bound flow. Frequently they start and end suddenly. When these rhythms prevail, the two-year-old enjoys stop-and-go games (such as opening and closing faucets, playing with switches, shooting and traveling games, squirting water and aiming) rather than passive immersions. As he practices in this manner he learns to bulge gradually when he initiates tension increases and to hollow when he suddenly stops with a jerk. As he gains control over the forward-backward dimension of the sagittal plane, he not only loves to run ahead of his mother, but also run away from her. He no longer thinks of himself as very steady and takes less pride in showing off what "he has got." Having become ambitious, he rather wants to show what he can do.

The Urethral Body Ego

The two-year-old loses the distinct and firm shape of the vertically aligned toddler. He is bubbling over with fluids, ideas, and words which threaten to burst or transcend his body boundaries. This promotes a feeling of advancing to his mother, whom he expects to find wherever he goes. He is dismayed when, running on and on, "he loses himself" as well as his mother (Freud, A., 1967a). He needs her to contain him, to dry his tears and pants, and to help him reestablish body boundaries by holding and patting him (Mahler *et al.,* 1965). His body image may grow out of bounds when he protrudes into space, reaching out and running into it. He becomes deflated when he has to stop and retreat, or to hollow instead of bulge. Soon, he begins to appreciate that his mobility shapes his body in a new way. His body image changes from a static to a mobile elastic unit. He may not only feel like a human locomotive, an animated choo-choo train or truck, but also like an agile "slinky" that proceeds in a magic way by changing its tension and size as well as its shape. When his body image becomes mobile after having been stable, he experiences his mother, too, as a mobile, jointed, shape-changing, displaceable object. Yet his mother is much better able to restabilize than he is. At the end of his run she contains him. When he leads, she follows, watching over his safety from a distance. She teaches him to stop and go in accordance with safety rules. As he gains control over timing, he enjoys the game of stopping and going, of shooting, aiming, falling and retreating, getting up and advancing. Yet he still needs his mother. Together they form a *mobilizing-containing* system of operation which incorporates the previous "prehension-release" and "stabilization-release (mobilizing)" systems. Not only does mother take him places, she also makes him rest before he is exhausted. The child seems to watch over his mother also. He pulls her to take him out and he points to a seat when he wants her to sit down "here and now." Venturing out on his own, he seems to feel that everything is due to his initiative. He makes everything move or stop. He pulls, he leaves things behind, he animates immobile objects and makes them run or stop as he wishes. The mobilizing quality of his body ego initiates a new ego organization. Timing becomes an ego function, and anticipation of sequence starts to bring secondary-process order into actions, words, and thoughts.

Urethral Ego Organization

When he takes *decisions* into his own hands, when he is capable of slowing down or hurrying up, the toddler becomes *time*-conscious. He begins to *anticipate* what will happen next, and his actions become goal directed. He starts a puzzle and finishes it without help. He guides toy trucks and trains to their delivery places and stations. He becomes an efficient little operator who gets things done, or pretends he has done them (denial in fantasy, Freud, A., 1936). He now can understand his mother's absence in terms of sequential events ("Mommy will be back after nap"). He develops a new type of object constancy, namely, *constancy in time* (see note 3). Having experienced "time" as a factor that governs his life, he now can endow his self- and object-representations with continuity in time. He and his mommy have a history, a yesterday, a present, and a tomorrow.

The two-and-a-half- or three-year-old has become an effective little fellow who can help or refuse help, can advance or retreat, initiate play or stop it. He can communicate, present his intent (inform), and operate (tell a short story or play a short game), all achievements dependent on his ability to maintain object-constancy in space, weight, and time. He has yet to learn to integrate these ego attitudes into meaningful behavioral phrases. Having gained control over each pregenital drive, he still needs to integrate them into his early infantile genitality (see Chapter 13). Having achieved object constancy in space, weight, and time, he still needs to integrate these part-functions into the complex but still dyadic relationship with his mother, which precedes triangular forms of relating. In a phase which has been called "inner-genital" his object constancy will remain mother-oriented and his relationship preoedipal until he leaves his babyhood behind and enters the world of oedipal relationships in the phallic-oedipal phase (see Chapter 10).

Excerpts from a Discussion
by Margaret Mahler, M. D.

New York Psychoanalytic Society Meeting, 2–23, 1971

Dr. Kestenberg's research has placed psychoanalytic observation in a truly new key. Without thorough familiarity with this "new key," I thought it would be most appropriate to use this opportunity to compare some of Dr. Kestenberg's research findings on a few points, chosen at random, with some of our own.

I feel that research work such as our own will gain immeasurably from complementation by consensually verifiable data that Dr. Kestenberg and her team's work has opened up. On the other hand, I shall point out in what follows a very few of the authors' many findings which our research appears to verify and thus render, I believe, ever so much more convincing.

I should like to highlight also some of the similar findings of developmental steps which we have conceptualized somewhat differently.

Finally, I cannot but suggest the great advantage that the efforts of such observational research by psychoanalysts like Dr. Kestenberg, ourselves, and several others may, with time, provide to supplement our present psychoanalytic metapsychology.

The aim of both Dr. Kestenberg's and our research has been identical: To decipher the meaning of preverbal phenomena and to draw valid inferences from these phenomena within the framework of psychoanalytic metapsychology. Our methods have, of course, been different.

Dr. Kestenberg's team devised an ingenious method—a kind of alphabet—whereby notation and study of the infant's body language alone allowed her far-reaching conclusions about his body image and id-ego development.

We, on the other hand, prejudiced as we were by our main hypothesis of the "symbiotic origin of human development," have used what I have called a bifocal approach: *looking simultaneously* at mother and infant, thereby emphasizing the fact that we regarded the "mothering mother" as the *continuous counterpoint* to the infant-child's developmental process during the first years of life. For this reason, we needed to look simultaneously at the mothering half's contribution to all the transactional patterning.

The patterns of growing and shrinking that the authors derive from the rhythm of inhaling and exhaling would mean to us primarily and essentially that *inhaling* diminishes the distance between the *holding* mother and the *held* infant's body and promotes molding, whereas exhaling might be the prototype of some distancing of the bodies. Thus, in term of our observational focus, growing and shrinking would correspond to the basic elements of approach and distancing patterns on all levels— purely biological, psychobiological, and ultimately psychological.

All along our focus was on this dual reference: We noted the attraction outside the body (even in plant life there is chemotaxis) that calls for approach, and we stressed also the importance of readiness to let go of the grip of the familiar; in short, that one has to distance oneself from one point to be able to approach another point.

Our special attention to the phenomena of attraction and approach allowed us to emphasize the bipolarity of most phenomena in most patterns of early human development. We recognized, for example, the ubiquity, running parallel with and complementing the more or less conspicuous apprehension about the stranger, of the equally conspicuous—in normal infants indeed, obligatory—positive interest and curiosity about the stranger, and the efforts on the part of the child to find out about the stranger. This accompanies even the most glaring manifestations of stranger anxiety.

In this connection, we have also learned the great developmental and clinical significance of the concept—individually so different—of the "optimal distance" between mother and infant-child, between subject and object, and finally between "patient and analyst."[7] These side remarks should serve merely to exemplify the complementing value of psychoanalytically oriented research.

Let me now highlight a few of the authors' inferences, derived from their study of the epigenetic sequence of the oral, anal, and urethral body-image manifestations of zonal development.

What they have observed at the outset or during the course of the oral-sadistic rhythms was borne out by Spock's extensive observations, as well as by our intensive mother-infant studies. We found that, at the point of beginning teething, it was not only and not mainly the mother

211

who was occupied with disengaging herself from the biting infant; the infant himself was starting to differentiate, in terms of pulling away from the nursing mother; loosening the hitherto adhesive closeness with her body; squirming out of the narrow confines of her enveloping arms; standing up on the lap of mother to look at her and also to look around him. In other words, the infant at that time seemed temporarily to have lost interest in the hitherto uniquely gratifying close contact with the mother. He displays this tendency in the form of protest against symbiotic confinement.

The author's findings also draw out attention to and enrich our understanding of what we had until now only begun to notice—namely, the toddler's active experimentation with his facial expressions, his mimicry. This "enables the toddler to display emotions like an actor." I remember one or another of our junior toddlers who, at that point in his development, most indefatigably sought interaction with the adults around him, especially with his mother, by what amounted to veritable clowning.

For us, who were able to observe these mechanisms and saw them only in their broad outlines, the essential meaning of these patterns, as far as developing object relationship and individuation were concerned, was the dramatic shift of libidinal cathexis—from the mother, as symbiotic half of the self to the child's own rapidly emerging autonomous ego functions, especially locomotion and reality testing. This begins around nine to ten months at the onset of "the practicing period" and coincides more or less with the anal phase. In the "peek-a-boo" and "bye-bye" games, which have a gradual and interesting development to which the author has also contributed a great deal through her careful study of the minutiae of movement patterns, our focus has been on the infant's subphase-specific and rapidly growing awareness of, need for, and quest for mastery along with concomitant enjoyment of his newly emerging sense of separateness.

It would be difficult to overestimate the significance of what the author describes as the child's bodily "alignment" in the *vertical plane*—especially because this achievement matures and thus becomes the essential basis for his free upright locomotion. As I have emphasized in several as yet unpublished papers, this achievement of free upright locomotion, coupled with the beginning of representational intelligence, constitutes the most decisive contributor to, and organizer of, the psychological birth of the human being.

I concur with and can substantiate the author's drawing our attention to the importance of a distinct urethral phase or patterning. Purely impressionistically, I am able to verify the predominance of urethral patterns and predilections in the play activities of boys and girls alike at around two years of age. At a time when, in our setup, the junior toddler is graduated to the toddler nursery by his own choice, he is consistently and preferentially engaged in endless *water-play* of his own choosing, whereas playing with dough or with finger paint has to be suggested to him, if he is to enjoy it.

It will probably take time for work of the kind the author has done to be adequately understood, learned, appreciated, and finally integrated. But I am convinced that the day will come when the author's "new key" will be adopted, her alphabet and grammar will be learned and will be more generally appreciated and utilized. Most importantly, her interpretations of the kind of body language that she is gifted enough to decipher, to communicate, and to apply in analytic treatment will, I think, become a source for enriched understanding of psychoanalytic theory and practice.

NOTES

[1] Even five-year-old children move their tongues in the direction of the lines they draw. (For a study of the tongue see Bonnard, 1960.)

[2] Channeling and wandering are examples of movement patterns called "precursors of effort." Mastery of space is achieved through the use of adaptive motion factors, the "efforts of directness and indirectness" (Kestenberg, 1965, 1967a; Laban, 1960).

[3] Anna Freud places the stage of object constancy after the phase of anaclitic, need-fulfilling relationships (1965). We believe that object constancy develops in successive steps, beginning in the oral phase (Kestenberg, 1967a). The study of movement patterns, which are correlated with various ways of relating to objects, suggested to us that we should distinguish between object constancy in space, in weight, and in time (see Chapter 10).

[4] Although Freud described urethral-erotic drives very clearly, he never postulated a separate urethral-erotic phase (Freud, S., 1905a, 1908, 1930, 1932), in which urethral drive components predominate over others. Observation and notation of the older toddler's movement patterns has suggested to us that there exists a phase at the end of the second year, and extending over a variable part of the third year, in which urethral discharge modes and their derivatives are dominant (Kestenberg, 1966, see also Chapters 9, 10, and 13). Generally speaking, one can look upon the first year as primarily oral, the second as primarily anal, and the third (at least the first half of it) as primarily urethral. This division is artificial to the extent that children progress at different rates, and phases may overlap for long periods of time. In addition, the continuance of outmoded forms of gratification, such as sucking, may mislead the observer into thinking that a phase organization, such as the oral (Freud, A., 1965), still persists. Derivatives and remnants of behavior which is no longer phase-specific are commonplace. To appraise

213

phase dominance one must examine the drive- and ego-organization rather than single behavioral items.

[5]These terms have been suggested by M. Blumenthal, who discussed our papers on movement patterns in a workshop on methodology, chaired by L. Rubenstein at The New York Psychoanalytic Institute, 1969.

[6]It would take us too far afield to discuss here the differences between boys and girls during this phase. Differences exist in every phase, but are especially noticeable in the urethral and phallic phases.

[7]We noticed with great pleasure that we reached consensus even where our focus has been different from that of Dr. Mahler. We have derived insight about the infant's range of comfort and discomfort, as related to primary, environmental objects (Balint, 1960) from patterns of shape-flow, exemplified in respiration. In contrast, asymmetrical shape-flow is an apparatus for responsiveness to stimuli, on which attraction and rejection are based. From these inborn motor mechanisms there evolve advanced movement patterns, serving the expression of complex relationships through approach to and withdrawal from objects (Kestenberg, 1967 a, b, 1973 a, b, c; see also Chapters 10 and 17).

CHAPTER 9

From Organ-Object Imagery to Self- and Object-Representations

Our present ego-feeling is . . . only a shrunken residue of a much more inclusive—indeed, an all-embracing—feeling which corresponded to a more intimate bond between the ego and the world about it. If we may assume that there are many people in whose mental life this primary ego-feeling has persisted to a greater or lesser degree, it would exist in them side by side with the narrower and more sharply demarcated ego-feeling of maturity, like a kind of counterpart to it [Freud, S., 1930, p. 68].

Mahler explains so well what little children feel because of her superior capacity to retain "this primary ego-feeling" side by side with a sharply delineated "ego-feeling of maturity." With a very special gift, she expands the primary ego feelings of those she teaches, and transforms the study of infancy for them into a life experience.

More than thirty years ago, in a paper on the Rorschach of amputees (1938), Mahler and I explored the connections between feelings of object-belonging and the love of the drive object. We noted the intrinsic unity between organ and object in the case of an amputee whose fiancee was killed in the accident that maimed him. In accepting the loss of his love object he also accepted the loss of his limb and developed no phantom.[1]

The basic assumptions of my thoughts about organ-object images were cradled in my early work with Mahler. They took shape in my work on development of movement patterns and were formulated and presented in other versions elsewhere (Kestenberg 1945, 1965, 1967a,

First published in *Separation-Individuation*, Papers in Honor of Margaret Mahler, ed. McDevitt, J.B. *et al*. Pp 75–99 (New York: International Universities Press, 1971). Reproduced here by permission in a slightly revised version.

1968, 1971; see also Chapters 1, 8, 10, and 17). Although substantiated by clinical material derived from analyses of young children and acting-out adults, the thesis to be presented cannot be fully documented here without leading the reader too far afield into specialized study of movement patterns and body attitudes. As Ferenczi wrote in 1912:

> It definitely looks as if one could never reach any real convictions at all through logical insight alone; one needs to have lived through an affective experience, to have—so-to-speak—felt it in one's own body, in order to gain that degree of certain insight which deserves the name of "conviction." [pp. 193-194]

This chapter will deal with the nature of *symbiotic bonds* throughout development, with special emphasis on prephallic phases. Each developmental phase is distinguished by a heightened cathexis of a dominant organ, by a zone-specific pleasure and phase-specific contact with the drive object from which a united *organ-object* image emerges. At the end of each phase, new shapes of self and object representations differentiate from the global imagery of a united organ-object. The separation between the pleasure-seeking organ and ʳhe satisfying object, the prototype of which is weaning from the breast, is experienced as a loss. Two basic mechanisms which maintain the integrity and continuity of self and object despite this loss, are: (1) the replacement of the lost dual unity between between organ and object by a new unity, albeit less symbiotic in nature; (2) the establishment of symbiotic bonds which link organ and object anew through such *bridges* as body products (intermediate objects), external possessions (transitional objects, [Winnicott, 1953]) and people (accessory objects), all of which the child shares with his mother. The sequence of symbiosis followed by separation-individuation repeats itself in an increasingly attenuated form in each developmental phase, until in adulthood a periodic union with the love object can be attained in orgastic experience.

Organ-Object Images in Cycles of Separation and Merging in Pregenital Phases

Through successive phases of separation-individuation, the child forms self and object representations from the images of his own and his mother's satisfying bodies (Freud, S., 1905, 1910a, 1912, 1915a, 1917b, 1926, 1930, 1932–36, 1940; Ferenczi, 1912, 1924; Jekels, 1913; Fenichel, 1926, 1928, 1945a; Schilder, 1935; Benedek, 1949,

1956; Hoffer, 1952; Mahler, 1960, 1961, 1963, 1965, 1966, 1967; Mahler and Elkisch, 1953; Mahler and Furer, 1963; Mahler and LaPerriere, 1965; Mahler and McDevitt, 1968; Sandler and Rosenblatt, 1962; Jacobson, 1964; Freud, A., 1965, 1967a; Joffe and Sandler, 1965). The "satisfaction in something that we may call 'organ-pleasure' " (Freud, S., 1932–36, p. 98) depends on the intactness of sources of pleasure, of the pleasure-giving organ and of the need-satisfying object. Each abatement of pleasure is connected with a loss of organ-object unity. Through contact with the mother's need-satisfying body, the drive object becomes "part of the subject's own body" (Freud, S., 1915, p. 132). In autoerotism, the "object is negligible in comparison with the organ . . . and as a rule coincides with that organ" (*ibid.*). The part played by the dominant organic source is so decisive that the form and function of the organ not only determines the activity and passivity of the instinctual aim (Federn, 1913; Jekels, 1913), but also shapes the image of the body (Schilder, 1935).

During nursing, the rapid oscillations between prehension and release (between closeness to the mother during milk intake and removal during swallowing) blur rather than sharpen body boundaries. The oral image of "mouth-body-object" is not well defined until later stages of orality. Its functional modality is based on prehension and release. At first, the flow of milk merges with the rhythm of sucking. With the introduction of solids, milk and food are associated with the mother as links between the infant's primal cavity (Spitz, 1955) and the body of the feeding mother. Food as the heir of symbiotic dual unity preserves mother-child unity despite separation. It is looked upon as a bridge to the oral image of the mother, a bridge that maintains the integrity of the oral organ-object image as a functional unit. Throughout life, a drink or sweet can restore the long-lost well-being intrinsic in oral organ-object unity.

When swollen gums and teething pain spoil the pleasure in sucking, the oral mucosa loses its exquisite sensuality. When biting impulses interfere with the flow of milk, the infant becomes disgruntled. He sucks, bites, and chews on things, then drops them and calls for his mother to retrieve them. The feeling of loss of oral organ-object unity occurs without weaning because the nature of early sensations fades through maturation. The softness and blurriness of the sucking rhythms, which pervaded the oral organ-object image, gives way to sharpness and distinctness of biting rhythms, which contribute to the sharpening of body boundaries. The feeling of separateness through cleavage between early self and object is experienced in the context of biting off, chopping, and destroying.

These conceptualizations, derived from my own studies, run parallel

217

to those arrived at by students of cognition. Important as it is to distinguish between drive object, object-representation, and the "object" of psychologists, it is equally important not to overlook parallelisms in their formation. Elkind (1967) states: "During the first few months after birth objects are really not distinguished from the actions associated with them" (p. 384). Gradually the object "is coming to be regarded as something which exists independently of the infant's perceptual and motor activity" (*ibid.*) Not until the second year of life does the child ". . . deal with objects as independent of his own perception and as having independent positions and trajectories in space" (p. 385).

The firmness of the standing infant's body helps him achieve a new "one-piece" unity of his body self. As he acquires a dependable center of gravity, his body becomes steady, centered, and solid. The oral nursling is transforming into the anal toddler. Carrying his own weight, he identifies with the mother who held him and protected him against falls and injury. Because verticality gives him a new, species-specific spatial perspective, the child begins to appreciate the mother as a solid but separate unit. Through acquisition of locomotion, he begins to practice and enjoy intentional separation from her. Yet the practicing infant "crawls to his mother, rights himself on her leg and touches her, or merely stands leaning against her leg" (Mahler and La Perriere, 1965, p. 485). He now tends to merge with the lower part of his mother's body. The focal area of his body image has also shifted downward.

When the toddler squats, his pelvis acts as a stabilizing base for differentiating between the upper, prehensile part of his body and the lower, supporting part. When he stands up, he uses his arms for balance. He must stop, sit, or squat again before his arms recover their prehensile function. The lower part of his body contains him and holds him in place. The primal cavity extends downward; its content becomes the child's own as he struts and exhibits his belly with an air of self-importance. The anal rhythm of retaining and expelling gives a phase-specific feeling tone to the functional image of the anal child's body. He tends to stand when he retains and to squat when he expels. He becomes aware of his mother's interest in his "making."

As soon as the toddler recognizes that feces, once they leave his body, are not his any more, he begins to treat them as a bridge to the mother. When he "makes," they act as a magic signal to summon his mother and reinstitute organ-object union. When he begins to understand that she discards his feces and makes them disappear, he suffers from a feeling of loss.

When the toddler leaves his mother to explore the world or to spite her because she left or rejected him, he does not burn his bridges. His newly developed intentionality and self-sufficiency are far ahead of his ability to maintain separation from his mother (Mahler and La Perriere, 1965). He seeks her out again, brings her things to look at, woos her with his feces, feigns that he "made," and gets her to toilet him more often than he needs. If he ventures too far afield in his explorations, he calls his mother, and he panics if she does not hear him.

Toward the end of the second year, anal sensuality may be spoiled by discomfort in defecation produced by diarrhea and constipation. He blames his mother for real or imaginary pains which she does not alleviate. The unity of the anal organ-object is disrupted and a new, sharply defined distinction between self and object emerges. By taking over maternal functions, the child becomes partially independent of the mother. He enters a new phase in which he enjoys running off into the endless space into which things and people used to disappear.

The rhythm of early running is consonant with the rhythmic flow of urine. The child who frequently wets himself while running goes through a phase of urethral dominance which, although it overlaps the anal and genital phases, should be clearly distinguished from them (Kestenberg, 1966; Chapters 8, 10, 13). During urethral dominance, the child's body image becomes fluid rather than solid. His body boundaries become uncertain. His new mobility threatens his equilibrium and subjects him to falls and injuries. The distance he traverses in the sagittal plane (forward-backward) represents a new peril of separation and loss. When he loses sight of his mother, he may not know which of them is lost (Freud, A., 1967a). When he cannot stop himself, he needs his mother's solid body to contain his mobile body and restore its integrity. He enjoys melting into her when she carries him and protects him from injury. His passive surrender within the confinement of maternal embrace may be indistinguishable from letting go and allowing the stream of urine to flow and wet his body and that of his mother as well. This feeling of unity re-creates old organ-object images within the new framework of flowing into one another. The memory of such a union with the drive object creates a bridge between mother and child out of warm urine.

Fear of passive surrender to melting with the mother, fear of temporary loss of body boundaries, coupled with the mother's reluctance to accept urine as a gift all reinforce the toddler's need to regain initiative and move on. As he practices locomotion, he learns to stop and to go as he wishes. His feeling of self begins to acquire an operational quality and his functional body image, at first primarily prehensile, then primarily stable, now becomes primarily self-propelling. He becomes acquainted with the distinction between front and back, his own as well as his mother's. The highly cathected front of his body becomes associated with urine as "number one," and his "tushy" that gives out feces becomes "number two" in the hierarchical ascendance of values. His body image gains in depth as his oral-gastric cavity, which had extended into the abdomen, protrudes into the pelvic-vesical region. His new shape of self representation generates pride in achievement and self-initiative. The "do-it-myself" child separates himself from his mother as a distinctly delineated operational unit. However, urine can bridge the separation when it is used to restore closeness. During long separations, letting go and wetting will, in fantasy, bring back the mother of the past to receive the fluid and wipe the child dry (Freud, A., and Burlingham, D., 1942).

In pregenital phases, the mother becomes immersed in the infant's total functioning; she selectively stimulates specific body zones in feeding, cleansing, and diapering. Unity of stimulation, excitation, and abatement of pleasure are most pronounced in the oral phase and recede in importance as physical contact diminishes and communication through distance receptors increases. Within the totality of the infant's experience, there emerge specific dominant shapes of orally, anally, and urethrally centered organ-object units from which new self- and object-representations differentiate. With the passing of a developmental phase, the original qualities of dominant zones and phase-specific objects are irretrievably lost. However, traces of original feelings of unity with the object are retained in affective components of self feelings and object love, and in unverbalized substrates of creativity.

Each loss of organ-object unity brings pain. The ensuing estrangement from the once so pleasurable zone leads to its desexualization and to its use as a neutralized functional organ. The estrangement from the object promotes separation and individuation, and the loss of symbiotic unity challenges the child to find new ways to retrieve what has been lost.

The loss that occurs with the passing of urethral eroticism is probably least conspicuous to the observer because the urethral zone adjoins the genitals, and sensations from one tend to spread to the other. However, the budding enjoyment of genital sensuality is spoiled by the removal of maternal hands from the genital area once toilet-training has been successfully accomplished. Regressive longing for all past forms of object-organ unity characterizes the transition from pregenital to early genital phases. Maternal failure to revive what has been lost is experienced as object loss.

Each intrapsychic loss is based on a real loss, the loss of organ-object unity that occurs with shifts of dominance from one zone to the next.

Early changes in mood are related to organ-object pleasures—their loss and their retrieval. It is not only the mother's behavior, but also the child's congenital apparatus (frustration tolerance, special sensitivities, etc.) and maturational level that determine whether separation is tolerable or experienced as a "catastrophic threat" (Mahler and Furer, 1963; see also Chapter 6). In normal development, the child has at his disposal a number of resources which safeguard him against depression (Mahler, 1966). Among these resources, externalization stands out as a prime method of object-seeking. The ambiguity with which external and internal losses are presented (Mahler, 1966) results from the fact that, in the process of differentiation of self and object from organ-object images, the child alternates externalization and internalization. He frequently uses external bridges to the mother as aids to maintain the inner image of the absent object. The use of these adjuncts to the drive object upholds the unity and integrity of self and object and allows for a smooth transition from thing to object-representations (Freud, S., 1917b), that are only shadows of the past.

Retrieving the Past Through Intermediate, Transitional, and Accessory Objects

The adult mourner consoles himself for his loss by holding on to mementos and heirlooms as external links to the lost object. Damage to these bridges to the past, or their real loss, is experienced as a personal injury (Freud, A., 1967a) and a desecration of the memory of the deceased. Although the world of things familiar to the infant, created by mother and himself, loses its intense cathexis in time, the "house we lived in," certain toys and furnishings, as well as people from one's childhood retain their special quality as meaningful landmarks in the recollection of the past (Searles, 1960). As isolated fragments of memory which withstood repression, they bridge the discontinuity created by developmental changes, and become intermediate links in reconstructions from screen memories. The "coherent self that has continuity and remains the same in the midst of changes" (Jacobson, 1964, p. 68) cannot be maintained without periodic revival of the past by use of external bridges to lost objects. As carriers of narcissistic and object libido, these bridges prevent delibidinization of self- and object-representations (Fenichel, 1928) and function as buffers against self- and object-destruction. Despite their variety, their origin can be traced back to three principal infantile patterns of erecting "symbiotic bridges" between organs and objects through (1) intermediate, (2) accessory, and (3) transitional ob-

221

jects. This classification, albeit incomplete, will, I hope, eliminate the semantic confusion between drive objects and other libidinized objects. Neither people nor the "stuff" of transitional phenomena (Winnicott, 1953; Reik, 1953; Hannett, 1964) from which dreams are made, can be reduced to the status of things. They are adjuncts of the drive object.

1. *Intermediate Objects:* Food and bodily products associated with organ pleasure seem to belong to the infant's and the mother's body. They help to maintain the sense of dual unity in the absence of the object. For that reason, the child feels a keen sense of loss when he discovers that bodily products lose their live quality upon separation from his body. To reestablish them as bridges between himself and his mother, he reanimates them and treats them as intermediate objects. Pleasure in things that belong to the total experience of organ-object unity helps the infant to combine the enjoyment of exteroceptive perceptions and sensuality of mucous membranes with intense kinesthetic and visceral sensations. In playing with food, feces, urine, and other bodily excretions, the child displaces their qualities and condenses them with all inanimate things that he felt and saw in the intimate space he shared with his mother (fingering her clothing during feeding, feeling the texture of sheets, diapers, bath water and soap, etc). The need to reanimate body products overflows to the many inanimate things which the child actually never felt inside of his body. He treats them as if they too had come out of his body and externalizes upon them qualities of feelings from the inside of his body. They too become intermediate objects. Some toys and utensils derive their cathectic value from the overestimation of the magic quality of bodily products. The interest in these objects is marked by a feeling of urgency, an almost physical need to have "right now" and not a moment later. Sometimes even pets and people are used as intermediate objects: craved for the moment, they become devaluated and discarded when no longer needed. This differs from the use of people as external accessories to the intimacy with the mother.

2. *Accessory Objects:* People who assist the mother in the care of the infant are frequently fused in memory with the image of the mother (Mahler, 1966). Such fusion may be accomplished by treating nurses, grandmothers, siblings, and even the father as bridges to the mother, who may disappear in the background but is summonable and controllable through accessory objects. The disappearance of such an object can represent an indirect threat of separation from the drive object. Underneath the depression about the loss of a nurse or a grandmother, in infancy, there always lurks a latent feeling of loss of a symbiotic organ-object. Unlike the intermediate object, the accessory object is held on

222

to as a temporal link of the past with the future ("when Nannie goes, mother will come").

3. *Transitional Objects:* While intermediate objects serve the momentary re-creation of the past and accessory objects create a continuity between past and future, transitional objects (Winnicott, 1953) serve the preservation of the old, within the newness of the present, into the future. They are the child's own creations, invented out of a variety of sensorimotor modalities. They not only evoke the illusion of unity with the mother but also unite body parts and integrate simultaneous, yet different needs (see Chapter 2). Transitional objects give continuity to the succession of self and object images and allow the child to be partially independent of the real drive object. A transitional object need not be a smelly blanket or a wooly animal. Pets and people, sounds and words, melodies and rhythms, colors and shapes become part of the world of transitional phenomena and may be treasured as personal possessions which re-create "something old" within the context of "something new."

As he progresses and regresses the child changes the value sign of external objects many times. A cherished transitional object can become devalued when it is "used up," washed, or damaged. Intermediate objects can become cherished and unrelinquishable possessions. A new person may be endowed with qualities of the mother and the child and thus can fulfill the function of a transitional object. Intermediate objects become prime targets of aggression in the process of denigration of self and object. By entering the world of transitional phenomena, intermediate objects can become divested of instinctual cathexis and change their function to become tools of creativity. Transitional objects can become so distorted that their sole function is to re-create the past without creating something new. Thus they can become fetishistic objects (Wulff, 1932b) or fossilized vestiges of the past which serve acting out and prevent joyful play and creative expression (Winnicott, 1967; Kestenberg, 1968).

The developmental line from intermediate objects leads to play with toys, interest in tools and to the valuation of means of consumption and production. Cathexis of accessory objects widens into interest in playmates, teachers, comrades, and friends, and the community at large. Transitional objects and their derivatives open up avenues for novel approaches and for the creation of external models for the internalization of the past and its preservation in the present and the future. Artists often refer to their creations as bridges, and some, especially poets, become aware of their meaning as links to the mother of their infancy. With the passing of pregenital phases, all these bridges to the primary

223

drive object contribute their share to the formation of illusory babies, to be created in illusory genital union with the love object.

Seeking of Organ-Object Unity in the Development of Genitality

The principle of biological unity between genital sexuality and reproduction becomes manifest as soon as early genital drive components begin to assert their dominance over pregenital forms of expression. Under the influence of genital excitement, the child seeks genital union with the drive object and hopes to create a baby with his mother, and later with his father. Although the image of a baby as bridge to the love object undergoes phase-specific transformations (Chapters 2, 11, 13), its persistence through development prevents the total cleavage between self and object during separation-individuation. The continuity and irrevocability of this image distinguishes man from all species in which maturation leads to object loss and estrangement between parent and offspring. The inner-genital organs (vagina, uterus, ovaries, tubes or prostate, seminal vesicles, vasa deferentia and testicles) are intrinsic to adult sexual performance and reproduction. The development of genitality in childhood cannot lead to integration of sexuality and reproduction in adulthood without cathexes of both. The sequence in which psychic representations of genital needs appear in childhood has been clearly specified by Mack Brunswick (1940): "Contrary to our earlier ideas, the penis wish is not exchanged for the baby wish which, as we have seen, has indeed long preceded it" (p. 311). The preoedipal phase in both sexes is also prephallic; its phase-specific erogenous zone adjoins sources of pregenital pleasure but is not identical with them.

Analyses of adults and children and analytic observation of young children suggest that inner-genital structures (such as the vagina in the girl or the vasa deferentia in the boy) become the dominant sources of infantile sexual excitement before the intense cathexis of external genitalia, in particular the phallus or the clitoris, achieve dominance in the phallic phase. For that reason I have found it useful to distinguish two successive phases of childhood genitality: (1) the inner-genital preoedipal phase and (2) the outer-genital phallic-oedipal phase.

Inner-genital Preoedipal Phase

This phase follows pregenital phases and precedes the phallic. Pregenital component drives become integrated into the dominant form of inner genitality, and the wish for a baby becomes evident in both sexes, more so in girls than in boys.

When the toddler nears nursery-school age, physical contact with his mother diminishes considerably. Looking back longingly at his lost baby-hood, the child reconciles his regressive and progressive wishes by identifying with the mother of his past and creating a baby of his own (see Chapters 1, 2, 11, 13). He embarks on his developmental task of re-creating the past within the newness of his strivings for genital organ-object union. Images from his past, derived from synesthetic, syncretistic experiences, become subject to evaluation and clarification, as increasing verbalization aids conceptualization on a secondary-process level (Katan, 1961). With the help of his mother, the child can now create an integrated image of himself out of the chaos of his past.

Dorie, at the age of three, could neither conceptualize nor put into words what she felt and remembered from the past. Using newly learned concepts of color and shape, she constructed out of circles and color blobs integral parts of a baby, built in the image of her mother. This was embedded in a reconstruction of her past out of intensely cathected fragments of colors, shapes, and things that served as structural components of what was to become an integrated memory.

Acting out the traumatic event of moving and "losing" all possessions, Dorie introduced the theme in the process of finding the right hue for an organ she had seen during a primal scene experience. Experimenting with the reproduction of this organ she also found the right tint and shape for a chair that belonged to her old house. From similar reproductions of body parts and possessions she was led to the acting out of the event of moving, without yet understanding how it all happened. She emptied the contents of a shelf in my office and looked at me questioningly as if to say: "That's all I know, you tell me the rest." Only her parents could tell us that, at the age of twenty months, Dorie saw movers packing contents of drawers into cartons but did not witness the loading and unloading of the van. By incessant acting out, playing, imagining, and learning of new concepts and words, Dorie found out what became of people and things from her infancy and where they were now. All that had happened to her was important within the framework of her psychophysical needs which merged with those of her mother and extended to her father, her nurse, her grandparents, neighbors, and visitors, all perceived as accessories to her mother.

In her effort to recapture her lost babyhood, Dorie literally wanted to reproduce herself. She regressed to bottle feeding, soiling, and wetting. She used food and excretions as intermediate objects with which she tried to recapture the lost unity with her mother. The new baby she was trying

225

to create out of food and excrement was conceived and nurtured by inner-genital sensations which she could neither localize nor describe. At first I knew about them only from the colors she chose to represent various types of sensuality. Not until a year later could Dorie explain to me what she felt was inside of her that differed from food, feces, and urine.

Dorie's analysis shows how a three-year-old masters the loss of pre-genital organ-object images by re-creating them in a new form, suitable for the expression of inner-genital drives. The integrative task of the preoedipal-prephallic toddler can be accomplished only when the child has experienced undisturbed organ-object unity in infancy. How difficult it is for a child to erect an image of his body and a concept of self on the basis of fragmented organ-object images can be seen in the case of Mortimer, who hated babies.[2]

Unlike Dorie, Mortimer at the age of two and a half did not seem to need his mother. He ran to and fro and periodically reminded himself to ask, "Where is mommy?" without waiting for an answer. He rapidly shifted his attention to switching lights, patting dogs, touching all kinds of things, and repeating words and phrases in an endless stream of unrelated "communication." Foremost, Mortimer wanted to achieve mastery over objects of the external world. When it came upon him that he could not master screws, lights, and all things that closed and opened, Mortimer would break up furniture, scatter toys, and threaten me: "I will break you." When he went outdoors with his mother he threatened to break up her friendships with neighbors by selectively attacking their babies. I first realized that Mortimer was preoccupied with insides of things when he began to explore the inner workings of a flashlight. Pulling wires and switching the light on by touching the battery fascinated him. However, when I tried to take out the batteries to show him the empty case, he protested anxiously: "Don't do that, the *hole will run out.*" All little parts were allowed to come out, but the space-filling batteries had to remain inside undisturbed.

At three, Mortimer wanted me to help him to be a big boy. However, only when his mother held him on her lap could he pay sufficient attention to profit by my observation: "Things fall out of your hands; your fingers, your arms and legs 'fly' and don't stop. You need your mommy to pick all the pieces up for you. They are yours. They must stay with you all the time." His mother said with sudden insight: "I used to tell him all the time that either he will break me or I will break him."

Mortimer began to "break" his mother before he was born. Stricken by a life-threatening illness during her pregnancy, she was advised to keep calm to prevent a relapse. After his birth, Mortimer's existence continued to threaten her body integrity; he made her excited, frustrated, and helpless. Moments of organ-object unity became anxiety-laden and had to be broken up.

Mortimer disrupted everything: he could not draw a unit and when I drew for him (a square, a circle, a letter, a body), he interrupted me, connected unrelated pictures, and distorted the Gestalt of things by scribbling over them and around them. The sight of a tiny baby-doll evoked in him an irresistible urge to pull off its arms and legs. He hated babies. I asked whether Mortimer wasn't a nice baby once himself. He retorted that he was a "big boy" and never had been a baby. When he consented to draw a baby and mother, he put one inside the other, and it was not clear which contained which. Crisscrossing scribbles and smudges extending to the outside gave a feeling of depth to this combined mother-baby image. We shall see later that scribbling of this nature may represent the image of undescribable genital sensations.[3]

The three-year-old begins to form an image of his body from past and present sensations and observations. The disappearance of food into the body and the emergence of excreta and secretions from it focus the child's attention on what is inside him. It is his responsibility now to control input and output. He knows that a feeling of impending evacuation will subside when things from inside of his body materialize outside. Yet, he feels crisscrossing waves of excitement which neither food intake nor elimination can relieve. They spread outward and inward and all over, merging with pelvic-abdominal contractions, coming and going in an unaccountable manner. They go, but no product appears. When they come, they create a desire or need hitherto unknown. These undefinable inner-genital sensations initiate object love. They may be evoked by the mere sight, touch, or voice of the object.

The inner-genital feelings of the three-year-old revive earlier nonverbal, noncognitive experiences of genital stimulation which had become submerged in phase-specific pregenital sexuality. The three-year-old becomes unaccountably disgruntled, nagging, and dissatisfied because he does not know what he wants. He looks to his mother for relief of genital tensions and struggles to find a new type of organ-object union which will not only bring satisfaction but also a tangible product of the union, to be used as a permanent bridge between organ and object. Since he cannot form a clear concept of his inside, the child condenses the images of himself, the baby, and the mother to represent the inner structure of his body. The need to form an image of the inside genital is much more urgent and more manifest in the girl than in the boy.[4] However, the boy too is beset by disquieting sensations and pelvic contractions that accompany genital excitement (Mahler, 1968a). Sensations from the base of the penis, where it meets the scrotum, from the sides in which something moves upwards and inwards (movement of vas deferens), and the feeling that the penis is emptying to the inside when it shrinks draws the boy's attention to the mysterious inner-genital apparatus that is hidden from his view. He looks upon this "inside motor" of his genitality as a substructure that makes external genitals stay in place or move. He too anthropomorphizes the live "something" inside of him and thinks of it as a little creature that stirs and pulls invisible strings or lets go so that the penis or scrotum can become loose and fall. He too wants a baby, but he is more prone than the girl to look at baby objects from the viewpoint of an explorer of mechanisms. Because of the equation baby = mother = inside, he fears that the delivery of this baby may not only pull out the attached external organs but will, at the same time, sever his genital symbiotic bonds with his mother.

With a mixture of reality and unreality the three-year-old "knows" that he has something inside his "house" that calls for expression not yet available to him. He gets angry at his mother who does not help him to materialize his inside "furnishings." He uses old and new methods to create a live baby out of things from his inside, the way mother created him out of hers. The live quality and permanency of the baby image that is created out of products and things is traceable to externalization of inner-genital sensations. These unclear feelings call for union with the object. They are elusive, to be sure, but so intensely alive and spreading that they overflow and animate the world of objects.

> Dorie created babies out of colors and shapes, out of bags of colored candy she stuffed herself with, out of fluids she craved, out of masses of feces she retained to make into a big and well-shaped baby, and out of urine or water which made designs on the floor. At night she had to arrange three dolls from her infancy to fit under her head. When she awoke she called for Mommy but accepted Daddy whom she used to call "Moddy" in moments of need. Her pictures were full of designs which did not fit anything she really knew. She dedicated them to her mother and added her name to them. She created letters out of baby shapes: D was a belly and R was a belly with legs. They were her letter-babies, not to be shared with other children.
>
> Dorie accepted me as a fellow shaper who could make wholes out of fragments she could not put together herself. I could draw what she wanted to create and provide the words that made sense.
>
> Despite our excellent therapeutic alliance, Dorie always hated me and

called me "stupid" when I had to confront her with the fact that she could not make babies. My explanation that she had a place for a baby inside brought relief only to the degree that it accounted for the feelings that spread inward from her vulva and introitus. Because she had to wait for a baby until she was grown up, Dorie was angry. Nevertheless she explored her vulva and lovingly accepted it as a flower that grew out of the introitus. But not until she reached the phallic phase could she explain the difference between inner and outer genital sensations and their meaning.

In transition to phallic dominance, Dorie alternated two manners of jumping on the couch. When, after a long time of exploration, I asked her to show me the difference, she first showed me the button on the couch to symbolize the clitoris. To explain how the other type of jumping felt, in contrast to one that came from "button" feelings, she drew two pictures. The nonbutton way of jumping was represented by a baby-house in which she placed a baby that she quickly transformed into a mother at whose side another baby materialized. The base of the house was thickly shaded and the entire house framed by rhythmic undulatory patterns which intruded inside.[5] The contrasting drawing also began as a house but became dominated by concentric circles, from one of which lines emanated, radiating outward like the rays of a sun.

In transition from pregenital phases to the phallic, dominant innergenital, sensorimotor feelings evoke a need for a genital organ that can be united with the object. The child incorporates long-lost pregenital organ-object images into his new creation. To give substance to an unrealizable wish, the child creates out of external objects "bridges" between the invisible inner-genital structures and his mother. The "baby" he thus creates, be it a doll, a teddy bear, a design, or train, helps him to maintain the inner image of himself as well as of his mother. The externalization of what he feels inside and the seeking of shapes and qualities for the baby image on the outside bring about desexualization of inner-genital sensations. This eventually leads to denial of the existence of the inside genitalia (see Chapter 13). A new sense of reality helps the child to use external models for the construction of separate, "true" self- and object-representations. External reality becomes truly real and the illusory baby is relegated to the make-believe play world of the phallic-oedipal child.

Outer-Genital Phallic-Oedipal Phase

This phase is characterized by the subordination of preoedipal wishes for a baby to fantasies of phallic-genital union with the oedipal object.

229

The repudiation of pregenital wishes and the denial of inner genitalia devaluates the whole inside of the body. The phallic body image is a closed system that does not allow for body openings other than those serving a currently useful function. The sharp differentiation between outside and inside, true and false, live people and inanimate things, leads to a tightening of body boundaries and to a distinct separation between self and object. Although the child himself is afraid of organ-object unity because of its fear-evoking loss of individuality, he blames his mother for cutting off access to her body. His estrangement from the preoedipal mother makes separation-individuation an unequivocal reality. The realization that mother has to depend on daddy to create babies further devaluates femininity. The father becomes transformed from an accessory object into an idealized phallic figure, the heir and successor of the idealized preoedipal mother. This shift can be seen in both sexes but is much more obvious in girls.

> When Dorie accepted that she could not make a baby for mother and could not woo her with her phallic jumping stunts she told me: "I hate you and never want to see you again." She informed me that she and her daddy would plant seeds together in the garden. It was daddy now who could provide seeds for growth. He was not "moddy" anymore.

The persistence of old images within new fantasies gives continuity to the child's ego feelings and guarantees the survival of object constancy despite angry death wishes that are generated in the process of separation-individuation. The phallus and, in some measure, the little "button" clitoris manipulated in masturbation becomes the successors to all previous bridges to the mother. Out of the phallus a baby can be made. As instinctual cathexis is withdrawn from the inside, and external objects, onto which inner-genital impulses had been externalized, lose their magic value, one can observe in *statu nascendi* how phallic symbols are formed out of intermediate, transitional, and accessory objects. Food, feces, urine, babies, toys, pets, and people become means to aggrandize or multiply the phallus.

The phallic wish to penetrate or to be penetrated seeks to restore organ-object unity with the mother or her successor, the father. Fear that the real or imaginary penis will be cut off or will fall off always contains the latent apprehension that the object will be lost as well. Castration fear is the heir of fear of disintegration of organ-object unity which injures both mother and child. To safeguard his bodily integrity, the phallic child gives up the image of the phallus as a concrete bridge to the mother's inside. During his solitary masturbation, he maintains closeness to the object and creates babies only in fantasy. Fantasy as a bridge to the love object becomes highly sexualized. Through repression, even this bridge to the object is partially given up and self- and object-representations become desexualized. Their separation is reflected in the clear differentiation of the superego from the ego. The superego is heir to the oedipus complex, but it always bears traces of lost organ-object unity and its disruptions. Feeling of ego and superego unity is derived from early, peaceful ego states, experienced through organ-object unity. Loss of self-esteem and guilt derive their archaic features, which equate active attempts at cutting symbiotic ties with the destruction of self and object, from past feelings of object-loss.

Latency

The passing of the phallic-oedipal phase is characterized by a new feeling of loss. The magic of preschool age is waning. In transition to latency proper, the child veers between regressive revivals of pregenital organ-object unity and progressive steps toward separation. When the schoolchild accepts the teacher as a temporary substitute for the mother, his play gives way to games of skill, and work becomes differentiated from play. The latency child uses achievement as a bridge to his mother. Words and grammar become vehicles for the flow of externalization and internalization. Seeking of union with the love object is transformed into communication with the desexualized, real parent. Repression upholds the separation between self and object. To reinforce repression and separation the latency child becomes estranged from the adult world (see Chapters 10, 11, and 13).

Prepuberty

The appearance of secondary sex characteristics begins to approximate the child's body to that of the adult. Progressive signs of sexual maturation make the child feel like an intruder into the adult world. Children and parents begin to seek new bridges for rapprochement by intruding upon each other's privacy. The onrush of inner-genital sensations (uterovaginal in the girl, primarily prostatic in the boy) fuse with and overflow into external genital structures. Old modes of discharge and old wishes for organ-object unity are revived in transition to the formation of new ones. Bewildered by and unable to cope with the variety of excitations, the child feels that he is not only becoming an open system again but also a disorganized one (described as "prepuberty diffusion" in Chapter 14). He would like to be contained and given direction so that he can integrate all fragments of his past and present into a new meaningful image of himself, as he did in the early inner-genital phase. Despite his wish for autonomy he seeks unity with his mother once more.

Within the framework of adolescent pseudoindependence, all the characteristics of earlier separation-individuation phases put in their appearance. From a safe distance, the prepuberty child shadows his mother, provokes her to shadow him, and projects upon her his need for closeness. Practicing skills with a fervor comparable to that of the toddler, he forgets to come home on time. He overwhelms his mother with the urgency of his physical needs, his ravenous appetite, and his messy habits, then rushes away and refuses to help or be helped. Suddenly he tires. Collapsing onto chairs and couches he leans against furniture as he used to when he was a baby. He calls his mother and forgets what he wanted. He turns to her with real or imaginary "growing pains" which give him a legitimate excuse for his wish to be mothered. He becomes enamored of objects of the external world which, in analysis, frequently reveal themselves as baby substitutes. He constantly involves his mother in keeping his "baby" in good condition. He reasserts his phallic narcissism by his lack of consideration while, at the same time, he uses phallic fantasies as bridges to the object. He creates transitional objects out of friends and reduces his father to the status of an accessory object by accusing him of being merely a shadow of the phallic mother. A renewal of intimacy with the father has oedipal features, but is also used to reach the mother. By excluding her he expels her and excites her all at once, a method familiar from the ambitendent activity of the toddler (Mahler and McDevitt, 1968).

Massive externalization of inner-genital sensations reinforces the child's phallic position and rescues him from utter confusion. However, this method cannot be upheld when menarche or ejaculation becomes tangible proof of the existence and importance of inside genitalia. At last the long-coveted product from which a baby can be made has materialized. The new product becomes a phase-specific bridge to the love object, uniting the mother's inside with the child's own. The wish for the mother to touch menstrual blood or the ejaculate leads to acting out. These new bridges become devaluated because they carry incestuous wishes in unacceptable infantile forms of physical rapprochement. In adolescent masturbation, fantasies once more become bridges between body and object.

Puberty and Postpuberty

Working through of losses incurred in infancy on the way to childhood, and in transition from childhood to physiological puberty, estab-

232

lishes a new level of separation-individuation. Puberty fantasies become increasingly removed from primary objects. Revived oedipal wishes are repressed once more and eventually abandoned. The wish to attain organ-object unity with a new object becomes highly cathected. Identifications form the basis of sex-specific identity and replace symbiotic bonds with infantile objects.

Relinquishing of primary objects is accomplished through desexualization of their images. The adolescent appraises his parents' past and current behavior and becomes resentfully aware of their continuous need to treat him as a bridge between them. To stress his separateness he exaggerates their unity. Not only through identification with his father but also through identification with the preoedipal mother, the young man prepares himself to love and provide for a new unit—a family of his own. The young woman tends to retain old bridges to the mother, which she redirects from the mother to the father and from him to a new love object. Her longing for a child is not only due to the need, shared by both sexes, to create a permanent tie to the new love object but, more so than in men, to her persistent yearning to recreate organ-object unity with the mother of her infancy. For her, and to a considerable degree for the new father, separation-individuation begins all over again.

The detachment from primary objects "burns old bridges," but from their ashes there emerge new methods of reaching and holding new objects. Periodically, body boundaries blur in the merging of self and object as genital organ-object union materializes in the orgastic experience of the adult. Relibidinization through symbiotic dual union reaches its developmental peak. Refueling is still needed to assure the maintenance of constancy of self and object (Mahler and Furer, 1963); from each union evolves a new working through of separation-individuation. Loss and retrieval of organ-object unity continues throughout adulthood in the periodicity of constant adult-genital relationships and in the cycles of gain and loss, when children change their phase-specific identity and build a new identity for their parents (Chapter 11; Benedek, 1959).

NOTES

[1] Note Ludwig Uhland's intuitive understanding of organ-object unity in his poem about a lost comrade, *Der Gute Kamerad* [The Good Comrade]. "Er liegt zu meinen Fuessen als waer's ein Stueck von mir [Now at my feet he is lying, Oh, part of me is gone]."

[2] For further material from the analyses of these and other preschool children, see Kestenberg, 1969, 1971, 1972, and Chapters 2 and 5.

[3] For the use of the scribbling game as means of exploration of the child's body image, see Elkisch (1948, 1952).

233

[4]Brunswick (1940) describes an often overlooked preoedipal phase in the male which "despite its comparative brevity, is perhaps less dramatic than the woman's but equally far reaching (p. 317). Independently of Brunswick, Lampl-de Groot (1947) also discovered the importance of this phase in the male.

[5]Compare this structure with Mortimer's drawing of a crisscrossed and smudged mother-baby unit (p. 15).

CHAPTER 10

The Development of the Young Child From Birth Through Latency, as Seen Through Bodily Movement, II

The basic movement patterns, observable from birth, are rhythms of *tension-flow* (used to express needs, drives, and feelings), and rhythms of *shape-flow* (used to express self-feelings such as comfort-discomfort and attraction-repulsion, e.g., modes of relatedness to the environment).

Tension-flow refers to the continuity created by changes in muscle tension from bound (inhibited) to free (uninhibited) movements. In addition to bound and free flow, we observe the: (1) holding of tension on an even level or adjustments of levels; (2) high or low intensity of tension, and (3) abrupt or gradual changes of tension. Tension-flow rhythms consist of certain sequences of tension qualities which are well suited for biological needs, such as sucking, defecating, urinating, and others.

Shape-flow refers to changes in body-shape from shrinking to growing, as exemplified in exhalation and inhalation and in shying away from noxious, and seeking our pleasant stimuli. In addition to these basic shapes we observe more specifically narrowing and widening, shortening and lengthening, as well as hollowing and bulging.

The role of these patterns in the development of children under three years of age was discussed in Chapter 8. Here I shall add to the vocabulary of movement and review development from birth through latency by extrapolating developmental trends from motion factors, which I shall briefly define below and discuss more fully in separate sections. They will be used to illustrate how our understanding of progressive developmental phases can be deepened through the study of movement.

Readers who may not be able to follow precisely the description and interpretation of movement can still derive insight into the nature of inferences made from movement observation and can form opinions as to whether the hypotheses proposed here are helpful for the understanding of development.

Brief Definitions

Body attitude is the somatic core of the body image which changes in accordance with each new developmental phase. *Efforts* are used to cope with external reality. Their *precursors* are genetically and functionally related to tension-flow and are the motor mainstays of learning and defense mechanisms. *Shaping of space in directions* is genetically related to shape-flow and is used to establish or discontinue bridges to objects. *Shaping of space in planes* reflects more complex relationships.

One can deduce the degree of harmony or conflict between the ego and the superego from the way effort or shaping patterns are used in parts of the body, through *gestures*, and in the whole body, through *postures*. The latter are advanced motion factors which are not clearly structured before mid-latency.

Body Attitude[1]

The term "body attitude" refers to the way the body is shaped, how it is aligned in space, how body parts are positioned in relation to one another and to the favored positions of the whole body. It also denotes all the patterns and phrases of movement for which there is readiness at rest. In addition, it indicates the qualities of movement which, through frequent use, have left their imprint upon the body.

Efforts and Their Precursors

Efforts are motor apparatus used to express attitudes to environmental forces (space, gravity, and time) which are the essential factors of our external reality. We classify efforts in the following way:

> We use direct direct efforts when we approach space in order to direct our attention to stationary objects, and *indirect* efforts when we follow moving objects and pay *attention* to them wherever they are going. However, our attitudes to space denote the scope of our attention, not our interest in objects.

We use *strong* efforts to lift heavy *weights* and for other activities that require determination. We use *light* efforts for activities requiring a "light touch." Our attitudes to weight denote the degree of our *intent*.

We use the effort of *acceleration* to attend to urgent matters and of *deceleration* when we have plenty of time. Our attitudes to time denote modes employed in *decision*-making.

Precursors of effort are motor apparatus which mediate between tension-flow and effort. Inasmuch as they control tension, they are body-oriented; to the degree that they attempt to deal with space, weight, and time, they are reality-oriented. We use precursors of effort when learning new skills, a process that requires control over the body before learned patterns become automatized through mature efforts. We also use precursors of effort in the service of defenses. We classify precursors of effort in the following way:

Precursors of approach to *space* keep tension levels even as an aid in *channeling* pathways through space, and adjust tension levels to achieve *flexibility* in space. When an infant stares, he channels pathways into space without paying attention the way an older child does. When he follows sights or sounds he has to readjust his tension quite frequently to make roundabout flexible movements.

Precursors of dealing with *weight* increase the intensity of tension to produce *vehement* or *straining* actions when strength fails. They decrease tension to effect *gentleness*. To push in a door that is too difficult to open by strength, we use a good deal of free flow in actions so vehement that we may fall through the door while opening it. Before we have learned the light touch of fingertips for piano playing, we may approach the keys gently by reducing the intensity of tension. This happens almost invariably when the piano teacher tells the beginner to relax. Precursors of dealing with *time* change tension abruptly to produce *sudden* actions, and change tension gradually to effect *hesitation*. Told to hurry, a toddler may make a sudden move but not necessarily continue, because his sense of time is yet quite limited. Feeling unhurried, he may dawdle and proceed with hesitation, especially when he is reluctant to go ahead.

Shaping of Space in Directions And Planes

Changing of the shape of the body by shrinking or growing in width, length, and depth conveys alterations of states, but does not alter the space around us. By moving in lines and planes, we create new configurations in space.

When movement proceeds in *directions,* we divide space by lines which form bridges to objects or relinquish contact. When a child points by designing an imaginary line from his finger to an object, the observer can readily re-create this line so that he can interpret the child's movement correctly. We move in the following directions:

> Across and sideways, horizontally
> Downward and upward, vertically
> Backward and forward, sagittally

Movement in directions is unidimensional. *Shaping space in planes* requires the traversing of at least two dimensions. Shaping in planes follows an oval pathway in one plane or winds from one plane to another. By retracing these complicated shapes in our minds, we can interpret them and respond appropriately to what is conveyed by them. When we move in planes, we create concave and convex multidimensional shapes that express our attitudes toward real and imaginary objects. Each plane is used in a different way to best serve certain ego functions that play a role in our relationships.

> In the *horizontal* plane we *enclose* small areas of space or *spread* in a wide area of space (through moving across the body and backward or forward and sideways) in the service of *exploration* of objects. We enclose to hold and examine closely, and we spread for a more cursory survey or to allot more space to objects.
>
> In the *vertical* plane we *descend* or *ascend* (through moving downward and across or sideways and upward) in a manner most conducive for *confrontation* of objects. Descending can be used for expressing an attitude of looking down at others; ascending can be used for the expression of admiration.
>
> In the *sagittal* plane we *retreat* or *advance* (through moving backward and down or upward and forward) in *anticipation* of the attitudes of other people. For instance, we advance toward friendly people and retreat from those who threaten us.

There is a hierarchic ascendancy in the ego's control over motility. From the regulation of tension-flow there evolves control over precursors of effort and finally over the mature forms of effort. From the regulation of shape-flow there evolves control over the directions of space, followed by control of shaping space in planes. A coordination of affine sets of tension- and shape-flow, of precursors of effort and shaping in directions, and of effort and shaping in planes underlies the harmonious development of ego functions. As a result, feeling safe becomes associated with

238

the expression of well being and cautiousness with uneasiness; defensiveness is balanced by regulating contact with objects; and coping with external reality is structured by appropriate interpersonal relations. A lack of coordination between these patterns expresses conflict. The origin of these complex processes is revealed in infancy not only in characteristic sets of maturing motion elements, but also in corresponding body attitudes.

The Neonatal Phase

From Disequilibrium to Integration

At birth, the neonate is in a state of disequilibrium. His rhythmic centers are not yet mature. His movements are uncoordinated and often follow one another in unpredictable ways. For a few days or even weeks his genitals may be swollen and sometimes look inflamed. It is not clear at all what makes the boy's erections come, stay for a long time, and subside (see Chapter 5). He cries in discomfort not only when he is hungry. During various states in which his sensorium changes, he responds differently (Wolff, 1959, 1966). Gradually, under the guidance of his mother, who meets his maturational advances halfway, his various functions become integrated and his behavioral patterns become regular and predictable.

Body Attitude

A newborn baby's rounded shape, straight spine, short neck, and flexed limbs are all indicators of his recent confinement in the uterine cavity. As he tenses and releases tension, he exercises rhythmic shrinking of his body shape into a confined space and growing out into the space around him. In the upper part of his body, he alternates primarily between narrowing and widening which helps to get his hand into his mouth and take it away again. In the lower part of his body, he alternates between stretching with narrowing and shortening with widening. As he brings his heels up, the boy frequently hits or pats his scrotum and the girl comes close to her genital region. The upper part of the neonate's body seems to strive for mouth-hand-eye coordination (Hoffer, 1949), in the service of oral needs. The lower part coordinates the lower extremities with the pelvic-abdominal area in what appears to be an attempt to cope with stimuli from within. Activity in this region increases just before defecation or urination. Extension which increases inner pressure may also have an effect upon the infant's erections.

239

The division between the upper and lower part of the body is periodically undone when the whole body responds symmetrically through startles. The tonic neck reflex puts the baby into an asymmetric position that allows him to embrace his mother as he turns his head toward her breast (Robbins and Soodak, 1972). When she holds him, he coordinates the upper and lower parts of his body. Not only does his mouthing indicate his readiness for sucking, but the twiddling of his fingers and toes also keeps time with the rhythms of sucking, as if he were practicing the integration of body parts into one unit. His body attitude reflects the level of attainment in the developmental task of integrating body parts, positions, and movement into patterns that will be responsive to the opportunities, provided by the environment for his nurture and growth.

Characteristic Movement Patterns

Already in the neonatal phase there is a preponderance of oral rhythms over others.[2] Most striking is the great frequency of rhythms which we have classified as inner-genital (see page 248). It takes some time before they decrease to a moderate quantity. At the same time, oral rhythms develop their distinctive quality in mouthing, sucking of the fist, and of the nipple. At first there may be just a few sucking motions followed by sleep. Progressively, the infant achieves control over the continuity of sucking. There develops a regulation of bound and free flow, a regulation that can be used for the restraint or release of drive discharge through motor channels. From it there evolve feelings of caution and safety, especially those that are experienced in loss of balance and recovery from it through safe holding. Concomitant with the regulation of bound and free flow, there develops a regulation of shrinking and growing of body shape which structures the distribution of drive discharge inward and outward, and into different body parts. From this regulation there evolve feelings of discomfort or comfort and of repulsion or attraction, which are probably the principal modes of self-feeling in the "narcissistic milieu interne" of the neonatal phase (Hoffer, 1949, 1950; Kestenberg, 1967a).

At first, tension-flow and shape-flow are not coordinated. Through the integrative influence of the mother, bound flow and shrinking, free flow and growing, as well as other attributes, such as keeping tension even and narrowing, become allied for optimum functioning. It seems likely that feelings of safety merge with feelings of comfort, and caution merges with discomfort. Thus, an infant, held securely, feels safe and comfortable, while inadequate support brings on caution (anxiousness) and discomfort. Safety and caution are even more clearly associated with feelings of attraction and repulsion, respectively. Attracted by a nipple before him, the infant feels free to seize it; repelled by a new taste he cautiously shrinks away from it. These and similar feelings become integrated in such a way that they can become meaningful to the mother through mutual attunement in tension-flow and accommodation in shape-flow. With the conclusion of the reintegration and adjustment to postnatal life, the infant is ready to learn new forms of self-expression in the oral phase.

Growth and Differentiation in Pregenital Phases

Body Attitudes

In the oral phase we see a steady growth of the control over positions of head and limbs in relation to the trunk. The alignment of head, chest, and arms in the horizontal plane makes it possible for the baby to reach his mouth at will and then reach objects in space by lateral grasp. The rudimentary control of approach to space is interrelated with the control of sucking and with the baby's capacity to soothe himself by settling down in a poised manner or by readjusting his position to changing stimuli. Shaping of his body through narrowing and widening (as in frowning and smiling, or in bringing his hands to his mouth and flinging them out) is the body-base on which he builds the skills of moving across and sideways.

When biting rhythms become more frequent, they interfere with sucking and soothing techniques. However, for the frustrated child they become a model for the sharp delineation and precision of movement patterns which make prehension possible. The progressive differentiation of basic positions of the body (prone and supine) and of limb movements (reaching and grasping) becomes the central core of his prehensile body image (see Chapter 8). The mobility of head and limbs and the progressive mobilization of the chest through twisting and turning facilitate the child's approach to space and its exploration. These are the basic ego functions which help differentiate the developmental task of the oral phase: the establishment of a primary system of communication.

In the anal phase, the child learns to control twisting anal-type rhythms before he can change positions with ease (as, for instance, in turning from creeping to sitting and vice versa). This involves a regulation of very small intensities of tension which cannot help maintain the erect posture, for which he strives. There is a growing trend toward stability of the trunk, with limbs used as adjuncts to maintain the alignment of the body in the vertical plane. An influx of anal-sadistic-type rhythms at this time becomes a model which the child uses for straining to pull himself up. By maintaining an even level of high intensity of tension, he averts the danger of losing his balance and falling.

When erect posture becomes habitual, the child's body-planes become aligned to the spatial planes through which the human species views the world. Having become a biped, he extends his length, solidifies the middle of his body, and uses arms and hands from the base of a steady, well-defined frame. The child's mastery over rhythms of defecation depends on his ability to control intensities of tension as well as on his capacity to lengthen and shorten his body shape at will. Through the maintenance of positions of sitting, squatting, and standing, he acquires a central core for a differentiated, yet stable body image. By carrying his own weight, he begins to understand the weight and mass of objects. By shaping his movement in the vertical dimension and plane, he shows his intent by gestures, such as pointing to the cupboard or climbing on a chair to reach it. Thus are born the ego functions of appraising and explaining which help complete the developmental task of this phase; the attainment of a basic form of presentation and representation of self and objects.

In the urethral phase, the child's advancing locomotor functions can be recognized, even while he is immobile, from the way his toes point forward rather than sideways and from the way his arms are held in readiness for walking. No longer does he take up a lot of space in the vertical plane. With the narrowing down of his stance and his arms balancing forward and backward instead of sideways, his shape has become arrowlike. He is aligned in the sagittal plane, the plane of locomotion.

At first, the mobile toddler moves in an uncertain, aimless way. He is just beginning to acknowledge his urethral rhythms and will let his mother know that he is wet. With the influx of urethral-sadistic-type rhythms, he begins to differentiate between the passive experience of wetting himself or being propelled into locomotion and the activity of precise aiming of urine or goal-directed walking. As he gains control over the urethral rhythms, he assumes positions that prepare for his impatient shooting out or for delaying. As he stands or walks, he manipulates his belly, making it bulge and hollow in succession. His budding sense of the timing of movement and his new ability to move forward and backward, to advance and to retreat, are imprinted upon his body attitude, which becomes the base for the fluid and yet boundaried body image of a "big" boy or girl. The developmental task of this phase, to put the yet immature ego functions of remembering, deciding, anticipating, mobilizing, and containing in the service of rudimentary operations, has been completed (see Chapter 8).

I have rephrased the development of the infant in terms of his changing body attitudes. Implied in its description, was the control over certain tension-flow and shape-flow attributes, as well as the beginning of more advanced movement patterns.

Characteristic Movement Patterns

In the oral phase, the harmonious interaction between mother and child becomes more and more intensified. The control over sucking rhythms culminates in the infant's ability to find his hand and suck a finger of his choice. Smiling becomes more frequent and other expressions of pleasure, such as cooing, gurgling, and laughing become more pronounced. At the same time, the baby's attentiveness increases. He can keep an even level of tension for a long time when he looks at his mother's face during nursing, stares at the corner of his crib and later at his hands. While staring, he narrows down his field of exploration. He is not yet a gazer into distant spaces. However, he can widen enough and readjust levels of tension sufficiently to follow his mother's movements with his eyes.

Angry moods begin to be frequent before the pain of teething becomes apparent to the mother. When he becomes irritable, the oral infant begins to use many more biting than sucking rhythms. The continuity of his nursing suffers. At first, he cannot really choose whether he will suck or bite; then, he gains control over oral rhythms and bites at will and sucks, as he pleases. At the same time his patterns become increasingly more differentiated. He learns to discriminate between channeling pathways in space and moving flexibly. He can cross over to the other side of his body or reach sideways. Having learned to differentiate between his mother and strangers, he now employs precursors of effort and directional movements in the service of defenses. For instance, he avoids a stranger who faces him directly by readjusting the level of his tension and flexibly veering away to the side; or, keeping tension on an even keel he channels his attention away from the stranger, reaching across and turning to look at his mother.

When he begins to use mature efforts, his body tension becomes subordinated to the aim of the ego to pay heed, either by directing his attention to specific issues or taking an indirect route to foster general investigation. In addition to localizing objects in space through directional movement, across and sideways, the older infant becomes capable of enclosing a small segment of space by traversing an arc across the body and backward (in the horizonttal plane) and of spreading in space by reversing the course of the movement. Shaping of space in this plane serves the exploration of small and large segments of space. Attention and exploration combine to promote the development of self- and object-representations and of self- and object-constancy through recognition of sameness in nearness and distance. These rudimentary mental structures are requisite for the beginning of communication between mother and child.

The early anal phase can be best characterized as a period of polymorph growth (Kestenberg, 1966). The child practices what he has learned and acquires a great many more skills. A preponderance of anal (twisting type) rhythms, which are modeled after sphincter contractions, becomes apparent. These are mixed with other rhythms, especially the sucking and biting ones. The child twists away from the breast and demands it again after a few minutes. As he sucks, he may twist or lick the nipple and he may also use a combination of sucking and biting with a bit of tongue twisting added to it. To be a good twister he needs to gain control over tension levels in small intensities. This type of control comes also in good stead for picking up small objects and releasing them. He lowers his tension a bit to drop objects on the floor. He watches their trajectories (Piaget, 1948), then looks up at his mother trying to induce her to reverse the direction of the movement from downward to upward.

On his way to conquer new dimensions of space, and ready to oppose gravity as well, the child becomes overstimulated by all the things he is experiencing from a new vantage point. His intent to do more than he can actually accomplish overwhelms him; he becomes cross and unable to control his temper. It is interesting to note that the influx of anal-sadistic type of rhythms at this time becomes the primary incentive for the child's recovery from his growth crisis. He can accomplish more by using high intensity of tension and keeping it on an even level for some time, which are the principal qualities of the anal-sadistic type of rhythm. Soon, he begins to differentiate between twisting and straining; at the same time he begins to regulate intensities of tension and related shape changes. He foreshortens when he strains and he lengthens, lowering his tension when he stops straining.

From the control of intensities of tension there evolve the precursor of strength (vehemence or intentional straining), and the precursor of lightness (a gentle, easy touch). The same patterns are used for defenses,

244

vehement temper serving as identification with the aggressor and defensive stubbornness, while gentleness is used as the motor counterpart of reaction formation against aggressive impulses. Associated with these patterns are directional movements downward (as in stamping feet) and upward (as in looking up to mother with tenderness). A rudimentary control over weight begins now, with the toddler becoming capable of lifting relatively heavy objects with strength and playing with little whisps of thread, for which lightness is needed. Not only does he practice pointing downward and upward at that time, but he also begins to shape in the vertical plane in sequences of descending and ascending. He practices taking possession and relinquishing in games of picking up things from the floor and throwing them down again and he becomes an indefatigable furniture climber. His intentionality reveals itself in his incipient use of strong or light efforts. He coordinates it with incessant confronting of objects in the vertical plane, as if to say that he knows what to do and what object he needs to do it to. Representation is now modeled after the ability to present concrete objects, which initiates symbolic thinking.

In the ensuing urethral phase, the toddler practices walking, running, and vocalizing as if he were talking. It is difficult to contain him. He loves playing with water and spills things for lack of control. Despite his great mobility, he prefers to use urethral rhythms which are characterized by a gradual and small increase or decrease of tension. He tends to bulge his abdomen and lengthen his torso as he proceeds, moving ahead incessantly, unable to stop even when he is tired. Once more he is undertaking more than he can master and he becomes impatient with his lack of accomplishment. An influx of urethral-sadistic-type rhythms (Kestenberg, 1963, 1965, 1966) increases the child's agility and helps him overcome his new developmental crisis. He gains control over sharp or abrupt changes of tension in low intensity, which are the principal qualities of urethral-sadistic rhythms. He learns to differentiate between graduality and abruptness at the same time as he becomes able to change his bulging shape and hollow at the waist. When precursors of effort become operative and shaping in directions becomes possible, abruptness changes into suddenness and graduality into hesitation; at the same time hollowing presages moving backward and bulging presages moving forward. The same patterns are used for defenses. Moving back suddenly is one of the ingredients of an escape action. Moving forward with hesitation is not an infrequent reaction of the toddler to a feared stranger. Concomitantly with the acquisition of a rudimentary control over time through acceleration (as in hurried running) and deceleration (as in leisurely walking), there develops shaping in the sagittal plane, effecting

245

clarity of retreat and advance. At first the toddler walks around uncertainly, pointing his finger and extending his arm forward, before he reaches the person he is seeking. Then, he begins to advance and offer objects to people in a leisurely manner; empty-handed, he retreats hurriedly to find another object. Time begins to play a role in his decision-making; his initiative determines when he needs to accelerate or decelerate. Retreating and advancing in the sagittal plane become the mainstays of the ego functions of sequencing, ordering, and anticipating. Combined, his favored efforts and shaping help endow his self- and object-representations with continuity in time and mobility. His speech and thought can now become operational.

In each of the developmental phases discussed above, the child practices certain motor patterns incessantly, sometimes to the exclusion of all others. For instance, the attentive infant wants to watch things all the time and may fight sleep to do so; the creeper and climber are intent on getting their way and oppose passive submission to diapering; and the child who has just begun to walk skillfully wants to be always on the go and has no time to sit down for a meal. In the next phase, the child ceases to be a "specialist." The task before him is to combine what he has learned and practiced into complex behavioral entities and phrases.

The Inner-Genital Phase:
From Disequilibrium to Integration

At the beginning of this phase, the child suffers from a disequilibrium produced by divergent trends, persistent pregenital needs vying with early genital urges and with incompatible ego interests. He may still need his bottle, especially at night; he may not yet be toilet-trained. At the same time he wants to get a baby—a wish arising from ill-defined inner-genital tensions. He wants to be big, but he still clings to his mother. His body-attitude veers from one position to another. Under the guidance of internal and external organizers, the divergent trends become integrated, allowing the toddler to give up pregenital wishes in subordination to his early genital organization.

Body Attitude

The two-and-a-half-year-old may be rounded and curled up with his toy or bottle clutched to his body, but may soon turn and twist, trying to move out of the horizontal alignment by getting up and realigning himself in a vertical position. He may then proceed to throw his bottle away, only to retrieve it later. He may advance toward it with an arrow-like body attitude, bulging as he seizes it and already hollowing in preparation for a retreat. After being weaned from the bottle, he may continue to soothe himself by sucking his fingers. If he combines sucking with stroking or clutching of a blanket or toy, he will lie down in a habitual body shape, into which the transitional object fits in a special way. When he stands up or walks with it, he carries or drags it, incorporating it into his manner of standing or walking, so that it becomes a part of the space close to him, and a part of his body as well, e.g., his baby (Winnicott, 1953).

If the toddler in this phase still needs diapers, he will lie down to be changed, with his trunk flat on the table and his limbs spread out symmetrically. However, he will attentively follow his mother's motions and will often raise his head, straining to see what is going on below. During and after training, he may resort to withholding of feces, striding with a distended, heavy belly, big enough to carry an imaginary baby.

The boy, standing up to urinate, proudly bulges forward, displaying an arrowlike attitude, in alignment with his urinating penis. The girl may sit on the toilet with a hollowed belly; at times, she is intent on hiding her genital, and at other times she bends down to look at it or touch it.

Common to all the divergent body-attitudes, which are reminiscent of those assumed in earlier developmental phases, is the focus on the inside of the body. Characteristically, the toddler will pull up his shirt, point to the umbilicus or pat his abdomen.

Only gradually we witness the child's transformation into a little girl or boy. From an uncertain-looking, lordotic straggler who veers between progression and regression, the girl develops into a dainty, miniature "lady." The boy, however, may take on feminine characteristics before he too can develop sex-specific qualities.

Both, girls and boys, become multidimensional in their appearance. They develop clear waists, with the division between chest and pelvis acting as an organizer of two coordinated units: (1) shoulder-girdle-chest-upper extremities, (2) pelvic-girdle-abdomen-lower extremities. Through swinging, rolling, swaying, and almost imperceptible shifts of weight, there develops an integration between all parts of the body that provides the core of an integrated body image. The shape of the body is characterized by curves, bulges and hollow spots, lines and waves, tense and relaxed areas, with head and limbs positioned so as to be complementary to the trunk. The observer can detect a composition that creates unity between the shape of the body and the shape of the space around it. The integrating influence of phase-specific, inner-genital types of rhythms can be recognized even during rest and sedentary activities: the acute observer can see ripples and waves that radiate from the inside of the body, outward and inward, with gradually increasing and decreasing intensities of tension. The predominant use of this rhythm is reinforced by the child's identification with his mother, whose feminine-maternal rhythms are of the same order. They may be especially pronounced when she alternates between letting him become independent and inviting him to be her baby again by opening up the flow from the inner spaces of her body to him. Her influence helps create the body attitude, which reflects the subtle integration of inside and outside in the body image of the three- to four-year-old child.

Characteristic Movement Patterns

In each developmental phase, the phase-specific, dominant rhythm of tension-flow becomes more clearly differentiated (pure rhythm) and is used more frequently than others. In addition, the favored rhythm tends to merge with or organize the course of other rhythms in accordance with its own prevailing qualities (mixed rhythm). Some rhythms, especially those which operate with even flow or gradual flow changes, are better organizers than others. The inner-genital type of rhythm exerts an integrative influence upon the many oral, anal, urethral, and phallic types of rhythms that vie with one another for dominance in the beginning of this phase.

The subtle, inner-genital rhythm is characterized by very gradually increasing and decreasing intensities of tension in bound and free flow. It can be recognized without notation by the undulating, finely graded changes that lend a feminine character to movement. Robbins (1969) discovered the subtle inner-genital type of rhythm in the horizontal ripples that traverse the scrotum of the newborn. From wavy scribbles of little girls and from descriptions of sensations by older girls and women, we have deduced that similar undulations are characteristic of "waves" of vaginal excitations (see Chapter 9). Toward the end of this phase, one can observe some swaying motions in which very gradually a high intensity of tension is reached. This intense inner-genital-type rhythm is perceived in terms of large waves of long duration. We have encountered this type of rhythm in the myographic recording of uterus contractions during labor. It can be noted with increasing frequency during adolescence (see Chapter 17).

Because the subtle undulatory rhythms, which seem to arise from cryptic parts of the genitals, are all-pervasive in this phase of development, the term "inner-genital" has been used in referring to the phase and to its characteristic rhythm as well. The latter gives a languid quality to the motility of the three-year-old.[3] Its influence is felt in all behavior and all modalities. The following example illustrates its effect on zones, associated with pregenitality.

> The transient retention of feces or urine—which recurs in this phase—is often accomplished by a very gradual filling and distending of the rectum or bladder without any awareness of a need to eliminate. Owing to the graduality and low intensity of changes, the child experiences little pressure and does not feel uncomfortable until a great amount of excreta has accumulated in his rectum. In contrast, during regressive bouts of withholding feces in a purely anal-sadistic way, tension mounts greatly and is held on an even level for a long time. At such times, the child spitefully refuses to release the tension and let go of the feces. In the passive, gradual distension we encounter a combination of retention and incontinence. A very gradual release of small quantities of tension is frequently the cause of the child's lack of awareness that he had stained or wet his underwear.

When subtle, inner-genital types of rhythms spread through the body in waves, it is difficult to localize their origin. The gradual and fine differences in tension interfere with the acuity of perception. Nevertheless, the tensions are felt and have a disquieting effect upon the psyche. As described in other chapters, the child in this phase becomes confused by the vagueness of his kinesthetic sensations and, at first, assigns their origin to the stomach, the rectum, or the bladder.[4] Distensions of these organs, experienced as "tummy-aches," are used to master unclear tensions of unknown origin. However, through pressures on the adjoining genitals, the distensions increase rather than relieve the inner-genital waves of excitement.

Rhythmic changes in the shape of the body, which are coordinated with the inner-genital type of tension-flow rhythms, give them structure and direction. Almost imperceptible "shrinking" of body shape in the pelvic area alternates with combinations of lengthening and bulging of the abdomen. Through the former, tension waves seem to flow centripetally into the inside of the body, where they become contained for a while through inhibition of flow; through the latter they reverse their direction, flowing freely to the outside of the body and beyond. They crystallize in space as "spatial tensions" created by movement (Laban, 1966). This traffic between inside and outside facilitates the externalization of kinesthetic percepts and impulses from the inside of the body to its periphery and to external objects.

249

In the process of passing on the inner excitement through externalization, the child becomes a nagger, and does not cease to bother his mother until she too becomes excited (Chapter 4). It is interesting to note how often a mother experiences the same waves of excitement as the child, and meets his nagging with "counter-nagging." If the excitement does not become too intense, the subtle interplay of mildly sexual and desexualized transactions between mother and child creates a fertile ground for the mother to become the external organizer of the child's drive-derivative play with objects. When there is attunement between them, mother and child play together, share, touch, and manipulate objects in the intimate space between their bodies which Winnicott (1953) called the "in-between-space" of transitional phenomena. The typical transitional object of that time, created by the child for himself and his mother is the baby: usually a three-dimensional, inanimate object, enlivened by a fantasy evolving from inner-genital excitement. Even though boys in that phase may roll cars to their mothers, rather than play with dolls, their movement patterns betray that they too have the kind of excitement that creates babies not only out of dolls and teddy bears but also out of machines.

During practical activities and play, we encounter in this phase a great many effort and shaping elements, the former used as tools of dealing with external reality and the latter as ways of expressing relationships. There is a decided preference for handling things with lightness and deceleration and with rising and advancing, which gives a maternal tinge to activities with and without objects. All effort and shaping elements are in use, but the most frequently combined patterns are those that most resemble maternal movement. Because of the increasing identification with the preoedipal mother (Mac Brunswick, 1940), verbalization is beginning to replace wordless gestures such as pointing. Only when the mother herself persists in using many directional movements does the child continue to use mime in lieu of communication through words. To reinforce speech the child creates two- and three-dimensional shapes in the space, not too far from his body. They provide complementary configurations to the shapes assumed by the body. Shaping in space helps to delineate three-dimensional objects by direct touch and by imaginary mimetic manipulation. Using movement to create shapes in external space helps the child construct models for the unseen "inner shape" (Barnett, 1966, 1968; Fraiberg, 1972) inside the body. In this phase, this particularly refers to the imagined shape of the inner genitals, which is equated with the shape of a cherished baby-object.

With increasing externalization and the help of the integrative influence of the mother, the interests of the toddler become deflected from

250

bodily functions to playing with objects. Experimentation with retention of body contents to produce pregenital-type babies decreases, and fantasies about having had a baby inside and having delivered it replace manipulations of the belly. Taking care of the baby and doing things like mother, although more frequent with girls, lies also in the center of boys' interests.

Toward the end of this phase inner-genital tensions may become so intense that externalization can no longer relieve them. This is especially true in those instances in which overstimulation, seduction, and genital irritations have produced inner-genital pressures and sensations much earlier. Even though these causes of excitement are long past, they are revived, acted out, and relived at this time. Since desexualization is failing now, the child tries to contain his inner-genital excitement through tensing and hollowing (knotting inside). In hidden masturbatory activities, the girl, more than the boy, "squeezes" the thigh muscles and visibly shortens the distance between pelvis and thighs. This type of containment produces genital engorgement through the cutting off of the venous supply of blood. There is enough clinical material from analyses of women and girls to provide a fairly accurate impression of the localization of this mode of excitation in the vagina (Fraiberg, 1972). Some data from analyses of men and boys and observations of boys corroborate the impression of movement observers that male inner-genital excitation travels inward and outward via the testicular-inguinal route (see Chapter 5). Inner-genital sensations are reported when boys press their pubic-inguinal region against a hard surface. Simultaneously, the spermatic cords contract and the testicles are raised.[5] The nature of the sexual excitement betrays itself in a facial expression of stillness with glazed eyes, which results in the shutting off of stimuli and loss of focus. However, the notation of tension- and shape-flow—revealing repeated gradual increases of tension to a high plateau with simultaneous bulging and shortening of the pelvic-femoral shape—is a more reliable indicator of the inner-genital nature of the sexual excitement.

Under favorable circumstances, high waves of gradually rising excitement are rare. Instead, one notes that efforts of strength and deceleration, fleeting at first, are becoming more pronounced. Their combination makes the child appear determined and decisive. It is also used in skills requiring desexualized pressing and squeezing, as in handling clay. However, resexualization does occur; at such times efforts becomes subservient to tension-flow rhythms rather than subordinating the latter to their own aims. Strength is then used for destructive purposes, especially when it is not tempered by deceleration and is regressively infiltrated by anal-sadistic discharge forms. Shaping, through small excursions of advancing and descending, becomes dominated by changes in body shape that bring the child's hands closer to the lower part of the body. Whereas before baby-objects were held and cuddled at the shoulder and chest area, now they are frequently placed close to the thighs or between the legs, and treated roughly.

Regressive episodes are individually variable as to duration and intensity. Only in pathological development does one see a preponderance of aggression, anxiety, and defensiveness over recoveries through sublimation. The following, condensed account is extrapolated from analyses of young children and reconstructions from analyses of older patients. However, all of it, in an attenuated form, reveals itself through movement studies in typical end stages of the inner-genital phase.

Deliberate damage to toys and attacks upon others are occasioned by feelings that the inside is intolerably tense and should be eliminated. The child wishes to expel this disturbing "inside" which, in his mind, is taking on the concrete shape of a live object. Such wishes evoke fears of losing pelvic-abdominal content, becoming incontinent and empty. They are frequently reawakened in fears of delivery. It is not easy to elicit the expression of these fantasies and anxieties, unless one first understands the underlying kinesthetic sensations. High waves of tension, combined with shrinking of the pelvic region—used to contain excitement—increase it instead by concentrating it in a small area. Correspondingly, fears increase and evoke regressive defenses. The child's behavior may deteriorate into an oral-type hair-plucking, anal twisting, balling, smearing, or throwing, urethral-type sogging and similar activities. These are frequently performed with mixed inner-genital and pre-genital rhythms and immature effort and shaping patterns. Vehemence, combined with shortening and directing movement downward and away from the body, is used for identification with an aggressor, who threatens from within and is externalized to an outsider. Sudden backtracking, combined with gentle lifting of the head and chest away from the lower part of the body, is one of the ways denial is expressed through movement. Straining, combined with hesitant reluctance is the motor counterpart and forerunner of repression, in response to anxiety regarding the delivery of an imaginary baby—an attacker from inside. The revengeful destruction of this imaginary baby is reflected in the use of aggression with objects, other children and parents, who are sometimes embraced and "squeezed to death." There is dual anger, at the "unruly baby inside," and at the mother who does not relieve the inner excitement, does not punish the baby to "make it nice," and may even get her own real baby instead. Precursors of the superego reveal themselves in rhythmic alternations of blaming the mother for the "death" of the imaginary baby (see Chapter 1) and blaming oneself for its destruction, attitudes which condense with similar wishes regarding a real sibling baby. In such instances, hitting the mother may be followed by self-hitting, in which the total body of the child is involved.[6] Provoking the mother to hit the baby (Freud, S., 1919) alternates with "begging for punishment" and depressive withdrawal.

The better the integration of pregenital with the dominant genital drives, the less intense the child's aggression and the less prolonged his depression will be. Data from movement profiles suggest that the integration of rhythms of tension-flow (as seen in mixed rhythms) has a positive correlation to the increase of libidinal discharge forms. The better the integration of the child's approach to reality—as expressed through efforts—and his achievement of object constancy—as expressed through shaping in space—the more access he has to sublimations. The identification with the mother decreases in importance, enabling the child to pursue his interest in nursery school and play with other children, whom he emulates. This helps him to assume and confirm a sex-specific identity on the basis of his own movement, his own body build and a comparison with his peers.

The need to retain genital dominance, turning to reality, and the stabilizing influence of object constancy (based on a sex-specific attitude to the mother), all help the child to resolve conflicts, centered on inner-genital types of fantasies and wishes. The denial of the existence of inner genitals (Horney, 1933) and a transfer of inner-genital interests to the external genitalia put an end to sado-masochistic fantasies about the inside of the body. Fingers which come close to the introitus or groin, flit away abruptly and dart to the clitoris or penis. There is a tendency to "close" the introitus by pulling it upward and backward and making it disappear. As a compensation the clitoris "jumps out" coming down from hiding, and bulging out. A similar tendency in the boy (pulling the testicles upward and backward) often leads to an erection or "wiggling" of the penis. Keeping up these "pull-up" positions leads to a compactness of body shape in preparation for the phallic child's new body attitude.

The Outer-Genital (Phallic) Phase: From Global Growth to Differentiation

The developmental task of the first part of the phallic phase is to unify the increased drives, profuse interests, and intensified relationships that make the young phallic child's love and hate all-encompassing, yet capable of changing from one oedipal position to another. In the later part of the phallic phase, the increasing discrimination between opposing wishes, identifications, and ego-attitudes becomes a prelude to the ensuing differentiation of psychic structures, especially of the superego from the ego. Correspondingly, the motor patterns of the early phallic phase differ from those prevalent in its later stages.

Body Attitude

The young phallic child tends to use his whole body as a global unit, with head and limbs acting as extensions of the trunk. The impression of a rounded shape containing a space inside, which was the distinguishing mark of the three-year-old, is lost. The child (the boy more than the girl) looks as if he were hewn out of one solid piece without hollows. The center of gravity is stable and body boundaries are clearly delineated through increases of tension centrally and peripherally. The whole body seems to be in readiness to propel itself abruptly into space. Strength and acceleration soon become imprinted in the body attitude of the boy. The girl develops comparatively less strength; she may be light and springy instead. Both sexes enjoy jumping up and down as a pastime.

The unity of head, limbs and trunk and their intrusive quality are the core of the body-phallus image (Lewin, 1933) on which phallic fantasies are built. The boy's wish for a giant phallus like his father's evokes ideas that the penis is the outer extension of the spine, or that a gigantic inner network of wires or strings keeps the penis in place. The boy will lengthen and flatten his tummy to keep this apparatus intact. The girl's fantasy of an inner penis (Jacobson, 1936), which fills her whole body from top to bottom, stems from a condensation of penis, child, and breast envy. She too lengthens to give room to her secret possession, but she tends to bulge to emphasize her fullness. Both sexes, at that time, tend to feel superior and to assume condescending airs as if they as individuals were big and others were small.

When fantasies of penetration with aggressive intent begin to predominate, the child's movements become sharp and his aimless jumping is replaced by a leaping through the air and landing safely. This requires a precise balance between limbs and trunk. As he veers between wanting to penetrate (in identification with his father) and wanting to be penetrated (in identification with this mother); from hurting others and being hurt to loving and being loved; from shooting games to games of skill; and, from identification with the aggressor to reaction formation—all along his movement reflects the continuous differentiating processes, now in operation. Their effect on the body attitude is that of

254

a sharp differentiation between head, limb, and trunk, each functionally different and serving specialized aims. As a result, the child becomes more skillful in tasks requiring fine motor coordination and he is less infatuated with gross motor feats, which had dominated his life in the earlier phallic phase. The relation between head and limbs becomes accentuated, and both are used more and more in coordinated gestures. As repression of genital wishes increases, the child's attention withdraws from the middle and the lower parts of his trunk. The increasing desexualization of functions liberates the hands, which will now forgo masturbation and perform useful, approved tasks. Busy hands attest to the child's purity and alert eyes watch others on whom "badness" is projected. Needless to say that this occurs much earlier in the girl than the boy.

In the beginning of the phallic phase the child was primarily action-oriented. By the end of this phase, he has become capable of planning his actions in accordance with his ego interests and consideration for others. With it he has attained his developmental task of differentiating between action-thinking and word-thinking.

Characteristic Movement Patterns

The phallic, "jumping" rhythm is characterized by abrupt increases and releases of tension. When the sadistic aspect of his phallic wishes predominates, the child darts and leaps with sharp reversals between free and bound flow and with an exaggerated intensity of tension and a considerable drop in releasing it.

In the early part of the phallic phase, the unity between drive-demands and ego-attitudes is expressed in the harmony between tension-flow attributes and efforts. For instance, high intensity of tension and the abruptness of its increase or decrease are synchronized with strength and acceleration. There is also, at that time, a close interrelationship between narcissistic self-feelings and relationships to objects. This is expressed in movement through the harmony between shape-flow changes and the shaping of configurations in space. For instance, lengthening will synchronize with ascending and bulging (protruding) with advancing in space. However, there is frequently a conflict between drive-demands and narcissistic self-aggrandizement, and a concomitant intra-systemic conflict between ego interests and relationships to people. These conflicts are expressed in a disharmony between tension- and shape-flow rhythms, and a mismatching between effort and shaping respectively. Because of the frequent use of such discordant patterns, the phallic child becomes accident-prone. For instance, he rams into people and things with abruptly increasing intensity and exertion of strength. At the same time he protrudes into space, lengthens his body, and ascends, trying to reach and surpass something or someone much taller than himself. Eventually, he will resolve these clashes by proper sequencing of gestures, in which tension-flow and shape-flow, effort and shaping will be coordinated.

As he learns to discriminate clearly between opposites, the older phallic child becomes an expert in preparing for actions through the sequential use of contrasting patterns. For instance, in preparation for a leap, he flexes his legs and hollows the abdomen in a position of retreat, from which he ascends and advances in conjunction with lengthening and bulging into space. He flexes his legs with intensity and strength, providing a springboard for the subsequent shooting out into the air with a lightness that makes him feel like the "daring young man on the flying trapeze." His fantasies are becoming clearer now and his needs and aspirations more object-centered.

The fine discrimination between antagonistic patterns promotes such defenses as turning into the opposite, undoing, and reaction formation. For instance, to cope with vehement expressions of aggression, the child becomes gentle and affectionate. The differentiation between aggressive and friendly actions is also revealed in sequences of gestures which, in play, become the mimetic representations of fantasies. Playing a daring intruder, the boy shoots his adversary; he may then retreat a step or two and put his gun back into the holster in a gesture of peace. However, soon after, his hand and gun leap out and the old or new opponent is killed in a daring surprise attack. With increasing differentiation, he becomes more skillful in expressing realistic and more complicated story sequences in words and actions. The girl uses appropriate sequences of gestures in her favored games of being tied, put into a dungeon, and rescued. However, both sexes show the veering between masculinity and femininity by alternating the roles of pursuers and victims, as for instance shooting and being shot at, tying up a victim and being tied. Appropriate movement patterns emphasize and affirm these sex-specific differences.

As latency approaches, one encounters, singly and in combinations, a great many patterns that seem to reinforce repression through movement. Channeling of actions into restricted areas of space (which reflects the curtailment of exploration) frequently combines with vehement, downward-directed actions (which may accompany a forceful lowering of aspirations) and with hesitating while progressing (which may reveal a restriction put on advancement). At the same time, effort and shaping of space, which serve to express curiosity, investigation, and communication, are reduced in frequency. The child begins to be more reticent and demands more privacy for himself. An influx of immature forms of total body involvement in postural movement (Lamb, 1965) betrays the increasing influence of the incipient superego on the ego's control of motility.

Latency: From Regression to Stability and Consolidation of Functions

In latency, the child attains a stable equilibrium through the consolidation of ego- and superego-functions. However, before he can progress in this direction, he undergoes a regression that revives pregenital impulses and immature forms of ego-functions (Bornstein, 1951; Chapters 11 and 13).

Body Attitude

In early latency, the child frequently assumes babylike attitudes, as he giggles, waves limbs, and loses control over the stability of the trunk. This occurs more often in company of other children, who egg each other on to use "improper" anal language or mess food and spill fluids. The influx of pregenital-type rhythms of tension-flow and frequent changes in shape alter the contours of the child's body in such a way that he seems smaller than he was, rounder and inordinately mobile. However, each time he recovers from a bout of regression, he appears more stable than before.

The permanent body-attitude of latency proper is characterized by a one-piece trunk that only infrequently twists at the waist and is isolated from the well-proportioned, mobile wrists, finger joints, and ankles by an inhibition of movement in proximal joints (shoulders and pelvic-femoral junctions). This division between trunk and periphery of the body is temporarily lifted when the body seems ready to employ all its parts in the service of a pattern (postural movement). Despite the habitual isolation between head and limbs, cooperation between them becomes immediately operative not only in postures, but also when the child plans to move in well-coordinated, useful gestures. For instance, the right hand is in front of the left, ready to move, while the left one (already somewhat inhibited) prepares for the holding of an object, which the right one will act upon. At the same time, the head is tilted to allow for maximum vision in the area in which the action will take place. The solid trunk may be ready to move forward or sideways as a unit to give support to the above gestures (see also page 262).

The latency child gives the impression of stability and dependability. His striving for conflict-free functioning is reflected in the clarity with which his gestures are coordinated and his effort and shaping interact harmoniously when he gets ready for action. His developmental task is concerned with the achievement of a social sense and its partial incorporation into his superego as a social conscience. This is reflected in the way his body blends with his surroundings when he moves in gestures or postures and rests in intervals between them.

Characteristic Movement Patterns

During the regressive episodes in early latency, pregenital types of rhythms gain dominance over phallic and inner-genital. Recovery from regression brings about an even distribution of all rhythms, in their pure form and in mixed varieties. One observes modulations of tension- and shape-flow while at the same time repetitions are less frequent. Gestures reinforce speech and provide a melody of their own in accordance with the aims of concomitant effort and shaping elements. This reflects the ego's control over all aspects of motility.

The increasing independence from drives, from self-centered needs for immediate approval, and from interrelated affects frees the latency child so that he can devote himself to the consolidation of his ego-function by:

1. *Combining* two or three coping mechanisms in one action, and thus becoming more efficient; using more than one mode of relating to objects, and thus structuring relationships on a higher level.
2. *Harmoniously matching* coping methods with optimal ways of dealing with people in single actions, and thus being able to function economically within socially acceptable limits.
3. *Planning* a sequence of isolated *gestures* in several actions, all devoted to an ego-syntonic aim, and integrating all body parts in a single *postural* action, reflecting the unified aims of all psychic structures, including the superego.

1. Combinations of Patterns. The effectiveness of his action depends on the child's ability to select combinations of two or three elements of a given pattern, in adaptation to a given task. His versatility allows him to vary elements, as is necessary for the maintenance of his work. For instance, he will select a direct, strong, and accelerating stroke for hammering or punching, but will vary these patterns, reverting to lightness, indirectness, or both, in preparation for the next strong and direct stroke. It follows that he must be capable not only of combining elements but also of eliminating them and practicing them in isolation from another. Concerned primarily with time, he may want to decelerate only, but he is capable of combining deceleration with other effort elements, such as directness and lightness, which together produce a gliding motion (Laban, 1947).

When the child combines two or three shaping elements in one action, he can convey several attitudes to a person all at once. For instance, by combining spreading, descending, and advancing in one gesture, he may proffer an invitation in a condescending way as he comes forth to greet someone. He may then choose to ascend, changing condescension to admiration, and add to it an enclosing gesture that expresses a wish to embrace.

The latency child is an avid and efficient learner. One can teach him to keep several variables in mind all at once. He uses two or three precursors of effort in learning new skills. For instance, he will start off as a novice skater, giving himself a sudden push with enough vehemence to enable him to traverse some distance before he falls. Similarly, he can combine several spatial directions and move in diagonals so that he can get where he wants to go by cutting corners without losing his way. We shall see later how he matches precursors of effort and shaping in directions in complex clusters, which he can use for learning and for defensive behavior as well.

2. Harmonious Matching of Patterns. Coping with external environment is structured by relationships to objects. Correspondingly, specific effort elements are structured best by related (affine) shaping in planes. Directness is well matched by enclosing, indirectness by spreading in space, strength by descending, lightness by ascending, acceleration by retreating, and deceleration by advancing. This implies that a direct approach is best executed in close contact with one or two people; an indirect approach functions best in large areas of space, which provide room for many people to express themselves. A strong determination is useful in dealing with subordinates; a light touch may be more convincing with people to whom one looks up for guidance. Rushing against time can be accomplished better if one stays away from people who might impede one's speed; decelerating in a leisurely fashion is more enjoyable when one anticipates meeting people on the way. Combining an effort with mismatched shaping (as for instance lightness with descending) produces clashes, reflecting intrasystemic conflicts in the ego. Matching direct and indirect efforts with shaping in the horizontal plane provides an optimal motor base for paying attention and exploring. These are the necessary ingredients for successful communication, which began in the oral phase. Matching of strength and lightness with shaping in the vertical plane

259

confronts people with the intent of the mover. These are the principal qualities, which facilitate the presentation of objects and ideas, which began in the anal phase. Matching of acceleration and deceleration with shaping in the sagittal plane combines timing and anticipation of actions in ways most suitable for conflict-free operations, which began in the urethral phase. Because of the restriction he puts on his curiosity, the latency child limits the scope of his communication; he can present and explain quite well with the aid of practical examples; his greatest forte is his talent for concrete operational procedures. This pertains primarily to skills he has learned and can use without fear.

It has been noted before that defense mechanisms and learning patterns are interrelated through their common use of precursors of effort and directions in space. For instance, isolation, restraining, and delay are used together to uphold repression of forbidden wishes and thus maintain contact with the love object without fear. These defenses are reflected in the use of simultaneous channeling, straining, and hesitating (all precursors of effort) in combination with moving in a diagonal across the body, downward and forward. The same combinations can be used in learning. Thus, channeling will maintain focusing and help exclude extraneous stimuli; straining will reflect the degree of willingness to learn, and hesitating will counteract the disturbing influences of impatience. Directing movement across the midline of the body, down and forward will bar access to it, keep down physical temptation and maintain continual contact with the learning aids, placed in front of the student.

Once the child has learned a skill, he automatically uses effort and shaping in planes to practice what he has learned. Instead of channeling he will approach his task directly, and instead of straining and hesitating he will act in a determined and unhurried way. By enclosing, descending, and advancing he will help define the scope of his task, bring it down to its essentials, and carry it to conclusion. This example concerns only one possible combination of effort and shaping patterns, used in one action; it illustrates the high adaptive value of combining several patterns into matching clusters.

In latency, conflicts between the ego and the id are largely in abeyance. Intrasystemic harmony in the ego tends to bring about an intrasystemic harmony in the id as well. This can be seen in motor behavior in the following way.

Efforts regulate rhythms of tension-flow and determine the selection of tension qualities in accordance with the aim of the action. Shaping in planes regulates rhythms of shape-flow and has an influence over the selection of dimensional changes in the body. When effort and shaping in planes are well matched, they exert an integrative influence upon tension- and shape-flow. The harmony between effort and shaping is instrumental in coordinating adaptive patterns with those serving relationships to objects. Such a coordination fosters the harmony between tension- and shape-flow, which reflects a synthesis of drive demands and affects related to them with feelings of comfort or discomfort and of attraction or repulsion. Under those circumstances, the child performs well in the knowledge that his actions are approved by parents and teachers. Many of the patterns he uses are modeled after various people with whom he has identified in the past and continues to do so at present. Matching of effort and shaping elements reflects the synthesis between identifications with actions (through effort) and identification with attitudes to objects (through shaping). For instance, a child who emulates his father's frequent use of strength and his mother's prospensity for deceleration will experience no conflict if he can structure his actions by descending and advancing. One of these he may have chosen in identification with his grandfather's attitude to people and the other by emulating a teacher and on the basis of a personal preference. The most harmonious combinations occur when personal preferences coincide with those of people with whom the child identifies. Another source of equilibrium and stabilization of functions is the latency child's ability to subordinate needs and bodily states to the aims of the ego. The degree to which this is possible depends on various factors including identifications with adults' attitudes toward their body.

The synthesis of various types of identifications within the ego allows the latency child to act in a conflict-free, socially accepted manner. At this time his "social sense" *(Gemeinsinn)* is still solely a function of the ego (Freud, 1921). Not until mid-latency does it differentiate from the social conscience as a component of the superego. This is reflected in the differentiation of so-called posture movements from gestures that occurs at the same time.

3. Gestures and Postures. In a *gesture,* only some parts are put into the service of a given pattern. For instance, we can bang our fist on a table, developing strength in one upper limb only; we lift our eyes, looking up while the rest of the body remains immobile; or we may advance with one leg only, leaving the rest of the body behind. When all parts of the body, become involved in an action that serves the implementation of one and the same pattern (or patterns), we speak of a *posture* movement, a term coined by Lamb (1961).[7] For instance, all body parts participate in developing strength, in moving upward or advancing. A posture movement requires the temporary removal of the latency child's typical isolation between the center and the periphery of the body. Generally speaking, gestures depend on the functional isolation of

261

body parts while postures are based on their unification or integration. The latency child's skills are controlled by both the isolating and the synthetic functions of the ego. This is expressed through the capacity to isolate gestures from one another and nevertheless coordinate them in the service of a complex activity, governed by rules. For instance, playing jacks, the child may throw the ball up with the left hand; at the same time the right hand will gather the jacks up from the floor and, under the guidance of the head and the eyes, will move upward in time to catch the ball. Arms and head will participate in the action while the chest remains relatively stable, acting only as an isolator between the three active body parts. The latter are coordinated with one another as regards spatial directions, approach to a mobile and to stationary objects (jacks), appraisal of their number and weight, and the timing as well as the sequencing of gestures, all of which makes this particular operation possible. The planning and regulation of such combinations and sequences of isolated, and at times contradictory, gestures (one arm going up while the other comes down) serves the ultimate unification that occurs when all jacks and the ball are held by one hand.

To uphold the unification or integration of body parts in postures, appropriate tension-flow changes pave the way for the development of postural effort and appropriate shape-flow changes make postural shaping in space possible. The inhibition between the center of the body and its periphery has to be relinquished to allow for an unimpeded flow of impulses from one part of the body to another. As a result, changes in tension-flow pass through the body in a sequence that aids the development of an effort pattern throughout the whole body. For instance, a lowering of tension that travels upward from the pelvic region to the chest and head, paves the way toward experiencing lightness in the whole body. The reestablishment of the connection between body parts allows also for a consistent change in the shape of limbs and trunk which, through flexing and stretching, involve the whole body in the creation of concave and convex shapes in space. For instance, lengthening simultaneously or successively throughout the body makes postural ascending possible.

The comparison between movement profiles and clinical assessments suggests that effort and shaping in gestures are primarily regulated by the ego, and that movement in these patterns in postures reflects the superego's influence on the ego's control of motility. Each postural action gives the mover a chance to reorganize his body attitude and its psychic representative, the image of the body, in accordance with certain aims, which are syntonic to the id-ego and approved by the superego (Schilder, 1935). However, in latency, attempts at reorganization of the body attitude, run counter to the prevailing trend toward sameness and stability of structures. To uphold this trend and reestablish his typical body attitude, the latency child isolates gestures and postures from one another in the following ways:

> Postural use of effort or shaping occur sporadically without adequate preparations by gestures. For instance, as if out of nowhere, the child's whole body engages in light motions of skipping or hopping; a postural advance often emerges from a resting position. More detailed observation reveals that gestures do precede and follow postural movements, but they become isolated from the latter by pauses or by the interpolation between them of tension- or shape-flow changes. An arm retreats; the child pauses and resumes movement by retreating or advancing posturally; then his progress is impeded by an influx of bound flow into the trunk and by a constriction of body shape. He still will retreat or advance with his head, an arm or a leg, but the connection of this gesture with the preceding postural action has been interrupted.

The latency isolation between postures and gestures disappears in adolescence (see Chapter 17). The reorganization of the body image in adolesence requires a fluid type of communication between all structures that participate in its rebuilding. In contrast, latency children persist in retaining their old body image even when anatomical changes already call for its restructuring (see Chapter 11). The latency isolation between postures and gestures suggests the possibility that, in latency, there is a trend to counteract the sporadic unification of structures (when id, ego, and superego aims become syntonic) by a renewal of isolation between them. The latter may be used to uphold and consolidate the differentiation of structures that has been achieved in prelatency years.

We recognize the influence of the synthetic function of the ego in the latency child's capacity to work effectively by combining several motion factors in one action. His ability to choose one new pattern to vary an action rather than continue using two or three at once, reflects his versatility in undoing combinations, using isolated patterns or combining them, as is necessary for a given task. A special form of synthesis plays a role in the way he achieves intrasystemic harmony in the ego by matching patterns used for specific defense or coping mechanisms with related modalities of interpersonal adjustment (pp. 238-239). Mismatching of patterns indicates specific conflicts, but using effort and shaping separately (either one or the other) signifies a split between coping with the environment and relating to objects. Isolating and synthetic functions operate simultaneously in the coordination of gestures. They alternate in sequences of gestures which become disconnected from postures. We are tempted to infer from the above that the latency equilibrium depends on a balance between the synthesizing and isolating functions of the ego.

Over and beyond the ego's capacity to synthesize, there is a general tendency toward unification of structures which expresses itself periodically when all parts of the body simultaneously or successively act to develop or uphold a pattern of movement. A harmony between ego and superego that is longer lasting than the one achieved in such a postural movement, is revealed in the use of the same patterns in gestures and postures (Chapter 17). For instance, advancing to greet someone by first extending the arm and then following with the whole body to a proper distance and then, once more, extending the hand only, is a phrase which expresses a conflict-free relationship to the greeted person. When a pattern is used in a gesture which is incompatible with that used in a subsequent posture, we can infer from it a conflict between the ego and the superego in regard to the actions under consideration. For instance, balling a fist with strength, when followed by a light movement of the whole body, implies a change of aims. Under the influence of the superego, the ego has given up its original aims; however, it may revert to it quickly, as evidenced by a renewal of fist-balling in the next gesture. The latency child is not able to tolerate intersystemic conflicts; he tends to obviate an overt clash between his ego and superego by isolation or symptom formation.

The consolidation of the ego and superego in latency depends not only on the degree of harmony between these structures. It also depends on the frequency and degree of recovery from intrasystemic conflicts in the ego and the superego as well. We have discussed earlier how the syntheses of various types and modes of identification express themselves in the harmonious matching of effort and shaping patterns. When multiple efforts and shaping in postural movements are matched harmoniously, we infer that the superego has incorporated and given its stamp of approval to previously established consonant identifications. The latency child has begun to crystallize and consolidate his identifications and to extrapolate from them general rules and guidelines for proper social behavior, which are the intrinsic qualities of social conscience.

Our investigations suggest further that the use of efforts in postures is an indication that the punitive or permissive components of the superego participate in the regulation of motility, serving adaptation to external reality. For example, the total commitment to strength or lightness in postural movements, reflects the mover's superego attitude to aggression or indulgence respectively. The use of shaping in space in postural movements appears to be a sign that the ego-ideal has become part of the superego. For example, the total commitment to ascending or descending in a postural movement reflects the mover's lofty aspirations or his self-depreciation, which can be experienced in relation to the self alone or to objects as well. When effort and shaping in postural movements are harmoniously interrelated, we infer that certain punitive or permissive aspects of the child's conscience and related guidelines—determined by the ego-ideal—have combined to create an intrasystemic harmony in the superego (Hartmann, 1939). The latency child is capable of coordinating some internal prohibitions against bad behavior with internal admonitions to be a good child. However, the major task of incorporating and integrating the ego-ideal into the superego is left to adolescence.

The latency child emerges from the regression that initiated this phase through the introduction of a balanced distribution of the structural components in his behavior. Pregenital and early genital-type rhythms contribute an equal share to movement and can thus balance one another. The reduction of tension- and shape-flow rhythms increases the stability of the body attitude. An isolation between trunk and limbs and head upholds the repression of sexual interests in the child's own body. The synthetic function of the ego coordinates isolated gestures in the service of skills; it combines several motion elements into actions, serving clusters of adaptive, defensive, or object-centered mechanisms; it provides harmony in the id-ego by matching related patterns in an optimal way. An overall trend toward unification and consolidation can be recognized in the newly won ability to move all parts of the body consistently in the service of one or more patterns, e.g., posturally. Potural movements reflect the capacity to integrate motion factors, controlled by the id-ego under the influence of the superego.

Matching of effort and shaping in gestures reflects lack of conflict between identification with actions and with attitudes to objects. In postures, it indicates also a harmony between certain punitive or permissive aspects of the superego and related guidelines and aspirations of the ego-ideal. When several effort and shaping elements combine into matching sets, we infer from it the confluence of several identifications that underlie the child's social consciousness. When these harmonious combinations occur in postural movements we take it as a sign that a social conscience (a function of the superego) has differentiated from the social sense (a function of the ego).

A balance between synthesis and isolation in latency can be deduced from the way isolated gestures are organized into adaptive sequences and from the way postures are isolated from preceding and succeeding gestures. Not until adolescence does the child become capable of establishing a continuity between postures and gestures which provides the basis for a reorganization of the body image in sequences of clashes and reconciliations between the id-ego and the superego. Until then the body image of the child remains stable. Attempts to reorganize it are regularly counterbalanced by inhibition and isolation. The latency child is intolerant of conflict. The consolidation of his structures depends on the degree and frequency with which he can achieve balance between opposing functions and can establish intrastemic harmony and ward off intersystemic conflicts.

NOTES

[1]The concept of "body attitude" was originated by Laban (1950) and developed in a way somewhat divergent from the one used here by Bartenieff and Paulay (Lomax *et al.*, 1967). Effort and shaping are terms originated by Laban (1947), and the distinction between postures and gestures by Lamb (1961). Additions, modifications, definitions, and interpretations of patterns evolved from joint research of the Movement Study Group (1960–1974) of Child Development Research, Sands Point, N.Y.

[2]It is interesting to note that, throughout life, oral rhythms tend to be used more frequently than others (Kestenberg, 1967a).

[3]In contrast to the inner-genital rhythm, the phallic, outer-genital rhythm that prevails in the phallic phase is characterized by an onrush of excitement, emanating from the outer parts of the genitalia.

[4]For the shift of cathexis from the testicles and scrotum to the anal region, see Bell, 1964.

[5]When this form of masturbation continues into or is revived in adolescence, it sometimes leads to ejaculations without erections.

[6]As will be seen later, effort or shaping patterns in which the whole body supports an action (Lamb, 1965) are considered to be a motor reflection of the influence of the superego. The immaturity of this structure is indicated in the immaturity of the pattern.

[7]It is likely that this term was chosen because movements of the whole body in one pattern tends to lead to a change of posture.

CHAPTER 11

The Effect on Parents of the Child's Transition into and out of Latency

Each transition from one childhood phase to the next presents a challenge to both parents and children to give up outdated forms of interaction and to adopt a new system of coexistence. The ability of a parent to meet his side of this challenge depends on his inner preparedness to accept the new image the child forms of him and to erect a new image of his child. Only with flexibility in shifting roles and assigning the child a new identity, based on the actuality of his maturational advances, does parenthood become a developmental phase (Benedek, 1959; Furman, 1969). Through successive subphases of parenthood the parent's own identity undergoes a continuous transformation until parenthood assumes a subordinate position in the individuality of a new life of "parents without children."

Latency has been defined as a phase in which childhood sexuality is dormant. It is more useful to look upon latency as a phase dominated by desexualized, drive-derivative behavioral patterns. Instinctual breakthroughs and sexualization of adaptive behavior do occur but are subordinated to the overall dominance of desexualized psychic structures. The developmental task of latency is the progressive consolidation of the newly acquired psychic agencies, which is assured by the maintenance of desexualized, relatively autonomous ego-and superego-functions. The latency child's independence from id strivings and drive objects is reinforced by his partial separation from his parents. Ability to separate from the child and to surrender him to teachers, who act as guardians of desexualization, enforcers of independence from parents, and organizers of systematic skills, is an indicator of the parents' acceptance of the child's latency.

First published in *Parenthood,* eds. E. J. Anthony and T. Benedek (Boston: Little, Brown, 1970), pp. 290–304. Slightly revised and reproduced by permission.

In transition to latency, parents must take the lead in the institutionalization of desexualized functioning. This constitutes an important step in their own separation-individuation process (Mahler and La Perriere, 1965). To highlight the crucial transition into "part-time parenthood" in latency, let us survey problems of transition in general and glance at the succession of past transformations that paved the way for the current one.

Parents in Transition

An intermingling of progression and regression characterizes transitional periods. To cope with the confusion created by conflicting clues in the child's behavior, parents use four sets of reference as aids in the adjustment to the changing identity of the child. They rely on tangible signs of maturation such as visible physical changes or acquisitions of skills. They follow ritualized customs of child-rearing, such as those prescribed for specific ages for weaning, training, school entry, etc. They act on the basis of positive and negative identifications with their own parents and adapt these practices to current views of influential authorities such as physicians or teachers. The younger the child, the greater the parents' reliance on intuitive understanding, an understanding based on memory traces of similar childhood states, now revived through closeness to the child and identification with him. In this manner parents can regress and progress with their children (Fries, 1944). But their regression is held in check by their ability to maintain their identity as parents and to use clues other than those transmitted by the child's change of state. Their emphatic understanding is tempered by their knowledge, foresight, and a stability born from adult constancy of object relationships.

In transition from one phase to the next, the child threatens the continuity of the parent's working ego. In transforming himself and demanding that parents also change to suit the needs of his next developmental phase, the child seems to reject the parents. As a result parents feel hurt and inadequate. They too become estranged from the child and, so to say, reject him. Before they can erect a new, egosyntonic identity as parents, they must give up the Johnny they know to become acquainted with the new Johnny. But once the strange child loses his strangeness and becomes "familiar" again, the discontinuity of the relationship is bridged over and the period of alienation has passed.

A transition is in progress when a parent makes a remark such as the one Gesell and Ilg attribute to mothers of six-year-old children

(1946): "He is a changed child and I do not know what has gotten into him." We sense that a transition has been accomplished when we hear parents say: "We don't have a baby anymore. Glenda goes to school. She is a big girl and does not need us the way she used to." The child has changed, she is not the same anymore, and neither parent can remain the same (Fries, 1944). There is regret, but pride in the child's advancement is there too.

Every transition from one phase to the next generates aggression. Parents and children blame each other for each step in their progressive separation, but each new phase brings on a reconciliation, a rapprochement on a new level of coexistence (Mahler and La Perriere, 1965). A successful transition dissolves not only the barrier between parent and child but also the isolation of the parental ego from the rest of the adult ego (Furman, 1969). Before a new isolation sets in, the parent has developed not only as a parent but also as an individual. Intrinsic to this progress is the task of every transition: to give up not only the real child—as he was and is not anymore—but also to revise and re-form the revived imaginary baby of one's own childhood.

The Changing Image of the Child

The image of the child changes throughout development in accordance with the shifting dominance of drive components and their organization. In this image we find the most concise and brief representation of the totality of psychic functioning in a given phase. As an aid to the understanding of the following synopsis of successive child images, my classification of phases prefaces this section of the chapter (see also Chapters 10, 13, 14, 15):

1. *Neonatal* phase.
2. *Pregenital* phases (oral, anal, urethral).
3. *Inner-genital* phase during which inner-genital tensions predominate over others. At this time the child becomes capable of giving ideational content to oral, anal, urethral, and inner-genital representations of the inside structure of his body, in accordance with their specific products. Externalization of inner-genital impulses helps the child to integrate pregenital and genital component drives before he can cathect his external genitalia, and thus subordinate other bodily pleasures to the urgency of phallic needs, dominant in the next phase.
4. *Phallic* phase during which the whole body serves phallic modes of expression, and impulses from the inside genitalia are externalized and

condensed in the child's body-phallus representation of himself. The growth and differentiation of this phase become the organizational base of psychic structure formation.

5. *Latency* is a phase of dominance of drive-derivative functioning and is characterized by a consolidation of newly acquired psychic structures.

6. *Prepuberty* revives the organization of the prephallic, inner-genital phase. Its developmental task is the reintegration of pregenital, inner-genital, and outer-genital drive components and patterns of organization suitable for genital dominance.

7. *Puberty* repeats the growth and differentiation patterns of the phallic phase on a genital level, and results in a reformation of psychic structure that becomes the basis for adult autonomous functioning.

8. *Preadult* phase of consolidation repeats on a higher level the organization of latency, thus establishing the dominance of drive-derivative functioning over expressions of untamed sexuality and aggression.

9. *Adulthood* phases subordinate drive expression to a variety of demands so that needs can be fulfilled without the loss of a normal degree of independence from drive tension and from fixation on primary objects.

A long and circuitous road leads from early concepts of babies to the reality of being a parent of a real infant, soon a toddler, and now a schoolchild. Can one define what a child *is,* how his image remains constant and yet keeps changing through the developmental phases, from one's own childless infancy through the vicissitudes of real parenthood to the childless state of senescence? A scientific definition may not do justice to the feeling that pervades the creativity of parenthood through all ages.

> A child is part of me and part of you, a link between us . . . a bond of constancy that holds us together when we are apart. Something of you and something of me . . . it belongs . . . it's ours. Created with our insides and our outsides, in our own image . . . in the image of our parents . . . and yet different . . . strange, new, forever changing . . . a possession . . . a new life and now a separate being with a life of his own.

Giving vent to our own feelings brought us closer to the infant's feelings about his first possession—a transitional object—he created out of his bodily needs, his closeness to his mother and his emerging self-realization (Winnicott, 1953). The transitional object is in a more real sense the infant's first baby than are the toddler's symbolic equations of the baby with food, feces, and urine that leave their imprint on the inner-genital" image of the baby of the two- to three- or four-year-old (see Chapters 2, 8). Equated with the mother's and the child's own inner genital, and externalized onto the toddler's cherished, desexualized possessions—his toys—the inner-genital baby belongs to mother and child. In contrast, the phallic baby is a gift received from the father or given to the mother, the fruit of a forbidden union, a shared sin. With the resolution of the oedipus complex emerges the image of the acceptable, desexualized child, a schoolchild to be shared with a teacher. The latency child transfers much of his allegiance to school (Freud, S., 1914b, 1923a), and, even in his play at home, he often assumes the role of the teacher rather than that of the parent.

In adolesence parenthood is anticipated with a mixture of reality and fantasy, with love, repudiation, and fear. In prepuberty, increased inner-genital tensions, vying with regressive pregenital and phallic urges, resexualize and distort the baby image at the same time that the child's image of his parents and his own self becomes distorted. Even though a more realistic child image emerges out of this chaos (see Chapters 2, 13–15), it undergoes repression with the revival of oedipal wishes in puberty. When fertility becomes a reality in adolescence, the realization of the wish for a child is postponed and the image of the child is once more desexualized in the final phase of adolescence which is similar in organization to latency. The new wish for a child grows out of a need for a permanent love relationship with a nonincestuous object in a new home and a new family.

The removal from primary objects (Katan, 1951) is sealed, so to say, when the young adult can become a parent not only by virtue of his biologic readiness but also with the full approval of society.

The real "approved" child draws his acceptable qualities from the desexualized child image, created in a preadult phase of adolescence and its precursor in latency (Chapters 13–15). But these qualities are never free from traces of earlier baby images that emerge from repression and resexualize the parent-child relationship. These unconscious roots of parenthood exert a regressive pull from which empathy to the real child arises. They form the id core of ego repression in the service of adaptation to the child's needs. In normal parenthood, the ego's adaptive regression to the phase of the child's maturity is confined within the limits of this specifically parental form of adaptation that is isolated from the remainder of the parents' ego and superego (Furman, 1969).

The nursing mother feels relieved when the child is satiated, and uncomfortable when he is hungry. She may even feel like "eating up the baby, he is so cute." But she does not radically change her own eating habits. She does not become a baby herself. As her child grows older, she allows her parenthood to encroach less and less into her life as non-parent. In this she finds support from her husband, who can split off his fatherhood from the rest of his life much better than she can split off her motherhood.

With the passing of the child's pregenital phases, the parents give up their control over his bodily functions and relinquish him as a possession. At the time the preoedipal toddler invents his own baby and identifies with the "lost" mother (Freud, A., 1967a) of his babyhood; parents too feel a need for a new baby as they give up the image of the toddler as a baby. Sharing a real or toy baby with his mother, the three-year-old child involves her and the father in the process of integration of pregenital and early genital drives he must accomplish before entering the phallic-oedipal phase. By a shift of cathexis from the inside of the body to the outside, parents and children re-form the "inner-genital baby image" and build the image of a child as a phallus. The resolution of the child's oedipus complex gives parents a chance to revise their own. A sensible, desexualized "brainchild" becomes the heir to the phallic child, conceived with a parent. The desexualization of the parent-child relationship creates a distance between them in more ways than one.

Transition into Latency

With the onset of their child's latency parents not only give up the forbidden phallic-oedipal child, but they become "partially childless" in reality as they release the child—his body and mind—to teachers who represent their own parents (Freud, A., 1952b, 1965; Freud, S., 1914b). With this crucial separation, children and parents also go their own ways in divergent organizations of their lives. Consolidation of the newly formed psychic structure is the developmental task of latency (Chapter 13). Parents assist in this process but, in contrast to preceding phases, their own pattern of organization is different. The liberation of large quantities of narcissistic cathexis invested in the child as a possession, the confrontation with extrafamilial authorities and with expressions of the child's new autonomy, all call for a reintegration of old and new attitudes as well as a working through of the revision of the parent's own oedipus complex.

The five-and-a-half-year-old child acts like an older edition of the two-and-a-half-year-old child (Guthrie, and Jacobs, 1966; Inhelder and Piaget, 1958). For parents, both of these periods represent successive steps in relinquishing the child as a possession. But latency initiates a much more crucial phase of parenthood that will later serve as a model for the reorientation to the "state of childlessness" when parents separate from their grown sons and daughters.

Some societies regard the three-year-old child as the adult's helper, but all societies entrust the six-year-old with responsibilities. The three-year-old child's autonomy was based on his new ability to verbalize and channel his thoughts into secondary-process thinking (Katan, 1961); But the six-year-old child has real "sense" (Guthrie and Jacobs, 1966). He should not only give lip service to what is right and wrong, he should know it. Although his thinking is syncretistic and concrete, he can reason and communicate in an adultlike manner (Piaget, 1950); but parents are disappointed because he is losing the ability to remember and integrate the past with the present he had acquired as a toddler (Schur, 1966), and the scintillating, creative mind he exhibited at five years gives way to the prosaic concreteness and reticence of latency. Repression reduces his passionate interests and his daydreams lack vitality. In addition, his new achievements are easily undone by regressive processes. Adults doubt his reliability when they discover his "lies" or small thefts, find evidence of "accidents" in his underwear, and discover his enchantment with "duty (bathroom) talk." They doubt his advances even more when they realize that he behaves "as though he were living by the rules of the secondary process" (i.e., conforming to reality) only to please them (Bornstein, 1951).

In relinquishing the phallic-oedipal child, parents shift much of their narcissistic investment in the child as their phallus upward to the child as their "brain"; from the child as proof of their guilty incestuous sexuality to the child as representative of their morality. They hope to exhibit a precociously bright, well-brought-up extension of themselves to the admiring eyes of the teacher. But at the very point when the six-year-old child becomes ready to be exhibited and subject for evaluation, he lets his parents down. Their shame and guilt become tinged with regressive wishes to hide the evidence of "sins" they had committed against the child. Analysis of their fear of exposure to the teacher reveals parents' guilt about masturbatory practices, which the child's deficiency will disclose. The physician, who examined the child's body, was the parents' trusted ally who repaired the damage they might have caused. The teacher is a stranger who tests the child, judges his performance, and grades him publicly.

Parents and Teachers

The image of the teacher varies (Ekstein, 1967; Freud, A., 1952b). She is sometimes thought of as a good fairy who rescues children and transforms them into angels who purify their parents. On the other hand, she is sometimes thought of as a cruel, witchlike stepmother who kills bad parents and castrates their children.

"No Gentleman Talks That Way." A mother, observing in the classroom of her not yet six-year-old first-grader, noted tht her son was restless and not as well behaved as the other children. She felt publicly exposed when the teacher singled out Paul for reprimand and demanded that he stop scratching his leg. All eyes focused on little Paul but he kept on scratching. In a dulcet voice the teacher suggested that the offending leg might have to be cut off so that Paul could stop scratching and the classwork could be resumed. Paul stopped instantly. The teacher regained her leadership, and the children learned what might happen if they "move in a forbidden way."

Paul's mother regarded the teacher's threat as an attack upon herself. She had hoped to find her own beloved grammar school teacher, an idealized mother image. Instead, she found one resembling her punitive older sister who had enjoyed exposing her and undermining her relationship to their mother. She looked to her husband for help. Paul's father reminisced about his early failure in grammar school. He had not become a star pupil until his father had tutored him in second grade. He advised his wife to stay out of the situation. She too responded by a feeling long familiar. There was nothing else to do but placate the teacher as she had in the past placated her "castrating" sister. She advised Paul to behave himself in school. But Paul's battle with the teacher continued.

While the teacher was out of the classroom, Paul told the children that they were all "full of duty." The children "snitched" on him and heard the teacher tell him: "No gentleman talks that way." Thus Paul was publicly branded as already "castrated" as a result of his sinful persistence in masturbation substitutes and regressive rebelliousness. However, Paul did not give up. After a while he pulled down his pants and thus proved to his audience that he was indeed still a "gentleman." The stunned teacher consulted the principal who agreed with her that the boy's outrageous behavior was the result of a misguided, progressive education at home. Paul's parents were advised to have the child "tested."

Needless to say, the conflict between school and home varies with the individuality of child and parent. Paul's mother wanted to share a good teacher with him. Another mother was competitive with the teacher. When she offered to give a guitar recital to the first-graders, the teacher agreed reluctantly and reported the problem to the principal. He summoned the "delinquent mother" and told her that, even though a performing artist and a teacher herself, she was not a teacher in *his* school but *merely* a mother. Reduced to tears, the mother not only resolved to retreat from the school as enemy territory but spread the word around and thus helped the principal to quash the parent-rebellion.

The foregoing examples illustrate how "bad teachers" can enforce parent-child separation and the surrendering of the child to them by castration threats and aggressive setting of boundaries, which delineate the role of the child and mother in relation to school authorities. The next vignette of parent-child-teacher interaction will serve to illustrate how "good teachers" can hinder parent-child separation by fostering use of the child's school status to prolong the parents' narcissistic investment in the child, and how a "bad teacher" can help establish a proper balance between family and school.

> *"The Biggest and the Most Beautiful Ribbon."* Glenda's parents prepared themselves for the separation from their baby girl by having a new baby. They not only accepted but accelerated their daughter's growing up. They made her give up her transitional object to qualify for admission to kindergarten. As an older sister and a schoolchild, Glenda vied for the teacher's attention in lieu of recapturing her position as a favorite child at home. She became the teacher's pet. Her mother shared in her glory when the teacher gave Glenda "the biggest and the most beautiful ribbon." In first grade, Glenda was restless but her cute appearance and the compliments she paid the teacher assured her continuation of her role as teacher's pet. Despite her gratification, Glenda's mother betrayed her anger at her daughter's liaison with the teacher by occasionally neglecting to be home when Glenda returned from school. The dormant battle between home and school was climaxed in second grade, when a "bad, old teacher" summoned the parents to complain about their child's poor performance. Both parents became greatly upset and the father cried in sympathy with his daughter. But the "bad" teacher helped change the relationship between Glenda and her parents. They began to rely less on the teacher as source of narcissistic supply. They ceased to regard Glenda as an object of display, they accepted her femininity, and were later able to ease her transition from latency into puberty.

It is tempting to explore further the role of the teacher in the development of parents. Suffice it to say that to many parents she represents a voice of the superego, superordinated over their own. As keeper of desexualization in the form of learning and acceptable behavior, the teacher contributes to the redistribution of parents' instinctual and neutralized cathexis and to the reorganization of parental superego.

A Prize for Attendance and Neatness. Nancy's parents, living in dire circumstances, neglected their home and children. As a baby, Nancy was never brought to the hospital for a change in formula or routine injections. In the first grade, when the teacher gave her a prize for attendance and neatness, both parents felt commended not only as parents but also as people. When she failed in school, Nancy's father took it upon himself to drill her until she could pass. The total readjustment of the family during their youngest child's latency brought an unprecedented order into their home.[1] Mother went to work and the whole family began to attend church. When standards fell short of the desired appearance, a code of concealment was invoked. When Nancy was reluctant to reveal to the interviewer that she shared her bed with her brother, her father praised her for her reticence. Despite these superego lacunae, the reorganization of parental ego and superego attitudes brought a new dignity to the whole family. Never before did Nancy feel ashamed, and never before did the father feel as calm facing an intruding strange visitor (the author) who represented the hostile society that had victimized him.

This example illustrated the beneficial influence of school on parental attitudes toward the child which, otherwise uncensored and unsupervised, might hinder desexualization and retard development. The next section will exemplify how the child himself contributes to the reorganization of parental ego—and superego—attitudes by invoking extrafamilial authority.

God and the Parents

The child's early superego is fraught with archaic features derived from his own id strivings. These combine with old and new teachings in a form that may be alien to the parent.

"Nancy is bad," her mother told the interviewer. "Recently her conscience bothered her. She asked me: "When a child does something bad to her mother and father, does God fix that?" Nancy's mother reacted to the question with a mixture of amusement and surprise but seemed pleased with the unexpected help given by God to parents of "bad" children.

Charlie, at the age of six, punished his mother for interfering with the repression of his curiosity by introducing rituals into homework that deadlocked both mother's and teacher's endeavors to help him. One morning he surprised his mother by saying: "Oh, mother, the sun came out. It is beautiful. Come to the window. Let's pray." Thanking God for the beauty of the sun, Charlie ingratiated himself with his religious father and invited his mother to join in bowing to the father's superior phallic force. Charlie was teaching his mother to give him up as a phallic object and to accept him as subordinate to father figures. His mother "got a charge out of it" but also felt a new respect for the unteachable child who was becoming her teacher.

The six-year-old child who invokes God in his dealings with parents seems endowed with special powers that make him appear wise beyond his years. The awed parent may feel that out of the babe's mouth speaks the voice of the omnipotent parent of his own childhood.

The invocation of extrafamilial authority challenges the parents to revive their everyday working conscience to conform to the child's high ideals. As the child's superego becomes reinforced by principles of fair play, impartiality, justice, and consistency of standards, learned in school, he gradually relies less and less on archaic superego demands. He imparts to the parents what he learned and becomes their guide at home. At no point in the parents' development are they more forcefully confronted with their double standard of morality. To protect the young from too harsh a reality, to maintain the myth of parents' omnipotence, and foremost, to deny evidences of adult sexuality, parents tend to deceive their young children. Latency morality challenges them to become honest for the sake of their children.

Parents and the Regressed Child

The six- or seven-year-old moralist who has made honest people out of his parents is neither consistently honest himself nor able to conform to other ideals he holds the parents to. He regresses as he progresses.

To combat his masturbatory impulses he resorts to pregenital modes of behavior. In the process of transforming them into desexualized patterns of work he seesaws precariously between pleasing and displeasing adults. Adult desexualization of pregenital components of good work habits is far beyond his meager beginnings. Neither parents nor teachers accept what is self-evident to six- and seven-year-olds: the connection between work and "do your duty," between effort and straining, between ambitious aspirations and "aim your sissy in the toilet." A long time has elapsed since parents themselves introduced these links. They demand an isolation between these original and derivative functions that the young latency child cannot consistently uphold. To him the teacher takes on the quality of the training mother, especially since the strange adult things he must learn (incorporate), memorize (retain), and produce

277

on command (eliminate) seem as important to the adult world as his toilet training once was. "Duty" talk and anal jokes offend adult sensibilities more, the more they feel degraded and caricatured by the child.[2]

The average parent understands and even welcomes the child's regression when he comes home from school. But the pleasure in the return of the "lost child" (Freud, A., 1967a) may be overshadowed by the intrusion into the house of school in the form of homework for which parents are made responsible. Even the many illnesses of early latency are not entirely free from the shadow of school life (Gesell and Ilg, 1946). In providing reports to school, the physician loses his status as the parents' trusted ally and sharer of the child's body (Freud, A., 1967b). But he can still alleviate parents' guilt by mediating between them and teachers and taking responsibility for the child's temporary removal from school.

As illnesses renew bodily closeness between the child and the parents, the parents become more tolerant of his regression. Their unsupervised intimacy gives parents a new chance to identify with the child's way of thinking. They may, for instance, help the child to transform pregenital interests into jokes. Latency witticism, as strange as it is to adults, teaches parents to be more tolerant and less concerned with the child's regressive reactions to his learning experience. As they revise the image of their child, they also revise the image of their own parents and feel freer to pursue interests renounced in the past.

Parents' Readjustment During Their Child's Latency

As parents reintegrate their ego ideals and superego demands, they can assist the child in strengthening, amplifying, and making concrete his self-image as a schoolchild and his self-esteem as an achiever. To keep up with their children, in identification with them or with their teachers, parents reorganize their own learning patterns and integrate new knowledge with the core of learning automatized in childhood. Many become students themselves to make up for past deficiencies in their education. Fathers revive old interests in hobbies and sports they share with their children. Mothers have time now to paint or write, to resume old friendships, to join clubs, or go back to work. The children's own widening social contact and outlets for sublimation also guide their parents' socialization. Scouting and parent-teacher organizations are among the many fields of activity in which parents of latency children meet people from several social groups and assume new identities as members of the community. Whatever these new interests, they do give parents wider perspective which promotes reintegration of old and new cultural influences.

After the initial reorganization of parental attitudes and activities, life becomes peaceful and settled. The child in late latency has made great strides in the development from bodily needs to physical and intellectual skills, from play to work, from dependence to self-reliance, and from proneness to regression to a consistency in progression (Freud, A., 1965). Parents have learned to rely on his stability. They treat infractions and disturbances of peace, such as sibling fights or school setbacks, as temporary phenomena that can be settled by proper handling and reasoning. To continue the peaceful coexistence with their children, parents try to prolong latency and tend to ignore signs of impending adolescent changes.

Transition into Prepuberty

In late latency the body begins to change in structure and function. Physical complaints become more frequent and habits begin to deteriorate. Parents tend to ignore or deny the significance of these changes. Even prodromal syndromes of disorders do not disquiet them until they become fulminant in prepuberty.

Belinda, Was Obedient. Belinda, an only child of loving parents, began to lose weight at the age of ten. Her parents attributed her loss of appetite, her decrease in sociability, and the decline in her schoolwork to their having just moved from another state. By the time Belinda was eleven she had become so haggard that the pediatrician suspected Simmond's disease. When this was ruled out, the parents were relieved and accepted the child's thinness. They helped her with schoolwork and encouraged her to call friends. But they did not notice Belinda's depression.

She did all that was expected of her, but reduced it to "daily minimum requirements." Only with the onset of prepuberty did she become negativistic to a degree that alarmed her parents. They seemed unprepared for what they now accepted as their child's illness. They had forgotten how sensitive she had been as an infant and how easily hurt and frightened as a toddler. They reiterated what an outstanding student she had been when they lived in Florida; how industrious and adult she had been at home, in school, and in church. They were so impressed with her high religious and ethical standards that they considered becoming more observant Catholics to please her. The whole family had become involved in the child's illness as long as she perpetuated and exaggerated a latency pattern.

279

When parents cling to the peace of latency, even normal young adolescents may contain their inner turmoil. They give the appearance of stability and solidity by maintaining empty latency forms to disguise their nagging unrest. Politeness without consideration, conversation without content, and mechanical performance without personal involvement can mask the early signs of prepuberty diffusion and feign the persistence of latency.

Once parents become engaged in the process of transition out of latency, they resexualize the image of the child. Approaching adolescence emphasizes the dichotomy between sexes not only in children but in parents as well. Physical development and preoccupation with the body meet a responsive feeling tone in the girl's mother. She lets the father participate in her observations without involving him directly. A boy's fears about his changing body, especially concerning his inner-genital maturation, are often scoffed at by both parents, who consider such concerns feminine. Mothers are embarrased to talk about them and fathers, more often than not, are too threatened by homosexual temptations that may beset father and son in intimate talks about the body. But fathers, less involved with children's bodies than mothers and more inclined to maintain distance from their older children, regress less at this time than mothers do. Consequently they act out less and reject their children less in transition into adolescence. Father's longer persistence in "parental latency" and his better composure help mother to endure prepuberty sexuality. Maternal poise in turn assists the father when he regresses in response to aggressive or asocial acts or unreasonable outbursts of "independence" that foreshadow adolescence.

The changing image of the child creates problems for which parents are not prepared. What children feel inside their bodies calls for an outward expression that is not available. Girls want brassieres before they need them. Boys tell their mothers with disgust: "Gee, mom, you don't know nothing about what guys wear." Parents are discarded for friends, who serve as mirror images for self-observation (Chapters 14–15).

> Through a successful reintegration of her body image and identity, Glenda's mother was able to guide her out of latency with a smoothness born out of her native gift for harmonizing with the child. But she did discourage friendships and held on to the closeness with her daughter. In accepting the child's femininity, she tended to exaggerate it. Glenda began to pout and complained, "She makes me wear dresses." In retaliation she attacked her mother's physical appearance: "You could not wear clothes like me, even when you were my age." She missed a mirror image of herself. She yearned for a close girl friend.

THE CHILD'S TRANSITION INTO AND OUT OF LATENCY

Many parents become annoyed by exaggerated expressions of friendship in latency. But the loss of the child to a friend has its compensations. Bouts of diffuse, undirected excitement that grow out of incipient inner-genital sensations are contagious to parents and evoke archaic fears. A transient dissolution on body boundaries, a beginning diffusion of thought, and a greater need to externalize all add up to mutual dissatisfaction between children and parents. Regressing with the child, parents often blame each other for the waves of unrest created by the child. After a rainy afternoon at home, parents are only too glad to surrender their intimacy with their child to his bosom friend. Listening to preteen conversations from a safe distance, they become acquainted with the new customs of the "almost adolescent," which differ from those in their own childhood. A temporary estrangement from the child allows parents to regain their equilibrium and accept the waning of latency. The more deeply rooted the reintegration of psychic structure in the parents during their child's latency, the better prepared they are to participate constructively in their children's adolescent struggle.

Latency stands out as a period of "part-time parenthood" during which parents learn to share their child with the community and in which distance from the child facilitates the desexualization of his image as well as a phase of redistribution of cathexis and reorganization of ego and superego attitudes that prepares the ground for the paradoxical ultimate goal of child-rearing, the state of "childless parenthood" at the end of the child's adolescence.

NOTES

[1] Even though the examples used concern children from families of more than one child, the comments in this chapter are geared to the first and only child. It is not possible here to discuss the complexities of parents' developmental phases when several children present them with problems from different developmental phases. Neither is it possible to consider the variations stemming from relationships to first, second, youngest, or only children. Only passing references could be made to the differences between fathers and mothers, as each of them relate in a sex-specific way to different children and different age groups.

[2] In this category also belong moron jokes and riddles of later latency in which the child caricatures the wisdom of teachers who belittle children = morons. These also make fun of the literal approach to learning the children have just overcome.

281

PART III

Phase Development in Adolescence

CHAPTER 12

Menarche

Anna Freud (1958) commented on how little we know from analysis of adolescents, and how little we can reconstruct, from adult analysis, about adolescence, even though the experiences of that time may not have been heavily repressed.

It is therefore not surprising that the menarche, an event specific to adolescence, has been predominantly discussed in the literature within the framework of feminine development in general, and of reactions to menstruation in particular. In an issue of the *Zeitschrift für psychoanalytische Paedagogik* (1931), devoted entirely to menstruation, most authors did focus on the anticipation of menarche and reactions to it, but only one dealt with material from analyses (Schmideberg, 1931). At that time the prevailing lack of preparation for the first menstrual period was deplored by educators.

A survey of literature conveys the impression that the menarche has been considered one of the traumata within the female castration complex. The positive aspect of the menarche as a turning point in the acceptance of femininity has been greatly overshadowed by the emphasis placed on the "trauma" of the first and even subsequent menses.

H. Deutsch (1944–45), as well as others, have pointed out the girl's own contribution to her lack of preparedness. Her own repressions and distortions of what she was told were felt to be important factors in the complex experience of menstruation as a trauma. The mother's role in the girl's expectation and evaluation of her menarche and subsequent menstruations was considered crucial. Some authors, principally Daly (1931), stressed the male attitude toward menstruation. Anthropological data, as well as analyses of male patients, tend to confirm the view that men are inclined to regard menstruation as a dangerous traumatic event (Chadwik, 1931; Landauer, 1931). The role of the father

First published in *Adolescents: Psychoanalytic Approach to Problems and Therapy*, eds. Lorand and H. I. Schneer (New York: Haeber, 1961). Slightly revised and reprinted by permission.

and male siblings in the girl's evaluation of her menses has not been sufficiently clarified.

There is general agreement that menarche initiates a critical period in the girl's life; that she will cope with this conspicuous change in her body with a variety of reactions acquired earlier in life and now revived and intensified.

Reactions to the Menarche

Data gathered from analyses of adult women, analyses of adolescents, or observation of adolescents, suggest that there are manifold reactions to menstruation, running the gamut from the extreme of suicide and psychotic breakdown to joy over the attainment of maturity. Yet a careful review of adult and adolescent analyses of my own experience reveals a dearth of data on the effect of the first menstruation on the patients' development. I can recollect many facts elucidating particular brands of penis envy, attitudes toward siblings, and special features of the oedipus complex as well as preoedipal relationships. Patients have revealed in great detail their early and later masturbation struggles and the impact of their first sexual experiences with others. Some had particular difficulties in the first years of life that stand out vividly in my mind. I am quite aware of fluctuations of mood and attitude in various phases of these patients' menstrual cycles. I do not have a comparable series of data in regard to menarche. I do know that menarche initiated in these girls a personality change of which they were not aware and which did not become the focus of analysis because it constituted, in all cases, an improvement rather than a regressive development.

Three girls whom I analyzed at the time of their menarche stand out in my memory. All three were enlightened partly by their mothers, partly by their friends, and partly in their analyses. Menarche did not constitute, for them, a traumatic event. Also, in dealing casually and sporadically with a group of average girls who were being brought up by what is called progressive education, I gained the impression that the first menstruation was not considered by them a traumatic event. Apparently, their parents, teachers, nurses, and physicians had done what was recommended a quarter of a century ago for preparing girls for their first menstruations. None of them was unprepared; none was left to her own devices. Not only did the mother or the school or camp nurse help physically when menses started, but they also made sure that the previously enlightened child was still enlightened. By enlightenment I do not mean that the children understood the full significance of menstruation, but

286

they did know that the appearance of menses was normal and to be expected at a certain age, that it was part and parcel of feminine maturity and a prerequisite for having children in the future.

For example, a twelve-year-old who has known about menstruation for some time has shown, in the last few months, all the signs of beginning feminine development, such as breast growth, pubic hair, and feminine hiplines, as well as the unpredictability of behavior expected of the prepubertal child. Questioned casually as to whether she still knew what menstruation was for, she replied impatiently, "Of course, I know." When I asked her to tell me what she knew, she answered quickly and with obvious scorn for my naïveté, "It's the bed for the baby that you don't need any more because you don't get the baby." She said she knew positively that she would not get her period before she was thirteen-and-a-half years old. When her period did arrive at the time she predicted, she did not tell her mother about it until the matter came up in connection with going swimming. In regard to time of appearance of menses, she was guided by what happened to most of her girl friends. When she later discussed the irregularity of her menses, she reassured her mother that "most girls' periods are irregular at first—this is normal." The topic had been fully discussed in school, especially its usefulness as an excuse to be absent from gym. Striking was her practical approach to the problem—an approach typical of the group to which she belonged.

In contrast to these youngsters, children brought up by old-fashioned methods of education frequently regard menstruation as a traumatic event. There is also a direct correlation between emotional disturbance and proneness to view menarche as a threat or calamity. Dr. Helen Schur, through skillful interviewing, has collected responses to questions about the prospect as well as the experience of menarche from random samples of children hospitalized in the Psychiatric Division of Kings County Hospital. From the following examples one can readily recognize the severity of these children's problems as well as their lack of carefully thought out preparation for the first menstrual period.

Case Reports

Case 1. The subject is ten years old and the diagnosis is adjustment reaction of childhood with conduct disturbance. She has not started to menstruate. Asked about it she says, "You bleed." But she does not know from where. She goes on: "It means that you grow up and get older and older. You just get it; it's normal. The first time you get it, it lasts three to four weeks. Then you get it every week, no every month. It lasts about one week and you have it until you die. You wear a Kotex and you have to be very careful that you don't drop it. I only want to get it when I know more about it. What puzzles me is how you get pregnant by yourself. The matron at the police said it's bad when girls fool around with each other, you know—Lesbian, they touch each other. It's worse when boys and girls get together. It always needs a female and a male, a dog and a dog, a cat and a cat so they have to be just next to each other. I don't want to wear slacks, I am not a boy."

Case 2. A ten-year-old's diagnosis is adjustment reaction with habit disorder. She has not menstruated yet. She first stated that she had never heard of menstruation, period, or monthly. But on later questioning she revealed that menstruation meant that blood came from the vagina. She was "surprised that she has not got it." She had previously thought that "period" meant vaginal examination, because her older sister goes to the doctor to get a checkup and she gets a vaginal examination. She knows about that because her sister told her, and once, when she went with her sister and mother to the doctor, the doctor sent her out. Now that she knows that "period" does not mean vaginal examination, she says, "I have nothing to worry about." She thinks that her sister has a crooked pelvis and that the doctor has told her that a baby will straighten it out. Her eleven-year-old sister always goes to the bathroom to see "if she has got it." While talking, she had to go to the bathroom herself. She then wanted to know whether one can have a baby if one does not menstruate, or if the baby would die, because one of the neighbors had eight children who all died at birth and one child who is crazy.

Case 3. The patient is eleven years and nine months old. The diagnosis is schizophrenic reaction, paranoid type. She had her first period about six months ago. Nobody had told her about it before. She had pain in the lower abdomen. While menstruating, she also has headaches. She never knows when she will get her period but gets a headache before. The first time she noticed blood was when she wiped herself. She felt scared because of the pain but did not tell anybody. She did not know where she was bleeding from. She felt too ashamed to ask. She could not explain why she felt ashamed. The bleeding was light, and she washed her underwear herself. A girl friend explained it to her spontaneously after her first period. She felt relieved that somebody else had it too. The girl friend only told her that one bleeds. She is not sure if boys get it too. She never wondered why a person gets it, and never asked for more information. In the hospital she only confided in one girl who got napkins for her. She never told the nurse. She usually restricts her activity on her own initiative, because if she gets excited she gets pain.

Case 4. A sixteen-year-old, diagnosis schizophrenic reaction, catatonic type, has not menstruated for the last five months. She thinks it has something to do with the change of climate—mountain air. She thinks she menstruated twice at the age of fourteen but is not sure. Her mother had told her long before—she does not remember when—that it is natural and nothing to hide. She thinks that she saw her mother's bloody napkins, as her two-year-old cousin does his mother's. Her aunt always sends him to the window to look for his daddy because he might get frightened (apparently on seeing the bloody napkin). She does not like the period in summer because of the sweat and odor, which disturb her.

Case 5. The patient is thirteen years old with a diagnosis of schizophrenic reaction, childhood type. She does not menstruate. She was embarrassed when a male doctor asked her about it previously. Her mother had told her about it when the child was three-and-a-half years old. The mother explained to her that when she gets older she will bleed, and that's called a period. This reminded her of an accident, at the time the mother told her, in which the mother closed the lid of the piano on her fingers. She bled and needed several stitches. The patient does not know what period is. It means "that you have gotten into womanhood." She is glad that she has not gotten it because it is a big nuisance. She thinks the blood comes from the rectum. She denies wanting to know more about it but says that when she asks her friends they answer her, "It's none of your business." All during the interview she asked to be fed.

Case 6. A fifteen-and-a-half-year-old has a diagnosis of depressive reaction. She has had her period since age twelve or thirteen but does not remember exactly. Her mother had told her about it long before. She had told her what to do, "that you become a lady," and not to be afraid or ashamed. In the beginning she had no pain and seldom has it now. Would not know when she would get pain. She feels happy about it. This way she knows that she can have children and that she is healthy. But she feels moody during the period, has cramps one week before, sharp pains in her rectum, and often "after cramps." The period lasts three days. She used to get crying spells before the period and felt very tired. She does not exactly know what "period" is, although in the seventh grade the hygiene teacher explained; but she cannot remember—something about leftover and waste, but she does not know where from. During the period she also had "funny feelings" like being high up, like being very tall and looking down, which made her dizzy. She would ask for milk and wanted to be petted. She then described her emotional upset, during the period, which brought her to this hospital last year. She would "holler and scream" and tried to kill herself. She also had at those times "terrible and stupid" dreams which she could not recall. Her mother also gets cramps, as does her sister. The mother calls it "period," "monthly," or "her friend."

Case 7. A fourteen-year-old is diagnosed as having an inadequate personality. Menarche occurred at twelve. She said she felt funny and her pants were wet. She knew that she had her period. The mother, when explaining it to her, had told her that she herself did not know when she was a girl. She had fallen down and injured herself. The patient had thought one would bleed much more; that she would have to change every hour. One friend thought it would come like a river. The patient gets pain in her back before menstruation. She does everything, although she has been told that doing certain things can stop it. She says that she is glad she got it and was scared that she might not get it, because then she would not be able to have children. She wants to become a nurse because she can look at disgusting things, such as cuts on hands or head, or vomit. She had a vaginal examination a year ago.

Case 8. The subject is fifteen-and-a-half years old, with a diagnosis of adjustment reaction of adolescence with paranoid features. She menstruated for the first time for one day at age ten, a day after an appendectomy. She was frightened, could not imagine what it was, and thought she had been cut at the operation. The nurse explained it to her. She had her period regularly at eleven. She did not worry in between because she thought that "you only get it once." She is unable to explain what menstruation is. She feels happy that she got it, because she "is a young lady." She has cramps—at times bad—and then she wishes that boys would have it too. She does not discuss it with her friends; she thinks it is disgusting that some girls talk about it.

Discussion

In each of these reports one notices a mixture of information, misinformation, and fantasy. In some it is evident that instruction as to the nature of menstruation has been either repressed or denied and substituted for with ideas stemming from individual problems. In some, oral regressive features stand out; in others, the problems of injury are strongly cathected. All derive a great deal of elaboration from observations of mothers and siblings. Superimhosed upon the struggle inherent in the acceptance versus nonacceptance of menstruation as the girl's model of womanhood, we can see, in this disturbed group, features similar to those described in the more normal adolescent group. Here, too, menarche has its positive aspects in terms of group identity, in terms of an ego-ideal of growing up and becoming a lady, and in terms of identification with one's mother.

We encounter a variety of reactions: the unprepared girls who are shocked by menarche and can only rely on fantasies to explain what is happening—the old fashioned type; those who had been prepared but act as if they had not; those who had been prepared and seem to understand it, but retain their own fantasies along with what has been told them, with resultant confusion; and, last, those girls who give no evidence of keeping their old fantasies, having either repressed them or disposed of them.

In the more normal group many girls tend to accept menstruation as a necessary nuisance in maintaining their group identity as girls and future women and mothers. On the surface, complaints about the need to endure menstruation for the sake of feminine maturity would seem justified. The periodic bleeding, feeling of weakness, pain, and inconvenience in terms of additional bodily care and restriction of activity—all this does sound more like a sickness than a wholesome part of mature well-being. No wonder, one may argue, that the girl protests against the cruelty of nature and asks why a more pleasant way could not have been invented to get her ready for motherhood and femininity. Were we to accept such complaints at face value, we would have to ignore the normal feminine masochistic attitude toward pain and discomfort.

Feminine Masochism in Prepuberty and Puberty

After Freud, it was primarily Deutsch (1944–45) who described the normal feminine masochism that makes women enjoy the literally bloody experiences to which they are subjected in the normal course of development (menstruation, defloration, and childbirth). On the other hand, much of feminine penis envy and resentment of men has been ascribed to the woman's lack of acceptance of a "bleeding hole" which she refuses to enjoy. The girl's discovery that she lacks a penis and the experience of her menarche are classified as *the* traumata in feminine development. Masculine identification, which goes hand in hand with denial of femininity, is used temporarily or permanently to master the traumatic situation. It is less well known that feminine masochism not only represents a specifically feminine genital-drive endowment but is also employed in the service of mastery. Pain of all shades and intensities can sharpen and define body boundaries and is used as a landmark in the process of incorporating an invisible body part into the image of one's own body.

Undefined, unlocalized inner sensations promote anxiety. They are the no-man's-land between the girl herself and the outside in which projections and introjections continuously operate, thus preventing a sharp delineation of the girl's body image, and increasing the diffuseness of body boundaries. The girl, in prepuberty, experiences spurts of intense but poorly defined sensations which flow into each other.

Helene Deutsch (1944–45) defines prepuberty as "that last stage of the latency period in which certain harbingers of future sexual drives may be discerned, but which in the main is the period of greatest freedom from infantile sexuality" (p. 4). Deutsch is aware that other authors believe prepuberty is characterized by intensified sexual needs. At times, she does concede considerable interest in sexuality in the prepubertal child: "During prepuberty her intense curiosity about sexual processes in general directs her interest toward her own body" (p. 25). Greenacre (1950a and b) and Blos (1958) accept Deutsch's concept of prepuberty as the phase of greatest freedom from infantile sexuality. All three authors seem to be guided by the observable fact that girls in prepuberty show very little actual interest in the opposite sex. The girl's sexual interests at that time primarily center on her own growing body. This is a highly narcissistic state in which objects, male and female, serve as anchor points for exploration of the girl's body by comparison. The male sex is rejected because of its unsuitability for elucidation of secrets concerning the female body.

It is interesting to note the variety of definitions of prepuberty throughout the literature (see especially Fraiberg, 1955; also Deutsch, H., 1925b; Meng, H., 1931). Similarly, another transitional phase, that between anality and phallicity, has been variously assigned to either the pregenital or the phallic stages of development. In this early transitional stage (see Chapter 1) the child's heightened interest in her body expresses itself in a medley of pregenital and genital fantasies. The same mingling is characteristic of the transitional phase of prepuberty.[1]

Menarche brings relief, providing the girl with fixed points of reference upon which she can now organize many of her experiences. It is important to distinguish between enjoying the discomfort of menstruation and making use of it for orientation. In prepuberty, masochistic enjoyment of unpleasure only heightens anxiety, spreads diffuseness, and counteracts organization—both frustration and disorganization become sources of masochistic pleasure.

To illustrate the difference between feminine masochistic adjustment and prepuberty like masochistic enjoyment of diffusion, I shall describe two mothers with whom I have regular contacts for research purposes, Mrs. A. and Mrs. B., each living in similar circumstances, each busy with housework and the care of several children. Each of them has an apartment to clean; each has to cook, shop for food and clothing, and perform other household necessities. Each has to take the children to the doctor and dentist. Each goes out only on rare occasions, leaving the children with an obliging relative. The children of both women are lively and quite capable of making a great deal of mess and creating general bedlam. The children fight among themselves and with other children, insist on having pets, get sick from time to time, and are naughty more often than not.

To Mrs. A., my proposed visit always appears to come at the most inconvenient time, as she has a lot of work to do, someone in the family is sick, or it is just the one day when she has a chance to go out. She lets me know that I can come anyway but that my visit will give her a lot of trouble. When I arrive, she invariably complains, in response to my queries, about one child or the other, or scolds them. They are fighting too much, she says. They do not give her a moment's peace. Her oldest daughter has been talking in school; the little one is a devil, she is so active. Her older boy has never been like this. She wishes she had another boy, instead of so many girls, because boys are so much more quiet. She may proceed to tell me about an outstanding achievement of one daughter, using it to disparage her other children by comparison. Then she may go on to tell me that they had to give the cat away because she was too much trouble. Without any transition that I can detect, she may tell me her delivery had been painful, and her cousin has not been treating her right.

Poor Mrs. A—she cannot report anything pleasurable of which she may be proud without immediately adding a negative, unpleasant, even disastrous piece of news. Her verbal productions flow into each other in a steady stream of complaints and pleasure.

Let us take a look at Mrs. B. When I phone her she is very pleased to hear from me and invites me to come at any time. Her attitude denotes her feeling that I am conferring an honor upon her. When I arrive, she interrupts her work to chat with me or to do something for one of the children who may happen to need her help at the moment. When she reports misbehavior or difficulty with one or the other child, she never puts emphasis on how much trouble it has been for her, although many times she finds herself too tired to cope with the problem that has arisen, and she lets her husband do it. She is quite eager to find out how to handle these problems, although she is not always able to carry out the advice. She is by no means a perfect wife or mother. Her children have their share of neuroses, partly because of her way of handling them.

293

In her everyday living Mrs. B has as many difficulties as Mrs. A., but she does not suffer as much. She tolerates the displeasure and uses it to formulate questions and ideas as to how to make things better. Speaking of her daughter, she may report, "I never realized that she is scared of dogs until the whole trouble with the dog started that day. Then I began to wonder whether she would be less scared if I got her a pet."

Mrs. A. would have expressed it in this way: "She was so scared of this dog. My boy was never like that. We had so much trouble. She screamed and cried. It was just like that time when she got scared of the pumpkin, but I must say she is not scared to cross the street like her cousin. I watch her from the window and she is perfect. Now, my boy, he is very careless and he will get run over yet . . ." and so on and on.

Mrs. A. is confused, confusing, diffuse, unprecise. Her tough life, her feelings of frustration are a necessary by-product of her masochistic outlook. As she continuously interrupts herself, an additional interruption coming from the outside jars her and makes her feel overwhelmed by too much pressure. She is an anguished soul, forever trying to find a way out of her misery, forever hoping to finish what she had set out to do. Her complaints attempt to shift onto an outside agent her inner discontent. She seems to revel in pain, disaster, suffering, frustration, and many other shades of displeasure. One gains the impression that she finds all too brief relief in focusing on a structured experience which helps her to formulate, at times, what it is that is "too much for her." Her child is too active, which is too much for her. Or her neighbor has offended her and that was too much. Mrs. B., on the other hand, does not seem to suffer so much. She finds continuous relief in the sharpness and directness with which she acts and expresses herself. Whatever bothers her has a beginning, and there is at least an end in sight, so that she can take each new obstacle in her stride.

Mrs. A., then, is an example of a woman who cannot find lasting relief in the feminine type of enjoyment of pain but, instead, relishes the endless complaints. Her attempts to find relief are short-lived and unsuccessful. Mrs. B., on the other hand, uses painful experiences to find direction and organization in her life, and she gets pleasure in so doing.

The cases of Mrs. A. and Mrs. B. have been used here to differentiate between masochistic pleasure in pain on an instinctual level and the use of pain to bring about relief through mastery on the ego level. The first one leads to disorganization of ego functions; the second promotes organization. Desexualization is implicit in the transformation of uncontrolled masochistic pleasure into pleasure specifically derived from the localizing and differentiating qualities of pain.

The normal girl, who does not suffer unduly from menstrual discomfort, also attains a degree of organization which distinguishes her markedly from the disjointed child in prepuberty. Adolescents who suffer with menstruation and attach fearful fantasies to it are unable to accept or retain clear explanations. They exhibit various degrees of masochistic complaining about their discomfort. They try to combat their masochistic surrender and, like Mrs. A., they cannot succeed. Mrs. A.'s case represents an example of the continuation of prepubertal behavior in an adult woman. It is more usual to find that the menarche promotes some degree of organization, even in disturbances which are characterized by diffuseness of thought and masochistic tendencies.

If we survey the data collected by Dr. Schur, we find that Patients 1, 2, and 5, who had not begun to menstruate, are much like Mrs. A. in their productions. Their thoughts flow into each other. There is no clear beginning or end to what they are saying. When patients 3, 7, and 8 talk directly about menstruation, their expressions are much more clearly defined than those of the other girls. Patient 4, who suffers from amenorrhea, is vague about her menarche. Patient 6, who had been suicidal during a menstrual period, seems best organized when talking about her cramps.

All the patients are, of course, disturbed by their problems and also by the questions put to them. They all have fantasies about menstruation, and fears as well. The difference lies not so much in content as in the way they are able to talk about it. Although Patients 6, 7, and 8 tend to speak in a more diffuse fashion than other girls who have experienced menstruation, they do offer much more circumscribed data about menstruation than girls who have not had the experience. Patient 7 gets pains in her back before menstruation sets in; patient 8 has bad cramps during it. Patients 3 and 6 can even indicate precisely where they have pain, namely in the lower abdomen and rectum respectively. Even though they too, like Patients 7 and 8, relate a great deal of misinformation about menstruation, they are able to tell a much more coherent story than the uninitiated girls.

Patient 4 becomes more incoherent than Patient 3, but this is due more to omission than to diffusion of thought. Patient 6 feels moody during her period, has cramps one week before, etc. Although she has a great many sensations in connection with her period which may frighten and disturb her, she is able to describe them in a relatively organized fashion. In contrast, the three girls who have not achieved menarche tend to "talk a blue streak." Patient 1 says, "It means that you grow up and get older and older. You just get it; it's normal. The first time you get it, it lasts three to four weeks. Then you get it every week, no every month. It lasts about 1 week and you have it until you die . . ." Whatever discomfort this girl anticipates and experiences never becomes clear-cut, and it seems to go on forever. A similarly unstructured story is told by Patient 2 when she explains her confusion between vaginal examination and menstruation. Patient 5 shows diffusion and lack of organization in her story about when and how she was enlightened.

Even in this highly disturbed group of girls, those who had had the experience of menstruation exhibit some direction toward organization derived from the specificity of their physical complaints. They have a great deal of anxiety, to be sure, and many more fantasies than the prepubertal girls, but their thoughts regarding menstruation take on a concrete quality.

Menarche as a Trigger Mechanism for Organization

The difference in organization in the patients who had achieved menarche and those who had not may not seem convincing, because many of the children whose data have been collected here exhibited various confusions owing to the disturbances which led to their hospitalization. It might be well, therefore, to turn to an example of the so-called average normal girl, for reexamination of the differences between premenarcheal and later behavior.

The premenarcheal girl may come home from school and say to her mother, "You know what happened? This man came to school—we giggled terribly and we had to stay after school which is very unfair because after all he did this and it was not our fault. So that's why I'm late and you don't have to get mad because everybody had to stay after class on account of this man. . . ."

By this time even the most patient mother might interrupt and ask who the man was and what was he doing in school and what made the children giggle.[2] I doubt, however, that she would get far in her attempt to ask these questions. The child would cut in, saying, "You're not letting me finish. You're interrupting me. I'll tell you if you listen. You never listen to me, nobody does. Remember when I had a bellyache and I tried to tell you but you wouldn't let me finish and finally I had to vomit and it was your fault because you wouldn't listen?"

Since it is obvious that we will never find out what "this man" did, let us turn to another example of typical prepubertal behavior. A girl of between ten and thirteen is getting dressed in the morning. She has absolutely nothing to wear because all the girls are going to wear brown dresses to school that day. This has been carefully established on the telephone the evening before. She has only three brown dresses and they are "no good." One is too tight and "my you know what will show and don't say the word for it." Another dress is "too childish and everybody will think I'm a baby and the last one I would wear, it's okay, but you will start saying it's dirty, I know, and I only wore it for one week and I can't help it if I perspire. Every girl comes to school with some spots on her dress and no mother makes so much fuss about it. It's positively disgusting to make so much to-do about dirt."

I have selected the modes of vague, disjointed, profuse communication as examples of the overall disorganized behavior in prepuberty, but the same is true of movements, actions, approaches to problem-solving, and other aspects of functioning in prepuberty.

Mothers, exhausted, and bewildered because they feel guilty about the accusations hurled at them, come asking for advice from teachers, guidance counselors, and psychiatrists. They are able to cope with many things, but not with this avalanche of confusion. They explain that they try so hard to please their daughters. They really try to understand them. Are they failing as mothers? they ask. They have no recollection of going through a phase like this. Some add that *they* really did have nothing to wear when they were young girls, and *their mothers* really did not understand them.

One has the impression that prepubertal behavior is more contagious to mothers than to fathers. Fathers do get angry. They become upset because they feel their children are losing command of their native tongue. They try, with occasional fleeting success, to elicit clear, grammatical statements. Thus the father's attitude frequently becomes a model for attempts at organization.

Girls who have experienced menstruation may dwell on the painful physical symptoms accompanying menses and may indulge in a number of conflicting fantasies about this event, but their language is usually clear and organized. They find an outlet in the newly developed ability for clear thinking, regardless of what unpleasant experience they may discuss. They are able to start, explain, and finish what they have to say, of course within the limits of their individual personality problems; for instance, they may have difficulties in finishing their work, owing to an anal type of delaying. After menarche, average so-called normal girls act very much like Mrs. B. They use various unpleasant experiences for purposes of organization. They become more settled after menarche, and increasingly more so when their cycles become regular. In mid-adolescence they evidence the typical mood swings, often changing from one extreme to another. These may relate to their cycles or to difficult, groping, interpersonal relationships with parents, teachers, and their peers. They may be *himmelhochjauchzend zu Tode betrübt* (sky-high happy— deadly depressed). Still, we can understand them much better because, in contrast to prepubertal affects, conflicting feelings are not only well defined but even grossly exaggerated in their delineation. We may not feel empathy with the intensity and the rapid fluctuations of such affects, but we know clearly the kind of affect with which we are confronted.

In reexamining the data from analyses of children who went through menarche during analysis, I wonder whether the paucity of my recollection of reactions to menarche is not due to the fact that the main change could not be classified in terms of content of material. The fantasies had not changed, they had become clearer. The conflicts had not changed, they had intensified and become more analyzable because of the sharper delineation of opposites which menarche brought about. Analyzing girls in prepuberty is a much more difficult task than working with girls who have reached puberty (Geleerd, 1957). One gets the same impression in going over Fraiberg's (1955) examples, as many of the children she refers to belong to the prepubertal group. When analyzing both girls and boys during puberty, we must be prepared for a vehemence of resistance which may interrupt treatment. We may, as Anna Freud (1936) pointed out, lose some adolescent patients in this fashion. On the other hand, we may spend weeks and months with prepubertal children without making headway in understanding them. Prepubertal boys often become quite uncommunicative to adults. Prepubertal girls are usually quite talkative, but it is difficult to pin them down long enough to get the material clarified or to interpret it to them. The exceptions in both sexes are those children in prepuberty who suffer from definite long-standing symptoms, such as phobias or inhibitions of functions, which make these children feel different from their group. The frequency with which so-called mental breakdown occurs after menarche highlights the fact that the current struggles intensify conflicts. In these cases we encounter an increase of organization of symptoms rather than personality organization. Even in psychoses, one frequently gains the impression that maturation brought about exaggerated manifestations of previously loosely woven trends toward psychotic regression. (Cf. Eissler, 1958)

The onset of menstruation makes it possible for the girl to differentiate reality from fantasy. What she knew and what she anticipated can now be compared with how it happened to her. The sharpness of experience, the regularity of it, the well-defined way of taking care of it, the sameness of the experience as compared with her own anticipation of it and the experience of others—all these provide relief. It helps the girl to structuralize her inner and outer experiences, to regain her ability to communicate and to perceive in an organized fashion. The girl, however, is hardly ever aware of this change. She does not know that her communications were confusing, and she does not notice that she has now become clearer in her thinking.

She may now focus on the pain of menstruation to the point where it seems to us that she is enjoying it. In reality, she enjoys the sharpness of this painful experience in terms of quantity, localization, and quality of pain. I am not speaking of an intolerable pain which, by its nature may dull the senses and bring about a state akin to loss of consciousness. I am referring to the mild cramps of uterine contractions. They are localized in the lower abdomen and have a beginning, an end, and a definite quality which makes them recognizable as menstrual cramps, in contradistinction to intestinal cramps. Some girls may have only a dull ache, less defined in quality but still relatively well localized. Although this type of pain has a less sharp beginning and ending than a cramp, it has certain time limitations, because it is usually felt on a certain day of the menstrual cycle. Girls report a regularity in the pain appearing on the first day, the second, the fourth, or the day before menstruation. They know when the pain will start and when it will go away. Or they know when their menstruation will start because the pain is a preparation for it. They seem to miss the pain when it does not come and are disturbed when it changes in quality. Their special menstruation pain is their friend rather than their "curse." Girls frequently refer to menstruation as "falling off the roof." This may sound as if they are thinking in terms of suicide, injury, bleeding, and death. But we must not forget that they also hint at a sudden sharply delineated experience where, to be sure, one loses equilibrium but where one eventually lands on safe ground, coming from uncertain heights. It connotes a feeling that something definite has happened and is over with. Not only pain but the nature of the menstrual flow and its definite source, the regularity of the period, and the establishment of regular habits for body care at that time all add to stabilization, in contrast to previous diffuseness; to organization, in contrast to previous confusion.

Benedek (1952) speaks of pain as being an integrative part of women's psychosexual experience (p. 356). She says: "It is as if menarche were a puberty rite cast upon woman by nature itself " (p. 329).

Differences Between Boys and Girls

For boys, their first ejaculations are frequently not as traumatic nor as stabilizing events as first menstruations are for girls (Chapter 13).

299

Still their erections as well as their ejaculations seem to them to come from nowhere, unless produced by masturbation. And even then they wonder how long the erection will last each time, how soon they will ejaculate, and how profuse the ejaculation will be. Boys give a great deal of thought to the establishment of regularity in the sexual activity of their genital organs. They are forever trying to gain control over the production of erections and ejaculations, whereas girls adapt themselves and their mode of life to what is happening regularly in their bodies. Much of the boys' preoccupation with methods of genital control becomes diverted, by crude displacement or sublimatory activity, to inventions of gadgets, push-button controls, and the creation and improvement of remote-control machines which produce a predictable quantity of material.

Boys who have not begun to ejaculate are hampered in their experimentation and are apt to master the mystery of genital function by gross motor outlets—throwing, pushing, punching, and falling—which reproduce all variations of the mysterious activity of the penis and testicles. They don't think as much as do the boys who have ejaculated already; they try out more. The road to understanding these younger boys lies in observation of and participation in their activities.

Once ejaculation has occurred, the gross experimentation slowly gives way to more refined methods of exploration. To a varying degree here too, as in menstruation in girls, ejaculation seems to structuralize the experience. A product is discharged which definitely ends the erection, either immediately or in a short time. With a certain amount of reassurance from this source, the boys have more peace of mind even though they are beset by masturbation conflicts and intense castration fears. They can grapple in thought and action with intricate problems requiring more patience than they had before.

For girls there is less room for experimentation, less room for sublimation than we see in boys. Masturbation, with the main emphasis on exploration and experimentation, is rare in girls and frequent in boys. Similarly, intellectual curiosity wanes in girls and increases in boys at that time. In their latency years, girls pride themselves on being far better students than boys. With some variations, this state of affairs lasts through the junior-high-school years. In the last year of junior high school and in senior high school a significant change seems to take place. The once "dopey boys" now know more than the girls, can think better than the girls, and excel in mathematics and science, whereas the majority of girls are ready to acquiesce and acknowledge the boys' superiority in these subjects.

The girls may continue with their good language skills, their fine

300

feeling for literature and poetry and for art and history. They are still conscientious about their homework. They are more settled and, despite their similar changes, more conservative than boys. They can use their intuition well, but they do not become adventurous experimenters. Throughout life they remain a steadying influence, upholding the sameness of tradition, but still able to serve many masters creatively as mothers, wives, and teachers.[3] They tolerate pain better than men and may even seek pain in moments of stress and uncertainty. Pain provides them with a definite relief for a surplus of varying tensions arising from fleeting and undefined stimuli for which controlled localized discharge is not always available (Chapter 1).

Menstrual Disturbances

To the members of a hospital staff, who work with very neurotic and many psychotic girls having problems of delinquency and psychopathy, normal development may seem less impressive than pathological development. For them it may be useful to focus on the irregularity in menstruation so frequently associated with emotional disturbance. This irregularity, though often the result of emotional difficulties, also contributes further to states of anxiety, depression, and disorganization of ego functions (Fenichel 1945b).

It may be necessary to know the patient for quite some time before one becomes acquainted with her type of menstrual disturbance. Her data of menstruation may be uncertain; she may suffer from excessive pain or prolonged and profuse bleeding; she may have periods of amenorrhea. Some patients persistently ignore premenstrual and menstrual changes. They seem unable to admit the usual proneness to fatigue and the lowered resistance that come with menstruation. They may even begin to menstruate without noticing it and may not care where the blood comes from. When the denial of feminine experience, the estrangement from the happenings in their bodies, is lifted, anxiety or depression may set in. Many patients who do not suffer from menstrual irregularity have isolated the physical from the emotional experience. They are surprised to discover that their unexplained, seemingly unprovoked upsets, their tendency to get into trouble periodically, coincide either with the menstrual period or with the even more difficult premenstrual time (Horney, 1931).

A chart of patients' cycles reveals a high correlation between flare-ups of certain problems and hormonal changes. The irregularity of menstruation seems to be, at least in part, produced by unconscious fantasies and defensive reactions to sensations stemming from changes in the vaginal mucosa during various parts of the cycle. As noted, the irregularity, in turn, adds to anxiety, promotes fantasies, and strengthens the defensive positions. One of the signposts of improvement in a patient is the establishment of a regular and normal cycle, a regularity which foreshadows steady progress in ego organization.

The severity of adolescent problems is directly correlated to the length and extent of cycle instability so common at that time. In turn, the menstrual irregularity is correlated to earlier development. A girl who in earlier childhood was able to find definite, well-defined repetitive modes of discharge does invariably suffer during prepuberty from a decrease in organization of discharge modes, but she recovers and uses the earlier patterns for reorganization on a higher level. She will have a relatively brief and easy transitional menstrual irregularity. Conversely, the girl who, during latency, did not evidence a stable adjustment of definitely patterned repetitive modes of adaptation to inner and outer needs, in prepuberty tends to suffer from severe disorganization which sometimes continues into mid-adolescence and later. She may have long periods of amenorrhea, prolonged irregularity of cycle, and severe reactions to various phases of the cycle.

Amenorrhea with conversion symptoms, amenorrhea of the anal-retaining type, masochistically tinged dysmenorrhea, and menstrual irregularity produced by an omnipotent wish to gain control over the timing of physical events are but a few of the other variations in pathology. Stunting of the development of maternal feelings as well as violent wishes for pregnancy, fantasies of oral impregnation, of having a child with one of the parents—all these play a role in menstrual disturbances and in difficulties in accepting the menarche.[4]

Brief Review of Some Physical Aspects of Feminine Development

In this section I shall summarize briefly the views of endocrinologists on the development of the female from birth to maturity and shall follow this up with descriptions of early and later modes of genital discharge. Suggestions for a correlation of these findings with the psychological development in childhood and adolescence will be given in subsequent chapters.

The genital tissues of the majority of newborn female infants manifest a transient precocity. The labia majora and minora undergo hypertrophy during the last weeks of intrauterine life and are relatively large at delivery. The vaginal epithelium is thickened and contains glycogen; a whitish discharge containing Doderlein's bacilli is present. The uterus of the newborn is congested and approximately 40 percent heavier than that of a one-year-old girl. There is a gradual recession of these changes over a period of 3–4 months (Talbot *et al.*, 1952).

This precocity of the infant is attributed largely to stimulations by estrogen from the mother. Prolactin, which is demonstrable in the urine of infants before and during the periods of lactation, may play a role in the frequent milk production from infants' breasts. Whether this hormone is fetal or maternal in origin is unknown. We are told that, between the third and fourth months of life until the eighth to eleventh year, sexual development is largely in abeyance. Estrogen and androgen excretions in urine are demonstrable at the age of three, remaining more or less steady for both sexes, but with more androgen in boys and more estrogen in girls. A small increase of sex-specific hormone appears at about seven to eight year, and there is a gradual increase up to age ten or eleven. At this point the boys' estrogen level in the urine rises to another small peak, and then there begins a small decrease in estrogen; in girls, the estrogen level rises rapidly to a high peak, falling rapidly until age thirteen to fourteen and then rising abruptly again.

It is not too clear what happens in the hormonal household between four months and three years of age. It is also not known whether there is a periodic or sporadic fluctuation of hormone levels from the age of three on. Gonadotropin first becomes demonstrable in girls' urine at the age of eleven. The menarche is associated with progressive increases in the amounts of gonadotropin and in the frequency with which it can be detected in the urine.

As the endometrium develops, it exhibits proliferative phases paralleling the ovarian estrogen cycles. Eventually, the oscillations of the estrogen levels become sufficiently pronounced to induce a vascular crisis in the endometrium, and the first menstrual period occurs. Finally, the rising peaks of estrogen production reach a level adequate to stimulate release of appreciable quantities of luteinizing hormone from the pituitary, and ovulation takes place, initiating the luteal phase of the menstrual cycle. It is believed that the release of gonadotropin in adolescence is dependent upon a neural or neurohormonal mechanism inhibited in childhood. Removal of this inhibition is thought to be dependent upon the maturation of hypothalamic centers of the nervous system, which ordinarily occurs about the turn of the first decade.[5]

In the mature menstrual cycle, the uterus and vagina undergo definite changes which consist of a relatively long period of growth and differentiation and a short period of regression, manifested externally by menstrual bleeding. The state of the uterine mucosa is continuously changing, except for about 48 hours after menstruation has ceased. As

303

the follicle matures, the estrogen secretion rises rapidly, and the endometrium proliferates at an increasing rate until ovulation occurs. Under the influence of progesterone, the mitotic activity ceases, and differentiation begins. The stage of premenstrual regression reflects the withdrawal of growth stimuli from the endometrium. Blood flow decreases, and the arterioles, by becoming more tortuous, accommodate themselves to the restricted space caused by the shrinking of endometrium. The stasis thus induced is held to be responsible for the necrosis of the endometrium and the weakening of the vessels, culminating in hemorrhage. Progesterone promotes a slight to moderate retention of sodium chloride and water and is, in all probability, more important than estrogen in the production of premenstrual edema. After ovulation, changes also take place in the rhythmical contractibility of the uterine and tubal musculature. Not known for humans but studied in lower animals is the change in uterine motility characterized during the follicular phase by low-amplitude, high-frequency waves and a tonic type of spontaneous contraction. This rhythm alters with the changing of hormone combinations and levels.

Clinical studies by Benedek (1952) established a high degree of correlation between phases of the menstrual cycle and psychological manifestations. It must be left to future research to discover what physical changes contribute to the vicissitudes of psychosexual attitudes before maturity. Whether such changes are really minimal until prepuberty and only become activated by external stimulation is difficult to ascertain, both because the available methods of testing may be too gross, and because one cannot yet conduct such studies without undue traumatization of the children involved (see Chapters 13, 14, 15, and 17). As discussed below, genital discharge has been observed in infancy and childhood (Chapter 5). Its correlation with anatomical and hormonal changes is yet to be explored.

Analysis and observations of small children and reconstructive analysis of childhood experiences in adults suggest that sporadic waves of sexual excitation pervade the little girls' genitals, provoked by either inner or outer stimuli. Evidence of pleasure from genital sensations can be seen as early as the first year of life. Observable genitally derived states of excitement occur sporadically before intense genital preoccupation culminates in masturbatory experiences of the phallic-oedipal phase.

As the little girl does not have an adequate organ of discharge at her disposal, she tends to externalize her undefined sensations. She seems to meet with some measure of success in the period in which she uses clitoral manipulation, producing a lightning-rod type of discharge. Although a rapid and well-defined mode of discharge offers her temporary

304

relief, she is soon subjected again to ever-changing undefined, slow waves of excitation which seem to stem from vaginal sensations.

The little girl uses alternate ways of discharge through anal and urethral channels. The urethral pathway is chosen not only because of the proximity of the bladder to the vagina but also because changes in the vagina are associated with similar if not identical changes in the lowest part of the urethra. Deep pressure in clitoral masturbation frequently involves pressure on the distal part of the urethra. Children occasionally are able to distinguish the different sensations coming from the clitoris proper and the tissue deep underneath. The lower part of the urethra, like the lowermost portion of the vagina, is a derivative of the urogenital sinus. Both are responsive to estrogenic stimulation. In maturity the lower part of the urethra exhibits cyclic epithelial growth and cornification simultaneously with such changes occurring in the vagina. Thus this part of the urethra in itself is a source of stimulation, but it also serves as a discharge vehicle both in the pleasures of retention and elimination of urine and in the various ways of exerting pressure on the urethra through manual and pressure-of-thighs masturbation.

Many are the ways of stimulation to the vagina, and many ways of discharge are open and used simultaneously and alternately by different children and in different phases of genital needs (see Chapter 10). Seductions can enhance it. Vaginal fluor of unknown origin can act as a stimulus but may also be a method of discharge of genital sexual tension. The multitude of stimuli of various rhythmical qualities act upon each other. Vaginal, anal, urethral, and clitoral rhythms, as well as the diverse rhythmic ministrations in physical care are added to stimuli of a kinesthetic nature which also evoke vaginal sensations. These various frequencies and intensities of stimuli sequences add to each other, combine with each other, and very frequently interrupt each other. In addition, as the little girl uses a number of pathways for discharge both simultaneously and alternately, her discharge rhythms frequently interrupt each other as well. Oral, anal, urethral, clitoral, secretory, and skin discharges are used sometimes in wholesale fashion, with the resulting feeling of being flooded with stimuli and flooding the world in response. Fear of incontinence from all orifices accompanies such feelings and adds to the girl's tendency to interrupt one discharge after another.

The diffusion, created by the many stimuli and discharge modes, used to provide relief for cryptic genital tensions, is pronounced at the onset of the phase that precedes the phallic. It becomes even more marked when latency gives way and prepuberty begins.

Menarche focuses the girl's attention on one special feminine way of discharge, serving as a model for a vaginal orgastic discharge pattern. The experience of the menstrual flow enhances the integrative function which eventually subordinates the various sources of stimuli and discharge ways to the primacy of the vagina (Freud, S., 1905a; 1931).

Reports of vaginal orgasm in very disturbed women, as well as mention of many vaginal orgasms following each other, seem to contradict the foregoing thesis (Greenacre, 1952). One wonders, however, whether such experiences are not representative of a flooding with sexual stimuli in which the vaginal sensations and partial discharges have become conscious, possibly along with conscious acknowledgment of other simultaneous or successive locations of stimulation and discharge. Psychotic women may become aware of intense sensations in the vagina, whereas neurotic women repress them. This in itself does not indicate vaginal primacy. In the rare instances when neurotic patients describe flooding with stimuli as they experience it on the analytic couch, we hear that sensations in one organ are quickly followed by sensations in another. They are retrospectively understood as waves of excitement going through the whole body, with varying wavelengths and intensities. The result is that, at some points, one organ is especially highlighted, and in the next moment there is simultaneous sensation in two or more organs. Attempts to hypercathect one organ to counteract free-flowing shifts of cathexis often produce conversion phenomena.

One such patient would become aware of vaginal sensations, then quickly wonder whether she needed to urinate or defecate, and at times oral sensations would follow. Patients with disturbances of the vaginal rhythm frequently refer to vaginal sensations as "flies, mosquitoes, birds." They seem to be describing the scattering of sensations. Their fears that, with relief, they will lose everything that is contained in their body betray that the stimuli have flooded the inside. In some patients only the analysis of a transitory conversion symptom leads to the understanding of the nature of their vaginal sensations. When vaginal primacy has been established, these patients are able to live through the experience of a vaginal rhythm which incorporates in one unit various previously interfering rhythms from other organs and organ systems.

The complex adult vaginal-uterine organization presupposes a high degree of integration. A preliminary basic step toward such an organization is the menarche, which paves the way for the pattern of vaginal-uterine discharge. Through frequent repetition, menstruation facilitates the specific feminine discharge rhythm which subordinates other rhythms to its main theme. Although a certain amount of inhibition of other excitation waves is operative in this subordination, the principal achievement of feminine genital maturity is the coordination and integration of various rhythms to a point where unity and continuity of the sexual experience are accomplished.

Not only are the various excitations from organs other than genital gathered and discharged without interrupting each other, but the simultaneous and successive excitations of different parts of the female genitals are synthesized in the same fashion. The excitability of the clitoris, urethra, labia, introitus, and the upper and lower parts of the vagina are all of a different order. During childhood, stimuli from these regions tend to jar each other rather than flow together. During successive stages of masturbatory experimentation, little girls try to focus on one or another region. If one area (most frequently the clitoris) becomes hypercathected at the expense of others for a long time, stimuli from the others undergo a lasting inhibition. At menarche this strong inhibition is suddenly disrupted, with resulting shock and disorganization. Some girls then recover the primacy of an accessory genital part and hold on to the infantile organization of dominance of the previously overcathected genital part over the vagina. This type of dominance is mainly established by inhibition.

When the childhood experiences leading to the selection of a genital part other than the vagina have been analyzed, patients go through a phase of disorganization—flooding by various stimuli accompanied by anxiety. A reorganization under vaginal dominance, which evolves during further analysis, includes the establishment of a regular menstrual cycle and the ability to adapt to changes occurring during different phases of the menstrual cycle. Still, under stress, regressive disorganization and subordination of rhythm to a pregenital or early genital level do occur.

Premenstrual edema often gives rise to such sensations as bursting. These promote anxiety, irritability, and depressive moods. The form of premenstrual reactions is determined by previous fixations; for instance, depressions are typical of women who tend to regress to the oral phase. No matter what mood changes occur premenstrually, this is the time of relative disorganization and the lowest level of adaptation in the feminine cycle. The onset of menstruation provides relief and fosters reorganization under vaginal dominance. The postmenstrual time is then used for renewed stabilization and preparation for the more intense excitations to follow in the subsequent phase of the cycle.[6]

Organizers of Feminine Development

Changes in adaptation during the menstrual cycle are a miniature of the happenings of the prepubertal, pubertal, and postpubertal periods.

The disorganization in prepuberty is followed by a period of restructuring heralded by the menarche. Not only the first, but each successive menstruation acts as an organizer. At first, the cycles may be irregular and organizational attempts may come in spurts, sometimes varying to the point of extremes during different parts of the adolescent menstrual cycle. Not until the last phase of adolescence does the young woman consolidate her organization in preparation for the intense challenges of her first mature sexual experiences.

Menarche (and the menstrual cycle) is only one of the organizers in the girl's life. Another, that may even counteract the development of menarche as an organizing agent, is the girl's mother.

The mother ministers to the girl's physical needs and, in so doing, she conveys to her how she feels about her genitals. When she sees the child touch her genitals, she gets excited or angry or she may look away. When the preoedipal girl identifies with her mother and plays with dolls, we recognize from the way she treats them how she feels about herself. When, at the end of this phase, the girl discovers her introitus, the degree of her upset and the efficiency of her denial of its existence depends a great deal on the attitude of her mother toward her own femininity. Turning to her clitoris for consolation, the phallic girl believes that the mother values a male organ more than her own. She gives up clitoral masturbation for psychological reasons, such as wishes to be penetrated by her father and reawakening of vaginal tensions, fears of loss of love, or depreciation of her tiny organ as compared to that of the father and the boy. The renunciation is also facilitated by lack of physical relief. All these factors present themselves in analyses of girls, along with continual reference to the girl's mother as having encouraged one of the components over the others. Some mothers promote penis envy; others, fears of injury; still others, feelings of dissatisfaction. The influence of the mother is twofold. The mother's educational approach to the child's sexual problems is added on to the child's identification with the mother's observed attitudes toward the same sexual problems. If the mother's own solution of conflicts corresponds with the advice she offers the girl, the child is enabled to go through latency with a minimum of regressive behavior.

The girl proceeds into latency by keeping up her previously established denial of the introitus (see Chapter 1; and Horney, 1933) and by reactive overcompensation of the angry feelings against her parents for not having provided a definite satisfaction for her diffuse needs. But her proneness to be quarrelsome, to have secrets, and to form cliques against one child or another betrays the continuing lack of gratification; hence the need to find a scapegoat on whom she can transfer her own feelings of inadequacy. Her successful striving for clear-cut experiences that will counteract the vagueness and diffuseness of her various needs expresses itself in her practicality, her conforming behavior, and her focusing on learning in a precise, systematic way. Here, the mother and the teacher help in the achievement of satisfaction. If guidance in terms of preciseness and definiteness is lacking, the latency girl tends to regress and has difficulties in learning (see Chapter 10).

In the prepubertal stage the young girl experiences an onrush of a greater quantity of genital excitation. She is subject to rapid changes of hormone levels, to the various internal and external stimuli stemming from the growth of different organs. Her previous latency adjustment still gives her a background of steadiness, but her new moods and her new ways of relating to others, as well as her new way of expressing herself, all betray a partial breakdown of ego organization. She tries to focus on some fad or craze (movie stars, anonymous boys, wrestling, horses, clothes, telephoning, etc.). In her great effort to find relief from tensions, she seeks pain and provokes punishment, but it fails to do the trick. At this point the mother may either promote masochistic solutions or she may help by being tolerant and encouraging structuralization of experiences.

No real intensity of affects is involved in prepubertal "crazes." The repetition and never-ending demands of the girls during such crazes mislead many parents into thinking that they are dealing with an intense experience. Furthermore, parents, especially mothers, judge the quantity of their daughters' affects by the intensity of their own disapproval of them.

Intolerance of fads facilitates masochistic solutions instead of preventing their further development. Tolerance may be used constructively. The mother who has a benevolent interest in the child's feelings for a rock-and-roll singer, for example, will help her to distinguish between his style and the features used by other types of singers. The introduction of categories thus acts as an organizer and may convert the craze into a meaningful experience in growing up.

When menstruation, with its relief-bringing qualities, finally arrives, the girl patterns her reactions in identification with her mother. We see the double influence of previous infantile solutions then guided by the mother and that of present maternal behavior. The girl who has been severely traumatized by her discovery of the vaginal opening, who clings to penis envy, and maintains a homosexual libidinous position will be retraumatized by the sight of her menstruation and will tend to repeat her earlier denials of femininity. She may revert to renewed external masturbation, but more often than not she is unable to obtain relief that way because of its painful reminder that she lacks a penis. A mother who treats menstruation as a shameful experience, a "curse," and does not, except by lip service, foster the pride of growing up and being a woman, disrupts the girl's budding efforts at feminine organization and promotes regressive behavior. Most frequently, the mother's earlier behavior is continued at the time of menarche, thus consolidating previously established fixations. A girl who, in identification with her masochistic mother, has already established a martyr complex, will exploit her menarche masochistically, magnifying and enjoying the unpleasant aspect of menstruation rather than deriving relief from the clarity of the new experience.

One type of girl, influenced by an ever-dissatisfied, nagging mother, holds onto the lack of satisfaction, to the diffuseness and fragmentation of excitation and discharge, because she identifies excitement with possession of precious goods which she is afraid to lose. She envies her mother's ability to maintain the upper hand by continuously flowing excitement. She is forever excited, without reaching an orgasm or real achievement in other areas. She mistakes continuous excitement for aliveness and vivacity. She misuses the stimulations of the menstrual and premenstrual periods to gain and retain more excitement. Her fixation stems from the beginning of the early genital phase, when oral envy, anal possessiveness, and urethral ambition vied with vaginal yearnings.

Another type, given to depressions and even suicide in reaction to premenstrual and sometimes menstrual experiences, belongs to the group of oral-sadistic disorders. In some of these girls premenstrual feelings of swelling evoke intense biting responses. Others react to the sight of menstrual blood with cannibalistic fantasies. (Cannibalistic tendencies are evidenced to a small extent in normal development, as remainders of an archaic reaction to the sight of blood.) Schmideberg (1931) pointed out that oral-sadistic impulses of the menstrual period are influenced by the girl's oral-sadistic interpretations of the primal scene. In all these cases the mother's oral behavior—and here we must lay special stress not only on eating and feeding behavior but also on speech and choice of words— paves the way through identification for oral-sadistic solutions. The seemingly enlightened girls who are unable to use the information given to them often report that their mothers, by their tone of voice and choice of words, have given away the fact that they themselves do not believe what they are explaining. Many mothers, by such subtle means, convey to their daughters their own fears and fantasies concerning menstruation.

Not only mothers but other family members and close girl friends influence the girls' attitudes toward the menarche. Sometimes they reinforce existing fears; at other times they help allay them. Especially important is the father's benevolent interest and his own freedom from fear of blood.

Girls who look forward to menstruation as a "friend" change markedly after menarche, establish regularity soon, and become steady within the limits of their cycles, and also accept their inner reproductive organs and the mode of vaginal rhythm. They adjust to changing bodily stimulations, being more energetic before ovulation, more passive after, excited premenstrually, relieved with menstruation, and quiescent for a short time thereafter (Benedek, 1952). This continuous readjustment to inner needs becomes a model for adapting to the changing needs of their future husbands and children of different ages and different sexes.

A discussion of the roles of defloration, pregnancy, and childbirth, as well as the role of husband and children as organizers of feminine development, is beyond the scope of this chapter. The considerable contribution of the father and of siblings to the girl's acceptance or rejection of herself as a woman is interrelated with and subordinated to the mother's influence. The way she reacts to the rest of the family in relation to herself and in relation to her daughter will have a lasting influence upon the child. It is important to note that successful adjustability, although governed by the models of changing inner rhythms, is possible only where a flexible mother provides the model from outside.

Summary

Menarche is presented as an organizer in feminine development. Diffuse [premenarcheal] behavior is contrasted with the more sharply delineated [postmenarcheal] organization. Feminine masochism, usually intensified after menarche, is considered normal where it leads to pain tolerance and appreciation of the relief qualities of sharp sensations. Attitudes toward menarche are described as determined by earlier infantile solutions, the identification with the mother being the guidepost in the establishment of early and present solutions. It is stressed that the mother acts throughout development as the organizer from the outside, providing models for organizing of stimuli stemming from the inside.

NOTES

[1] For a definition of prepuberty as a phase, beginning with the onset of secondary sex characteristics, and ending at the time of onset of fertility, see Chapter 13.

[2]Note here the frequency of giggling attacks in prepuberty. To the adult, such behavior appears to be a never-ending exuberance of spirit for which no adequate explanation is forthcoming. Although the sexual tinge of giggling is unmistakable, no concrete sexual idea is attached to it. Any word or situation connected with sex may bring on a giggling attack in a group of prepubertal girls.

[3]The fact that women demand and achieve equal rights and have pursued many careers and professions does not detract from this statement.

[4]Further examples of menstrual disorders are given on pp. 309-310.

[5]For a divergent theory see Chapter 16.

[6]Compare the change in uterine contractility during the follicular phase in animals mentioned on p. 304. Most likely, the rhythm of excitation in humans follows the same pattern. The excitation processes in the vagina may well be correlated to uterine contractility rhythms.

Phases of Adolescence with Suggestions for a Correlation of Psychic and Hormonal Organizations

I: Antecedents of Adolescent Organizations in Childhood

Adolescence is a prolonged period of development. It is a stage of reorganization of the past and preparation for the future. Earlier developmental phases are revived, but a more complex ego, a more advanced intellect, a trained superego, and a much less restricted social situation give a new color to old strivings. There is a new organization, to be sure not an adult one, yet quite different from its precursors in childhood. This difference is dependent on hormonal maturation which triggers anatomic, physiological, and psychological changes as a final step toward attainment of adulthood.

I shall focus in this and the two succeeding chapters on the changing organization in adolescent development. I shall sketch out some suggestions for a correlation of psychic and hormonal organizations, based on data I have collected before 1967. These will be supplemented and enlarged to include newer insights derived from movement studies in three chapters on adolescent rhythmicity (written with Dr. Esther Robbins), which conclude this book.

First published in *J. Amer. Acad. Child Psa.* 6:426–6, 1967. Slightly revised and reproduced by permission.

In this chapter, I shall lay the ground for the subsequent discussion of adolescent phases by outlining their antecedents in childhood and by presenting a review of anatomical and hormonal changes from birth to young adulthood.

Introduction

Before attempting to suggest possible correlations of phases of psychic organizations with hormonal changes, one must stress the hazards and uncertainties involved. Some of the data on the anatomy and physiology of reproductive organs in childhood are even more open to question than comparative data on adults; they are vastly more in need of revision by repetition of old and institution of new investigative procedures (Masters, 1959; Masters and Johnson, 1966). Hormonal studies of children are cross-sectional or sporadic. The data given in reports of assays are related to ages rather than developmental levels and many of the available reports are based on unreliable techniques (Eberlein, 1966; Paulsen, 1966). A correlation of hormonal and psychic changes based on existing data must be considered premature. In addition, the suggested chronology and interpretation of developmental phases which were extrapolated from analyses and observations have not been scientifically validated. My formulations are only tentative and require reevaluation and critical scrutiny by investigators of psychoanalytic child psychology.[1]

My decision to present suggested lines of inquiry for a correlation of psychic and hormonal changes on so scant and uncertain a basis was prompted by the following considerations. When I began to explore dominant modes of organization in phases of psychic development (Chapter 12; 1963), I discovered striking parallelisms between some of the data and views published by endocrinologists and my own expectations, which were based solely on clinical observations and interpretations of behavior. At the same time it became apparent to me that misunderstandings and obstacles to a better understanding of total development were created by the lack of systematic cooperation between researches pursuing similar interests. Even where endocrinologists made assays on children drawn from longitudinal studies of development, the respective findings were presented in different journals and isolated from one another (Stuart, 1939; Nathanson et al., 1941). Extensive research projects on sex behavior were carried out without a clear understanding of allied disciplines. As a result, Kinsey et al. (1953) did not find a correlation between levels of sex hormones and sex interest, while Benedek (1952), in a much less extensive but well-thought-out project, demonstrated in great detail how specific attitudes were interrelated with specific hormonal constellations during phases of menstrual cycles. Fifteen years ago Benedek stressed the need for similar interdisciplinary studies in children, yet none was attempted. If my suggestions of areas of correlation between psychic and hormonal changes in development succeed in stimulating interdisciplinary investigations, my effort will be well spent, despite the paucity of data presently available for such a correlation.

In order to make this presentation comprehensive, I had to select pertinent findings from older and newer anatomical reports, and those data on hormonal assays which, even though based on outmoded techniques, did not significantly differ from newer findings, were most complete, and based on chronologically arranged averages rather than on single individual assessments (Tables 1-3, pp. 333-335). To establish a common denominator for phases of psychic, anatomic, and hormonal changes I had to adopt definitions of prepuberty and puberty that are applicable in both contexts.

Prepuberty begins with the onset of secondary sexual characteristics and with considerable increase in the production of sex-specific hormones. These coincide with a breakdown of latency organization which will be referred to as "prepuberty diffusion." Menarche and first seminal emissions are not to be taken as evidence of puberty. First menstruations are anovulatory and first emissions do not contain mature spermatozoa. They are landmarks in the "prepuberty integration" of childhood sexuality into puberty genitality. The term "puberty" refers to the time at which ovulation or discharge of mature spermatozoa begins to occur and reproduction becomes possible (Talbot et al., 1952; Wilkins, 1965). But the adult mechanism of sex hormone production does not stabilize until the end of the second decade (Paulsen et al., 1966). The transformation of puberty genitality into an adult form occurs in several stages which will be referred to as "puberty growth" and "differentiation" and the "preadult phase of consolidation."

Although the emphasis in this chapter is on the correlation between activities of sex hormones, sex organs, and behavior, it is understood that this represents only one segment of the total psychosomatic organization in a given phase. Psychoanalytic nomenclature for the designation of phases originated in Freud's first formulations about infantile sexuality (1905), but even then referred to the total psychic organization. To each dominant pregenital or genital organization there belongs a phase-adequate maturational level that provides a basis for drive differentiation, for crystallization of adaptive modalities (Hartmann, 1939; Erikson, 1950) and defense mechanisms (Freud, A., 1936) and related advances in individuation (Mahler, 1965; Mahler and La Perriere, 1965) and iden-

315

tity formation (Erikson, 1959; Jacobson, 1964). In the classification of childhood and adolescent phases proposed in this paper, an attempt is made to describe states of imbalance in development from which new patterns of equilibrium emerge, and to detect the predominant mode of progression within a given phase (growth, differentiation, integration, consolidation). All these are intrinsic to development in every period of life. But there also seems to be a sequential arrangement of prevailing modes of organization over longer spans of time. This arrangement gives a broad direction to developmental progression in the first ten year of life and is repeated in the advancement toward adulthood in the second decade.

The revival and reorganization of childhood sexuality in adolescence are generally recognized, but the parallelism in the dominant modes or organization in specific developmental phases of childhood and adolescence has been explored only recently (Blos, 1967). Endocrinologists look upon the first decade as a period of latency, but they refer to steroids produced in childhood as precursors of hormones whose sex-specific metabolism begins in adolescence. The following presentation of antecedents of adolescent organization will attempt to unify both points of view.

Disequilibrium and Integration in the Inner-Genital Phase (Precursors of Prepuberty Diffusion and Integration)

Prepuberty is characterized by a curious mixture of pregenital and genital trends. It contains features of every preceding developmental phase; at the same time it anticipates puberty traits. It is initiated by states of diffusion of thought processes and other signs of disequilibrium which may become manifest even before the appearance of secondary sex characteristics. A new integration of psychic functions resolves the initial disequilibrium in transition to puberty.

The phase in which the transition from pregenitality to phallic genitality is accomplished in childhood evidences similar characteristics. This early phase, too, shows mixtures of pregenital and genital trends. It contains features of all preceding pregenital phases and at the same time it anticipates phallic genitality. It is initiated by states of disequilibrium which may coincide with an increase of hormone production and an upsurge of tensions arising in the inner genitals. An integration of pregenital, inner and outer genital drive components, stabilizes psychic functioning in transition to the phallic phase.[2]

The dominant drive component in the prephallic stage, as well as in prepuberty, can be best described as *inner-genital* in contradistinction to "outer-genital." The child deals with his inner-genital sensations and interests by externalizing them from the inside of the body to the outside. The externalization of impulses stemming from diffuse, unlocalizable inside tensions enhances the desexualization of the inside of the body and facilitates processes serving the integration of pregenital and genital drive components. In this manner the child deals not only with current problems but also erects integrated psychic representations for more primitively organized experiences of the past. Examples from pregenital phases during which genital activity is incorporated into dominant phase-specific organizations will illustrate this point.

The infant boy's erections and testicular-scrotal movements and the infant girl's vulvovaginal engorgements are incorporated with and subordinated to the oral frustration-gratification cycle. Genital tensions as a background of hypercathected oral experiences contribute to the fantasies about oral intercourse and impregnation which are conceptualized in the prephallic phase of integration.

Toward the second part of the first year, when the child becomes aware of the lower part of his body and anal needs begin to predominate over others, genital stimuli are absorbed into the anal frustration-gratification complex. In sitting up and walking, the one-year-old boy may connect the sight of his genitals with the previously experienced tactile and kinesthetic sensations. But as the anal-sadistic impulses of retaining and throwing away come into the foreground of his experience, genital and anal feelings merge, providing a foundation for the subsequently developed penis-feces (Freud, S., 1917c) and testicle-feces (Bell, 1964) equations. The girl, who cannot see her genitals, senses only vaguely that "down there" there are varieties of tensions which she wants to retain up to a certain point and then eject. But the representation of a "cloaca" cannot be formed until much later.

In the succeeding pregenital phase urethral preoccupations become the center of attention (Freud, S., 1908; Sadger, 1910; Kestenberg, 1966). The boy who begins to urinate standing up regards his penis as a "pee shooter." It may take six months or a year before he begins to wonder about the origin of babies and may think that they are made out of urine. The exploration of the consistency and location of testicles and scrotum provides a foundation for the subsequently developed idea that the testicles contain urine. Observations of erections during urine retention and their loss with the release of urine give rise to incipient castration fears which vie with the newly developing feelings of organ constancy and organ belonging. The girl during the urethral phase begins to look whence the urine came. Even though she is aware that defecation and urination feel differently, she does not begin to erect a division between the anovulval "cloaca" and the urethral-clitoric "bump" until a later time when spatial concepts and localization become more meaningful to her. At the height of the urethral phase children of both sexes tend to discharge genital tensions through vesicourethral channels.

The divergent discharge forms and discharge zones in pregenital phases of development (Kestenberg, 1966) had deflected genital discharge into phase-specific channels. By the time the child enters the inner-genital phase he has achieved partial control over pregenital discharge zones. His pregenital drives have been tamed to a degree and have been so modified that their derivatives can be used for useful and accepted activities such as speech, work, and play. The child has become civilized to the extent that he is usually weaned and toilet-trained, can communicate verbally, and can distinguish between socially acceptable and undesirable actions. To be sure, regressions are frequent. Speech can deteriorate into screaming, cleaning up into messing, washing into flooding (Kris, 1955). A new kind of interest in the genitals is anxiety-provoking, fosters regression, and adds to the instability and *disequilibrium* of the two-and-a-half-year-old. The confusion between genitals and excretory organs flares up over and again. As genital feelings become progressively centered upon genital discharge zones, they seem to have a quieting effect upon the child who is beset by so many conflicting progressive and regressive impulses and reactions. Boys tend to embark upon this phase of transition from pregenitality to phallicity later than girls. Before they achieve phallic dominance they seem to be more burdened than girls by the disequilibrium created by clashes between pregenital and genital interests, between being a baby and growing up. At times their training is not accomplished before four or four and a half. The transition to phallic dominance is consequently delayed with a corresponding retardation of the onset of latency. These boys enter school at the height of their phallic excitement and do not settle down to latency before seven or eight.

The child of about two and a half and three has become aware of his identity as "I," but he is confused by the changing image of himself. At one moment he is a big boy, proud of his newly acquired controls; but soon after, or even simultaneously, he may whine like a baby, call for his mother, suck his thumb, mess with food, stain his pants with feces, splash water all over, and drip urine in his pants. Confronted with a small baby, he takes pride in having teeth, in being able to walk and jump, and in being clean. At the same time he is not averse to snatching the baby's bottle, to crawling on all fours, and crumbling cookies all over the floor. Veering from activity to passivity, he refuses to hold his mother's hand, will run ahead of her with great vigor, and then demand to be picked up and carried. Whereas his identity as a baby was defined by the boundaries between the mother-child unit and the outside world (when he was successively "baby," "Johnny," and "you"), his new feeling of himself as "I" is blurred by the inconsistency of his needs and actions (Mahler, 1963; Jacobson, 1964). Not only does he want conflicting things at the same time, but he does not always know what is expected of him. He loses the intimate contact with his mother which used to give him a steady direction. The estrangement he feels towards his mother, because he is "I" and she is "you," makes him feel abandoned and alone. He reaches back to the oneness with her and finds himself unable to regress fully to what was once at least togetherness. He blames his mother for his confusion and turns away from her. Defensively, on the rebound, so to say, he overemphasizes his independence. His mother's feelings sharpen the conflict. She is both sad because she lost her baby and proud tht her child is growing up. She too has lost some of her earlier intuitive understanding of the child since she neither feels him often enough close to her body nor is she any longer a continuous participant in his intimate bodily activities. She, too, may become defensive and may overemphasize the separation between herself and her big boy or girl. Anna Freud's (1958) observation that the parents of adolescents may need more help than the adolescents themselves pertains also to the mother of the growing toddler. This is probably true in all phases of transition in development.

In transition from babyhood to being a boy or big girl, the child works out his problems by identification with the mother who used to tend to his bodily needs. He has separated himself from her by disengaging each of his body parts from her ministering hands. The distinction between himself and his mother provides the core for the discrimination between inside and outside. This brings into focus the polarity between his own inside and outside. Food, feces, and urine, which comprise what is inside of him, are now becoming his own rather than shared with his mother (Freud, A., 1965). Nevertheless the "inside" is associated with the mother whose demands have so often coincided with inside pressures (Kestenberg, 1966). But the "inside" with its obscure needs is also connected with impulses disapproved by the mother and now rejected as babyish. Thus, an equation is formed of inside = mother = baby. This condensation is based on such bodily experiences of the past as the child has experienced syncretically, namely, "hunger sensation—inside-mother-baby-food," "peristalsis inside rectal pressure—mother-baby-feces" and "full bladder-inside distension—mother-baby-urine."

To cope with these inside feelings, as mother did, the child must take mother's place. He must take care of himself the way mother took care of him. This replaces the previous oneness between the child and the mother and forms the core of future identification (Jacobson, 1964; Mahler, 1963). The integrated behavior of the mother becomes the model for the child's *integrative* efforts. As the mother now decreases her attention to the child's bodily needs and stimulates him much less than before, the child himself takes over this role. In doing so, he becomes aware of the distinctive quality of genital sensations. But he still misses his mother's touch and will occasionally ask for it. He may still get his mother to feed him, wipe him or wash him, but he begins to understand now that she will not purposively enhance his genital excitations.

In preceding pregenital stages the attention of the child has been diverted from sensations of the inside to products of the inside. In the process of establishing controls, "where, how much, and what" has been produced became more important to mother and child than the feeling that accompanied the production. The image of the inside is modeled after the visible product of the inside. Inner-genital sensations share diffuseness and lack of boundaries with other sensations from the inside of the body, but they yield no valued product.

Through contact with the discriminating hand, the outer genitals gain distinction. At times they yield secretions, more so in the girl than the boy. But inner-genital sensations, though resonant with outer-genital excitation, are neither localized nor productive. Vaginal sensations of a nagging quality are elicited by excitation of external genitals in ordinary bodily care, by pressures from neighboring organs, and by occurrences of vulvovaginitis, a frequent by-product of respiratory infections (Nelson, 1959). The boy too has to contend with some unclear inner-genital feelings that may result from resonant excitation of the proximal parts of the penis (bulb, crura), movements of testicles, contractions of spermatic cords, and pressures on the prostate and seminal vesicles. Whether these organs become inflamed during ordinary childhood colds is not known.

Children of both sexes solve the problem posed by the vagueness of inside sensations by externalizing them to the outside. The girl seems to experience periodically recurring vaginal tensions as something unfocused, "nagging" her from the inside. She tends to nag others, especially her mother, and, in identification with her mother, her baby-doll. The unclear tensions inside give rise to fantasies that she has a baby there, but she transfers her inner-genital impulses to dolls and toys. The boy at that time equates his testicles with male babies; but the testicles can be palpated, moved, and even visually observed through the thin scrotal sac. Consequently, the girl's need for fondling on the outside that which cannot be reached inside is much more imperative than that of the boy. The boy is much bolder in experimenting with the inside of objects (see Chapter 2) and chooses a greater variety of models of his inside. He becomes interested in everything that moves and he tries to find out how it works. He is trying to solve on objects the intricate mechanics of erections and testicular movements, which he interprets as imposed on him from the inside of the body.

Children of both sexes now become outside-oriented. Unable to investigate their own inside, they investigate animate and inanimate objects. They integrate what they see, hear, smell, and touch. They form analogies between organs and objects in space through symbolization. Although they verbalize as they play, they are not able to put into words their theories about the inside of their body. Everything that moves, appears to move or can be made to move, seems alive and can be used to represent inside stirrings. The interest veers from excretory functions to genital preoccupation, externalized to objects. The shift to the outside accomplishes a desexualization of the inside, which promotes desexualized parental behavior. Transitory and reversible in the girl, a tendency to desexualize inner genitality becomes a permanent characteristic of male integration. As "live" genital excitement progressively condenses in the external genitals and becomes more intense, handling of inanimate objects becomes less suitable for mastering inner-genital impulses.

Transition to the Phallic Phase

As the magic of live dolls and animated choochoo trains breaks down, both sexes (but girls more than boys) become disillusioned and temporarily depressed. The boy gets over this disappointment quickly as he withdraws a good deal of the externalized genital cathexis from objects and cathects his penis as *the* representative of his genitality, in fact of his whole body (Lewin's body-phallus, 1933). The girl in her disappointment with dolls, which are not live babies after all, also cathects her external genitals. In exploring her genitals, she searches for something to replace her "lost" baby-doll. In doing so she discovers the introitus. She hopes that this door leads to a secret "garden" which may contain a live baby or a hidden penis (Burnett, 1938). At the same time, she becomes frightened by the thought that the introitus is a wound rather than a door. She hides and denies the existence of the introitus, isolates the now overcathected clitoris from the rest of her genitals, and spreads inner-genital excitement all over her body surface. She devaluates her inside and interprets all inner sensations as oral, anal, or urethral. She becomes secretive and ashamed of all body functions and envies the boy who displays his body with pride (Freud, S., 1923b). Earlier, sometimes violent, displays of penis envy have a different character. They express oral greed, anal possessiveness, urethral competitiveness or inner-genital nagging in phallic terms.

The boy enters the phallic stage with a full narcissistic appreciation of his phallus and a devaluation of his inside, which he identifies with femininity and pregenitality. He divides pregenital urges and inner-genital wishes and representations into shameful anal-infantile-feminine wishes and highly valued functions and possessions which enhance his phallic masculinity. In this process he begins to ignore and devaluate his testicles and scrotum. He may fuse them with anal representations (Bell, 1964), he may go on looking upon them as bladders, he may think of them as a background cushion for his penis, equate them with breasts or fuse them with the thighs or the clothing they touch. Each child integrates these representations, some more and some less cathected, with corresponding images of oral, anal, urethral, and phallic babies. In the boy's mind the phallic baby may be transformed from the penis or grow out of a testicle. Twins are often taken for the offspring of the right and left testicle. No matter which of these fantasies predominates, the outcome of the prephallic, inner-genital integration phase is a denial of the scrotum, the testicles, and all dimly felt inner sources of external genital excitement. Inner-genital sensations are externalized upon the phallus and the whole body seems to serve phallic needs (Lewin, 1933).

The girl enters the phallic stage with a denial and a desexualization of inner-genital sensations, with a devaluation of femininity, and a concentration of libidinal cathexis on the clitoris. Her angry disappointment is mitigated by her hope that she, like the boy, will grow a penis. She renews her interest in a baby by equating it with a penis.

There is something distinctly different between the shapeless and awkward two-and-a-half-year-old and the three- to-four-year-old who exhibits a new balance in the movements of body parts in relation to each other and to the outside (Chapter 10). Both sexes begin to look like miniature adults rather than babies. At first, both move in a somewhat feminine way, but soon one begins to distinguish between boys and girls from the way they act and move. At four or five when phallic trends become prominent, masculine qualities become conspicuous, but more so in boys than in girls. The sex-specific identity which was initiated in the inner-genital phase is stressed in the phallic boy and partially erased in the phallic girl.

The similarities of the sequence of disequilibrium and integration in the prephallic phase and the diffusion and integration in prepuberty suggests the following lines of inquiry:

Is there already in the prephallic phase a sudden or irregular influx

322

of sex hormones that is followed by a stabilization of hormonal constellation?

Can the hidden genital tensions in the inner-genital phase influence or be influenced by estrogens?

Is the increasing externalization of inner-genital tensions in this phase and the subsequent phallic phase interrelated with progressive increments of precursors of male sex hormones?

Growth and Differentiation in the
Phallic Phase (Precursors of Puberty)

The two-and-a-half-year-old lacked a steady direction and could not cope with his divergent urges. The four- to-five-year-old child may veer from one activity to another, but each of these activities serves the expression of his dominant phallic drive. His is a growth crisis. The three- to five-year-old child's task is to first integrate and then unify clashing needs and goals. The five-to six- or seven-year-old child resolves his growth crisis by a process of differentiation of psychic structure which becomes consolidated in latency.

The similarities between the behavior in the phallic and in puberty phases become strikingly apparent in Gesell's descriptions of the four-year-old child's "growthsome stage" and the more "defined" traits of the five-year-old:

> The key of Four's psychology is high drive combined with a fluid mental organization [Gesell, 1940]. Four years is above all an age of going out of bounds. This kind of behavior is observed in all fields physical, language, personal-social [Gesell and Ilg, 1943].
> [Five's] motor coordination, his image and sentences, even his personal-social relations, his concept of himself, his adjustment to home, school and community are better defined [Gesell, 1940].

The same distinctions can be made between the "growthsome" fluidity of the fifteen- and sixteen-year-old and the progressive differentiation of the seventeen- and eighteen-year-old.

The four-year-old child's overflowing activity seems to be an expression of undifferentiated phallic sexuality. In this period of *growth* his body and mind become increasingly sexualized. His exhibitionism may become excessive; he brags, clowns, exaggerates, and shows off: he knows no bounds. He jumps for jumping's sake until exhausted; he leaps and rams against people. His motor urges, global, undefined, and crude, do not allow for subtle approaches. As adults and playmates recoil from his

323

wild advances, the phallic child is especially vulnerable to rejections. His exuberant joy can turn into inconsolable crying when his feelings are hurt or his knees abraded. He frequently hurts himself and others primarily because he seems to want to master things with his total body. It is not easy to distinguish whether he enjoys cruelty or hurts pets and friends by accident. His moods change from wild aggression to anxiety, terror, excessive laughter, and depressive preoccupation with injury and death. Even though he asks innumerable questions, he seems to have a great many ready-made, rapidly shifting answers. His theories are based on concepts developed in the preceding phase, which he now verbalizes in imaginative play and conversations. His sensations have become extremely intense, his fantasies overwhelming, and his communications governed by primary-process thinking. He does not distinguish clearly between love and hate, friendliness and hostility, sex and aggression, as he urgently seeks out objects and outlets for his global drive. But he seeks out his parents not only to satisfy his needs but also to help him to distinguish between fantasy and reality and to tame the overwhelming excitement he cannot control by himself.

Children of both sexes switch rapidly from one parent to another, but in each activity or fantasy they can express wishes related to both parents at once, as for instance getting between them, separating them, and having them both. But the girl's phallic excitement is not as pronounced as that of the boy; her behavior is not as exaggerated and her crises less acute. She is not as prone to motor excesses as the boy and she has a greater facility in verbalization; she communicates better and can maintain a more steady contact with reality. She maintains a more stable relationship with her parents, particularly her mother, which helps her to advance more quickly than the boy to the later phallic phase of predominant differentiation.

The boy's father has proven himself an interested partner in the exploration of moving objects. The anatomical similarity between father and son creates a lasting bond between them. When the boy's increasing genital urges draw a great quantity of libido to his phallus, in his fantasy this precious organ becomes further aggrandized at the expense of his father. As he fears retaliation from his father he turns to his mother passively for protection and actively, as a giver of satisfaction and babies. His wishes frustrated, disappointed and fearful he turns back to his father with feminine surrender or resigned abjectness (Freud, S., 1923b, 1924a). Not until he can differentiate between activity and passivity, between attack and surrender, between masculinity and femininity, can his oedipal conflicts crystallize sufficiently so that he can resolve them by identification with his father.

The four-year-old girl's phallic excitement is fraught with disappointment; her phallic orientation is largely defensive as it serves to discharge externalized inner-genital tensions. She still tends to nag and she argues excessively. She blames her mother for not giving her a live baby, for not loving her daughter as much as she loves her husband and son, for the lack of a penis, and a number of complaints which mask sexual frustrations.

I have never heard a little girl complain that she has no scrotum or testicles. Children and parents act as if in silent agreement to deny their importance, or that of the vagina. Even parents find themselves at a loss to explain what these organs are and may ignore questions about them. The girl may identify her labia majora with the scrotum, but she usually ignores testicles as she ignores what is inside her by denying the existence of the introitus. She hypercathects the clitoris defensively, but the clitoris resonates inner-genital sensations and may not offer protection against spreading of genital sensations inward. The girl soon becomes disappointed with her clitoris, disgruntled with the softness and lack of volume in the labia, and ashamed of the caseous secretion in the vulva. At first she may masturbate on the clitoris, pull on her labia, and bring them together, hiding the introitus and simulating a growing penis. She develops active phallic fantasies and she too, like the boy, wants to give her mother a child. As she encounters disappointment, she turns to her father to give her the phallus she does not possess and the baby she neither could get from her mother nor could create by herself. Her fantasy of the inner phallus seems to be derived from pelvic sensations during clitoric masturbation, and from concomitant wishes to be penetrated deeply by the father or brother. Because it implies castration of the male and admits inner-genital sensations, it is always a guilty secret. Inner excitement is equated with an inner penis that must not be shown lest it be taken away again. Where such fantasies predominate, the four-year-old girl may be unusually subdued and shy, fearful of exposure and punishment. When she is with boys and hoping to grow a phallus, she acts like a tomboy and likes to play with them. Not until she can define her conflicting wishes more clearly and weigh the alternatives, can she begin to resolve her oedipal conflicts and assume feminine attitudes in identification with her mother.

The *phallic phase of differentiation* evolves gradually or in spurts which follow crises. It is sometimes ushered in by seductions which not only evoke anxiety but also help to establish techniques for localized genital discharge. Earlier, masturbation is often disorganized as it easily overflows into generalized motor restlessness. In this later phallic phase both sexes, but the boy especially, learn to differentiate between various forms of excitement and establish a masturbatory technique which affords some

325

degree of relief. Fantasies become more specific. The bisexual orientation of the preceding phase of growth gives way to more consistent heterosexual strivings. Increase in object constancy paves the way for lasting identifications and the development of a sex-specific superego. Defenses become more constant and more specifically related to specific danger situations (Freud, A., 1936). Boys project their anal-feminine wishes upon girls; girls begin to identify the lack of a penis with lack of excitement and with lack of the aggressive rebelliousness that they project upon the male sex (see Chapter 1). This is altogether a stage in which everything is seen in terms of extremes; real and unreal, true and untrue, good or bad, male and female. An overzeal in differentiation is apparent in all activities. The five-year-old tends to be concrete and realistic. His understanding of his role as a child in contradistinction to his parents as adults make it finally possible for him to repress and give up his oedipal strivings (Freud, S., 1924a). As he distinguishes better between past and future he postpones wishes which can be gratified only in adulthood.

Because she has a less stormy phase of phallic growth and her earlier identifications with her mother merge with the one that follows the resolution of oedipal conflicts, the girl enters latency before the boy does. But her feminine strivings are not well differentiated from pregenital and phallic wishes and her sexual identity is less defined than that of the boy. The boy enters latency with a boyish rebelliousness, a spirit of adventure, and a greater independence than the girl, who embarks on it with a ready-made store of reaction formations. These overemphasize morality but do not necessarily reflect an independence of the superego as a structure (see Chapter 10). Throughout latency the girl remains more dependent on her mother than the boy.

One must wonder whether the similarities and the differences between boys and girls in the phallic phase are reflected in the hormonal constellations of that time. Is there a relationship between androgen excretion and phallic growth? Are there significant changes in hormonal constellations in the phase of differentiation which ushers in the more mature behavior of the latency child?

Consolidation of Psychic Organization in Latency
(Precursor of Preadult Consolidation)

In contrast to the phallic child who was "out of bounds," the latency child consolidates the controls acquired in the later phallic phase that keeps him "in bounds." But latency too can be divided into subphases

(Bornstein, 1951). In its early beginning one encounters shorter or longer-lasting revivals of regressive behavior reminiscent of the disequilibrium which followed the pregenital phase and will be seen again in prepuberty. A consolidation of earlier gains becomes the conspicuous feature of late latency. This phase is so well known and widely described that I shall touch upon its salient characteristics only briefly.

Having acquired a family conscience, the child in latency acquires a social code of behavior. Latency is the time of preponderance of *drive derivatives* over drive-dominated behavior (Kestenberg, 1963). The relative freedom from strong instinctual breakthroughs is achieved through automatizations and schematizations of defense mechanisms. The repression that ended the preceding phase is reinforced by a *consolidation* of defense complexes (Freud, A., 1936). Ego and superego become stronger and progressively more entrenched as lasting structures. Learning becomes disciplined and play more organized. Latency consolidation reinforces the integration of competing drive components and conflicting ego interests which preceded the phallic phase (see Chapter 10). The better the results of this early integration, the better does the child weather the storms of sexual excitement and fluctuating oedipal wishes of the phallic phase and the more pronounced does the consolidation of earlier gains become in latency. Where earlier integrative efforts failed to lay a foundation for an orderly development, more reintegration is required in latency and less time can be spent on consolidation of maturational gains.

Sexual differentiation continues throughout latency and becomes more prominent between the ages of eight and eleven. Much of the girl's latency is spent on strengthening her defenses against phallic drives which overshadow her feminine strivings. Sex play occurs sporadically but more frequently in boys than in girls. It is masked by play such as wrestling, jumping at one another, and age-specific jokes. Sexual interest can be more easily hidden or controlled, not because of an absolute decrease in drive strength (Freud, A., 1965), but because a decreased rate of increment in drive intensity facilitates sublimation. This exerts an influence on late latency when physical changes may already become the center of attention, and children begin to vie with siblings and friends for group prestige, based on a more precocious development.

There is a consensus of older and more modern investigators that the onset of sexual differentiation coincides with a significant rise in hormone excretion and with the earliest beginning of an adultlike steroid metabolism at the age of eight or nine. The excretion of hormones before that is taken as a sign of predominantly adrenal rather than pituitary or gonadal activity. But small increases and differences in rates of excretion

327

do not necessarily reflect the qualities of steroid metabolism in tissues; they may prove to be more significant in the vicissitudes of total development than has been realized. If the older data about changes in the rate and quantity of hormone excretion (Tables 2-3) are even approximately correct, the hormonal constellation in latency may prove to be a miniature antecedent of the preadult consolidation during which the adult form of hormone production, initiated in puberty, becomes stabilized. Psychological changes during latency suggest that this phase of consolidation may be as much a necessary preparation for adjustment in adolescence as a similar period of consolidation of adolescent gains is for adult stabilization. The suggested correlation will become more meaningful in the ensuing discussion of neurohormonal research and the subsequent review of pertinent developmental changes, as well as in the more detailed description of adolescent phases in Chapters 14 and 15.

Discussion of Neurohormonal Research Up to 1966

The turbulent phases of adolescence are usually associated with a tremendous upsurge of genital drives (Deutsch, 1944–45; Freud, A., 1936; Spiegel, 1951). These are usually correlated with the influx of great quantities of sex hormones which guide physical and psychological sex-specific differentiation (Josselyn, 1952; Talbot et al., 1952; Wilkins, 1965). Earlier manifestations of genitality seem out of scale with the small changes in hormone levels and the inconspicuous physical changes that occur before latency (Benedek, 1952). Neither can the high hormonal levels and the size of reproductive organs at birth, nor the much less pronounced but similar constellation in late latency be easily reconciled with clinical observations.

Psychoanalysts have long been aware of the influence of neurohormonal and anatomic differentiation on psychic development in childhood (Freud, S., 1905, 1925). In stressing the importance of investigating psychosexual growth in relation to hormonal processes, Benedek (1952) pointed to the connection between sexual maturation and changes in the functions of the pituitary. Sexual precocity in patients with hypothalamic lesions suggests that the hypothalamic-hypophyseal connections have a decisive influence upon the development of primary and secondary sex characteristics. The hypophysis of the fetus contains gonadotropins and, in childhood, it is potentially capable of stimulating sex organs. The release of gonadotropins at the onset of adolescence may be dependent upon "a neurohormonal mechanism which is inhibited in childhood" (Talbot et al., 1952).

It may be that a maturation of "sexual hypothalamic" centers occurs

328

in spurts of growth and quiescence that influence not only the irregular small increases and plateaus in hormone production in childhood, but also the concomitant changes in psychic organization. Once established and consolidated, the postulated central control mechanisms may regulate sexual behavior with or without mediation of hormones. Infantile sexuality may draw its distinctive quality from the mutual influences of small quantities of precursors of adult hormonal mechanisms and maturing connections between the hypophysis, the hypothalamus, and the cortex. In transition from childhood to adulthood—in prepuberty and puberty— the conversion of the infantile hormonal and psychic constellations into integrated adult patterns covers another decade of development (Paulsen *et al.*, 1966). Both endocrinological and psychiatric studies suggest that childhood organizations pave the way for the adult mechanisms. Adolescence is an intermediate stage in which quantitative and qualitative changes in maturation reproduce in reverse order the genital crisis that occurs in transition from the fetal to the infantile organization. The regression in senescence revives earlier organizations and reverses the advances made in adolescence. But there is growing evidence of finer and more complex interrelations between hormonal constellations and phases of disequilibrium and reorganization in psychic development.

The interrelationship between various hormones and psychosexual and aggressive impulses not only in children but also in adults requires a great deal of study. Benedek's (1952) pioneering investigations, in which she correlated psychological and hormonal changes in female cycles, established a connection between psychological attitudes and levels of estrogen and progesterone production. Fluctuations in testosterone levels during menstrual cycles (Hudson *et al.*, 1964) and their relation to peaks of progesterone rise and to a dip of estrogen excretion after ovulation (Paulsen, 1965) are phenomena recently reported which she was not able to consider.

In the past two decades more refined techniques in the assays of steroids in urine, plasma, and tissue helped to identify twenty-one estrogenic substances in addition to the already known classical estrogens (estradiol, estrone, and estriol). Each of these compounds has been shown to attain levels differing in men, women, and children of various ages (Paulsen, 1965; Wilkins, 1965). Nevertheless assays of estrogens are not as reliable as those of 17-ketosteroids from which various metabolites can be isolated (Eberlein, 1966; Paulsen *et al.*, 1966). The chemistry and metabolism of steroids have led endocrinologists to believe that hormones are produced and transformed in a distinctly different way in men, women, and children (Diczfalusy, 1961; Dorfman, 1963; Paulsen *et al.*, 1966).

329

Adrenals can produce estrogenic and androgenic substances and the prevailing opinion is that much of sex hormone production in childhood is due to adrenal activity. (Talbot *et al.*, 1952; Wilkins, 1965). Moreover, the four main steroid-secreting organs (ovary, testicle, placenta, and adrenal) are only part of neurohormonal processes, involving the whole body. There is a "totipotentiality of endocrine tissues to produce all types of steroid hormones" (Ryan, 1963), and the "synthetic pathways for the formation of progesterone, cortiocoids, androgens and estrogens" (Dorfman, 1963) are intimately interrelated. The biosynthetic relationship between testosterone and estrogen can even take place "in peripheral tissues other than endocrine glands" (Dorfman, 1963).

These striking advances in endocrinology have not yet been correlated with neurophysiological or psychological studies. Benedek's work has remained unique and only few and sporadic attempts have been made to institute comparable interdisciplinary research. Even though steroids have for a long time been used to alleviate premenstrual distress and climacteric disturbances, there has been a surprising dearth of studies of their influence upon the psyche (Diczfalusy, 1961). This may be due to researchers' and therapists' disappointment in hormone therapy as a cure for psychosexual disorders. No correlation has been found between sexual desire and levels of sex hormones in the adult (Kinsey *et al.*, 1953; Diczfalusy, 1961). The psychic effect of androgens is said to be stronger than that of estrogens; still small estrogen doses help both men and women in senescence to feel better generally, become more active physically, and more alert mentally. In cases of congenital absence of ovaries, prolonged administration of estrogens enhances physical, psychic and mental maturation, but an increase in sexual maturation is not achieved. Sex hormones are important stabilizers of the vegetative nervous system (Diczfalusy, 1961) in adults. In all likelihood states of instability and stability in childhood can also be correlated with varying hormonal constellations. The parallelism in organization between childhood and adolescent phases suggests the possibility that, in critical developmental stages, not only quantity and quality of hormones but also their ratio and rate of increase and decrease significantly affect behavior. Even small quantities of hormones and even those hormonal constellations that precede the adult hormonal mechanism may affect psychosexual maturation before signs of anatomic sex differentiation become apparent.

In correlating behavior with neurohormonal changes one must bear in mind that infantile sexuality is a decisive but not the only factor in the development of psychic organization (Hartmann, 1939). Animal experiments substantiate the impression of clinical observers that estrogenic and androgenic substances have an influence upon neural activity, especially upon thresholds. Woolley and Timiras (1962) demonstrated that estradiol lowered certain thresholds while progesterone raised them in the female but not in the male animal, although there were effects in both. Testosterone significantly lowered these thresholds, but estradiol had a more marked central excitatory action. In certain critical developmental periods the administration of steroids produced irreversible acceleration of brain maturation (Heim and Timiras, 1963).[3]

Even though the hormonal assays in childhood have not yet established norms of hormone production in different developmental levels, both the older and the newer more reliable studies suggest questions such as:

Do sudden or irregular increases in hormone levels, small or large, lower thresholds for genital excitation before they can affect brain maturation sufficiently to permit integrated discharge of sexual tension?

Do such sudden or irregular increases account for states of disequilibrium in childhood? Does a steady influx over longer periods of certain hormones promote phases of integration of psychic functions?

Is there a relationship between small increments in estrogen production and increases in inner-genital tensions?

Do precursors of testosterone in childhood trigger aggressive impulses and phallic organization?

Do androgens and estrogens in certain proportions have a neutralizing effect upon each other which might be related to the special hormonal and psychic constellation in latency?

Is there a relationship not only between the adult hormonal mechanism in steroid metabolism and adult forms of genitality in men and women but also between its precursor in childhood and infantile forms of genitality in boys and girls?

Is the calming effect of progesterone due to its raising of thresholds? Does its absence or sudden reduction lower thresholds and thus produce the irritability and the diffuse sexual excitement, observed in premenstrual and menstrual phases or later in the climacteric? And is this type of sexual excitement comparable to that observed in immature phases of genitality when progesterone is not yet produced?

It is easier to describe the ideal hormonal study than to carry it out. There has so far been no study that meets all the requirements for correlations. In such a study population should be large and include all ages from birth to adulthood, of both sexes. The maturational level and chronological age of the individuals must be recorded. Reliable assays of a number of hormones on a frequent, if not daily, longitudinal basis would be required. We would still remain short of certainty unless anatomic and physiological data were compiled simultaneously, but the experimental situation itself would affect the results and make comparison difficult. At this time, when newer techniques of hormone assessment are being developed (Eberlein, 1966; Paulsen, 1966) and the results of older assays are found to differ quantitatively from those of new investigators (Paulsen, 1965), one can only suggest lines of inquiry for future interdisciplinary projects. To do so it is feasible to look at the older data that are available for comparison with psychic changes and allow for their deficiencies. If we focus on change rather than on absolutes, the problem is simplified. What we look for then is the nature, direction, and time of change. We will then find that some old studies, admittedly based on obsolete techniques applied to urine samples which do not fully represent the metabolites active in the tissues, will provide a clue to what we are seeking.

In appraising the tables used in the ensuing review of psychophysical changes (1, 2, 3,) one must keep in mind that they have been selected because they schematize the sequence of significant changes. They are to be taken as illustrative and not definitive. The hormonal assays especially are neither reliable nor complete, and are reproduced here only as a framework for tentative correlations with psychological phenomena.

Review of Anatomic, Hormonal, and Psychic Changes from the Neonatal Phase to Young Adulthood

The data selected for this review will extend beyond the phases that are the focus of this part of my presentation. They will serve as a background for the more detailed description of adolescent phases in the next chapters.

The Neonate

The flooding with maternal hormones and their withdrawal have a decisve effect on the sex organs of the newborn, but we do not know how this may affect the onset of psychic functioning.

In the neonatal period, hyperplasia of the breasts in both sexes and vaginal changes in the female are probably the result of estrogen received from the placenta or the maternal circulation. Withdrawal of estrogen or progesterone may account for the menstrual bleeding which sometimes occurs. Placental chorionic gonadotropin may account for the presence of Leydig cells in testes during the first four to six weeks of life and their disappearance afterwards until the onset of puberty. In both sexes, the plasma

17-ketosteroids are elevated in the newborn and fall to zero during the first two weeks. The urinary 17-ketosteroids are 1.5–2.5 mg per day during the first two weeks and then decrease to less than 0.5–1.0 mgs per day [Wilkins, 1965, pp. 195–196].

STAGES OF SEXUAL DIFFERENTIATION

Age	Boys	Girls
3-7	Infantile characteristics. Very small amounts of estrogen and 17-ketosteroids	
7-8	Excretion of estrogens and 17-ketosteroids increases. Ovarian follicles advance. Uterus growth.	
9-10	Low gonadotropin and testicular androgens in urine.	Growth of bony pelvis. Budding of nipples.
10-11	Growth of testicles and penis.	*perpuberty*. Public hair, Budding of breasts. Estrogen excretion accelerated.
11-12	Prostatic activity.	Remolding of the bony pelvis. Vaginal secretion, Ph changes, cornification, and glycogenization. Accelerated growth of external and internal genitals. Gonadotropins appear in urine. Estrogen excretion accelerated, and cyclic.
12-13	*perpuberty*. Pubic hair. Marked increase of gonadotropin.	Pigmentation of nipples. Mammae filling in.
13-14	*Active spermatogonia*. Rapid growth of penis and testicles. Subareolar node on nipples.	Axillary hair. *Menarche*.
14-15	*Axillary hair. Down on upper lip. Voice changes. Great increase in testicular androgens*.	*puberty*. Earliest normal pregnancies. Pregnandiol excretion in luteal phase. Great increase in estrogen excretion. Increase in 17-ketosteroids.
15-16	*puberty*. Mature spermatozoa. Marked testosterone rise.	Acne. Deepening of voice.
16-17	Facial and body hair. Acne.	Arrest of skeletal growth. Ovulatory cycles stabilize.
21	Arrest of skeletal growth. Increase of 17-ketosteroids and testosterone.	

Adapted from Talbot et al. (1952) and Wilkins (1965), used by permission. See also Table 3, lower section.

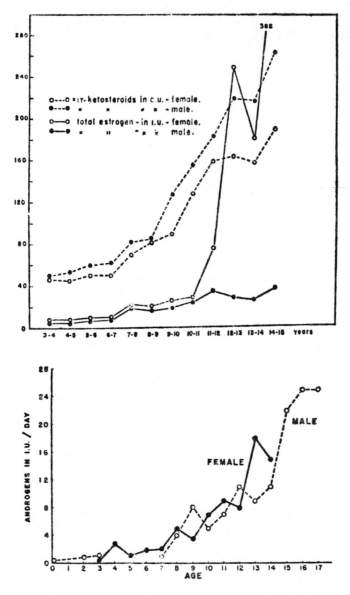

Fig. 1. *Upper Part: Averages from Urinary Assays of Estrogens and 17-ketosteroids;* reproduced from Nathanson et al. (1941). *Lower Part: Averages from Urinary Assays of Androgens;* reported by Dorfman (1948); reproduced from Kinsey et al. (1953).

Used by permission.

334

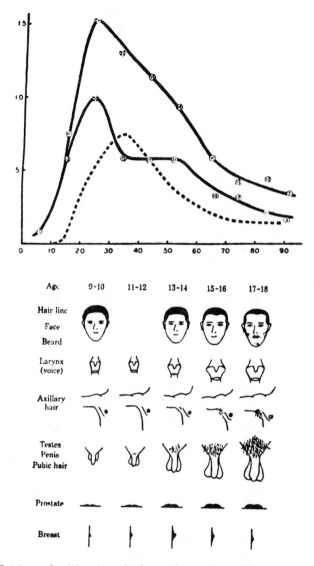

Fig. 2. *Upper Part: Averages from Urinary Assays of 17-ketosteroids in Men* (upper solid curve) *and Women* (lower solid curve); reproduced from Hamburger (1948). Dotted curve — difference between male and female curve — contribution by testes in 17-ketosteroid excretion. Figures in circles — number of subjects. Ordinate: mg/24 hours. *Lower Part: Stages of Sexual Development and Muturation.* Modified from Schonfeld (1943); reproduced from Wilkins (1965).

335

PHASE DEVELOPMENT IN ADOLESCENCE

The genital tissues of mature newborn females exhibit the following characteristics which vary in degree depending on the sensitivity of the target organs and the quantity of hormones present (compiled from Talbot et al., 1952; Nelson, 1959; Huffman, 1959):

> The labia majora and minora are hypertrophied. The hymen forms a thick, inverted cone with a central orifice about 0.4 cm. in diameter. The vaginal epithelium is thick, and contains glycogen for a few weeks after birth. The vaginal mucosa is pale, pink, and succulent; it is folded into high ridges and deeper crypts by rugae circularly arranged in the deeper portion of the vagina. The external os of the cervix is not distinct, and the boundaries between cervix and vagina are not definite. The uterus is large and congested and there is occasional bleeding. The ovaries are relatively large and congested and contain some large ripening follicles and some in the process of involution.
>
> Genital proliferation gradually recedes over a period of months. Involution of the neonatal layers of the vaginal epithelium occurs as the maternal hormones leave the child's body. The uterus shrinks slowly but resumes some growth after the first year of life. It does not regain its birth weight before the age of five.

Much less is reported about the genital tissues of the newborn male.

> A hyperplasia of the prostate of the newborn has been also ascribed to the influence of maternal hormones. Histologists report that the prostate and testicles are hyperemic and there is evidence of bleeding in the non-glandular tissue. The integument of the scrotum is thick. Leydig cells or alike cells as well as spermatogonia can be found in the testicles, and there is some secretion in the prostatic lumen (compiled from Hartmann, 1932; Schonfeld, 1943; Talbot et al., 1952; Nelson, 1959).

There has been considerable discussion about the source and nature of the steroids which may be responsible for these transitory phenomena.

Nelson (1959) attributes the transitory prostatic metaplasia to estrogenic substances of placental and ovarian origin. But a great many steroids have been isolated from the placenta, and the function of the majority of them is not known; nor is it clear in which manner different ratios of various steroids affect specific target organs (Wiele and Jailer, 1959). Hartmann (1932) points out that testicular function in the neonate may be incipient but does not develop further as there are already then signs of testicular involution. The secretion of the fetal testes is necessary to cause disappearance of the Mullerian duct and to promote

336

the development of the vas deferens and the seminal vesicles. With the development of these organs no further testicular secretion is indicated. Schonfeld (1943) ascribes the neonatal prostatic hyperplasia to the influence of androgens which are produced in the child's testes in response to chorionic gonadotropin. But these explanations make one wonder why changes are not reported for the penis, the seminal vesicles, and the vas deferens whose tissues respond sensitively to testicular androgens (Talbot et al., 1952). It has not been established whether the secreted hormones are maternal in origin, whether they are androgenic steroids or rather adrenal steroids that are found in adult concentrations throughout early infancy.

The time required for the involution of different signs of the genital crisis of the newborn varies from a few days, weeks to even months. The beginning of the involution coincides with a marked decrease in suprarenal weight after birth.

Neonates differ in degrees of alertness and excitability. The question arises whether the varying amount of hormones in their bodies play a role in these differences. One may also wonder how the rate of depletion of the massive amounts of hormones affects the rate of decrease in thresholds and the rate of maturation.

Cursory observations may throw some light on the differences in reactions of parents and attending personnel to the appearance and activity of male and female genitalia in the newborn and young infant. Swelling of the female genitalia and tumescence of the penis are frequently observed in the newborn nursery, but early masturbation is seen only in girls whose parents were concerned with vulvovaginal swellings, the appearance of the hymen, and vaginal bleeding. Considerable attention has been paid to erections and the lack or presence of testicles in the scrotum of the newborn, but hardly anything is known about the adultlike appearance of the neonatal scrotum and its activity.

> The infant's heels very frequently press on the scrotum without an immediate effect on testicular movements or tumescence of the penis. The scrotal sac is often pigmented and falls in loose folds not unlike the adult one. The tunica Dartos contracts with resulting horizontal waves of scrotal movements (Robbins, 1964). Preliminary inquiries did not reveal when the scrotum of the infant changes its appearance, and no data have been elicited on similar contractions in children. Only some adults who are cognizant of this occurrence describe the accompanying sensations as sensual.

Even though the neonatal period is physiologically a genital phase, and genital discharge forms can be observed in movements of neonates

337

(Kestenberg, 1965), it is likely that, in the absence of added external stimulations, central inhibitory mechanisms counteract the influence of large quantities of hormones sufficiently to prevent untoward effects of the neonatal genital crisis.

Pregenital Phases

There are more speculations than data on hormonal development from the uncertain time when the genital crisis of the neonate abates to the point, at the age of three, at which small increases in estrogen and ketosteroid excretion have been reported. Some tables and statements give the impression that it is not possible to demonstrate estrogenic substances or 17-ketosteroid (Nathanson *et al.*, 1941; Talbot *et al.*, 1952) in the urine of children under three; others suggest a gradual or sporadic increase of certain steroids before this age (Dorfman, 1948; Hamburger, 1948; Diczfalusy, 1961; Wilkins, 1965). After careful scrutiny of the data of most of these authors, I have come to the conclusion that beyond an occasional assay of steroid excretion in one or two children under two and a half there is nothing to indicate the hormonal status in pregenital phases. Various degrees of progressive development of ovaries and testicles begin in early infancy. But there is a paucity of data on the changes in the appearance and structure of reproductive and accessory sex organs after the involution of the "genitality of the newborn."

Halverson (1938, 1940) linked the erections occurring in early infancy with abdominal pressures and tensional states, especially oral frustrations. Wolff (1959) suggested a connection of neonatal erections with states of arousal which would imply that regulatory mechanisms of the reticular system play a role in the genitality of infants. The phase-specific discharge in pregenital stages may be centrally controlled through the reticular substance, the hypothalamus, and their maturing cortical connections.

Under circumstances of average bodily care, genital tensions are incorporated into the phase-specific modes of dominant discharge, but sporadic interest in the genitals occurs regularly at the end of the first year of life (Spitz and Wolf, 1949; Loewenstein, 1950; Kleeman, 1965, 1966). These occurrences seem to be directly related to maturation of the central nervous system in interdependence with environmental stimulation. There may well be corresponding temporary changes in hormonal levels and anatomical changes that produce organ tensions. There is, for instance, a convergence of several developmental factors at seven to eight months when boys first begin to poke at their scrotum, which undergoes a structural change (Hartmann, 1932) at the same time as the child becomes able to reach the lower part of his body. My own observations suggest that boys become aware of their external genitals much earlier than girls. They seem to connect their previous manual explorations with the visual experience once they see their genitals in sitting up and standing up. Because of the anatomical difference girls cannot reach their genital region proper for some time. Instances of very early masturbation in girls seem to pertain to thigh pressure rather than manipulation. A girl of eight months who saw her pubic region while bending over seemed puzzled by the sight but showed no further interest. A boy of the same age who habitually poked and pushed his scrotal region would accidentally touch his penis and then utter sounds which unmistakably expressed his pleasure. His mother understood him well, became quite excited, and removed his hand from the penis, admonishing him not to play with it.

There are references in the literature to the onset of growth in the uterus and of progressive changes in the structure of testicles at the end of the first year (Huffman, 1959; Talbot et al., 1952). These coincide with the functional development of pelvic and abdominal muscles and of anal sphincters. The dominant anal-abdominal interest in the second year of life normally absorbs genital excitations. In the urethral phase, an upsurge in the control of locomotion coincides with the beginning of organized control over urine and with an intensified interest in the genitourinary regions, but once more genitality is absorbed in the prevailing (vesicourethral) discharge forms.

There is some evidence that external stimulations can add enough fuel to endogenous genital tensions in infancy to produce specific effects. S. Freud (1905) discussed instances of quieting excited infants by rubbing their genitals. A child whose genital interest was aroused early by her mother's unusual preoccupation with her swollen genitals began at the age of four weeks to masturbate to the point of orgasm by thigh pressure and raising of legs. I followed her case through her latency and observed that she used masturbation compulsively to alleviate frustrations. A girl who began her equally compulsive orgastic masturbation at the age of three had uterine bleeding as a neonate, which had greatly distressed both of her parents. Since the young child's poorly formed labia majora and thin labia minora afford little protection to the introitus, vaginal infections in infancy are not infrequent (Nelson, 1959). A girl who at eighteen months suffered from a fungus infection involving her genitals became very excited and unmanageable. Her parents too had been greatly interested in her genitals at birth. This interest continued because the child had very thin and sensitive mucous membranes which were easily inflamed or abraded. Congenital differences in neural regulations, in the quality of target organs, and in the quantity of hormones may combine with the degree and frequency of external stimulations to focus children's attention prematurely on their genitals. This results in early disturbances which interfere with the orderly development of pre-genital phases (Greenacre, 1954) and gross exaggeration of the disequilibrium that initiates the early genital phase.

Inner-Genital Phase

Sporadic handling of genitals in conjunction with bodily care is common in pregenital phases, but genital interest proper begins between two and three years (Freud, S., 1905). At that time small amounts of estrogen and 17-ketosteroids appear regularly in the urine (Fig. 1). It is not certain that levels of sex hormones increase at the age of three since most authors did not make assays before that age, but isolated reports give credence to this view. Both the adrenal and the gonads attain a significant degree of maturity in the third year of life. Beginning in infancy, follicles mature periodically but become atretic before developing fully. An old report of a histologist indicates that he could not find ripe follicles in ovaries before the age of two and a half but then encountered isolated ripe follicles regularly (Waldeyer, cited by Hartmann, 1932). A report of a small amount of gonadotropin in the urine of a two-and-a-half-year-old boy (Talbot et al., 1952, p. 386) is another isolated finding that requires verification.

Young children cannot easily express what they feel and even adults find it difficult to describe intra-abdominal or pelvic sensations. One cannot easily prove impressions gained in the analyses and observations of young children that as early as at the age of two and a half tensions arising from the vagina or uterus and perhaps from the prostate, seminal vesicles, and spermatic cords make children concerned with what is going on inside of them that does not yield a visible product like urine or feces.

Three-year-old boys produce more 17-ketosteroids than estrogens; the reverse seems to be true of girls (Table 1). Although the differences are small, they are consistent with small changes in body contours and motor behavior which distinguish the sexes at that time. The quantities of hormone production are negligible and the body changes insignificant compared to adolescent upswings. If newer investigations will show that there is a sudden or irregular increase in these hormones at two and a half or three, this may prove to be one of the sources of the disequilibrium observed at that age. The subsequent plateau in estrogen excretion (Table 1) combined with an increase in androgens (Table 2) could be correlated with the increasing ability of the child between three and four to integrate divergent impulses by means of externalization of tensions from the inside of the body.

The Phallic Phase

Tables 2 and 3 indicate that estrogen production does not increase until six or seven, but androgen levels rise at four and remain steady from the age of five to seven (in the girl). Dorfman (1948), who conducted girls' assays himself, speaks of a dramatic rise in androgens of four- to five-year-old girls. One gets the impression that he assumes a sudden rise in girls and a more gradual increase in boys from birth on.

Dorfman's views on the differences between boys and girls as far as androgen production is concerned are compatible with clinical observations of increasing masculinity in boys from an early age. The somewhat feminine demeanor that seems to interrupt this steady trend in boys at the height of identification with the preoedipal mother is compatible with the view that estrogens become demonstrable in the urine of both sexes at the age of three (Talbot *et al.*, 1952). If a dramatic rise in 17-ketosteroid production at four or five could be demonstrated in both sexes (Table 2), this might account in some measure for the increase in muscular strength, aggression, and phallic excitement at that time. The plateau in hormone excretion between the ages of five and six to seven (Tables 2-3), if verified, may account for the more peaceful phase of differentiation in the late phallic phase.

Latency

This phase appears to be initiated by a moderate increase in all hormones. One can begin to note a widening discrepancy between estrogen and 17-ketosteroids in both sexes (Tables 1, 2, and 3).

The growth of primary sex characteristics in later stages of boys' latency coincides with the high rate of increase in 17-ketosteroids and androgens (Tables 1, 2, and 3). Changes in the ovary and uterus are preceded by a small increase in estrogens and can hardly be accounted for by the increase in 17-ketosteroids and androgens. Huffman (1959) states that from the time maternal hormones are withdrawn in early infancy until the growth of reproductive organs begins in later childhood the hymen is thin and flat with a delicate edge, the vulvovaginal mucosa thin and hyperemic, and the vagina grows only 0.5-1.0 cm. in depth. He implies that the girl does not produce her own endogenous estrogens until the age of eight. This view conflicts wtih all previous and later reports. A clear correlation between anatomic and hormonal changes is yet to be established.

341

PHASE DEVELOPMENT IN ADOLESCENCE

In a footnote added to the *Three Essays of Sexuality* in 1920, Freud wrote: "There is, of course, no need to expect that anatomical growth and psychical development must be exactly simultaneous" (p. 177). This may be applied to the relation between anatomical growth and hormonal changes.

A review of the most recent 17-ketosteroids assays (Paulsen *et al.*, 1966) shows a considerable variation from case to case with a trend characterized as a gradual rise between three and thirteen years of age. A detailed scrutiny of the assays by Paulsen *et al.* (1966) suggests that the absolute values in Tables 2-3 are too high; that Dorfman's (1948) report of an increase in androgen excretion in girls at the age of four is very likely applicable to boys too; that Nathanson's report of a gradual increase of ketosteroids between the ages of six and nine or ten is substantially correct; and that only a gradual increase of androgens occurs before the age of nine.

The data presented here offer a prospect for a correlation between hormonal and psychological changes in latency. A gradual increase in all hormones seems to reflect the struggles of beginning latency when progressive and regressive forces vie with each other as they do at the ages of two and a half or three and later in prepuberty. Based as it is on previous integration and differentiation of psychic structure, the development in early latency is smoother and does not produce disturbances equivalent to the disequilibrium of the two-and-a-half-year-old and the diffusion in prepuberty. If Nathanson's reports are confirmed and there is indeed a plateau in estrogen production during the later part of the girl's latency, a steady influx of small amounts of estrogen may prove to be an important organizer in the psychic development of children.

Latency consolidation of psychological gains reinforces the integration of psychic functions that, I believe, develops between the ages of three and four. It anticipates the phase of integration in prepuberty and seems to be a model for the final consolidation of psychic structure in transition from puberty to adulthood.

Prepuberty

This phase, as defined here, begins with the onset of secondary sex characteristics and ends at the time when reproduction becomes possible (Table 1). The correlation between anatomic and hormonal changes is more clearly established in this interval (Tables 1-3), apparently because gonadotropins are produced in sufficient amounts to stimulate sex-specific gonadal growth.

That an adultlike mechanism in hormone production begins in prepuberty is indicated in the findings of Hudson *et al.* (1964) who report a considerable increase in the plasma testosterone levels in ten-to-twelve-year-old boys. Nathanson *et al.* (1941) found that the tremendous upsurge in estrogen excretion of girls at the age of eleven is accompanied by cyclic changes.

The later onset of prepuberty in the boy than in the girl is evidenced in corresponding psychic and hormonal changes. Prepuberty diffusion seems to coincide with the sudden irregular upswings in sex-specific hormones in the girl and a much less pronounced but fluctuating increase in androgen production in the boy. Very likely various steroids that are important for the development of the adult steroid metabolism begin to occur sporadically rather than regularly.

The increasing changes in inner-genital structure (Table 1) precede and overlap with external manifestations of sexual differentiation. Inner-genital tensions and sensations have a disquieting effect upon the child in prepuberty. They seem to be a major factor in the diffusion of thoughts characteristic for that phase. The considerable alterations in bodily and psychic structure make the child especially vulnerable and prone to regressions. Landmarks of sexual differentiation such as budding of breasts and pubic hair promote externalization, which once more, as it did in the prephallic phase, can be put into the service of integration of psychic functions. Even though menarche and first emissions give rise to considerable anxiety, they promote the acceptance of sex-specific identity and enhance a reintegration of conflicting drives in preparation for puberty. Shorter and longer periods of reintegration in puberty may be correlated with the centrally controlled regularization in hormone production with precedes puberty.

Puberty

This phase begins with the appearance of pregnandiol in the urine of girls and first ripe spermatozoa in boys. It is then, I believe, that we can speak again of a growthsome phase. A rapid increase in adult forms of sex-specific hormones occurs at that time. The rapid maturation of the pituitary permits the development of the beginning constancy of interrelationship between hypophyseal and gonadal hormones. In the second phase of puberty the cyclic rise of progestin that initiated it in the female becomes increasingly regular and ovulatory cycles increasingly common. A similar regularization of testosterone production occurs in the boy, but at a later age.

The growth of sex-specific but not well-defined genitality is reflected in the intense feelings and impulses of girls between fourteen and sixteen and boys between fifteen and eighteen. Only gradually does a differentiation take place similar to that in the late phallic phase. However, sex-specific identity now becomes clearly established in both sexes, and the new differentiation of psychic structure is based on a much more secure foundation than it was in childhood. But not before a period of preadult consolidation is there an integrated heterosexual adjustment and a solid adaptation to the new social situation of an independent adult. This phase echoes and elaborates on the phase in latency when the child accepted the social values of a group that extended beyond the immediate family unit.

Conclusion

The similarity in the psychic organization of childhood and adolescent phases suggests a corresponding similarity of hormonal mechanisms.

From the data available, it appears possible that small changes in quantities, rates of increase, and ratios of sex hormones, although not sufficient to initiate substantial physical changes, may nevertheless be interrelated with alterations of psychic organization in childhood.

Sudden or sporadic changes of hormone levels may contribute to phases of disequilibrium in psychic development. Stabilization of estrogen levels in childhood may have an organizing effect upon the psyche.

The relationship between phases of stabilization of adult hormonal mechanisms and psychic development in adolescence will be pursued further in Chapters 14 and 15.

NOTES

[1]Since this was written, considerable progress has been made in hormonal assay techniques (see Chapter 16). However, no detailed data have been obtained on hormone production in young children. On the other hand, more data from psychoanalyses, from observations of children, and from movement studies have become available to give me a greater feeling of conviction about the usefulness and pertinence of my classification of developmental phases (Furman, R., 1973; Kestenberg, 1969; see also Mahler's discussion of Chapter 8 and Chapters 5, 9, 10, and 17.

[2]I first encountered evidence for the existence of this phase in girls (Chapter 1). Subsequently, I discovered that the maternal interest of the prephallic boy is also based on the externalization of inner-genital impulses (Chapter 2).

[3]For a review of generalized and localized actions of these hormones see Chapter 15, p. 383-388.

CHAPTER 14

Phases of Adolescence
With Suggestions for a
Correlation of Psychic
and Hormonal Organizations

II: Prepuberty Diffusion
and Reintegration

In the preceding chapter an attempt was made to show how changes in psychic and hormonal organization prepare the child for the fundamental alterations of psychosomatic organization in adolescence. Here I shall examine the prepuberty phase of adolescence in greater detail.

Introduction

While this chapter is devoted to the discussion of prepuberty, it may be advisable briefly to recapitulate the classification of childhood and adolescent phases that are used throughout.

1. *Childhood*

1. Neonatal phase of transition from fetal dependence on the mother to individuation. The adultlike hormonal state of the newborn is succeeded by a period of involution of variable duration.

2. Pregenital phases in which genitality is incorporated in the pre-

First published in *J. Amer. Acad. Child Psa.*, 6:577–612 (1967). Slightly revised and reproduced by permission.

vailing oral, anal, and urethral dominance, and rapid growth of body and brain far outweigh the changes in gonads and reproductive organs.

3. An inner-genital phase (between the ages of two and a half and four), in which neurohormonal changes may coincide with an initial state of psychic disequilibrium, and their subsequent stabilization following the disequilibrium may contribute to the integration of pregenital, inner- and outer-genital drive components.

4. Phallic phase, which may be initiated by an increase in androgens and can be divided into subphases of predominant growth and differentiation.

5. Latency, in which the predominance of drive derivatives over untamed drive discharge becomes increasingly consolidated, and an inhibitory factor seems to counteract the effect of increase in steroid production.

2. Adolescence

1. Prepuberty, initiated by a diffusion of psychic functions that is resolved in a phase of reintegration, in preparation for puberty genitality. The onset of prepuberty is marked by an activation of inner-genital organs and the appearance of secondary sex characteristics. Prepuberty diffusion coincides with a rapid increase in sex-specific hormones, and the subsequent reintegration parallels the regularization of sex-specific hormonal patterns.

2. Puberty begins with the maturation of gonads (mature spermatozoa and ovulation). It is divided into subphases of predominant growth and differentiation and is followed by:

3. A preadult phase of consolidation of previous gains during which the organization of adolescent genitality becomes transformed into its adult form.

There is growing evidence that the third year of life is characterized by changes reflecting a maturation of hypothalamic-hormonal pathways ushering in phases of childhood genitality. For instance, the adrenal gland, which is considered the principal source of steroids in childhood, loses half of its original weight in the third week of life and does not attain its almost adult character until about the third year (Watson and Lowrey, 1962). Some authors describe the ovary of three-year-old children in similar terms (Harman, 1932).

Growth of reproductive organs does not occur to any significant degree until the end of the first decade, but both estrogens and androgens seem to exert an influence upon earlier development in a manner not yet

346

sufficiently understood. There seems to be no doubt that the immature gonads secrete a certain amount of sex steroids but the change in metabolization of sex hormones is not simply a quantitative one. Endocrinologists tend more and more to regard the differences between hormonal constellations in childhood, adolescence, and adulthood as dependent on "the differential prevalence of metabolic pathways at different ages" (Van der Werff Ten Bosch, 1964).

The difference between sexes in childhood is reflected in the higher levels of estrogen in three-year-old girls and of 17-ketosteroids in boys (Table 2, Chapter 13). But only with the onset of a rhythmic interaction between gonadotropins and ovarian hormones in adolescence is the female mode of psychosexual functioning established. Conversely, we can think of the male mode of functioning as contingent upon a tonic type of relationship between the pituitary and testicular hormones. These changes are initiated in prepuberty. It is assumed that an inhibitory substance operative in childhood has been eliminated and a change has occurred in the hypophyseal sensitivity to steroids. Undoubtedly there is also an alteration in the complex interaction with the adrenal as prepuberty's most reliable sign is the appearance of pubic hair. A substantial rise in 17-ketosteroid excretion already begins in latency, and changes in the inner-genital organs precede the appearance of pubic hair (Tables 1, 2 and 3, Chapter 13).

Both the phase of transition from pregenitality to phallicity, between the ages of two and a half and four, and prepuberty seem to be landmarks in the reorganization of psychological and hormonal constellations, and both phases appear to be initiated by an influx of diffuse innergenital sensations that increase the need for externalization. Externalization, used as means to find or regain a focus for body-image formation, becomes prevalent in the phases of integration that precede phallic dominance in childhood and puberty genitality in adolescence.

Prepuberty Diffusion and Reintegration in Both Sexes

The disequilibrium which follows latency in both sexes occurs under conditions strikingly similar to those which initiated the phase of transition from pregenitality to phallic genitality (Chapter 13). A new psychosomatic constellation may trigger aggression as well as inner- and outergenital excitations (Tables 1, 2, and 3).

Progressive and regressive trends vie with each other as tensions from the inside of the body and changes in body contours disrupt the child's body image. Diffuse and unlocalized inner-genital tensions evoke regressive discharge through pregenital channels at the same time that changing sensations in outer genitals call for another form of genital discharge. Instinctual impulses invade adaptive behavior as drive diffusion, breakthroughs of pregenital impulses, and a primary as well as a defensive use of aggression disrupt the cohesiveness of the ego. With the changing identity of the child, the relationship to parents becomes strained. Parents once more become the primary targets of immature sexual and aggressive drives, and they become embroiled in the child's conflicts between independence and dependence, between activity and passivity, and between sadistic attacks and masochistic suffering.

The disequilibrium in prepuberty, as in its childhood antecedent at two and a half, may be followed by a phase of integration, or a series of crises may be resolved by successive integrative efforts. Whether there are two distinct phases or two distinct trends within one progressive phase seems to depend on sequels of earlier developmental stages, the individuality of growth cycles and the relative stability of the environment. A failure to resolve pregenital problems in early childhood results in a deviant integration that prevents the development of true phallic dominance and distorts the resolution of the oedipus complex. This in turn leads to a deficiency of the superego and a corresponding maladjustment during latency. Symptoms and undesirable traits that seemed only mild during the latency period become considerably increased with the breakdown of an already shaky organization. Fortunately, favorable conditions in prepuberty give the child a second chance to create a new organization which may lead to a more wholesome redistribution of psychic forces.

It is important to treat children who suffer from poor integration of psychic structure before puberty sets in. However, treatment initiated in prepuberty is difficult and prolonged for many reasons, two of which I shall single out here. The child at that time is normally estranged from adults and does not and cannot share confidences with them. He is so busy trying to put together the pieces of things falling apart that he cannot bear to look at undesirable parts of himself for any length of time. If the therapeutic alliance has been firmly established beforehand, the analyst has a chance to cope with the stormy resistances of prepuberty. Under these circumstances the youngster's need to recover his equilibrium by reintegration of various opposing forces may make him an interested and willing participant in analysis. But even then the analyst has to be forever on guard to refrain from interpretations which concern regressions until the child is himself in the process of progressive reintegration.

Prepuberty disequilibrium is much more intense than its predecessor in early childhood. It is more aptly called *diffusion* because of the characteristic lack of focus that colors the experiences in beginning adolescence. A veneer of latency solidity may mask the diffusion of thinking characteristic of prepuberty, but the analysis of the child's feelings, hidden thoughts, and fears reveals a profound disintegration of latency attainments. Changing moods and inappropriate affective outbursts are more disquieting to the child himself and to the environment than they were in the young child. Bodily changes are more substantial and progress more rapidly than in the young child. Sensations from the inside of the body are stronger and more frightening, and regressions to pregenitality are perceived as more shameful. Nevertheless, the description in Chapter 13 of the two-and-a-half-year-old fittingly characterizes prepuberty behavior as well: "Speech can deteriorate into screaming, cleaning up into messing, washing into flooding."

The latency child was dependable and predictable. He maintained a steady, affectionate relationship to his parents. With the onset of prepuberty there is an increasing tendency to withdraw from the parents, to exaggerate friendships with peers, and to idealize adults other than the parents. Affective restraint and personal habits that had been acquired and maintained for the parents' sake begin to deteriorate. Unaccountable giggling, laughing, and crying fits, and unexpected coarseness in behavior contrast sharply with the composure of latency. Eating jags interfere with the orderly routine of meals, washing of unexposed body parts becomes abhorrent, underwear gets stained from occasional dripping of urine and secretions from genitals. Overshooting of movements, especially in boys, coupled with the fact that clothes do not grow to accommodate rapid changes in body proportions, makes children of this age appear careless and disheveled. A disproportionate investment of certain body parts at the expense of others may result in endless grooming of hair, unreasonable demands for special articles of clothing, and refusals to relinquish dirty or ill-fitting garments.

Parental alarm and reproaches are met with argumentativeness. Communications veer from short, cryptic sentences to floodlike, confused, and incoherent accounts of grievances. Personal feelings become all too easily injured as the mother is expected to be at the beck and call of changing needs but must not refer to childish habits by name. Children are, in turn, revolted by previously tolerated parental habits such as "eating too loud," "smacking of lips," kissing and using words referring to the body. Mothers become desperate and fathers put a foot down. Misunderstood and rejected, the child may feel like a stranger in his own home.

PHASE DEVELOPMENT IN ADOLESCENCE

At the beginning of prepuberty, the incipient changes of the outer contours of the body can be discussed by mother and child; in later stages children rely more and more on information from siblings and friends. Sophisticated as many of them seem and enlightened for some time, they now become overwhelmed by the shocking discovery that their parents engage in sex for its enjoyment. They associate sex with the inside of the body and its secretions that signify pregenital pleasures and forbidden early forms of masturbation. They struggle against urges which they had learned to control in early childhood in order to be deserving of parental love and protection. It took them a long time to forget that the mother used to participate in such infantile excitements, which she successively evoked by her bodily care and forbade when they became play. Now that they know her "guilty secret" they do not trust her affectionate approach and her "false" utilitarian interests in their bodily functions and external appearance. Mothers respond with regressive spiteful remarks such as: "You are a dirty pig, Johnny" or "You look like nothing, Mary." Shocked and deeply hurt, the youngsters may turn to the father for protection and support. Disappointed by him, they may turn to recover the idealized mother image of their childhood. They turn their wrath and contempt upon the father who "makes mother do it" not just once to get a child but "all the time" to suit his pleasure. The disillusionment with parental objects enhances a projection of revived pregenital and early genital wishes upon the parents. Phallic-oedipal identifications with one or the other parent are linked with derivatives of primal scene experiences and fantasies. A new insight into the nature of adult relationships calls for a reorganization of memories that emerge as repression is weakened. Regressive fantasies of rape may be reenacted in an effort to master actively the passively experienced seductions that occurred in early childhood (Greenacre, 1950a). Delinquent behavior may be used to test the validity of earlier prohibitions; it can also serve to degrade the unmasked parents in dramatic, sadomasochistic scenes in which the forbidden act leads to mutual recriminations. A revival of archaic demands of the superego leads to the establishment of compulsive rituals, reminiscent of those initiated in the third year of life. Phobic avoidances of objects and things that evoke incestuous or aggressive wishes alternate with secret deals in which forbidden actions are allowed by bribing the superego with good deeds, advance punishment or masochistic submission through penance. The rejection of ego ideals, modeled after parental objects, is often counterbalanced by idealization of adults (athletes, performers) who meet the standard of skill and achievement valued by peer groups. A rebellious rejection of conventions and values imposed by society may be coupled with a submissive accep-

350

tance of external attributes imposed by prepuberty fashions. Not only hair and clothing styles, but poses, mannerisms, and favored phraseology are mirrored and shared in groups whose common aim is the externalization of disturbing inner sensations and feelings. Stylized attitudes do not prevent incidents of excessive loss of control, and these can be followed by a defensive shallowing of affect. A contagious spreading of excitement may be used as a method to get rid of tensions or may be the expression of an unfocused general state of excitation. Attempts to get rid of irritating feelings and thoughts by passing them on to others bring about provocative, nagging, and silly behavior (see Chapter 4).

The dissolution of previously established body boundaries and the upsurge of secondary narcissism, the invasion of adaptive behavior by regressive infantile wishes and early defenses, the breakdown of reaction formations, and the disintegration of the latency superego are all transitory characteristics of prepuberty. Only in pathological development do they become permanently established. In normal children, they fluctuate in intensity and mingle with features of latency as well as with progressive strides. The absurd effects of some such combinations resemble slapstick comedy, often abhorrent to parents. The diffusion of body boundaries is more noticeable in boys than in girls. Boys' limbs seem to grow out of proportion to their bodies while their motor skill increases. Girls and boys sprawl all over as if they were fusing with couches and chairs, but girls appear less awkward than boys.

> Shuffling his feet and waving his arms, a boy in prepuberty may approach the baseball field in a manner suggesting that his arms and legs are not really his own, his shirt belongs to his father, and his pants to his younger brother, while his hairdo seems borrowed from his mother. Unexpectedly, he grips the bat and executes superbly coordinated movements with a precision in aiming, and with strength and timing he had not been able to achieve in latency (see Chapter 17). His task accomplished, he reverts to hip wiggling, shaking, swinging, and shuffling, in the midst of which he may stop to hitch up his pants or to groom his hair.
>
> A girl in prepuberty may make a grand entrance, posing as an actress, ribbons in her hair, all dolled up in a new attire, even wearing makeup, all ready to have her grown-up qualities admired and approved. Invited to sit down, she may practically fall onto the couch, and extend her arms and legs in an unladylike gesture, revealing scratches on her knees, and dirty streaks in the hollow of her elbows.

Both sexes tend to externalize inner tensions. They use live friends

351

more than inanimate objects to mirror their feelings. Both sexes reorganize oral, anal, urethral, inner-genital and phallic needs, fitting them into a new genital organization. They are aided in this reorganization by bodily changes (breast development, vaginal secretion, pubic hair, uterine cramps and menarche; growth of penis and testicles, prostatic secretion, pubic hair, scrotal changes, testicular sensitivity and emission (see Table 1 in Chapter 13), which orient them toward sex-specific individuation.

Prepuberty diffusion is resolved by *reintegration,* guided by the organizing influence of clear-cut physical and intellectual maturation, and by the identification with parental attitudes toward these changes (Chapter 12; Spiegel, 1951). Where parents, through their own attitude, convey respect for growing up and look upon the change in the boy's or girl's body with approval rather than regret, the child looks forward to each anticipated landmark of advancing development. One can easily paraphrase again what was said in Chapter 13 about the three-year-old: "As he separates each sphere of bodily functioning from his mother's executive guidance, the distinction between himself and his mother and father provides the core for discrimination between inside and outside." The equation "inside-mother-baby" is counterbalanced by the equation derived from the late phallic period: "outside-father-penis-baby." The estrangement from parents becomes more and more focused on the genitals as the parents themselves single out genital functioning to be discussed in secret or not at all.

While the early integration phase ends in phallic dominance, prepuberty integration incorporates pregenital, inner-genital, and phallic drive components into the newly acquired puberty genitality. The acceptance of the difference in sexual characteristics between boys and girls puts an end to infantile illusions about the existence of a female phallus. In preparation for genital functioning in which reproduction becomes a reality rather than a child's fantasy, boys and girls first exaggerate and then accept the dichotomy between sexes. A maturation of hypothalamic-cerebral connections provides a basis for a new sex-specific organization, in which the cyclicity of woman stands in marked contrast to the greater steadiness of reactions in man.

Female Prepuberty

The girl's external genitalia do not grow nearly as much as those of the boy's do in late latency, but the growth of uterus and ovary begins before the external changes characteristic of prepuberty (Table 1, Chapter 13). During latency this growth of internal organs may be counterbalanced by rises in androgenic substances (Table 2), which probably reinforce phallic trends that may neutralize inner-genital tensions and interests. The great upsurge of estrogens with beginning of prepuberty and the cyclic changes in gonadotropine levels eventually bring on menarche. Long before menarche the girl has to cope with changes inside her body. These enhance regression to pregenital phases. To combat pregenital and inner-genital fantasies the girl reverts to a phallic position. Veering between preoccupations with the inside and the outside of her body, she finds it difficult to establish a steady attitude. The visible changes on the outside of her body and the irregular cryptic changes inside her body lead to a diffusion of body boundaries and a dispersal of sensations.

The ten- to eleven-year-old girl is prepared for the budding of her breasts, whose erectility and conic shape she equates with similar attributes of her clitoris (Sarlin, 1963). In a parallel displacement upward she hides her pubic masturbatory activity and displays an exaggerated interest in her hair. She shares these interests with her girl friends and her mother, but hides them from her father and brother. Impulses from her inside genital disquiet her, but may not reach the level of cognitive perception (Greenacre, 1950b; Mason, 1961). It is easy for her to externalize them and to maintain the denial of her introitus—which persists after the onset of the phallic phase—by reinforcement of a regressive phallic position. To maintain the isolation between the outer and inner genital, she not only displaces upward, but tries to prove herself equal to boys and gives only lip service to the significance of inside female organs. Forever trying to get rid of diffuse inner sensations, she rushes forth without focus. Her intellectual functioning suffers, as denial, lack of attention, and diffusion of identity between herself, other people, and objects invade her conceptualizations. Her identity diffusion (Erikson, 1959) becomes quite apparent in a regressive use of pronouns and unstructured use of grammar (Chapter 12). Devoid of syntax, her speech may become reminiscent of the verbal productions of the four-year-old:

> The teacher said it does not matter. I only made a mistake. That is true indeed because I know very well that one writes "ihn" [him] with an "h." We were both dressed in white with pink ribbons and everybody thought we were sisters, or at least cousins. Such a cousin I wouldn't mind. But as a friend it is even better, one can confide in her with everything. [Production of the eleven-year-old writer of Hug-Hellmuth's disputed diary (1919; my translation).][1]

As gonadotropins increase, the irregular estrogen production becomes cyclic, breasts advance to the primary mamma stage, and the pelvis re-

353

molds. The external and internal genitalia grow appreciably, the vagina begins to show epithelial changes (Table 1, Chapter 13) and lubrication occurs spontaneously. Even if the girl knows about the existence of the vagina, she periodically distorts her knowledge to aid her denial. She is much better equipped to deal with the growth of her labia and her clitoris than with her internal changes. She confuses sensations stemming from the inside of the vagina with anal, urethral, and clitoric feelings. She revives oral, anal, urethral, and phallic cathexes to cope with vaginal tensions. Since her image of herself as a good girl is much more important to her than the corresponding ideal is to the prepuberty boy, the girl suffers more from the reappearance of pregenital impulses. She tries all avenues of escape to retain her self-esteem and the approval of her parents. She is much more prone to lie about overeating, retention of feces and urine, messing and occasional soiling or dripping of urine. Masturbation is much more threatening now than it was in latency because excitation of external genitals so easily spreads into the vagina. Vaginal feelings and occasional uterine cramps make the girl feel injured, babyish, passive and dirty, and inferior to the boy. Acceptance of genital impulses now means not only passivity, being a baby and inferior, but also masochistic surrender to her own body and to the oedipal seducer. To counteract the breakdown of inhibition and repression, she defends herself by a flight into activity that is usually associated with masculinity (Deutsch, 1944–1945; Harley, 1961a).

The girl can focus on her growing breasts to counteract or escape her genital tensions. But the genital excitement can be so great that sensations in the breasts spread to the vagina. She tingles all over when her breasts are touched. She veers from clitoric masturbation to handling of her breasts. Preoccupied with their growth, she watches and "measures" them day by day. But the other parts of her body also become a source of excitement, in rapid succession or simultaneously. Sensations flow into each other, come and go with a relentlessness which may make focusing impossible. Intellectual functions become sexualized. Anxiety spreads to schoolwork, and the girl finds it difficult to pursue her studies as consistently as she did in latency. Dissatisfied with herself, she becomes disgruntled and argumentative.

Unable to get rid of her excitement, she becomes "contagious." Once calmed down, however, she feels void, "like nothing," and attempts to regain excitement by contact with a friend. The diffusion of body boundaries easily leads to fusion with anyone available and becomes a basis for transient identifications. Crushes on women frighten her by their intensity. Adulation of unapproachable male idols provides protection from physical contact with an adult and yet affords her opportunity to express pent-up feelings. In everyday conversations about the idol she may be able to keep her feelings down to the desired shallowness, but in a group demonstration the intense love for a popular star may deteriorate into an aggressive attack upon him. When excitement becomes too great, the boundaries between love and destruction of the loved object can become obliterated and feminine slavery may change into "masculine" rape. As she veers from a sadistic to a passive masochistic position, the girl begins to eye boys from a distance, but actual contact with them often ends with disappointment. Feeling hurt, she may confide in her mother with the stipulation that her secret be kept from the males. As she approaches her mother she begins to envy her mother's complacent acceptance of femininity and she wishes to explore the mother's body, but the mere sight of her mother's exposed arm or neck may induce sexual excitement. Fantasies of touching her mother's breast erupt into consciousness. The girl becomes defensively aggressive and runs away. Her sporadic turns to her father evoke a flood of masochistic fantasies to which she once more reacts with flight or attack.

The girl becomes acquainted with her own body by experimenting with her mirror image and by comparing herself with her girl friend. As she exchanges news about brassieres, skirts, idolized or despised teachers, popular singers, dating of boys and parental habits she seems to talk incessantly in what appears to an adult as empty chitchat. But all along she compares her ideas as well as bodily characteristics with those of her girl friend. Based on sameness, this relationship is typical of homosexual love (Kestenberg, 1962). Mutual grooming, measuring, dressing, combing, touching, and looking, which may begin with breasts or hair, may lead to transient homosexual episodes. Longer liaisons occur with older idolized girls. Sporadic sex play with a "twin" friend leads to violent quarrels in which guilt is projected upon the sex partner and attached to irrelevant issues. Reconciliation is contingent upon the friend's submission to a stylized scheme of values ("If you never use that word again, stop ignoring me at lunch, don't talk to me when I am with a boy, stop wearing that horrible dress," etc.). To disguise homosexual urges and channel sexual excitement to distant objects, conversation between friends can shift to endless recounting of having seen an adult idol or a boy admired by both girls. To make herself more attractive to the girl friend, a girl may engage in petting with boys and premature dating.

As menarche approaches, the long-practiced desexualization of the vagina and identification with maternal feelings for babies may suffer a setback. Usually dependable as a baby-sitter, the girl may suddenly become seductive with her wards. She may treat them as she did her dolls. Turning to her girl friend she feels more secure as her "twin" or "double" shares not only her excitement but also her guilt. Transient episodes of sex play with a girl friend may alternate with interest in boys, with reverting to doll play, and with more persistent interest in animals.

An exaggerated interest in horses frequently serves the externalization of intense inner sensations and bisexual needs as well. This sometimes very intense fad can become an important step in feminine integration. No doubt horses are symbolic of a powerful father. The most important use of horses, however, is connected with the wildness of this animal, which represents the quality of untamed genital impulses. Riding affords real relief as some of the horses' gaits correspond in rhythm to the rocking type of vaginal contractions and releases. The taming of the horse—the control the rider exercises over the animal—are welcome practice in the taming and channeling of genital sensations. The integration necessary in good equitation encompasses coordination and adjustment between the rider and the horse. Much of this coordination is achieved through the control of pelvic and abdominal muscles in relation to the animal's movement.

But girls are not only interested in riding; they love to look at horses, feed them, and groom them.[2] They develop a maternal, desexualized interest in them. One of the girl's greatest fears is that her inside is too small to hold a penis or a baby. During this period of growth of inner genitals, the image of the huge horse that depends on the care of a slight girl has a reassuring value, as it indicates that she can cope with something much larger than herself. But horseback riding is not only reassuring, it also creates anxiety. The Trojan horse seems to contain unseen enemies and one must be wary. It may be Pandora's box. Riding may bring the genitals into too close contact with a "runaway" horse. The masturbatory quality of such an experience brings about disorganization and lack of control that can end with falls and injuries. The conquering of the fear and the regaining of control are contingent on the girl's ability to desexualize both the anxiety and the pain associated with falling.

Tolerance for pain and the facility in handling states of high tension are akin. Pride in achievement and confidence in her ability to recover her equilibrium, based on past experiences, help the girl to desexualize inner and outer dangers, provided she can lean on her mother's constancy of feelings toward her. Her mother's attitude toward pain and injury, toward tensions and setbacks, influence the girl's attitude toward loss of control, tension, anxiety, frustration and pain.

The more regular her cyclic hormonal changes have become, the more the girl learns to anticipate relief after periods of tension. It is interesting to note that phases of high tension are associated with a lowering of hormone levels in premenstrual states, menopausal syndromes, and premenarchal states (Sutherland and Stewart, 1965; Southam and Gonzaga, 1965). As reported for the premenstrual and menstrual phases, genital sensations mount and impinge upon consciousness shortly also before menarche (Benedek, 1952; Kinsey *et al.,* 1953). Girls seem to experience premenarchal states periodically before menstruation does occur. They become irritable, tired or depressed. In analysis they reveal their awareness of inside swelling to the bursting point. The breasts ache and the abdomen becomes tender. In telescopic fashion they now repeat and reorganize fantasies and ideations that originated in the early inner-genital phase (Chapter 13, pp. 316-321).

To master actively what they experience passively as an attack from the inside, girls may overeat and retain their feces and urine. This only increases inside pressures; the eventual discharge of products held back does not bring total relief and may even bring the previously blurred vaginal sensations into clearer focus. An attempt to eradicate a gnawing pressure from inside may lead to a violent handling of external genitals during wiping or masturbation. These may produce abrasions and pain. An intense desire to get rid of the unexplored "monster" inside brings about fears that everything will fall out of the abdomen. One device for protection against such dire consequences is continuous tensing of thighs and pelvic muscles. During all these operations, representation of inside genitals, revived from the inner-genital stage, change from oral, anal, urethral to inner-genital models. As urethral and clitoric excitations produce swelling that spreads to the labia, the introitus and the distal portion of the vagina, and reverberate into deeper genital parts, fantasies about a penis growing outside alternate with ideas that a penis is hidden inside. All real and imaginary products of the inside are equated with babies, and the internal upheaval is equated with pregnancy and delivery. The introitus is rediscovered and denied again, but not until menstruation takes place does it become incorporated into the body image.

In the process of accepting and rejecting her total genital, the girl equates excitement with an organ belonging to her and the subsiding excitement with organ loss. Wishing to get rid of the high tension and the organs that produce it, the girl both desires and dreads aphanisis (Jones, 1935a). When the exciting swelling subsides, she experiences an organ loss that evokes a wish for a constant visible external object, a baby or a baby-producing penis. The girl can no longer find a representation for the loss and recovery of the "baby-vagina" in the numerous variations of "lost doll" theme in doll stories of her latency literature (Chapter 5). In the way she sometimes acts out the loss and the retrieval of her pocketbook, she telescopes feelings similar to those she evidenced when her "live" baby doll "died" and became inanimate at the end of the prephallic phase and was reaccepted as a "practice" baby in later stages (Chapters 1 and 2).

The advent of menstruation establishes the existence of the introitus as a door through which the blood passes and a baby will follow suit in the future. Physical relief and the feeling of purpose and pleasure that "it did come" bring about a peaceful interval during which the many divergent fantasies about menses can be reevaluated in a positive way. However, this occurs only if both parents currently enhance previously established feminine integration. The actual experience of menarche is organized by the sharpness of physical sensations and by the past and present attitudes of important people in the child's life (Chapter 12). An externalization of inner sensations produces an acuity in visual and acoustic perception that is selectively applied to shapes symbolizing parts of genitals, now accepted. Past and present events come into sharp focus that brings about new insights. Pregenital representations become subordinated to the total genital Gestalt. Previous experiences, linked to recent events, may suddenly attain a new meaning. It is this sudden understanding of the past through the eyes of the present that can make the experience of menarche a trauma or an illumination.

Rumer Godden, a writer of enchanting stories about children and dolls sensitively described the complex integrative process of the first menstruation (1958).[3]

> All through the summer Cecil, whose mother was sick and father dead, helped her older sister, Joss, to supervise the younger children. At the same time she observed and interpreted the strange doings of grownups and took great interest in Joss's flirtations with older men. One of them, Elliot, was old enough to act as a father protector to the mistreated children and to carry on an affair with an older woman, but still young enough to admire Joss. [He thus could represent an idealized father figure whose unmasking as villain takes up the better part of the story. Implied in the plot is Cecil's interpretations of sex with the older woman as wicked and the love for a young girl as pure.]
>
> Cecil suspected for some time that Elliot was planning a sinister deed, but on a memorable day she found evidence for her suspicions in the "cove." Busily describing all the exciting things that were going on around her, Cecil suddenly became aware of a pain which may have been plaguing her for some time. She tried to explain it away as due to overex-

posure to the sun, prolonged bathing or as the effect of the shocking "discovery" of Elliot's misdeed. [As the pain increases, Cecil's attention is forcibly turned to her own body. Nevertheless, she finds a framework for her intense sensations in familiar external objects, suitable for symbolic representation of her inner organs. In addition, she externalizes inner tensions to her legs, back and head:]

"I slowly crossed the *little room* and shut the *door*. Whether because of long bathing that afternoon or the *shock* in the *cove,* I seemed *filled* with pains in my *legs* and back and head, pains that hurt, and I did not want to *hear* any more ugliness. I thought I could sense that there was something ugly—and I wished I were with Hester and the Littles on the other side of the *door.*"

[To escape the adult ugliness that fills her with fears, Cecil wished to be young again, unknowing and not faced with the secrets on the "inside of the door." In the detailed account of her reactions to the rhythmically recurring pain, one notices how Cecil alternates between turning for guidance to her older sister, whose sexuality she condemns, and turning to Elliot, whose sinister scheme she has discovered. Thus we see here a beautiful example of the role played by both mother and father substitutes, in organizing the girl's femininity, which is initially repudiated.]

On seeing Joss who was dressing for a party, Cecil attacked her sister's bareness saying tersely: "It shows." [Joss's empathic understanding helped Cecil to focus on herself and she could confess that she had "pains" that were "everywhere." Joss's reassuring and concise definition "growing pains" guided Cecil later when she experienced a new attack of pain shortly after another encounter with Elliot:]

"I went back to the *landing* where I had another pain and with it such a sense of desolation that I could hardly bear it. If this was growing—Joss said that was what the pains were—I did not like it."

As the cramp seemed to ease, Cecil became melancholy, listening to the noises of the party from which she felt excluded. She then tried to get into her brother's room, but mysterious Elliot kept her out of it. Then suddenly she had to go to the bathroom which she called "the Hole."

"I went to the Hole because something has happened to my pain. There wonder overcame me. Wonder and fear. 'I shivered with reluctant feet, where the brook and river meet,' Mr. Stillbotham [a teacher] had said. No matter how reluctant, one was pushed into a *full tide.* Dazed, I came out of the *Hole* and went into *Joss's room* and found what I needed in a drawer."

[When she could neither deny, undo, nor externalize any longer, Cecil could find a few apt words and a quotation to describe her experience. She could focus on wonder and fear and she could become practical all at once,

359

as she used her knowledge to find the right place where sanitary napkins were stored. Almost immediately after the integration of old experiences with the new one, after the crystalization of her feelings, memories and sensations, she began to exaggerate her newly found femininity in a masochistic self-pity:]

"I had to manage for myself with those strange first necessities of being a woman, and it was inexpressibly lonely. When I was comfortable, I began to cry with excitement and self-pity. I was still crying when I went back to the landing." Despite the memory of her mother's warning to be discreet about these private matters, she had to tell Elliot: "I . . . have turned into a woman." [Now mysterious Elliot became explicit as he brought forth a man's point of view:] "It does not hurt if you consider how exciting it is." [Being a woman is only worthwhile if a man opens the road to it:] "Because now you are ready for love." To prove his point, Elliot kissed her, but soon he sent her to a motherly woman to be fed as he himself rejoined the grownups. [In this episode we recognize the position of the young adolescent girl who is not grown yet, but can merely see a guideline to the future of womanhood. Cecil was not quite ready for "love" yet; she needed the reassurance that women still loved her and would feed her. Accepted by a father substitute she began to crave the kind of food her mother used to give her. Acceptance by feeding is the equivalent of approval by mother.

The experience of Cecil's menarche was organized by recurring uterus cramps, by the flow of blood, and the relief it brought. At the same time memories, fantasies, and attitudes carried over from latency morality, began to merge and alternate with reevaluations of the past and a new attitude to the present. Cecil used her sister and Elliot as substitutes for parental objects. She used them for regressive and progressive assertions of femininity. Veering back to childhood, attempting to care for her siblings in an asexual maternal way, identifying with them, all alternated with positive and negative oedipal feelings, with an awkward attempt at rejoining her phallic brother and with a repudiation of femininity as pregenital in nature. The unmasking of adult sexuality as "ugly" and sinful reinforced her refusal to grow up. But, in turning to reality and away from the idealized parental world of the latency child, and by exaggerating what she now felt and perceived, she found a framework for the organization of diffuse sensations and uncoordinated memory fragments which confused and bewildered her. The parts of the house which she wandered in stood out as definite shapes and landmarks for the more focused experiences of menarche; the people encountered seemed fraught with the same mystery she felt in her body. They were ugly and naked as she felt degraded and exposed; they were helpful and accepting as she accepted her new body image and her new identity. In her mind past and present merged and her feelings crystallized. The discovery of adult "ugliness" made her tolerant of her own "ugly" sexuality. She could rise from the contemptuous dirty "hole" to feeling comfortable, womanly, loved and fed.]

The organizing experience of the first, yet anovulatory menstruation helps the girl to localize her inner sensations and to gain a more realistic representation of her unseen inner organs. Symbolic images of her inside are revived from the early inner-genital phase; they now become more sharply delineated and unified with the representations of external genitals whose hypercathexis, established in the phallic phase, recedes. At the same time the contributions of pregenital zones to genital representations are reexamined and, so to speak, relocated in their relation to sexual needs. The reevalutation of the inside and outside of the body goes hand in hand with a reevaluation of the meaning of childhood and adulthood and of the roles men and women play in relation to each other and to children. Although this new integrative effort is based on revivals of representations from the early phase of integration (early inner-genital phase), the early images can be clearly distinguished from their new editions.

A three-year-old gave two finger paintings to her parents. Father's picture was easily identifiable as "Waterfalls"; mother's picture was not clear except that one could detect a central hollow part surrounded by a mass of rounded finger strokes. Asked why this picture was selected for the mother, the child replied in amazement: "Can't you see? It is a triangle." The three-year-old identified maleness with the vertical strokes of a forceful waterfall. To her, a triangle was a shape that she once fitted into an appropriate hole on the form board. The surrounding circular strokes may have indicated a connection to the anus as the water had to urine in the male picture.

Eleven-year-old Cecil used symbolic expression in a similar, but more complex way. Cecil felt pain as she slowly crossed the "little room" and shut the "door." In the next attack of pain she went to the "landing" and at last she went to the "Hole." Smelly though it was, it helped her to clarify the junction between external and internal genitals which reminded Cecil poetically of the place "where the brook and river meet." Here the smelly hole symbolized the rectum as well as the vagina. The familiar quotation applied to the difference between the flow of urine and of blood, the "place" (introitus) being now clearly localized between the anus and the urethral opening.

361

The menstruating girl knows and understands a great deal more than the three-year-old, but she has to experience a great many cycles before she can become accustomed to her total "floor plan" and can begin to reconcile her physical needs with love.

As the cycles of estrogen production become more regular and the ratio between androgens and estrogens becomes more dependent on particular phases of the cycle (Hudson *et al.*, 1964) than it was before, the girl learns to anticipate her changing moods, levels of activity as well as alternations between states of sexualization and desexualization of her inside. Although she has not yet experienced the typically feminine receptivity of the luteal phase of the menstrual cycle, she seems to have enough of a foreboding of it that she can anticipate it by empathic identification with her mother and older sister. These states may be fleeting as she tends to regress to pregenital or early genital fantasies before each menstruation. At those times she becomes irritable, and reverts to denial and repudiation of femininity, but her integrative efforts become stabilized in successive cycles that repeat themselves with increasing regularity.

Parents, teachers, physician, older siblings and friends, now near-equals, help her to look forward to an adulthood which realistically includes good and bad, pretty and ugly. Her feelings toward adults change. She may even get close to her mother with whom she shares her secrets. She begins to understand why her mother is subject to mood changes, similar to her own. However, her oedipal wishes and shifting identifications impede the continuity of contact with her parents. She tries to direct her parents to conform to the new image she is creating of them. She identifies with them in a positive and a negative way. She becomes similar to her mother while she professes to be very different. She tests her father in an effort to discover his true feelings toward her. The relationship to her favored girl friend becomes less intense, but continues to be based on sameness, in contrast to the attraction of boys and men, which is based on difference. In the process of libidinization of her body she demands that others give her unlimited love, on her own terms. But her preoccupation with herself and the changes in her body as well as in her moods can make her insensitive to finer shades of feeling which do not correspond to her own. Through many shifts of identification she manages to construct an identity based on hidden identification with her family members and open allegiance to her peer group.

The repeated experience of the cycle regularizes the girl's feelings about herself, and she becomes less diffuse. She focuses on her genitals and is able to subordinate conflicting impulses to this central part of her body. In the interval between menarche and the first ovulatory cycle she becomes accustomed to the changes produced by the regular rises and falls in estrogen levels. She seems to coordinate her plans and her moods with her biological time schedule. Phases of desexualized interests alternate with direct preoccupation with genitals, especially in premenstrual and menstrual phases. In accepting the cyclicity of her existence the girl prepares herself for her role as woman.

The girl in prepuberty may have had a foreboding of cyclicity earlier in life. Analysis and close observation of three-year-old girls suggest that there may already be cycle changes at that age. Mood swings, episodes of nagging and irritability alternate with phases of contentment. Whether these changes are interrelated with sporadic or more regular fluctuations of estrogen production cannot be ascertained without daily hormonal assays, but clinical investigations suggest a connection with recurring inner-genital tensions. In prepuberty the girl's greatest task is to unify and to libidinize the various parts of her genitals. She realizes that her genital excitement can be triggered by external stimuli of various parts of her body (breast, neck, clitoris, labia, pubic hair or thighs) and may be related to internal changes as well. In this process she may temporarily reject, even condemn, any one part of her genital chain reaction. By necessity at this time of her life she still transfers genital excitement from the vagina to the outer genital, but she becomes increasingly aware of the function of the clitoris as a trigger and resonance organ of the vagina (Chapter 5). In masturbating she successively explores various stimuli and sensations resulting from them and tries to unify clitoris, labia, and the distal portion of the vagina with the unexplored internal part of it. She becomes acquainted with the hymen that she perceived only vaguely in earlier childhood. Now she worries that she may have injured it. Because of this fear and the inaccessibility of the proximal portion of the vagina she often gives up overt masturbation altogether and finds more hidden forms of discharge.

Fantasies triggered by inner-genital tensions veer from ambitious plans to breed multitudes of animals to dressing up for dates, going to a wedding, becoming engaged and raising children in a manner superior to that of her mother. Sewing dresses and buying the right kind of brassiere or sweater may take up a inordinate amount of time and care. The image of the vagina and uterus changes at that time; it frequently becomes deflected from the shape of a baby to the shape of manikins and their apparel. The preoccupation with externalizing of impulses from inside is much more varied now than in the early maternal phase of three to four years of age. Focusing on breasts is of course aided by localized mammal sensations and nipple erections, but this too spreads to articles of clothing, materials, costumes, and sketching of female bodies. The interest in pubic hair shifts to changing hair styles, which become expressive of changing moods and of trial identifications with idealized romantic figures. Transitory creativity is expressed in activities which serve the rebuilding of the body image. It plays a consistent and lasting role as sublimation only in children with special talents.

Whether the girl accepts or rejects the clitoris, the vagina, and the uterus depends to a large extent on the attitudes of her family. If her mother keeps telling her that she looks like "nothing," she feels that she has nothing worthwhile to please with. If she still feels that her brother is favored because he is a boy, she devaluates her vagina and either favors her clitoris or rejects it as too small. She may repress fantasies of penetration because of her oedipal feelings or she may interpret as a rejection of her femininity her father's refusal to treat her as a grownup. She may condemn her clitoris and isolate it from the rest of her genitals because of her repudiation of negative oedipal feelings, prohibitions of masturbation, and a defensive overemphasis on femininity. A permanent rejection of the clitoris leads to total frigidity rather than vaginal sensibility (Harley, 1961b), to a passive masochistic position rather than an active receptive feminine attitude. In normal development, the vagina is accepted as an organ and other parts of the genitals begin to assume an accessory and preparatory function in the total genital excitation. The vagina becomes the more precious the more it is felt as desirable for a love relationship the girl looks forward to.

The increase of inner-genital tensions, the changes in body boundaries and in the image of the outside and inside of her body disturb the equilibrium of the girl in prepuberty. The intermingling of regressively revived pregenital, early inner-genital, and phallic impulses with sporadic, irregularly repeated, ill-defined sensations from uterine contractions and genital congestions undermine the stability the girl has acquired during her latency. Diffusion of sensations and thoughts accompany the nagging, unfocused genital excitement and evoke wishes to get rid of what is inside and to find a focus in the external world. Estranged from grownups, half child, half woman, she finds a double in her girl friend and seeks a new identity by maintaining bonds with a peer group. She draws on the model of integration accomplished in her childhood, but the growth of her internal sex organs and external accessory sex characteristics paves the way for a reinforcement of a feminine position in identification with her mother. Menses help her centralize her diffuse sensations and direct her attention forcibly to woman's double role as sex partner and mother. Repeated cycles and their regularization, the sharpness of pain preceding or accompanying menstruation, and the associated bodily care routines focus her attention on the inside of her body and help her to form a new female body image. On the basis of a new self-representation, she enters puberty identified with her mother and yearning for her father's acceptance to consolidate her role as near woman. But foremost she has learned to accept the cyclicity of woman's existence which will grow in complexity and become the basis for sexual differentiation in later phases of adolescence.

The outcome of prepuberty integration differs from that of the early integration in the prephallic phase. The little girl abandons her inside genital and pronounces it nonexistent; the adolescent girl rediscovers it with live excitement. The little girl turns to her mother with phallic wishes; the adolescent girl directs her genital feelings toward her father and father substitutes. The little girl hopes to get a penis from her father; the girl entering puberty looks for her father's approval of her growing femininity. Whereas the little girl succeeds in desexualizing her inner genital, the adolescent girl is now less capable of desexualization of vaginal sensations than she was in latency. With the onset of puberty, that is, with the beginning of ovulatory cycles and cyclic progesterone, more and more she will experience feelings of peace, contentment, and hope, and will become more sensitive to the needs of her love objects. Her emotional understanding of feminine cyclicity will grow, and her heterosexual strivings will become powerful. Because she develops earlier than the boy, she will act as an activator of his sexuality. But only in a relationship with an adult male will she be able to achieve her full feminine potential.

Male Prepuberty

Male development appears to be more gradual than the female. The male hormone has a decisive influence on male differentiation already *in utero* (Burns, 1964) and the newborn's genital crisis may well be generated, at least in part, by testicular activity. There seem to be changes in the degree and in the quality of androgen production throughout childhood and, beginning with adolescence, male hormones increase in quantity until adulthood. In contrast, male estrogen production, steady in the adult (Paulsen, C. A., 1965), undergoes changes at about three years of age, with beginning latency and in prepuberty. The evaluation of Nathanson's 1941 data, on which this conclusion is based, must await the results of newer investigations now in progress (Paulsen, E. P., 1966; Eberlein, 1966). At present, hormonal assays in children are often interpreted in terms of studies of adults:

> The inherent risk of such comparisons must be borne in mind, especially in regard to androgen metabolism. The adult has reached a fairly sta-

365

ble and maximal level of activity, while the child is undergoing constant changes and even at fifteen to sixteen years of age has not attained adult levels of androgen synthesis (Paulsen, E. P., 1966).

Paulsen's words of caution are especially important with respect to male development. Rather than relying on quantitative data, we can regard hormonal changes at the ages of three and twelve as significant landmarks in the reorganization of hypothalamic-hormonal functioning in the male (Dorfman, 1963; Hudson *et al.,* 1964; Paulsen, C. A., 1965; Paulsen, E. P., 1966; Talbot *et al.,* 1952; Vesteergaard, 1965; Watson and Lowrey, 1962; Wilkins, 1965). Neurohormonal changes, initiating the prephallic "inner-genital" phase and a similar phase in prepuberty, may trigger off a psychosomatic disequilibrium which calls for a reintegration of psychic functions on which the formations of new male identities are based (Erikson, 1959).

In the early genital phase the boy is predominantly identified with his active preoedipal mother. In the phallic phase, he becomes primarily identified with his father. As he externalizes inner-genital tensions to his phallus, be also begins to master the passive experience of erections and testicular movements. From then on until the onset of prepuberty, the boy's predominant orientation remains phallic-active-masculine. In prepuberty the increase of inner-genital tensions activated by prostatic and testicular maturation (Tables 1 and 3, Chapter 13) threatens the boy's masculinity, revives the identification with the phallic mother, and enhances defensive exaggerations of aggressive aspects of the phallic position. The rise in androgen production triggers off muscular and skeletal growth in a manner conducive to the increase of unstructured aggression. These factors are largely responsible for the boy's identity diffusion and for his lack of differentiation between phallic masculinity and sadistic strivings. At times phallic aggression and castration fear are so outspoken at the onset of prepuberty that they overshadow hidden preoccupations with the disquieting changes inside the boy's body.

Generally speaking, throughout male development attention is centered upon the boy's external genitalia, and he changes neither his dominant discharge zone nor his sex object, as the girl must do before she can achieve sex-specific identity (Freud, S., 1924a). But the boy too has to cope with inner-genital tensions, experienced passively and therefore all too frequently mistaken for manifestations of femininity. The struggle between active and passive wishes plays an important role in the boy's shifts of identification with the preoedipal, phallic, oedipal, and desexualized mother image to the predominantly masculine identification with his father. Both during the early genital phases and in prepuberty, the boy behaves as if he knew that erections result from a relaxation of arteries in the corpora cavernosa and the return of tonus to the arterial walls makes erections subside (Dickinson, 1949). He repudiates the passive experience of involuntary erections and testicular movements and invents ways of stopping them. He looks upon active control as a symbol of masculinity when he manipulates his penis and scrotum so that he can become the originator and activator of genital changes he had experienced passively. The overwhelming experience of first emissions and spasmodic ejaculations becomes less traumatic because of earlier efforts at integration of inner-genital changes with outer manifestations of male genitality. These antecedents of prepuberty are the more important, the less parents and teachers prepare the boy for the fact that the inner structure of the phallus is visceral, that inner-genital activity and passivity are not necessarily feminine, but constitute an essential aspect of male sexual and reproductive functioning.

While girls nowadays are almost overprepared for menstruation, conception, and pregnancy, male sex education is neglected. Some pediatricians and some fathers discuss masturbation with growing boys, but only rarely are boys prepared for prostatic secretion and orgastic ejaculation (Balint, M., 1936; Landauer, 1935; Schonfeld, 1943). Our contemporary culture supports the externalization of inner sensations upon the phallus, not only in the inner-genital and in the phallic phase and not only in prepuberty, but throughout male development (see Chapter 5).

The breakdown of latency organization manifests itself conspicuously in the diffusion of body boundaries of twelve- to fifteen-year-old boys. The disproportion between torso and extremities, the lack of control over the voice that may emerge from the larynx or chest, the overshooting of movements in activities that are not governed by rules of skill, all these combine to make the boy ill at ease in unstructured social situations. In latency the boy was compactly put together, now he seems to suffer from an imbalance between periphery and center of his body. He becomes self-conscious with adults and sensitive to their criticisms of his manners. He feels either too tall or too short, too fat or too thin, too strong or too weak. His impulse to move with excessive free flow, with strength and speed, is so great that he temporarily loses control over fine movements or has to fidget and shift his uncertain weight from one foot to another. Outbreaks of unprovoked aggression frequently alternate with attempts to control the unruly arsenal of the body by rigid holding on to steadying objects (see Chapter 17). Even boys who do not appear overwhelmed by a surplus of motor push find it necessary to accompany verbal teasing with shoving, pulling, and pushing. Sexual impulses are expressed through aggressive channels, and sexuality is regarded as a sadistic attack

367

upon the body. Disquieting sensations from the inside of the body (Table 1), likened to femininity, give rise to hypochondriacal fears of illness and enhance a defensive shift to an active phallic-aggressive masculine position. A regressive pull toward pregenital fantasies brings about instinct defusion and revives the autoerotic practices characteristic of the three- to four-year-old.

Vague inner feelings fuse with "growing pains" experienced as threats emanating from the mysterious changes occurring inside the body. A voracious attitude to food is generally connected with the rapid growth of the prepuberty boy. The boy revives the oral magic of early childhood, reexperiences the pleasure of biting, tearing, and gulping food, and indulges in excessive drinking as he experiments with sensations of fullness, feeling, "blown up," and similar practices. Anal retention, manual pressure on the perianal-anal region, or insertion of fingers into the rectum, may occasion the first prostatic secretion. At the same time the boy may rediscover the fact, already sensed in the early inner-genital stage, that contraction of the anal and urethral sphincters can produce small movements in the penis, and that changes in intra-abdominal pressure and in the tonus of pelvic muscles can make the penis protrude or retract. But the boy tends to confuse "wet dreams" with urination and begins to doubt the efficacy of urethral sphincters that play uncanny tricks on him.

> A patient in his early thirties was still convinced that he had been a bed wetter in his early teens until he discovered in analysis that he had been deeply ashamed of stains on his bed sheets which were really produced by nocturnal emissions. Rather than face his mother's disapproval of his awakening masculinity, he had preferred to think of himself as a small child.

In contrast to early prostatic emissions, boys may experience "dry runs" in which they reach orgasm before they are capable of ejaculation. They become alarmed by the spasms they feel in the pelvis and scrotum and associate the new experience with long-familiar bellyaches, anal-feminine surrender or menstrual cramps. Dimly aware of scrotal contractions (Bell, 1961) and the rise of testicles during sexual excitement (Masters and Johnson, 1966), they fuse these sometimes noncognitive perceptions with anal-prostatic sensations and the contractions of the spermatic ducts. If they had a previous history of small or undescended testicles or inguinal hernias, they tend to associate the new sensations with the earlier discomfort and interpret them as manifestations of illness (Blos, 1960). Early traumatic handling by frightened parents and thoughtless physicians may be revived in an acting-out type of psychosomatic complaint. Testicles are looked upon as feminine and referred to as "eggs" or "jewels." They tend to fuse with thighs and are equated with breasts, especially during prepuberty gynecomastia. Boys seem convinced that the removal of the penis will make them into women as they deny the maleness of their gonads. One adult patient, when faced with the existence of testicles, aptly characterized the denial of his testicles and scrotum by saying: "They don't count." Such denial of testicles and scrotum seems to begin at the end of the early inner-genital phase and becomes reinforced at the onset of prepuberty.

Some boys, especially obese ones, begin to show signs of gynecomastia and of spurious smallness of the penis which is embedded in fatty tissue. Such changes as well as a dissatisfaction with the downy quality of the incipient pubic hair provoke frightening fantasies of transformation into a woman. Masochistic wishes and defensive evoking of dreaded castration combine with consolation fantasies that women have a hidden large phallus. The identification with the active mother, revived from the preoedipal stage, leads to an initial closeness to the mother and an estrangement from conspicuously boyish friends. Active wishes for pregnancy and delivery reinforce pregenital regression (Bell, 1961). Masturbation at such times is rarely acknowledged as such as it consists largely of experimentation with breasts, contraction of sphincters, squeezing of testicles, pushing them in and making them jump out, invaginating or hiding the penis between the legs, and similar games. Interest in female clothes may camouflage these games, especially when a boy is brought up in a matriarchal family setting.

In normal development, the increasing acuity of sensations in the penis shifts the focus of attention from inner pelvic and scrotal testicular sensation to the erect phallus. Ejaculation can be a frightening experience for the unprepared youngster, but has an organizing effect upon the boy who has looked forward to it with eagerness. Even then the new excretion is associated with messiness, infection, and female secrets. Despite his better knowledge the boy is afraid that the ejaculate is a sign of injury produced by masturbation. He receives little help from adults who themselves look upon the emission as evidence of the boy's masturbation. Discussing the matter with other boys or masturbating in company brings relief as guilt can be projected upon the playmate and a lot can be learned from techniques observed in others. In adult recollection of first ejaculations, one frequently encounters a report of seduction by another boy that brought about the discharge. Firsthand accounts in prepuberty analysis often reveal that roughhousing and wrestling evoke genital excitement which gives rise to subsequent solitary masturbation ending in ejaculation. Prepuberty homosexual practices are largely based on attempts to externalize genital sensations, to explore oneself through the medium of another boy, and on defensive exaggerations of a phallic cult that upholds the repudiation of femininity.

> A carry-over of prepuberty homosexuality into later phases of adolescence and adulthood frequently results from a failure in the desexualization of inner-genital sensations, and more generally from a failure in the integration of childhood bisexuality into a predominantly heterosexual orientation. Homosexual practices cover a wide range of activity such as pregenital forms of perversion, or seductions of children who are used very much the same way as toys and teddy bears were treated in the prephallic phase. These can include fellatio, anal penetration, and mutual masturbation with or without role playing. The need to penetrate another male may be prompted in part by a wish to explore his inside instead of one's own. Simultaneous experiencing of similar sensations reinforces early genital practices which are based on mirroring rather than mutual adjustment. The partner takes the place of the prepuberty pal whose penis is added in fantasy to aggrandize one's own. A defensive exaggeration of feminine traits serves the maintenance of the illusion of the female phallus.

The sharpness of orgastic sensations and their relief-bringing quality acts as an organizer of male integration. They help the boy to distinguish between pregenital, phallic, and genital masculine discharge forms. They allow him to accept sequences of activity followed by passivity. They give rise to intellectual curiosity about the inner trigger mechanism that evokes emission and convulsive motility. At the same time, they promote the externalization of inner sensations upon the phallus and stimulate an orientation to objects. The inside of the body, acknowledged as the initiator of orgastic discharge, is looked upon as an internal mechanism that operates in the service of phallic activity. A masculine body image is formed through elaborations of inner-genital and phallic theories about growing and moving objects.

The growth and movement of the penis and testicles (Bell, 1961) stimulate the boy's interest in ball playing, flying models, construction kits, and machines that can serve as models for the functional image of his body. Insight gained from biology and science helps him to elaborate and rationalize fantasies, about the connection between the inside and outside of his body, revived from the early inner-genital stage. The unseen motility that triggers various degrees of orgastic discharge helps the boy to distinguish between pregenital and inner-genital sensorimotor patterns. The penis, in which the pleasure is concentrated, becomes the core of the overall design of the male body. The most frequent conceptualization is that of the phallus growing out like a tree from roots inside the body. Fears of skeletons, revived from earlier phases, are often connected with the image of the penis-bone (erection) growing out of the spine and supported by it. Growing pains, felt in the bones, seem to lend support to this thesis. The realization that thoughts can produce erections, spontaneous discharge, and tingling sensations that can spread over the body gives rise to the idea that electrical wires (nerves) lead from the brain to the penis and set off an explosion.

Interest in the inner machinery of erections and testicular movements evokes the desire to get inside and direct them from there to the surprise of the innocent spectator. It promotes interest in magic tricks and puppetry, traditionally a male occupation. Pulling strings, as with marionettes, provides a pattern for actively inducing movements and sensations rather than being overwhelmed by them. Ignoring changes in the scrotum and testicles and denying their participation in the sexual experience is no longer possible. Sensitivity of the testicle and the sweaty and itchy sensations in the scrotum can produce discomfort that evokes an urge to get rid of the baggy loose "feminine" appendages (Bell, 1964). Irritations of the foreskin, of the ridge where the foreskin once was, playing with the smegma, irritations of the urethra, are fused with feelings about the scrotum (Nunberg, 1947). Looseness, stickiness, and pendulousness are identified with infants and women. An erect penis, a tight scrotum become symbols of masculinity. Tight pants create an illusion that the skin itself is stretched and taut (Bell, 1965). At times the boys feel a need to separate the scrotum from the penis, to relegate it to the back. The use of the term "balls" to express disdain, grabbing each other by the balls, and goosing are playful expressions of debasing this part of the body that defies direct control.

Once a boy can set up a system in which he can assign functional significance to the inside of the genitourinary tract and to the appendage of this inside in the scrotum, he can again ignore these accessory parts of the machinery which are subordinated to the central position of the phallus. In working with tools, sports equipment, and machinery, boys in prepuberty can elaborate on and give a practical and scientific background to representations (originated in the early inner-genital phase) that all moving objects can help to solve the mystery of the body. But at this age the boy has the intellectual and physical equipment at his disposal to master actively what he has experienced passively. Using motors as models, he looks upon secretions as the grease that makes for smooth operations of gears, he likens fuel to food and exhaust to flatus. This kind of ideation is evidenced in the jokes and typical expressions of twelve- to-sixteen-year-old boys as they communicate with each other, in a language which excludes adults. This material may be evaded in analysis, and the analyst must take the first step by showing familiarity with the appropriate idioms before the boy can begin to use his secret language in the therapeutic sessions.

The boy's ability to conceptualize as well as his control over movements by gauging aim, speed, and strength become a source for the mastery of aggression and of the genital mechanics he is learning to use. The narcissistic investment in the boy's body and its extensions such as bats, racquets, boats, and bicycles leave little over for the maintenance of relationships with others who do not share these interests. The science, shop or physical education teacher often becomes the center of admiring affection. Older boys and contemporaries are useful in explaining and sharing secrets and tricks in sports, work, and on their bodies directly. Parents seem too old-fashioned and girls too different to understand the miracles of the new experiences. Adults are threatening when they are incestuous objects or when their approach forebodes a passive experience. Boys long to be taken care of, yet dread the passive surrender which they anticipate when the adult becomes a seducer. Their response is a sadistic attack upon the would-be seducer (Fraiberg, 1961). Girls are dreaded, despised, tortured, and teased not only because they have no phallus but also because they are seductive. One can look at them and giggle about them with other boys, making jokes about their mysterious anatomy, but one must not go near them without a defensive weapon. The boy has to master his feelings about his own inside before he can approach that of the girl. The externalization of inner-genital impulses upon the phallus is aided by the externalization of inner-genital sensations upon the heterosexual object. Early sex play between boys and girls involves the boy's handling and exploring the girl's body and avoidance of activity by the girl. The girl, however, often plays the role of the initiator and organizer of the experience. She must be forever watchful to avoid getting hurt by the clumsy approach of her youthful partner. It is interesting to note that mothers of boys in prepuberty often admonish them to be nice to all girls, not only to their sisters.

The working through of the changed body image and of the new sensorimotor genital and aggressive impulses and of passively experienced "attacks from within" is contingent on previous solutions of similar problems, on the maturation of the central nervous system, on the integrative effect of a steady supply of steroids, and on the current behavior of parents and teachers who act as external regulators of inner upheavals.

In his adjustment to his new role, the boy begins to doubt his masculine potential. He fears that suppression of masturbation and the storing up of semen, which he pictures as occurring in the testicles, will burst these organs. He fears that excessive ejaculation will deplete the testicles and lead to infertility and lack of potency. These fears give rise to revival and elaboration of equations of testicles with breasts, kidneys, and bladder, and of semen with milk and urine. Prostatic-anal and testicular-phallic condensations also play a role in wishes to be impregnated and deliver a baby. The inability to achieve ejaculation, modeled after anal retention, may bring about prolonged manipulations of the penis that lead to abrasions of the skin and irritations of the urethra, producing reflex anuria, familiar to some boys from childhood. At such times the boy profits from confidential talks with his father who by recollecting similar events from his own youth provides a basis for a transitory pallike relationship. Communication with the mother about these matters increasingly takes on the form of nonverbal communication through secret messages. The boy leaves evidences of ejaculations on his bed sheets, pajamas, and underwear, and covers them up with ritualistic ceremonial actions which frequently become fixed habits. Lubricating of the penis with soap, spit or creams, urinating right after ejaculation to wash out the semen from the urethra, masturbation only during showers, in front of the toilet, and other masturbatory patterns are related to fantasies of the past and present bodily care, provided or demanded by the mother. Mothers who react with hostility to the secret messages and draw the fathers into the battle with the growing son enhance sadomasochistic behavior and perpetuate the myth of the powerful, all-seeing, and unforgiving female phallus. Only rare fathers become disquieted nowadays by masturbatory practices at that age, but both parents may begin to inspect the child with greater care than before. Paternal threats, if they do occur, are more direct, while mothers tend to make veiled remarks, admonishing the boys to be careful, to keep their hands out of their pockets, over the blankets, and keep them clean. Positive responses of parents, optimally expressed are: tolerance of transitory regressions and confusions; being available for help and enlightenment and allaying fears while keeping a benevolent distance from the boy's genital urges; approval of motor and intellectual achievements.

The processes of externalization of inner tensions and of extensions of the image of the phallus reshape the boy's body image. A male inside structure underlies the new identity which continues to be elaborated in later stages of masculine development. At the same time the boy becomes able to desexualize pregenital urges and inner-genital sensations that cannot be fused with phallic representations. In this he is greatly aided by the achievement of satisfactory and dependable, well-timed masturbation techniques. His discharge form is still phallic, and he attains only inadequate control over his erections and ejaculations. Nevertheless he is prepared to face the "wildness" of genital urges and the frequency with which masturbatory impulses will overcome him when the sudden steep increase of androgens will bring on puberty.

The outcome of prepuberty integration differs from the results of the early inner-genital phase of integration. Whereas the little boy turns away from his inside genital, the adolescent boy acknowledges the continuity of inside and outside sensations in the orgastic experience. He enters puberty with a successful externalization upon the phallus, but the early denial of the testicles has been succeeded by a subordination of these organs, as well as those hidden inside his body, to the supremacy of the phallus. The four-year-old phallic child is all body-phallus, the adolescent boy brings into puberty an integrated functional structure of his puberty phallic-genital organization. He embarks now upon a prolonged period of further growth and differentiation in which his neophallic genitality transforms into a constant genital-heterosexual organization.

Conclusions

Prepuberty is a phase of preparation for the more definitive changes in puberty that initiate the reproductive period of adult life. The hormonal and psychic changes that occur in transition from pregenitality to phallicity in childhood and in transition from latency to puberty in adolescence create an imbalance in the psychosomatic organization. The ensuing regularization of the newly acquired hormonal mechanisms can be correlated with the integration of psychic forces that follows the disequilibrium in the prephallic phase and the diffusion in prepuberty. These phases of integration prepare the growing child as transitions from infantile to childhood sexuality, and from childhood to postpubescent genitality. In the early integration phase, children seem to cope with unclear genital tensions by externalization. Both sexes deny the existence of inner-genital organs when they enter the phallic phase. In prepuberty the problems of the early inner-genital phase are revived and reinforced by the impact of sensations stemming from the maturing sex organs on the inside and the outside of the body. Prepuberty reorganization of childhood sexuality elaborates on mechanisms initiated in the inner-genital phase. The advent of menstruation or ejaculation counteracts the denial of inside genitalia and their repetition gives direction to sex-specific reorientation.

The frequent changes in feminine development prepare the girl for the cyclicity of her adulthood which she begins to experience in prepuberty. The question arises whether cyclic fluctuations in estrogen production may not occur in earlier phases, especially at the age of three when mature follicles seem to develop with greater frequency. It is assumed that follicles which become atretic contribute to estrogen production in adult women. Since not only adrenal but also ovarian estrogen is already operative in childhood, there is a likelihood that an irregular rise and fall in estrogen levels occurs as follicles ripen and become atretic. That follicles do not develop further is generally assigned to an inhibitory factor which prevents the secretion or activation of gonadotropins in sufficient amounts to allow for the completion of ovulation. Prepuberty represents an intermediary stage in which rhythmic estrogen cyclicity becomes established before the maturation of the full reciprocal pituitary-ovarian feedback mechanism that is necessary for corpus luteum formation. The existence of irregular cyclic alterations of steroid levels in childhood is open to question. There seems to be no doubt that the transition from an immature form of hormonal interaction to the adult estrogen and progesterone cycles occurs in prepuberty, and culminates with the advent of ovulation in puberty (see Chapter 15).

In contrast to feminine development, males develop in a more uniform pattern. There is little change in male gonads until an increase of gonadotropins in prepuberty initiates a significant rise in testosterone production and spermatogenesis. The growth of male sex characteristics depends on the presence of active androgens. Animal experiments suggest that estrogen has a markedly trophic effect on muscular tissues of the entire male genital system and some slight effect on glandular secretion in the prostate (Thorborg, 1948). The question arises whether estrogen plays a similar role in human development, especially in the phases called here inner-genital, at the age of three and in prepuberty. Undoubtedly, testosterones and their metabolic precursors, epiandrosterones, gain significance in male development at the onset of prepuberty, while estrogen production lags behind (Hudson et al., 1964; Paulsen, E. P., 1966). But not until the advent of puberty do testosterones, in interaction with gonadotropins, reach high levels, and only then can fertilization take place. It is probably then that the adult mechanism of testosterone production—from progesterone—begins to operate (see Chapter 15). Whether the full reciprocal pituitary-testicular regulation in the male is "tonic" rather than cyclic (Gorski and Wagner, 1965) or whether there is a special type of periodicity characteristic of the male (Southren et al., 1965) cannot be established at this stage of hormonal research.

The increase in gonadotropins and in sex-specific hormones at the onset of prepuberty precedes or coincides with the state of psychic imbalance, referred to as prepuberty diffusion. The ensuing integration of precursors of adult hormone metabolization with the incipient adult mechanisms parallels the integration of pregenital, inner-genital, and phallic drive components with puberty genitality.

In transition from childhood to puberty, the originally small difference between sex-specific and opposite sex hormones increases significantly, and from then on estrogens in the male and testosterones in the female are produced in quantities comparable to their childhood levels. These findings are in keeping with psychoanalytic formulations about the differences between childhood and adult sexuality. Childhood sexuality is bisexual in nature; overt homosexual episodes in childhood are part of normal development. These trends become regressively exaggerated in prepuberty, in transition to the heterosexual orientation of puberty genitality. In adulthood, psychologically based deviations from adult heterosexuality and from adult sex-specific organization are due to persistence, or regressive revival, of immature strivings, organized in a manner reminiscent of the transitory organizations in the early inner-genital phase and in prepuberty.

NOTES

[1]The error pertains to a confusion between *ihn* meaning "him" and *in*. The latter reference brings about an increased need to externalize and spread her excitement. In the flood of ideas the child confuses the female teacher, her error, and her girl friend, and comes forth with a rapid change of wished-for identities, ending in ungrammatical sentences.

[2]See Anna Freud's (1965) lucid remarks on the little girl's "horse craze."

[3]In the following account of Cecil's description of her menarche, the direct quotes within the synopsis are identified by quotation marks and interpretations are set off in brackets. All italics are mine.

CHAPTER 15

Phases of Adolescence with Suggestions for a Correlation of Psychic and Hormonal Organizations

III: Puberty Growth, Differentiation, and Consolidation

Chapter 13 dealt with childhood antecedents of psychic and hormonal organizations in adolescence. In Chapter 14, prepuberty was presented as a phase of transition from childhood to the onset of reproductive functioning in puberty. In this chapter the psychic organization of three subphases initiated by puberty and preceding adulthood (growth, differentiation and consolidation) will be discussed against the background of earlier and concomitant anatomic and neurohormonal changes.

Introduction

There is considerable disagreement in the literature about the onset of puberty. Some authors regard the appearance of secondary sex characteristics as manifestations of early puberty, others look upon menarche or first emissions as the boundary lines between childhood and adolescence (see Chapter 13). Male puberty has been defined as the time of the second stage of pubic hair development (Table 3, Chapter 13) which terminates pubescence and initiates postpubescence (Schonfeld, 1943). In

---

First published in *J. Amer. Acad. Child Psa.*, 7:108–48 (1968). Slightly revised and reproduced by permission.

377

trying to correlate changes in psychic organization with their anatomic and hormonal counterparts, I found most useful the views of Selye (1950) and Talbot *et al.* (1952) who regard puberty as the time when fertilization becomes possible (Chapter 13).

It is not easy to establish the onset of fertility in adolescence. The connection of painful menses with ovulatory cycles cannot be used as a criterion because many girls experience pain during menarche, at a time when progesterone does not yet affect uterine motility. A more reliable index is an increased flow of menstrual blood and the shedding of considerable amounts of endometrial tissue. It is likely that the onset of male fertility coincides with an increase in the volume of and a change in the consistency of seminal fluid and with considerable intensification of ejaculatory spasms. At puberty, neither ovulatory cycles nor the production of large amounts of mature sperm cells are permanently established, and even in adulthood their occurrence depends to a great extent on psychological factors.

The onset of fertility in adolescence is contingent on a convergence of maturation and psychological readiness. It occurs at the conclusion of prepuberty reorganization which prepares the ground for the growth, differentiation, and consolidation of adult mechanisms. At the end of prepuberty, girls become accustomed to regular cyclic changes and boys overcome the difficulties presented by early ejaculations. Both sexes establish preferences for certain fantasies and for overt or concealed masturbatory habits. Both sexes look forward to the progressive increase in sex-specific characteristics. In prepuberty, irregular spurts of feelings tend to dissipate quickly; in puberty, they rise to a high intensity. In prepuberty, body boundaries become diffuse and the body image distorted; in puberty, body boundaries expand and the body image grows out of proportion to actual physical changes. In the early phase of puberty, everything seems exaggerated. Sensations soar, perceptions attain a high degree of acuity; and impulses, emotions, and ideas assume an unprecedented intensity (Freud, A., 1958; Jacobson, 1961). These phenomena seem to coincide with the onset of fertility in adolescence. In prepuberty, problems of the pre-phallic, early inner-genital phase are revived, intensified, and resolved on a higher level (Chapter 14). Developmental phases, initiated by puberty changes, repeat and restructure phallic-oedipal and latency organizations.

The period of growth, initiated by puberty, bears a striking resemblance to that of the four-year-old: "high drive combined with a fluid mental organization" (Gesell, 1940), or "an age of going out of bounds in all fields physical, language, personal-social" (Gesell and Ilg, 1943). Because of the growth of body and intellect, of needs, drives, fears, and defenses during this early phase of puberty, adolescents at that time have a global approach to problem solving. The ensuing phase of progressive differentiation can be aptly characterized by Gesell's (1940) description of the five-year-old: "his personal social relations, his concept of himself, his adjustment to home, school and community are better defined." The revival of the oedipus complex in puberty is followed by a process of detachment from parental objects during which drives, emotions, adaptive attitudes, and defensive constellations become increasingly differentiated. A newly acquired sense of values and a new morality usher in a preadult phase of adolescence which is similar in organization to latency. This is the time when defenses and sublimations become consolidated and adult character traits are established.

The changing trends in the organization of developmental phases are reflected in all aspects of development, in childhood and adolescence. Because of the paucity of data on the role of neurohormonal changes in childhood, one can only speculate about the nature of their interrelationship with concomitant psychic changes (Chapter 13). The interdependence of neurohormonal and psychic advances in adolescence is generally recognized, but not yet sufficiently explored. Nevertheless one can detect a common denominator in the processes that lead to the restructuring of psychic and neurohormonal mechanisms on the road to adulthood.

Review and Discussion of the Influence of Neurohormonal Maturation on Development

Successive stages of maturation of the nervous system are responsible for the activation of hormonal chain reactions, which in turn serve as feedback mechanisms for brain development. Postnatal growth differentiation and integration are influenced by the growth hormone of the anterior pituitary, by the thyroid hormones, by androgens, and estrogens, both derived from the adrenal and the testis or ovary. Thyrotropin, adrenocorticotropins, and gonadotropins, released by the pituitary, manifest their major effects at different periods of life and in different ways (Talbot et al., 1952; Wilkins, 1965). The complex interrelation between psyche and soma employs direct and indirect channels of communication, through which neurohormonal and psychic organizations mutually influence one another.

So little is known about the role of hormones in the development of psychic structure that an attempt of correlation such as this must be taken only as a suggested approach to the problem rather than a definite proposition. It is not possible to qualify each statement about data from

379

hormonal literature and the manner in which behavior may be influenced by progressive steps in neurohormonal maturation. But the uncertainties and questions involved must be borne in mind throughout. While details of correlation have a certain heuristic value, they are used here only to illustrate the postulated common trends in the organization of neurohormonal and psychic stages of development. These do not necessarily coincide with phases of growth and differentiation of single organs or systems, nor can one detect a simple one-to-one, temporal or quantitative, relation between somatic and psychic changes (Freud, 1905a).

Wilkins (1965) compares the maturational changes in the central nervous system which trigger sex-specific development in adolescence to those "responsible during infancy for motor performance, speech development and sphincter control." The possibility of a more definite parallelism in the progression of psychic and hormonal development in childhood and adolesence suggests various avenues for inquiry. In many ways childhood phases appear to be small-scale models for what is to come in adolescence. If there is indeed an influx of estrogens and androgens at the onset of the genital activity at the age of three, if there is indeed a dramatic rise in androgens at the beginning of the phallic phase (Dorfman, 1948),[1] and if a widening discrepancy between estrogen and 17-ketosteroid excretion does mark the onset of latency—then childhood development in both sexes proceeds on a scale more like that of male than female adolescence (Tables 1–2, Chapter 13), as suggested by Freud (1917b, 1925, 1931, 1932–1936). But there may be subtler changes in childhood which anticipate the cycles that will become pronounced in female adolescence and, in both sexes, prepare for the significant contribution of internal genital organs to psychosexual and reproductive functioning (Chapters 13, 14).

The way various hormones—in small and large quantities; through steady or cyclic secretion; through particular forms of metabolization; through agonistic, antagonistic, and reciprocal interaction—promote growth, differentiation, integration, and consolidation in development depends to a large degree on the maturational stages of the anterior pituitary. This central gland mediates between soma and psyche, and between the central nervous system and almost every organ of the body. Hypothalamic regulations control pituitary activity and thus affect indirectly total body economy.[2] The rate of growth of a structure or activity of a gland is proportional to the nature and intensity of pituitary stimulation. Peripheral glands emit messages which in turn affect the nature and level of pituitary functioning. The adrenal and the gonads have to attain a level of maturity before they can play a role in the regulation of pituitary output.

It is likely that a maturation of hypothalamic-pituitary pathways at the age of two and a half or three results in the activation of the adrenal, which is the principal supplier of androgens and estrogens in childhood. Through them the adrenal may exert an influence on brain activity and on the organization of childhood sexuality (Chapters 13, 14). Once established, the feedback mechanism between adrenal hormones (excreted in the urine as 17-ketosteroids and 11-17-OCS) and adrenocorticotropins (ACTH), secreted by the pituitary, affords the organism a protection against the stresses of too rapid a growth. The psychic disequilibrium that can be observed at the age of two and a half or three may be an expression of a general state of imbalance, created by irregular oscillations between progression and regression. This occurs before a stability of the newly acquired mechanisms can be established. The integration of pregenital, inner- and outer-genital drives,[3] which, I believe, precedes phallic growth, may influence and be influenced by the progressive integration of hypothalamic-pituitary, adrenal and incipient gonadal activities. It seems likely that the growth and differentiation of psychic structure in the phallic phase and the subsequent consolidation of drive-derivative functioning in latency are interrelated with an increase in androgen production, a differentiation of adrenal and gonadal functions, and a consolidation of interactions between androgenic and estrogenic steroids. These maturational advances prepare the ground for the orderly development of reproductive functions in adolescence. A central inhibition prevents the secretion of high amounts of gonadotropins in childhood.[4] A multiplicity of safeguards against a premature development of reproductive organs is suggested by the discovery of a substance in the urine of children which counteracts the effect of gonadotropins (Landau et al., 1960).

It is not known what initiates the sudden increase in the production of gonadotropins at the beginning of adolescence. A maturation of the central nervous system may effect a release of inhibition and an activation of the pituitary through hypothalamic stimulation (Talbot et al., 1952). Genetic, nutritional, climatic factors and the general maturation of body tissues under the influence of growth hormones, all play a role in the complex mechanisms that transform steroid metabolization in prepuberty (Selye, 1950; Wilkins, 1965). The multiplicity of changes, such as the increase in adrenal androgen production, the growth of Graafian follicles or tubules under the influence of the follicle-stimulating hormone (FSH) of the pituitary, and the increase of estrogens in girls and of testosterone in boys (Tables 1 and 2) create an imbalance of a much greater order than the one described at the age of two and a half or three. It may be more comparable in magnitude to the genital crisis of the newborn

(Chapter 13). But the mode of progression in prepuberty seems to be modeled after the childhood sequence of disequilibrium, followed by integration of old and new mechanisms that lay the foundation for the growth, differentiation, and consolidation of maturational gains.

The growth of primary and accessory reproductive organs, a sharp rise of urinary excretion of epiandrosterone (a metabolic precursor of testosterone) and of testosterone concentrations in the plasma of boys (Paulsen, E. P., 1966; Hudson et al., 1964), and a cyclic high rise of estrogen production in girls (Table 2, Chapter 13) (Nathanson et al., 1941), all occur before external manifestations of sexual maturation become apparent. This developmental sequence may well be the basis for the psychic manifestations of prepuberty which led me to designate it as an inner-genital phase. However, anatomical and hormonal changes do not effect a breakdown of latency organization until the barrier to cognitive perception of inner-genital sensations is considerably weakened.

The unexplored maturational changes responsible for the release of inhibition in prepuberty may turn out to be the common matrix of the abrupt increase in gonadotropin production and of the disintegration of defense mechanisms that bring on the syndrome of "prepuberty diffusion." In the process of reintegration, children of both sexes have to contend with disquieting, cryptic inner-genital activity which culminates in first emissions or menstruations. These cause internal upheavals, but also act as organizers in the structuring of psychic forces in preparation for the expansive growth that follows the onset of puberty.

Anovulatory cycles and aspermatic emissions are external manifestations of advances in the hormonal reorganization that occurs in prepuberty. The follicle-stimulating hormone (FSH) of the pituitary promotes the growth of Graafian follicles or testicular tubules. Estrogens, secreted by the follicles, act as inhibitors of FSH production. The resulting decrease of FSH levels effects a lowering in estrogen production, which increases again under the influence of rising FSH. This type of cyclicity becomes increasingly entrenched in prepuberty. When the luteinizing hormone of the pituitary (LH) reaches effective levels, ovulation can be completed and the growing corpus luteum secretes progesterone and estrogen as well (Greenblatt, 1967; Talbot et al., 1952). This constitutes the beginning of the adult form of reciprocal interaction between the pituitary and the ovaries, a complex mechanism which grows in scope, becomes differentiated and consolidated before mature feminine cyclicity is established in adulthood (Table 4-b). A similar feedback mechanism between the pituitary and the testicles develops in the male. How it operates to assure the relative steadiness of high testosterone and low estrogen levels in adult functioning is not yet clear. But there is enough evidence for the assumption that the advent of puberty in both sexes depends on the successful initiation of the full pituitary-gonadal interaction, that is, when the influence of the follicle-stimulating hormone becomes supplemented by the reciprocal regulation between the luteinizing hormone and gonadal hormones. No doubt, the onset of significant progesterone production is a landmark of female puberty. New data about hormone metabolization indicate that progesterone plays a parallel, though different, role in the adult mechanism that becomes operative in male puberty (Dorfman, 1963).

The suggestion has been made that phases of adolescent growth, differentiation and consolidation of psychic functions can be correlated with parallel phases of advancement in the adult mode of hormone regulation, initiated by puberty. This general propostion is of necessity oversimplified, as are all previous suggestions about correlations between psychic and hormonal organizations. To highlight the complexity of hormonal interaction, it may be necessary briefly to review the general and localized actions of the hormones under discussion (Diczfalusy, 1961; Selye, 1950; Talbot et al., 1952; Wilkins, 1965). It must be understood, however, that this review cannot do justice to the intricacies of interaction between various steroids found in tissues, plasma, and urine (see Tables 4a-c).[5]

C19 + steroids, including testosterone, are obligatory metabolic precursors of *estrogen* (Duboff et al, 1964). The male adult produces steady amounts of estrogen in levels not too much higher than those of children. Estrogenic activity is antagonistic to that of testosterone. It is probable that the feedback mechanism between FSH and testosterone is mediated via estrogens as antispermatogenic agents (Talbot et al., 1952). High doses of testosterone inhibit FSH production, which results in an inhibition of spermatogenesis. Through its interaction with FSH in the female, estrogen limits its own level of production and thus regulates the extent to which proliferation of the endometrium can proceed. It acts as a primer for progesterone, which, in normal doses, has no effect on uterine activity without previous sensitization by estrogen. In sufficient quantities estrogens specifically stimulate the growth of female sex characteristics (Table 1, Chapter 13) and influence glandular and muscular development in the reproductive system not only in females but possibly also in males* (Thorborg, 1948). They cause changes in the vagina and uterus and are responsible not only for the mitosis and proliferation of the endometrium (Tables 4a, b), but also for the proliferation in buccal and gingival membranes. They effect peripheral vascular reactions similar to those in the uterus and are responsible for the engorgement and increased permeability of blood vessels not only in the genitalia but also

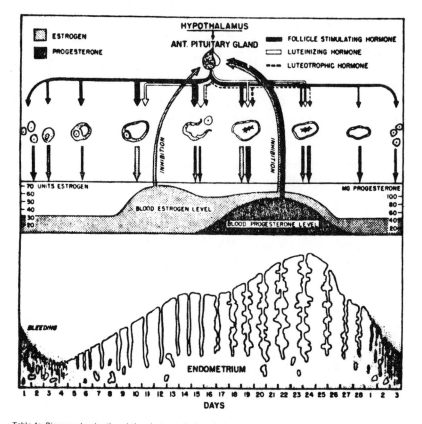

Table 4a. *Diagram showing the relations between the hypothalamus, the anterior pituitary, ovaries, and endometrium in mature female cycle,* reproduced from Talbot et al. (1952), by permission. Legend accompanying the diagram abbreviated and modified.

The growth and regression of the endometrium are indicated by differences in height. Note the change from tubular to saccular structure under the influence of progesterone. The progesterone levels were calculated from the pregnanediol content of urine. Different values are obtained by assays from peripheral plasma and ovarian veins.

A rapid rise, followed by a rapid fall, of progesterone levels in peripheral plasma occurs shortly after ovulation. The mean value of plasma progesterone through the 16th-25th day of the cycle is far below the level of this hormone in the ovarian vein blood (Runnenbaum et al., 1965). There is a cyclic variation in the quantity of different androgens (Hudson et al., 1964; Duboff et al., 1964), but plasma and ovarian testosterone levels are steady throughout the cycle. Urinary excretion of these steroids does not follow the same pattern (Tables 3b,c).

in other parts of the body, e.g., the nose (see footnote 7). They cause the skin to thicken and prompt the partial involution of sebaceous glands. Through their effect on the pituitary they inhibit bone growth, stimulate the release of adrenocorticotropins, inhibit the release of lactogenic hormones, and instigate ductal and lobubalveolar development in the breasts. Estrogens induce a slight retention of water and certain

384

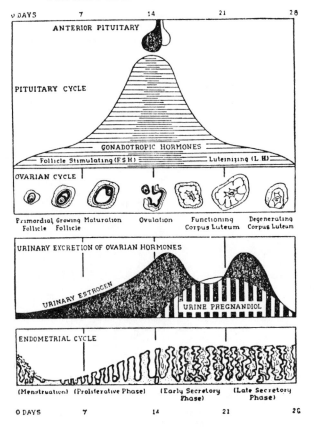

Table 4b. *Urinary Excretion of Ovarian Homones during the Menstrual Cycle.* Modified from Paschkis *et al.* (1954). Reproduced from Wilkins (1965, p. 200), by permission.

electrolytes. They help to liberate aminoproteins. Their actions are in some respects vagotonic and thus antagonistic to testosterone and progesterone. It is likely that some estrogenic compounds have an influence on brain maturation and may lower central excitation and thresholds* (see Chapter 13).

Progesterone promotes the retention of water and electrolytes, except potassium. By reducing the rate of estrogen degradation and inhibiting the release of the luteotropic hormone from the pituitary, progesterone acts as a regulator for a variety of functions. It is an immediate precursor of testosterone. In contrast to the route from epiandrosterone to testosterone which begins to be operative before prepuberty, the adult mechanism of testosterone metabolization from progesterone is probably initiated in

385

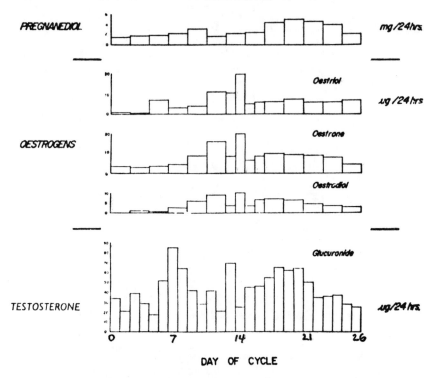

Table 4c. *Urinary Excretion of Pregnanediol, Estrogens, and Testosterone during the Menstrual Cycle.* Reproduced in part from Hudson *et al.* (1964), by permission.

Note the complex interrelationship between pregnandiol, estrogen, and testosterone levels of excretion. In addition, varying amounts of FSH and LH and of substances inhibiting their effectiveness are found in the urine during different phases of the cycle (Soffer and Fogel, 1964).

puberty. The principal local target of progesterone is the uterus in its function of nesting and nourishing the fertilized ovum. But progesterone can also act synergistically with androsterone or testosterone to stimulate prostatic activity* (Selye, 1950). Administration of progesterone relieves premenstrual tensions and may have a therapeutic effect on postpartum psychoses (Greenblatt, 1967).

The difference between estrogen and progesterone action is well illustrated in their effects on uterine motility in animals. Without estrogen the uterus has only a minimal isometric tension, shows no spontaneous motility, and hardly reacts to electric or oxytocin stimulation. Under the influence of estrogen the uterus muscles react to small stimuli with maximal tension and their spontaneous motility consists of small, frequent

386

contractions retaining a uniform level. In contrast, progesterone produces at first a reduced tension and only later a maximal one.

The influence of adrenal *androgens* on the growth of sexual hair in both sexes and of testicular androgens on the growth of these and other male characteristics is well established. Testosterone also promotes the growth of the clitoris. It seems to have a more specific effect on seminal vesicles than on the prostate.* It is largely responsible for changes in the laryngeal structure and skin texture and for adolescent acne. Testosterone stimulates substantial increase in musculature and skeletal growth, but its effect on growth is self-limiting. In contrast to the growth hormone of the pituitary, it accelerates ossification and closure of epiphyseal cartilages. Through its direct and indirect effect on pituitary output, it influences adrenal functions and regulates sperm production. It seems to contribute in some ways to brain development and it significantly lowers thresholds.* It stimulates appetitive sexual behavior in both sexes.

A great many metabolites are found in the urine and plasma of both sexes. Some of the metabolites may be inactive by-products of steroid conversion, others have specific effects on growth of organs and body economy. More refined methods of assaying hormones reveal new data which contradict earlier, and sometimes even contemporary findings. Recent investigations suggest that there is a diurnal variation in male testosterone levels which is related to cycles of rest and activity (Southren *et al.,* 1965). Pregnanediol has been found in the urine of women during the entire menstrual cycle (Table 4c). Plasma testosterone remains steady in women, but urinary excretion of testosterone undergoes cyclic changes (Tables 4a,c). The latter may be only a reflection of increased estrogen metabolization rather than an indicator of testosterone activity. "The type of quantities of steroids formed by the ovary at various times of the menstrual cycle may regulate activation or inhibition of enzyme systems. They may conceivably change cellular permeability to electrolytes, water, or nutrients, and thus may control development and growth" (Duboff *et al.,* 1964). One or more enzymes are involved in the conversion of pregenonolone to androgens and from these steroids to estrogen. Similar conditions prevail in the conversion of progesterone compounds to testosterone in the male.

The specific role of progesterone fluctuations during mature cycles (Tables 4b, c) over and beyond its influence on nidation, is unknown. Neither is it clear what role it plays in the waxing and waning of sexual tension of the male. Much remains to be learned about the general effect of progesterone on the growth and differentiation of psychic functions in adolescence. Changes in the hypothalamic regulation of sex-specific progesterone metabolism seem to occur not only in female but also in male puberty. These changes must have have a foundation not only in genetic information but also in processes occurring in earlier critical developmental periods during which the hypothalamus has become irreversibly male or female* (Gorski and Wagner, 1965). The contribution of small quantities of opposite sex hormones, which stabilize in adolescence, is as little understood as is their role in the early development of both sexes. They may play an important role in reestablishing psychic equilibrium. It is possible that they regulate the levels of sex-specific hormones and counteract their excessive influence upon behavior. Such a mechanism may promote the secondary autonomy necessary for the consolidation of integration and differentiation of psychic functions, in latency and in the preadult phase of adolescence.

Puberty Growth

The upsurge of vitality and the expansive growth of the phallic child may coincide with small increases in the rate of urinary androgen excretion and of testosterone levels in the plasma (Hudson *et al.*, 1964). No rise in estrogen production has been reported for that time (Table 1, Chapter 13). In childhood, phallic excitement may depend on a rise of adrenal androgens and only in a small measure on testicular or ovarian androgens. Growing out of bounds in puberty coincides with an increase in progesterone, cyclic in the female and steady in the male, an end product of metabolization in the female and an intermediary step in testosterone formation in the male.

The onset of this adult mechanism in hormone metabolization in puberty constitutes an initial step on the road to adulthood. The first appearance of mature germ cells does not put an end to growth. But in contrast to prepuberty growth, during which limbs and trunk grow disproportionately, in puberty there is a continuous trend toward the attainment of adult proportions. The female uterus, ovaries, and vagina do not reach adult size until eighteen or twenty (Nelson, 1959) and the same is true of total body height (Kinsey *et al.*, 1953). In boys, the growth of principal and accessory sex characteristics and the increase in height continue for a few more years.

The boy between fifteen and seventeen or eighteen sees his penis and testicles grow in volume and length and his scrotum become looser and more pigmented. His erections are more frequent and last longer. His increasing capacity to ejaculate large amounts and in rapid succession fills him with pride and awe. His voice deepens persistently and his Adam's apple protrudes more and more. His shoulders broaden and his pectoral muscles bulge. His pubic hair spreads laterally and begins to form a line toward his umbilicus, his body and facial hair oegin to grow, and his scalp hair spreads along his ears. He may assist nature by shaving more often than necessary, by cultivating fashionable sideburns or a beard, or by letting his hair grow very long to indicate his "manliness." Bothered by his acne, he looks forward to the increasing coarsening of his skin and regular shaves, but he is less enthused by the growth of circumanal and scrotal hair.

The girl's breasts increase in volume and she experiences frequent nipple erections, which she may want to exhibit or conceal under a loose sweater. Her voice deepens gradually; she may change from a soprano to a contralto. She too suffers from acne and her skin becomes oily and may lose its infantile smoothness. In the contemporary American culture, she has been using cosmetics for some time and may now go to extreme lengths in "making up" or remaining natural. She worries about perspiration and uses deodorants, especially during menstrual periods. As her axillary hair grows and becomes curly and coarse and as down begins to appear on her legs, she may resort to shaving regularly. She becomes preoccupied with her weight, height, and figure and her changing "dress" size.

The four-year-old was in a "growthsome" stage (Gesell, 1940); the adolescent in prepuberty reacted to his irregular growth with diffusion; in puberty, he exaggerates his growth in an organized way. Drives increase in strength and the ego expands. Defenses are strengthened and apparatuses of adaptability mature. The intellect advances by leaps and bounds. Creativity blossoms and affects intensify and deepen. Symptoms crystallize and character traits become more marked (Eissler, 1958; Geleerd, 1961; Spiegel, 1961b).

In prepuberty, affects rose irregularly, were dissipated by spreading, and became shallow and inappropriate. Now feelings and affective states may appear enormously magnified, because they are fraught with meaning derived from an almost hyperpathic acuteness of sensations and perceptions. Whereas in prepuberty adolescents felt all alike, in puberty the impact of their soaring sensations makes them feel unique.

Fourteen- to sixteen-year-old girls and fifteen- to seventeen-year-old boys love and hate intensely. They devote themselves to causes and solve problems in sweeping gestures. They defend their individuality with fervor. Their beliefs become convictions as they think in absolutes and lack the capacity for modulation. To underscore their differences from their parents they identify with outgroups, but their need for solitary individuality stands in opposition to group discipline.

The change from sameness with the group to being very special and unlike the others may produce feelings of depersonalization ("Who am I") (Spiegel, 1961a). The transient loss of identity may be followed by a state of narcissistic introspection (Jacobson, 1961) in which exhibitionistic and voyeuristic tendencies are realized in mirror-gazing and in intense observations of one's own thought processes. The need to look and be looked at encompasses friends and strangers, parents and teachers, and may lead to transient ideas of reference. Unsolicited attention embarrasses the teenagers and makes them blush. They feel "discovered." Adults must not understand them until they are ready to reveal themselves. Sudden illuminations that bring about feelings of exuberance, awe, nostalgia or mortification sometimes have the character of recovery of long-forgotten memories. Sharing such experiences with a parent can lead to new insights which can put unresolved conflicts of the past into a new perspective.

The renewal of mutual trust in heart-to-heart talks between parents and adolescents is a periodic phenomenon in girls as well as in boys. To their parents' chagrin the youngsters go back to their solitary daydreams that cannot be shared with others until they bring about creative productivity. Teachers show little respect for their reveries and demand immediate performance in the classroom. Parents invade the privacy of their rooms and disturb the continuity of thought processes by insisting that they perform household chores or come for dinner on time. The lack of conformity in early adolescence is largely due to the discrepancy between the inner and outer time schedule. Masturbatory impulses and practices and thinly disguised positive and negative oedipal fantasies can be more easily correlated with activities of peers than with school and family routine.

The exaggeration of individuality colors the puberty oedipus complex. Daydreams are more personalized and less practical than they were in prepuberty. At the same time they gain in significance not only because of the depth of feeling involved but also because they deal with events realizable in the not too distant future. A girl may spend a great deal of time elaborating on what seems to her a uniquely romantic way to meet a boy. With a typical phallic directness a boy may fantasy sexual intimacies bestowed on him and him alone. But there are also dreams of a more distant future. The girl thinks of love, marriage, and children; the boy of exciting adventures such as joining the navy and getting to know half-naked exotic girls. Boys, more frequently than girls, dream of fame and heroism. In girls, such dreams are often connected with being admired by an audience as an actress, or rescuing ill-treated children as teacher, social worker or nurse. The boy's heroic deeds are concerned

390

with rescuing women, saving his country, conquering enemies, and courageously performing great deeds against tremendous odds.

Boys, more than girls, use sports as outlets in which they learn to channel instinctual discharge. But the intimate contact in bathrooms and locker rooms stimulates homosexual urges to which a boy may react with a defensive emphasis on heterosexual fantasies. The increased castration fear leads to preoccupation with the genitals, which in turn evokes masturbatory impulses. In an effort to combat temptation, a boy may settle down to do his homework "in peace," but the slightest noise or interruption weakens his self-control. The nature of his excitation-discharge processes is such that sexual excitement strikes like lightning and a frantic form of masturbation quickly brings about ejaculation and relief. A technique, already automatized in prepuberty, is readily available. But the frequency and intensity of the need for immediate discharge are new. Prepuberty genital practices were linked to mechanical stimulation in showers, bathrooms, and the bed. Now arousal occurs in response to all kinds of stimuli, and masturbation rituals acquired in prepuberty can clash with the strong desire to "come" as quickly as possible. Ritual lubrications of the penis and planning for the disposal of the ejaculate, preparatory to masturbation, become obstacles to immediate gratification. A mother's voice both interrupts and adds to the excitement. Painful physical sensations during delays of discharge evoke hypochondriacal fears of illness. The awareness that the whole body and "brain" have become involved in the genital excitement aggrandizes castration anxiety, frequently expressed as fear of insanity or fear of death. Masturbation fantasies become the more important, the more they can direct the boy's attention away from the acceleration of his heartbeat and respiration rate, away from feeling hot all over and from the disquieting internal contractions and "shrinking" of his scrotum. Even though he does not know that he has reached puberty, he does recognize the newness of the all-encompassing quality of his excitement and its relation to forbidden wishes, whose fulfillment is imagined during orgasm. But orgasm may bring about letdown instead of release, especially if fantasies are mistimed in relation to the brief excitation and discharge cycle. The ensuing lassitude is interpreted as a depletion of vital energy. Genital secretions evoke disgust when postorgastic passivity promotes regressive dependence on the mother. Defensively, thoughts turn to girls. In fortuitous circumstances, sex play with girls can teach the boy to delay immediate discharge and to vary levels of sexual excitement between foreplay and end play. This is greatly facilitated by his easy projection of castration fears upon the girl. But he becomes anxious in the face of the girl's continuing excitement after he has attained orgastic release. He may abandon her suddenly and seek out male companions. Under conditions of decreased sexual tension he can practice subtler changes in levels of sexualization and intellectualization with members of his own sex.

From prepuberty, the girl adjusted her masturbatory techniques to the spreading quality of her genital excitement. In direct masturbation she tried to unify sensations from the clitoris, the labia, and the vagina, and to centralize them on the now accepted introitus. The erotization of the introitus and the distal portion of the vagina focused her attention on their division by the hymen. She became fearful of injuring it, especially when her efforts to penetrate herself were accompanied by masochistic fantasies. When she begins to experience ovulatory cycles, she becomes aware of the new distinctness of uterine contractions and of the chunks of tissue discharged in her menstrual blood. She associates these changes with the anticipated pains of defloration, penetration, and delivery. In identification with the aggressor who represents the father, his large penis and the baby, she may attack her genital with ferocity and really injure herself. Fear of being torn to pieces, not unlike those discharged in the menstrual flow, prompts her to give up direct masturbation. Indirect masturbatory techniques, in which she defensively tenses her thighs and maintains tonic contractions of pelvic muscles and sphincters, are already familiar to her from earlier developmental phases. Organized more clearly in prepuberty, they serve not only defense but also stimulation and prolonged tonic discharge. The maintenance of some degree of genital excitation is as important to the girl as awareness of the phallus is to the boy. It counteracts fears that all of her inside has fallen out. It promotes the development of organ constancy that is necessary to incorporate the inner genital into the feminine body image. But the girl's excitement may occasionally mount high enough to produce a series of "spontaneous orgasms." The state of "nothingness" that follows such a sexual discharge increases her need to be revived by stimulation from outside sources. Stimulus-hungry, she becomes seductive to both parents and friends. She wants to regain the feeling of organ constancy through the maintenance of some degree of genital excitation. When faced with overstimulation by a disproportionate response to her advances, she makes attempts to delay discharge in herself and others. Labeled a flirt or a tease, she feels rejected and finds solace in endless solitary fantasies of unrequited love that maintains sexual excitement on a foreplay level. Because of the defensive masturbatory inhibition of discharge, she both hampers and sexualizes the flow of motility and thought. Consequently her physical and intellectual progress becomes relatively retarded. The ratio of sexualization and intellectualization of her ego functions varies with the state of her cycles, and with the source and degree of external stimulation. Her performance may veer from one extreme to another. To maintain her self-esteem, she may compensate for her lack of achievement by easy success with boys. But the speed and freedom with which a boy gets rid of his sexual tension and regains his phallic independence make her feel rejected and envious. She turns to her girl friends and sometimes to her mother to whom she passes on the excess of her excitement, frustration, and envy.

The unsteadiness of heterosexual relations between girls and boys in early puberty triggers off bouts of excitement and depression. When parents actively lend a helping hand they may unwittingly interfere with the spontaneous cures of adolescent distress. The adolescent in puberty does not quite shun his parents as he did in prepuberty, but he approaches them on his own terms and in his own good time. He needs time in which he can redirect his sexual feelings and fantasies from the parental to substitute objects. Even though physical intimacy with parents of either sex becomes repulsive to adolescents, they become very curious about their parents' sex life and make direct or indirect inquiries about it. When parents respond with too many revelations, they contribute to a breakthrough of incestuous wishes which can evoke panic. It invariably leads to acting out in a manner which calls for severe punishment. But even without parental seduction, masturbation conflicts intensify sporadic needs for punishment. When provocative behavior is designed to test the parent-castrator, parents begin to feel with desperation: "I could kill him (or her)"; "I wish he (or she) was gone already." The wish for separation becomes mutual. It is strengthened by a revival of intimacy between the parents who seek each other to avoid the incestuous wishes toward their children. By the same token, the children, beset by forbidden heterosexual and homosexual wishes toward their parents, turn to age-adequate substitutes to discharge their sexual tensions and guilt feelings as well as pent-up aggression.

Overt masturbation conflicts are more typical for puberty boys than girls. Sadistic and masochistic interpretations of sex prevail. The boy thinks of raping, the girl of being raped. Yet analysis of such outspoken attitudes reveals that the dreamer identifies with both partners in the violent sexual act. Sex play among adolescents helps them to divert their oedipal feelings to real objects. They gain a sense of reality when they contrast experience with fantasies. They do tend to torture each other in innumerable ways, but not to the extent of their fantasies. Guilt is often projected upon the partner in sex play and quarrels occur after the most sublime moment of bliss. The boy tries to prove his masculinity by recounting his conquests to other boys. The girl feels betrayed and un-

393

loved, although she herself may have discussed her intimacy with a girl friend. The homosexual feelings which play a role here are latent rather than overt. Boys engage in transient homosexual episodes more often because their sexual urges tolerate little delay. Girls sublimate a great deal of sexual drive into ideation about romantic love which makes it easier for them to hope and wait for fulfillment. Being in love and going steady are no longer mere playing at being grown up. Girls are quite capable of maintaining intense relationships for long periods of time. They accept their dependence on a man for the awakening and reaffirmation of their femininity. Boys resent being dependent as they identify dependence with childhood and castration. They are ashamed of their passive strivings which make them yearn for a mother substitute.

In analysis girls tend to develop intense love for their male therapists, a love which may make treatment impossible (Katan, 1951). Boys are less apt to transfer their genital feelings onto a female therapist. However, boys do leave treatment when their incestuous wishes come too close to the surface, when they begin to resent the regressive dependence inherent in analysis, or when their castration fears become intense. Both girls and boys in puberty are introspective, but they tend to sexualize introspection and proceed with analytic work at too rapid a pace. It is difficult to get them to recognize finer shadings of feelings. A father, for instance, may be a villain and none of the expressions of interst and sacrifice he may have shown in the past can modify this negative image. At the same time, descriptions of parents can be amazingly insightful. Caricaturing and underlining traits can easily become contagious and the therapist may react with overidentification with the adolescent patient. It is safer at such times to stay away from parents because the adolescent will not tolerate the analyst's neutrality. He demands that the analyst be partial to him and cannot otherwise endure treatment. The analyst, deliberately or intuitively, sides with the patient so that he is in danger of acting out himself when confronted by irate parents who tend to make demands on him which are meant for the child.

States of excitation in puberty evoke fears of castration, of passive surrender, abandonment, and death. Periodic feelings of emptiness in which the world seems to stop make the teenagers yearn for continuity in all aspects of life. They seek out vast expanses in nature and become intensely preoccupied with the infinity of time and space in the universe. They exaggerate the lasting values of their current interests and achievements. Parents, teachers, and siblings become envious of the exalted positions of the "geniuses, star players, revolutionaries, virtuosos, philosophers, and star gazers" amidst them and, consciously or unconsciously, provoke regression by bringing the teenager down to earth. These interferences are felt as intrusions into the ego boundaries and as constrictions of the body image, as disruptions of identity, and as debasements of ego ideals. Methods to delay sexual discharge collapse in such *puberty crises* in children and some adults as well. Mutual hostility, both driven and defensive, extends the battle front and weakens the existing fortifications that had been erected in prepuberty. Episodes of acting out may represent attempts to regain the organization achieved in prepuberty.

Delinquent acts occur more frequently in boys than in girls. This difference is largely due to the boy's much greater need for immediate discharge through motor channels, for action rather than daydreaming, and for flights into actuality rather than planning for the future. The sharp contrast between the lofty dreams of fame and love and the degrading surrender to lowly physical outlets revives earlier fears of "intruders in the dark." The kinesthetic memory of recently experienced convulsive "attacks" by their own orgasms makes the teenagers keenly aware of resonant discharge forms in their parents' behavior: "My father had a fit when he found out"; "My mother will give it to me." Boys and girls begin to look upon their fathers as "master criminals" and their mothers as "glorified prostitutes" (Glover, 1943). They envy them their freedom to seek pleasure without restriction. They make up for all the times they were left alone and excluded from adult parties. Now they have their own "secret cult of fun."

The teenager may embark on thrill-seeking adventures; only analysis reveals that his driven actions had already been organized in a distinct pattern in prepuberty. Fantasies constructed in prepuberty from a network of unresolved infantile conflicts now erupt into consciousness as irrepressible urges. They are triggered off by current actions of adults which give the youngsters a final proof of long-suspected parental immorality. It is as if the period of isolation imposed before the puberty initiation (Landauer, 1935) has ended and all the defects in the parental superego must be exposed to society. The asocial acts of adolescents put the parents on trial before a tribunal of justice that overrides the territorial confines of family law. Puberty adulation of the master criminal who flaunts and denies the guilt of the primal sin both exposes and defends the untamed infantile instinctual drives of the parents. The manner in which the parents meet the challenge of their child's puberty crises plays a crucial role in the resolution of the oedipus complex and the differentiation of the superego.

The unmasking of parents frequently ties in with the grandparents' appraisal of the teenager's mother and father, in the past and in the present. Grandparents contribute their share in trying to retain the authority they had lost when their own children grew up. The revival of the oedipus complex in adolescence is aggravated by the fact that the parents too are stimulated to revive their own incestuous wishes. The teenager is apt to repeat the revolt of his own parents, but may also identify with a grandparent, uncle or aunt as represented in the fantasies of his parent. For instance, a girl in her late teens may exaggerate the traits of the grandmother with whom her father had identified her from early childhood on. Her oedipal seductiveness and her adult features bring a semblance of reality to the fantasied relationship to her father, who begins to exhibit infantile traits in relation to her. In brief, he now acts as if she were his mother and may elevate her as an authority over himself, his wife, and the younger children. In her efforts to detach herself from her father, the girl may begin to appraise the father as infantile and dependent: "My father is nothing but a baby." In the phase of rapid growth of drives and defenses such a relationship may lead to a great many crises which involve the whole family. When in later adolescence the girl becomes analytic, she begins to recognize that her father sees in her the traits of his own mother and does not crave his own daughter in an adult fashion. The situation is even more complicated when the child represents the oedipal objects of both parents. A boy, for instance, viewed by his mother as a replica of her father and faced with his father's expectations that he fulfill the role of the father's brother, may have a difficult time in establishing his identity. In postpuberty differentiation, however, he has a chance to work through the ego ideals, appraisals, and condemnations of his parents who act out their infantile conflicts in relation to him.

Postpuberty Differentiation

The phase of expansive growth is usually followed by a phase of differentiation during which differences between infantile and adult sex-specific forms of steroid metabolization become more clearly defined. This is also the time of finer differentiation of anatomic as well as psychological sex characteristics.

Facial features, hair distribution, and body shape become adult in appearance, and acne subsides. About 50 percent of seventeen-year-old boys have reached the stage of postpubescence, and 83 percent by the time they are twenty or twenty-one (Schonfeld, 1943; Talbot et al, 1952). Shaving becomes routine, and masturbatory habits are more and more replaced by heterosexual play and coitus. Girls begin to look and act like adults earlier than boys. By nineteen or twenty they usually have regular ovulatory cycles, and the characteristic differences between phases of the menstrual cycle become apparent. These are based not only on local but on systemic changes which affect total body economy. There are alterations in body temperature, pulse, blood pressure, respiration, weight, skeleton, blood cytology, the gastrointestinal tract, vitamin utilization, and endocrine glands other than the pituitary and the ovary (Southam and Gonzaga, 1965).

Parents are now seen as near equals. New positive and negative identifications are made on the basis of self-appraisal and comparison with parents as members of adult society. There is increasing differentiation between these mature identifications and the much less realistic identifications of childhood and early adolescence. The removal of libido and aggression (Katan, 1951) from incestuous objects, which is the developmental task of this phase, allows for a rapprochement to parents as real objects.

Under normal circumstances the boy tends to give up his positive and negative oedipal wishes out of fear. He tends to project incestuous wishes upon his parents and to supplant internal conflict by a clash with the demanding father or mother. A sadomasochistic relationship to parents is frequently used to repudiate regressive, active and passive, pregenital wishes. The girl too resolves her oedipal conflicts in a sadomasochistic struggle with her parents. Her masochism is often regarded as an integral part of her femininity (Bonaparte, 1953; Deutsch, 1944–45). The pain involved in menses, defloration, and childbirth is cited to substantiate this view. But in the sadomasochistic crises in puberty, the girl is as much an attacker as the attacked. It is undoubtedly true that pain fosters a masochistic position. It is also true that a new type of pain connected with the maturation of reproductive functions begins in puberty. It is often overlooked, however, that the boy too is initiated into puberty with physical pain. His testicles become extremely sensitive; the excruciating pain of a "kick in the balls" gives rise to a revival of sadomasochistic fantasies of torture. While the girl is periodically subjected to pain which prepares her for similar experiences in the future, the boy absorbs testicular pain, as all pain, into his castration complex. While the girl connects pain with feminine functioning and thus becomes more tolerant of it, the boy begins to associate pain in his reproductive organs with sexual frustration—equated with dreaded castration. He tends to elaborate on hurts with feminine masochistic, often anal fantasies. His testicles hurt when he is abstinent; ejaculation proves his masculinity as it relieves the pain. The normal girl sublimates masochistic wishes and develops an adaptedness to pain which is part and parcel of her feminine integration. Where prepuberty integration has failed to incorporate adaptive responses to pain, the girl in puberty becomes overwhelmed by masochistic fantasies which become enhanced by premenstrual tensions,

397

menstrual pain, and drawing sensations in breasts. Sexualization of pain is one of the most important causes of frigidity.

Under favorable circumstances, the excessive instinctual demands of adolescent growth can be tamed by a guided distribution of sexual and aggressive cathexes. Partially detached from oedipal objects, they flow simultaneously and successively from parents to siblings, from men to women, and from boys to girls, all of whom compose society at large. The images of parents as members of society differentiate from the images of childhood parents that were erected in various developmental phases in accordance with the then prevailing organization of psychic structure. However, adolescent ego and superego gains can suddenly vanish when the young individual is exposed to leadership or other conditions which facilitate defusion of instincts (Freud, S., 1921). Epidemic or isolated contagion can lead to riots, teenage orgies or isolated crimes when the "unmasked" parents relinquish their supervisory role before a social conscience has been consolidated (see Chapters 17 and 18).

In normal development, the increasing detachment from parents makes the earlier exaggeration of their negative traits redundant. Whereas in the early puberty crises parents may have become a global entity (referred to as "they"), the older adolescent appraises each parent with some objectivity as a human being who has assets and faults. Positive and negative identifications begin to be based on selectivity and fine discrimination. The older adolescent becomes not only observing but also analytic. His own identity becomes less global, less independent, less unique. Biographical scrutiny leads him to a retrospective evaluation of himself and his parents. He gains a continuity of identity as he sifts and weighs his own and his parents' behavior in the past. The result is a finer differentiation of the superego leading to greater flexibility and tolerance.

The seventeen- to eighteen-year-old looks forward to physical separation from home, not because he must flee it as he felt he must in earlier phases of adolescence, but because he is eager to test his newly acquired independence in a society of his peers. The distance from his parents makes the process of mourning for the lost objects of his childhood more meaningful (Katan, 1951; Freud, A., 1958). In a parentless society adolescents work through their solutions of the oedipus complex.

In desexualized relationships with other boys the adolescent learns to cope with homosexual urges by delay of sexual discharge and by sublimations. He has lost some of his earlier cockiness, which made it seem so easy to do things better than his parents. He deflects his aggression from parents and siblings and tries to prove himself in competitive behavior.

The fervor of sports events, the need to excel in intellectual pursuits, and the race for the most desirable heterosexual object extends oedipal conflicts into everyday life. In repetition of the past and in rehearsals for what is to come, he involves himself in triangular relationships. At a safe distance from his home he can maintain the identification with the parent of his own sex without loyalty conflicts. By maintaining object constancy in prolonged friendships with his own sex he can endure the frequently acted-out and worked-through loss of a heterosexual object. Relationships between girls and boys vary from long liaisons, in which they step out from the intimacy of home to the protection of a planned new one, to short-term experimentations with object gain and object loss.

Relations with nonoedipal objects help adolescents to define their roles. This brings about finer differentiations between activity and passivity, between sadism and masochism, between aggression and love. But in the laborious process of achieving sex-specific identity in distance from parents, young people still need adult leadership to protect them against castration and separation anxiety. The less cohesive and therefore more pliable feminine superego (Lampl-de Groot, 1933) is based on the identification with the mother and molded by the love for the father and his successors (Freud, S., 1923b, 1924a, 1925). The finer differentiation of the ego and superego in the male proceeds more through group identification with leaders.

Male societies afford mutual protection against the "castrating" father and the "phallic" mother (Muensterberger, 1961). In the phase of transition to adult genitality they reinforce masculine identity by reaffirmation of masculine phallic dominance and projection of "inner genitals" upon women. The neutralizing effect of organized groups and individual friendships on homosexual strivings is particularly important for those young men who respond to castration fears and separation anxiety by identification with the mother. The daring and gambling spirit of male groups provides a strategic technique against fears of the "castrated" female genital. In preparation for the final unmasking of the phallic mother as a castrated woman, jokes about female anatomy and pictures of nude women are passed around. Invasions of the female territory are sometimes planned by groups and executed in gangs. The phallic fantasy of multiple penises is acted out under the motto *"in pluribus vis."* In this setting, the adolescent boy "fearlessly" sets out to meet a "doll," who symbolizes the complexity of the accomodating inside of the female genital (Chapters 1 and 2).[6] He behaves in a manner reminiscent of his early phallic behavior when he broke dolls open to see what is inside, but also played with them seemingly to please his sister or little girl companion.

The girl who meets the "guy" prepares for this meeting with the help of her friends by stressing the external attributes of her femininity. Her hairdo, her clothing, and her jewelry become part of her foreplay fantasies. They serve as protections against too rapid an attack upon the inside of her body. They communicate to her "date" which parts of her body are libidinized and ready to be used as landmarks in foreplay. They have a reassuring effect on the boy who, himself afraid to go too far and too fast, welcomes signs of externalization of inner sensations, familiar to him from his own experience. He, too, fusses with his hair and slicks it up with "lubricating" creams or makes it bushy. Impatient as he is, he still welcomes a step-by-step foreplay in which he can take time to explore the girl's body and reassure himself that he indeed is built differently. The girl's ready acceptance of his body allays the remnants of earlier fantasies and fears that his face is too pimply, his body not hairy enough, his breasts too pronounced, his penis too small, his scrotum just a loose skin like the external labia, and his testicles too "scroungy" in comparison with the fullness of breasts (Bell, 1964; Nunberg, 1947). The girl focuses on her own breasts to make up for the smallness of her clitoris. She is afraid of ridicule and may defensively "condemn" her clitoris as out of bounds or stress her role as a phallic mother by offering her nipples to be sucked.[7]

Mutual exploration in late adolescent sex play helps to resolve anxieties that arose in the earlier phase of rapid growth. Boys project their feminine wishes upon the girls and suffer less from fears of homosexuality. Consequently the relationships take on a more permanent character. The boy becomes more tolerant of the girl's divergent discharge form and learns to cope with the cyclic changes in her behavior. In interaction with the boy, the girl becomes better acquainted with her body and becomes more aware of the connection between her moods and her menstrual cycle. A telescopic account of the vicissitudes of relationships during successive stages of her cycle (Tables 4a,b,c) may serve to illustrate the development toward constancy in adolescence.

The girl's premenstrual distress calls for immediate relief and causes her to become demanding and nagging. She may seek a rapid discharge, reminiscent of phallic masturbation. But the feeling of engorgement and swelling does not subside. Her insatiability frequently endangers her relation with a boy because he tends to interpret her nagging and continuous excitement as a sign of her transformation into a dangerous phallic mother figure. Thus, temporary estrangements between boy and girl frequently coincide with the girl's premenstrual phase. The greater her premenstrual tension, the more vulnerable she is to hurt and disappointment. She needs the boy's tolerance for the diffuse, regressive behavior she exhibits at that time.

As the advent of menstruation brings relief and she recovers from her diffusion, her progressive reintegration makes her more cheerful and confident, and prepares her for a reconciliation with the male sex. By the end of the menstrual period she engages in flirtatious advances designed to lure the boy back. The boy may interpret her menstruation as castration. This increases his fears and makes him reluctant to re-establish a relationship. He may, on the other hand, be relieved by the realization that she is not a dangerous phallic woman after all. He may pity her and magnanimously forgive her, especially since the period of separation has increased his positive or negative oedipal strivings, from which he can escape by a renewal of dating.

In the girls' preovulatory phase boys and girls resume their courtship activities, dominated by the boy's preferences. The girl's excitement becomes increasingly focused as her estrogens mount, her uterus and vagina undergo rapid changes, and ovulation occurs. In reaction to the wished-for penetration and impregnation, she identifies with the aggressor at the same time as her masochistic fantasies evoke sadistic responses in the boy. In an integrated adult relationship this period can bring about a peak of heterosexual adjustment; in adolescence it frequently leads to violent quarrels and change of partners on a rebound.

The rising progesterone production mitigates the storm of the preceding days. Neutralization of aggression and partial desexualization of the relationship initiates calmer behavior. The girl's fantasies turn to the future as she plans her home, discusses the sex and names of her future children, and generally behaves as if she were building a nest. The boy becomes the recipient of her maternal feelings. If he is not afraid of her becoming too "serious," he becomes increasingly comfortable in her presence and joins in planning for their future. These are the times in which "doll house" play is revived, relations become steadier, and marriages are not only planned but sometimes even consummated.

This description of the influence of differentiated cycles (Tables 4a,b) on late adolescent relationships is based on extrapolations from analyses of adolescent girls and older women who behaved like adolescents. It is also derived from cursory observations of adolescent interaction. It may be unduly weighted by the fact that its primary sources were analyses of neurotic girls. Benedek's (1952) scientific correlation of hormone levels with changes in behavior of adult women undoubtedly crystallized my thoughts. It must be noted, however, that our interpretations differ somewhat regarding the luteal and the menstrual phase of the cycle.

The sexual differentiation of the adolescent girl is determined by the reciprocal relation between her menstrual cycles, the degree of detachment from oedipal objects, and the current relation to a love object. Current conflicts disturb her cycle, and a disturbance in her cycle revives past conflicts and makes her vulnerable to current stress (Benedek, 1952; Deutsch, 1944–45; Josselyn, 1952). Because of her multifaceted adjustment she takes on the values and interests of her love objects in adolescence and later. However, unless she transfers her oedipal feelings to an older man who becomes her teacher, her greater maturity challenges her to guide her adolescent companion. She suffers from the inconstancy of such a relationship because she is vulnerable to object loss. She needs the guidance of steady love to neutralize her own changes in feelings and to become independent of her mother. Not until she can feel secure in her relationship to a man, so that she need not fear impregnation, can she successfully project her masculinity upon him and become truly feminine.

The adolescent boy gradually achieves control over the timing of his genital excitation-discharge cycle. He libidinizes the inner genital of the woman, externalizes inner urges upon her, and projects onto her representations of the inside of his body. This is reflected in Federn's classification of men wl.ose orgasm arises in the penis alone as masculine, and those who localize the orgasmic trigger mechanisms in the pelvis as feminine (1913–14). The boy becomes acquainted with the multilocal nature of the girl's arousal which may change with successive phases of her sexual cycle, with her moods, and with variations of her trust in him (Chapter 5). As he adjusts to the periodic changes in her attitude, he penetrates retrospectively through the iron curtain of his mother's mysterious shifts in attitudes. In his dealing with his girl friend he recognizes the various images of maternal handling: tender and giving, aggressive nagging, depressive suffering, active organizing and supporting, seductively exciting, loving and punishing, which comprise the memory of his mother. As he reacts to these new insights, he begins to understand and forgive not only his mother, but his father as well. This helps him to work through his detachment from oedipal objects.

At the end of this phase an integrated adult personality is not yet established. At the end of the teens and in the early part of the twenties a progressive consolidation of masculine and feminine interests, of sexuality and love, and of passion and tenderness effects a constancy of object relations characteristic of adulthood.

402

Preadult Consolidation

All through development, maturational changes can be delineated only by age ranges rather than ages, and even these limits can be narrower or wider without necessarily implying precocity or retardation. There is considerable variation depending on genetic, ecological, nutritional, cultural, and other differences. The most difficult time to define by age is the last phase of adolescence in transition to adulthood. It usually begins with a regression of shorter or longer duration. Attempts at recovery may be interrupted by new bouts of regression. The rate of consolidation of previous gains may be slow and the attainment of adult maturity delayed. Analysis of patients in their twenties frequently reveals the persistence of adolescent traits which do not allow for the development of an adult type of transference neurosis (Freud, A., 1965). Kinsey's (1953) studies, indicating that higher educational aspirations may retard adjustment to adulthood may be interpreted in two ways. The longer the years of schooling required to qualify for self-supporting positions within our contemporary society, the longer is the period of dependence upon parents and teachers. A need to prolong one's identity as a student may be the expression of a continuing need for dependence; on the other hand, it may be due to culturally determined parental rearing practices which retard individuation.[8]

The questions are similar to those which arise in discussions of latency, especially in boys. Stormy transitions into latency may occur when a rise in hormone production does not keep pace with maturational advances, responsible for the inhibition of the effect of gonadotropins. An influx of phallic-genital impulses may be the occasion for the regression that normally initiates latency. As a result, some boys do not enter latency proper before they are seven or eight years old. Physiologically, latency ends at the age of nine or ten, but there are only gradual changes in sex differentiation before the onset of prepuberty. The period of latency consolidation can be prolonged or shortened depending on the interaction between physical and psychological factors.

The preadult phase of consolidation repeats many features of latency. Like latency it begins with a regression which ushers in a longer or shorter period of consolidation of previous gains. In this phase, there is a close interrelationship between the stabilization of adult mechanisms of hormone production and metabolization and the stabilization of sex-specific character traits. When one of these processes is disturbed or there is a desynchronization between their rates of advancement, the regression that initiates this phase may be prolonged or stormy. The time required for consolidation to become entrenched is variable. It depends not only on internal but also on external circumstances which may favor or hinder the consolidation of maturational gains. Much depends on the maturity and attitude of available love objects and outlets for sublimation, especially so in females. Consolidation of the multifaceted aspects of adult feminine integration can hardly be achieved without adequate guidance by a man (Chapter 5).

Neither in childhood nor in adolescence does the girl repress her oedipal attachment as definitely as the boy does (Freud, S., 1924a, Lampl-de Groot, 1928). Correspondingly, her superego is less differentiated and her ego more subject to regression. She reacts sensitively to inner and outer changes and tends to lean on love objects to maintain her equilibrium and to reestablish her self-esteem. It is interesting to note that a high degree of psychological infantilism in women is often accompanied by a delay in the maturation of reproductive organs. Thus pregnancy does not occur until the end of the third decade. The male, whose development is slower than that of the female, frequently finds it easier to consolidate autonomous adjustment, once he has achieved a sufficient degree of differentiation in his adolescence. In this, he is very much aided by a greater stability of hormonal levels and by his progressively increasing ability to withstand stress in the last stage of adolescence and in young adulthood. Even after completion of sexual differentiation, his physical strength and endurance continue to increase. Not only do his striate muscles develop further, but so do his heart muscle (Nelson, 1959) and the musculature of his reproductive organs. He achieves greater control over the timing of ejaculations; nevertheless a general tendency to rapid discharge persists. More active and more prone to reach high peaks than the girl, he still spends himself more quickly than he likes to acknowledge. His intellectual and sexual performance and the degree of his creativity and fertility fluctuate, depending on states of rest and fatigue. This clinically observable phenomenon supports Southren *et al.*'s (1965) preliminary findings that plasma testosterone levels in men rise after a period of sleep and fall after a period of activity.

The consolidation of sex-specific character traits in preadulthood provides for the constancy of identity, which must be maintained throughout adult developmental phases (marriage, pregnancy, parenthood [Benedek, 1952], climacterium, grandparenthood, and senescence). Flexibility of ego and superego attitudes, attained in preadulthood, facilitates progressive readjustment of identity within the narrow sphere of achievement in work, skill, and position and in the larger sphere of changing economic, political, and social structures.

During the phase of preadult consolidation the girl develops a constancy of attitudes to self and to objects by maintaining steadiness despite the changes in cycles. This constancy allows her to tolerate and profit from the repeated revival of earlier developmental organizations during successive phases of her cycle. Premenstrual distress is reminiscent of the states of disequilibrium, heralding the inner-genital phase in childhood and prepuberty. Menstruation and the immediate postmenstrual phase provide the framework for a reintegration, modeled after the reorganizations that follow the imbalance in the early inner-genital phase and in prepuberty. The increasing activity in the preovulatory period, culminating in ovulation, repeats the growth periods of the early phallic phase and puberty. The luteal phase revives phases of differentiation and consolidation, already familiar from the later phallic phase and latency in childhood, and from postpubescence and preadulthood in adolescence. These revolving cycles of regression allow for repeated working through of unresolved infantile conflicts without which the control of adaptive regression (Hartmann, 1939; Geleerd, 1965) required for successful feminine adjustment, could not be achieved.

Woman's integration is based on acceptance of all parts of the body and all pregenital and genital urges, since all of these are involved to some degree in the intimacy of her relationship to her love objects. Her ability to change from tolerance and enjoyment of immature behavior to encouragement of control must keep pace with progressive maturational advances of her children. This adaptation is based on past and current adjustment to varying periods of alteration in psychosomatic states. A superego more loosely structured than the man's, a pliable ego based on less defined body boundaries and a greater ease in oscillation between regression and progression, between narcissistic and object cathexis—all are features of woman's adaptation. The form and degree of her adjustment depends on the organizers of the past, but continues to be molded by the organizers[9] of the present: the stimuli emanating from her body during different phases of her cycle and during longer-lasting alterations of state (pregnancy, lactation, etc.), and the stimuli provided by her intimate love objects and desexualized relationships. Models from early and later phases of reorganization are readily available to her when she needs to shift rapidly from sexual to desexualized activities. Such desexualization continues to be achieved by externalization of inner tensions and impulses upon objects. Flexibility in shifting allows for feminine adjustment to various roles as wife, mother of different-age children, teacher, cook, cleaner, wage earner, social organizer, etc. This characteristic is most vulnerable to stress, which accounts for the contradictory appraisal of women as mainstays of family and social structures as well as fickle, changeable, and enigmatic creatures men cannot understand.

If the control over the ratio and degree of sexualization and desexualization is disturbed, the last phase of adolescence consolidates pathological, rather than reinforces normal, feminine integration. Frigidity, which resists conditioning and training of genital organs by repeated coitus with a constant partner, is frequently due to a failure in resexualization of inner-genital sensations, a rigid persistence of externalization and masochistic elaboration of repressed oedipal fantasies. Various degrees of sexualization of relationships to children are caused by a failure in desexualization and unsuccessful or partial externalization. A defective or distorted integration of pregenital, phallic, and inner-genital drives underlies character deviations, frequently manifested in conspicuous rejection of feminine identity.

Consolidation of man's characteristics is difficult to achieve under conditions which favor a perpetuation of dependence on parents, whether they be his own or those acquired through a premature marriage. The success of male integration is contingent on active striving for independence and autonomous achievement. A man functions best at work when he is temporally and spatially separated from his love objects. His reality-oriented, desexualized activities consolidate when his oedipal competition and homosexual temptations are replaced by a well-integrated ego ideal and a constant superego. The developmental delay in maturation of sexual characteristics and of adult genital discharge provides the male with a long period of time to establish a wide range of desexualized interests. His adult genital organization is predicated on the previous externalizations of inside sensations which establish the primacy of the phallus. In continuation of earlier trends, his need for a child is delayed by his creative interests. He achieves adult genital organization when he becomes capable of delaying discharge and of adjusting his discharge form to one suitable for interaction with a constant love object.

Mutual projections and identifications between partners consolidate their partial independence from the past and bring about a steadiness of relations. Their new relationships are to a great degree independent of external influences and of the changes of state which occur during the psychic and hormonal reorganizations of adult developmental phases.

Conclusions

In examining predominant trends in the organization of adolescent phases, we look back at their antecedents in childhood and take a glimpse at their outcome in adulthood. The repetition of childhood organizations in adolescence cushions and protects the growing individual from too sudden an exposure to problems involved in the developmental task of adjusting a new psychosomatic identity to the requirements of a complex society. The interpolation of adolescence between childhood and adulthood allows for a more gradual and therefore less traumatic transition which gives a foundation for complex integrations in adult developmental phases (Benedek, 1952).

The sequence of disequilibrium and reintegration followed by growth, differentiation, and consolidation of psychic functions (described in the prephallic–inner-genital, phallic and latency phases) repeats itself in adolescence. With the breakdown of latency organization, a state of imbalance (prepuberty diffusion) brings on a regression to earlier phases, repeating the disequilibrium of the two-and-a-half-year-old. The integration which follows the disequilibrium of the toddler leads to phallic dominance. In prepuberty, the sex-specific reintegration which follows the renewal of inner-genital excitations and the diffusion of psychic functions becomes the foundation for puberty genitality.

In a phase of rapid growth initiated by puberty, oedipal urges are revived and intensified. Exaggerations of feelings, attitudes, and defenses become excessive in puberty developmental crises.

In postpubescence, the process of detachment from oedipal objects directs libido and aggression toward heterosexual objects outside the family. Ego-superego differentiation leads to a sharp delineation of differences between male and female identities.

A constancy of character traits and of object relationships characterizes the end of the phase of preadulthood in which the final transition from adolescence to adulthood takes place.

When we correlate the progressive reorganization of psychic structure with the concomitant hormonal changes in adolescence, we are tempted to explore the possibility that these interactions are anticipated in childhood. A tentative scheme for such a correlation is presented, in the hope that future interdisciplinary research will clarify the progressive psychosomatic changes in development toward adulthood.

It is postulated that stages of cortical-hypothalamic-pituitary maturation are responsible for the mutual influence of psychic and hormonal constellations during development. Up to prepuberty there are only small changes in reproductive organs and small quantities of steroids are produced primarily in the adrenal. The decisive difference between childhood and adolescence lies in the appearance of gonadal hormones in amounts sufficient to initiate sex-specific alterations. The release of central inhibition, which initiates this neurohormonal reorganization, seems to create an imbalance in the total psychosomatic economy of the young adolescent. The establishment of a reciprocal regulation between gonadotropins and gonadal hormones in later stages of prepuberty parallels the progressive reintegration of psychic functions at that time. Important landmarks are the first, still anovulatory, menstruations and the first, still aspermatic, ejaculations.

Prepuberty is a stage of cortical-hypothalamic-pituitary maturation through which cyclic changes in estrogens cause cyclic changes in female reproductive organs. Inner-genital stimuli become dominant somatic sources of psychic reorganization in female prepuberty. These may have been anticipated by sporadic rises and falls in estrogens during follicular maturation and atresia in childhood. Male prepuberty is initiated by a rise in testosterone, by prostatic activity, and by an increased activity in spermatogonia. These somatic changes enforce male acceptance of internal genital organs as essential for adult male functioning.

In puberty sex-specific germ cells reach maturity but not yet a regular rate of production. The influence of progesterone marks the beginning of adult hormonal mechanisms in puberty. Progesterone plays a central role in the girl and an intermediary role in the boy.

Physical growth and psychic expansion accompany the substantial increases of gonadotropins and adult sex-specific hormones in early puberty.

A progressive differentiation of physical and psychological traits parallels the differentiation of sex-specific hormonal constellations in post-pubescence. When the influence of progesterone on feminine attitudes gains in importance, ovulatory cycles become regular and testosterone production stabilizes at low childhood levels. Male differentiation leads to the preponderance of testosterone metabolization from progesterone, to an increasingly higher rate of testosterone production, and to a stabilization of estrogen at low levels.

The consolidation of adult sex-specific attitudes in the last phase of adolescence is interrelated with a consolidation of sex-specific adult mechanisms of hormone production and metabolization.

In adulthood, character traits and relationships become relatively independent of the past. At the same time, psychic functioning becomes less dependent on hormonal fluctuations (in female cycles and in male forms of periodicity) and less dependent on changes of states in adult developmental phases.

NOTES

[1]Fraser et al. (1969) published a table on plasma concentration of testosterone and androstenedione in boys between the ages of four and fifteen and a half. It appears that there is a higher concentration of both hormones in children under six than in those be-

tween the ages of six and ten and a half. The mean in the younger group for testosterones is 50 ng/100mg, for the latency child about 32. The mean in the younger group for androstenediones is 90ng/100ml, for the latency child 50. This seems to corroborate older, less reliable findings which showed relatively high values of male hormones in the phallic phase. However, these assays cannot be compared with those for younger ages; the differences are small as compared with increases in puberty; the data are cross-sectional and done on too few children to be statistically reliable. Endocrinologists pay too little attention to small differences, but they do agree that longitudinal studies are needed.

[2]For newer views on hypothalamic-pituitary interaction see Chapter 16.

[3]Component drives have been traditionally named after the bodily zone which is the somatic source of the drive and the primary location of need satisfaction (Freud, S., 1905a). The division of early genital drives into "inner and outer" helps to sharpen distinctions between female and male, and between cryptic and apparent sources of genital tension and discharge (Chapters 5, 13).

[4]For a newer view on the role of the hypothalamus see Chapter 16.

[5]In this account all data on hormones derived from animal experiments and not necessarily applicable to humans will be marked by an asterisk.

[6]The root "dol" is contained in the Latin words: *dolium* (barrel), *dolor* (pain), as well as in *dolo* (hidden dagger) and *dolus* (deceit). The German and French words for dolls are derived from the Latin word *pupa* (girl). The corresponding Polish word *lalka* shares its first syllable with the Latin words: *labea* (lip), *labes* (fall, destruction, spot of shame), *labor, labyrinthus, lac* (milk), *lacero* (tear), *lacrima* (tear), lacuna (hole), *lacus* (basin), *laedo* (beat, injure, offend), *laetifico* (give pleasure, impregnate, fertilize), *laevus* (left, silly), and many others. See also Bradley (1961) and Veszy-Wagner (1965).

[7]These observations pertain to transitory phenomena during the phase of differentiation in adolescence. Permanent condemnation of the clitoris occurs in cases of excessive penis envy and is usually associated with total frigidity (Harley, 1961b). The nipple-clitoris equation stressed by Sarlin (1963), is based on the parellelism with which these erectile tissues act as trigger mechanisms for the spreading of sensations to the vagina and uterus. Contrary to Sarlin's view, successful nursing is contingent on the desexualization of nipples and breasts which occurs periodically in end play. A prolonged period of desexualization of these and other organs during pregnancy and lactation may well be due to the influence of pituitary hormones. The erectile tissue of the nose that Freud mentioned is similarly affected by hormonal changes. In both sexes it atrophies after the climacterium, and in both sexes it acts as a trigger mechanism to evoke genital excitement probably already in the inner-genital phase (Daly, 1928; Schering, 1941–42).

[8]For a fuller treatment of the regression that initiates the preadult phase of consolidation see Chapters 17 and 18. For the discussion of a connection between early social isolation and the prolongation of adolescence see Chapter 18.

[9]This term denotes here an organizing influence; it is not to be confused with the concept of biological organizers.

Rhythmicity in Adolescence

Coauthored by Esther Robbins, M.D.

Introduction to
Chapters 16, 17, and 18

Our understanding of adolescence has been greatly enriched by ideas put forth to explain the current behavior of our youth. There is a consensus that adolescence is now prolonged and is marked by deeper regression than in previous generations, but that it has not basically changed. Exaggeration of normal behavior has served to point up issues vital for clarification.

One of the phenomena upon which our attention has focused is the trend from the relatively tonic, stable structures of latency, through the mobile rhythmicity of adolescence, to a new stable consolidation leading to adulthood. The appreciation of the effects of rhythmicity on vital bodily functions, psychic constellations and behavior has made it incumbent upon us to extend observation beyond the treatment hour. Our studies of movement patterns, used in the expression of psychic qualities and structures, promise to facilitate explorations of rhythmic changes in the adolescent "behavior-day" that have been brought to our attention by recent insights in endocrinology.

The discovery that rhythmicity is inherent in the nature of social relationships drew our attention to early forms of socialization that we were able to discern through observation of groups of young children and

---

Read in part at the Panel on "Adolescence: A Reconsideration of Current Concepts" at the Meetings of the American Academy of Child Psychiatry, New Orleans, La., October 14, 1972.

Chapters 16–18, as well as this Introduction, are coauthored by Esther Robbins, M.D., Director of the Sidney L. Green Prenatal Project of Child Development Research, Sands Point, N.Y.

411

adolescents who were behaving in a regressive fashion. Our hypothesis, that the developmental task of adolescence is the crystallization of a community spirit from elaborations of earlier rhythmic relationships, arose not only from our own method of movement assessment, but also from conventional clinical observations and concepts available in endocrinology, sociology, education, and psychoanalysis.

As in previous chapters, we shall consider adolescence as comprised of four subphases, defined primarily by the distinguishing (1) physical changes and (2) organizations governing the total behavior:

1. *Prepuberty,* characterized by: (a) an irregular influx of sex-specific sex hormones and the appearance of secondary sex characteristics, followed by menarche and first ejaculations; (b) a breakdown of latency organization (prepuberty diffusion) which is followed by reintegration.

This phase is referred to by some authors as pubescence, and by others as early adolescence.

2. *Puberty growth,* characterized by: (a) a rise of hormones to high levels, and the onset of the ability to reproduce; (b) a psychological growth, with great increase of drives, soaring of affects and an augmentation of ego interests.

This phase is referred to by some as postpubescence and by others as mid-adolescence.

3. *Puberty differentiation,* during which: (a) ovulatory cycles and mature sperm production become regular and progesterone and testosterone attain near adult levels; and (b) drives, ego interests, and superego become highly differentiated as the removal from primary objects is accomplished.

This phase is often referred to as late adolescence.

4. *Preadult consolidation,* in which: (a) sex-specific hormone metabolism becomes stabilized; and (b) the sex-specific adult character is crystallized and settled (see Chapters 5, 15).

In the following chapters we shall view adolescence from three vantage points:

Rhythmic Patterns in Hormonal Secretion (Chapter 16)

We shall examine some questions posed by recent discoveries concerning the rhythmicity of hormone production and regarding the interplay of physical and emotional factors involved in the development of adolescents.

Rhythmic Patterns in Motility (Chapter 17)

We shall show that certain modes of rhythmicity in adolescence are operative not only in movements, but also in other forms of behavior, extended over longer periods of time; that adolescent movement patterns reflect a new cognitive style and new ways of relating to people, as well as changes that occur in the ego ideal and superego proper; and that all of the foregoing functions, including relationships with people, are governed by a rhythmicity that undergoes successive transformations as development proceeds.

From Early Rhythms of Socialization to the Development of Community Spirit (Chapter 18)

We shall propose that the developmental task of adolescence is the establishment of a community spirit that incorporates rhythmic and stable relationships on different levels, including the young and the old, kin and neighbors, friends and strangers, fellow countrymen and foreigners. In latency, constancy and consolidation of altruistic love evolves from the rhythmic forms of relating in early childhood. This process is reversed in adolescence; rhythmicity is revived and reorganized into new forms of constancy. Socialization in early childhood provides a basis for the development of a social conscience in latency and community spirit in adolescence. As a result of early isolation from social contacts, occasioned by the current privatization of the middle-class family unit, an extensive social experimentation is required during adolescence. Under those circumstances, adolescence is prolonged and sometimes distorted; it can be concluded only when an adult community spirit has been finally acquired.

CHAPTER 16

Rhythmic Patterns in Hormonal Secretion

Coauthored by Esther Robbins, M.D.

New Data About Hypothalamic Regulation

The discovery that neuroendocrine releasing factors are of hypothalamic rather than pituitary origin has given rise to the reconsideration of previous concepts regarding neurohormonal regulation. The hypothalamus, long recognized as a central regulator of vital functions such as respiration, temperature, hydration, hunger, sleep-waking cycles, and as the mediator between hormones and emotions, must now also be considered the conductor of endocrine gland performance, with the pituitary relegated to first violinist (Sussman, 1972). Recent insights into neurohormonal hypothalamic interaction suggest that the "sensitivity" of the hypothalamus to quantities of sex hormones diminishes in adolescence (Zondek, 1972). It is likely that, because of the alteration in the feedback mechanism between gonadotrophins and sex hormones, not only does a considerable increase in sex hormones occur, but a new type of rhythmicity in their release is initiated.

Hormone Secretion as a Dynamic 24-Hour and Cyclic Process

Because of the recent improvement of radio immuno-assay techniques, data have become available regarding diurnal variations in hor-

---

We are grateful to Dr. Benjamin Sussman of New Hyde Park, N.Y., and to Professor Theodor Zondek of London, England, for their generous sharing with us of information about recent progress in neuroendocrinology and for supplying us with pertinent bibliographic information.

415

mone concentrations in older children, adolescents, and adults. The cyclic (as opposed to pulsatile or episodic) secretion of cortisol has been known for some time. More recently, episodic secretion has been' demonstrated for adrenocorticotropic hormones (ACTH), thyroid-stimulating hormones (TSH), cortisol, prolactin, the luteinizing hormone (LH), and the human-growth-hormone (HGH). The frequency and magnitude of spikes of secretion is controlled in part through rhythms mediated by the hypothalamus, that are related to time of day and the sleep-wake cycle (Sassin *et al.*, 1972) and to stages of neurohormonal maturation. Boyar *et al.* (1972) stress "the importance of considering hormone secretion as a dynamic, 24-hour process characterized by widely fluctuating plasma concentration and periods of episodic secretion." The diurnal and circadian rhythhs exist within the framework of lunar cycles, which Richter (1967) claims are evidenced by changes in bodily activity, temperature, pulse rate, urine output, hours of sleep, mood concentration, and other physical and psychic phenomena, not only in women but in men as well. On the more encompassing scale of an individual lifetime, the maturation of systems proceeds from conception through childhood and adulthood and a gradual senescence. Of course, all of the preceding should be considered in the context of periodicity in societal species and planetary evolution, which is not within the purview of this chapter.

Many more systems than we have hitherto acknowledged obey the laws of periodicity and are dependent on hypothalamic regulation and mediation. One cannot help but be impressed by the apparently rhythmic nature not only of somatic processes and emotions which arise from bodily needs and states, but of cortically controlled cognitive functions as well. We must not be misled into thinking that phenomena recurring at irregular intervals are not rhythmic. Biological rhythms are marked by recurrence and alternations in features, elements, and qualities at regular or irregular intervals. The factors determining the intervals of recurrence have not been discovered, except for those rhythms which are governed by circadian or lunar cycles.

The Effect of External Influences on Hormone Production

We do know that external influences profoundly alter the periodicity in all organisms. Students of the psyche have long been persuaded that internalization of external traumata, i.e., emotional responses, affect neurohormonal functioning. Current research has begun to provide information on the mechanism involved. For example, in the maternal deprivation syndrome (Spitz and Wolf, 1946), failure to grow, secondary to anaclitic depression, is accompanied by the lack of human-growth-hormone (HGH) secretory response to hypoglycemia. After a period of good psychological care, HGH secretion, which also normally increases with emotional arousal, is restored and growth resumes dramatically. Severe depression in adults may also lead to a lack of HGH response (Sacher *et al.*, 1971). It is known that certain types of amenorrhea and infertility can yield to resolution of emotional conflicts.

External influences can affect larger spans of periodicity. For instance, poor nutrition and overcrowding delay maturation. The quality of feeding in early childhood sets the pace for later neurohormonal development. Children from small families are said to mature earlier than those raised in large groups (Hubble, 1969; Tanner, 1969). We have known for some time that the adolescents of our affluent society (Bernard, 1961), have matured quite a bit earlier than the previous generation. A recent estimate suggests that about 50 percent of the girls in menarche are already ovulating (Altcheck, 1971). The rate of maturation varies a great deal, as is indicated in Tanner's (1969) description of several fourteen-year-old boys, who vary greatly in height and in the degree of sexual differentiation. The same is true for girls. There is a wide span over which girls achieve menarche—from eleven to fourteen years of age or more. Emotional factors also play a role in the delay of acceleration of maturation. The transmission of early parental attitudes about maturation to their children (Noshpitz, 1970; Friedman, 1972) is further reinforced at puberty by the parents' current image of adolescents (Anthony, 1970a). All these, combined with communications from siblings and peer groups, create an atmosphere of fear or hopeful expectation that has a direct or indirect effect upon neurohormonal metabolism.

The Mutual Influences
of Sexual Maturation
and Behavior

Sexual maturation influences behavior in a number of ways. For instance, the more mature adolescents begin to look down on the stragglers, and the latter frequently suffer from a deflated self-image which may in turn have a dilatory effect upon maturation. Animal experimentation has led us to expect that the influx of certain sex hormones would accelerate brain maturation (Dalton, 1968). However, adolescence may not be the critical stage for such a development. The question arises as to whether brain maturation, which effects the development of operational thinking in early adolescence (Piaget, 1943, 1953) has a direct or indirect influence on sexual maturation. It is interesting to note that the change in adrenocortical function in adolescence is "coincident with and presumably related to the development of the zona retucularis in man" (Rosenfield *et al.*, 1969, p. 932). However, the lack of normative data regarding neuroendocrine development has made it difficult to study the mutual influence of neurohormonal status and psychological development. Even the relationship between the somatic manifestations of adolescence and the plasma concentrations of adrenal and gonadal steroids is difficult to detect by cross-sectional studies which mask individual changes. Endocrinologists agree that a longitudinal study will resolve these problems (August *et al.*, 1972; Frasier *et al.*, 1970). However, the data recently made available through improved radio immuno-assay techniques suggests a complex diurnal correlation between hormonal and psychic rhythmicity in adolescence.

For a few weeks after birth the plasma level of the human-growth-hormone (HGH) is markedly elevated, but after that it falls to a tonic level which is so low that it becomes almost immeasurable. However, there are one to three small secretory episodes which occur only during sleep. This pattern changes markedly during adolescence (Finkelstein *et al.*, 1972). At prepuberty, the number, magnitude, and duration of the secretory episodes increases, and they take place during the day as well as at night. Maximal secretion occurs early at night, primarily in a deep, slow-wave sleep. The young adult returns to the childhood pattern and with aging may cease to have any unstimulated secretory episodes.

Boyar *et al.* (1972) found similarly that with the increase of luteinizing hormone (LH) secretion at the beginning of adolescence there is also a change in excretory mode specific for this developmental phase. The mean plasma LH concentration at prepuberty is significantly higher during sleep than in waking. The secretion of LH during sleep is uniformly initiated during NREM sleep and terminated in close promixity to or during REM sleep. In later phases of adolescence, which coincide with postpubescent growth and differentiation, the LH concentration increases, but there is progressively less distinction between sleep and waking averages of plasma LH levels. Children and adults differ in the quantity of LH secreted, but the averages seem to be constant day and night. We note here the similarity with the HGH secretion pattern. Southern *et al.*, (1965) found that testosterone quantities in adult males vary between day and night; Boon *et al.*, (1972) found the same as regards androgens. There is a diurnal cycle in the serum concentration of the follicle stimulating hormone (FSH) in adult males (Fayman *et al.*, 1967), but no comparable data are available on children and adolescents. There are indications that FSH follows a course similar to that of LH. It is also probable that the day and night rhythmicity of estrogen, progesterone, and testosterone is greatest in adolescence, with the highest concentrations occurring during deepest sleep, when there is both motoric and psychic inactivity. It is interesting to speculate further upon the possibility that such a hormonal distribution serves as a physical and psychic protection for an organism under the duress of rapid anatomical growth and greatly increased sexual and aggressive drives (Blos, 1962) that threaten to propel it into immediate unsublimated drive discharge.

There are other mechanisms known to serve the protection of adolescents against acting out on the basis of drive increase. The rise in hormone levels and the concomitant breakdown of latency organization are counterbalanced by a simultaneous increase in reality testing and reasoning. The ability to think operationally (Piaget, 1948, 1953) allows for the reorganization of psychic structure before the full influx of hormones and drives emerges in middle adolescence. Most of the gross reshaping of the adolescent body is completed before reproduction becomes possible (Tanner, 1969). As his feelings surge to great heights, the fifteen- to sixteen-year-old, who is capable of reproduction, can fall back upon his newly established integration of cognitive and defensive functions—an integration based on the foundation of a unity of body-ego and self-representation created in prepuberty (Chapter 14). This protective resource tempers the expansiveness of the mid-adolescent's self-representation. The mean hormone concentration begins to equalize between waking and sleeping as the mid-adolescent becomes better able to deal with hormonal increases during the daytime. This capacity increases in late adolescence when differentiation predominates. Finally, during the preadult phase of consolidation (see Chapter 15; Spiegel, 1961; Blos, 1973), the stabilization of psychic functions seems to be correlated with the stabilization of diurnal levels of gonadotrophin, sex hormone, and growth hormone production.

What happens when one of the mechanisms that protects the adolescent from acting out is deficient is exemplified in investigations made by Cobliner (1970) and Cobliner et al., (1972). These authors found that pregnant teenagers from low socio-economic groups tended to use figurative rather than abstract thinking, which led to the disregard of the consequences of their actions. In conjunction with normal cognitive and emotional development, the knowledge that impregnation has become possible constitutes a protection against adolescent acting out. The "sophisticated" adolescent girl, who takes contraceptive pills almost as soon as she begins to menstruate, obviates the fear of impregnation, but runs the danger of becoming promiscuous. Jaffe and Midgley (1969) suggest that "oral contraceptives may have, as one of their major mechanisms, the ability to disrupt the normal patterns of serum LH and FSH during the menstrual cycle" (p. 207). The diagrams in their publication indicate that normal female cyclicity is suppressed. This raises questions as to whether the contraceptive pills so widely administered to adolescents in recent years have the effect of infantilizing or masculinizing our adolescent female generation and whether the development of sex-specific identity, of womanliness in general and motherliness in particular, is endangered by it.

Some investigators believe that human sex differences are irreversibly imprinted on the hypothalamus prenatally or perinatally (Hubble, 1969). Others feel that sex differentiation is established at the age of two and three mainly via parental methods of imparting gender roles to children (Money, 1965). Our clinical data, obtained from patients at the various developmental levels and correlated with known neuroendocrine timetables (Chapters 13, 14, 15), suggest that sexual differentiation is an ongoing maturational and emotional process not completed before adulthood. The interplay between hormonal and psychic influences has not been adequately explored. However, it appears to be a crucial factor in the formation of sex-specific self-representation in adolescence. The reshaping of the adolescent body, the tremendous endocrine and psychic upheaval and the changes in susceptibility to nonfamilial influences make the adolescent ego particularly vulnerable to abnormal conditions. Tampering with the adolescent girl's cycles endangers her on serveral counts. She is not challenged to develop ego strength through dealing with her sexuality and through enforcing of defenses; she does not become prepared for normal feminine cyclicity; moreover the flattening of her hormone-secretion curve provides a physical core for a masculine identification. Preliminary impressions are that she is inclined to be more aggressive and less maternal than her predecessor. She is thereby less prepared for motherhood.[1] Moreover, her mode of secretion of progesterone may contribute to the lessening of receptivity and the decrease in nurturing capacity. It would be important to study the effect of masculinization of the girl and the loss of the fear of impregnation on the adolescent boy's image of himself as a male. Such a study would require complex interdisciplinary research, based as it must be on a multiplicity of periodical changes in both sexes (cyclic, pulsatile, brief, diurnal, lunar, etc.). For now, however, we shall have to confine ourselves to the much less ambitious project of studying adolescent behavior with due consideration for the rhythmic changes characteristic of this developmental phase.

Conclusions

Drive endowment and regulation have been understood as somatically based and rhythmic in character. In view of the rich, complex interrelation of soma and psyche, it seems to us unparsimonious to regard cognitive functions and object relations as outside the pale of rhythmicity. We might be better equipped to help the adolescent, if we were able to comprehend the obligatory nature of his life cycle as related to the episodic nature, not only of his sexuality and aggressiveness, but also of his productivity and social interaction. The infant's behavior-day (Gesell and Ilg, 1943) and the variations in his states (Wolff, 1966; Escalona, 1962) have been studied in the past. We might do well to extend our observations of adolescents beyond the 50-minute hour, paying particular attention to changes in states in terms of a dynamic 24-hour process, characterized by widely fluctuating feelings, arousal, and attention. Our own studies have led us to the understanding of rhythmicity through the observation of movement (Chapters 8, 10). We have learned that the rhythmicity of infancy diminishes progressively and reaches a low ebb in latency. In the next chapter we shall turn our attention to the resurgence of rhythmicity in adolescence, as revealed by the study of movement.

NOTES

[1]In adult constancy, the artificial disturbance of cycles does not notably detract from the previously established character of maternality.

CHAPTER 17

Rhythmic Patterns in Motility

Coauthored by Esther Robbins, M.D.

The pathway for the mutual influence of neurohormonal and psychic correlates in adolescence has begun to be elucidated (Chapter 16). In this chapter, we shall explore adolescent development through the study of motility, which provides another avenue of approach to those aspects of the psyche to which verbal investigation has no access. Unfortunately, the somatic mechanisms for the transmission of the mutual influence of motility and psyche remain obscure. Thus, as we draw conclusions about the psyche from investigations of movement, it must be borne in mind that they rest upon the hypothesis that the way we think influences how we move and vice versa.

We should like to emphasize that we do not suppose a simple relationship between motility and psyche. Rather, we shall attempt to draw inferences about the psyche from movement patterns, just as we draw inferences about the psyche from verbal productions. In order to convey the means by which we arrive at our developmental data, it will be necessary to introduce the terminology we use to categorize movement patterns (see also Chapters 8 and 10). We shall define briefly some of the movement patterns that are subject to *rhythmic repetition* as contrasted with *body-attitude,* which represents the more stable, unchanging aspect of motor patterning. Special attention will be given to the rhythmicity

Our views on movement are extrapolated from joint discussions with the members of the Movement Study Group of Child Development Research; Dr. J. Berlowe, A. Buelte, T.M.N., Dr. H. Marcus, and M. Soodak, M.A., 1962-1973. We are especially grateful to Irma Bartenieff of the Dance Notation Bureau, New York, and to Warren Lamb, London, who shared with us their views on the development of adolescent motility.

versus tonicity in the expression of object relationships.[1]Data from movement studies will be correlated with data from clinical observation of behavior over varying spans of time.

A change in predominant rhythms and in body-attitude marks the onset of each new developmental phase. In contrast to typical rhythms and sequences of movement patterns that are the dynamic aspect of the developmental phase, body-attitude represents the more constant base upon which the "morphostatic" image of the body is built (see Chapter 8). Self-representation is based on the schema of both the moving and the still-positioned body. The latter contributes a greater share to the permanency of shapes of self-representation (Sandler and Rosenblatt, 1962).

Rhythms of motility reflect and affect minute-to-minute variations in state. These represent, in miniature, a periodicity which governs the "behavior-day" of the child, adolescent, and adult. The rhythms, inherent in the repetition of needs and object-seeking in short and long spans of time, decrease under the influence of sustained ego-interests and superego-demands. In early adolescence, there is a renewal of the frequency with which needs and object-seeking recur. This presents a challenge that is met by adolescents by extending the scope of rhythmicity to the reiteration of phrases, serving the solution of current problems. In later phases of adolescence, there is a progressive trend toward repetitions of sequences, which are organized to meet complex demands of reality and social requirements.

After a brief review of typical motor patterning prior to adolescence we shall describe in some detail the body attitude and the rhythmicity in successive subphases of adolescence.[2]

Body Attitude and Rhythms of Movement Prior to Adolescence

Body Attitude

Movement patterns, used habitually, leave an imprint on the body that can be seen even at rest. For instance a person who is in a habit of rushing, may look rushed, even though he is not going anywhere. His body has assumed an attitude of rushing.

Body attitude is the composite of preferred positions, body alignments, relations of head, trunk, and limbs, body shapes, as well as of a structure of "engraved" tension areas, which are the remainders of frequently used rhythms (Chapter 8). Each developmental phase is characterized by the predominance of certain patterns of moving and their reflection in a corresponding body attitude.

In some developmental phases, the young child is so much on the go that he is always ready to take off, whereas in others, stability is of prime interest. Early mobility, which promotes the exploration of space with head, eyes, and limbs is succeeded by tonicity, which is required to counteract the effects of gravitational pull upon the body. The new mobility of the toddler, whose locomotor strides give him a new sense of time, is succeeded by the relatively greater stability of the three-year-old who coordinates head, limbs, and trunk as he begins to explore the inside and outside of the body. The phallic child's total body mobility springs from the base of a solid, one-piece trunk with arms and legs acting as its extensions. The latency child's repression and inhibition of interest in the body, reinforced by the defense of isolation, is reflected in a body attitude in which the body center is separated from the mobile limbs. A distinct zone of bound tension (tonicity) isolates the solid one-piece trunk (center) from the dynamic rhythmicity of the distal joints (periphery). When the latency child puts his entire body into the service of an action *(postural movement)*, the inhibition between center and periphery is temporarily removed. The reestablishment of the inhibition, immediately after a postural movement is completed, leads to an isolation of postures from the ensuing action, which is performed with one part of the body only *(gestural movement)*. Because of his stable body attitude the latency child is capable of performing several coordinated gestures simultaneously or in sequence, in such a way that they support one another despite their isolation (Chapter 10).

Rhythms of Movement

The basic and ubiquitous forms of rhythmicity that are part of the congenital motor apparatus, consist of repetitions of changes in tension *(rhythms of tension-flow)*, and changes in the shape of the body *(rhythms of shape-flow)* (Chapter 8). Tension-flow is used to express needs and their psychic counterparts, the drives. The apparatus of shape-flow is used for the intake or expulsion of environmental substances (Balint, M., 1959; Kestenberg, 1967a) as well as for the seeking or avoidance of stimuli. These are the motor nuclei of the incorporation and expulsion of objects. With maturation, tension-flow and shape-flow rhythms become subordinated to the following motion factors which come under the control of the ego:

425

1. *Efforts,* which are used to cope with *space, weight* and *time.*
2. *Shaping,* which conveys the form of relationship through movement in spatial *planes.*[3]

In that efforts deal with relatively unchanging forces of nature and shaping with constant self- and object-representations, they tend to stabilize motility and reduce the rhythmic repetition which is dictated by needs and triggered by hormonal-metabolic changes in the organism.

Effort and shaping appear in the first year of life in fleeting, rudimentary forms. With progressive ego development, they become clearer, more complete, and more frequently used. They are firmly established in the latency child's movement repertoire. In counteracting excessive repetition of tension- and shape-changes, they serve to transform motoric discharge of drive and object-seeking into ego attitudes and object relationships.

The harmonious matching of related effort and shaping elements would seem to bespeak the latency ego's capacity to deal with external reality (expressed through efforts) in accordance with socially approved standards (expressed through shaping). Movement profiles indicate that the matching of complex patterns of effort and shaping is interrelated with the development of a social conscience, derived from past and present identifications with the actions and aspirations of various important objects. During latency this ego-controlled structure becomes incorporated into the superego. In terms of movement, this is correlated with the occurrence of matching of several effort and shaping elements during postural movements (Chapter 10).

The ability to put the entire body into the service of tension-flow and effort, or shape-flow and shaping in postures, appears to be correlated with the capacity to use all of the psychic agencies in the service of combined id-ego and superego demands. Postural efforts and shaping do not attain their mature form before mid-latency (Lamb, W., 1970). This is the time when values are consolidated, and identifications stemming from the most various sources become unified, internalized, and restructured in the superego.

As indicated earlier, in latency the coordination of all body parts in a postural movement is isolated from preceding and successive gestures, in which only one part of the body moves in a given pattern (Chapter 10). When adolescence begins, the breakdown of the gesture/posture isolation is heralded by the flow of gestures and postures into one another, providing a new continuity in the evolution of the integration between head, trunk, and limbs.

426

Adolescence: Prepuberty Diffusion and Reorganization

Body Attitude

In prepuberty, the hallmark of a change in body attitude is the acquisition of a supple, mobile waist. The trunk no longer moves as one piece but is clearly divided into an upper and lower segment. The changes that occur in the upper and lower parts of the body (in girls, mamma budding and hip enlargement and in boys, somewhat later, broadening of shoulder and relative narrowing of hips) are accentuated by the division at the mid-trunk.

When the latency isolation between trunk and limbs disappears, it is at first replaced by a looseness in the waist, which results in an imbalance between body parts. There is an uneven growth of trunk and limbs; they may be positioned and move without relation to one another, sometimes in opposition, at other times in unison. Formerly harmonious combinations of patterns, which promoted stability, may now be replaced by clashing combinations. For instance, if an arm shoots out abruptly in an indirect fashion and, instead of hollowing in the clavicular area and spreading out in the horizontal plane, it bulges in the shoulder and crosses over to the midline of the body, the youngster—who was awkward to begin with—may now end up hitting himself. The gangling look of the young adolescent is due to the dissolution of trunk tonicity and to frequent derailments in limb motions. As in the neonate and toddler, just when limbs overshoot their mark and seem to fly away from the body, they are anchored by an inhibition of flow. This binding, especially as it occurs in the pelvis, where the center of gravity is located, guards against loss of control.

The renewal of untamed rhythmicity and the veering between derailment and rigidity call for a fresh integration between limbs and body center which will serve as a base for a new body image, encompassing current and anticipated sex-specific differences. Head and limbs are now positioned to facilitate the inclusion of pelvis and chest when movements in gestures are followed by postural changes. These evolve frequently from the pelvis and spread into the chest, head, and limbs. At the end of this phase, the young adolescent's equilibrium is maintained by sequences of stability and mobility which originate in the pelvis. His reintegration allows him to tolerate conflict and find new ways to resolve it.

Rhythms of Movement

The even distribution of pregenital and genital-type rhythms in la-

427

tency is now replaced by a disorganized vying of various rhythms for dominance. One of the first signs of the breakdown in ego functions in prepuberty is the sporadic loss of control over rhythms of tension- and shape-flow. These may run rampant (as seen in bouts of restlessness and aimless horsing around), or combine in unusual ways (as seen in outlandish gesturing and disruptions of biological functions, such as regurgitating while eating). Owing to the diminishing influence of the synthetic function there is a temporary loss of control over combinations and sequences of gestures. Lack of harmony results in a frequent mismatching of effort (used for dealing with reality) and shaping (used for dealing with objects) in gestures as well as postures (see Chapter 10). The youngster finds himself acting in a way which clashes not only with what adults and peers expect of him, but also what he expects of himself.[4]

The de-differentiation of the formerly stable psychic structures produces a fluidity in psychic functioning that allows the youngster such an array of possibilities as to lead to a diffusion in thinking that parallels the diffusion in motility. He is rescued from this disorder by a growing ability to think operationally (Piaget, 1948, 1953) and to solve problems independently. The new cognitive style has as its motor counterpart a newly matured capacity for continuity between postures and gestures. In contrast to the latency isolation of gestures from postures, the young adolescent's rhythmic style is characterized by repetitions of fluid gesture-posture-gesture sequences. The reintegration of the released rhythms of tension- and shape-flow occurs within the framework of the alternations between gestures and postures.

If the same pattern is used in a gesture as in the posture that follows it, we speak of *gesture-posture-merging* (Lamb, 1965; Ramsden, 1973). When the patterns are in opposition to one another, we speak of *gesture-posture-clashing*.

In gesture-posture-merging, the initiating gesture is frequently used as a trial action, which accompanies thinking it over. The posture, which merges with this gesture, e.g., uses the same pattern as the preceding gesture, reflects total commitment to the chosen action. For instance, we might begin an action by stepping up on a ledge with one foot only and then follow suit by committing the whole body to the ascent of the elevated area. The trial action has been adjudged ego-syntonic and the commitment results from the approval by the superego.

When a posture merges with a gesture which ends the phrase, what is implied is that the aim has not been given up but the extent of the commitment has been reduced. For instance, in climbing we may reach a point where to continue in this way (posturally) might result in a loss of balance. To avoid it, we may extend an arm and resume postural ascent when it becomes safe again, as (when through the arm gesture) we find something to hold on to for a while.

We speak of gesture-posture-clashing when an initiating gesture uses a pattern that is opposite to the one used in the posture that follows. The implication is that the trial action has been met by rejection of the aim through a process of turning it into the opposite, i.e., the total commitment is now to an aim which is incompatible with the one originally initiated. It would appear that the superego had intervened and directed the ego to do the exact opposite of what it intended. For instance, a gesture of strength may be followed by a posture using lightness. The strong action has been rejected as unsuitable and its opposite imposed on the id-ego. However, if the postural lightness is followed by an end-gesture employing strength this would reflect the ego's disobedience to the superego—a conflict between them.

In prepuberty, we encounter: (1) frequent conflicts between the id and the ego, as evidenced by the clash between rhythms of tension-flow with effort and shape-flow with shaping patterns; (2) conflicts between the ego and the superego, as reflected in gesture-posture clashing in effort and shaping; (3) intrasystemic conflicts between ego attitudes and relationships, as reflected in mismatching between effort and shaping patterns; and (4) conflicts between the superego's punitive components and the ego-ideal, as reflected in the mismatching between effort and shaping in postures. Through repeated clashes and reinstitutions of harmony, the prepuberty child reorganizes and restructures his psychic agencies. Coordinated tension, effort, body shape and shaping patterns, in merging gesture-posture-gesture sequences, are most frequently encountered in clearly structured tasks, such as the narrowly defined requirements of specific sports. However, shortly after a superior sports performance, mismatching between effort and shaping and infantile forms of rhythmicity may return. This can be detected in awkward actions, marked by such alterations of body shape as are incongruous with the concomitant tension changes. Gesture-posture patterning may disorganize in such a way that individual unrelated gestures occur simultaneously, interrupting rather than continuing into a postural movement. For instance a youngster may, at such times, narrow his shoulders, wiggle his hips, and drum with his fingers and begin to punch posturally, interrupting the punch by pointing upward. This disorganization may be followed by an attack of limpness and shapelessness, out of which there emerges a sequence of gesture-posture clashing, followed by a beautiful sequence of gesture-posture-gesture merging. All this can occur within a period of minutes.

A parallel periodicity may pervade the young adolescent's behavior-

429

day. High group performance in school and sports is frequently followed by "fiddling" around and aimless lounging that interrupts important tasks. The evening may be ushered in by a renewal of productivity, beginning with a conflict which is resolved, as the evening progresses. Though both sexes are subject to brief as well as diurnal variations of this kind, the boy's rhythm of activity is more pulsatile, whereas the girl tends to develop changes more gradually and be more sustained. In both sexes, inner-genital rhythms have an organizing effect upon behavior. They subordinate pregenital forms of discharge to their aims and mitigate the abruptness of phallic rhythms. In both sexes, inner-genital and outer-genital (phallic) rhythms combine at times to serve the incipient needs of adolescent genitality. However, in boys these combinations show the greater influence of phallic rhythms and the opposite is true of girls.

At the same time as hormonal, physical, and mental growth becomes more regular, the young adolescent gains control over the distribution of brief and prolonged periods of achievement and rest. However, there is an additional task before his new body image can emerge with clarity. Not only do his drives and coping patterns require reintegration, but also his ways of relating to people.

In early infancy, object-seeking is related to needs and drives. It is rhythmic in nature because it is tied to rhythmic bodily phenomena. Through desexualization, there develops a constancy in object-representations which is instrumental in making needs and relationships independent of one another. As a result, rhythmicity in object-seeking is reduced, but social needs begin to evidence a rhythm of their own. The need to be alternately alone, with a loved one, a friend, or group is repeated in regular or irregular intervals. In latency, with its increasing tonicity, there is a corresponding decrease in rhythmic alternations of various social needs. Thus, one type of relationship can be sustained over a longer period of time; however, a new increase in rhythmicity marks the onset of adolescence.

The revival of infantile forms of rhythmicity in need satisfaction and in social interaction in prepuberty is followed by their reintegration into a new form of rhythmic phrasing through repeated sequences of gestures and postures. We described how these phrases reflect the youngsters' new ways of problem-solving, as for instance through repeated sequences of trial actions, followed by total commitment and ending in a reduction of commitment that restores equilibrium. This type of problem-solving applies not only to methods of coping with concrete and abstract problems, but also to methods of dealing with people. For instance, trying out a new approach to a friend may be followed by an unqualified devotion and may end in a reduction of total commitment. Repetition of such sequences may lead to a balanced relationship.

Out of prepuberty diffusion, a reintegration of need, work, and social rhythm evolves. This enables the mid-adolescent to withstand the crises of growth that threaten to disrupt body boundaries and the cohesiveness of psychic structures.

Adolescence: Puberty Growth

Body Attitude

In this phase of adolescence, everything seems to intensify and to become exaggerated. The new body attitude is based on narcissistic overemphasis of sex differences. In order to stress their manly alignment in the vertical plane, boys widen at the shoulders and stick their elbows out sideways. They may cross their legs to emphasize the narrowness of their hips. As they walk, they frequently stomp, emphasizing their strength by descending upon the ground in the attitude of a conqueror. Girls show off their curves by spreading at the hips and bulging their chests. They sway as they walk, holding their heads high with pride in their new womanliness. The relatedness between boy and girl is apparent in the complementarity or fit in their body shapes. This new style of relating can be noted in groups as well, where there can be contact without touching. Relationships are formed not only via verbal expression, not only through the "fit" in their body shapes, but also through the use of the space "in-between" (Winnicott, 1953) them to create shapes, which carry meaning through the language of movement.

In contrast to the average mid-adolescents who emphasize their differences, there are some whose body attitude and attire betray yearning for unisex. Prepuberty has not provided them with the opportunity for a reintegration of body-shape and self-feelings, which ordinarily form a base for the subsequent narcissistic expansion of sex-specific identity. Thus, the boys deny the uniqueness of their male individuality by hollowing their chests, narrowing their shoulders, and presenting themselves as flat and unspecific as far as the distribution of body mass is concerned. Girls hollow to hide their breasts and attempt to narrow their hips in order to look like flat parallelograms rather than multidimensional, rounded shapes. In contrast to the usual exuberance of the mid-adolescent, these young people are unable to experience the joy of growth as a positive incentive for living. While they tend to gather in groups just as their more mature peers do, their interaction is reminiscent of the type of socialization one finds in young infants who make contact by playing with the same toy (Freud, A., 1962). The group may be held together, with distance overcome by shared transitional, intermediate, or fetishistic objects (Greenacre, 1960, 1969) such as guitars, records, camping equipment, marihuana, alcohol, etc. (see Chapter 18).

Periodically, the intensity and expansiveness of the unimpaired mid-adolescent's body attitude also gives way to the opposite traits. Recovery occurs when the accompanying bout of depression lifts. Thus, even the most stable of the motor apparatus, the body attitude, is subject to the rhythmicity typical of this period.

Rhythms of Movement

In the phase of puberty growth, there is a considerable increase of pulsatile, masculine and cyclic, feminine type of rhythmicity. Rhythms of tension-flow, used for the discharge of genital drives, are frequently characterized now by high rises in tension which reverse into states of low tension. The phallic mode consists of abruptly rising and falling tension. The inner-genital (feminine) mode consists of gradually rising and falling tension. Both modes are accompanied by alternations in shrinking and growing of body-shape, the change occurring more sharply in boys and more smoothly in girls. All these rhythmic changes are experienced as being all-encompassing and so unique that the youngster feels alienated unless his rhythms are met by a similar one. Pairing and friendships are frequently initiated by the experience of synchronization and attunement of rhythms during which boundaries merge and the body image expands. New, adult-genital discharge forms evolve from the confluence of phallic-type and inner-genital type rhythms, which began in prepuberty. Increase in free flow is then neither abrupt nor gradual; after it peaks, it reverses into bound flow, where the same pattern repeat themselves (Marcus, H., 1966). A primacy of adult-type genitality is beginning at this time.

The veering between excited elation and depletion (Freud, A., 1958; Jacobson, 1961; Anthony 1970b) is expressed motorically in extreme alternations between high an low intensity of tension, coupled with equally extreme variations in body shape. This type of rhythmicity may overpower effort and shaping in gestures and postures. The latter will cease to subordinate tension- and shape-flow to their own aims and instead will become subservient to them. For example, a youngster who experiences great frustration and discomfort, as observed in an increase of tension and shrinking of body-shape, may give vent to his frustration by attacking others. The attack will be carried out employing efforts suitable for organized fighting and appropriate shaping, which are motor elements of the ego apparatus. To take this a step further, if the action is performed posturally, we can take it as a sign that the superego has been induced to participate in the acting out. On such occasions, extremes of angry depreciation—usually directed against the oedipal object—may reverse without visible transition into infatuated idealization. In movement, this is reflected in the startling succession of clashing postural actions. Behavior, observable over longer spans of time, also demonstrates this type of rhythmicity. The mid-adolescent, without visible transition, may abandon one cherished cause for another or one love object for another, frequently coming to hate the very same person he had adored or falling in love with someone he had hated.

Equally startling as a series of clashing postures which follow one another without transition, are those postural actions in which effort and shaping are mismatched or occur without one another. For instance, one might picture how curious it would seem if the efforts of the entire body were employed to pound furiously upward at the ceiling rather than down upon the table or floor, or if there were no directions at all to the "show" of strength. The lack of cohesiveness between postural effort and shaping as described above is indicative of a split between the superego proper and the ego-ideal (Blos, 1973; Lustman, 1972; Settlage, 1972).[5] However, the progression toward unity is such a dominant aspect of this phase that almost every split (as reflected in the mismatching of patterns) is followed by a restoration of unity (expressed through rematching of effort and shape). Over larger spans of time we see such alterations between split and reunion in behavioral sequences. Thus, for example, the adolescent may at first fight for a cause detrimental to the people he loves and wants to emulate. Soon after, in accordance with his aspirations to be a hero and a benefactor of mankind, he may become immersed in goal-directed activities which, he feels, will benefit his loved ones.

As he recovers from disharmony of movement patterns, the mid-adolescent practices unifying and combining tension-flow and shape-flow, and effort and shaping in harmonious postural actions. This reflects his capacity for uniting all psychic agencies in order to resolve conflicts. His method of problem-solving stands in contrast to the young adolescent, who thinks things over before he commits himself and still can change his mind on the basis of reality-testing or in consideration of other people. When he reaches mid-adolescence, he begins to suffer from total clashes, which he resolves by total synthesis.

433

A reunification of the id, ego, superego, and ego-ideal at this time restores infantile omnipotence and self-aggrandizement (Kohut, 1971; Settlage, 1973), which will differentiate in the next phase into self-tolerance and self-confidence. Before this can even begin, there is still another task of unification required in the phase of puberty growth. The formation of a dynamic undivided self-concept (identity) calls for re-synthesis of past and current identification, which include not only familial but peer and other adult objects. In movement, this development, which had begun in latency, can be recognized in the evolution of complex effort and shaping patterns from combinations of several simple effort and shape elements. The latency child has begun to use two or three effort or shaping elements in one action. In this phase of adolescence each motion may be overloaded with various qualities of movement. The latter are expressions of partial identifications which, when combined, lead to a high degree of dynamicity reflecting the dynamic rather than static nature of adolescent identity (see also Chapter 10).

Unbounded growth and synthesis of so many aspects of functioning puts such a strain on the organism that there is the danger of depletion and collapse. It is very likely that a progressive differentiation in modes of hormone secretion, which brings on the regularization of ovulatory cycles and of sperm production, contributes its share to the new organization which ushers in the next developmental phase of adolescence. The differentiation which will prevail will rescue the adolescent from the perils of growth crises.

Adolescence: Puberty Differentiation

Body Attitude

In this phase, the attitudinal configuration of head, trunk, and limbs becomes indicative of the finer orchestration of sequential use of joints in movement, which is different for men and women.

In mid-adolescence, a rhythmicity of contrasting traits overshadowed the individuality of body attitude. In the phase now under consideration, the body attitude becomes individually distinctive and adultlike. Body boundaries are clear-cut, with different body parts varying in the sharpness of their delineation, reflecting a differentiated, sex-specific body image. For instance, the male shoulders may stand out as an important landmark of the body, with hands positioned in relation to them. In the female there may be a distinctive wrist-fingers relationship, with the "physiognomy" of hands almost as important as that of the face.

RHYTHMIC PATTERNS IN MOTILITY

One can frequently tell, from the individually distinctive configuration of body parts, which of them will assume the lead, which will follow, and whether movement will begin with gestures or postures, with flow, effort, or shaping. The differences in individual preference for certain sequences and combinations of movement, which will be discussed below, influence the respective configurations of sex-specific and yet individualized body shapes.

Rhythms of Movement

In contrast to the startling sequences of postures, following one another without transition, which occurred frequently in the preceding phase, there is in this phase a return to phrasing in sequences of gestures-postures-gestures. In addition, we see a finer modulation of phrases, with qualities of patterns increasing or decreasing in graduated sequences. For instance, instead of a strong action being followed immediately by a light touch, the force may decrease and increase several times or decrease successively before lightness emerges. A distinctive sign of individuality derives from the preferential repetition of certain patterns in a well-defined tripartite type of rhythmicity that gives an overall organization to sequences of movement patterns: (1) preparation for an activity; (2) its execution; and (3) its resolution, which may be also used for transition into another activity. As an example of individual differences which can be detected within the framework of such differentiated sequences, we may use two ways of punching.

> One person will prepare for the punch by raising an arm with a moderate degree of strength, which increases greatly while the arm is held in bound flow; he will then execute the punch by narrowing and bringing the arm down, forward, and across, with free flow and acceleration and with a sequence of diminishing, increasing, and diminishing strength; he will conclude by dropping the arm in fine gradations of free flow, allowing it to veer sideways to a resting position. Another person will prepare for a punch by suddenly widening and raising the arm indirectly in free flow, holding it there for a second, and bringing it further back; he will then execute the punch with free flow, increasing strength, acceleration, and directness, bringing the whole body down and across with such a swing that he will turn, veering backwards; from there he may raise his arm again in the same manner as before, to prepare for the next punch.

When we examine the rhythmicity inherent in the behavior-day of both sexes in late adolescence, we are impressed with the regularly recur-

435

ring cycles of preparations, executions, and resolutions or transitions to new tasks that make individual behavior regular and predictable. Relationships with people improve, when the new capacity to differentiate, modulate, and compromise is applied not only to work projects but also to the consideration for the participants. The more clearly defined personal style enables family and friends to react with differentiated responses. Dealing with people he knows, the late adolescent is quite dependable. In addition, he is becoming sensitive to changes and he is beginning to react to different people in different ways.

The late adolescent's psychic structures are becoming highly differentiated (Blos, 1973), without the rigid isolation which was characteristic in latency. This has become possible because of a new form of resolution of the oedipus complex. The successful transfer of commitments from the family to new ties can be sustained only when physical maturation, neurohormonal, and motor patterning support the progressive differentiation which enables the older adolescent to find his place in the community. However, his progress in this phase is not yet stable. Before he can achieve a consolidation of gains in the last phase of adolescence, he has to contend with a regression that is very similar in nature to that which shocks parents in early latency (Chapter 9).

Adolescence: The Transition to the Preadult Phase of Consolidation

The regression which follows the steady progression of the preceding phase consists either of a few bouts or a long period of disorganization of body attitude and rhythmicity in movement.

Regressive Body Attitude

The principal signs of regression in body attitude at this time are a loss of vitality, a decrease in the clarity of body-shape and boundaries of the body and the de-differentiation of the functions of head, limbs, and trunk. The latter counteracts stability and makes the young individual subject to passive propulsion into unplanned and sometimes bizarre positions and changes of tension.

Regressive Rhythmicity

There is an influx of rhythms of tension-flow, suitable for the discharge of pregenital and early genital drives with a consequent loss of primacy of the adult genital discharge forms, which has begun in early adolescence. Rhythms which have become clearly differentiated in specific developmental phases may now undergo de-differentiation, so that they become difficult to classify. A return to very frequent repetitions characterizes both the tension-flow and the shape-flow rhythms. Thus, general restlessness and changes in shape are so frequent that the observer becomes confused, finding it difficult to interpret their meaning. There is a return to moving in gestures only, and there are long periods of time in which neither effort nor shaping are being used. Tension-flow and shape-flow seem to predominate. These motoric regressions indicate that drives are stronger and ego functions as well as superego demands are breaking down.

> The observation of large congregations of young people who are in this phase of regression, and who seem to be pursuing a common interest or are in revolt without a clear aim, reveals that they move every which way, with limbs thrashing about and bodies moving in disorganized rhythms without respect for the territory occupied by other people. They lose track of spatial directions and seem unable to cope with weight, space, and time, giving rise to an unruly mass of dysrhythmic, undifferentiated body parts.[6] If a regular rhythm is superimposed upon them through song or the shouting of slogans, this primitive organization, through contagion, brings order into the chaos. One can then see global mass movement based on a common rhythm rather than individual differences. In this and further transformations of chaotic contact seeking, one can recognize earlier forms of social interaction from which there will emerge an adult form of joining the community (see Chapter 18).

Adolescence: Preadult Consolidation

(From the chaos of regression to reconstitution and consolidation of previous gains.)

Body Attitude

An *adult* body attitude becomes solidly established. It contains traces of earlier body attitudes, portions of which have been preserved without change. Characteristic configurations of head, limbs, and trunk relationships, plus preferred alignments of the body and its shape, determine styles of sitting, standing and lying down. Body boundaries are restored and made more solid than before, as habitually used patterns of tension- and shape-flow become permanently imprinted upon the body attitude.

437

Readiness to move in certain efforts and positioning of the body in definite vectors of space is so constant that it can be considered a stable, somatic core of adult self-representation and identity.

Rhythms of Movement

As neurohormonal periodicity acquires greater dependability, rhythmicity of movement ceases to dominate behavior and is evoked, modified, and consolidated primarily in the service of adaptation to external reality and relationships to people. While the rhythmic centers in the hypothalamus are still highly influential, they cease to conduct the totality of life as the young adult gains a wide margin of control over biological clocks and rhythms.

There is, in this phase, a greater stability in the drive organization and much less variability in self-feelings, which are reflected in a general decrease of rhythmic repetition altogether and in a greater differentiation of rhythmic patterns. There is steady progress in the establishment of adult genital primacy over other drive components. This is expressed in movement by an influx of genital-type rhythms, which have an organizing effect upon other rhythms. Phrasing of sequences of tension-flow rhythms becomes very distinctive with well-developed preferences for certain tension qualities and for certain pregenital or early genital rhythms to initiate and precede adult genital discharge forms.

A return of the primacy of the ego over the id is steadily reinforced by a greater complexity and solidity of coping with reality, of defense mechanisms, and of relationships to objects.[7] In terms of movement, we see the return of the subordination of rhythms to the aim of effort and shaping. Individually distinctive, frequently repeated phrases in gestures and postures reflect the typical conflicts and typical solutions of a given individual. These can be seen in movement patterns as well as in other aspects of behavior.

A new tripartite organization, which Lamb (1961; Ramsden, 1973) detected in sequences of adult movement, also influences behavior in short and long cycles of adult life-style. Superimposed upon phrasing in gestures and postures and upon the order of introduction, execution, and resolution of activities, is the periodic repetition of:

(1) *Investigating-exploring-communicating* (as reflected in combinations of spatial efforts, which are used for attention, and shaping in the horizontal plane of space, which gives attention to its structure).

(2) *Determining-explaining-presenting* or representing objects or intentions (as reflected in combinations of efforts, coping with weight, and shaping in the vertical plane, which gives structure to intentionality).

438

(3) *Deciding-anticipating of progress and setting into motion of an operation* (reflected in combinations of effort, which deal with time, and shaping in the sagittal plane, which gives meaning to progression in time).

These sequences, which can be inferred from detailed notation and interpretation of movement phrases, are typical of the complex clusters of ego functions, which govern behavior in short and increasingly longer periods of adult work schedules and long-standing relationships to people. The division into communicating, presenting and operating parallels the classification into orienting-perceptual, processing-conceptual, and executive-motor structures which are the adult's tools, available to the ego processes (Hartmann, 1939, Rapaport, 1951). The individual style is revealed by preferences for one or another of the three modes of functioning. However, the inability to use one of these or the incapacity to follow their logical order indicates a pathological outcome of adolescent development. No doubt, negative as well as positive traits also become consolidated and distinct in this last phase of adolescence (Blos, 1973).

Under the aegis of the new organization, there develop higher forms of sublimation and new values, based on institutionalized distributions of work, leisure, and sleep or on individually controlled alternations of periods of solitude, group-life, friendship, and intimate relationships. As a reasonable means of achieving aspirations comes to match realistic, short- and long-term goals, the conflict between the superego and the ego-ideal is healed and the solidification of a cohesive superego guides the ego into the establishment of an indelible sense of identity based on a new sense of "I" and expanded into a new sense of "we" (Erikson, 1970).

Conclusions

We have examined some contributions to the understanding of adolescent development made through observation and notation of movement. Both the tonic and the rhythmic aspects of motility were considered. Changes in body attitude and rhythmicity, respectively, were seen to accompany each new phase and to parallel psychic development. A detailed description was given of the progression from the revival of infantile rhythmicity in prepuberty to the relative stability in adulthood.

We found that the rhythmicity of the motor expressions of needs, drives, and self-feelings in prepuberty is reintegrated in a new form with gestures and postures becoming the main rhythmic components in which are embedded the ego- and superego-controlled movement patterns, serving adaptation and object relations.

439

PHASE DEVELOPMENT IN ADOLESCENCE

During the phase of puberty growth, the frequency of postural movements, which follow one another in rapid succession and without transition, suggested that the correlated increase in physical growth, in hormone levels, drives, affects, ego interests, superego, and ego-ideal strivings had contributed to the unification of psychic structures.

In the ensuing phase of puberty differentiation, we noted the establishment of a new form of organization, namely, phrasing in sequences of preparation, main theme, and resolution or transition into next phrase. The capacity for such phrasing reflects the higher level of differentiation attained by psychic structures.

Lastly, in the preadult phase of consolidation, we observed that regressively revived infantile forms of repetition become incorporated by a hierarchically higher organization of rhythms. The periodic repetition of sequences proceeding from investigation through concept formation to operation is the hallmark of adult functioning, which is established in this phase.

The adolescent is prepared for an adult life style in which individual, family, and community needs are coordinated with one another and with consideration for the exigencies of space, the priority of values, and the perspective afforded by the concepts of time, past, present, and future. We have alluded to and shall develop further, in the next chapter, the role of rhythmicity in object-seeking, as it proceeds from dyadic through triadic to the manifold relationships encompassed in adult community spirit.

NOTES

[1]"Tonicity" is used here to connote sameness, stability, permanence as contrasted with alternations, variation, and repetitions. Endocrinologists use this term in the same manner. For instance, Gorski and Wagner (1965) characterize pituitary-testicular regulation as "tonic" rather than "cyclic." In psychoanalysis we postulate a binding which prevents the dissolution of structures (Freud, S., 1915b,c; Rappaport, 1960). This implies a tonicity which holds them together through inhibition.

Stable psychic structures are primarily tonic. Their functions, organizations, and boundaries do not alter. However, in the process of development we see rhythmic cessations and alternations of structural components before a structure is "settled" or consolidated.

[2]In order not to obscure the orderly presentation of phase-specific changes in body attitude and rhythms we will have to omit references to the manner in which individual preferences for certain movement patterns influence development (Fries, 1935, 1937, 1946; Fries and Woolf, 1953; Kestenberg, 1965).

440

[3]A discussion of precursors of effort and shaping in spatial directions, described in Chapter 10, had to be omitted in this presentation.

[4]In the face of increasing anxiety, he finds himself defenseless at times because the clusters of defenses he had used during latency are falling apart (see Chapter 10).

[5]On the basis of data derived from movement notation and correlated clinical assessments, we have concluded that postural efforts are used in the service of the superego, both in its permissive and punitive aspects, and that postural shaping is used in the service of the ego-ideal (Chapter 10).

[6]For a masterful description of such a crowd, see Greenacre (1973).

[7]Much can be deduced from movement patterns as regards the nature of defense mechanisms. However, this area of our study has not been included in this chapter (see Chapter 10).

CHAPTER 18

From Early Rhythms of Socialization to the Development of Community Spirit

Coauthored by Esther Robbins, M.D.

In the preceding chapters, we gathered data from endocrinology and from movement studies to show the vicissitudes of rhythmicity in adolescence. Before establishing the primacy of stable over rhythmic structures the adolescent must balance the rhythms of drives and ego attitudes with rhythms in relationships. Out of the early modes of relating to objects, through successive stages of constancy, there develops the stable social conscience of latency. Through the reorganization of rhythmic relationships in adolescence, a stable structure of adulthood evolves: the *community spirit,* which keeps rhythmicity in check and safeguards the individual and his community from the excesses of drive-dominated behavior. The social conscience and its successor, the community spirit, become incorporated into the superego, the former in latency and the latter in the last phase of adolescence. They are interrelated with the moral aspects of the superego—to which they belong—but not identical with them.

We are indebted to Gideon Lewin, Ada Lewitt, and to members of Kibbutz Lahavot Bashan, Barkai, Kfar Blum, Hatzor-Ashdod and Shamir collectively for allowing one of us (J.K.) to observe in their children's houses and for introducing her to kibbutz culture.

Freud's Distinction Between
Social Conscience and Morality

Freud maintained that group spirit is the result of reaction formation against sibling rivalry (1921). Demands for equality and justice for all are derived from defenses against the wish to possess all and oppress others. While religion and moral restraint evolve through the process of mastery of the oedipus complex, social feelings develop through the necessity for overcoming the rivalry that remains between the members of the younger generation (Freud, 1923a). In tracing the development of social conscience *(Gemeinsinn)*, Freud described a path that "leads from identification by way of imitation to empathy, that is to the comprehension of the mechanism by means of which we are enabled to take up any attitude at all towards another mental life" (1921, p. 110). He explained that we limit aggressiveness toward those with whom we identify. These identifications rest upon the acknowledgment of a common substance as, for instance, a meal eaten in common. On a somewhat higher developmental level, identifications and friendships are maintained under the influence of a common affectionate bond with a person outside the group. While identifications with siblings and peers are the basis for group-belonging in latency, each individual in his adulthood, is "bound by ties of identification in many directions, and has built up his ego ideal upon the most various models" (1921, p. 129).

The Need for "Various
Models" of Social Experience

Observation of socialization among infants lead us to believe that the primary root of identification is the recognition of sameness, which is based on the attunement of rhythms between mother and child in the symbiotic phase (Mahler, 1968b). During the second part of the first year, identification is based on imitation. Creepers, observed in groups, explore one another, play with the same toys and vie for interest of the same adults. Gideon Lewin (1971a) feels that this early type of group formation is based on the sharing of sensorimotor experiences and should be termed "perceptual group life." Observations in our Center for Parents and Children in Port Washington, L.I., N.Y., suggest that even at an early age children use the companionships of peers to identify on a horizontal ("here and now") level, rather than on the vertical ("looking-up-to" or "someday I will too") level through which they identify with older siblings and adults.

444

Gideon Lewin (1971b) contrasts the isolated or lonely child, who has been raised in a family and is unprepared for social experiences, with the kibbutz child, who lacks privacy and is seldom alone. He describes the eagerness with which the kibbutz adolescent, bored with his *kkvutzah* (peer group), looks forward to its enlargement in the *mosad* (the high school shared by several communes). He speaks of the adolescent's need for attaining an equilibrium between privacy, pairing, and grouping. The facility with which such an equilibrium can be attained depends on the early activation of social rhythms.

We have long known that biological needs, and consequently drives, obey the laws of periodicity. It should not be surprising, therefore, to discover that the object relationships through which we structure and tame our drives cannot operate in isolation from biological clocks. In fact, they seem to have their own periodicity. The younger we are the more frequently we require phases of withdrawal. The need for respite never disappears entirely. However, as we grow older, our ability to maintain relationships without recourse to periodic withdrawals increases. It is never totally attained except in dreams of young children who hope that their mothers will love them continuously, with unvarying intensity and enduring freedom from hostile wishes. Overcrowding and its opposite, social isolation, which do not allow for rhythmic alternations between closeness and distance, breed destructive or hostile behavior. A "tonic" type of intimacy which excludes others also generates aggression. For instance, a pair of lovers isolated from others for a long time will begin to quarrel. During a long day of lonesome-togetherness, mother and child become annoyed and angry at each other. Separating enhances identification as a safeguard against the destruction of the absent object. New identifications are formed when children separate from their peers and return to their parents. These multiple identifications are enduring qualities of the mind which evolve from rhythmic alternations of contact with different people. In these structures are deposited remnants of relationships, shadows of the past. However, current life experiences are needed for their reinforcement or modification. Especially during adolescence, in which the transition to the permanency of adulthood takes place, do we require "objects as external referents for internal reorganization" (Ritvo, 1972). In latency, the ego-ideal begins to merge with other components of the superego. Not until late adolescence, however, does the superego attain a high level of complexity. In it are embedded not only the identifications with the dicta and goals of oedipal parents but also the aspirations and values acquired through contact with siblings, friends, teachers, current parents, various groups, and community institutions.

445

PHASE DEVELOPMENT IN ADOLESCENCE

The developmental task of the adolescent is to become capable of enduring intimate relationships with love objects within the framework of his latest achievement, an adult community spirit. There is no safety in the family without the maintenance of such a spirit. The danger of destruction threatens the individual both from within and without. To keep the object intact, he needs to separate and seek less-intense, desexualized social relationships which are the heirs to narcissistic self-sufficiency. These new relationships become reinforced through the sharing of activities which foster neutralization and dilution of aggression. Rhythms of need-satisfaction, of love and hate, of sublimated and drive-determined activities, of altruistic and egoistic attitudes, and of community spirit and isolation are structured by the periodicity of social contacts: togetherness-solitude, intimacy-distance, dyadic-pairing–triangular, siblings-parents, home-oriented–extraterritorial, casual-planned, friends-strangers, and allies-rivals, in love, in play, and at work.

Settlage (1973) describes the incorporation of what we defined as "community spirit" into the superego in adolescence as follows:

> While the superego represents the familial and cultural values and traditions taken in during childhood years, it must also come to represent values and traditions unique and appropriate to the experiences of the individual in his own generation and his own particular socio-cultural times.

According to him, this modification of the superego takes place in the last phase of adolescence, when some values are retained and others are discarded. He looks upon this modification as a creative act which occurs in what Winnicott (1953) called the "in-between space" (between mother and baby), the prototype for this being play with the transitional object. Settlage proposed that there is a progression from the play with one's own body and that of the mother in earliest infancy to playing roles, to fantasy without play, and finally to thinking. Observation of babies in groups suggests to us that this progression includes play with other children as well (Freud, A., and Burlingham, 1942).

> In the Center for Parents and Children in Port Washington, N.Y., we have begun to study the infants' first steps in developing a community feeling through the manner in which they use space and rhythms in their handling of animate and inanimate objects. The first signs of interest in one another were discernible in the very young infant's fascination in watching children at play. Mutual touching could be observed at four to five months of age. When inspection of faces began, babies clutched, pressed, and pushed other infants. Soon, hair-pulling became so intense

that it was difficult to disengage the fingers from the hair. The crying of victims was disregarded at first, then watched with curiosity. Pulling of doll-hair was rarely accepted as a substitute. Listeners or onlookers would pucker their lips or cry themselves when another child cried.

When, at the end of the first year, babies began to feed their mothers, they also offered food to other infants who sat next to them in their high chairs. Some of this sharing was simply a game of giving and taking back ("Indian giving"). When a child took what had been offered, the giver would be surprised and would look around for the lost cracker or carrot. At first, he would accept a substitute quite readily and resume eating. However, sometimes no substitute would suffice and he would become inconsolable when his "gift" was not returned or his cracker permanently removed by another infant. It seemed that giving was beginning to be experienced as losing. Giving and yet retaining was experienced through the sharing of toys as several babies would touch and handle the same toy. When there was a distance between giver and receiver, the sharing became "ball-play," with the object remaining visible as it was sent away and returned in rhythmic fashion. Mothers and other adults would adjust to each child's individual rhythm of giving and taking, but the infants could not adjust to each other in this manner. They would leave the game and avoid contact with other babies for a while. To alleviate the distress of discordant rhythms while still keeping children in close proximity, we gathered them around a common large object, such as a piano, which they could bang while a staff member played. They were held by their own mothers or other mothers and staff. They alternated between banging on the keyboard, and looking at and investigating one another and the adults near them and opposite them, on the other side of the upright. A crowd—as described by Greenacre (1973)—was created: a touch-crowd, feel-, look- and hear-crowd. Soon, it became united by the pulse of the music, which provided a common rhythm for all participants. As they began to subordinate their own rhythms to the shared one, there were moments in which they became a group rather than a crowd.

Through the alternation between attunement and discord, spatial closeness and spatial distance and through practicing of giving and taking away, there developed a sense of play in less-casual contacts and in more extended spatial areas. Toddlers walked around with their arms outstretched, ready to give something to a child or an adult whom they had spotted from a distance. They walked away and came back with another gift. The need for periodic rapprochement (Mahler, 1968b) extended from mothers to other adults and children. When older children visited, they enjoyed greater popularity than adults or infants. By the middle of the second year, sharing and giving were often disrupted by an intense sense of possession,

447

expressed through holding on, screaming, and hitting. Soon, they were able to invent games in which roles were changed and a division of labor had begun. For instance, several children alternated between pushing a playpen and being given a ride in it. Organized games of holding hands for "Ring Around the Rosy" or marching together followed solitary play, play with one's own or someone else's mother or a staff member. Games such as jumping together or playing hide-and-seek began to arise spontaneously. Just as spontaneously the two-year-old toddlers introduced "make-believe" games. Sharing ideas and fantasies had already begun, but their disruption through periodic recurrence of shoving, pushing, hitting, or biting and other forms of assault brought into focus the aggressive aspects of group formation. By the middle of the third year, we saw the beginning of friendships and lasting identifications with friends. Indicative of this was a child's intervention when an adult deprived his friend: "Leave him alone, he is my friend." In transition from play through fantasy toward identification, a three-and-a-half-year-old whose friend moved out of town created an imaginary companion, named after the absent child.

In social groups, the dyadic relationship with the mother is extended to identifications with other children and to role-playing in which the relationship between mother and child is worked through at a distance from the mother. Similarly, the intense triadic relationship of the phallic-oedipal child can be deflected from parents and diluted in play with siblings, friends, and groups. Periodic changes in social contact from home to friends and groups provide a fertile ground for the resolution of conflicts with parents. Giving up a parent as an exclusively possessed love object or rival is facilitated by the acquisition of friends who share the child's problems and help find solutions, under the guidance of an adult who himself is not involved in the oedipal struggle. Varieties of social contact alternating with homelife are requisite for the development of a social conscience in latency and of community spirit in adolescence.

The Role of Regression
in the Development of Community
Spirit in Adolescence[1]

Community spirit grows upon a base of early relationships, which evolve from rhythms of sharing objects and space. The developmental line from sharing to creating new social structures is fraught with regressions out of which progressions arise. Behavioral standards are often split because group pressures and parental values differ from one another. Aspirations change with each developmental level not only in consequence of maturational advances and the expansion of social horizons, but also because of regressive responses to social pressures. In early adolescence, new patterns of interaction, evolving out of the revival of regressive forms of social contact, bring back long-forgotten rhythms of touching and inspecting, by means of which separation-individuation is achieved anew (Chapter 9). Adolescents rediscover sensory pleasures of old; they relive wanting what others have, taking away, giving and taking back, sharing, changing interests and friends; competing in pairs and groups alternates with outracing one another for fun or just running together; hostile exclusions of outsiders, who may have been friends until recently, alternate with the renewal of old or creation of new friendships and their coordination with group membership; violent, possessive infatuations alternate with altruistic love; individual and shared rebellion against adults alternates with coordinating the interests of family, friends, and community; all of these have to be reworked in progressively changing rhythms. Reorganized and elevated to an adult, constant level of behavior, they constitute the ingredients of an integrated adult community spirit.

Regressive behavior is especially prominent and prolonged in those who, because they were deprived of early opportunities for socialization, have failed to develop standards of behavior that are precursors of social conscience and community spirit. In their belated involvement in group activity, they are subject to contagion and a vitalizing sensual rejuvenation of shared sameness (Greenacre, 1973), sometimes expressed in terms of ideals which are only thinly disguised successors to narcissistic overvaluation of merged self- and parent-images (Kohut, 1971).

In those young people who are self-reliant and possessed of a more mature form of social conscience, the regression which normally initiates the last phase of adolescence (the preadult phase of consolidation) is even more startling to adults than was the regression in early latency (Chapter 11).

The young people who were beginning to exhibit clearly organized, differentiated behavior with their time regulated for eating, cleaning, working, socializing, and sleeping, now begin to sleep through the day, eat irregularly, disregard the accumulation of a mess in their rooms, and renege on work schedules and social obligations. Intense preoccupation with sexuality may elevate masturbatory practices to indiscriminate masturbatory forms of intercourse (Greenacre, 1973). Buttressed by group approval and driven by new aspirations, young people sometimes pursue aims in a manner contrary to their own standards of behavior. Unbridled aggression unleashed against elders or opposing groups comes as a shock to parents who considered their son or daughter grown and civilized. Groups and crowds promote these unexpected outbursts of "shared," untamed, driven actions. A loss of individuality, a deterioriation in secondary-process thinking and submerging of self-representations into group-representations may lead at times to a primal-horde ideology (Freud, S., 1913, 1921).

Shared acting out revives and reinforces both pregenital and oedipal wishes. The taking over and messing of "sanctified" institutional buildings may be not only symbolic of pregenital possession-taking, but also of encroaching upon inner sanctums, permitted only to adults. The aggressive-fighting commotion is reminiscent of the phallic-oedipal child's conception of the primal scene. The use of explosives may not only express anal-sadistic wishes but also a genital form of aggression which occurs in response to the feeling of bursting arising from accumulation of sexual tension.

Frequently, mature social actions, based on secondary-process thinking, but derived from regressive wishes, cannot be distinguished (outside of analysis), from those which arose directly out of consideration for social change. Taking over of forbidden places may be only the means of attaining a goal such as equality. An example of the latter was the sit-in by blacks at southern lunch counters. Self- and group aggrandizement at the expense of the dreaded, now-denigrated adversary is a sign of a phase of aggressive rebellion arising from within. In a modified form, it may constitute an individual or group response to the victimization by oppressors. In aggressing against father figures, young people identify with their elders, who organize periodic ritual wars (Escalona, 1963; Wangh, 1968, 1972), unconsciously designed to decimate the younger generation.

Out of the last adolescent regression, there arises a consolidation of old and new values, through which the development of the community spirit, the adolescent's prime developmental task, can be completed. In the phase of preadult consolidation, the adolescent, reaping the fruit of his break with primary objects, gives up pregenital and early genital wishes and ceases to yearn for intermediate, accessory, and transitional objects (Chapter 9) that are only bridges to the past. However, traces of the past remain in his love, work, and social relationships, in his habits and hobbies, in the way he manipulates objects in his work and at home, in fantasies and memories, and in the cultural configurations he creates through social action and new art forms. The better his object relationships, the less clinging his libido, the less obligatory his aggression and the more flexible his ego and superego, the more capable does he become of replacing cultural rituals by free forms of community spirit.

As we sought a definition of "community spirit" that would encompass the earliest to the most advanced form of social nexus, the anthropologist W. Torry (1972) suggested the following: "Community Spirit? I know it, I have seen it. It is a visible expression by a defined, bounded group of people, with common interests and involvement in a set of activities or ideas, which relate to the welfare of every one in the group." Such a community spirit is based on special forms of group belonging that are subject to ritualization of customs. Our own form of community spirit grows beyond it; it institutes diversified controls over the style and periodicity of relationships. When these prevail, trust in one's community need not be reinforced through distrust of strangers, that is, provided that there is enough experience in enlarging spheres of interests and in diverting shared aggression from strange people to adversaries in nature (e.g., conquering mountains, outer space, oceans, and others).

Social Deprivation and Its Consequences

It is our impression that, in modern times, our children have not been given enough opportunity to distribute libido and aggression within gradually expanding, rhythmically repeated social contacts. Social isolation has thrust our young children into prolonged stranger anxiety and our adolescents into alienation from the community.

Commenting favorably on the counteraction offered by collective living in Israeli kibbutzim, Bettelheim (1962) suggested that privatization of middle-class life was a consequence of social isolation. To compound the problem, privatization caused the social deprivation of the young. In addition, many of our institutions have been geared toward disruptions rather than furtherance of lasting friendships and social continuity.

Granville Hicks, in reviewing Vance Packard's book, *A Nation of Strangers* (*New York Times Book Review,* September 10, 1972), said:

> We are all aware that our friends and neighbors are constantly moving around, even if we ourselves stay put. But the totals he [Packard] tabulates are overwhelming; at least 40 million Americans change their residence every year; in many cities and towns more than 35% of the population changes annually; it is not unusual to find a junior executive who has moved fifteen times in twenty years of marriage; a different school each year is commonplace for kids.

451

We might wonder whether a father commissioned to overcome new rivalries on an annual basis can help his children to transform sibling rivalry into friendship and fair play. The disruption of social continuity to which scores of families are subjected is aggravated by the frequent disregard of children's social needs in schools. Children who may have learned to socialize in nursery schools lose their feeling of group belonging as they join strange children in a strange, large building which houses their kindergarten. Many latency children are subjected to yearly regrouping through which they lose teachers, friends, and groups and must acquire new ones. For many this annual loss is dreaded. The entrance into junior high school, where subjects and groups change with each period, is frequently the occasion for an outbreak of neurosis in early adolescence. Similarly, the entry into college may become too much to bear for the young person who, having been habituated to expect abandonment, looks with distrust upon strangers. When young college students drop out of school for a while, one can observe how they proceed, sometimes on home territory, to engage in group experiences they have never had before.

Many adolescents, from all social strata, are lonely and need alcohol, cigarettes, and other "companionship-drugs" (Deutsch, 1967) to assist their sociability. More toxic drugs are employed by those who would retreat into the pre-object world of early infancy. Some young people worship distortions of perceptions and loss of boundaries instead of seeking mastery over their new body-ego. Pseudomastery over frightening "attacks of passivity" is achieved by others through a self-imposition of lassitude and idleness, which is interrupted only by relibidinization of the self through sexual need-satisfaction of an anaclitic nature (Williams, 1970).

The indiscriminate use of contraceptive pills in adolescence has arisen from the substitution of sex for friendships and love. It has, in turn, contributed to the shallowing of relationships in both sexes and has deprived girls of the opportunity to reorganize their psychic apparatus in accordance with the sex-specific cyclicity of feminine existence. It seems to us that girls have become less motherly and have not been able to counteract boys' propensities for untamed eruptions of aggression, as they used to in previous generations. Indeed, they are inclined to emulate boys and to join in aggressive acting out. In their unisex attire and advocacy of sex without affection, they even resemble boys in appearance and demeanor. Bisexual pairing, open idealization of homosexuality, masculinization of women, and feminization of men go hand in hand with the growing trend toward infanticide and child battering.

In the midst of a breakdown in bourgeois community values, the individual adolescent is forlorn, distrustful, and often rejected by the very group he seeks to join. Normal rhythms of adolescence call for the periodic breakthrough of untamed drives and regressive outbursts, which ultimately serve adaptation (Geleerd, 1961; Blos, 1971). However, this will be delayed in those young people who have been primed by years of social deprivation and artificial pacifiers. Alienated from their communities, some of them seek social outlet through embracing new religious and supernatural beliefs that have a curative effect on their neuroses (Freud, S., 1921). Many of them have recently been "blending the physicality of Eastern mysticism with the Mosaic injunction to serve the People, whose well being is the measure of all truth" (Miller, 1973).

Other youngsters, because of their lack of experience in overcoming sibling rivalry and their inability to find a structure on which to build communal feelings, envy strange brotherhoods, from which they feel excluded. They strive to join groups which have been cohesive through common deprivation. Belonging to an out-group may provide goals for unstructured ideals and offer protection against the adolescent's own aggression and that of the group he befriends. The uneasy truce between the individual and the group may lead to periodic changes in allegiance, as he continues to seek people from whom he can borrow social values rather than build his own. Some young people, who temporarily engage in senseless destruction in order to please and appease the feared group, may eventually find their way to engaging in the kind of social action that restores psychic equilibrium by providing a balance between individual and group demands.

Some Speculations on the Structure of the Isolated Family

Psychiatrists, and especially psychoanalysts, have been accused of aggrandizing the importance of individual adjustment and offering as cure the conformance to old values. No doubt, some of our limitations lie in the fact that we deal primarily with individuals. Our interest in social interaction may also suffer from too great a concentration on the role of parents as models for identification and a corresponding neglect of other sources of identifications. In more recent years, the decrease of paternal authority and the increasing dependence of mothers and children upon each other's company has brought about more and more protracted and more intense dyadic relationships. Our attention has been drawn to early mother-child interaction and away from oedipal problems. For instance, our interest in stranger anxiety has exceeded the earlier focus on the castration anxiety of the phallic-oedipal child. It would seem that the period of stranger anxiety has been prolonged and perpetuated in new forms. A prolonged adolescence may well be the inevitable outcome of these psychosocial changes.

At every age level there are rumblings of discontent at the loneliness resulting from a lack of community interaction. Chafing from social isolation, economic pressures, and the drain of total responsibility for child care, young mothers have begun to clamor for day-care centers. Before our society settles on supplanting family ties with early peer interaction, there are many vital questions to answer. Enough data must be gathered on the age at which a child is ready to alternate home with group life, and in what doses and settings. Much can be learned from the distribution of work, child care, and other interests in Israeli kibbutzim, where both community spirit and devotion to children flourish side by side. In addition, mothers and fathers may be visited while at work and have enough time to spend with their children to provide models for identifications. Adolescents assume responsibilities early, not only as workers, but also as youth leaders. In our own social setting, we can, at this time, only speculate about the factors that have led to the loss of parental authority and to children being deprived of companionships and lasting friendships, both of which have made the task of removal from oedipal objects in adolescence such a difficult one.

The American adolescent has come a long way from his previous exaggerated devotion to team sports and careers at the expense of interest in social issues and active engagement in public affairs. Undoubtedly social consciousness has increased in the community at large as technological advances have forced us into communication with the rest of the world. It is no longer possible for our young people to remain remote from oppression, enslavement, war, and abuse, wherever they occur. The "grandchildren of Depression," unimbued as were their fathers to undo its effects on their family through personal success, have begun to follow their European and Asian predecessors and contemporaries in helping to shape our society. Before they could do so, many had to undergo a profound transformation, which was made possible by the progressive forces that bring adolescents out of chaos into realism. To gain some notion how this came about, we need to understand the dilemma of their fathers, whose childhood or adolescence was blighted by the Great Depression, and whose young adulthood was shaken by the upheavals of World War II and the McCarthyism of the postwar years.

From many analyses, one gains the impression that the Depression was felt by the parent of that day as a personal rather than national disaster. Arthur Miller (1973) described how the tragedy discredited the whole older generation:

> I was about 14 when the Depression hit, and like a lot of others who were more or less my age, the first sign of a new age was borne into the house by my father. It was a bad time for fathers who were suddenly no longer leaders, confident family heads, but instead men at a loss as to what to do with themselves tomorrow. The money had stopped, and these men were trained by American individualism to take the guilt on themselves for their failures, just as they had taken the credit for their successes.

Commenting on the disillusionment of the young with his elders, he wrote: "It was that nothing one had believed was true, and the entire older generation was a horse's ass." Miller's feelings of obligation to make good were identical with those conveyed in many analyses of sons who resented their fathers' "failures."

> I was listening only for what I wanted to know—how to restore my family. How to be their benefactor. How to bring the good times back. How to fix it so my father would again stand as the leader, instead of coming home at night exhausted and guilty.

The drive to make good was encouraged by parental aspirations for the son and by adolescent ambitions to outdo the father in the eyes of the mother. It was the mother who, very often, kept the family going and browbeat the children into helping her. Sometimes the oldest child was made the confidant of the mother, who blamed the father for his failure and his dejected attitude. She often pushed her son to a success which would be credited to her and her family's superiority over father and his lineage. Thus, the boy was shamed into rejecting his paternal origins and identified with a phallic-masculine mother. In line with the desire to outdo the father was the aspiration to give a better life to one's own children. They should never suffer hardship and no undue demands would be made upon them. They must grow up healthy and happy in good neighborhoods, far away from the streets on which their parents were raised in continuous social interaction with other "children of Depression." In some instances, it seemed that the neighborhood itself was tainted by failure, in others there was a desire to escape old family ties and make "better-class citizens" out of the children. In the move to the suburbs, the disruption of social rhythms (alternations between contacts with parents, peers, and adult relatives; between home, school, and street influences) was compounded by their ostracism as newcomers who "invaded" other people's territories and by the large distances between neighbors (Wynne, 1973). Even larger distances separated children from their father's work-life and kept him from them for long periods of time. The mother found herself alone with her small children, who demanded her undivided attention. Grandparents often remained in the old neighborhoods, dependent on their children financially and emotionally, and unable to offer companionship to their grandchildren. The worship of the old was replaced by the worship of the young. Parents became afraid of their own children who, in their eyes, had become the successors of the once dreaded fathers of their own youth.

Afraid of new financial disasters and yet unable to refuse the demands made upon them by their children, fathers began to treat their money affairs with great secrecy. In order to provide generously for their offspring, they restricted the size of their families to one or two children.

Not only because of social isolation but also because of parental attitudes toward siblings, the child was unable to develop group spirit. The dire circumstances of his parents' youth had hampered their own attempts to overcome sibling rivalry. They felt guilty at bringing forth "another mouth to feed," one of which the older child will be "justly" jealous. Alleviation of parental discomfort at introducing a sibling to the previous child was often sought through offering the latter excuses and bribes. Instead of requiring the children to share, parents took on the job of eliminating the need to share or to give up something. Moreover, when a child was required to be altruistic in extrafamilial groups, parents tended to take his side against those adults and children who were "making him unhappy" by their demands. Thus, normal rhythms of alternations between possessing, sharing, giving, participating, and cooperating were disrupted and corresponding phases of social interaction were distorted. Tonic holding on to parents and to their possessions—given to children by these very middle-class parents—stifled the natural will to share as a precursor of social justice. Partly, because of the exaggerated importance placed on the child's right to personal happiness, the understanding of other people's needs and feelings fell by the wayside.

The tendency for problems in the nuclear family to be interwoven and to parallel national and world dilemmas may be best seen in the manner in which aggression was expressed and countered in the family and in community institutions. Because their fathers had survived the outbursts of unmitigated, large-scale destruction in World War II, children felt safe. They were the "good guys" who were rewarded by invincibility. Wangh (1972) suggested that the disaffection of youth began with our use of the atomic bomb. Escalona (1963) has written with foreboding about the effects on children of living in a society in which there was the ever-present threat of annihilation. However, from the analyses of middle-class children one could glean that they felt safe and sheltered by the notion that the atomic bomb was a weapon which would destroy "bad guys," not them. Even in the era of McCarthyism, when many livelihoods were threatened, children still believed in the intrinsic justice that would prevail. In retrospect, it appears that they felt privileged and did not have adequate understanding of what constitutes oppression and danger to life. One of the reasons for this failure to empathize was the manner in which projection of guilt was fostered in the family and the nation.

Under conditions of social isolation, the young child began to alternate between playing with a family member and watching television. All demands were centered at first on the mother and then on the father. Thus, aggression was concentrated on the family members. The idealized child, in the eyes of his parents, had no faults. In his own eyes, he was a hero whose aggressive acts were justified because he fought the "bad guys." It seemed incumbent upon the parents to help the child deny and project his failures. His nagging, his provocations, and his encroachment upon the rights of others were met with patience lest he think that he was rejected or unloved. When siblings fought, parents could not contain their childrens' aggression; instead they veered between reassuring one or the other of the young adversaries. Parental indulgence and the suppression of their anger could not last definitely. A new type of rhythm arose, consisting of defensive abandoning of the children to television, long periods of forbearance and periodic outbursts of anger. The eruptions occurred when parents could no longer control themselves, and therefore, to the child, they seemed to be unrelated to his misdeed. Even discipline through deprivation had to be avoided. It evoked too much guilt and empathy in parents; the former, as the children came to represent their own distressed parents and the enemies they had conquered, and the latter, as they relived their own economic privations. At the same time as media taught the children about the enemies of World War II, the onetime adversaries were treated with kindness. Thus, even identifying with aggressors did not evoke fears of retaliation. The problem was compounded when the school system bowed to parental pressure and surrendered outmoded disciplinary methods without offering an adequate replacement. Even teachers began to lose their tempers and thus put the blame upon themselves. At the same time the ability of the authorities to prevent violence and destruction of property also diminished markedly.

Growing up as a lonely and blameless idol, the child had difficulty in giving up infantile omnipotence and narcissistic self-aggrandizement. Their successor, the ego-ideal, became so unrealistic that it was impossible to attain. Giving up such standards in adolescence resulted in self-depreciation and lack of trust in a world that did not fulfill one's expectations. By projecting guilt upon others, especially their parents, the youngsters could construe their own failures as acts of revenge upon their elders. Instead of experiencing rivalry and changing aspirations in identifications with teachers and friends, the entire problem of personal achievement was sometimes battled out with parents alone.

We have previously described the attempts at social adaptation in adolescence. In its last phase, as adolescents could form groups that offered them power, they were forced into a regression which was deeper than the one usually seen in the preadult adolescent. On every level, oral through oedipal, they had been able to defeat the goals of their parents and other adults. Now the real danger of destroying their love objects had to be further defended against. Thus, one observed apathy, depression, alienation, or aggression, in which there was a loss of individuality, disorganization, and pseudostupidity. Many adults were quick to pick up the latter and to accuse the young people of being critical and violent without having real solutions to offer. The irrational activities invited containment and punishment by authorities. The adult counterreaction shocked the nation. As in the individual family, permissiveness and patience with the young people's aggression suddenly changed its course and anger obscured the judgment of the adults who tried to contain the youth. The effect on the adolescents was varied. Some had used rebellion from the start to institute constructive social action (Lustman, 1973). Some began to emulate the others only after the shock of retaliation had worn off. Still others became apathetic and subdued. Whether this apathy is but a prelude to renewed outbursts of aggression remains to be seen.

To achieve an adult form of desinstinctivization and to avoid entering adulthood with a readiness for periodic loss of impulse control, the adolescent must learn to integrate his own, his family's and group needs and strengthen his ability to identify on the basis of common interests. At times, he transfers his home life into group or pair living before he can stand on his own two feet and become a contributor to society rather than its dependent. That he may achieve this in devious ways is not surprising, since he must experience various immature forms of group belonging at a time when he is already an adult in the physical sense. When he becomes capable of giving up old ties and exchanging them for new ones within the framework of an adult community spirit, he chooses a suitable periodicity in the distribution of relationships. This serves to counteract boredom and prevents not only the release of untamed aggression against love objects and cherished values, but also the depression that must follow it.

Conclusions

In earlier chapters, we focused on changes in the rhythmic production of certain hormones and on rhythmic changes in motility, with special reference to the rhythmicity inherent in the behavior of adolescents. Applying this to the evolution of relationships, we found that there was a developmental trend from repetitive alternations between playing with mother, one's own body and things, through periodic repetitions of contact with various people and finally to adulthood, in which there are controlled variations between intimate and more remote objects, groups, and solitude.

During latency, relationships become more constant and intervals between changes longer. The need to vary relationships becomes obligatory in adolescence. While this is much less obligatory in adulthood, it is still necessary for the maintenance of psychic equilibrium. Even though the adult is capable of maintaining object constancy and a tonic type of relationship for considerable periods of time, there is a breaking point. Too intense, protracted closeness to one individual, with isolation from others, breeds hatred and destructive behavior. Through the attainment of community spirit in adolescence, the adult becomes capable of viewing his relationships within a broader context, and, under normal circumstances, allows himself the luxury of separation from loved ones without guilt. On the other side of the ledger, the adult is capable of postponing extrafamilial contacts in consideration of demands made by love objects, especially in response to the requirements of the young infant, who needs his mother at very frequent intervals.

We have suggested that too great an isolation of the nuclear family and the resulting social deprivation of children, who need varying social contacts, may be responsible for the extended regression to a childhood rhythmicity in present-day adolescence. We have all seen the prolonged period of aimlessness of the adolescent group we have discussed: their need to "drop out" in order to catch up. They have been attempting to organize their own runaway rhythms through a great deal of contact with one another and the earth, through rebelling and reveling in excesses, through leaving home and country to force themselves into independence, and through immersing themselves in their own music, their manual skills, their art, their own social alienation, and their own social action. We should hope to find a way to help them bring their journey toward adaptive competence and a community spirit much earlier, that we might spare them so long a time of being lost to themselves and to the society which needs their vitality.

Obviously, a solution which offers to exchange early parental ties for early social relationships, primarily with peers, is exchanging one disruption of social rhythms for another, one form of deprivation for another. We would like to find ways to undo the isolation of the nuclear family, which makes child-rearing a chore rather than pleasure. Certainly, parents today require a review of the nutrients involved in raising a child, which should include not only the consideration of the rhythms of needs, but also of the phase-specific distribution of social contacts for their children and themselves.

NOTES

[1]The data on which our descriptions are based stem—unless otherwise specified—from therapy or observations of middle-class adolescents.

Bibliography

Abraham, K. 1920. Ausserungsformen des weiblichen Kastrationscomplexes. *Int. Z. f. Psa.* 7:422–52.

———. 1924. A short study of the development of the libido, viewed in the light of mental disorders. *Selected Papers*. New York: Basic Books, 1953, pp. 418–501.

Aldrich, C., and M. Aldrich. 1944. *Babies Are Human Beings*. New York: Macmillan.

Almansi, R. 1964. Ego-psychological implications of a religious symbol. *The Psychoanalytic Study of Society*. New York: Int. Univ. Press, pp. 39–70.

Altcheck, A. 1971. Dysfunctional menstrual disorders in adolescence. *Clin. Obstetrics & Gynecology* 14 (4): 975–87.

Anthony, E. J. 1970a. The reactions of parents to adolescents and to their behavior. *Parenthood*, eds. E. J. Anthony and T. Benedek. Boston: Little, Brown, pp. 307–24.

———. 1970b. Two contrasting types of adolescent depression and their treatment. *J. Amer. Psa. Assoc.* 18(4):841–59.

August, G. P., M. M. Grumbach, and S. L. Kaplan. 1972. Hormonal changes in puberty: III. Correlation of plasma testosterone, LH, FSH, testicular size, and bone age with male pubertal development. *J. Clin. Endocr.* 34:319–26.

Balint, A. 1933. Ueber eine besondere Form der infantilen Angst. *Z. f. Psya. Pead.* 7:413.

———. 1939. Die Liebe zur Mutter und Mutterliebe. *Int. Z. f. Psa* 24:33–4.

Balint, M. 1936. The adolescent's fight against masturbation. *Problems of Human Pleasure and Behaviour*. London: Hogarth Press, 1956, pp. 49–68.

———. 1959. *Thrills and Regression*. New York: Int. Univ. Press.

———. 1960. Primary narcissism and primary love. *Psa. Q.* 24:6–43.

Barnett, M. C. 1966. Vaginal awareness in the infancy and childhood of girls. *J. Amer. Psa. Assoc.* 14:129–41.

———. 1968: "I can't" versus "He won't". Further considerations of the psychical consequences of the anatomic and physiological differences between the sexes. *J. Amer. Psa. Assoc.* 16:588–600.

Bartenieff, I. 1962. *Effort Observation and Effort Assessment in Rehabilitation*. New York: Dance Notation Bureau.

———. 1970. *Four Adaptations of Effort Theory*. New York: Dance Notation Bureau.

BIBLIOGRAPHY

———— and M. Davis. 1971. *Effort-Shape Analysis of Movement.* New York: Dance Notation Bureau.

Beach, F. A., and C. S. Ford. 1952. *Patterns of Sexual Behavior.* New York: Paul Hoeber.

Bell, A. 1961. Some observations on the role of the scrotal sac and testicles. *J. Amer. Psa. Assoc.* 9:261–86.

————. 1964. Bowel training difficulties in boys: prephallic and phallic considerations. *J. Amer. Acad. Child Psychiat.* 3:577–90.

————. 1965. The significance of scrotal sac and testicles for the prepuberty male. *Psa. Q.* 34:182–206.

Benedek, T. 1949. The psychosomatic implications of the primary unit: mother-child. *Amer. J. Orthopsychiat.* 19:642–54.

————. 1952. *Psychosexual Functions in Women.* New York: Ronald Press.

————. 1956. Toward the biology of depressive constellations. *J. Amer. Psa. Assoc.* 4:389–427.

————. 1959. Parenthood as a developmental phase. *J. Amer. Psa. Assoc.* 7:389–417.

————. 1960. The organization of the reproductive drive. *Int. J. Psa.* 41:1–15.

————. 1961. In panel: Frigidity in women, rep. B. E. Moore. *J. Amer. Psa. Assoc.* 9:571–84.

————. 1970a. Motherhood and nurturing. *Parenthood,* eds. E. J. Anthony and T. Benedek. Boston: Little, Brown, pp. 153–65.

————. 1970b. Fatherhood and providing. *Parenthood,* eds. E. J. Anthony and T. Benedek. Boston: Little Brown, pp. 167–83.

Benjamin, J. 1961. Some developmental observations relating to the theory of anxiety. *J. Amer. Psa. Assoc.* 9:652–68.

Bergler, E. 1947. Frigidity in the female: misconceptions and facts. *Marriage Hygiene* 1:16–21.

Bernard, J. 1961. Teen-age culture: an overview. *Annals Amer. Acad. Pol. & Soc. Science* 338:1–12.

Bettelheim, B. 1962. Does communal education work? *Commentary* 33:117–25.

Blos, P. 1958. Preadolescent drive organization. *J. Amer. Psa. Assoc.* 6:47–56.

————. 1960. Comments on the psychological consequences of cryptorchism. *Psa. Study of the Child* 15:395–429. New York: Int. Univ. Press.

————. 1962. *On Adolescence: A Psychoanalytic Interpretation.* Glencoe, Ill.: Free Press.

————. 1967. The second individuation of adolescence. *Psa. Study of the Child* 22:162–86. New York: Int. Univ. Press.

————. 1971. Reflections of modern youth. *J. Jewish Board of Guardians, Psychological Process Issues in Child Mental Health* 2(1):11–22.

————. 1973. The epigenesis of the adult neurosis. *Psa. Study of the Child* 27:106–35. New York: Quadrangle Books.

Blumenthal, M. 1969. Personal Communication.

Bonaparte, M. 1935. Passivity, masochism and frigidity. *Int. J. Psa.* 16:325–32.

————. 1953. *Female Sexuality.* New York: Int. Univ. Press.

462

Bonnard, A. 1960. The primal significance of the tongue. *Int. J. Psa.* 41:301–7.

Boon, R., R. E. Keenan, W. R. Slaunwhite, Jr. and T. Aceto, Jr. 1972. Conjugated and unconjugated plasma androgens in normal children. *Pediat. Res.* 6:111–18.

Bornstein, B. 1951. On latency. *Psa. Study of the Child* 6:279–85. New York: Int. Univ. Press.

———. 1965. Personal communication.

Boyar, R. et al. 1972. Synchronization of augmented LH secretion with sleep during puberty. Unpublished paper presented in part at the Annual Meeting of the *Amer. Soc. of Clin. Invest.,* Endocrinology Section.

Bradley, N. 1961. The doll: some clinical, biological and linguistic notes of the toy-baby and its mother. *Int. J. Psa.* 42:550–56.

Brierley, M. 1932. Some problems of integration in women. *Int. J. Psa.* 13:433–48.

———. 1936. Specific determinants in feminine development. *Int. J. Psa.* 17:163–80.

Buelte, A. and J. S. Kestenberg. 1971. Holding the baby. Presented at the meetings of the Am. Psa. Assoc. in New York. *Unpublished.*

Burlingham, D. 1935. Die Einfühlung des Kleinkindes in die Mutter. *Image* 21:429–44.

Burlingham, D. T., and A. Goldberger. 1968. The re-education of a retarded blind child. *Psa. Study of the Child,* 23:369–90. New York: Int. Univ. Press.

Burnett, H. F. 1898. *A Little Princess.* New York: Scribner's, 1953 ed.

———. *The Secret Garden.* New York: Grosset & Dunlap, 1938 ed.

Burns, R. K. 1964. Role of hormones in the differentiation of sex. *Sex and Internal Secretions,* ed. W. C. Young. Baltimore: Williams & Wilkins, 1:76–158.

Call, J. D. 1968. Lap and finger play in infancy, implications for ego development. *Int. J. Psa.* 49:375–78.

Chadwick, M. 1931. Menstruationsangst. *Z. Psa. Paed.* 5:184–189.

Child Development Research. 1971. Training films: *Movement Patterns in Development.*

Cobliner, W. G. 1970. Teen-age out-of-wedlock pregnancy. *Bull. NY Acad. Med.* 46(6):438–47.

———, H. Schulman, and S. L. Romney. 1973. The termination of adolescent out-of-wedlock pregnancies and the prospects for their primary prevention. *Amer. J. Obstetrics & Gynecology.* 115(3):432–44.

Coleman, R. W., E. Kris and S. Province, 1953. The Study of variations of early parental attitudes. *Psa. Study of the Child* 8:20–47. New York: Int. Univ. Press.

Cunningham, D. J. 1964. *Cunningham's Textbook of Anatomy,* ed. G. J. Romanes. 10th ed. London: Oxford U. P.

Daiken, L. 1953. *Children's Toys Throughout the Ages.* New York: Praeger.

Dalton, K. 1968. Antenatal progesterone and intelligence. *Brit. J. Psych.* 114:1377.

Daly, C. D. 1928. Der Menstruationskomplex. *Image* 14:11–75.

BIBLIOGRAPHY

————. 1931. Zu meinen Arbeiten über die weiblichen Tabu-Verschriften. *Z. Psa. Paed.* 5:225–228.

Deutsch, F. 1953. Analytic posturology. *The Yearbook of Psychoanalysis,* ed. Lorand. New York: Int. Univ. Press. pp. 234–49.

Deutsch, H. 1925a. The psychology of women in relation to the functions of reproduction. *Int. J. Psa.* 6:405–18.

————. 1925b. *Psychoanalyse der Weiblichen Sexualfunktionen.* Vienna: Int. Psa. Verlag.

————. 1930. Der feminine Masochismus und seine Beziehung zur Frigiditaet. *Int. Z. f. Psa.* 16:172–184.

————. 1933. Homosexuality in women. *Int. J. Psa.* 14:34–56.

————. 1937. Folie a deux. *Psa. Q.* 7:307–18, 1938.

————. 1944–45. *The Psychology of Women.* 2 vols. New York: Grune & Stratton.

————. 1961. In panel: Frigidity in Women, rep. B. E. Moore. *J. Amer. Psa. Assoc.* 9:571–84.

————. 1967. Selected problems of adolescence with special emphasis on group formation. New York: Int. Univ. Press.

Dickinson, R. L. 1949. *Atlas of Human Sex Anatomy.* Baltimore: Williams & Wilkins.

Diczfalusy, E. 1961. *Oestrogene beim Menschen.* Berlin: Springer Verlag.

Dorfman, R. I. 1948. Biochemistry of androgens. *The Hormones,* ed. G. Pincus & K. V. Thimann. New York: Academic Press, 467–548.

————. 1963. Steroid hormone biosynthesis. *Proc. 5th Int. Cong. Biochem.* 7:335–46.

Duboff, G. L., et al. 1964. Patterns of steroidogenesis of androgens in the normal human ovary associated with rhythmic processes of the menstrual cycle. *Fertility & Sterility* 15:661–74.

Eberlein, W. 1966. Personal Communication.

Eichhorn, D. 1970. Physiological development. *Carmichael's Manual of Child Psychology,* ed. P. H. Mussen. New York: John Wiley, 1:157–283.

Eissler, K. R. 1939. On certain problems of female sexual development. *Psa. Q.* 8:191–210.

————. 1958. Notes on problems of technique in the psychoanalytic treatment of adolescents. *Psa. Study of the Child* 13:223–54. New York: Int. Univ. Press.

Ekstein, R. 1967. The child, the teacher and learning. *Young Children* (Nat. Assoc. for Ed. Young Children) 22:195–209.

Elkind, D. 1967. Cognition in infancy and early childhood. *Infancy and Early Childhood,* ed. Y. Brackbill. New York: Free Press, pp. 361–97.

Elkisch, P. 1948. The "scribbling game"—a projective method. *Nerv. Child* 7(3):247–56.

————. 1952. Significant relationship between the human figure and the machine in the drawings of boys. *Amer. J. Orthopsychiat.* 22(2)379–85.

————, and M. S. Mahler. 1959. On infantile precursors of the "influencing machine" (Tausk). *Psa. Study of the Child* 14:219–35. New York: Int. Univ. Press.

Ellis, H. 1936. *Studies in the Psychology of Sex.* 4 vols. New York: Random House.

Erikson, E. H. 1950. *Childhood and Society*. New York: Norton.

———. 1959. *Identity and the Life Cycle*. New York: Int. Univ. Press.

———. 1964. Reflections on womanhood. *Daedalus* 2:582–606.

———. 1970. Reflections on the dissent of contemporary youth. *Int. J. Psa.* 51:11–22.

Escalona, S. 1962. The study of individual differences and the problem of state. *J. Amer. Acad. Child Psychiat.* 1(1):11–37.

———. 1963. Children responses to the nuclear war threat. *Children* (Dept. of Health, Educ. and Welfare, Children's Bureau). Washington: USGPO.

———. 1967. Developmental needs of children under two-and-a-half years old. *Children's Bureau Research Reports* 1:7. Washington: USGPO.

———, and P. Bergman. Unusual sensitivities in very young children. *Psa. Study of the Child* 3–4:333–52. New York: Int. Univ. Press.

Fayman, C., and R. J. Ryan. 1967a. Diurnal cycle in serum concentrations of follicle-stimulating hormone in men. *Nature* 215:857.

Federn, P. 1913, 1914. Beiträge zur Analyse des Sadismus und Masochismus. *Int. Z. f. Psa.* 1:29–49, 2:105–30.

Fenichel, O. 1926. Die Identifizierung. *Z. Psa.* 12:309–25.

———. 1928. Ueber organlibidinoese Begleiterscheinungen der Triebabwehr. *Z. Psa.* 14:45–64.

———. 1934. Further light upon the pre-oedipal phase in girls. *Collected Papers*. New York: Norton, 1953, pp. 241–88.

———. 1945a. Neurotic acting out. *Psa. Rev.* 32:197–206.

———. 1945b. *The Psychoanalytic Theory of Neuroses*. New York: Norton.

Ferenczi, S. 1912. Transitory symptom-construction during the analysis. (In Eng. trans.) *Selected Papers of Sandor Ferenczi*. New York: Basic Books, 1960, 1:193–212.

———. 1919. Cornelia, the mother of the Gracchi. *Further Contributions to the Theory and Technique of Psycho-Analysis*. London: Hogarth Press, 1950.

———. 1924. *Thalassa: theory of genitality*. Albany, New York: *Psa. Q.* ed., 1938.

———. 1929. Das unwillkommene Kind und sein Todestrieb. *Int. Z. f. Psa.* 15:148–53.

Finkelstein, J. W., et al. 1972. Age-related change in the 24-hour spontaneous secretion of growth bormone. *J. Clin. Endocrinology & Metabolism* 35:665.

Fraiberg, S. 1955. Some considerations in the introduction to therapy in puberty. *Psa. Study of the Child* 10:264–86. New York: Int. Univ. Press.

———. 1961. Homosexual conflicts. *Adolescents,* ed. S. Lorand and H. I. Schneer. New York: Hoeber, pp. 78–112.

———. 1968. Parallel and divergent patterns in blind and sighted infants. *Psa. Study of the Child,* 23:264–300. New York: Int. Univ. Press.

———. 1973. Some characteristics of genital arousal and discharge in latency girls. *Psa. Study of the Child* 27:439–75. New York: Quadrangle Books.

BIBLIOGRAPHY

Frasier, S. D., F. Gafford and R. Horton. 1969. Plasma androgens in childhood and adolescence. *J. Clin. Endocr.* 29:1404–408.

Freud, A. 1936. *The Ego and the Mechanisms of Defence.* London: Hogarth; New York: Int. Univ. Press, 1946.

———. 1949. Über bestimmte Schwierigkeiten zwischen Eltern und Kindern in der Vorpubertät. *Die Psychohygiene,* ed. M. Amande-Pfister. Zurich: Hans Huber, pp. 10–16.

———. 1952. The role of the teacher. *Harvard Educ. Rev.* 22:229–34.

———. 1952b. Studies in passivity. *The Writings of Anna Freud,* 4:245–59. New York: Int. Univ. Press.

———. 1954. The concept of the rejecting mother. *Parenthood,* eds. E. J. Anthony and T. Benedek. Boston: Little, Brown and Co., 1970. pp. 376–86.

———. 1958. Adolescence. *Psa. Study of the Child* 13:255–78. New York: Int. Univ. Press.

———. 1962. The emotional and social development of young children. *The writings of Anna Freud* New York: Int. Univ. Press, 1969, 5:336–51.

———. 1963. The concept of developmental lines. *Psa. Study of the Child,* 18:245–65. New York: Int. Univ. Press.

———. 1965. *Normality and Pathology in Childhood: Assessment of Development.* New York: Int. Univ. Press.

———. 1967a. About losing and being lost. *Psa. Study of the Child* 22:9–19. New York: Int. Univ. Press.

———. 1967b. Panel Discussion: The role of physical illness in the emotional development of children. Cong. Int. Psa. Assoc., Copenhagen.

———, and Burlingham, D. 1942. *Young children in war-time.* London: Allen & Unwin.

——— ——— ——— 1943. *Children without families.* London: Allen & Unwin.

Freud, S. 1905. Three essays on the theory of sexuality. *Standard ed.* London: Hogarth Press, 1953, 7:125–245.

———. 1905b. *Jokes and their relation to the unconscious. Standard Ed.* London: Hogarth Press, 1960, 8:3–242.

———. 1908. Character and anal eroticism. *Standard Ed.* London: Hogarth Press, 1959, 9:167–75.

———. 1909. *Analysis of a phobia in a five-year-old boy. Standard ed.* London: Hogarth Press, 1955, 10:5–147.

———. 1910a. Five lectures on psychoanalysis. *Standard Ed.* London: Hogarth Press, 1957, 11:3–56.

———. 1910b. Leonardo Da Vinci and a memory of his childhood. *Standard Ed.* London: Hogarth Press, 1957, 11:59:137.

———. 1911. Formulations on the two principles of mental functioning. *Standard Ed.* London: Hogarth Press, 1958, 215–26.

———. 1912. On the universal tendency for debasement in the sphere of love. *Standard*

Ed. London: Hogarth Press, 1957, 11:178–90.

———. 1913. Totem and taboo. *Standard Ed.* London: Hogarth Press, 1955, 13:1–162.

———. 1914a. On narcissism. *Standard Ed.* London: Hogarth Press, 1957, 14:67–104.

———. 1914b. Some reflections on school-buy psychology. *Standard Ed.* London: Hogarth Press, 1955, 13:241–44.

———. 1915a. Instincts and their vicissitudes. *Standard Ed.* London: Hogarth Press, 1957, 14:109–40.

———. 1915b. Repression. *Standard Ed.* London: Hogarth Press, 1957, 14:141–158.

———. 1915c. The Unconscious. *Standard Ed.* London: Hogarth Press, 1957, 14:159–215.

———. 1917a. The taboo of virginity. *Standard Ed.* London: Hogarth Press, 1957, 11:191–209.

———. 1917b. *Introductory Lectures on Psychoanalysis. Standard Ed.* London: Hogarth Press, 1963, 15 & 16.

———. 1917c. On transformations of instinct as exemplified in anal eroticism. *Standard Ed.* London: Hogarth Press, 1955, 17:125–33.

———. 1919. A child is being beaten. *Standard Ed.* London: Hogarth Press, 1955, 17:175–204.

———. 1921. Group psychology and the analysis of the ego. *Standard Ed.* London: Hogarth Press, 1955, 18:67–143.

———. 1923a. The ego and the id. *Standard Ed.* London: Hogarth Press, 1961, 19:1–66.

———. 1923b. The infantile genital organization: an interpolation into the theory of sexuality. *Standard Ed.* London: Hogarth Press, 1961, 19:141–45.

———. 1923c. A seventeenth-century demonological neurosis. *Standard Ed.* London: Hogarth Press, 1961, 19:69–105.

———. 1924a. The dissolution of the oedipus complex. *Standard Ed.* London: Hogarth Press, 1961, 19:173–79.

———. 1924b. The economic problem of masochism. *Standard Ed.* London: Hogarth Press, 1961, 19:157–170.

———. 1925. Some psychical consequences of the anatomical distinction between the sexes. *Standard Ed.* London: Hogarth Press, 1961, 19:243–58.

———. 1926. Inhibition, symptoms and anxiety. *Standard Ed.* London: Hogarth Press, 1959, 20:75–175.

———. 1930. Civilization and its discontents. *Standard Ed.* London: Hogarth Press, 1961, 21:57–145.

———. 1931. Female sexuality. *Standard Ed.* London: Hogarth Press, 1961, 21:225–43.

———. 1932. The acquisition and control of fire. *Standard Ed.* London: Hogarth Press, 1964, 22:183–93.

BIBLIOGRAPHY

———. 1933. New introductory lectures on psychoanalysis. *Standard Ed.* London: Hogarth Press, 1964, 22:1–182.

———. 1937. Analysis terminable and interminable. *Standard Ed.* London: Hogarth Press, 1964, 23:209–53.

———. 1940. An outline of psychoanalysis. *Standard Ed.* London: Hogarth Press, 1964, 23:139–207.

———. and J. Breuer. 1893–95. Studies on Hysteria. *Standard Ed.* London: Hogarth Press, 1930.

Friedman, D. D. 1972. Childbirth education for the adolescent. Unpub. paper presented at the *Israel Int. Cong. on Sex Ed.,* Tel Aviv, July, 1972.

Fries, M. 1935. Interrelationship to physical, mental and emotional life of a child from birth to four years of age. *Amer. J. Disturbed Child* 49:1546–63.

———. 1937. Factors in character development. *Amer. J. Orthopsychiat.* 7:142–81.

———. 1944. Psychosomatic relationship between mother and infant. *Psychosomatic Med.* 6:159–62.

———. 1946: The child's ego development and the training of adults in his environment. *Psa. Study of the Child,* 2:85–112. New York: Int. Univ. Press.

———. 1947. Diagnosing the child's adjustment through age level tests. *Psa. Rev.* 34:1–31.

———. 1958. Some hypotheses on the role of the congenital activity type in personality and development. *Psa. Study of the Child* 13:48–64. New York: Int. Univ. Press.

———. and P. J. Woolf. 1953. Some hypotheses on the role of the congenital activity type in personality development. *Psa. Study of the Child,* 8:48–62. New York: Int. Univ. Press.

Furman, E. 1957. Treatment of under-fives by way of parents. *Psa. Study of the Child* 12:250–62. New York: Int. Univ. Press.

———. 1969. Theoretical and clinical considerations in the assessment of parents. *Therapeutic Nursery School,* eds. E. Furman and A. Katan. New York: Int. Univ. Press, pp. 66–79.

Galenson, E. and H. Roiphe, 1971. The impact of early sexual discovery on mood, defensive organization, and symbolization. *The Psychoanalytic Study of the Child* 26:195–216. New York: Int. Univ. Press.

Gates, J. S. 1905. *The Story of the Lost Doll.* Indianapolis: Bobbs-Merrill.

Geleerd, E. 1957. Some aspects of psychoanalytic technique in adolescents. *Psa. Study of the Child* 12:263–83. New York: Int. Univ. Press.

———. 1961. Some aspects of ego vicissitudes in adolescence. *J. Amer. Psa. Assoc.* 9:394–405.

———. 1965. Two kinds of denial: neurotic denial and denial in the service of the need to survive. *Drives, Affects, Behavior,* ed. M. Schur. New York: Int. Univ. Press, 2:118–27.

Gero, G. 1939. Zum Problem der oralen Fixierung. *Int. Z. f. Psa.* 24:239–57.

BIBLIOGRAPHY

Gesell, A. 1940. *The First Five Years of Life*. New York: Harper.

———, and F. L. Ilg. 1943. *Infant and Child in the Culture of Today*. New York: Harper.

———. 1946. *The Child from Five to Ten*. New York: Harper.

Gill, M. M. 1963. Topography and systems in psychoanalytic theory. *Psychological Issues* 3/2. Monograph 10. New York: Int. Univ. Press.

Glenn, J. 1965. Sensory determinants of the symbol *three*. *J. Amer. Psa. Assoc.* 13:422–34.

Glover, E. 1943–1957. The psychopathology of prostitution. *The Roots of Crime*. New York: Int. Univ. Press, pp. 244–67, 1960.

Godden, R. 1958. *The Greengage Summer*. New York: Viking Press.

Gorski, R. A., and J. W. Wagner. 1965. Gonadal activity, sexual differentiations of the hypothalamus. *J. Endocrinology* 76:226–39.

Gray, P. 1962. Personal communication.

Greenacre, P. 1941. The predisposition to anxiety. *Psa. Q.* 10:66–95.

———. 1947. Child wife as ideal: sociological considerations. *Amer. J. Orthopsychiat.* 17:167–71.

———. 1948. Anatomical structure and superego development. Amer. J. Orthopsychiat. 13:636–648.

———. 1950a. The prepuberty trauma in girls. *Psa. Q.* 19:298–317.

———. 1950b. Special problems of early female sexual development. *Psa. Study of the Child* 5:112–38.

———. 1952. Pregenital patterning. *Int. J. Psa.* 33:410–415.

———. 1953. Certain relationships between fetishism and the faulty development of the body image. *Psa. Study of the Child* 8:79–98.

———. 1954. Problems of infantile neurosis. *Psa. Study of the Child* 9:18–24.

———. 1955. Further considerations regarding fetishism. *Psa. Study of the Child* 10:187–194.

———. 1960. Further notes on fetishism. *Psa. Study of the Child*, 15:191–207. New York: Int. Univ. Press.

———. 1969. The fetish and the transitional object. *Psa. Study of the Child*, 24:144–64. New York: Int. Univ. Press.

———. 1973. Crowds and crisis: Psychoanalytic considerations. *Psa. Study of the Child*, 27:136–155. New York: Quadrangle Books, 1973.

Greenblatt, R. B. 1967. Progestational agents in clinical practice. *Med. Sci.*, 18:37–49.

Guthrie, G. M., and P. J. Jacobs. 1966. *Child Rearing and Personality Development in the Philippines*. University Park: Penn State Univ. Press.

Halverson, H. M. 1938. Infant sucking and tensional behavior. *J. Genet. Psychol.* 53:365–430.

———. 1940. Genital and sphincter behavior of the male infant. *J. Genet. Psychol.* 56:95–136.

BIBLIOGRAPHY

Hamburger, C. 1948. Normal urinary excretion of neutral 17-ketosteroids with special reference to age and sex variations. *Acta Endocrinology* 1:19–37.

Hannett, F. 1964. The haunting lyric. *Psa. Q.* 23:226–69.

Hann-Kende, F. 1933. Über Klitorisonanie und Penisneid. *Int. Z. f. Psa.* 19:416–427.

Harley, M. 1961a. Masturbation conflicts. *Adolescents,* eds. S. Lorand and H. I. Schneer. New York: Hoeber, pp. 51–77.

———. 1961b. Some observations on the relationship between genitality and structural development in adolescence. *J. Amer. Psa. Assoc.* 9:434–60.

Harlow, H. F. 1965. Sexual behavior in the rhesus monkey. *Sex and Behavior,* ed. F. A. Beach. New York: Wiley, pp. 234–66.

Harman, I. M. 1932. *Textbook of Embryology.* Philadelphia: Lea & Febiger.

Hartmann, H. 1932. Zur Anatomie der Geschlectsorgane Neugeborener. *Arch. Gynäk.* 148:708–23.

Hartmann, H. 1939. *Ego Psychology and the Problem of Adaptation.* New York: Int. Univ. Press, 1958.

———. E. Kris, and R. M. Loewenstein. 1946. Comments on the formation of psychic structure. *Psa. Study of the Child* 2:11–38.

Hediger, H. 1965. Environmental factors influencing the reproduction of zoo animals. *Sex and Behavior,* ed. F. A. Beach. New York: Wiley, pp. 319–55.

Heim, L., and P. S. Timiras. 1963. Gonad-brain relationship: precocious brain maturation after estradiol in rats. *Endocrinology* 72:598–606.

Heiman, M. 1963. Sexual responses in women: a correlation of physiological findings with psychoanalytic concepts. *J. Amer. Psa. Assoc.* 11:360–85.

Hicks, G. 1972. Review of Vance Packard's *A Nation of Strangers. New York Times Book Review,* September 10.

Hitschmann, E., and E. Bergler. 1934. *Die Geschlectskälte der Frau.* Vienna: Ars Medici. Eng. tr., *Frigidity in Women.* New York: Nervous and Mental Disease Publ. Co., 1936.

Hoffer, W. 1941. Mouth, hand and ego-integration. *Psa. Study of the Child,* 3/4:49–56. New York: Int. Univ. Press.

———. 1950. Development of the body ego. *Psa. Study of the Child,* 5:18–24. New York: Int. Univ. Press.

———. 1952. The mutual influences in the development of the ego and the id. *Psa. Study of the Child* 7:31–42. New York: Int. Univ. Press.

Hollos, S. 1922. Über das Zeitgefühl. *Int. Z. f. Psa.* 8:421–39.

Horney, K. 1926. The flight from womanhood. *Int. J. Psa.* 7:324–39.

———. 1931. Die praemenstruaellen Verstimmungen. *Z. Psa. Paed.* 5:161–67.

———. 1932. The dread of woman. *Int. J. Psa.* 13:348–60.

———. 1933. The denial of the vagina. *Int. J. Psa.* 14:57–70.

Hubble, D. 1969. Endocrine control of growth and skeletal maturation. *Pediatric Endocrinology.* Philadelphia: F. A. Davis, pp. 29–333.

Hudson, J. P., et al. 1964. The measurement of testosterone in biological fluids in the evaluation of androgen activity. *2nd Int. Cong. Endocrinol.* (London), pp. 1127–34.

Huffman, J. W. 1959. The structure and bacteriology of the premenarcheal vagina. *Ann. Amer. Acad. Sci.* 83:227–36.

Hug-Hellmuth, H. 1919. *Das Tagebuch eines halbwüchsigen Mädchens.* Vienna: Int. Psa. Verlag.

Huschka, M. 1941. Psychopathological disorders in the mother. *J. Nerv. & Mental Dis.* 94:76.

Inhelder, B., and J. Piaget. 1958. *The Growth of Logical Thinking from Childhood to Adolescence.* New York: Basic Books.

Jacobson, E. 1936. Beitrag zur Entwicklung der Weiblichen Kindeswunsches. *Int. Z. Psa.* 22:371–79.

———. 1937. Wege der weiblichen Überichbildung. *Int. Z. Psa.* 23:402–12.

———. 1950. Development of the wish for a child in boys. *Psa. Study of the Child* 5:139–52.

———. 1954. The self and the object world. Vicissitudes of their infantile cathexes and their influence on ideational and affective development. *Psa. Study of the Child,* 9:75–127. New York: Int. Univ. Press.

———. 1961. Adolescent moods and the remodeling of psychic structures in adolescence. *Psa. Study of the Child* 16:164–83. New York: Int. Univ. Press.

———. 1964. *The Self and the Object World.* New York: Int. Univ. Press.

Jaffe, R. B., and A. R. Midgley. 1969. Current status of human gonadotrophin Radio-Immunoassay. *J. Obstet. & Gynecology Survey* 24:200–13.

Jekels, L. 1913. Einige Bemerkungen zur Trieblehre. *Int. Z. Psa.* 1:439–43.

Joffe, W. G., and J. Sandler. 1965. Notes on pain, depression and individuation. *Psa. Study of the Child* 20:394–424. New York: Int. Univ. Press.

Jones, E. 1927. The early development of female sexuality. *Collected Papers.* London: Baillière, Tindall & Cox, 1938, pp. 556–70.

———. 1933. The phallic phase. *Int. J. Psa.* 14:1–33.

———. 1935a. Early female sexuality. *Papers on Psycho-Analysis.* London: Baillière, Tindall & Cox, pp. 485–95.

Josselyn, I. M. 1952. *The Adolescent and His World.* New York: Family Service Assoc. Amer.

Kaplan, E. 1963. Observations on the congenital absence of the vagina. Paper presented at the Long Island Psa. Soc., June.

Kaplan, E. B. 1965. Reflections regarding psychomotor activity during the latency period. *Psa. Study of the Child* 20:220–38.

Katan, A. 1937. The role of "displacement" in agoraphobia. *Int. J. Psa.* 32:41–50. 1951.

———. 1961. Some thoughts about the role of verbalization in early childhood. *Psa.*

BIBLIOGRAPHY

Study of the Child 16:184–88. New York: Int. Univ. Press.

Keiser, S. 1947. On the psychopathology of orgasm. *Psa. Q.* 16:378–90.

———. 1952. Body ego during orgasm. *Psa. Q.* 21:153–66.

Kestenberg, J. 1945. Early reactions to tensions. Unpublished paper presented to New York Psa. Assoc.

———. 1953a. History of an "autistic" child. *J. Child Psychiatry* 2:5–52.

———. 1953b. Notes on ego development. *Int. J. Psa.* 34:111–22.

———. 1954. Report on observations from a longitudinal study. Panel of Infantile Neurosis, New York Psa. Assoc. and Inst., E. Kris, Chairman.

———. 1962. Panel on Theoretical and Clinical Aspects of Overt Female Homosexuality, rep. C. W. Socarides. *J. Amer. Psa. Assoc.* 10:579–92.

———. 1963. *Birds-Eye View on Development.* Unpublished lectures given at the Psa. Division, Downstate University, New York. (Summary)

———. 1965. The role of movement patterns in development. I Rhythms of movement. II Flow of tension and effort. *Psa. Q.* 34:1–36, 34:517–63.

———. 1966. Rhythm and organization in obsessive-compulsive development. *Int. J. Psa.* 47:151–59.

———. 1967a. The role of movement patterns in development. III The control of shape. *Psa. Q.* 36:356–409.

———. 1967b. *Self Environment and Objects as Seen Through the Study of Movement Patterns.* Unpublished.

———. 1968. Acting out in the analysis of children and adults. *Int. J. Psa.,* 49:341–46.

———. 1969. Problems of technique of child analysis in relation to the various developmental stages: prelatency. *Psa. Study of the Child.* 24:358–83. New York: Int. Univ. Press.

———. 1971. A developmental approach to disturbances of sex-specific identity. *Int. J. Psa.* 52:99–102.

———. 1972. How children remember and parents forget. *Int. J. Psa. Psychother.* 1/2:103–23.

———. 1973a. *The Role of Movement Patterns in Mother-Child Interaction.* Unpublished.

———. 1973b. *Movement Patterns in Development IV. Epilogue.* Unpublished.

———. 1973c. *Glossary of Movement Patterns.* Unpublished.

———. and H. Marcus. *Notes on Bisexuality,* based on a psychoanalytic interpretation of movement patterns. Unpublished.

Kinsey, A. C., et al. 1953. *Sexual Behavior in the Human Female.* Philadelphia: Saunders.

Kleeman, J. A. 1965. A boy discovers his penis. *Psa. Study of the Child* 20:239–66.

———. 1966. Genital self-discovery during a boy's second year: a follow-up. *Psa. Study of the Child* 21:358–92.

———. 1967. The peek-a-boo game. I Its origin, meanings and related phenomena in the first year. *Psa. Study of the Child,* 22:239–273. New York: Int. Univ. Press.

Klein, M. 1928. Early stages of the oedipus conflict. *Int. J. Psa.* 9:167–80.

————. 1932. *The Psycho-Analysis of Children*. London: Hogarth Press.

————. 1948. *Contributions to Psycho-Analysis, 1921-1945*. London: Hogarth Press.

Kohut, H. 1971. *The Analysis of the Self*. New York: Int. Univ. Press.

Kramer, P. 1954. Early capacity for orgastic discharge and character formation. *Psa. Study of the Child* 9:128—41.

Kris, E. 1951. Some comments and observations on early auto-erotic activities. *Psa. Study of the Child* 6:95—116. New York: Int. Univ. Press.

————. 1955. Neutralization and sublimation. *Psa. Study of the Child* 10:30—46. New York: Int. Univ. Press.

Laban, R. 1950. *The Mastery of Movement*. 2nd ed., revised and enlarged L. Ullman. London: MacDonald & Evans. 1960.

————. 1966. *Choreutics*. Annotated and edited by L. Ullman. London: MacDonald & Evans.

————, and F. C. Lawrence. 1947. *Effort*. London: MacDonald & Evans.

Lamb, W. 1961. *Correspondence Course in Movement Assessment*. Unpublished.

————. 1965. *Posture and Gesture*. London: Gerald Duckworth.

————, and D. Turner. 1969. *Management Behavior*. New York: Int. Univ. Press.

Lampl-de Groot, J. 1928. The evolution of the oedipus complex in women. *Int. J. Psa.* 9:332—45.

————. 1933. Problems of femininity. *Psa. Q.* 2:489—518.

————. 1947. The preoedipal phase in the development of the male child. *Psa. Study of the Child* 2:75—113. New York: Int. Univ. Press.

Landau, B., et al. 1960. Presence of gonadotropic inhibiting factor in urine in young children. *Metabolism* 9:85—87.

Landauer, K. 1931. Menstruationserlebniss des Knaben. *Z. Psa. Paed.* 5:175—89.

————. 1935. Die Ich-Organisation in der Pubertät. *Z. Psa. Paed.* 9:380—420.

Langer, M. 1951. *Maternidad y Sexo*. Buenos Aires: Ed. Nova.

Levy, D. 1939. Maternal overprotection. *Psychiat.* 2:99—128.

————. 1942. Psychosomatic studies of some aspects of maternal behavior. *Psychosomatic Med.* 4:223—227.

Lewin, B. D. 1933. The body as phallus. *Psa. Q.* 2:24—27.

————. 1950. *The Psychoanalysis of Elation*. New York: Norton.

Lewin, G. 1971a. Personal communication.

————. 1971b. In *Children in the Kibbutz* by Mutsuharu Shinohara. Tokyo: Seishin Shobe, pp. 1—23.

Loewenstein, R. M. 1935. Phallic passivity in men. *Int. J. Psa.* 16:334—40.

————. 1950. Conflict and autonomous ego development during the phallic phase. *Psa. Study of the Child* 5:47—52.

Lomax, A., Bartenieff, I. and Paulay, F. 1967. Choreometrics. In *Folksong Style and Culture* by Lomax, A. New York: Amer. Assoc. Adv. Sci.

BIBLIOGRAPHY

Lorand, S. 1939. Contribution to the problem of vaginal orgasm. *Clinical Studies in Psychoanalysis*. New York: Int. Univ. Press, 1950, pp. 148–58.

Lownsberry, E. 1946. *Marta the Doll*. New York: Longmans, Green.

Lustman, S. L. 1973. Yale's year of confrontation. A view from the master's house. *Psa. Study of the Child* 27:57–73. New York: Quadrangle Books.

Mack Brunswick, R. 1940. The preoedipal phase of libido development. *Psa. Q.* 9:293–319.

Mahler, M. S. 1942. Pseudo-imbecility: the magic cap of invisibility. *Psa. Q.* 11:149–64.

———. 1960. Perceptual dedifferentiation and psychotic object-relationship. *Int. J. Psa.* 41:548–53.

———. 1961. On sadness and grief in infancy and childhood: loss and restoration of the symbiotic love object. *Psa. Study of the Child* 16:332–51.

———. 1963. Thoughts about development and individuation. *Psa. Study of the Child* 18:307–24. New York: In. Univ. Press.

———. 1965. On the significance of the normal separation-individuation phase. *Drives, Affects, Behavior,* ed. M. Schur. New York: Int. Univ. Press, 2:161–69.

———. 1966. Notes on the development of basic moods: the depressive affect. *Psychoanalysis, a General Psychology,* ed. R. M. Loewenstein et al. New York: Int. Univ. Press, pp. 152–68.

———. 1967. On human symbiosis and the vicissitudes of individuation. *J. Amer. Psychoanal. Assn.,* 15:10–67.

———. 1968a. Discussion of Lofgren's paper, Castration anxiety and the body ego. *Int. J. Psa.* 49:410–12.

———. 1968b. *On human symbiosis and the vicissitudes of individuation.* New York: Int. Univ. Press.

———, and J. Silberpfennig. 1938. Der Rorschach'sche Formdeutversuch als Hilfsmittle zum Verständnis der Psychologie Hirnkranker. *Schweitz. Arch. Neurol. & Psychiat.* 40:302–27.

———, and P. Elkisch. 1953. Some observations on disturbances of the ego in a case of infantile psychosis. *Psa. Study of the Child* 8:252–61. New York: Int. Univ. Press.

———, and M. Furer. 1963. Certain aspects of the separation-individuation phase. *Psa. Q.* 32:1–14.

———, and K. La Perriere. 1965. Mother-child interaction during separation-individuation. *Psa. Q.* 24:483–98.

———, and J. B. McDevitt. 1968. Observations on adaptation and defense *in statu nascendi*. *Psa. Q.* 37:1–21.

———, F. Pine and A. Bergman. 1974. *The psychological birth of the human infant. Symbiosis and individuation.* New York: Basic Books.

Marcus, H. 1966. Personal communication.

————, and J. Berlowe, 1965. *Erections in Newborn Infants.* Research of the Movement Study Group, unpublished.

Marmor, J. 1954. Some considerations concerning orgasm in the female. *Psychosom. Med.* 16:240–45.

Mason, R. E. 1961. *Internal Perception and Bodily Functioning.* New York: Int. Univ. Press.

Masters, W. H. 1959. The sexual response cycle of the human female: vaginal lubrication. *Ann. N.Y. Acad. Sci.* 83:301–17.

————, and V. E. Johnson. 1965. The sexual response cycle of the human male and female: comparative anatomy and physiology. *Sex and Behavior,* ed. F. A. Beach. New York: Wiley, pp. 512–35.

————. 1966. *Human Sexual Response.* Boston, Little, Brown.

McGinley, P. 1950. *The Most Wonderful Doll in the World.* New York: Lippincott.

McGraw, M. 1943. *The Neuromuscular Maturation of the Human Infant.* New York: Columbia Univ. Press.

Mead, M. 1949. *Male and Female.* New York: William Morrow.

————. 1956. Personal communication.

Meng, H. 1931. Pubertät und Pubertätaufklearung. *Z. Psa. Paed.* 5:167–74.

Millar, S. 1968. *The Psychology of Play.* New York: Aronson.

Miller, A., 1973: Miracles: A political letter to the young, from the author once young himself. *Esquire,* Sept., 1973.

Money, J. 1965. Psycho-sexual differentiation. *Sex Research, New Developments.* New York: Holt, Rinehart & Winston, pp. 3–24.

Moore, B. E. 1964. Frigidity: a review of psychoanalytic literature. *Psa. Q.* 33:323–49.

————. 1968. Psychoanalytic reflections on the implications of recent physiological studies of female orgasm. *J. Amer. Psa. Assoc.* 16:569–87.

————. 1971. Opinion: what is the most comon cause of frigidity. *Sexual Behavior* 1(6):28–9.

Muensterberger, W. 1961. The adolescent and Society. *Adolescents,* eds. S. Lorand and H. I. Schneer, New York: Hoeber, pp. 346–68.

Müller, J. A. 1932. A contribution to the problem of libidinal development of the genital phase in girls. *Int. J. Psa.* 13:361–68.

Nathanson, I. T., et al. 1941. Normal excretion of sex hormones in childhood. *Endocrinol.* 28:851–65.

Nelson, W. E. 1959. *Pediatrics.* Philadelphia: Saunders.

Noshpitz, D. 1970. Certain cultural and familial factors contributing to adolescent alienation. *J. Amer. Acad. Child Psychiat.* 9(2):216–22.

Nunberg, H. 1947. Circumcision and problems of bisexuality. *Int. J. Psa.* 28:145–79.

————. 1949. *Problems of Bisexuality as Reflected in Circumcision.* London: Imago Publ. Co.

BIBLIOGRAPHY

Packard, V. 1972. *A Nation of Strangers.* New York: David McKay.

Paschkis, K. E., et al. 1954. *Clinical Endocrinology.* New York: Hoeber.

Paulsen, C. A., ed. 1965. *Estrogen Assays in Clinical Medicine: A Workshop Conference.* Seattle: Univ. Washington Press.

Paulsen, E. P. 1966. Personal communication.

————, E. H. Sobel and M. S. Shafran, 1966. Urinary steroid metabolites in children. 1: Individual 17-ketosteroids in children with normal sexual development. *J. Clin. Endocrinol.* 26:329–39.

Payne, S. A. 1935. A conception of femininity. *Brit. J. Med. Psychol.* 15:18–33.

Petö, E. 1937. Saeugling und Mutter. *Z. Psa. Paed.* 11:244.

Piaget, J. 1937. *The Construction of Reality in the Child.* New York: Basic Books, 1954.

————. 1948. *Language and the Thought of the Child.* London: Routledge & Kegan Paul.

————. 1950. *The Psychology of Intelligence.* New York: Harcourt Brace.

————. 1950. The Origin of the Intelligence of the Child. London: Routledge & Kegan Paul.

———— and B. Inhelder. 1948. *The Child's Conception of Space.* New York: Basic Books, 1960.

Pratt, K. C. 1954. The Neonate. In L. Carmichael's (ed.) *Manual Child Psychology.* New York: Wiley, pp. 190–254.

Rado, S. 1927. Eine aengstliche Mutter. *Int. Z. Psa.* 13:283–289.

————. 1933. Fear of castration in women. *Psa. Q.* 2:425–75.

Ramsden, P. 1973. *Top Team Planning. A Study of the Power of Individual Motivation in Management.* New York: John Wiley.

Rapaport, D. 1951. Consciousness: a psychopathological and psychodynamic view. *Problems of Consciousness.* Transactions of the second conference, March 19–20. New York: Josiah Macy, Jr. Foundation, pp. 18–57.

————. 1959. The Structure of psychoanalytic theory. *Psychol. Issues,* 2(2), Monograph 6. New York: Int. Univ. Press. 1966.

Reich, W. 1927. *Die Funktion des Orgasmus.* Vienna: Int. Psa. Verlag.

Reik, T. 1953. *The Haunting Melody.* New York: Farrar, Straus & Young.

Richter, C. P. 1967. Periodic phenomena in men and animals. *Endocrinology and Human Behavior.* London: Oxford Univ. Press, pp. 284–300.

Ritvo, S. 1972. Late adolescence: developmental and clinical considerations. *Psa. Study of the Child* 26:241–63. New York: Quadrangle Books.

Riviere, J. 1934. Review of Freud, *New Introductory Lectures on Psychoanalysis. Int. J. Psa.* 15:329–339.

Robbins, E. 1964. Rhythmic scrotal contractions in the newborn. *Research of the Movement Study Group,* Sands Point, New York. Unpublished.

———— and M. Soodak, 1973. Personal communication.

Roheim, G. 1945. Aphrodite, or the woman with a penis. *Psa. Q.* 14:350–90.

Rosenblum, L. 1968. Personal communication.

Rosenfield, R. I. and W. R. Eberlein 1969. Plasma 17-Ketosteroid levels during adolescence. *J. Pediat.* 74:932–36.

Ross, J. M. 1968. Pierre as sequel to Moby Dick: a study of Herman Melville. Unpublished.

Runnenbaum, B. et al, 1965. Steroids in human peripheral blood of the menstrual cycle. *J. Steroids,* Suppl. 2, pp. 189–204.

Ryan, K. J. 1963. Biogenesis of estrogens. *Proc. 5th Int. Cong. Biochem.* 7:381–94.

Sacher, E., et al. 1971. Growth hormone responses in depressive illness. I Response to ITT. *A.M.A. Archives of Gen. Psychiatry,* 25:263.

Sadger, J. 1910. Über Urethralerotik. *J. Psa.* 2:409–50.

Sandler, J., and B. Rosenblatt. 1962. The concept of the representational world. *Psa. Study of the Child* 17:128–45. New York: Int. Univ. Press.

Sarlin, C. N. 1963. Feminine identity. *J. Amer. Psa. Assoc.* 11:790–816.

Sassin, J., et al. 1972. Human prolactin 24-hour pattern with increased release during sleep. *Science,* Sept., 1972, p. 1025.

Selye, H. 1950. *Textbook of Endocrinology.* Montreal: Acta Endocrinologica.

Schering 1941–42. *Male Sex Hormone Therapy. Female Sex Hormone Therapy.* Vols. I & II. Medical Research Div.

Schilder, P. 1935. *Image and Appearance of the Human Body.* New York: Int. Univ. Press, 1950.

Schmideberg, M. 1931. Psychoanalytisches zur Menstruation. *Z. Psa. Paed.,* 5:190–202.

Schonfeld, W. A. 1943. Primary and secondary sexual characteristics: study of their development in males from birth through maturity. *Amer. J. Disturbed Child* 65:535–49.

Schur, H. 1966. An observation and comments on the development of memory. *Psa. Study of the Child* 21:468–79.

Searles, H. 1960. *The Nonhuman Environment in Normal Development and in Schizophrenia.* New York: Int. Univ. Press.

Settlage, C. F. 1973. Cultural values and the superego in late adolescence. *Psa. Study of the Child* 27:74–92. New York: Quadrangle Books.

Sherfey, M. J. 1966. The evolution and nature of female sexuality in relation to psychoanalytic theory. *J. Amer. Psa. Assoc.* 14:28–128.

Silving, H. 1964. The oath. *Essays on Criminal Procedure.* Buffalo: Dennis, pp. 1–188.

Sofer, L. J. and A. M. Fogel, 1964: Urinary gonadotropic (ICSH) inhibition substance during the normal menstrual cycle. *J. Clin. Endocrinol.* 24:651–55.

Southam, A. L., and F. P. Gonzaga. 1965. Systemic changes during the menstrual cycle. *Amer. J. Obstetrics & Gynecology* 91:142–65.

Southren, A. L., et al. 1965. Plasma production rates of testosterone in normal adult men and women and in patients with the syndrome of feminizing testes. *J. Clin. Endocrinology* 25:1441–50.

BIBLIOGRAPHY

Spiegel, L. A. 1951. A review of contributions to a psychoanalytic theory of adolescence: indivudual aspects. *Psa. Study of the Child.* 6:375–93.

———. 1961a. Identity and adolescence. *Adolescents,* eds. S. Lorand and H. S. Schneer. New York: Hoeber, pp. 10–18.

———. 1961b. Disorder and consolidation in adolescence. *J. Amer. Psa. Assoc.* 9:406–16.

Spitz, R. A. 1955. The primal cavity. *Psa. Study of the Child* 10:215–40. New York: Int. Univ. Press.

———. 1959. A Genetic Field Theory of Ego Formation. New York: Int. Univ. Press.

———, and K. M. Wolf, 1946. Anaclitic depression: An inquiry into the genesis of psychiatric conditions in early childhood, II. *Psa. Study of the Child* 2:313–42. New York: Int. Univ. Press.

———. 1949. Autoeroticism: some empirical findings and hypotheses on three of its manifestations in the first year of life. *Psa. Study of the Child* 3/4: 85–120.

Stevenson, O. 1954. The first treasured possession. *Psa. Study of the Child* 9:199–217.

Stuart, H. C. 1939. *The Center for Research in Child Health and Development, the Group under Observation, and Studies in Progress.* Monographs of the Society for Research in Child Development. Washington: National Research Council.

Sussman, L. 1972. Personal communication.

Sutherland, H., and I. Stewart. 1965. A critical analysis of the premenstrual syndrome. *Lancet* 1:1180–83.

Talbot, N. B., et al. 1952. *Functional Endocrinology from Birth through Adolescence.* Cambridge: Harvard Univ. Press.

Tanner, J. 1969. Normal and abnormal growth patterns. *Endocrinology and Genetic Disorders of Childhood,* ed. L. I. Gardner. Philadelphia: Saunders, pp. 19–60.

Tausk, V. 1919. On the origin of the "influencing machine" in schizophrenia. *The Psychoanalytic Reader,* ed. R. Fliess. New York: Int. Univ. Press, pp. 52–85.

Thorborg, J. V. 1948. On the influence of estrogenic hormones on the male accessory genital system. *Acta Endocrinol.* Suppl. 2:97–98.

Torry, W. 1972. Personal communication.

Van der Leeuw, P. S. 1958. The preoedipal phase of the male. *Psa. Study of the Child.* 13:352–74.

Van Ophuijsen, J. W. 1920. On the source of feeling persecuted. *Int. J. Psa.* 1:235–39.

Van der Werff Ten Bosch, J. J. 1964. Control of puberty by endocrine and other factors. *2nd Int. Cong. Endocrinology.* Lecture 5/2:833–46.

Vesteergaard, P. 1965. Urinary excretion of individual 17-ketosteroids in children. *Acta Endocrinol.* 49:436–42.

Veszy-Wagner, L. 1965. The equation: baby= girl= doll. Unpublished paper read at *Brit. Psa. Soc.,* Feb..

Wangh, M. 1968. A psychogenic factor in the recurrence of war. *Int. J. Psa.* 69:319–23.

———. 1972. Some unconscious factors in the psychogenesis of recent student uprisings. *Psa. Q.* 61:207–33.

Watson, E. H., and G. H. Lowrey. 1962. *Growth and Development of Children.* Chicago: Year Book Med. Publishers. 1962.

Webster's New International Dictionary. Second Edition. 1955. Unabridged. Springfield, Mass.: Merriam Co. Publ.

Weiss, E. 1962. Theoretical and clinical aspects of female homosexuality. Panel: Theoretical and clinical aspects of overt female homosexuality, rep. C. W. Socarides. *J. Amer. Psa. Assoc.* 10:579–92.

Wiele, P. C., and J. W. Jailer. 1959. Placental steroids in the uterus. *Ann. Amer. Acad. Sci.* 75:889–94.

Wilkins, L. 1965. *The Diagnosis and Treatment of Endocrine Disorders in Childhood and Adolescence.* Springfield: Thomas.

Williams, F. S. 1970. Alienation of youth as reflected in the hippie movement. *J. Amer. Acad. Child Psychiat.* 9:251–63.

Wills, D. M. 1965. Some observations on blind nursery school children's understanding of their world. *Psa. Study of the Child,* 20:344–64. New York: Int. Univ. Press.

Winnicott, D. W. 1949. *The Ordinary Devoted Mother and Her Baby.* London: Tavistock.

———. 1953. Transitional objects and transitional phenomena. *Int. J. Psa.,* 34:89–97.

———. 1963. Dependence in infant-care, in child-care and in the psychoanalytic setting. *Int. J. Psa.* 44:339–44.

———. 1967. Discussion of Kestenberg's paper "Acting out in the psychoanalysis of children and adults" at the Int. Psa. Congress, Copenhagen.

Wittels, F. 1934. Mutterschaft und Bisexualität. *Int. Z. Psa.* 20:313–322.

Woolley, D. E., and P. S. Timiras. 1962. The gonad-brain relationship: effects of female sex hormones on electroshock convulsions in the rat. *Endocrinol.* 70:196–209.

Wolff, P. H. 1959. Observations of newborn infants. *Psychosom. Med.* 21:110–18.

———. 1966. The causes, controls and organization of behavior in the neonate. *Psychol. Issues* 5, No. 17. New York: Int. Univ. Press.

Wulff, M. 1932a. Die Mutter-Kind-Beziehungen als Ausserungsformen des weiblichen Kastrationskomplexes. *Int. Z. Psa.* 18:104–9.

———. 1932b. Über einen interessanten oralen Symptomenkomplex und seine Beziehung zur Sucht. *Int. Z. Psa.* 18:281–302.

———. 1946. Fetishism and object choice in early childhood. *Psa. Q.* 15:450–71.

Wynne, E. 1973. Can suburban kids really grow-up? *Newsday,* Sept. 16, 1973.

Yazmajian, R. W. 1966. Reactions to differences between prepubertal and adult testes and scrotums. *Psa. Q.* 35:368–76.

Zondek, T. 1972. Personal communication.

Bibliography to the Preface
to the Second Printing

Phases of Feminine Sexuality. Psychotherapy Tape Library, 1976.

Prevention of Emotional Disorders in Infancy. Contribution to the Workshop "The Vulnerable Child," meetings of the Amer. Psycho-Analytic Assoc., N.Y., December 12, 1973. Published in *Psychiatric Enfant* 19:516-542, 1976a.

Regression and Reintegration in Pregnancy. *J. Amer. Psycho-analytic Assoc. Supplement* - Female Psychology, 24:213-250, 1976b.

Psychoanalytic Observations of Children. *Int. J. Psychoanal.*, 58(4), 1977a.

Holding Each Other - Holding Oneself Up (with A. Buelte). *Man-Environment Systems*, 7:275-278, 1977b.

Prevention, Infant Therapy, and the Treatment of Adults. I. Toward Understanding Mutuality. II. Mutual Holding and Holding Oneself Up (with A. Buelte). *Int. J. Psychoanal. Psychotherapy*, 6:339-396; 369-396, 1977c.

Manifestations of Aggression (with A. Buelte, E. Schnee, M. Sossin and J. Weinstein). In Workshop *The Vulnerable Child*, chaired by T. Cohen. Meetings of the American Psychoanalytic Assoc., N.Y., December 1977d.

The Development of Patterns of Aggression (with A. Buelte). *Presented at the Int. Dance Therapy Conf.*, Toronto, Oct. 30, 1977e.

Transensus Outgoingness. The Psycho Physical Aspects of Feeling. In: *Between Reality and Fantasy - Transitional Objects and Phenomena*, Grolnick and Barkin, eds., 61-73. New York: Jason Aronson, 1978a.

Transitional Objects and Body-Image Formation (with J. Weinstein). In: *Between Reality and Fantasy - Transitional Objects and Phenomena*, Grolnick and Barkin, eds., 75-95. New York: Jason Aronson, 1978b.

Pregnancy as a Developmental Phase. *Presented to the Dept. of Obstetrics*, McGill University, Montreal, Oct., 1978c.

From Movement Studies to Prevention. Contribution to the workshop in History of Psychoanalysis, meetings of the Amer. Psycho-analytic Assoc., December, 1978d.

Prevention or Infant Therapy. Signs of Vulnerability in Transitional Phases. *Address given in Prevention Program in St. Francis Hospital*, Pittsburgh, Pa. 1978e.

Child Development Research Newsletters 1978-1979.

Hypothetical Monosex and Bisexuality - A Psychoanalytic Interpretation of Sex Differences as They Reveal Themselves in Movement Patterns of Men and Women (with H. Marcus). In *"Psychosexual Imperatives,"* The Self-in-Process Series. N.Y.: Human Sciences Press, 1979a. Ed. Colemna Nelson M. and Ikenberry J.

Notes on Parenthood as a Developmental Phase. In *"Volume Commemorating the 25th Anniversary of the Psychoanalytic Division of Down State University,"* ed. Orgel, S., and Fine, B. N.Y., Jason Arons, 1979b.

Movement Patterns in Development II. Epilogue and Glossary. N.Y.: Dance Notation Bureau, 1979c. With Mark Sossin.

Ego Organization in Obsessive-compulsive Development. A study of the Ratman, based on the Interpretation of Movement Patterns. In *"Volume Commemorating the 25th Anniversary of the Psycho-analytic Division of Down State University."* ed. Kanzer, M., and Glenn, J. N.Y.: Jason Aronson, 1979d.

Prevention and Infant Therapy. Presented in the *Jamaica Center for Psychotherapy 1978* and in the *Munich Psychoanalytic Society.* 1979e.

A Multimedia Project for Infants and Toddlers. Presented at the *New England Council of Expressive Therapies.* Rhode Island, June 1979f.

The Multiple Facets of Work. To appear in the *Psychoanalytic Q.* 1980a.

The Three Faces of Femininity. To be published in the *"Development of the Female Child,"* ed. Mendell, D., 1980c.

Eleven, Twelve, Thirteen. Years of Transition from the Barrenness of Childhood to the Fertility of Adolescence. In *"Human Development"* ed. Greenspan and Pollock. Washington, D.C. Office of Health and Education, 1980d.

Maternity and Paternity in the Developmental Context. Contributions to integration as a procreative person. In *"Sexuality Issue"* of Psychiatric Clinics of North America, ed. Meyer, J.K. 1980e.

The Development of Parental Attitudes in the Boy. To appear in *"Anthology on Fatherhood,"* ed. Cath, S., Gurwitt, A., and Ross, M.J. With Marcus, H., Sossin, M., Stevenson, R., and Tross, S. N.Y.: Little Brown, 1981.

INDEX

INDEX

INDEX

trated by doll theme in children's literature and, 111-14

infantile genitality and, 108-9

orgastic discharge and, 104-7

pseudoadult femininity distinguished from adult feminity, 120-21

psychoanalytic and biological views on, 102-4

similarities and dissimilarities between male and female, 141-51

transition from adolescence to adulthood and, 119-20

transition from latency to adoscence and, 117-19

transition from pregenitality to phallicity, 114-15

Inner genitals, 127-33

acceptance of, as basis for achieving adult genitality, 152

becoming active at puberty, 75

children as externalization of, 130

denial of

elements counteracting, 7, 232, 374

inner genitals equated with immaturity, 127-31, 144, 322

in inner-genital phase, 143, 146

growth of

in prepuberty, 143

at puberty, 388

models of male, 133-35

neonatal, 337

prepubertal, 343

growth of, 143

representations of, 94

See also Ovaries; Testicles; Uterus; Vagina

Inner male sexual development, 127-41

avoidance of male inner genitals and, 132-33; *see also* Inner genitals

development sequence in, 130-32

infantile attitudes toward women in, 135-41

male dominance and, 127-30

models of male inner genitals, 133-35

orgastic discharge and, 104-7

psychoanalytical and biological views on, 102, 104

similarities and dissimilarities between female development and, 141-51

Inner-genital image of the baby, 271, 272

Inner-genital impulses

adult males externalizing, 60

anxiety-provoking nature of, 102

clitoris and, 91, 124

coping with, 87

by adult women, 99, 123

in latency, 93-94

at puberty, 95-96

desexualization of, 90, 97

externalization of, 119

doll play as, 116

in inner-genital phase, 142-43

in latency, 143, 146-47

by males, 60, 128, 129

orgastic discharge and, 106-7

penis envy and, 122

in prepuberty, 143

in inner-genital phase

dissimilarities between male and female

handling of, 145-46

externalization of, 142-43

in phallic phase, 59, 321, 322

in pregenital phases, 316-17, 320-21, 323

prepubertal, 316-17, 348

dealing with, 366-67

estrogen production and, 147-48

fantasies triggered by, 363

as source of motherliness, 52

urges fused with, 54

See also Vaginal excitations

Inner-genital phase

antecedents of adolescent organization in, 316-23

bodily movement in, 246-53

characteristics of child image in, 269

denial of femininity in, 143

dessimilarities between male and female, 144-45

first and second, 152

hormonal organization in, 323, 340, 346

masturbation in, 251

psychophysical changes in, 340-41

similarites between male and female, 141-51

Inner-genital preoedipal phase

defined, 192

organ-object unity in, 224-29

Inside, developing concept of, 88

Intellectual curiosity at puberty, 300

Intensity factors of tension, defined, 196

Intermediate objects

defined, 216

retrieving the past through, 221-24

Investigating-exploring-communicating, defined, 438

Isolated family, structure of, 453-60

Jacobs, P.S., 272, 273

Jacobson, E., 3, 17, 92

bodily movement and, 199

denial of vagina and, 124

development of maternal feelings and, 47, 50

male development and, 127, 135

organ-object images and, 217, 221

psychic and hormonal organizations and, 316, 319, 320

puberty and, 378, 390

rhythmicity and, 432

riddle of female sexuality and, 102

vaginal orgasm and, 103

Jaffe, R.B., 420

Jailer, J.W., 336

Japanese doll festival, 56-57

Jekels, L., 216, 217

Joffe, W.G., 217

Johnson, V.E., 81, 91, 110, 122, 124

activity-passivity problem and, 5

defense mechanisms and, 125

discoveries made by, 103-4

feminine sexual responses and 76, 77

infantile genitality and, 109

libidinization of vagina and, 126

male development and, 133

orgastic discharge and, 104-5

psychic and hormonal organizations and, 314, 318

transition from latency to adolescence and, 118

treatment of frigidity by, 151

Jones, Ernest, 3, 102, 119, 122, 357

Josselyn, I.M., 328, 402

Kaplan, E., 109

Kataw, puberty and, 394, 397, 398

Keiser, S., 105, 122, 130

Kestenberg, J.S., 5, 8, 9, 102-4, 110

bodily movement and, 189, 192, 193, 196-98, 210

in anal phase, 203, 244

in neonatal phase, 241

in urethral phase, 245

early fears and defenses and, 184

infantile genitality and, 124

male development and, 139

maternal feelings in early childhood and, 52

mother-child interaction and, 158, 159, 167

INDEX

male development and, 133
orgastic discharge and, 104-5
psychic and hormonal organizations and, 314, 368
transition from latency to adolescence and, 118
treatment of frigidity by, 151

Masturbation
adolescent, 232
in prepuberty, 94, 147, 354, 363, 369, 373-74
in puberty, 23, 300, 390-93
clitoric, 80, 81, 83, 305, 308, 325
in early maternal phase, 14-15
in inner-genital phase, 251
in latency, 20, 110
orgastic discharge and, 106
in phallic phase, 17, 49, 50, 91-93, 110, 143, 325-26
in phallic-oedipal phase, 230
in pregenital stages, 339
pubertal, 23, 300, 390-93
as viewed by genuinely anxious mothers, 69-70

Maternal behavior
as example of femininity, 4
externalization of inner impules in, 124
loss of, 452; see also Masculinization of women
as trait of both sexes, 52

Maternal feelings, development of, 23-62
anal-baby concept and, 30-34
basis for, 23-24
in boys, 51-55
in early maternal stage, 34-39
maternal instinct and, 27-28
transitional objects in, 29-30
vaginal stimulations in oral phase and, 29

Maternal instinct, 27-28
Maternal love, 26
Mead, M., 56, 57, 97, 128, 135
Melville, H., 105
Men, see Father-child interaction; Father-daughter interaction; Father-son interaction; Fathers; Male sexual development; Masculinity
Menarche, 285-312, 400-1
acceptance of femininity and, 148
body image formed on basis of, 98, 365
case reports on, 287-89
"death of the baby" situation compared with trauma of, 22
denial of inner genitals counteracted by, 7, 232, 274
effects of cyclicity of, 362-63
as form of discharge of inner-genital sensations, 143
increase in menstrual blood flow as sign of fertility, 378

integration process of first menstruation, 358-61
masochism in prepuberty and puberty and, 291-96
menstrual disturbances in, 301-2
organizers of feminine development and, 307-11
parents and, 362
physical aspects of feminine development and, 302-7
organizers of feminine development and, 307-11
parents and, 362
physical aspects of feminine development and, 302-7
as trigger mechanism for organization, 296-99, 306-7
Meng, H., 292
Menstruation, see Menarche
Mental functioning, problems involved in nonverbal expressions of, 188; see also Bodily movement
Middle-class life, privatization of, 451
Midgley, A.R., 420
Miller, A., 455
Miller, E., 453
Mobilization-containing system of urethral phase, 209
Moby Dick (Melville), 105
Moodiness
in adolescence, 99
of adult women, 97, 99
inner-genital tensions and, 87
in latency, 98
in neonatal phase, 87-88
related to internal discomforts, 88
See also Nagging
Moore, B.E., 75, 102, 104
Morality
latency, 276-77
social conscience and, 444
Mother-child interaction, 157-70
attunement in, 160-65
complete, 160, 161
one-sided attunement, 161-63
partial attunement, 164-65
selective attunement, 165
as basis for development of community spirit, 448
bodily movement and, 189, 199-212
in anal phase, 204-6
in neonatal phase, 199
in oral phase, 200-2
in urethral phase, 208-9
clashing in, 165-69
early fear development and, 185-87
generalized clashing, 165-67
partial clashing, 167-68
selective clashing, 168-69

development of early fears and, 184-87
difficulties arising from, 64, 72-73
effects of husband-wife relationship on, 66-67
factors affecting, 63
functioning for the other in, 163-64
partial clashing and, 167
in isolated family, 453
subordination in, 127
Mother-child unity in pregnancy, 63-64, 72, 319-20
Mother-daughter interaction
doll play to reverse, 25
in latency, 21
mothers as organizers of daughters' development, 308
in phallic phase, 17, 49-50, 324, 341
in prepuberty, 22
in projection phase, 20
at puberty, 95-96
Mother identification
doll play and, 12, 14, 37
identifying with pregnant mother, 55
in latency, 20
menarche and, 310-11
mirroring as form of, 168
in phallic phase, 18
in preoedipal phase, 308
Mother-son interaction
Freud and, 27
in prepuberty, 373
at puberty, 148-49
Mother types, 63-74
anxious mothers, 64, 66-68
distant mothers, 72
genuinely anxious mothers, 68-73
openly aggressive mothers, 64-66
Motherhood
biological vector of, 59
effects of oral contraceptives on, 420
as sublimation of masculinity, 46
Mothering, see Maternal behavior
Mothers
behavior of depressed, 48
in isolated families, 455-56
missing the mother, as earliest known fear, 174
rejecting, in development of early fears, 183-84
role of, in menarche, 309-10
Motility, rhythmic patterns in, 412-13, 423-41
in preadult consolidation, 436-40
in prepuberty diffusion and reorganization, 427-31
prior to adolescence, 425-26

490

INDEX

Dr. Kestenberg is a clinical professor of psychiatry at Down State University, Brooklyn, New York and a training analyst for adults and children in the Division for Psychoanalytic Education, New York University. She has been in psychoanalytic practice since 1939, has taught psychoanalysis since 1959, and has pursued longitudinal studies of children since 1963. She originated the Kestenberg Movement Profile and is the author of "Movement Patterns in Development," which is widely used in expressive therapy teaching centers. She has helped found *Child Development Research*, an organization devoted to *prevention* of emotional problems. It operates in two areas of research, service and education: the Sidney L. Green Prenatal Project and the Center for Parents and Children in Roslyn, Long Island, N.Y. Because of their innovative methods, applying psychoanalytic and movement principles to prevention, both projects have become models and training sources for health professionals, working with parents and children. Royalties for this volume help support these facilities.